TOWARD AN INFRAMARGINAL REVOLUTION

Over the past fifteen years, there has been a surge of interest among legal scholars in altering legal rules to redistribute wealth. Many believe that neoclassical economic theory stands in the way. A growing number of progressive scholars are showing that it actually reveals the way forward. *Toward an Inframarginal Revolution* offers a fresh perspective on the redistribution of wealth by legal scholars who argue that the neoclassical concept of the gains from trade provides broad latitude for redistribution that will not harm efficiency. They show how policymakers can redistribute wealth via taxation, price regulation, antitrust, consumer law, and contract law by focusing on the prices at which inframarginal units of production change hands. Progressive and eye-opening, this volume uses conservative economic concepts to make a compelling case for radically redistributing wealth. This title is part of the Flip it Open program and may also be available open access. Check our website Cambridge Core for details.

Ramsi A. Woodcock is the Wyatt, Tarrant & Combs Associate Professor of Law at the University of Kentucky Rosenberg College of Law.

Toward an Inframarginal Revolution

REDISTRIBUTING THE GAINS FROM TRADE

Edited by

RAMSI A. WOODCOCK

University of Kentucky

CAMBRIDGE
UNIVERSITY PRESS

CAMBRIDGE
UNIVERSITY PRESS

Shaftesbury Road, Cambridge CB2 8EA, United Kingdom

One Liberty Plaza, 20th Floor, New York, NY 10006, USA

477 Williamstown Road, Port Melbourne, VIC 3207, Australia

314–321, 3rd Floor, Plot 3, Splendor Forum, Jasola District Centre, New Delhi – 110025, India

103 Penang Road, #05-06/07, Visioncrest Commercial, Singapore 238467

Cambridge University Press is part of Cambridge University Press & Assessment, a department of the University of Cambridge.

We share the University's mission to contribute to society through the pursuit of education, learning and research at the highest international levels of excellence.

www.cambridge.org
Information on this title: www.cambridge.org/9781009306775

DOI: 10.1017/9781009306720

When citing this work, please include a reference to the DOI 10.1017/9781009306720

First published 2025

A catalogue record for this publication is available from the British Library

A Cataloging-in-Publication data record for this book is available from the Library of Congress

ISBN 978-1-009-30677-5 Hardback

Contents

Figures

Tables

Contributors

Reuven S. Avi-Yonah University of Michigan Law School

Zvikomborero Chadambuka Wayne State University Law School

Faisal Chaudhry University of Massachusetts School of Law – Dartmouth

Matthew Dimick University at Buffalo School of Law

Brian L. Frye University of Kentucky Rosenberg College of Law

Inge Graef Tilburg University Law School

Daniel J. H. Greenwood Hofstra University Deane School of Law

Michael D. Guttentag Loyola Marymount University's Loyola Law School

Behrang Kianzad School of Economics and Management, Lund University

Adrian Kuenzler The University of Hong Kong, Faculty of Law

Przemysław Pałka Jagiellonian University Faculty of Law and Administration

Vijay Raghavan Brooklyn Law School

Ramsi A. Woodcock University of Kentucky Rosenberg College of Law

Acknowledgments

I thank the John S. and James L. Knight Foundation for providing funding for Inframarginalism & Internet, a conference held online on February 18 and 19, 2021, that brought together the contributors to this volume. (The conference program and recordings of the presentations may be found at https://inframarginalism.net/.)

I would trace the origin of the "inframarginalism" name, the conference, and this volume to a conversation with Michael Guttentag in the atrium lounge of the Marriott Wardman Park in Washington, DC, during the 2020 annual meeting of the Association of American Law Schools. I had always been an inframarginalist, in part thanks to the left-wing law and economics that I had absorbed from Duncan Kennedy while at Harvard. But I had given little thought to institutionalizing the approach. That afternoon, however, I learned that Michael and I shared the view that the emerging Law and Political Economy movement was missing something vital: an appreciation for the distributive freedom afforded by the gains from trade and the power of that freedom to tame conservative economics. It was Michael who suggested the name "inframarginalism" – no doubt to his great chagrin, because he prefers the term "surplus." Michael also shared his experiences with the institutionalization of ideas in other fields. He joined me in introducing the conference, and his enthusiasm for publishing work from the conference ultimately induced me to undertake the creation of this volume. I must therefore thank Michael, too.

1

Introduction to Inframarginalism and This Volume

Ramsi A. Woodcock[*]

CONTENTS

[*] *The author wishes to dedicate this chapter to the Palestinians killed by Israel during the chapter's preparation.*

I INTRODUCTION

The progressive lawyer very often feels himself placed at a disadvantage by economics. He proposes that the government intervene in a market and the conservative replies that the intervention will prevent buyers and sellers from transacting. He is told that these lost transactions will prevent goods and services from flowing to those who value them the most. He is told, in short, that justice has an economic cost. He must now explain to those prevented from transacting why the good he wishes to do should take precedence over their appetites. The experience of the progressive with economics is, thus, one of constraint. The economist pulls the progressive away from the language of justice with which he feels most comfortable and forces him to converse in terms of efficiency – a concept that has no intuitive appeal to him whatsoever.

Let us say, for example, that the progressive is a first-year law student and that he has just read the case of *Williams v. Walker-Thomas Furniture Company*,[1] in which a seller repossesses all of a poor woman's furniture when she misses a payment on a single item. It is obvious to the progressive that this is unfair. But the conservative explains that prohibiting the practice of foreclosing on earlier, paid-off purchases will force down the effective price of the seller's furniture, as now the seller will receive less in the event of a default. But, as a consequence of the decline in price, the seller may no longer be able to cover the cost of selling furniture to impoverished buyers who often fail to pay. And once the seller has exited the market, the poor woman may be unable to purchase furniture. The progressive's well-intentioned intervention has a cost, one that is exacted on those whom the progressive seeks to help. It is enough to make any lover of justice cry.

The progressive does not know how to overcome this economic argument. But, at the same time, he trusts his intuition regarding justice, and so he is led to the conclusion that he must simply reject economics.[2] Like a man tempted by the devil, he cannot explain precisely why the argument is wrong, but he can say for sure that it must be wrong because to accept it would require that he go against his conscience. His rejection of economics is, however, a catastrophic result. For the economic system is not devoid of morality but in fact based upon a morality that has the greatest popular appeal today, even to the progressive himself. The progressive thinks that he must forsake economics in order to retain moral authority. In fact, in forsaking economics, he compromises that authority.

The trouble is that the economist is on the side of liberty. He is anxious to ensure that transactions into which parties wish to enter are not precluded. When the progressive forsakes economics, he therefore concedes the terrain of liberty to the

[1] Williams v. Walker-Thomas Furniture Company, 350 F. 2d 445 (D.C. Cir. 1965).

[2] *See, e.g.*, Jedediah Britton-Purdy et al., *Building a Law-and-Political-Economy Framework: Beyond the Twentieth-Century Synthesis*, 129 Yale L.J. 1784, 1800 (2020); Elizabeth Popp Berman, Thinking Like an Economist (2022).

other side. He concedes that his proposed government regulations will preclude transactions. That is a big concession because in the modern world there is no universal measure of value and so no basis for telling others what to do. God is dead.[3] All that remains is the multitude of little gods whose individual preferences society is supposed to honor as much as possible. In the modern world, if two people say they want to do something, society is supposed to try its best to let them do it. When the progressive acts to preclude such apparently voluntary behavior, he appears to impose his own personal set of preferences on others. But one is never supposed to do that in a world without a universal measure of value. When the economist chides the progressive for pricing the poor woman's only source of furniture out of the market, the economist stands up for individual liberty. He says that if the poor woman is willing to accept the risk of losing everything upon default in exchange for receiving a price she can afford, then she should be allowed to do that. When the progressive prevents her from making that choice, he imposes his own personal set of preferences – that the poor not experience foreclosure – on poor women who would rather risk foreclosure in order to furnish their homes.

Once upon a time, the progressive could have appealed to universal moral principles residing, immutable, behind the world to justify his view that the poor should escape foreclosure no matter what the poor themselves might think. He could have argued that foreclosure is simply *wrong* or *inherently* inconsistent with human dignity. But that is no longer possible. The most that the progressive can do today is to insist that the poor woman does not really prefer to buy subject to such punitive terms. But this hardly cuts the stink of paternalism. Normally, the progressive is a friend to individual liberty. He cries out for democratic governance. He champions the rights of people to live according to conscience. In rejecting economics when confronted with arguments about the liberty of the poor woman to transact, the progressive seems to reject his own credo. It is not a pretty sight, and the progressive knows it, making him resent the economist all the more.

The American progressive wonders why in recent decades his policies have been on the retreat nearly everywhere. Tax rates have fallen.[4] Consumer protections have been cut.[5] The regulation of industry has been rolled back.[6] The progressive thinks that perhaps the cause is a conspiracy of monied interests,[7] lobbying, the racism of

3 Friedrich Nietzsche, The Gay Science: With a Prelude in Rhymes and an Appendix of Songs § 125 (Walter Kaufmann trans., 2010).

4 *See* W. Elliot Brownlee, Federal Taxation in America: A History 182–290 (Cambridge University Press 3d ed. July 2016).

5 *See* Ramsi A. Woodcock, *The Obsolescence of Advertising in the Information Age*, 127 Yale L.J. 2270, 2290–98 (2018).

6 *See* Joseph D. Kearney & Thomas W. Merrill, *The Great Transformation of Regulated Industries Law*, 98 Colum. L. Rev. 1323, 1329–63 (1998).

7 *See, e.g.*, *The Lewis Powell Memo: A Corporate Blueprint to Dominate Democracy – Greenpeace USA* (July 16, 2015), https://perma.cc/7FJS-6CDD.

working-class voters causing them to vote against interest,[8] or the brainwashing of students or judges with economics.[9] But it is not these things. The progressive has lost because he has offered no rejoinder to the economist.[10]

This is a great shame because economics is not an insurmountable intellectual obstacle for the progressive. As soon as one has ventured into the economic thicket by even a few steps, it becomes clear that in fact economic theory – neoclassical, mainstream economic theory – is a friend to the progressive. To see why, it will be helpful to think for a moment about notches and lines.

In neoclassical economics, every commercial transaction can be represented by a vertical line that measures pleasure in dollar terms. We put a notch in the line to represent the pleasure that a buyer gets from buying a good. We know where to place the notch because we make the admittedly unreasonable assumption that the maximum the buyer is willing to pay for the good measures the pleasure he gets from consuming the good. We place the notch at the point on the line representing the maximum that the buyer is willing to pay for the good in dollar terms. Now, consider the seller. He would have derived pleasure from consuming the good if he had not sold it. Or, if he manufactured the good, he would have derived pleasure from spending his time and money on some other productive project. We assume that the minimum amount of money he would be willing to accept for the good reflects the loss of pleasure to him of producing and giving up the good when he sells it. Call it his cost of production. We make a corresponding notch on the line. We now have two notches. The result is shown in Figure 1.1.

Now, it should be evident that the two notches could appear anywhere along the bar. If a seller greatly values the good, then the seller's notch will appear very high up. If the seller values the good only a bit, the notch will appear close to the bottom. The same is true for the buyer. There is no necessary relation between the buyer's valuation and the seller's valuation, and hence between the buyer's notch and the seller's notch, other than this: In order for a transaction to take place, the buyer's valuation must be at least as high as the seller's valuation – the buyer's notch must be at least as high as the seller's. Otherwise, the minimum the seller is willing to accept will be greater than the maximum that the buyer is willing to pay and the two will, therefore, be unable to agree on a price.

Now we come to the place in neoclassical economics where justice lives: The buyer's notch can be anywhere at or above the seller's. It can be a little bit higher or a lot higher. The buyer and seller will negotiate a price and that price will necessarily

8 *See, e.g.*, Mehdi Hasan, *Time to Kill the Zombie Argument: Another Study Shows Trump Won Because of Racial Anxieties – Not Economic Distress*, The Intercept, https://perma.cc/NZQ2-DP4Z (last visited July 12, 2024).

9 *See* Elliott Ash et al., *Ideas Have Consequences: The Effect of Law and Economics on American Justice* (June 26, 2017), https://perma.cc/CK37-9N4J; Berman, *supra* note 2.

10 *See* Ramsi A. Woodcock, *A Progressive Critique of the Law and Political Economy Movement* (Mar. 31, 2023), https://osf.io/twbrk.

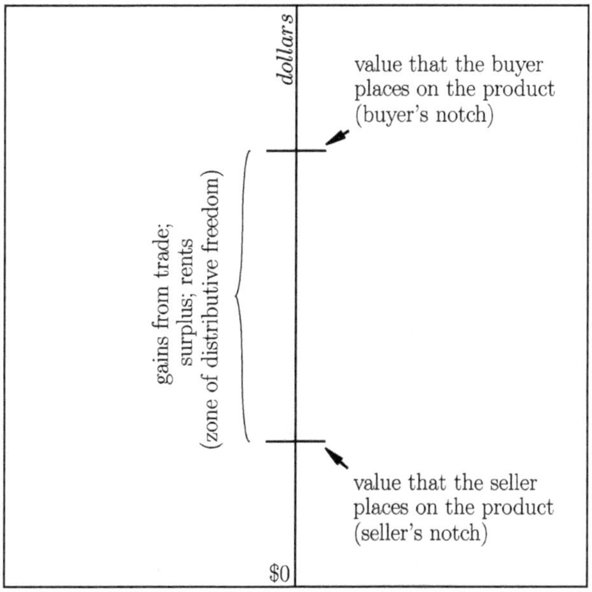

FIGURE 1.1 The gains from trade depicted with a line and two notches

fall at or between their notches because it must be above the minimum the seller is willing to accept (the seller's notch) and below the maximum that the buyer is willing to pay (the buyer's notch). But so long as price remains between them, an increase or decrease in price will not interrupt their transaction. Over the expanse of the gap between the notches, efficiency is irrelevant. Price can be high, in which case the seller benefits, or price can be low, in which case the buyer benefits. But wherever the price may be, the transaction will take place. The notches pose the problem of efficiency. Price must fall between them in order for a transaction to take place. But the gap between the notches poses a pure question of distributive justice. Price can fall anywhere within the gap without discouraging the transaction.[11]

This means that the progressive can reject the assumption of the economist that driving down the price of the furniture seller will prevent the seller from selling and the poor woman from buying. There must be a gap between the furniture seller's notch and the poor woman's notch, and there is no reason to suppose that at the outset the price of furniture is at the furniture seller's notch. If it is not, then there must be room to push price down without driving price below the furniture seller's notch and so rendering the seller unwilling to sell to the poor woman. To be sure, a price reduction that is too great will make the transaction impossible. But so long as the reduction is not too great, the

[11] *See, e.g.*, WILLIAM J. BAUMOL, ECONOMIC THEORY AND OPERATIONS ANALYSIS 593 (Prentice-Hall 4th ed. 1977) (defining "surplus" as "any payment in excess of the amount necessary to have the input in question supplied").

transaction will take place. The furniture seller can be prevented from imposing oppressive terms on the buyer, and the effective price of the furniture can be reduced, without preventing the poor woman from getting her furniture.

The economist may respond that the progressive must nevertheless concede that the price reduction *might* preclude the transaction, and he is right to say this. But one must step back and appreciate what a weak position this is relative to the one that the economist initially wished to occupy in relation to the progressive. The economist wished to maintain that justice deprives the poor woman of furniture. Now he can maintain only that it might possibly do so. The economist wished to maintain that as a matter of theory the progressive's intervention is unjust, because it takes from the poor woman. Now the economist maintains only that it might be unjust if pushed too far. In neoclassical economics, markets are efficient when people actually enter into all transactions into which they want to enter given their budgets.[12] The economist wished to maintain that efficiency *requires* that the market for furniture operate without the progressive's intervention, else a poor woman who would otherwise buy a bed ceases to find willing sellers. Now he maintains only that the progressive's intervention might drive sellers from the market. Moreover, he must now also concede that it might not.

II THE MAGIC IN NEOCLASSICAL ECONOMICS: THE GAINS FROM TRADE

A *The Gains from Trade as a Locus of Distributive Freedom*

What is this gap between the notches that strikes such a devastating blow against the economist? It is what economists call the "gains from trade," "surplus," or sometimes "rents." The progressive discovers to his astonishment and delight that this concept accomplishes everything that a progressive might wish to accomplish in economics, almost as if it were created by progressives themselves. Even better, this concept is absolutely essential to the economic project and so cannot be avoided by economists. The gains from trade are the increase in pleasure created by the movement of resources from sellers to buyers. They are the difference between the greater pleasure that the buyer takes from the good and the lesser pleasure that the seller would take from keeping it or from not producing it at all. As such they are the economist's justification for encouraging trade – they represent the net gain created by transactions. The economist cannot do without them.

What makes the gains from trade inherently progressive is that in principle they can be redistributed without discouraging buyers and sellers from transacting. They

[12] This is what it means for an economy to achieve pareto efficiency. *See* Hal R. Varian, Intermediate Microeconomics: A Modern Approach 306–8 (W. W. Norton & Company 7th ed. 2006).

are the place in economics in which the progressive can do justice without harming efficiency.[13] What makes the gains from trade redistributable without precluding transactions is that, from the perspective of the buyer and the seller, a gain is a gain whether it is large or small. If one wishes to give all of the gains from trade to the buyer, one can set price so close to the seller's costs of production that the seller will receive only a vanishingly small share of the gains from trade. By choosing such a low price, one can allocate nearly all of the gains from trade to the buyer, who pays a price close to the cost of production and retains all of the rest of the value he derives from acquiring the good as surplus. The seller will not, however, be discouraged from transacting. The seller will receive very little of the gains from trade, but so long as the seller receives something, the seller will be content to sell. He will cover his costs, and then some, and that is better than not transacting and receiving no part of the gains from trade. A gain is a gain whether it is large or small.

By the same token, if one wishes to give all of the gains from trade to the *seller*, one can set price so high that the buyer will receive only a vanishingly small share of the gains from trade. By choosing such a high price, one allocates nearly all of the gains from trade to the seller. The buyer will pay a price almost equal to, but slightly below, the value the buyer places on the good, and the buyer will therefore receive very little of the gains from trade. But the buyer will not be discouraged from transacting. So long as the buyer receives some part of the gains from trade, the buyer will be content to buy. He will derive more value from the purchase than he pays out for it, and that is better for him than not transacting and receiving no part of the gains from trade. For the buyer, as for the seller, a gain is a gain whether it is large or small.

The implication of all this is that how the gains from trade are sliced up and distributed between the buyer and the seller has no bearing on whether the parties will transact. The gains from trade can be given entirely to the seller, entirely to the buyer, or divided between them in any proportion without dissuading them from doing a deal. Indeed, the gains from trade need not even be distributed to the buyer or the seller. They can be taxed away from both and given in toto to others, as we shall see in a moment. The great irony of economics is that economics' basic efficiency proposition – that markets create wealth – simultaneously opens up a vast field upon which distributive justice is free to roam unmolested by questions of efficiency: that field consists of the gains from trade.

B *Redistribution in Terms of Notches*

We can show that price distributes the gains from trade between the buyer and the seller using our notched line. As already noted, the gap between the buyer's notch

[13] I have touched on this idea in several earlier works. For a discussion in the context of corporate governance, see Ramsi A. Woodcock, *The Antitrust Case for Consumer Primacy in Corporate Governance*, 10 UC Irvine L. Rev. 1395, 1403–26 (2020).

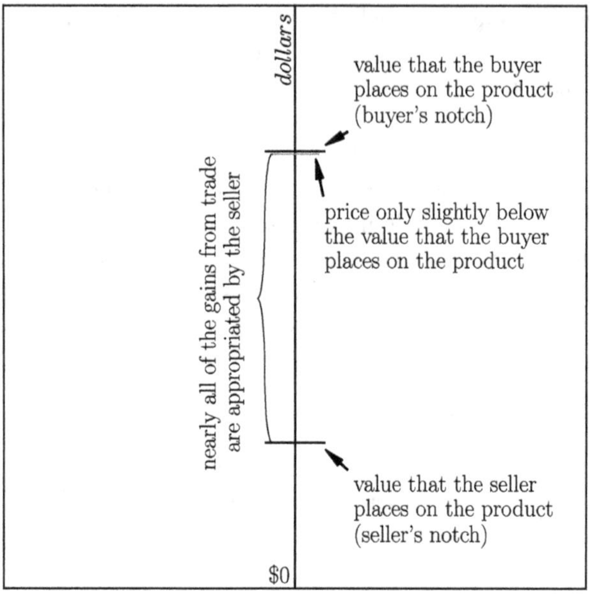

FIGURE 1.2 A price nearly equal to the buyer's value enables the seller to appropriate all of the gains from trade

and the seller's notch measures the gains from trade. If price is at the level of the seller's notch, then the buyer pays out only an amount equal to the seller's cost of production. The buyer keeps the entire gain for himself (Figure 1.3). If instead price is at the level of the buyer's notch, then the buyer pays out an amount equal to the value the buyer places on the good to the seller, including both the gain from trade and the amount necessary to compensate the seller for the cost of production. The seller keeps the gain from trade (Figure 1.2). A price anywhere between these extremes divides the gains from trade between the buyer and the seller (Figure 1.4). A numerical example may help drive home the point. If, for example, the buyer is willing to pay $10 at most (i.e., places a $10 value on the good) and the seller is willing to accept $2 at least (i.e., places a $2 value on the good), then the gains from trade are $8 (the difference between the value the buyer places on the good and the value the seller places on the good). A price of $10 leaves the buyer with no gain. He pays $10 to receive a good he values at $10. But, at that price, the seller receives an $8 gain because the seller receives a payment of $10 less his $2 cost of production. If price is $2, the buyer gains a good he values at $10 in exchange for making a payment of $2, so he enjoys an $8 gain. The seller, who receives the $2 payment to cover costs of $2, enjoys no gain. If instead price is $6, the seller receives a gain of $4. He receives a $6 payment but must deduct his $2 cost of producing the good. The buyer enjoys a gain of $4 as well. He receives a good he values at $10 at a price of $6.

Now, if price falls precisely at the buyer's notch, the buyer will be indifferent between doing the transaction and not, for he will pay out the value to him in dollars

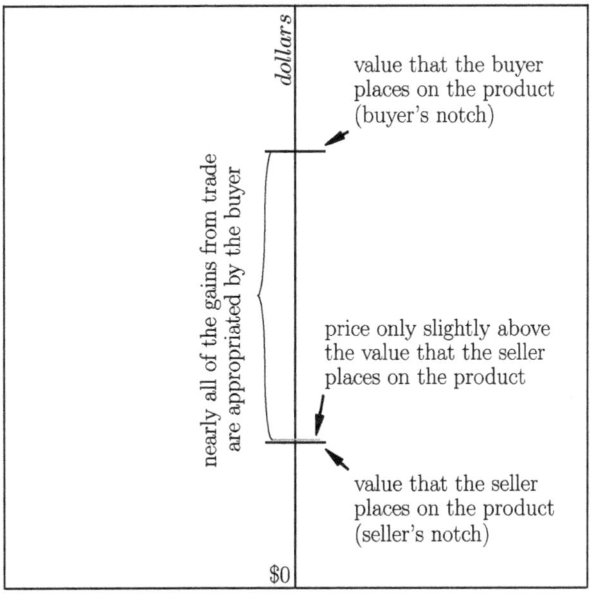

FIGURE 1.3 A price nearly equal to the seller's value enables the buyer to appropriate all of the gains from trade

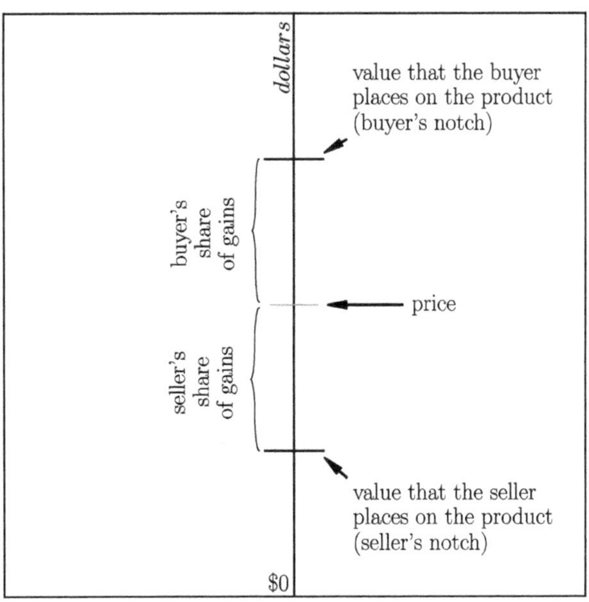

FIGURE 1.4 A price between the buyer's value and the seller's value divides the gains from trade between the buyer and the seller

of what he consumes. And if price falls precisely at the seller's notch, the seller will be indifferent between doing the transaction and not, for he will pay out the value to him in dollars of what he consumes. To make sure that each will have an incentive to transact, we must make sure that each obtains a share of the gains from trade. But the amount of that share does not matter. It can be vanishingly small, as will be discussed in detail in the next Section. It follows that so long as the price is below the buyer's notch and above the seller's notch, even if vanishingly close to one or the other, the buyer and the seller will have incentive enough to transact. From this it follows in turn that the progressive do-gooder can put the price anywhere between the notches and so distribute the gains from trade in any fashion, without precluding the transaction and so without harming efficiency.

Indeed, the state can even tax away the gains from trade and redistribute them to a third party without harm to efficiency, so long as the amount of the tax is slightly less than the gains from trade. A sales tax on the buyer's payment to the seller would do the trick, so long as it were set at a rate slightly less than the gains from trade as a share of the value placed by the buyer on the good. For example, suppose again that a buyer places a $10 value on a good and a seller places a $2 value on it, creating $8 in gains from trade. If the state were to tax the transaction at a rate of 79.9 percent, the state would extract $7.98 of the $8 of gains from trade and still leave buyer and seller with two pennies of gains from trade to divide up. The buyer and the seller will not be dissuaded by the tax from carrying out the transaction because they will still be able to split some gains from trade, and any gain is better than what would result from a failure to complete the transaction, which would be no gain at all for either. The seller would need to charge $9.99 in order to have an incentive to transact. After paying $7.98 in taxes (79.9 percent of $9.99), the seller would be left with revenues of $2.01 – a penny more than the value of $2 that the seller places on the good. That penny would give the seller an incentive, however small, to carry out the transaction and improve her lot. The buyer, too, would have an incentive to transact at a price of $9.99 because that price is a penny less than the value of $10 that the buyer places on the good, creating a penny of gain for the buyer. (If the buyer were to pay $10 for a good upon which the buyer places a value of $10, then the buyer would enjoy no net gain from the purchase.) The state could pay its $7.98 in tax revenue out to the neediest – without having prevented the buyer and the seller from transacting.

C *Addressing Conservative Denial and Objections*

1 Sometimes Conservatives Are in Denial about Gains from Trade

It is the conservative economist's rejection of the existence of the gap between the notches that gives him so much misguided confidence in debates and which so often leads him into embarrassing error. Perhaps the most famous example is the minimum wage.

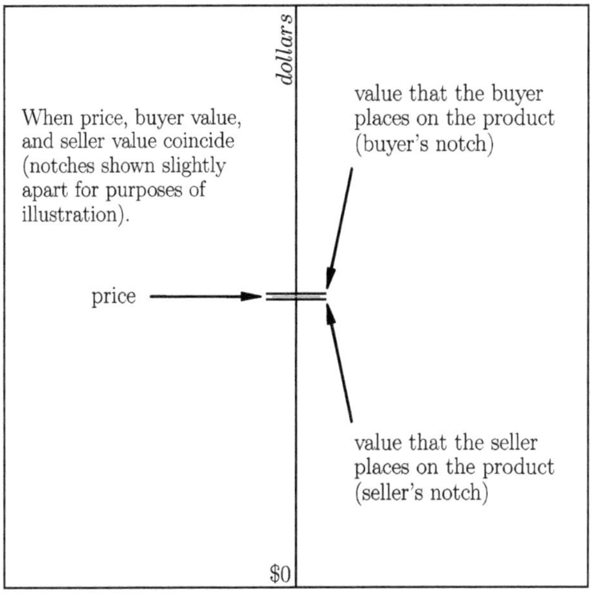

FIGURE 1.5 When buyer and seller place almost the same value on a product, the range of prices at which they can transact is severely limited

For the economist who assumes that there is no gap between the notches, raising wages must throw some people out of work. For if there is no gap, then the notch of the buyer of labor is coextensive with the notch of the seller of labor. Price (the wage) must be at the level of the notch for the employee to be hired. Raising price drives price above the maximum that the buyer (employer) is willing to pay, causing the employer to eliminate the position (Figure 1.5).

This is what in other contexts economists call a knife's edge argument: It depends on the assumption that a single one of many possibilities holds. In order for the employer and the employee to transact, the notch of the employer as the buyer of labor must be above that of the employee as the seller of labor. It need not be right above. It could be very much above or anywhere in between. But the conservative selects out of this infinity of possibilities a single one: that the employer's notch is just above the employee's. And the conservative economist then proceeds to balance his entire argument on that blade.

When empirical economists in fact went out and showed that there was a gap between the notches in labor markets and that in some cases an increase in the minimum wage created no job losses,[14] conservative economists were at a loss. One Nobel Prize winner published an editorial accusing the empiricists of rejecting the

[14] David Card & Alan B. Krueger, *Minimum Wages and Employment: A Case Study of the Fast-Food Industry in New Jersey and Pennsylvania*, 84 Am. Econ. Rev. 772 (1994).

laws of supply and demand.[15] This they had not done. They had merely shown that the labor market works in the same way as theory predicts that virtually every market should: that there is a gap between what buyers will pay and what sellers will accept – and that price may safely be renegotiated within that gap in order to do distributive justice.

2 The Abuse of Incentives Arguments

Sometimes economists who have not spent enough time interrogating the foundations of their economic models will try to deny the importance of the gap by arguing that the greater the amount of surplus that one offers to a particular party – say, a seller – the greater the party's incentive to conclude a transaction.[16] The implication is that any price other than the one that allocates all of the surplus to the party requiring the incentive will reduce the likelihood that a transaction will take place and therefore be inefficient.[17] The trouble with this argument is that it selectively departs from the simplifying assumption of rationality upon which economists otherwise feel quite comfortable relying. If a seller would obtain a certain amount of pleasure from consuming a good and is presented with the opportunity to receive a greater amount in compensation for selling the good, then a rational seller would accept the compensation, whether the net gain to the seller is small or large.[18] A rational seller should be willing to transact whether his share of the surplus is great or vanishingly small. If in fact he is less likely to transact in return for a smaller share, then he is not a rational actor. The calculus would be different were the seller given a choice between obtaining different amounts of surplus. In that case, the seller would, of course, choose the larger amount, and, in this sense, more would be required to induce the seller to sell. But the question we face is that of determining how much surplus might be needed to induce the seller to sell if we limit the seller's options. If we can impose a single price on the seller, how high must it be to avoid discouraging the transaction? The answer is that the price need be only slightly higher than the seller's notch – only slightly higher than his costs.

Even if we reject the assumption that buyers and sellers are rational, and consider actual human behavior, we do not find that more gain translates into a greater incentive to transact. Rather, it is self-evident that the motivational gains from

[15] James M. Buchanan & Merton H. Miller, *Minimum Wage Addendum*, WSJ, Apr. 25, 1996, at A20.

[16] *See* Richard M. Brunell, *Appropriability in Antitrust: How Much Is Enough?*, 69 ANTITRUST L.J. 1 (2001).

[17] These arguments are often arbitrarily asymmetric. The economist assumes that the seller needs an incentive to sell but not that the buyer needs an incentive to buy. As a result, these arguments arbitrarily support giving the full surplus to the seller rather than splitting it or giving it all to the buyer.

[18] *See* VARIAN, *supra* note 12, at 334 ("[T]he firm chooses a production plan so as to maximize its profits.").

increasing rewards fall over time until further increases have no effect.[19] We can take account of any additional rewards that do have a motivational effect by increasing the seller's notch to take them into account. That is, we can treat them as necessary to compensate the seller for the pain of giving up the good. They become a part of the seller's costs. Once the notch is adjusted, we can once again say that it reflects the amount of payment required to induce the seller to transact. But we have no reason to suppose that this adjustment must eliminate all of the freedom that we have to divide up the gains from trade. In other words, we have no reason to suppose that, after increasing the seller's notch, the gap between the seller's notch and the buyer's will disappear and the two will be coextensive in every market. There will still be gains from trade and so there will still be freedom to redistribute them without harming efficiency. (A similar analysis can be carried out in the case in which the economist argues that the buyer requires all of the surplus in order to be induced to buy – although economists rarely make this sort of argument.[20])

3 Interlude on the Rationality Assumption as a Red Herring for Progressives

The ability of the progressive to charge the economist with ignoring the assumption of rationality when the economist argues that more surplus means more incentive to transact is one way in which the progressive gains power from engaging with economics rather than fleeing from it. Engaging with economics enables the progressive to point out instances in which the economist misapplies his own concepts. The critical legal studies movement called such misapplications the "abuse of deduction."[21] The progressive who flees economics gives up the opportunity to show that economists fail to abide by their own rationality assumption.

Progressives sometimes argue that they can safely ignore the rationality assumption – and forego the opportunity to demonstrate how conservatives abuse it – because the assumption is unrealistic.[22] But this reflects a misunderstanding of the role that the assumption of rationality plays in conservative economic thought. The assumption of rationality is not a claim about how people behave in fact. Rather, it is an expression of respect for individual liberty. The conservative economist accepts that people do not always make decisions that are in their best interests, as the rationality assumption insists. We become enraged; we self-destruct; we sacrifice for others; we become confused; we are seduced; we make mistakes. For economists,

[19] This is the basis for the assumption commonly made by economists that there is declining marginal utility of wealth. *See* Sarah B. Lawsky, *On the Edge: Declining Marginal Utility and Tax Policy*, 95 MINN. L. REV. 904, 905 (2011).

[20] *See supra* text of note 17.

[21] *See* Duncan Kennedy, *The Hermeneutic of Suspicion in Contemporary American Legal Thought*, 25 LAW & CRITIQUE 91, 99 (July 2014) (borrowing the phrase from Francois Geny).

[22] *See, e.g.*, Christine Jolls et al., *A Behavioral Approach to Law and Economics*, 50 STAN. L. REV. 1471, 1476 (1998).

that is beside the point, however in their view, liberty requires that policymakers *pretend* that people are rational. To assume that people act in their own best interests is to treat them with dignity. It is to assume that they know best what pleases them. It is to accord weight to their choices. It is to choose liberty over paternalism. The appeal of the assumption of rationality to economists is not descriptive, but normative. When the progressive rejects the rationality assumption, the progressive rejects individual liberty. As already observed, that puts progressives out of step with the spirit of a godless age.[23]

The progressive may reply that he is no enemy of liberty, but believes that buyers and sellers make better choices at the ballot box than in markets the regulations for which people freely vote are a better indicator of what people want than are their purchase decisions in markets. Therefore, if the progressive can convince a legislature to support his proposed interventions in markets, he implements the will of the people instead of substituting his own will for theirs. Never mind that in recent decades progressives have had great difficulty convincing legislatures to support intervention in markets.[24]

The economist can defeat this reply, however, because he can repurpose all of the progressive's arguments for the irrationality of buyers and sellers to demonstrate the irrationality of voters. They are swayed by politicians. They are cognitively impaired. They make mistakes. The implication is that the people cannot be trusted to vote any more than they can be trusted to buy or sell. Even if people happen to vote for progressive intervention in markets, how can the progressive be sure that the vote reflects the people's true preferences? If the progressive protests that this should not matter so long as the people choose progressive policies, then he finds himself implicitly endorsing an enlightened dictatorship. Someone will need to make sure that a manipulable populace chooses the right policies. The only alternative is for the progressive to surrender to the conservative by embracing the assumption of rationality on normative grounds. The progressive ought to do the latter, because the progressive shares the economist's respect for the dignity of the individual. Unfortunately, he too often flees economics, conceding, as we have already observed, the moral high ground to economists.

By contrast, when the progressive accepts the assumption of rationality and engages with economics, good things follow. The freedom of the progressive to choose any distribution of the gains from trade is, as we have just seen, consistent with the assumption of rationality. By embedding his arguments in economic theory, the progressive shows that the economist's (and his own) commitment to individual liberty is in fact consistent with the redistribution of wealth.

4 More on the Difficulty of Denying the Existence of Gains from Trade

All this works only if there is in fact a gap between the notches. For a transaction to take place, the buyer's notch must be at or above the seller's. If the buyer's notch is

[23] *See* Ramsi A. Woodcock, *Wealth and Happiness*, What Am I Missing? (Jan. 14, 2023), https://perma.cc/SD9A-GYGZ.

[24] *See* Kearney & Merrill, *supra* note 6, at 1329–63.

above the seller's, then we have a gap and room for justice. If the buyer's notch is at the level of the seller's, then there can be only one price at which the buyer and seller transact – a price at the level of the notches (Figure 1.5). And because in this case the notches are coextensive, there will be no gains from trade and so nothing for the progressive to distribute. In this case, the requirement of efficiency fully determines economic outcomes. But this case does not represent a model of the world that an economist would ever seriously espouse, for it is a world in which economic activity promises nothing for society. There must be gains from trade for economic activity to be desirable.

Indeed, in this world there would be no guarantee that the buyer and seller would ever transact because there would be no gains from trade available to induce them to transact. At a price equal to the buyer's notch, the buyer is indifferent between transacting and not because he pays out a price exactly equal to the value he places on the good. And at a price equal to the seller's notch, the seller is indifferent between transacting and not because he receives a price exactly equal to his cost of selling the good.

5 Uncertainty about Costs to Sellers or Benefits to Buyers and the Problem of Regulatory Capture

It should be clear from the foregoing that the economist who wishes to deny scope for distributive justice in economics faces a daunting challenge, because a space for efficient redistribution lies between the notches in virtually every transaction. An economist hoping to hold on to the view that redistribution precludes transactions will typically respond that progressives do not know with certainty what a seller's costs might be or what the maximum price that a buyer is willing to pay might be. Progressives do not know exactly where the notches are located. As a result, there is always a danger that the progressive might dictate a price that falls outside of the notches, precluding a transaction. Indeed, the more the progressive dictates prices, the more likely it becomes that the progressive will make such a mistake. Intervention in markets therefore harms efficiency after all.

It is true that the progressive cannot initially know where the notches lie, and that creates a risk that he will preclude transactions. But he can learn by doing, much the way an engine builder learns, over time, how to maximize an engine's output without making it explode. The progressive dictates an initial price and observes the outcome. If the seller leaves the market, the price is too low, and the progressive increases it. If the seller flourishes, the price may be too high – it may redistribute too little to the buyer – and the progressive reduces the price. In this way, through a process of negotiation with the seller, the progressive learns what prices redistribute without precluding transactions. Buyers and sellers go through the same process when they negotiate with each other. The seller may initially quote a price that the buyer cannot afford. Over time, the parties learn what prices make trade between them possible. So long as the progressive is no less likely to choose viable prices than buyers and sellers negotiating privately, the progressive's intervention in the market will not harm efficiency.

The conservative will respond that the progressive will, however, be less likely to choose viable prices than would the buyer and seller negotiating privately in a free market because in practice the progressive will delegate the task to a government official. And that official may be purchased by a special interest. Unfortunately, progressives who flee from economics often fail to appreciate the importance of this argument. It calls into question all progressive interventions in markets by suggesting that they are subject to the same market forces that progressives hope to avoid through regulation. Progressives' inability to engage with this argument has rendered virtually all of the arguments for greater regulation that they have deployed in recent years without real force.[25]

That is a shame because this capture argument is highly vulnerable when considered in its own, economic terms. For while the argument suggests that the progressive may not get the redistribution he wants, it does not suggest that any transactions will be precluded – and the conservative professes to care only about enabling transactions. No transactions will be precluded, even if the regulator is captured, because the special interests that have the greatest investment in the market, and are therefore most likely to capture it, are those of the buyer and seller themselves. But both the buyer and the seller have an interest in finding prices that facilitate transactions – so that each can appropriate for himself all of the surplus that transactions create. It follows that whoever controls the regulator will strive to dictate prices that encourage transactions. The prices will favor either the buyer or the seller (depending upon which has captured the regulator), rather than the public, thereby frustrating the progressive's aim of redistributing wealth. But the prices will not preclude transactions.

The conservative may try to argue that the buyer and the seller will waste resources in trying to capture the regulator, but the conservative ignores that the buyer and the seller will at the same time save resources that they might otherwise have used to bargain directly with each other over price in an unregulated market. To the extent that regulators are subject to capture, the locus of price negotiation shifts, but the cost of such negotiations does not necessarily change. The greatest threat to regulation is that special interest capture will thwart redistribution, returning markets to the status quo. It will not, however, harm efficiency – and efficiency is, again, all that the conservative professes to care about. Capture threatens the progressive's project, not the conservative's. But the progressive will persevere so long as he believes that capture will not always be complete or effective.

[25] *See* Woodcock, *A Progressive Critique of the Law and Political Economy Movement*, *supra* note 10.

III THE FAILED ATTEMPT TO USE MARGINALISM TO DENY THE GAINS FROM TRADE

A *The Attempt*

Perhaps the most important way in which conservative economics has sought to flee from the basic fact of the gap between the notches is through a strong form of marginalism – specifically, the view that the valuations of the marginal buyer and seller coincide, and that competition renders price uniform within a market. If that view holds, then the marginal buyer and seller can transact only at a single, unique price and any progressive attempt to change price for any other buyer and seller in the market will change price for the marginal buyer and seller, preventing them from transacting. Intervening in markets turns out to be inefficient after all.[26]

Let us take a closer look at this argument. The conservative concedes that there is a gap between the notches for every buyer and seller in the market – except for one buyer and seller. This unique pair consists of the marginal buyer and seller. As a general matter, a buyer and seller are marginal if the buyer places the lowest value on the good of any buyer in the market and the seller places the highest value on the good of any seller in the market. Their notches are the closest together of any buyer or seller in the market, but need not coincide. Any change in price will preclude them from transacting before it precludes any other buyer and seller from transacting (this is why they are called *marginal*). But small price changes, which fall within the gap between their valuations (their notches), will not prevent them from transacting. (For simplicity, the discussion in this Introduction assumes that each unit has a unique seller and buyer. But the argument applies with equal force to markets in which a particular seller may sell more than one unit of the good and a particular buyer may buy more than one unit of the good. In that case, one speaks of a marginal unit rather than a marginal buyer and seller.)

The conservative imposes a further requirement: that the marginal buyer and seller's valuations not only be the closest together of any buyer and seller but so close that they exactly coincide. The conservative assumes that the notches of the marginal buyer and seller are located at precisely the same point. When the buyer's notch and seller's notch precisely coincide, the buyer and seller can transact only at one price: the price that precisely equals the common valuation that they place on the good. Any other price will be either too high for the buyer or too low for the seller. Price must be at the same level as their notches. It follows that an increase or decrease in price of *any* amount will drive the marginal buyer and seller from the market. Only a single unique price is capable of keeping them in the market and therefore of keeping the market efficient (Figure 1.5).

As we have already noted, it is difficult to believe that the valuations of any particular buyer and seller would ever happen to coincide. Lightning never strikes

[26] This argument is rehearsed in every mainstream intermediate economics textbook, mostly in implicit fashion, in sections on the inefficiency of taxation. *See, e.g.*, Varian, *supra* note 12, at 301.

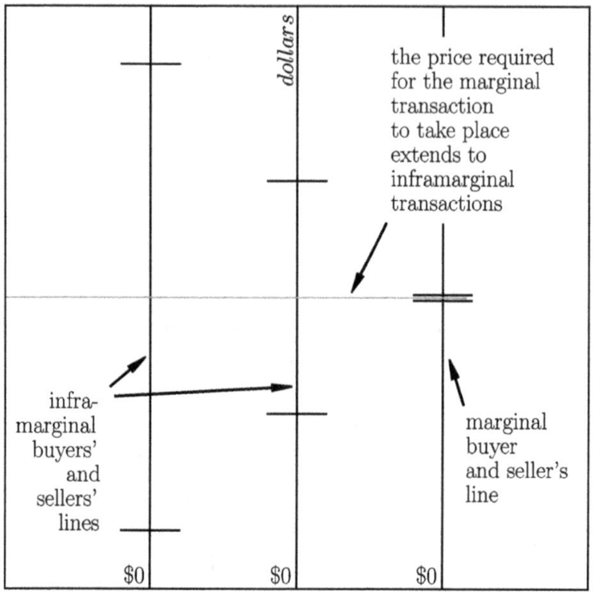

FIGURE 1.6 Competition causes the price required for the marginal transaction to take place to govern inframarginal transactions as well

the same spot twice. The conservative's response is to concede that this is true for nearly all buyers and sellers in any given market, but to insist that in every market there is nevertheless one buyer and one seller for whom valuations do, in fact, coincide. The conservative's case for this concession is that if a market is large enough, sheer chance will be sufficient to ensure that at least one buyer's notch will equal a seller's – or at least be sufficiently close to render the gap between the notches of no policy significance. If you randomly make two marks on a line over and over, the argument goes, a moment will eventually come when you will draw both marks on top of each other – or at least very close to each other. Given enough time, lightning does strike the same spot twice. By assuming that markets are in general very large – indeed, to really make the argument, *infinitely* large – the conservative can recover at least one buyer and one seller in any given market for which valuations coincide.

Once he has achieved this concession, the conservative then deploys the logic of competition, which drives all prices charged in a market to the same level, to argue that the unique price at which the marginal buyer and seller must transact must also be the price at which all other buyers and sellers in the market – the "inframarginal" buyers and sellers – including those with widely divergent valuations, transact (Figure 1.6). It then follows that any attempt to redistribute wealth by changing the prices at which buyers and sellers with divergent valuations transact must change the price at which the marginal buyer and seller transact. But because the marginal

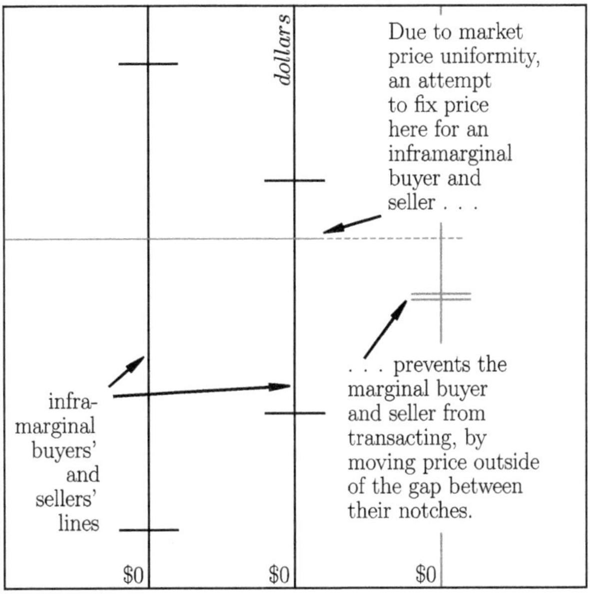

FIGURE 1.7 In a competitive market, altering price for an inframarginal transaction also alters price for the marginal buyer and seller, preventing them from transacting

buyer and seller can only transact at the single unique price that coincides with the unique valuation that they both put on the good, any price change will drive them from the market. Any price change will preclude their transaction and will therefore be inefficient (Figure 1.7). Thus, the assumption that the marginal buyer and seller have the same valuation, combined with the view that competition imposes a uniform price on the market, rescues for the conservative the contention that attempts by progressives to dictate prices will preclude transactions. In this way, the conservative snatches victory from the jaws of defeat.

Inframarginalism's name is a response to this attempt by conservatives to deny the freedom to redistribute gains from trade. Marginalism in the strong form identified here is the view that there is a unique price required for the marginal buyer and seller to transact and that this price must be the price at which all market participants transact. Inframarginalism is the view that the prices at which all other market participants transact can and should vary from that at which the marginal buyer and seller transact.

Let us look more closely at the role of competition in the argument that the gain from trade cannot be redistributed. Why exactly do conservatives believe that competition renders price uniform for the entire market, such that any attempt to change price for a particular buyer and seller would change it for all buyers and sellers, including the inframarginal buyer and seller? The answer is not really clear. Economists love to assume that competition renders price uniform. They say that it makes all market participants into "price takers." But they have never been able to give a good argument about why that must be the case, as some economists themselves have acknowledged.[27]

What economists have in the backs of their minds might be a story like this. In a competitive market, buyers and sellers have good information about the prices at which other buyers and sellers are going to transact. Buyers hold out for the lowest price that any other buyer will receive and sellers hold out for the highest price that any other buyer will receive. As already observed, when the marginal buyer and seller place the same value on the good, there is a unique price at which they must transact. All the other buyers observe that price and insist on paying a price that is at least as low. All other sellers observe that price and insist on receiving a price that is at least as high. As a result, the only price that any of them can agree upon will be the price at which the marginal buyer and seller transact.

There is still no guarantee, however, that buyers and sellers will agree on that price. Indeed, economists have long recognized that there is never really any guarantee that any given buyer and seller will transact, because each may always wish to hold out for a more favorable price.[28] A buyer may wish to negotiate a price below that at which the marginal buyer and seller transact, and he may therefore refuse the entreaties of all sellers to sell at that price. If no seller changes his position, then the buyer will never transact – so long as he continues stubbornly to insist on a lower price. To maintain that trade will in fact occur, economists further assume that in a competitive market the number of buyers and sellers is so large that buyers can always find sellers who are willing to sell at the price at which the marginal buyer and seller transact and sellers can always find buyers who are willing to buy at the price at which the marginal buyer and seller transact. This eliminates the incentive of any buyer or seller to hold out for a different price, since the business will always simply go to another buyer or seller if the buyer or seller continues to hold out. It follows that no buyer or seller will hold out for a different price and all possible transactions will take place at a single, uniform price equal to the price at which the marginal buyer and seller transact. Thus, the

[27] David M. Kreps, A Course in Microeconomic Theory 315 (1990). Economists will sometimes rest the argument for price uniformity on the assumption that government officials will fail effectively to enforce the prices that they dictate. For example, economists sometimes argue that if the government dictates a high price to a particular buyer, the buyer will buy from other buyers to whom the government has not dictated a high price or from black market sellers who have found a way to evade the price regulation. *See* Ramsi A. Woodcock, *Personalized Pricing as Monopolization*, 51 Conn. L. Rev. 311, 333–34 (2019); Ramsi A. Woodcock, *The Case against Surge Pricing*, 76 U.C.L.J. — (2025) (forthcoming), https://osf.io/preprints/socarxiv/g8tym/. As a result, the price actually paid by all buyers remains the original uniform price. Buyers will have difficulty evading regulated prices in digital markets in which there is no anonymity. *See* Ramsi A. Woodcock, *Big Data, Price Discrimination, and Antitrust*, 68 Hastings L.J. 1371, 1406–7 (2017); Ramsi Woodcock, *Personalizing Prices to Redistribute Wealth in Antitrust and Public Utility Rate Regulation*, 2022 Wis. L. Rev. 1408, 1412–17 (2022). And all markets are becoming digital.

[28] *See* Robert Cooter, *The Cost of Coase*, 11 J. Legal Stud. 1, 17 (1982).

economist's argument for uniformity of price comes down to the assumption that buyers and sellers have perfect information about prices and that there are so many buyers and sellers (really, for the argument to work, buyers and sellers must be infinite in number) that transactions always occur.

We have an argument for why price must be uniform when it is at the level required for the marginal buyer and seller to transact. Must it remain uniform when the progressive dictates a new price to a particular buyer and seller in the market? If it does not, then a progressive market intervention will not affect the price at which the marginal buyer and seller transact and so progressive market intervention will not preclude transactions, contrary to what the conservative wishes to argue. The economist's argument that price must change uniformly is that when a progressive dictates a new price to a particular buyer and seller, the other buyers or sellers adjust their negotiating positions to reflect the new price, and because the new price is not the unique price that the marginal buyer and seller require to transact, at least one transaction is precluded, rendering the price change inefficient. If the progressive dictates a higher price, for example, all the other sellers, including the marginal seller, insist on receiving a higher price too. In order to transact, all the other buyers, including the marginal buyer, must now agree to pay the higher price. But because the marginal buyer is not willing to pay a higher price, but all sellers now insist upon it, the marginal buyer and seller will fail to transact.[29]

[29] One might ask why the marginal buyer and seller would feel compelled either to transact at the higher price or not to transact at all. One might suppose that in order for the two to have been willing to transact in the absence of a regulated price, they would have needed to be aware that they place a common valuation on the good. Otherwise, the buyer might have insisted on a price that was too low for the seller or the seller might have insisted upon a price that was too high for the buyer. But if the marginal buyer and seller are aware that they place a common value on the good, why would they feel compelled to follow the crowd and insist upon a price dictated by the progressive to a different buyer and seller when they know that such a price would prevent them from transacting at all?

The answer is that we have made a simplifying assumption that is not really required for the argument about price uniformity to hold. That assumption is that the marginal buyer and seller transact *with each other*. In fact, the marginal buyer might just as well buy from any other seller, and the marginal seller might just as well sell to any other buyer. In order for both the marginal buyer and the marginal seller to transact with *anyone*, price must just equal the common valuation that both the marginal buyer and the marginal seller place on the good. If price is higher, then the marginal buyer will not be able to transact with anyone. And if price is lower, then the marginal seller will not be able to sell to anyone. So we arrive back at the same conclusion at which we arrive when we assume that the marginal buyer and seller transact with each other. Assuming that they do simplifies the narrative, but it also obscures the fact that it is not necessary to assume that the marginal buyer must be able to identify the marginal seller or vice versa in order for both to transact. Both can transact with any counterpart, whether marginal or inframarginal. It follows that when the progressive increases the price, there is no guarantee that the seller with whom the marginal buyer deals will know that the marginal buyer is unwilling to pay the higher price. Even if the seller knew that, the assumption that there are infinite buyers in the market means that the seller will be able to find some other buyer who is willing to pay the higher price, so the seller has no incentive to compromise and pay the lower price demanded by the marginal buyer.

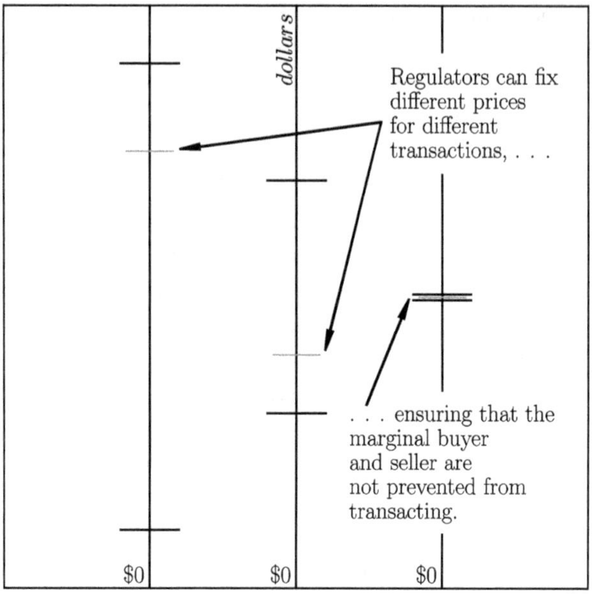

FIGURE 1.8 In actual markets, regulators can alter price for an inframarginal transaction without altering price for the marginal buyer and seller

B *Critique*

The trouble with the view that price cannot be regulated without precluding the marginal buyer and seller from transacting is that the assumptions required to maintain it are heroic. Consider a price increase dictated by a progressive government. Let us grant that buyers and sellers will tend to be informed about any regulated price dictated by progressives to the marginal buyer and seller. There is no reason to suppose that sellers will all insist on selling at the same price. And even if they do all insist at first on selling at the same price, there is no reason to suppose

More generally, when the progressive dictates a new price, either the marginal buyer or the marginal seller will be priced out of the market, but both need not be. If the progressive dictates a higher price, then the marginal buyer surely will not be able to pay and will leave the market. But the marginal seller will be happy to sell at the higher price and if he can find a buyer he will sell. Because the marginal buyer must leave the market, a seller must be forced out too, for lack of a buyer, but any seller may be forced out. (In the context of markets of infinite size, we encounter one of the paradoxes of infinity, which is that every seller can find a buyer who is willing to pay the higher price but at the same time there must be one seller in the market who is unable to transact because there is one buyer who cannot do a deal at the higher price and the number of buyers and sellers in the market must be equal (while also being infinite).) A similar argument holds in the case of a buyer when the progressive dictates a lower price.

that they will all be willing to hold out for that price ad infinitum. The marginal buyer will, therefore, be able to find a seller somewhere in the market who is willing to sell at the lower price that the marginal buyer is willing to pay (Figure 1.8). Sellers will have no incentive to hold out for the higher price ad infinitum because buyers are finite in number and sellers will not always be able to find another buyer who will accept the higher price if the marginal buyer refuses to pay it. Lacking alternatives, they will do business with the marginal buyer on his terms.

And even if sellers do all hold out ad infinitum, motivated purely by the vain hope that the marginal buyer will accept the higher price, there is no reason to suppose that this will be because the progressive intervened to raise price for a particular inframarginal buyer and seller. Sellers might have been willing to hold out ad infinitum anyway. Recall that economists acknowledge that buyers and sellers may squabble indefinitely over the proper division of the surplus, effectively precluding them from transacting, and that the only way to assume this problem away is to imagine that markets have infinite numbers of buyers and sellers – which, of course, they do not. The marginal buyer may be priced out of the market anyway due to the intransigence of sellers, quite regardless of whether the progressive intervenes to dictate a price to any particular group of market participants.

Similar arguments can be made in the case of a price *decrease* dictated by a progressive. There is no reason to suppose that when the progressive dictates prices to buyers and sellers the price changes will propagate to other corners of the market and prevent the marginal buyer and seller from transacting. Moreover, because the economist's assumption that the marginal buyer and seller place the same value on the good is itself unreasonable, the progressive can also change the price at which the marginal buyer and seller transact without driving them from the market either. Notwithstanding the best efforts of generations of conservative economists, the gains from trade remain a magical space in which progressives can do justice without harming efficiency.

C *A Note about the Partial Equilibrium Framework Employed Here*

I have presented the idea that there is space for justice within the economic system in a partial equilibrium framework.[30] It is a partial equilibrium framework because I have not taken account of the fact that the distribution of the surplus generated by a transaction changes the maximum a buyer is willing to

[30] *See* Eugene Silberberg, The Structure of Economics: A Mathematical Analysis 491 (2d ed. 1990).

pay or the maximum a seller is willing to accept. But the distribution of the surplus does in fact change the locations of the buyer's and seller's notches. The price the buyer pays in a transaction represents other goods that the buyer cannot purchase, and the amount the seller receives in a transaction represents goods the seller can now purchase. A buyer with a tighter budget may be willing to pay less for any particular good, and a seller with a looser budget may be willing to pay more for any particular good. So if, as a result of a decrease in price, a buyer obtains a smaller share of the surplus and the seller a larger share, then the buyer's notch might fall and the seller's might rise. Based on these changes, the buyer and seller might wish further to renegotiate the price at which they transact. If, for example, the buyer's notch falls below the original price, renegotiation will be required to ensure that the transaction takes place. The renegotiated price will itself feed back once again into new locations for the parties' notches and further renegotiation. This cycle need not go on forever – at some point the parties' notches may no longer shift or the parties may not wish to renegotiate price after a shift. But to be able to say whether a price change precludes a transaction, we must look at the final equilibrium. It is not enough simply to pick a price between the parties' original notches and assume that the transaction will take place or that the distribution of surplus implied by the price in relation to the original notches will be the actual distribution that will prevail once follow-on changes in the notches and the price are taken into account.

Despite these problems with the partial equilibrium framework, everything that I have said in the partial equilibrium context applies with equal force in the general equilibrium context. In particular, even in the general equilibrium context, there is complete freedom to redistribute gains from trade without harming efficiency. In the language of general equilibrium, there is a contract curve of efficient bargains and these exhaust all possible levels of utility that each party may enjoy consistent with carrying out the transaction.[31] By choosing the right (not always uniform) prices, policymakers can induce the parties to strike any of those bargains.[32]

[31] *See id.* at 579.

[32] General equilibrium provides the intellectual basis for a much more sweeping form of efficient redistribution than that described here: namely, the redistribution of endowments as opposed to gains from trade. Endowments determine the value that buyers and sellers place on products, so they ultimately determine the gains from trade and to some extent the distribution thereof. The Second Fundamental Theorem of Welfare Economics, a core tenet of neoclassical economics, holds that, if certain standard neoclassical assumptions hold, all distributions of endowments are efficient. *See* Varian, *supra* note 12, at 586–88. The implication is that government can engage in massive redistribution of property without harming efficiency. *See* Woodcock, *A Progressive Critique of the Law and Political Economy Movement*, *supra* note 10.

IV THE PAPERS COLLECTED IN THIS VOLUME

A *Inframarginalist Papers*

Inframarginalism is a new name for an old idea. The concepts of the gains from trade, surplus, and rents are at least as old as the early nineteenth-century classical economist David Ricardo.[33] Progressive lawyer-economists of the late nineteenth and early twentieth centuries recognized that these concepts created distributive freedom and used them to argue successfully for what became pillars of the New Deal state: price regulation, taxation, and unionization.[34] Unfortunately, this tradition was almost completely disrupted by the rise of conservative, Chicago School law and economics in the 1970s and 1980s – so much so that progressives all but forgot that neoclassical economics had once been a key progressive intellectual asset. Inframarginal analysis nevertheless remained an important component of a core subfield of neoclassical economics known as welfare economics, which occupies a central place in undergraduate and graduate economics curricula to this day.[35] Unfortunately, in the hands of conservative economists, the radical implications of welfare economics are often downplayed or ignored.[36] A self-consciously radical form of inframarginalism experienced a limited revival in the 1980s and 1990s, however, in the form of the "left law and economics" practiced by the Critical Legal Studies movement.[37]

This volume reflects a rekindling of interest in inframarginalism among progressives incident to a broader resurgence of progressive interest in the problem of wealth distribution over the past fifteen years. Unlike in the case of both the original progressive movement of a century ago and Critical Legal Studies, however, inframarginalism has not (yet) played a central role in the Yale flavor of the law and political economy movement – scholars associated with the Law and Political

[33] David Ricardo, Principles of Political Economy and Taxation 45–57 (Prometheus Books 1996).

[34] *See* Barbara H. Fried, The Progressive Assault on Laissez Faire: Robert Hale and the First Law and Economics Movement (Harvard University Press 1998).

[35] *See* Andreu Mas-Colell et al., Microeconomic Theory 545–73 (Oxford University Press 1995).

[36] *See, e.g.*, Varian, *supra* note 12, at 415 ("Often economic rents exist because of legal restrictions on entry into the industry.").

[37] *See* Duncan Kennedy, *Law-and-Economics from the Perspective of Critical Legal Studies, in* The New Palgrave Dictionary of Economics and the Law 465 (Peter Newman ed., Palgrave Macmillan UK 2002). For a recent paper that captures the spirit of the left law and economics approach, see Duncan Kennedy, *Law Distributes I: Ricardo Marx CLS* (Feb. 24, 2021), https://perma.cc/NED4-K8UT.

Economy Project,[38] its blog,[39] and manifesto[40] – which has dominated progressive debates over inequality in recent years. Indeed, Yale flavor law and political economy has often seemed unaware of the central role of inframarginalism in progressive intellectual history.[41] The papers collected in this volume, many of which were presented at or grew out of Inframarginalism & Internet, a conference held online on February 18 and 19, 2021, reflect both the promise of inframarginalism and its contested character in the present resurgence of progressive economic thought.[42]

Some of the contributions to this volume are squarely inframarginalist, although their authors do not always use that term to describe their work. In *A New Corporate Tax*, Reuven Avi-Yonah argues that the American corporate tax should be reformed to achieve the original vision of its creators, which was to tax rents. This can be done, he argues, by eliminating the current flat corporate tax rate and replacing it with a tax "set at zero for normal returns" (which reflect the cost of capital and so do not constitute rents) and set "at a sharply progressive rate for supernormal returns (rents)."

In *An Inframarginalist Argument for Mandating the Use of Pro-Consumer Boilerplate*, Michael Guttentag argues that boilerplate in consumer contracts often constitutes an implicit inframarginal price increase, redistributing surplus from consumers to firms. The implication is that boilerplate can be proscribed, and consumers favored, without precluding any transactions. Indeed, as Guttentag argues, removing boilerplate might improve efficiency. Removing it would eliminate "wasteful investment in efforts to include and enforce these kinds of provisions." Such investments are wasteful because, given boilerplate's character as an inframarginal price, the purpose of such investments is purely to redistribute surplus from consumers to firms rather than to produce more surplus.

In *Taxing Imputed Land Rent: A Historical Perspective and a (Modest) Contemporary Proposal*, Faisal Chaudhry takes on one of the most famous examples of inframarginal pricing: land prices, for which the game for both buyer and seller is to negotiate a transaction-specific price that maximizes his share of the gains from trade. Chaudhry argues that taxing the rent that homeowners implicitly pay themselves when they live in the homes they own is a better way of redistributing surpluses associated with land ownership than is the property tax system, which is the traditional method of taxation of land values. Because the value of a piece of

[38] *The Law and Political Economy Project*, LPE Project, https://lpeproject.org/ (last visited July 21, 2024).

[39] *Law and Political Economy Blog*, LPE Project, https://lpeproject.org/blog/ (last visited July 21, 2024).

[40] Britton-Purdy et al., *supra* note 2.

[41] Woodcock, *A Progressive Critique of the Law and Political Economy Movement*, *supra* note 10. For a critique of the progressive antimonopoly movement, which has shown a similar lack of understanding of inframarginalism, see Ramsi Woodcock, *The Progressive Case against Antimonopolism* (June 11, 2021), https://osf.io/jgucv.

[42] *Inframarginalism & Internet: The Distributive Perspective on Internet Governance*, https://inframarginalism.net/.

land is no more than the flow of rents that can be charged for its use, taxing the rents that can be imputed to homeowners who live in their properties amounts to the same thing as directly taxing the value of their properties. But the taxation of imputed rents has the advantage of being a tax on income that could be implemented at the federal level using rent data rather than property value assessments. This would avoid some of the problems associated with the current property tax system.

In *Inframarginalism and the Distributive Corollary of the Coase Theorem*, Matthew Dimick addresses a famous objection to the use of legal rules to redistribute gains from trade. According to the "double-distortion argument," the best way to redistribute gains from trade is by taxing them when they appear as income earned by individuals rather than when they are generated through transactions in other markets. That is because, according to this argument, taxing gains from trade when they are generated in other markets creates inefficiency in those markets and also alters individuals' incomes, creating further inefficiency in labor markets. According to this argument, taxation is never purely inframarginal but rather always harms efficiency to some extent. But despite this defect it remains the most efficient way to redistribute wealth. Dimick rejects the double-distortion argument. He shows that, even if we accept the view that taxation is never purely inframarginal and hence always causes some inefficiency, we do not need to accept that income taxation is always more efficient than other approaches. That is because the only way to distinguish gains from trade (which can be taxed) from costs of production (which should not be taxed) is by actually imposing a tax in the market in which the gains from trade are generated and observing the extent to which the tax precludes transactions. Tax authorities cannot generate this information through income taxation alone, however, because income taxes are imposed only on labor markets. It follows that tax authorities lack sufficient information to set the efficient income tax rate and might do a better job taxing other markets directly.

In *Self-Colonization in American Law: The Internet and Personal Information Example*, Daniel Greenwood marries a comprehensive critique of contemporary American political economy with an argument for property rights in personal information as "a small reform." Greenwood's paper is a good example of inframarginalism as internal critique. Throughout his sweeping tour of American economic policy failures, Greenwood leverages neoclassical economic models to show how contemporary policy operates to redistribute gains from trade from poor to rich. Given widespread public support for many of these policies, they are, in Greenwood's view, a kind of self-colonization.

In *The Progressive Case against Antimonopolism*, I argue that the current progressive love affair with antimonopolism is misguided because firms can appropriate a vast share of the gains from trade even when prices are perfectly competitive. I argue that progressive interest in antimonopolism is an unfortunate consequence of a combination of American anti-statism, pressure by the news industry for antitrust action against social media competitors, and progressives' frustration at being unable to influence tax policy as a political matter.

B *Inframarginalism-Adjacent Papers*

Another set of papers collected in this volume are inframarginalism-adjacent. They are deeply concerned with problems of wealth inequality or wealth redistribution but do not explicitly embed their arguments in the concept of gains from trade framed in neoclassical economic terms. They do not, in other words, appeal directly to the gap between the notches – a fact that does not detract from their quality.

In *(How) Does Competition Law Address Quality?*, Adrian Kuenzler argues that product quality is key to understanding the consequences of monopolization in tech markets in which products are distributed to consumers for free. Monopoly power enables firms to restrict the quality of the free services that they offer, reducing the value that consumers are able to appropriate from those services and hence the share of the gains from trade that they can extract from tech markets. In *The EU Regulatory Patchwork for Dark Patterns: An Illustration of an Inframarginal Revolution in European Law?*, Inge Graef looks at another problem that is closely related at an analytic level to that of product quality: dark patterns, which are digital techniques of manipulating consumers into acquiring products that they do not actually prefer. If we think about dark patterns as causing consumers to acquire products that have a quality level that is lower than what consumers expect (as a consequence of dark patterns' manipulative function), we see that dark patterns are a subcategory of the broader problem of firm manipulation of product quality to appropriate gains from trade. Graef surveys attempts by European regulators to limit the use of dark patterns.

In *Distributive Consequences of Regulating Boilerplate: Between Price Effects and Socialization of Risk*, Przemysław Pałka frames the problem of redistribution via consumer contracts in terms of insurance. Insurance deserves to play a much more important role in inframarginalist thought than it has so far because insurance is redistribution, albeit with a soft touch. Ex ante, no one knows whether he will prove to be lucky (and hence a victim of redistribution via insurance) or unlucky (and hence a beneficiary of redistribution via insurance). So insurance can attract support both from those who ultimately benefit from it and from those who do not. Perhaps for this reason, social insurance programs have proven to be the most enduring legacy of the New Deal state, persisting long after redistribution via price regulation and taxation was dismantled or rolled back.[43] Pałka deploys the insurance frame to argue that government regulation of standard terms in consumer contracts implicitly forces consumers to buy insurance. When the government bans class action waivers, for example, the government enables consumers to obtain redress in

[43] *Compare* David A. Moss, When All Else Fails: Government as the Ultimate Risk Manager 180–216 (Harvard University Press 2002); *with* Kearney & Merrill, *supra* note 6, at 1329–63.

the event that the manufacturer causes harm. The cost of this insurance is the higher price paid by all consumers for the product. Pałka argues that such insurance has progressive distributive effects because the poor have more to gain from insurance in consumer transactions.

In *Is Commodity Private Property Inherently Regressive?*, Zviko Chadambuka argues that the institution of property itself creates wealth inequality. The core of his argument is that because the poor value income more than the rich, they tend to place a lower valuation on property than the rich, causing the direction of transfer of property to tend to be from the poor to the rich. What is more, the rich tend to bargain for a larger share of the gains from trade in such transactions because their wealth enables them to hold out for better terms. These aspects combine to ensure that property ownership will concentrate in the hands of the rich and that the rich will appropriate most of the gains from trade. The result is an increase in inequality.

In *Hipster Antiplagiarism*, Bryan L. Frye takes the New Brandeisian movement in antitrust to task for failing to condemn academic plagiarism norms. He argues that plagiarism norms reflect an attempt by senior scholars to monopolize academic markets for ideas and the intellectual surpluses generated therefrom. Frye suggests that New Brandeisians have shied away from attacking plagiarism norms because creatives are a major New Brandeisian constituency. New Brandeisians have therefore tended to support monopolization of ideas despite their broader antimonopoly commitment.

C *Contrasting Papers*

Two of the papers collected in this volume provide important insight into the contested character of inframarginalism within progressive legal circles. In *A Neo-Kantian Approach to Competition Law? The Re-emergence of Fairness in Antitrust Law and Policy*, Behrang Kianzad argues that the concept of fairness is indispensable to a progressive approach to price policy and essential to a rejection of conservative law and economics. This approach contrasts with the inframarginalist view, which accepts, at least for purposes of critique, the neoclassical position that there are no universal values – including no universal value of fairness – and that value is purely a matter of individual preference as expressed in purchase decisions and voting behavior. The inframarginalist shows that redistribution can be carried out without preventing people from acquiring the things that they want. But the inframarginalist concedes that whether redistribution should be carried out is ultimately a matter for voters to decide based on their individual preferences. The inframarginalist will vote for redistribution, but he will not take the position, implicit in Kianzad's view that the law should be governed by a fairness norm. In other words, he will not take the position that fairness is required regardless of what voters happen to think.

In *Inframarginalism and Economism*, Vijay Raghavan delivers the first express critique of inframarginalism from the perspective of progressives who reject neoclassical economics as an analytic. He argues that economics creates a default presumption in favor of free markets that limits the vision of progressive policy-makers. The article provides a counterpoint to the critique of progressives' dismissal of economics that is offered in this Introduction.

V CONCLUSION

The inframarginal approach strikes the conservative economist on his own terrain and defeats him there. It denies him the high ground of deductive inference. He cannot argue that, a priori, any particular government intervention must be inefficient. The progressives' victory is all the more complete because economics is an authentic expression of the value system of a godless age. It is the only intellectual framework that honors the right of the individual alone to decide his fate whenever possible. In using neoclassical economics against the conservative, the progressive demonstrates that the progressive's paternalism is consistent with the ethic of individual liberty that characterizes the modern age. The gains from trade can be redistributed without precluding any transactions. No other progressive approach to political economy speaks so directly or triumphantly to contemporary values.

2

A New Corporate Tax

Reuven S. Avi-Yonah[*]

CONTENTS

If we can regulate our corporations simply through the medium of taxation, we can destroy every trust in a fortnight. It would be a great deal better for the Finance Committee to turn its attention to the imposition of such a tax upon corporations and the persons who actually need regulation, who are exercising powers that are injurious to the American people, destroying competition and invading our prosperity, than to attempt to levy a revenue tax upon all the little shareholders of all the little corporations throughout the length and breadth of the United States.[1]

* This chapter is a revised version of Reuven Avi-Yonah, A New Corporate Tax, Tax Notes 653 (July 27, 2020). I would like to thank Kim Clausing, Nir Fishbien, Ed Fox, David Miller, and Fadi Shaheen for helpful comments.

1 44 Cong. Rec. 3978 (1909) (statement of then Sen. Albert B. Cummins on enacting a corporate tax).

I INTRODUCTION: WHY TAX CORPORATIONS?

Should the United States (US) tax corporations? For many academic and political observers, the answer is no.[2] The corporate tax is a strange tax because by definition it is not borne by the corporate taxpayer, since corporations are legal entities and cannot economically bear the burden of taxation. Moreover, unlike other indirect taxes (e.g., consumption taxes that are passed on to consumers or the employer's portion of the payroll tax that is passed on to employees), economists after over fifty years of debate are not sure who bears the burden of the corporate tax: shareholders, all capital providers, corporate employees, or consumers.[3] The most likely answer is all of the above in varying ratios depending on the current elasticities of capital, labor, and demand in the global economy, and on the degree to which the US economy is open.[4]

The general public, on the other hand, is convinced that the corporate tax is borne by large corporations, and politicians respond by maintaining the corporate tax as a tax paid by someone other than the voters. But this fiscal illusion, the opponents of the tax pronounce, is hardly a valid reason to maintain a very complicated tax that is the cause of significant deadweight loss (changes in behavior caused by the tax) and transaction costs (tax compliance and avoidance costs).[5]

[2] *See, e.g.*, Yariv Brauner, *The Non-Sense Tax: A Reply to New Corporate Income Tax Advocacy*, 2008 MICH. ST. L. REV. 591 (2008); Edwin G. Dolan, *The Progressive Case for Abolishing the Corporate Income Tax*, MILKEN INST. REV. (Jan. 12, 2017), www.milkenreview.org/articles/the-progressive-case-for-abolishing-the-corporate-income-tax-2; Simon Constable, *6 Reasons Trump Should Abolish Corporate Income Tax*, FORBES (Dec. 19, 2016, 12:33 PM), www.forbes.com/sites/simonconstable/2016/12/19/6-reasons-trump-should-abolish-corporate-income-tax/?sh=9a66de854f59; Nathan Boidman, *Is Corporate Tax Abolition Unrealistic?*, TAX NOTES INT'L (Nov. 4, 2019); Nathan Boidman, *Boidman Offers Pillar 4: Abolish Corporate Taxes!*, TAX NOTES INT'L (June 8, 2020).

[3] *See, e.g.*, Alan J. Auerbach, *Who Bears the Corporate Tax? A Review of What We Know*, 20 TAX POL'Y & ECON. 1 (2006).

[4] In recent estimates, most of the burden of the corporate tax falls on capital and on rents. *See* Kimberly Clausing, *Who Pays the Corporate Tax in a Global Economy?*, 66 NAT'L TAX J. 151 (2013); Kimberly Clausing, *In Search of Corporate Tax Incidence*, 65 TAX L. REV. 433 (2012); Edward Fox, *Does Capital Bear the U.S. Corporate Tax After All? New Evidence from Corporate Tax Returns*, 17 J. EMPIRICAL LEGAL STUD. 71 (2020).

[5] Austan Goolsbee, *Taxes, Organizational Form, and the Deadweight Loss of the Corporate Income Tax* (Nat'l Bureau of Econ. Rsch., Working Paper No. 6173, 1997); Christopher Evans et al., *The Tax Compliance Costs of Large Corporations: An Empirical Inquiry and Comparative Analysis*, 64 CAN. TAX J. 751 (2016). All taxes except head taxes (assuming no interjurisdictional mobility) and Pigouvian taxes have some deadweight loss, but the corporate tax has more transaction costs than most. There is an entire industry of tax lawyers and accountants devoted to helping large corporations minimize their tax burden, and it employs some of the brightest minds who could have been contributing in more socially useful ways. On the corporate tax and economic growth, *see* ORG. FOR ECON. CO-OPERATION AND DEV., TAX POLICY REFORM AND ECONOMIC GROWTH (2010) (describing the corporate tax as the most destructive form of taxation).

This chapter will argue that we do need a corporate tax, but not for the traditional reason, which is that if we do not tax corporations, rich shareholders will be able to defer tax on their income. Instead, the chapter will argue that we should tax corporations for the same reason we originally adopted the corporate tax in 1909: to limit the power and regulate the behavior of our largest corporations, which are monopolies or quasi-monopolies that dominate their respective fields and drive their competitors out of business (the best example being Big Tech – that is, Amazon, Apple, Facebook, Google, and Microsoft). But if that is the reason to have a corporate tax, it should have a different structure from the current flat corporate tax of 21 percent. Instead, the tax should be set at zero for normal returns by allowing the expensing of physical capital, but at a sharply progressive rate for supernormal returns (rents), culminating at a rate of 80 percent for income above $10 billion a year.[6]

After this introduction, Section II of the paper discusses and rejects the traditional reason given for taxing corporations. Section III argues that the only reason to maintain a corporate tax is as a tax on monopolistic rents. Section IV develops this proposal in some detail. Section V provides a conclusion.

II THE CORPORATE TAX AS AN INDIRECT TAX ON SHAREHOLDERS

The traditional reason for taxing corporations is that if we did not, rich shareholders would be able to earn their income through corporations and defer the tax until there is a dividend distribution or they sell the shares, or even avoid the tax altogether by holding their shares until death and having their heirs sell at a stepped-up basis.

That is not a valid reason for keeping alive a tax as complicated and costly as the corporate tax, which is why many academic observers have called for its abolition.[7] Given that the corporate tax rate has been sharply cut to 21 percent and that the revenue from the corporate tax is at $230 billion (in 2019) and only a small fraction (below 7 percent) of total federal revenues of $3.4 trillion, it does not appear impossible that some future president could successfully argue for abolishing the corporate tax, despite its public popularity.[8]

There are three reasons why the corporate tax is not a valid way of taxing shareholders.

6 See below for more on the rate structure. Edward Fox & Zachary Liscow, *A Case for Higher Corporate Tax Rates*, 167 TAX NOTES 2021 (2020). The authors support a higher corporate tax rate for similar reasons but believe the rate should be limited by international considerations, which are addressed later.

7 *See* Edward Lane & L. Randall Wray, *Is It Time to Eliminate Federal Corporate Income Taxes?* (Levy Econ. Inst., Working Paper No. 979, 2020), www.levyinstitute.org/pubs/wp_979.pdf.

8 *Monthly Budget Review: Summary for Fiscal Year 2019*, CONG. BUDGET OFF. (Nov. 7, 2019), www.cbo.gov/system/files/2019-11/55824-CBO-MBR-FY19.pdf.

First, despite over fifty years of economic research, economists are still unsure of who bears the burden of the corporate tax.[9] Plausible candidates are (a) the shareholders, if the corporate tax reduces corporate profits available to them as dividends or is reflected in the price of their shares (although even that assumes that the tax was not priced in when they bought the shares, in which case only the original shareholders in an initial public offering bear the burden);[10] (b) all capital providers, if the tax causes capital to flow from the corporate to the non-corporate sector, which is influenced by the ever-changing relative tax rates on corporate versus passthrough businesses;[11] (c) employees, if the corporations can effectively reduce wages in response to the tax by, for example, threatening to move production overseas;[12] or (d) consumers, if corporations enjoy a monopolistic or quasi-monopolistic position and therefore can raise prices to include the tax without fear of being undercut by competition.[13] The true answer is probably that all of the above bear the burden in different ratios over time depending on the elasticities (response to the tax) of capital, labor, and demand.

Second, as economists have recently emphasized, many shareholders are tax-exempt. In fact, a recent study has shown that 70 percent of US equities are held by tax-exempt institutions or individuals (e.g., through retirement accounts).[14] The authors of the study argue that this is a reason to tax corporations because otherwise capital would not be taxed at all, but it seems to me that if we believe in the reason that we exempt these individuals and institutions from tax, there is no reason to tax

[9] For recent studies on the incidence issue, *see* Fox, *supra* note 4; *see also* Clemens Fuest, Andreas Peichl & Sebastian Siegloch, *The Incidence of Corporate Taxation and Its Implications for Tax Progressivity*, VoxEU (Oct. 10, 2017); Stephen J. Entin, *Labor Bears Much of the Cost of the Corporate Tax*, Tax Found. (Oct. 24, 2017), https://files.taxfoundation.org/20181107145034/Tax-Foundation-SR2382.pdf; Laura Power & Austin Frerick. *Have Excess Returns to Corporations Been Increasing over Time?* 69 Nat'l Tax J. 831–46 (2016); Clausing, *supra* note 4; Benjamin H. Harris, *Corporate Tax Incidence and Its Implications for Progressivity*, Tax Pol'y Ctr. (Nov. 2009), www.taxpolicycenter.org/sites/default/files/alfresco/publication-pdfs/1001349-Corporate-Tax-Incidence-and-Its-Implications-for-Progressivity.PDF.

[10] *See, e.g.*, Michael J. Graetz & Alvin C. Warren Jr., Integration of the U.S. Corporate and Individual Income Taxes: The Treasury Department and American Law Institute Reports (1st ed. 1998); Charles E. McLure Jr., Must Corporate Income Be Taxed Twice? (1979).

[11] *See* Arnold C. Harberger, *The Incidence of the Corporation Income Tax*, 70 J. Pol. Econ. 215 (1962).

[12] *See* William M. Gentry, *A Review of the Evidence on the Incidence of the Corporate Income Tax* (Dep't of the Treasury, Off. of Tax Analysis, Working Paper No. 101, 2007) (summarizing empirical studies on the incidence of corporate tax on labor); Lily L. Batchelder, *The Shaky Case* for a *Business Cash-Flow Tax over* a *Business Income Tax*, *70 Nat'l Tax J. 901, 917–920 (2017) (addressing the impact of a cash-flow tax, which entails a higher tax rate on rents, on labor).*

[13] *See* Marian Krzyzaniak & Richard A. Musgrave, The Shifting of the Corporation Income Tax (1963).

[14] Leonard E. Burman et al., *Is U.S. Corporate Income Double-Taxed?*, 70 Nat'l Tax J. 675 (2017).

them indirectly through a corporate tax (assuming that they do in fact bear the tax burden).

Third, even for taxable shareholders, there are better ways of taxing the shareholders directly, thereby eliminating the incidence issue. For closely held corporations, the answer is to tax the shareholders on their income earned through the corporation – that is, to make passthrough treatment mandatory – because there are no administrability issues for those corporations and most of them are passthroughs in any case. For publicly traded corporations and partnerships, passthrough taxation is not administratively feasible. Instead, the shareholders should be taxed on the changing value of their shares, because liquidity and valuation are not issues for publicly traded shares, and the same tax can be collected on a withholding basis on foreign shareholders and if necessary on tax-exempt domestic shareholders (the government can impose a lien on some of the shares and sell them if the tax is not paid by foreign shareholders).[15] Pre-enactment unrealized appreciation can be reached by applying the tax in the year of enactment to the difference between the end-of-year share value and original basis.

For these reasons, if the only rationale for having a corporate tax is to indirectly tax shareholders, it is not clear that it is worth fighting for against the many voices calling for its abolition. But that is in fact not the only rationale, as the next section explains.

III THE CORPORATE TAX AS A TAX ON MONOPOLISTIC RENTS

When the corporate tax was enacted in 1909, taxing shareholders was not the reason. In fact, taxing shareholders would in 1909 have been unconstitutional under the Supreme Court's 1895 *Pollock* decision, which both President Taft and Senate Majority Leader Nelson Aldrich believed precluded a tax on shareholders, although to placate the Progressives they also introduced a constitutional amendment to allow Congress to tax individual income, which neither expected to pass.[16] Instead, the corporate tax was designated as an excise tax on the privilege of conducting business through the corporate form, since the Supreme Court had held such excise taxes on corporations to be constitutional in 1898; but neither Taft nor Aldrich thought that was a good reason to impose a federal tax on corporations, because the privileges of the corporate form derived from state, not federal, law.[17]

[15] Alternatively, the tax can be collected only upon the payment of a dividend or a sale of the shares with an interest charge added to eliminate deferral, but that raises administrability issues for sales of shares between foreign shareholders.

[16] Pollock v. Farmers' Loan & Trust Co., 157 U.S. 429 (1895), *aff'd on reh'g*, 158 U.S. 601 (1895).

[17] 44 Cong. Rec. 3344 (1909) (statement of Taft) ("This is an excise tax upon the privilege of doing business as an artificial entity and of freedom from a general partnership liability enjoyed by those who own the stock."); Nicol v. Ames, 173 U.S. 509 (1899).

Instead, as I have shown elsewhere by examining the legislative history, the corporate tax of 1909 was primarily seen as a vehicle for limiting the power of and regulating the great trusts, such as John D. Rockefeller's Standard Oil Co. or J. P. Morgan's U.S. Steel Corp.[18] The Taft administration was at the same time litigating against Standard Oil and American Tobacco (among many other trusts) in order to break them up under the Sherman Act of 1890,[19] but the prospects of the litigation were uncertain (the government had lost the *E.C. Knight* case in the Supreme Court in 1895 and only narrowly won the *Northern Securities* case in 1904).[20] Thus, as President Taft said in his message to Congress, we should have a corporate tax in order to curb the trusts:

> Another merit of this tax is the federal supervision which must be exercised in order to make the law effective over the annual accounts and business transactions of all corporations. While the faculty of assuming a corporate form has been of the utmost utility in the business world, it is also true that substantially all of the abuses and all of the evils which have aroused the public to the necessity of reform were made possible by the use of this very faculty. If now, by a perfectly legitimate and effective system of taxation, we are incidentally able to possess the Government and the stockholders and the public of the knowledge of the real business transactions and the gains and profits of every corporation in the country, we have made a long step toward that supervisory control of corporations which may prevent a further abuse of power.[21]

The corporate tax of 1909 had several features that were considered potentially effective as antitrust measures. First, even though the tax rate was only 1 percent,[22] both supporters and opponents knew the rate could be increased (as it ultimately was, reaching 52.8 percent in 1968) and the threat of those changes might deter the trusts. Second, the tax returns were to be made public, thus alerting the press and the voters to which corporations were the most profitable and therefore the likeliest targets for antitrust enforcement actions.[23] Third, while intercorporate dividends were exempt (a controversial feature, because the trusts were holding corporations) there were no tax-free reorganizations and no consolidated returns.

Unfortunately, all of these antitrust features of the corporate tax were eliminated by 1928. The publicity feature was eliminated in 1910,[24] tax-exempt reorganizations

[18] *See* Reuven S. Avi-Yonah, *Corporations, Society, and the State: A Defense of the Corporate Tax*, 90 VA. L. REV. 1193 (2004).

[19] Standard Oil v. United States, 221 U.S. 1 (1911); United States v. American Tobacco Co., 221 U.S. 106 (1911).

[20] United States v. E. C. Knight Co., 156 U.S. 1 (1895); Northern Securities Co. v. United States, 193 U.S. 197 (1904) (resulting in a 5-4 decision).

[21] 44 CONG. REC. 3344 (1909).

[22] Payne-Aldrich Tariff Act of 1909, ch. 6, §38, 36 Stat. 112 (1909).

[23] Marjorie E. Kornhauser, *Corporate Regulation and the Origins of the Corporate Income Tax*, 66 IND. L.J. 53 (1990).

[24] *Id.* at 130–31.

were adopted in 1919,[25] and consolidated returns were made elective in 1928.[26] In addition, various pro-corporate provisions like accelerated depreciation, percentage depletion, and the foreign tax credit were adopted in the same period.[27] While the Franklin D. Roosevelt administration limited the dividends-received deduction and tax-exempt reorganizations in the 1930s, it never eliminated them,[28] and subsequent enactments, such as investment tax credits, reduced the corporate tax even further.[29] As for the rate, it never exceeded 52.8 percent[30] (as opposed to the individual rate, which reached 94 percent during World War II and was still as high as 70 percent when Ronald Reagan was elected president).[31] The effective corporate tax rate was much lower because of interest and depreciation deductions and investment tax credits. In 1986, the corporate rate was reduced from 46 percent to 34 percent (later raised to 35 percent),[32] and despite various base-broadening measures, the effective corporate rate remained low.[33] Corporate tax revenues consequently declined from 25 percent of total federal revenues in the 1960s to less than 10 percent in the 2000s.[34] Finally, in 2017, the corporate tax rate was reduced to 21 percent, and it was a flat rate – all the previous progressivity, which only applied to small corporations with revenues below $15 million, was eliminated.[35]

Other than the rates, we are unlikely to reverse these pro-trust features of the corporate tax, because they are old, well established, and benefit small as well as

[25] Revenue Act of 1918, ch. 18, § 202(b), 40 Stat. 1057, 1060 (1919); *see also* Treas. Reg. 45, art. 1567, 21 Treas. Dec. 170, 395 (1919) (promulgating the reorganization provision of the 1918 Act).

[26] Revenue Act of 1928, ch. 852, §§ 141–142, 45 Stat. 791, 831–33 (1928).

[27] Revenue Act of 1926, ch. 27, § 204(c), 44 Stat. 16 (1926) (enacting percentage depletion for oil and gas producers); Revenue Act of 1918, ch. 18, §§ 238(a), 240(c), 40 Stat. 1057, 1081–82 (1919) (describing foreign tax credits for US corporations and their foreign subsidiaries). On allowances for depreciation, *see, e.g.*, Revenue Act of 1918, ch. 18, §§ 214(a)(8), 234(a)(7), 40 Stat. 1057 (1919) (providing for "a reasonable allowance for the exhaustion, wear and tear of property used in the trade or business, including a reasonable allowance for obsolescence.").

[28] On the dividends-received deduction, *see* Steven A. Bank, *When We Taxed the Pyramids*, 41 FLA. ST. U. L. REV. 39 (2013); Steven A. Bank & Brian R. Cheffins, *The Corporate Pyramid Fable*, 84 BUS. HIST. REV. 435 (2010). On tax-free reorganizations, *see* Steven A. Bank & Ajay K. Mehrotra, *Corporate Taxation and the Regulation of Early Twentieth-Century American Business*, *in* THE CORPORATION AND AMERICAN DEMOCRACY 177 (Naomi Lamoreaux & William Novak eds., 2017).

[29] *See* Robert E. Rosacker & Richard W. Metcalf, *United States Federal Tax Policy Surrounding the Investment Tax Credit: A Review of Legislative Intent and Empirical Research Findings over Thirty Years (1962–1991)*, 9 AKRON TAX J. 59 (1992).

[30] *Marginal Corporate Tax Rates*, TAX POL'Y CTR. (Mar. 25, 2020), www.taxpolicycenter.org/statistics/marginal-corporate-tax-rates.

[31] *Historical Highest Marginal Income Tax Rates*, TAX POL'Y CTR. (Feb. 4, 2020), www.taxpolicycenter.org/statistics/historical-highest-marginal-income-tax-rates.

[32] Tax Reform Act of 1986, Pub. L. No. 99-514, § 601, 100 Stat 2085, 2249 (1986).

[33] *See* Reuven S. Avi-Yonah & Yaron Lahav, *The Effective Tax Rate of the Largest U.S. and EU Multinationals*, 65 TAX L. REV. 375 (2012).

[34] Auerbach, *supra* note 3, at 3–4.

[35] Tax Cuts and Jobs Act, Pub. L. No. 115-97, § 13001, 131 Stat. 2054, 2096 (2017) (amending I.R.C. § 11).

large corporations, which are not the proper subject of a corporate tax designated to limit the power of monopolies and quasi-monopolies.

Recent research by Edward Fox has shown, however, that most of the existing corporate tax falls on supernormal returns.[36] Fox shows this by demonstrating from corporate tax returns for 1995–2013 that if expensing of capital expenditures were allowed before 2017, corporate tax revenues would have been almost identical to actual revenues.[37] Because (as discussed later) expensing is equivalent to exempting the normal return, that means that the corporate tax has historically fallen primarily on supernormal returns, or rents. This finding is consistent with Laura Power and Austin Frerick's evidence from 2016 that excess returns to corporations have been increasing over time.[38] In the current environment, because expensing is in fact allowed until 2022, that finding is even more likely to be true.

In that case, and if the main reason to have a corporate tax is to tax rents and limit monopolies, then the tax should have a different rate structure than we have now. I would suggest that the effective tax rate on normal corporate profits be zero. On supernormal returns, because the main concern is monopolies and quasi-monopolies, the tax should be progressive, with a very high tax rate (e.g., 80 percent) for profits above a very high threshold (e.g., $10 billion). In between, there should be a series of graduated tax rates, similar to the individual rate schedule before 1980.

A *Normal Returns*

There is no reason to tax corporations on normal returns. Normal returns are the risk-free return from investing in, for example, US treasury securities. In recent years, these returns have been quite low, but they have historically been higher.[39] However, from the point of view of only applying the corporate tax to rents, these returns should be exempt. Also, there is the uncertainty about the incidence, which suggests that a tax on normal returns is less likely to contribute to the progressivity of the system. Finally, the deadweight loss from the corporate tax arises from the tax on normal returns, because a tax on pure rents does not generate deadweight loss (i.e., it does not change taxpayer behavior, because taxpayers not subject to any competition would derive net profit from rents even if 99 percent of them were taxed away).

Because from a political perspective a zero tax rate on normal returns is unlikely to pass, and because it is hard to determine what normal returns are, I would suggest that we keep the flat rate of 21 percent on corporations (with no de minimis

[36] Fox, *supra* note 4.

[37] *Id.*

[38] Power & Frerick, *supra* note 9.

[39] *See 3-Month Treasury Bill: Secondary Market Rate*, Fed. Rsrv. Bank St. Louis, https://fred.stlouisfed.org/series/TB3MS (last visited Mar. 18, 2021); *10-Year Treasury Constant Maturity Rate*, Fed. Rsrv. Bank St. Louis, https://fred.stlouisfed.org/series/GS10 (last visited Mar. 18, 2021).

exception, because small corporations are likely to be passthroughs), but allow for permanent expensing of capital expenditures. Under the Cary Brown theorem, as explained later, that expensing is equivalent to an exemption for the normal return to capital.[40] As elaborated later, however, we should not allow expensing for research and development (R&D), because that typically generates rents, nor a deduction for interest, because combining it with expensing generates negative tax rates.

The Cary Brown theorem demonstrates the theoretical equivalence, under specified assumptions, of expensing and exempting the normal return to capital.[41]

To take a common example, suppose a taxpayer earns 100 subject to a tax of 50 percent and can invest the after-tax income in a machine generating a return of 10 percent per year. Under an income tax, the 100 of earnings is subject to tax of 50, and the remaining 50 is invested in the machine, yielding 55 after one year; the 5 of income is subject to income tax, leaving the taxpayer with only 52.5.

In an exemption regime that exempts the normal return to capital from tax, the 100 of income is subject to a tax of 50 when earned. The remaining 50 is invested in the machine, but when the additional 5 of income is earned, it is exempt from tax, so that the taxpayer is left with 55.

In an expensing regime, the 100 of income is expensed, and the resulting deduction eliminates the tax on the 100, so that the taxpayer can invest the entire 100 in the machine. However, when the machine is sold for 110 a year later, because the basis is zero, the sale is subject to tax at 50 percent, leaving the taxpayer with the same 55 as in the previous example.

Hence, the Cary Brown theorem demonstrates that expensing the 100 is equivalent to exempting the normal return from tax.

The Cary Brown theorem makes two important assumptions. The first is that tax rates do not change between the time the income is expensed and the time the machine is sold. If the tax rate changes, the equivalence does not hold, because exemption applies the rate at the beginning of the investment and expensing the rate at the end. However, this assumption may not matter too much because rates can either increase or decrease over time, so that it is unclear which form of the tax is more beneficial to the taxpayer.

The other assumption, however, has clear implications. That is the assumption that the taxpayer can invest the savings from exempting at the same rate as the underlying investment. This holds true when the investment is a commonly available one, yielding what the economists call marginal (normal) returns. However,

[40] The following is based on Reuven S. Avi-Yonah, *Risk, Rents and Regressivity: Why the United States Needs Both an Income Tax and a VAT*, 105 Tax Notes 1651 (2004).

[41] *See* E. Cary Brown, *Business Income Taxation and Investment Incentives*, *in* Income, Employment, and Public Policy: Essays in Honor of Alvin H. Hansen 300, 301 (Lloyd A. Metzler et al. eds., 1948); *See also* Daniel Shaviro, *Replacing the Income Tax with a Progressive Consumption Tax*, 103 Tax Notes 91, 99–100 (2004) (discussing the Cary Brown theorem).

suppose the underlying investment is in a unique business opportunity, yielding what the economists call inframarginal (extraordinary) returns, or rents. In that case, the investor may be unable to invest the tax savings from expensing at the same rate as the underlying investment because the size of the unique investment opportunity is limited, and the Cary Brown equivalence does not hold.

For example, suppose in the earlier example the underlying investment yields a 50 percent return but the tax savings can only be invested in a bond earning 10 percent. In a regime that exempts the normal return, the taxpayer earns 100, pays 50 in tax, and invests the other 50 in the high-yielding opportunity, resulting after a year in a 25 return exempt from tax, for a net after-tax of 75. In an expensing regime, the investor earns 100 and does not pay tax because of expensing; however, of the 100, only 50 can be invested at a return of 50 percent, and the other 50 (the tax savings) is invested at 10 percent. The result is a yield after a year of 75 from the underlying investment and 55 from the tax saving, for a total of 130, and when that is sold and is subject to tax at 50 percent, the taxpayer nets only 65. To put it another way, in an expensing regime, only the normal yield is exempt from tax; the extraordinary yield is fully taxable. So how should those extraordinary yields (rents) be taxed?

B *Supernormal Returns (Rents)*

Economists are unanimous in supporting a tax on rents because (a) it does not create deadweight loss and is therefore efficient, and (b) it falls on the above-normal return to capital and is therefore progressive.[42]

Above the de facto exemption resulting from expensing, the corporate tax should be sharply progressive. In order not to create sudden jumps in the marginal tax rate, progressivity should be gradual, similar to the way the individual tax was structured when it was more progressive (before 1980).

The reason to have a progressive tax on rents is that in addition to targeting rents, we also want to discourage bigness, which is equivalent to monopolistic or quasi-monopolistic status. The less competition a business firm faces, the more profitable it is likely to be, because competition generally drives down prices. That is why our most monopolistic firms are also the most profitable, and why they engage in behaviors like "killer acquisitions" designed to eliminate competition.[43]

[42] For a discussion on taxing economic rents, *see* Joseph Bankman et al., *Collecting the Rent: The Global Battle to Capture MNE Profits*, 72 TAX L. REV. 197 (2019).

[43] *See, e.g.*, Naomi R. Lamoreaux, *The Problem of Bigness: From Standard Oil to Google*, 33 J. ECON. PERSP. 94 (2019); Kenneth A. Bamberger & Orly Lobel, *Platform Market Power*, 32 BERKELEY TECH. L.J. 1051 (2017); Axel Gautier & Joe Lamesch, Mergers in the Digital Economy (CESifo, Working Paper No. 805, 2020); Colleen Cunningham et al., *Killer Acquisitions*, 129 J. POL. ECON. 649 (2019); Marc Bourreau & Alexandre de Streel, *Big Tech Acquisitions: Competition & Innovation Effects and EU Merger Control*, CTR. ON REGUL. IN EUR. (Feb. 2020), www.cerre.eu/sites/cerre/files/cerre_big_tech_acquisitions_2020.pdf.

At the top, the corporate tax rate should be 80 percent for income above $10 billion.[44] In 2019, this rate would have applied to Big Tech: Amazon ($10.1 billion), Apple ($59.5 billion), Facebook ($22.1 billion), Google ($30.7 billion), and Microsoft ($16.6 billion). Other corporations that had profits exceeding $10 billion in 2019 include other major tech companies (Intel, Micron), Big Banks (Chase, Bank of America, Wells Fargo, Citi, Goldman Sachs, Visa), Big Pharma (Pfizer), Big Oil (Exxon, Chevron), Big Telecom (AT&T, Verizon, Broadcom), United Health, Boeing, and some major consumer brands (Johnson & Johnson, Home Depot, Disney, Pepsi).[45] All of those enjoy some degree of monopolistic or quasi-monopolistic status.

Such a high tax rate would make corporate regulation through the tax highly effective. It should enable Congress to grant deductions for activities it deems desirable, such as job creation during the current recession or in underdeveloped areas of the country, and impose high rates on activities it deems undesirable, such as invading consumer privacy.

In addition, the high rate may persuade the corporations subject to it to split up. Splitting up corporations to reduce their profits and therefore escape the 80 percent tax rate is actually a feature of the proposal and not a bug. As Lina Khan and others have proposed, we should ideally want to induce Big Tech companies to divest their anticompetitive acquisitions (e.g., Facebook's acquisitions of Instagram and WhatsApp). And if the tax structure also motivates an actual break-up of the core business (e.g., along geographic or business segment lines), any loss in efficiency would be more than compensated for by the removal of the threat to democracy posed by Big Tech.[46]

IV A NEW CORPORATE TAX

Besides the rate structure, the new corporate tax should have several other features missing from the current corporate tax.

A *The Tax Base*

The problem with using current definitions of the corporate tax base is that it allows large corporations like those in Big Tech to pay low effective tax rates because of

44 While we never had a corporate tax rate above 53 percent, the World War II excess profits tax, which applied to rents resulting from the war, was capped at 80 percent. *See* Reuven S. Avi-Yonah, *Taxes in the Time of Coronavirus: Is It Time to Revive the Excess Profits Tax?* (Univ. of Mich. Pub. L. Rsch. Paper, Paper No. 671, 2020, Univ. of Mich. L. & Econ. Rsch. Paper, Paper No. 20-008, 2020), https://ssrn.com/abstract=3560806.

45 2019 Fortune 500 Companies Ranked by Profit, FORTUNE, https://fortune.com/fortune500/2019/search/?profits=desc (last visited Mar. 6, 2021).

46 On Big Tech and democracy, *see* BARRY C. LYNN, CORNERED: THE NEW MONOPOLY CAPITALISM AND THE ECONOMICS OF DESTRUCTION (2010); TIM WU, THE CURSE OF BIGNESS: ANTITRUST IN THE NEW GILDED AGE (2018); Lina M. Khan, *Amazon's Antitrust Paradox*, 127 YALE L.J. 710 (2017).

three factors: profit shifting to offshore jurisdictions with low tax rates, expensing R&D, and deducting stock option compensation.

Profit shifting can be dealt with relatively simply by mandating consolidated returns (at the 50 percent level by vote or value, to prevent tax-motivated deconsolidation without giving up control) and including foreign corporations in the consolidation.[47] The standard objection that this will impede competitiveness does not apply because rents are not subject to competition by definition.

Research and development should not be expensed because unlike physical capital expenditures, it does not just generate future profits but specifically future rents.[48] Thus, it should be amortized over a fifteen-year term like acquired intangibles. Unsuccessful R&D can be deducted when it becomes clear that it will not result in future profits.

Stock options should be valued and deducted as wages when granted, as is done for book purposes. There is no reason to pretend that stock options have no value when granted. The same goes for restricted stock and other forms of stock-based compensation.

Interest should not be deductible because combining an interest deduction with expensing results in negative tax rates.[49] Also, under current conditions much interest is effectively guaranteed by the government so it should not receive a tax subsidy as well.

B *Anti-Avoidance Provisions*

The most important anti-avoidance provisions for public companies controlled by their founders are already in the Code: Section 367 imposes tax on all large shareholders in an inversion,[50] and Section 877A prevents the controlling owners of Big Tech from expatriating and selling their shares with no tax.[51] However, if the

[47] *See* Reuven S. Avi-Yonah, *Hanging Together: A Multilateral Approach to Taxing Multinationals*, 5 Mich. Bus. & Entrepreneurial L. Rev. 137 (2016) (proposing a tax on global profits for multinational enterprises (MNEs)).

[48] *See* Calvin H. Johnson, *The Effective Tax Ratio and the Undertaxation of Intangibles*, 121 Tax Notes 1289 (2008). Arguably, R&D generates positive externalities (mostly in the form of ideas that can migrate to other firms) but (a) there is less human capital migration than there used to be because of the above market rate salaries offered by Big Tech, and (b) there are significant negative externalities imposed by Big Tech. Research and development should be treated like any other expense – that is, matched to the income stream it generates.

[49] Assume the tax rate is 50 percent and a taxpayer borrows 100 at 10 percent interest and buys a machine which it expenses. The machine produces 10 in income each year. Before tax, the taxpayer has 10 (income from the machine) minus 10 (interest), or zero. After tax, the taxpayer has deductions of 100 (expensing) plus 10 (interest), or 110, and income of 10, so that produces a net loss of 100, which can offset other income, for a negative tax rate of −50 percent.

[50] I.R.C. § 367 (taxing shareholder-level gain on transfers of appreciated property from a US person to a foreign corporation).

[51] I.R.C. § 877A; *see also* I.R.C. § 877 (addressing expatriation to avoid tax).

mark-to-market proposal raised earlier is adopted, this will be irrelevant if it is applied to the entire unrealized appreciation. If that move is not politically feasible, a high tax rate (discussed later) of 50 percent should be applied upon expatriation.

Also, inversion transactions can be prevented, as the Obama administration proposed,[52] by (a) reducing the Section 7874 threshold to 50 percent, and (b) redefining corporate residence as the location of the headquarters. If that is not enough, the US can follow European Union (EU) countries by treating a move of the headquarters as a realization event and taxing both the shareholders and the corporation on a deemed sale of stock and assets.[53] Those "exit taxes" are the reason no EU countries have experienced inversions despite having similar effective tax rates to the US rate before 2017.[54]

C *Shareholder Taxation*

Ideally, shareholders in public corporations should be taxed on a mark-to-market basis, including on past unrealized appreciation. Also, accrual taxation should be applied to non-publicly traded property as well by adding an interest charge when the property is sold and abolishing the Section 1014 step-up. Those steps should enable the US to adopt a significantly more progressive system of individual taxation – up to, for example, 50 percent – for all income (including dividends).[55] Capital gains will not be taxed to domestic US shareholders, but stock buybacks as well as dividends should be subject to withholding tax for foreign shareholders not subject to the mark-to-market regime.

Taxing actual dividends in addition to mark-to-market may seem like double taxation, but in practice it is not, because the market value of stock is not a good proxy for underlying corporate earnings, and the receipt of dividends increases the ability to pay as much as capital gains (which will be taxable under either mark-to-market or the higher tax rates). Dividends as well as interest should not be deductible.

[52] *General Explanations of the Administration's Fiscal Year 2010 Revenue Proposals*, U.S. Dep't of the Treas. 1, 33–34 (May 2009), www.treasury.gov/resource-center/tax-policy/Documents/General-Explanations-FY2010.pdf.

[53] *See* Council Directive 2016/1164, art. 5, 2016 O.J. (L 193) (EU).

[54] Avi-Yonah & Lahav, *supra* note 33.

[55] Rates above 50 percent may induce the rich to work less, and we have never (except during World War II) had effective rates of over 50 percent on the rich (top 1 percent) even though nominal rates were much higher. That is why the corporate tax on rents should be higher than the top individual tax rate, which will also encourage moving businesses out of subchapter C and distribution of dividends, both of which make it easier to tax the rich on business profits. *See* Reuven S. Avi-Yonah, *Why Tax the Rich? Efficiency, Equity, and Progressive Taxation*, 111 Yale L.J. 1391 (2002) (reviewing Joel Slemrod, Does Atlas Shrug? The Economic Consequences of Taxing the Rich (2000)).

V CONCLUSION

This Chapter has sought to develop a new corporate tax that is appropriate for targeting rents earned by large, monopolistic, or quasi-monopolistic enterprises like Big Tech. Its main recommendations are that normal corporate returns be functionally exempt by allowing permanent expensing for capital expenditures, but that supernormal returns be taxable progressively (up to 80 percent above $10 billion in profit) and on a broad base that (a) includes foreign subsidiaries, (b) disallows current R&D and interest deductions, and (c) limits deductions for stock-based compensation to value on date of grant. Also, I recommend a mark-to-market regime for shareholders as well as full taxation of dividends at a progressive rate of 50 percent, but would allow for tax-free split-ups. These steps should complement antitrust enforcement to bring our large monopolies down to a normal size, without creating deadweight loss.

3

The Progressive Case against Antimonopolism

Ramsi A. Woodcock[*]

CONTENTS

[*] Faisal Chaudhry and participants at the 21st Annual Meeting of the Italian Association for the History of Political Economy, which was hosted by the Department of Historical Studies of the University of Milan, a Boston University Law Review Symposium on Law, Markets, and Distribution, a Yale Thurman Arnold Project workshop, and the conference titled "Should Wealth and Income Inequality Be a Competition law Concern?," which was hosted online by the Amsterdam Center for Law and Economics of the University of Amsterdam, provided helpful comments. This research was supported by a grant from the John S. and James L. Knight Foundation.

This chapter was written in 2021. The author slightly revised it in 2025, primarily to update references to cases to account for new developments. The arguments in the chapter have stood the test of time. However, readers interested in an update that accounts for Biden Administration developments may wish to consult Ramsi A. Woodcock, After Antitrust, Phenomenal World (Jan. 30, 2025), https://perma.cc/492T-LQHM.

I INTRODUCTION

Interest in some progressive policy circles in using antitrust to address the problem of wealth inequality largely results from political dysfunction in the United States – profound anti-statist resistance to reform of the tax system notwithstanding widespread popular discontent with wealth inequality – rather than from any insight into the sources of inequality, and should therefore be treated with caution by progressives and policymakers alike. Indeed, an enduring irony of the interest of contemporary American progressives in antitrust and inequality is that (1) the original progressive movement of a century ago rejected antitrust as a viable means of addressing wealth inequality and (2) the major theoretical effort that returned inequality to the global policy agenda, Thomas Piketty's *Capital in the Twenty-First Century*, rejects it as well.[1]

Both the original progressives and Piketty recognized that the primary source of wealth inequality is not due to monopoly rents – profits derived from the creation of *artificial* scarcity – but rather to *natural* scarcity, whether attributable to resource constraints (i.e., Ricardian scarcity) or technological limitations (i.e., Schumpeterian scarcity).[2] This means that inequality is not primarily a result of what antitrust practitioners call supracompetitive pricing: the sale of goods and services at prices above the prices that would obtain in a competitive market. Indeed, even were a perfect regime of antitrust enforcement to drive all prices to competitive levels, inequality would remain a major and, indeed, growing problem, because, thanks to scarcity, the profits that firms would earn in competitive markets would continue to be very large.[3]

The only way to get at scarcity – as opposed to monopoly – rents is to redistribute wealth through the tax system, which effectively democratizes ownership of scarce resources, ensuring that everyone gets a cut.[4] American progressives understood this

[1] *See* Thomas Piketty, Capital in the Twenty-First Century 537 (Arthur Goldhammer trans., 2017) ("Yet pure and perfect competition cannot alter the inequality r > g, which is not the consequence of any market 'imperfection.'"). For the original progressives, and more on Piketty, see *infra* Section II.B.1.

[2] *See* David J. Teece & Mary Coleman, *The Meaning of Monopoly: Antitrust Analysis in High-Technology Industries*, 43 *Antitrust Bull.* 801, 819–23 (1998); Piketty, *supra* note 1, at 269–72.

[3] *See* Thomas Piketty, Capital in the Twenty-First Century 441 (2014).

[4] *See infra* Sections II.B.1.e and II.B.2.

a century ago, which is why it is difficult to find much discussion of antitrust in the work of the major progressive theorists of the time, such as Robert L. Hale.[5] Instead, the original American progressives fought pitched battles to establish the income tax, the corporate tax, and rate regulation, which directly target scarcity rents.[6]

But, since the 1980s, a resurgent and uniquely American anti-statism has made it politically impossible for American progressives to achieve redistribution of wealth through the tax system and indeed has led to a major reduction in tax rates in the United States.[7] The hostility to taxation has remained remarkably popular even in recent years, despite broad public concern about inequality. The result is that American progressives have sought to carry out their redistributive project through an attack on monopoly as a kind of second- or third-best alternative to taxation. They have been encouraged in this endeavor by the appeal of antimonopoly rhetoric to an American public that is culturally distrustful of large institutions, public or private. And they have been greatly aided by a news industry that has been disrupted by innovation in advertising and content distribution by the Tech Giants and sees a rejuvenated antitrust as a means of protecting its competitive position.[8]

But interest in antitrust among progressives and in the press has far outstripped the ability of scholars to justify its use as a tool for solving the inequality problem, and unreflective pursuit of this policy route threatens to waste progressive energies and lead governments down a dead end, one that would be potentially quite destructive if a great many large, highly productive, and high-paying firms are pulled apart along the way.[9]

II SCARCITY, NOT MONOPOLY, AS THE MAJOR CAUSE OF INEQUALITY

A *Distinguishing Antimonopolism from Opposition to Inequality in Bargaining Power More Generally*

Antimonopolists' target is what they call "concentration of economic power," which they seem partly to dislike in itself – this is the "small is beautiful" strand of the

[5] For one of the few references to antitrust in Hale's work, see ROBERT LEE HALE, FREEDOM THROUGH LAW: PUBLIC CONTROL OF PRIVATE GOVERNING POWER 401 (1952).

[6] *See* BARBARA FRIED, THE PROGRESSIVE ASSAULT ON LAISSEZ FAIRE: ROBERT HALE AND THE FIRST LAW AND ECONOMICS MOVEMENT 40, 68, 160–205 (1998); Reuven S. Avi-Yonah, *Corporations, Society, and the State: A Defense of the Corporate Tax*, 90 *Va. L. Rev.* 1193, 1212–31 (2004).

[7] *See* ISAAC WILLIAM MARTIN, THE PERMANENT TAX REVOLT: HOW THE PROPERTY TAX TRANSFORMED AMERICAN POLITICS 2–15 (2008); W. ELLIOT BROWNLEE, FEDERAL TAXATION IN AMERICA: A HISTORY 182–83 (3d ed. 2016).

[8] *See* Ramsi A. Woodcock, Big Ink v. Bigger Tech, TRUTH ON THE MARKET, https://perma.cc/9P6J-UJF3/ (last visited Apr. 7, 2020).

[9] *See* ROBERT D. ATKINSON & MICHAEL LIND, BIG IS BEAUTIFUL: DEBUNKING THE MYTH OF SMALL BUSINESS 64–67 (2019); GERALD F. DAVIS, MANAGED BY THE MARKETS: HOW FINANCE RESHAPED AMERICA 67–72 (2011).

movement – and partly to dislike because they believe such concentrations to lead either to inequality of wealth or to political power.[10] Because antimonopolists believe that concentrations of economic power lead to political power through the wealth that they appropriate – in their view, those with economic power are able to dictate political outcomes mostly by buying support, rather than, say, by leveraging whatever charisma is associated with economic power in its own right – it seems reasonable to view antimonopolists' complaints about inequality and political power as essentially a single complaint about wealth.[11] It is this wealth-oriented strand of antimonopolism that will be considered here.

If by concentrations of economic power antimonopolists mean the possession of bargaining power in markets – the ability of one party to hold out for a better price because the other party needs a deal more than the first party does – antimonopolists are certainly right to view concentrations of economic power as the root of wealth inequality.[12] Virtually all wealth is valuable only to the extent that it can be exchanged. A rentier's parents might leave him a house and some cash, but the cash is useless unless he can exchange it either for consumption items or for paper rights to the proceeds of projects in which he wishes to invest. And the value of the house to him – assuming he is able to live in it – will depreciate away to zero as leaks develop in the roof and termites gnaw at the foundations, unless he is able to exchange some of the cash for repairs as well. But bargaining power determines the value for which wealth can be exchanged.[13] You might be the richest person in the world, but if you are desperate enough for a sip of water, and there is only one person who can provide it, you are, in fact, poor, because all your wealth will buy you no more than that sip.[14] The monopoly seller of water will insist on that price.[15]

But antimonopolists do not target all imbalances in bargaining power when they decry concentrations of economic power, as their emphasis on concentration and

[10] *See* Phillip Longman, *The Case for Small-Business Cooperation*, November/December 2018 WASH. MONTHLY (Oct. 28, 2018), https://perma.cc/5B5L-MVTK/.

[11] *See* Lina Khan & Zephyr Teachout, *Market Structure and Political Law: A Taxonomy of Power*, 9 *Duke J. Const. L. Pub. Pol'y* 57 (2014) ("[T]he wealth transfers in concentrated markets are political because they make big companies bigger and enrich their executives and shareholders, handing both the firm and top individuals more political power.").

[12] Recognition of the foundation of distribution in bargaining power dates at least to the original progressives. *See* Warren J. Samuels, *The Economy as a System of Power and Its Legal Bases: The Legal Economics of Robert Lee Hale*, 27 *U. Miami L. Rev.* 261, 309–23 (1973); Herbert Hovenkamp, *The First Great Law & Economics Movement*, 42 *Stan. L. Rev.* 993, 1022 (1990) (noting that Richard T. Ely argued that "[u]nregulated bargaining enhances power that already exists and creates increasingly greater economic inequality."); Duncan Kennedy, *The Stakes of Law, or Hale and Foucault Transformative Discourses in Postmodern Social Cultural and Legal Theory*, 15 *Legal Stud. Forum* 327, 328–30 (1991).

[13] *See* Duncan Kennedy, *Law Distributes I: Ricardo Marx Cls*, SSRN SCHOLARLY PAPER 29 (2021).

[14] *See id.*

[15] *See id.*

their self-described antimonopolism suggest.[16] They mean instead to link the maldistribution of wealth to inequalities in bargaining power associated specifically with breakdowns in the competitive process.[17] They hearken back to a midcentury golden age of antitrust enforcement in America in which enforcers broke up big companies, competition thrived, and wealth was more evenly distributed than it is today.[18] Although they generally make the connection between competition and equality only implicitly, the implication is clear: They believe that the increase in inequality over the past half-century in the United States is due in significant part to a decline in competition.[19] Or, conversely, they believe that restoring competition to American markets would go a long way toward solving the problem of inequality.

Critics on the right have long argued against a connection between monopoly and inequality on the ground that the relative wealth of buyers and sellers is indeterminate.[20] In some markets, the buyers are rich and the sellers are poor, so monopoly progressively redistributes.[21] In other markets, the reverse is true.[22] On average, then, it is a wash: The effects of monopoly on inequality are likely not significant.[23] Antimonopolists – who are mostly activists, not scholars – have so far dealt with this argument, as with all criticism, through denial and avoidance.[24] But law scholars belonging to the broader progressive community in antitrust respond by pointing out that shareholders tend to be relatively wealthy as a class, and they are the residual claimants on most of what is sold in the economy, apart from the labor services sold by workers.[25] Of course, workers are poorer than shareholders and breaking up any monopolies that workers in particular enjoy thanks to unionization, would tend to increase inequality, not reduce it.[26] But no one thinks workers have been using unions primarily to monopolize labor markets,

[16] *See* Longman, *supra* note 10.

[17] *See id.*

[18] *See* Sandeep Vaheesan, *The Evolving Populisms of Antitrust*, 93 *Neb. L. Rev.* 370, 383–95 (2014); Sandeep Vaheesan, *Resurrecting a "Comprehensive Charter of Economic Liberty": The Latent Power of the Federal Trade Commission*, 19 *U. Pa. J. Bus. L.* 645, 657–63 (2017); Longman, *supra* note 10.

[19] *See* Longman, *supra* note 10. Curiously, the clearest statement of this position (albeit with a twist) comes from a more centrist antitrust progressive rather than an antimonopolist. *See* Einer Elhauge, *Horizontal Shareholding*, 129 *Harv. L. Rev.* 1267, 1272 (2016) (arguing that horizontal shareholding in particular "helps explain why, as Professor Thomas Piketty has famously observed, income inequality has risen in … recent decades").

[20] *See* Daniel A. Crane, *Antitrust and Wealth Inequality*, 101 *Cornell L. Rev.* 1171, 1184–209 (2016).

[21] *See id.*

[22] *See id.*

[23] *See id.*

[24] *See* Woodcock, Big Ink v. Bigger Tech, *supra* note 8.

[25] *See* Jonathan B. Baker & Steven C. Salop, *Antitrust, Competition Policy, and Inequality*, 104 *Geo. L.J. Online* 1, 11–12 (2015) ("The returns from market power go disproportionately to the wealthy – increases in producer surplus from the exercise of market power accrue primarily to shareholders and the top executives, who are wealthier on average than the median consumer."); *cf.* Crane, *supra* note 20, at 1207–9.

[26] *Cf.* Fried, *supra* note 6, at 203–4; Crane, *supra* note 20, at 1208.

rather than to counteract attempts by employers to monopsonize those markets, and even if workers were monopolizing labor markets, the antitrust exemption for unions would prevent antitrust enforcers from touching the gains that workers derive from their power.[27] It follows that smashing monopoly and promoting competition through the antitrust laws should on average take money from rich shareholders and distribute it to everyone else, since competition drives down prices and hence profits for rich shareholders, and those lower prices constitute a transfer to the public at large, since everyone is a consumer.[28] That will tend to reduce inequality.[29] This is probably a good rejoinder to the right's critique, insofar as it establishes that a return to competition from a baseline of monopoly is likely to be progressive in its effects on the distribution of wealth.[30] The deeper question is, however: how progressive?

It is here that the critique of antimonopolism from the left, rather than the right, begins.

B *Two Scarcity-Based Critiques of Antimonopolism from the Left*

The trouble with antimonopolism is that its end goal of competition is unlikely greatly to reduce inequality or even to stop the West's current slide toward greater inequality.[31] There is a simple explanation for this, one that was advanced by progressive lawyers and economists in the first law and economics movement a century ago.[32] There is also a contemporary explanation, due to Thomas Piketty, the foremost student today of the growing wealth gap in the West. The contemporary explanation builds on the original progressive account.

1 The Original Progressive Critique of Antimonopolism

A. THE ORIGINAL PROGRESSIVES' REJECTION OF THE CONSERVATIVE CASE FOR ANTIMONOPOLISM. It is not without irony that the original progressive movement of a century ago – that of John R. Commons, Richard T. Ely, Robert L. Hale, and many others – developed its critique of antimonopolism partly in response to an attempt by a conservative economist – J. B. Clark – to advocate precisely what

[27] *See* Herbert Hovenkamp, *Is Antitrust's Consumer Welfare Principle Imperiled?*, 45 *J. Corp. L.* 101, 13 (2019); Suresh Naidu et al., *Antitrust Remedies for Labor Market Power*, 132 *Harv. L. Rev.* 536, 570 (2018).

[28] *See* Rory Van Loo, *Broadening Consumer Law: Competition, Protection, and Distribution*, 95 *Notre Dame L. Rev.* 211, 231–42 (2020).

[29] *See id.*

[30] *See id.*

[31] *See* PIKETTY, *supra* note 1, at 441.

[32] For overviews of the first law and economics movement, see FRIED, *supra* note 6, at 1–29; Hovenkamp, *supra* note 12, at 993–95.

progressive antimonopolists call for today: a world of perfect competition justified on moral grounds.[33] But unlike today's antimonopolists, who tend to assume without argument that the competitive price is the just price – or at least the lowest possible price that an undeserving monopolist can be made to charge – Clark tried to construct a detailed theory to explain why he thought competitive pricing was morally right.[34] The competitive price is just, he claimed, because the competitive price pays sellers an amount equal to their marginal contribution to the value they create for buyers.[35]

It is certainly true that the competitive price pays sellers an amount equal to their marginal contribution to the value they create for buyers. When markets are perfectly competitive, buyers enter the market until there are no buyers left who are willing to pay the market price but who have not had the chance to buy. Assuming the market is deep enough that there are some buyers willing to buy at every possible price, it follows that some buyers who place a value on the good that is just equal to the good's market price will buy the good. These are known as the marginal buyers in the market and the units they buy are the marginal units sold by sellers.[36] Assuming that all sellers charge the same, uniform price (of which more in a moment), the price paid to sellers on every unit they sell, including both the units sold to the marginal buyers and the units sold to all other buyers, must equal the marginal benefit contributed by the sellers to the market (Figure 3.1).[37]

It is as difficult today to understand why Clark placed moral significance on the fact of sellers being paid their marginal contribution to buyer value as it seems to have been for progressives to understand this argument a century ago.[38] Clark's

[33] *See* John Bates Clark, The Distribution of Wealth: A Theory of Wages, Interest and Profits 345 (1899) ("The entrepreneur who hires land does not make over the rent to the landlord because, after paying other claims, he has a certain remainder in his possession. That fact would never compel him to part with the remainder. He pays over this remainder, indeed; but he does it because each bit of land has a positive power to produce, and the landlord can make the tenant pay the value of the specific product of it. If this particular entrepreneur will not pay for a piece of land what it produces, another will. Competition forces the user of any productive agent to give to the owner of it the amount that it brings into existence.");
Fried, *supra* note 6, at 131–34; Hovenkamp, *supra* note 12, at 1022 & n. 159.

[34] *See* Longman, *supra* note 10; Clark, *supra* note 33, at 345.

[35] *See* Clark, *supra* note 33, at 345.

[36] *See* Hal R. Varian, Intermediate Microeconomics: A Modern Approach (7th ed. 2006).

[37] There is no cost curve drawn in Figure 1.1 because Clark's argument centered on the benefits conferred by production – the marginal product – not the costs of production. *See* Fried, *supra* note 6, at 133 ("The 'marginal product,' Hale argued, formally measured the value to the purchaser of a given input, not the cost to the supplier of providing it. In fact, Clark's marginal productivity theory contained no theory of costs at all.").

[38] *See* Hovenkamp, *supra* note 12, at 1022 & n. 159; Fried, *supra* note 6, at 132 (observing that "Clark's particular brand of naive apologetics was a source of embarrassment for most mainstream economists"). We can perhaps rescue Clark as follows: His argument is that the marginal benefit conferred by the seller, which in a competitive market equals the seller's own marginal cost of producing the marginal units, provides a reasonable baseline regarding what the market expects the costs of production *of all units* to be. *Cf.* Clark, *supra* note 33, at

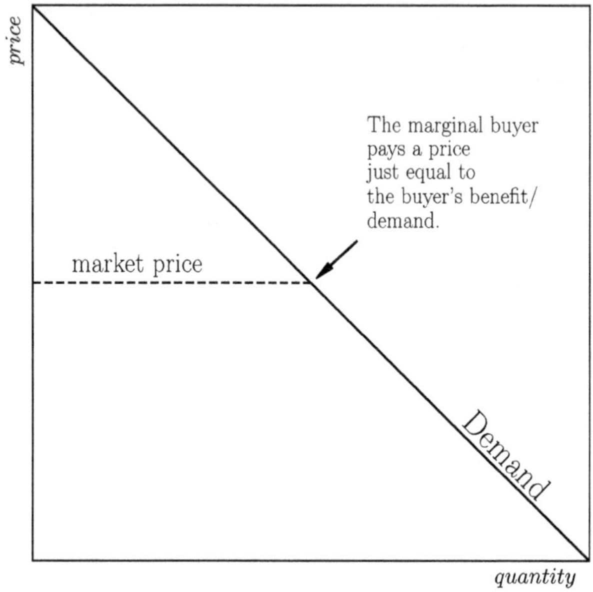

FIGURE 3.1 The marginal buyer pays a price just equal to the value the buyer obtains from the good

explanations read so much like restatements of the mathematics of marginalist economics, rather than moral arguments, that one is tempted to see him as the earliest victim of the tendency of economists to fetishize mathematical models.[39] Progressives responded, in any case, by pointing out that the marginal benefit conferred by a good is completely untethered from the distribution of wealth between buyers and sellers created by competitive pricing.[40] To see why, it is necessary to consider the concept of surplus and its relationship to price.

The wealth created in any market is the excess that the amount buyers are willing to pay for the product – a measure of the benefit the product confers on them – and

345. Certainly, it represents the maximum price that buyers in the market as a group (including the marginal buyers) are willing to pay for production: At a higher price, the market would buy at least one less unit since the marginal buyer would be priced out. It follows that any producer who is able to produce at a cost below the cost of producing the marginal units has excelled, in some sense, relative to the baseline, and so is entitled to keep the difference either as a just desert or an efficient incentive for excellence. It is the moral equivalent of a moral argument for price-cap regulation in public utilities law. *See* W. Kip Viscusi et al., Economics of Regulation and Antitrust (5th ed. 2018). Marginal cost pricing is the cap understood as the cost the seller is expected to have. Any profits the seller realizes by generating efficiencies that allow the seller to sell at a cost below the price cap are the seller's to keep because the seller is understood to have earned them by beating expectations.

39 *See* Clark, *supra* note 33, at 193; Deirdre McCloskey, *The Trouble with Mathematics and Statistics in Economics*, 13 *Hist. Econ. Ideas* 85, 90 (2005); Paul M. Romer, *Mathiness in the Theory of Economic Growth*, 105 *Am. Econ. Rev.* 89, 93 (2015).

40 *See* Fried, *supra* note 6, at 133–34.

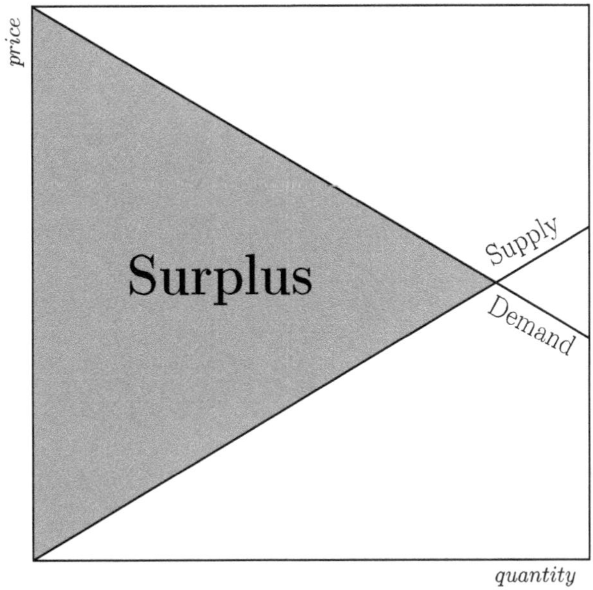

FIGURE 3.2 The excess of demand over supply is called the surplus

the cost to sellers of producing the product – cost being a measure of the value that sellers place on the product.[41] The benefits conferred on buyers are represented by the consumer demand curve, and the costs to sellers are represented by the producer supply curve.[42] The excess of benefit over cost is, then, equivalent to the excess of demand over supply and is called the surplus (Figure 3.2).[43]

Price divides the surplus between buyers and sellers because price is that which buyers give up to sellers to enjoy the benefits represented by the demand curve and therefore subtracts from the surplus that buyers enjoy.[44] And price is also that which sellers receive to compensate for the loss of the value to sellers represented by the supply curve, and the excess of price over that value is therefore sellers' share of the surplus they generate.[45] In a perfectly competitive market, price is driven to the point at which all willing buyers find sellers and vice versa – that is, to the point at which the market clears.[46] That market-clearing price is entirely determined by the

[41] *See* VARIAN, *supra* note 36.

[42] *See id.*

[43] *See* Michael D. Guttentag, *Law and Surplus: Opportunities Missed*, 2019 *Utah L. Rev*. 607, 609 (2019); Ramsi A. Woodcock, *The Antitrust Case for Consumer Primacy in Corporate Governance*, 10 *UC Irvine L. Rev*. 1395, 1403 (2020); Ramsi A. Woodcock, *Big Data, Price Discrimination, and Antitrust*, 68 *Hastings L.J.* 1371, 1380–81 (2017).

[44] *See* VARIAN, *supra* note 36; Woodcock, *Big Data, Price Discrimination, and Antitrust*, *supra* note 43, at 1380–81.

[45] *See* VARIAN, *supra* note 36.

[46] *See id.*

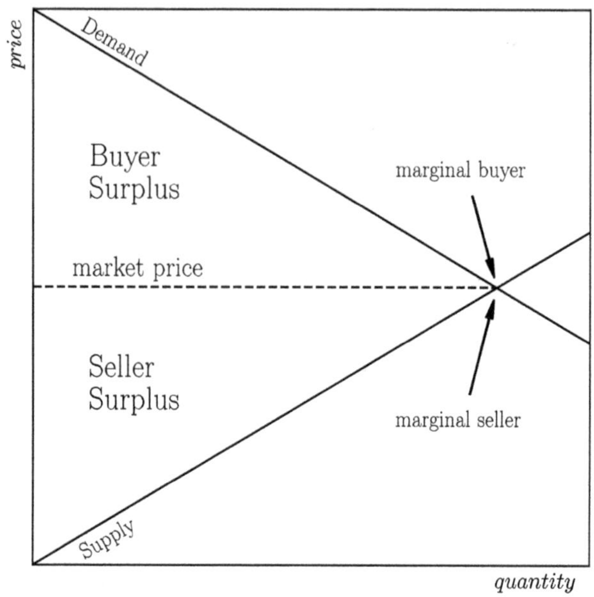

FIGURE 3.3 That market-clearing price is determined by the willingness to pay of the marginal buyer and the cost of the marginal seller

willingness to pay of the marginal buyer – the buyer with the lowest willingness to pay of all those who actually do buy – and the cost of the marginal seller – the seller with the highest cost of all sellers who actually do sell (Figure 3.3).[47]

But the division of the surplus created by the competitive price is not determined by the marginal buyer and seller alone, but rather by the relationship between the marginal buyer's willingness to pay and the willingness to pay of all the other buyers, and the relationship between the marginal seller's costs and the costs of all the other sellers.[48] That is, the distribution of wealth in a competitive market is determined as much by the *inframarginal* buyers and sellers as by the marginal buyers and sellers.[49] Consider this point from a slightly different angle. In a market in which there are some buyers willing to buy at every price and there are some sellers willing to sell at every price (though not always in the same amounts), the price that the marginal buyer pays for the good equals the cost of production of that good, because if not then some more costly goods could be brought to market and buyers willing to buy

[47] *See id.*

[48] *See* FRIED, *supra* note 6, at 134 ("Although marginal analysis gave an analytical structure for generalizing Ricardian rent theory to all factors of production, it said nothing about the actual incidence of rents – that is, the extent of producer's surplus accruing to a given factor. For that, one needed two things: a normative theory of what ought to count as a cost, and an empirical guess about the shape of the cost curve.").

[49] *See id.*

them could be found. But if the price that the marginal buyer pays for the good equals the cost of production of that good, then the surplus created by the transaction between the marginal buyer and seller is zero. So where is the surplus created by markets? Markets must create surplus in order for economic activity to make society better off, and in general economic activity has made society better off.[50] The answer is that the surplus is generated through all the transactions in the market between inframarginal buyers (who necessarily are willing to pay more than the competitive price because the marginal buyer by definition is willing to pay the least of any buyer in the market) and inframarginal sellers (who necessarily have costs below the competitive price because the marginal seller by definition has the highest costs).[51] Because the values inframarginal buyers place on the good exceed the market price and the costs incurred by inframarginal sellers are below the market price, there is an excess of benefit over cost for each transaction in which these buyers and sellers engage, meaning that surplus is created.[52]

How price divides that surplus is determined by how much more value the inframarginal buyers place on the good relative to the marginal buyer and how much lower the costs of inframarginal sellers are relative to that of the marginal seller.[53] If inframarginal buyers place a very high value on the good relative to the value placed on it by the marginal buyer, but inframarginal sellers' costs are not much below that of the marginal seller, then the competitive price will be close to sellers' costs for all units – yielding the sellers little surplus – but much below buyers' willingness to pay for all but the marginal unit, yielding buyers the lion's share of the surplus (Figure 3.4).[54]

By contrast, if inframarginal buyers place a low value on the good relative to the value placed on it by the marginal buyer, but inframarginal sellers' costs are much below the costs of the marginal seller, then the competitive price will be much

50 *See* Brad DeLong, *Estimates of World GDP, One Million B.C.–Present*, https://perma.cc/L9QA-XDPY.

51 *See* FRIED, *supra* note 6, at 26.

52 *See* Woodcock, *Big Data, Price Discrimination, and Antitrust*, *supra* note 43, at 1380–81.

53 *See* FRIED, *supra* note 6, at 134.

54 *See id.* at 126–27 ("As Wicksteed, Wicksell, and J. B. Clark saw, Ricardian land rents were just a special case of the general principle that rents will accrue to the more productive (that is, inframarginal) units of any factor that is not reproducible at constant costs. Thus, Ricardo's assumption of an absolutely fixed supply of land was just 'a limiting case of the infinite array of possible supply elasticities.' As Hale maintained, whenever supply cannot be readily altered at costs that do not increase with quantity, the 'owners of superior resources,' in the form of scarce land or capital equipment acquired for lower than reproduction cost, will realize a surplus return in excess of costs. While early marginalist analysis concentrated on rents accruing to land and other forms of concrete capital, the same logic suggested that rents should accrue to labor and pure capital as well. In Marshall's terms, there will be a 'worker's surplus' or 'saver's surplus' whenever one is remunerated for work or waiting, respectively, at a price [determined by the marginal productivity of one's labor or capital] that exceeds the minimum amount that one would have demanded to provide it – in short, whenever one is an inframarginal supplier.").

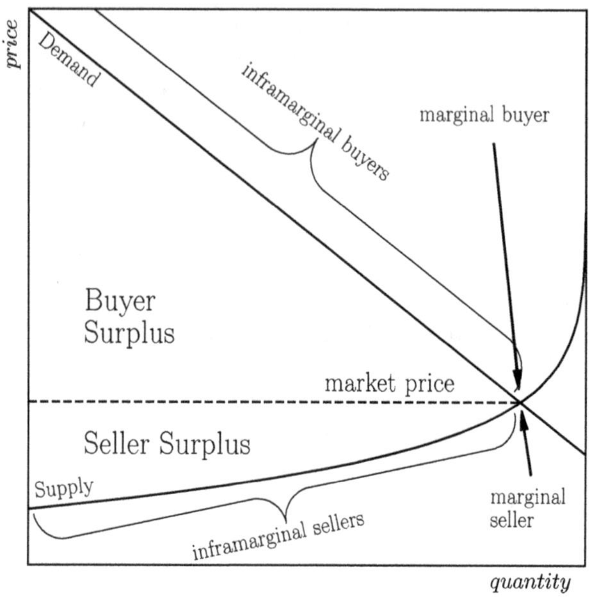

FIGURE 3.4 When buyers take most of the surplus

above sellers' costs for all but the marginal unit – yielding sellers the lion's share of the surplus – but not much below buyers' willingness to pay for all but the marginal unit, yielding buyers very little surplus (Figure 3.5).[55]

Whether the competitive price is fair in the sense that it divides the surplus equally between buyers and sellers, or fair in the sense that it minimizes the surplus enjoyed by sellers, or fair in any other distributive sense, depends on the value placed on the good by inframarginal buyers and sellers relative to the value placed on the good by the marginal buyer and seller. The fact that at the competitive price sellers are paid the marginal benefit they confer on consumers is just the starting point of the analysis and of no moral significance, at least insofar as distributive justice is concerned.[56] All that competitive pricing guarantees is efficiency in the sense that markets clear.[57] At the competitive price, all willing buyers will find willing sellers and vice versa, and so surplus will be maximized.[58] But how that surplus will be divided between buyers and sellers will be an arbitrary function of the relative magnitudes of the value placed on the good by the marginal buyer and seller and the values placed on the good by the inframarginal buyers and sellers.[59]

[55] *See id.*
[56] *See id.* at 134.
[57] *See* VARIAN, *supra* note 36.
[58] *See id.*; Woodcock, *The Antitrust Case for Consumer Primacy in Corporate Governance*, *supra* note 43, at 1409.
[59] *See* FRIED, *supra* note 6, at 134.

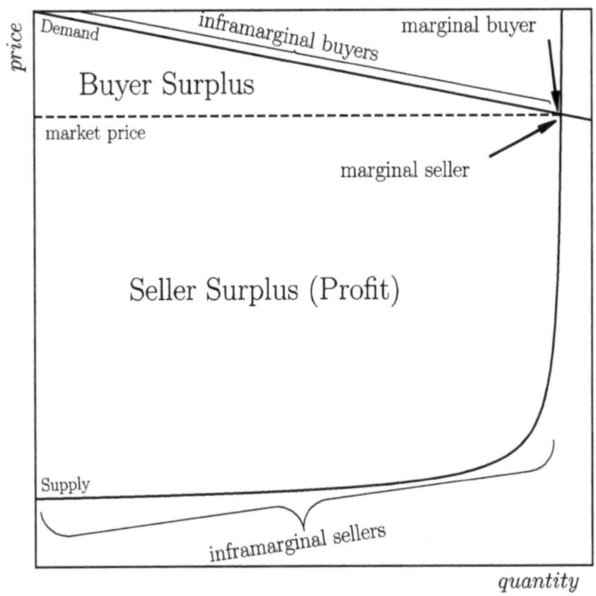

FIGURE 3.5 When sellers take most of the surplus

This critique dispatched Clark's claim to the abstract moral superiority of competitive pricing.[60] And it seemed to imply that antimonopolism, which at the time was a major political force in the United States, was wrongheaded: Promoting competition would not necessarily lead to a desirable distribution of wealth.[61] But this did not fully eliminate the appeal of antimonopolism. For just because competitive pricing *can* result in undesirable distributions of wealth does not mean that it *must* result in undesirable distributions. If costs tend to be uniform over all sellers, or nearly so (Figure 3.4), then competitive pricing will tend to allocate all of the surplus to buyers.[62] And if sellers tend to be richer than buyers, the result will be progressive redistribution that is potentially radical in magnitude if sellers are never able to extract much surplus from their transactions.[63] It is somewhat surprising how few progressive intellectuals of this era seem to have accepted this view, however.[64]

[60] *See id.* at 132–34.

[61] *See* RICHARD HOFSTADTER, THE AGE OF REFORM 227–56 (1960).

[62] *See* FRIED, *supra* note 6, at 134 ("Marginalism disproved the classical assumption that in competitive markets, prices would coincide with costs. More precisely, it showed that assumption held true only where inputs were reproducible at constant costs – in other words, where supply was completely elastic. In all other cases, the owners of scarce resources would receive 'economic rents' in excess of costs.").

[63] *See* Baker & Salop, *supra* note 25, at 11–12.

[64] *Cf.* FRIED, *supra* note 6, at 26 ("Hale and the other progressive rent theorists were sympathetic to the antimonopoly wing of progressivism .... But, beginning with the Fabian socialists in 1870s, they launched a third, distinct attack on the distributive justice of the market. Like the antimonopolists, they largely took as given the Marshallian bipolar model of the economy; however, they focused instead on the pole of so-called perfect competition."); William

Instead, progressives appear to have found it self-evident that this argument failed to take into account the problem of scarcity.

B. THE ORIGINAL PROGRESSIVES' UNDERSTANDING OF THE MEANING OF SCARCITY. Some inputs into the production process are scarce.[65] They may be raw materials, management talent, information, experience, or what have you.[66] Whatever input scarcity may strike, the result is the same: The sellers who have access to the input face lower production costs than the sellers who do not.[67] Those unfortunate sellers who do not must either pay a premium to acquire the resource or use an inferior substitute. The inferior substitute either costs more to acquire or results in a poorer quality product, which must be sold at a lower price to remain competitive and is therefore equivalent, from the seller's perspective, to a product that is less profitable due to higher costs.

It follows that production costs are unlikely to be approximately uniform over all producers in a given market, as would need to be the case to transform competitive pricing into progressively redistributive pricing (i.e., markets are unlikely to look much like Figure 3.4).[68] Some sellers will have high costs and others will have low costs, and so the competitive price, which is determined by the costs of the high-cost sellers (actually by the highest-cost, marginal seller), will be above the costs of the low-cost sellers, ensuring that the low-cost sellers take a potentially large share of the surplus (Figure 3.5).[69] (In the figure, I use "marginal" loosely to refer not just to the seller with the highest costs but also to those sellers with relatively high costs.)

Antimonopolism might push prices down from monopoly levels to competitive levels, and that might redistribute a substantial amount of surplus from sellers to buyers, but even were antimonopolism to be completely successful in creating perfectly competitive markets – itself a highly unlikely proposition – sellers would continue to command a share of the surplus, one that is potentially great.[70] If sellers

E. Kovacic, *Failed Expectations: The Troubled Past and Uncertain Future of the Sherman Act as a Tool for Deconcentration*, 74 IOWA L. REV. 1105, 1128–29 (1989) ("Most professional economists and academicians expert in corporate law initially treated the passage of the Sherman Act and its early enforcement with indifference or outright disapproval.").

65 *See* Harold Demsetz, *Industry Structure, Market Rivalry, and Public Policy*, 16 *J.L. & Econ.* 1, 2–3 (1973).

66 *See id.*

67 *See* Sam Peltzman, *The Gains and Losses from Industrial Concentration*, 20 *J.L. & Econ.* 229, 231–33 (1977).

68 *See id.*

69 *See id.*

70 *See* HALE, *supra* note 5, at 25–26, 401; FRIED, *supra* note 6, at 114 ("[E]ven in situations of competition, whenever supply could not be expanded at constant costs, the 'owners of the superior resources' in the form of land or capital equipment acquired for lower than reproduction cost – so-called 'inframarginal producers' – would realize a surplus return ['economic rent'] in excess of costs.").

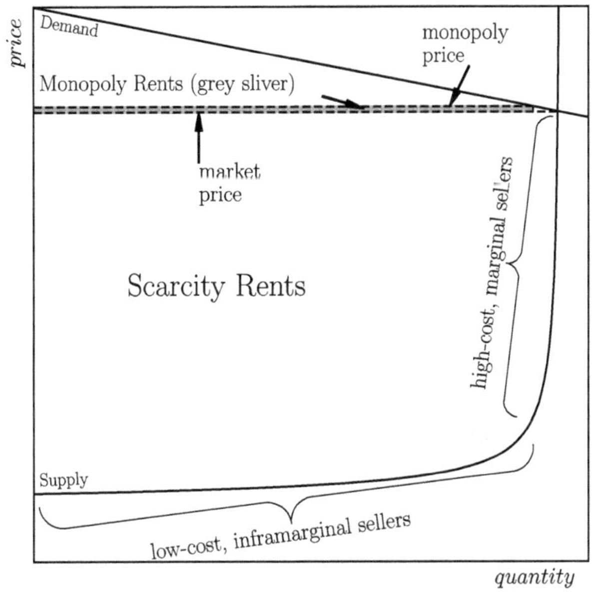

FIGURE 3.6 The problem of scarcity in relation to monopoly, as it was understood by progressives a century ago

are on average richer than buyers, then the surplus they appropriate makes the rich richer, and potentially much richer if costs vary a great deal more than demand. Robert Hale, probably the greatest of the original progressive lawyer-economists, put it thus:

> With the growth of trusts, there was some complaint of exorbitant charges, but the remedy which first suggested itself was, not direct regulation of the prices, but the enactment of anti-trust laws designed to restore free competitive conditions .... Even the classical economists realized ... competition would not keep the price at a level with the cost of all the output, but would result in a price equal to the cost of the marginal portion of the output. Those who produce at lower costs because they own superior [capital] would reap a differential advantage which Ricardo, in his well-known analysis, designated "economic rent."[71]

The problem of scarcity in relation to monopoly, as it was understood by progressives a century ago, is reflected in Figure 3.6.

C. MONOPOLY POWER AND SCARCITY POWER DISTINGUISHED. **i Scarcity Power** The power associated with scarcity is in an important sense indistinguishable from that associated with monopoly. Both are founded on an excess of demand relative to

[71] HALE, *supra* note 5, at 25–26, 401.

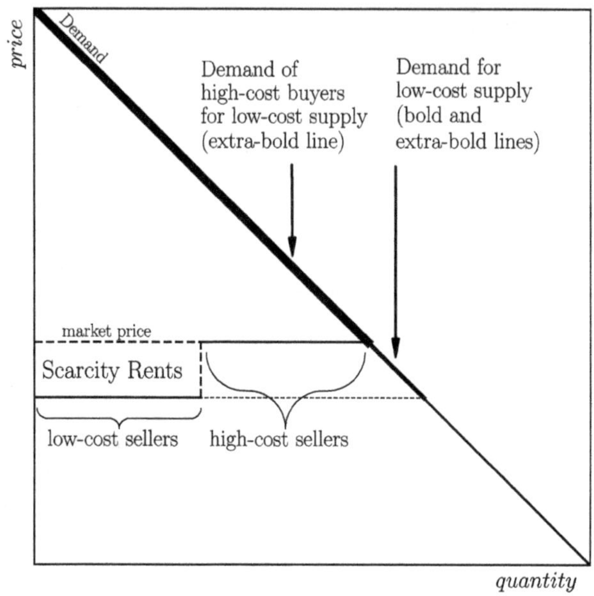

FIGURE 3.7 Firms enjoy scarcity rents when they have lower costs than other market participants

supply. In situations of scarcity, the reason the low-cost sellers are able to charge the same price as the high-cost sellers (and therefore to extract surplus for themselves) is that there are more buyers willing to pay the price necessary to cover the cost of the high-cost sellers than there are low-cost units available for sale. A low-cost seller can, therefore, refuse to sell to any buyer who insists on a lower price, secure in the knowledge that there is another buyer out there whose only option is to buy from a high-cost seller and who therefore would be just as willing to buy from the low-cost seller at the high-cost price (Figure 3.7, in which for simplicity sellers are represented as having only two possible costs).

Without this imbalance of demand and supply, which is baked into the concept of scarcity, there would be no reason for which low-cost sellers could charge the same price as the price charged by the highest-cost seller. The price line in Figure 3.6 could sag down to the level of the supply curve at every point except the point at which the marginal buyer and seller transact, for only at that latter point is a price equal to the marginal seller's high costs necessary for a seller to be willing to sell. Similarly, in Figure 3.7, the price line could step down to the level of the low-cost sellers' costs.

The price line is kept uniform in competitive markets only because scarcity in a competitive market implies that there must be more willing buyers than willing sellers with respect to the low-cost production. Indeed, if the market is not competitive, and there is, for example, a single monopoly buyer, then the price line will sag: The single monopoly buyer would insist on prices below the price at which the highest-cost seller would transact, and the low-cost sellers would have to accept the lower prices, because they could no longer be sure to find some other buyer willing to pay a price equal to the price at which the highest-cost seller would transact. Scarcity power derives from an excess of demand over supply that exists only when markets are fully competitive – a result that is at odds with antimonopoly intuition regarding the relationship between power and competition.

It is for this reason that personalized pricing – price discrimination – is impossible in competitive markets. A price line that sags represents a series of prices personalized to the cost of production of each unit of output – higher prices for units that are costly to produce and lower prices for units that are cheaper to produce. But in a competitive market, the price line cannot sag down to take account of the lower costs of those who control scarce resources, because competition between the buyers who would like to make the line sag enables all sellers, even those who have cost advantages due to control over scarce resources, to insist upon the same price. Thus personalized pricing is no solution to the problem of scarcity power in competitive markets. Personalized pricing is, instead, entirely a creature of monopolized markets in which agents can dictate prices.[72]

The nature of scarcity-based power is starkest in the extreme case in which a resource is so scarce that there are no high-cost sellers in the market at all and supply of the low-cost product is simply insufficient to meet demand[73] In this case, demand exceeds supply and any seller can insist on a price that rations access to the product to the buyers with the highest willingness to pay.[74] In particular, any seller can insist on a price equal to the value placed on the product by the marginal buyer – here the buyer who places the lowest value on the product of any buyer in the high-willingness-to-pay group of rationed buyers. The seller can reject any offer below that buyer's value, secure in the knowledge that there exist other buyers who place at least that value on the good and so are willing to pay a price equal to that value (Figure 3.8).

In such cases, in other words, the absence of high-cost sellers and the insufficiency of low-cost supply mean that the alternative faced by buyers to doing a deal with a low-cost seller is to do no deal at all, in which case buyers lose the value they place on the product. The marginal buyer who fails to acquire the good is willing to pay a price for the good equal to the marginal buyer's loss in value from not doing a deal, and so any seller can insist on a price from *any* buyer equal to that value lost by the marginal buyer, for otherwise the seller can simply sell to the marginal buyer at that price.

ii Monopoly Power The monopolist's power is identical to a seller's scarcity-based power to insist on above-cost (and so surplus appropriating) prices, but for

72 *See* Woodcock, *Big Data, Price Discrimination, and Antitrust*, *supra* note 43, at 1386.

73 *See* Ramsi A. Woodcock, *Toward a Per Se Rule against Price Gouging*, CPI Antitrust Chron. (Sept. 2020), at 51–52 (discussing this sort of scarcity when it arises from unexpected surges in demand).

74 *See id.* (discussing this sort of scarcity when it arises from unexpected surges in demand).

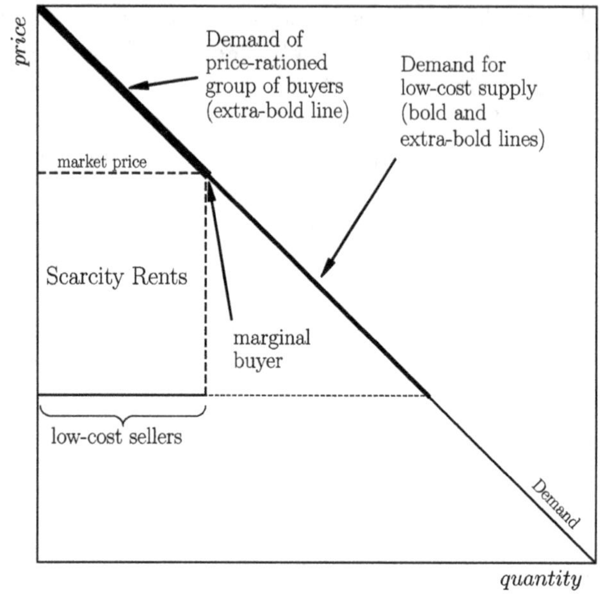

FIGURE 3.8 Firms enjoy scarcity rents when industry output is fixed

one important difference: The monopolist *creates* the scarcity – it is artificial – whereas the seller having scarcity-based power strives to *eliminate* the scarcity.[75]

Consider a seller that initially has power due to the presence of higher-cost producers in the market, as described in the previous section. At this stage, the seller has every incentive to expand the seller's (low-cost) production because competition from high-cost sellers prevents our low-cost seller from raising price above the price at which the high-cost sellers sell their products.[76] With price increases ruled out, our seller's only means of increasing profits is through increasing market share, because each additional unit the seller vends earns the seller the difference between the price of the good (competed down to the cost of the high-cost seller) and our seller's own lower costs (Figure 3.7).[77] The seller's power here to earn rents is due to natural, not artificial, scarcity. The seller has (natural) scarcity-based power but not monopoly power; the seller profits not by restricting output but by expanding it.[78]

As the low-cost seller takes market share from high-cost sellers, perhaps by selling at a price slightly below that at which the high-cost sellers are able to do business, the

[75] *See* Teece & Coleman, *supra* note 2, at 819–22; *cf.* FRIED, *supra* note 6, at 25 (describing "monopoly rents" as those "in which scarcity value [is] attributable to a naturally or artificially constrained number of producers").
[76] *Cf.* Peltzman, *supra* note 67, at 231–33.
[77] *Cf. id.*
[78] *See* Teece & Coleman, *supra* note 2, at 819–22; *cf.* Peltzman, *supra* note 67, at 231–33.

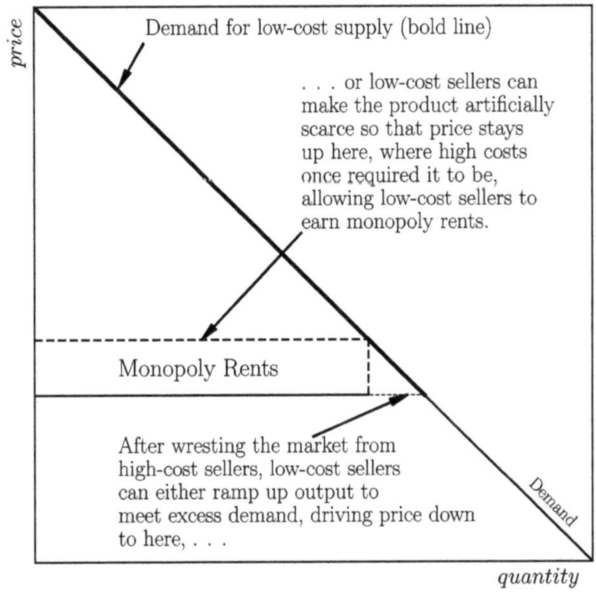

FIGURE 3.9 After wresting the market from high-cost sellers, low-cost sellers artificially limit output in order to enjoy monopoly rents

high-cost sellers exit the market until the low-cost seller is alone there.[79] Only at this point does monopoly power spring into existence. For only now does the seller face a choice regarding whether to increase output beyond the level of output that prevailed when high-cost sellers remained in the market and up to the level required to satisfy the excess demand that exists for the low-cost version of the product. That excess demand could not be satisfied when low-cost units were scarce and price was equal to the higher costs of high-cost sellers, even under perfect competition. But by expanding output, the low-cost seller has eliminated the scarcity of low-cost production. The seller can increase low-cost production further, increasing the size of the market and reducing prices down toward the firm's lower cost of production, in order to satisfy buyers who are willing to pay more than the cost of low-cost production but who were not willing to pay the cost of the high-cost sellers when they were still in the market (Figure 3.9).

Some amount of output increase may in fact be profitable for the low-cost seller; that depends upon whether the costs of the high-cost sellers were so high that they drove prices above the profit-maximizing price for a seller with low costs. But it will never be profitable for our low-cost seller to increase output to levels that would satisfy all of the excess demand, because that would drive price down to the seller's production costs, eliminating all of the seller's profits. The seller will instead choose

[79] *Cf.* Peltzman, *supra* note 67, at 231–33.

output to maximize profits, meaning that the low-cost seller will create artificial scarcity, transforming itself into a practicing monopolist. Our newly minted monopolist will create a market that looks just like the market described in Figure 3.8, in which there is demand in excess of supply of low-cost output and no high-cost alternatives. Indeed, Figures 3.8 and 3.9 are really the same picture. Only now the reason for which there are no high-cost alternatives will not be that the product is naturally scarce – that there is nothing that either the low-cost seller or high-cost sellers can do to make more – but will instead be that our low-cost seller has *chosen* not to make more low-cost products and high-cost sellers dare not return to the market because the low-cost seller can underprice them and take whatever business they wish to acquire.[80] The low-cost seller's power to charge above-cost prices is here due to an artificial scarcity created by the low-cost seller, not to a natural scarcity associated with the inability of the low-cost seller to increase output in the short run.[81]

Both scarcity power and monopoly power are vulnerable to dynamic competition, which here means competition from sellers that have found a way to produce at even lower cost.[82] A dynamic competitor may have chanced upon a new supply of a scarce natural resource, or, thanks to research and development, may have overcome a technological barrier to production that other sellers have failed to conquer.[83] If dynamic competitors enter the market, the cycle repeats: The market returns to one in which there are low-cost and high-cost sellers, only now the original low-cost seller becomes a high-cost seller in this new market, and the dynamic competitors are now the low-cost sellers seeking to run the high-cost seller out of the market. If this disruption occurs when our original low-cost seller is enjoying monopoly power (i.e., after our original low-cost seller has driven the original high-cost sellers from the market), then our original low-cost seller will no longer be able artificially to limit supply because buyers will simply buy from the new even-lower-cost dynamic competitors. Thus dynamic competition destroys the monopoly power acquired by our original low-cost seller (Figure 3.10).

If this disruption occurs before our original low-cost seller has become a monopolist (i.e., before our original low-cost seller has driven the original high-cost sellers from the market), then the dynamic competitors earn scarcity rents of their own, and those will be larger, on a per unit-basis, than those enjoyed by our original low-cost seller, because the dynamic competitor will have even lower costs (Figure 3.11).

What is more, once either the dynamic competitors or our original low-cost seller have taken market share from the original high-cost sellers, driving them from the

80 *See* F. M. Scherer & David Ross, Industrial Market Structure and Economic Performance (3d ed. 1990).

81 *See* Teece & Coleman, *supra* note 2, at 819–22.

82 *See* J. Gregory Sidak & David J. Teece, *Dynamic Competition in Antitrust Law*, 5 *J. Competition L. Econ.* 581, 603–7 (2009).

83 *Cf. id.*

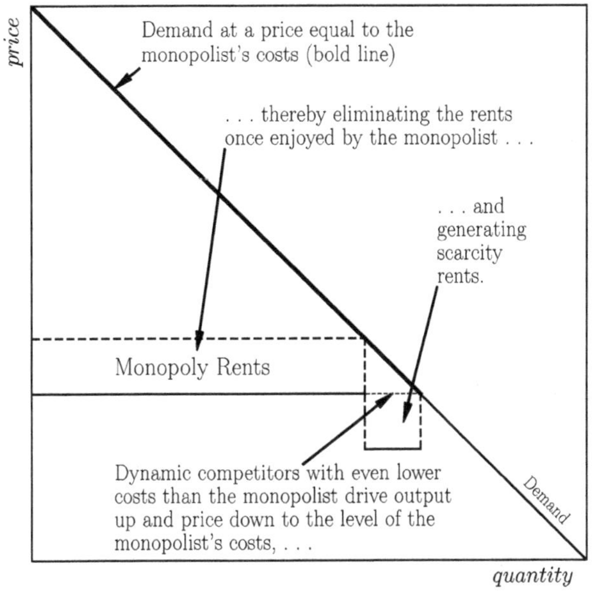

FIGURE 3.10 Dynamic competition replaces monopoly rents with scarcity rents

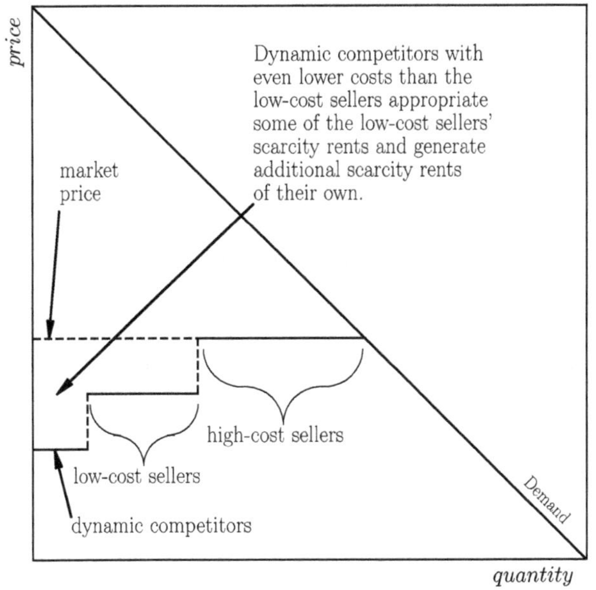

FIGURE 3.11 Dynamic competition shifts scarcity rents to the dynamic competitor

market, the cost of the marginal unit will fall to the level of our original low-cost seller's low costs and competition between our original low-cost seller and the dynamic competitors will push price down to our original low-cost seller's costs. Our original low-cost seller's products will no longer play the role of the scarce, relatively desirable products offered by the market. That role will now be played by the products sold by the dynamic competitors at even lower cost, explaining why competition is able to push price down and eliminate our original low-cost seller's scarcity rents.

It is evident that dynamic competition does not, therefore, destroy scarcity power in the way that it destroys monopoly power, but instead merely changes the identity of the firms that wield scarcity power, substituting dynamic competitors for the original low-cost seller as scarcity rentiers. The effects of dynamic competition are nonetheless good for consumers in both cases, because whether dynamic competition attacks monopoly power or scarcity power, dynamic competition reduces prices, and does so even though, in the scarcity case, it cannot eliminate scarcity-based power.

This point is worth repeating. While dynamic competition can eliminate monopoly rents in that it can make artificial scarcity impossible, dynamic competition can never eliminate scarcity.[84] The agents of competition – new firms with lower costs – bring competition to the market by bringing scarcity to the market. They beat out incumbents by lowering costs in ways that incumbents are unable to do. Thus competition eliminates scarcity-based power only in the sense of transferring it to new agents, whereas competition eliminates monopoly power entirely by preventing any one firm from enjoying a cost advantage for so long that it is able to drive all competitors from the market. Given the power of competition to snuff out monopoly, firms naturally try to slow competition, and the purpose of the antitrust laws is to prevent such

[84] To argue that scarcity power is an inherent part of competition is not to argue that the proceeds of that power – the scarcity rents – much less monopoly rents, are in any sense *necessary* to finance competition, to reward successful competitors, or otherwise to bring about the efficient operation of a market economy. *Cf.* JOSEPH A. SCHUMPETER, CAPITALISM, SOCIALISM AND DEMOCRACY 105 (1950) (arguing that monopoly profits are necessary to finance innovation); Verizon Commc'ns Inc. v. Law Offices of Curtis V. Trinko, 540 U.S. 398, 407 (2004) ("The opportunity to charge monopoly prices – at least for a short period – is what attracts 'business acumen' in the first place; it induces risk taking that produces innovation and economic growth. To safeguard the incentive to innovate, the possession of monopoly power will not be found unlawful unless it is accompanied by an element of anticompetitive conduct."). Rents are, *by definition*, not necessary to induce firms to produce and compete at optimal levels. *See* Woodcock, *The Antitrust Case for Consumer Primacy in Corporate Governance*, *supra* note 43, at 1412–26. The scarcity-based power to extract rents from buyers cannot be eliminated, but government can intervene to prevent the exercise of that power by, for example, dictating prices, taxing away rents, or weakening the ability of sellers to withhold access to their goods to buyers who refuse to pay full price for them. Each of these interventions will have an efficiency cost, but this cost is essentially administrative. It arises from the difficulty of identifying rents and enforcing their redistribution, not from the bare fact of their redistribution itself, for rents are, again, by definition, income not necessary to induce efficient behavior by firms. For more on taxation and rate regulation, see *infra* Section III.A. For more on weakening the ability of sellers to withhold access, see Kennedy, *supra* note 13, at 30–33.

behavior.[85] In promoting competition, the antitrust laws seek, in other words, to ensure that the only form of power in markets is scarcity power, not monopoly power.

D. THE GENERALITY OF THE CRITIQUE. The foregoing account of the origins of scarcity and monopoly rents may appear to apply only to markets in which economic growth takes place through cost reductions – otherwise known as process innovations – as in the case of the high-cost and low-cost sellers just described.[86] But in fact the account applies with great generality to all markets, including those for which growth typically takes place through the improvement of products rather than the reduction of costs.[87] That is because what really matters to buyers and sellers in any market is only the surplus created by the market transactions in which they engage, and that is determined by the excess of buyer value over seller cost. It follows that product improvements can be modeled as cost reductions without changing the results of the analysis. This can be done by measuring the surplus created by the product improvement and then reproducing that amount through a cost reduction with buyer value held constant.[88] Thus we can apply the supply and demand lines in Figure 3.2 to any differentiated-product market – as markets in which growth takes place through product improvements are known – so long as the space between the lines, which represents the surplus created by the market, accurately represents the excess of value over cost for the differentiated products involved.[89]

Once the generality of this account is understood, it becomes clear that what is often called "Schumpeterian rent" is really just a kind of scarcity rent and has therefore already been fully addressed by this account.[90] Schumpeterian rent is due to the power that comes from introducing into a market a technological advance that competitors are temporarily unable to reproduce.[91] It is, therefore, no more than the proceeds of the power enjoyed by the dynamic competitor that brings lower-cost production to a market and is able to earn scarcity rents thereby, until the next dynamic competitor with even lower costs comes along. Schumpeterian rent differs from scarcity rent more generally only in that Schumpeterian rent is defined to be short-lived.[92] A technological advance that no further dynamic competitor can

85 *See* Richard A. Posner, Antitrust Law (2d ed. 2001).

86 *See* Fried, *supra* note 6, at 26 (treating product differentiation and monopolistic competition as different in kind from the perfectly competitive markets considered by the original progressives).

87 *See* Frederic M. Scherer, *First Mover Advantages and Optimal Patent Protection*, 40 *J. Tech. Transfer* 559, 562–65 (2015).

88 This is the analogue of the quality-adjusted price concept, applied here to adjust surplus rather than price. *See* Keith Cowling & A. J. Rayner, *Price, Quality, and Market Share*, 78 *J. Pol. Econ.* 1292, 1294 (1970).

89 *See* Edward Hastings Chamberlin, The Theory of Monopolistic Competition: A Re-Orientation of the Theory of Value 71 (7th ed. 1956).

90 *See* Teece & Coleman, *supra* note 2, at 820–22.

91 *See id.*

92 *See id.*

reproduce over a long period of time, or the natural resource constraint that technology is not able to overcome for decades, are examples of scarcity that is not Schumpeterian in character because it is long-lived.[93] The historical transition of Western economies from markets characterized by short-lived Schumpeterian rents to economies characterized by long-lived scarcity rents plays an important role in the contemporary left critique of antimonopolism, as we shall see shortly.[94] But, for the original progressives of a century ago, it was enough to critique antimonopolism by pointing out that scarcity is an inherent feature of competition, and so the inequality created by scarcity rents of all kinds, Schumpeterian or otherwise, can never be touched by a policy focused purely on fighting monopoly.[95]

E. THE ORIGINAL PROGRESSIVE RECIPE FOR INEQUALITY. That was not to say, however, that scarcity rents could not be touched by anything. Indeed, sellers with low costs are not actually required to use their scarcity-based power to charge above-cost prices and appropriate surplus.[96] Costs in the economic sense include, by definition, all payments, including a reasonable return on investment, required to make a seller ready, willing, and able to sell whatever level of output is demanded by the market.[97] It follows that, if they wish to do so, sellers can choose to charge at-cost prices – prices that leave all of the surplus generated by the market to buyers – and still find it in their interests to remain in the market and continue to generate that surplus for others.[98] Sellers do not actually charge at-cost prices only because they like making profits, not because they need to make profits in order to survive.[99]

It also follows from the definition of economic cost that government can force sellers to charge at-cost prices, or can extract from sellers, via taxation, whatever surplus sellers do earn from charging above-cost prices and repurpose it to other uses, without reducing sellers' output (Figure 3.12).

The progressives who recognized competition's limitations a century ago understood this and therefore turned to rate regulation and taxation as alternative means of addressing the problem of inequality.[100] They pressed for regulation of prices in industries such as urban residential leasing in which scarcity was thought to be most enduring, in addition to pushing for price regulation not only in public utility industries characterized by massive economies of scale, for which the principal concern is monopoly power, but in a host of industries from airlines to trucking in which

93 *See id.*

94 *See infra* Section II.B.2.

95 *See* Hale, *supra* note 5, at 25–26, 401.

96 *See* Ramsi A. Woodcock, *The Antitrust Duty to Charge Low Prices*, 39 *Cardozo L. Rev.* 1741, 1753 (2018).

97 *See* Woodcock, *The Antitrust Case for Consumer Primacy in Corporate Governance*, *supra* note 43, at 1412–26.

98 *See id.*

99 *See id.*

100 *See* Fried, *supra* note 6, at 40, 68, 160–205; Avi-Yonah, *supra* note 6, at 1212–31.

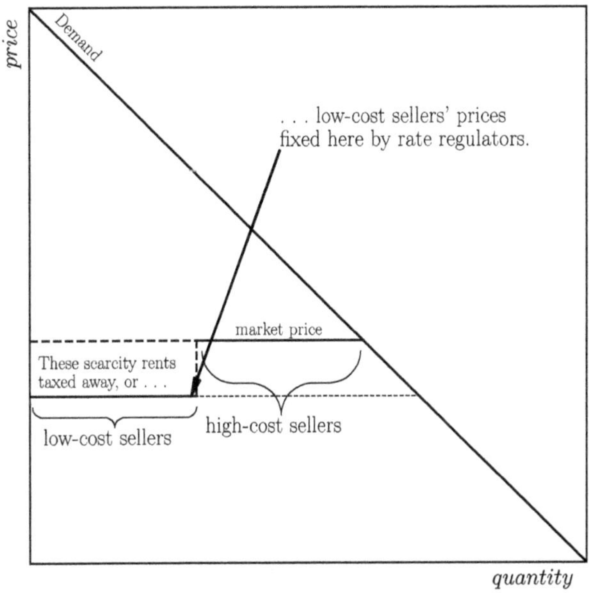

FIGURE 3.12 Both taxation and price regulation can redistribute scarcity rents

competition could be fierce.[101] Progressives also pushed for income taxation and, notably, corporate taxation, which tends to fall on scarcity rents directly because of deductions for interest on investment financing, which cover the cost of capital.[102] The answer to Richard Hofstadter's famous question – "what happened to the antitrust movement?" – was that progressives came to understand that what mattered were competition-immune (or, more to the point, competition-created) scarcity rents; and so taxation, and that special form of taxation for which buyers keep the proceeds that is known as price regulation, became progressives' preferred tool to address inequality.[103]

It is also worth noting that although progressive ardor for antitrust cooled early on, that did not prevent antitrust in America from institutionalizing itself and growing in power during the postwar period.[104] During that period, antitrust exhibited a tendency that one finds in antimonopolism today as well: a desire to go beyond the remediation of monopoly rents in particular to try to deploy antitrust remedies to attack scarcity rents. This was epitomized by the attempt in the 1970s of the American antitrust establishment to create a "no-fault" monopolization regime, meaning a regime that would have broken up a seller that earns economic profits even when the seller has

[101] *See* FRIED, *supra* note 6, at 124, 195–96, 204.

[102] *See* Reuven Avi-Yonah, *A New Corporate Tax*, TAX NOTES FEDERAL 653, 655–59 (2020); Avi-Yonah, *supra* note 6, at 1212–31; FRIED, *supra* note 6, at 203.

[103] *See* Richard Hofstadter, *What Happened to the Antitrust Movement?*, *in* THE PARANOID STYLE IN AMERICAN POLITICS AND OTHER ESSAYS 188 (1st ed. 1967); FRIED, *supra* note 6, at 24–25, 40, 68, 160–205; Avi-Yonah, *supra* note 6, at 1212–31.

[104] *See* Hofstadter, *supra* note 103; JOHN KENNETH GALBRAITH, THE NEW INDUSTRIAL STATE (2015).

not taken steps to block competition.[105] That would, of course, have swept in sellers that earn economic profits due to scarcity rather than monopoly.

Breakup is not, however, a good way to eliminate scarcity rents, as the Chicago School rushed to point out, causing the "no fault" movement to fizzle. The Chicago School argued effectively that breakup risks destroying whatever scarce resources – whether natural, technological, or experiential – make it possible for sellers to produce at lower cost and so to benefit from scarcity, or at least risks preventing firms with lower costs from increasing market share and spreading lower-cost production across the market as fast as possible.[106] Chicago contended that the solution to scarcity is the creation of more scarcity, in the sense of new firms with even lower costs.[107] It is not, argued Chicago, the breakup of existing low-cost sellers, for that merely risks increasing their costs.[108] One of the original progressives might well have added that such cost increases would be particularly unfortunate because they destroy surpluses that the government might otherwise tax away from sellers and put to good use. Chicago and the original progressives might well have agreed that only firms that have artificially created the scarcity from which they benefit can be punished without risk of raising costs, and then only by targeting the behaviors they use to undermine competition, rather than by breaking them up.[109]

There intellectual matters stood until Thomas Piketty embedded the original progressives' appreciation for the importance of scarcity and the need for taxation as remedy in a compelling historical account of inequality, one that again rejects antimonopolism as a redistributive vehicle.[110]

2 Piketty's Implicit Critique of Antimonopolism

The second, contemporary, left critique of antimonopolism, which is due, somewhat implicitly, to Thomas Piketty, builds on the original progressive insights regarding scarcity, but updates them with a dynamic story that explains the resurgence of wealth inequality over the past fifty years.

It is probably fair to say that Piketty's book, *Capitalism in the Twenty-First Century*, brought contemporary intellectual interest in wealth inequality into focus.[111] The book

[105] *See* Note, *The Industrial Reorganization Act: An Antitrust Proposal to Restructure the American Economy*, 73 Colum. L. Rev. 635, 637–40 (1973); Herbert Hovenkamp, *The Neal Report and the Crisis in Antitrust*, No. ID 1348707, 1–5 (2009).

[106] *See* Harold Demsetz, *Two Systems of Belief about Monopoly*, *in* Industrial Concentration: The New Learning 164 (Harvey J. Goldschmid et al. eds., 1974). Recall that firms that have scarcity power in a competitive market have an incentive to increase market share because they cannot raise prices. *See supra* Section II.B.1.c.

[107] *See id.*

[108] *See* Peltzman, *supra* note 67, at 262.

[109] *See* Posner, *supra* note 85.

[110] *See* Piketty, *supra* note 3, at 573.

[111] *See* Piketty, *supra* note 3; Idrees Kahloon, *Thomas Piketty Goes Global*, The New Yorker, https://perma.cc/DTD8-GTJ4 (last visited May 31, 2021).

did this not only by presenting the results of Piketty's painstakingly collected data on the growth of wealth inequality since World War II – data that established incontrovertibly that inequality has greatly increased in recent decades – but also by providing a theoretical account of how that inequality came into being and why it will continue to grow.[112] The theory is usually summarized by Piketty's conclusion that "$r > g$": The rate of return on capital in the long run is greater than the rate of growth of the economy.[113] The implication is that owners' share of the economic pie always ultimately grows faster than the pie itself, ensuring that in the long run the share of the pie going to labor will shrink and inequality will increase.[114]

Piketty's r > g argument is really an argument that scarcity rents drive inequality. That is because he views the 4 or 5 percent historical rate of return on capital that he identifies (his r in r > g) as a scarcity rent. If the return were to count as cost, in the sense that it were necessary to make the owners of capital ready, willing, and able to supply their capital, then that return would not count as scarcity rent.[115] But Piketty does not see the return on capital as a cost. Indeed, he makes clear that if part of his 4 or 5 percent figure for the rate of return were shown to be cost, he would deduct that part in order to determine the true rate of return. He accepts, for example, that landowners might incur costs in developing their land and that such costs should be deducted from the 4 or 5 percent figure for the rate of return, leading to a revised rate of 2 or 3 percent.[116] It follows that Piketty sees the return on capital as economic profit in the sense of a return not necessary to induce owners to supply their capital.[117]

Economic profits can, of course, be due either to monopoly power or scarcity power.[118] But Piketty flatly rejects the notion that monopoly power plays a significant role in juicing the rate of return on capital[119] According to Piketty, "pure and perfect competition cannot alter the inequality $r > g$, which is not the consequence of any

[112] *See* PIKETTY, *supra* note 3, at 1–49.

[113] *See id.* at 442–51.

[114] *See id.* at 443.

[115] *See* Woodcock, *The Antitrust Case for Consumer Primacy in Corporate Governance*, *supra* note 43, at 1412–26.

[116] *See* PIKETTY, *supra* note 3, at 445 ("Even if we accept a much lower estimate of the pure yield on capital – for example, by accepting the argument that many landowners have made over the years that it is no simple matter to manage a large estate, so that this return actually reflects a just compensation for the highly skilled labor contributed by the owner – we would still be left with a minimum (and to my mind unrealistic and much too low) return on capital of at least 2–3 percent a year, which is still much greater than [the] 0.1–0.2 percent [growth rate of the economy from antiquity through to the seventeenth century].").

[117] *See* Woodcock, *The Antitrust Case for Consumer Primacy in Corporate Governance*, *supra* note 43, at 1412–26.

[118] *See supra* Section II.B.1.c.

[119] *See* PIKETTY, *supra* note 3, at 537 ("[T]he fact that capital yields income, which in accordance with the original meaning of the word we refer to in this book as 'annual rent produced by capital,' has absolutely nothing to do with the problem of imperfect competition or monopoly.").

market 'imperfection.'"[120] It follows that Piketty sees the economic profits represented by his 4 or 5 percent return figure as scarcity rent.

Piketty does appear at one point to distinguish his return on capital from scarcity rent. He writes that scarcity magnifies the return on capital, suggesting that the return itself is not driven by scarcity.[121] And he argues that the return on capital is in a sense normal: Capital needs to be paid something, and that something just happens to be a high 4 or 5 percent.[122] But this distinction between scarcity as a booster of returns and a normal rate of return is not really tenable from the perspective of our definition of economic profit as payments in excess of amounts necessary to induce productive activity.[123] The only reason capital can earn any return at all in the sense of economic profit, assuming, as Piketty does, that this return is not comprised entirely of monopoly profit, is scarcity: the fact that some sellers have lower costs than others and so control scarce resources.[124] It follows that Piketty's 4 or 5 percent return is a scarcity rent and that what Piketty means by "scarcity" is *extreme* scarcity: markets for which the marginal buyer pays a price in excess of the cost of production of the marginal unit, because resources are so scarce that there is simply no production – not even high-cost production – available to satisfy demand. Piketty's scarcity is the extreme scarcity of Figure 3.8 and his return on capital is the less-extreme scarcity of Figure 3.7.

From this perspective, we can restate, as follows, Piketty's thesis that inequality will grow in the long term because the rate of return on capital exceeds the growth rate of the economy.[125] Piketty in effect argues that if national income (i.e., Picketty's g) is growing at a faster rate than scarcity rents (i.e., Piketty's return on capital, r), and we can assume that surplus grows at the same rate as national income (i.e., diminishing returns have not set in), then surplus, too, must be growing faster than scarcity rents. As a result, the very rich, for whom income is assumed to come primarily from scarcity rents, will be losing ground to everyone else. But if scarcity rents are greater than increases in surplus – if $r > g$ – then the rich, who as shareholders tend to enjoy the scarcity rents created by the economy, will pull away from everyone else.[126]

Thus Piketty's theory depends on the size of the scarcity rents generated by sellers. Because Piketty rejects the notion that these rents are due to monopoly power, he

[120] *See* Piketty, *supra* note 1, at 537.

[121] *See* Piketty, *supra* note 3, at 35 (arguing that the factors pushing up the rate of return on capital "can be aggravated by the Ricardian scarcity principle: the high price of real estate or petroleum may contribute to structural divergence").

[122] *See id.* at 536 ("If capital plays a useful role in the process of production, it is natural that it should be paid.").

[123] *See* Woodcock, *The Antitrust Case for Consumer Primacy in Corporate Governance*, *supra* note 43, at 1412–26.

[124] *See infra* Section II.B.1.c.

[125] *See* Piketty, *supra* note 3, at 442–51.

[126] *See id.*

rejects the notion that *r* can be driven down to *g* and inequality eliminated simply through competition policy.[127] Instead, he argues that only tax policy and other measures aimed at redistributing scarcity rents can drive *r* down.[128] Indeed, he argues that only two main factors have ever reduced scarcity rents historically, and then only once in the history of civilization, in the mid twentieth century.[129] The first is the world wars and the Great Depression, which in our schema would have reduced the amount of variation between low- and high-cost producers, wiping out all of the highest-quality and so lowest-cost assets, and so reducing the size of scarcity rents (i.e., transforming markets from that depicted in Figure 3.5 to that depicted in Figure 3.4).[130] This factor does not lend itself to future use by policymakers to reduce inequality. The second is the institution of the income tax with high marginal rates on large incomes.[131]

In the final analysis, the source of inequality, in Piketty's view, is that the rich own all the best stuff and it is better enough to ensure that even in competitive markets they can receive a sufficiently higher price for it to do better than the economy as a whole. In Piketty's view, Figure 3.6, with its depiction of large scarcity rents, is basically right. This is most obvious in the case of the very largest fortunes. Piketty notes that "[f]or the largest inherited fortunes, on the order of tens of billions of dollars or euros, one can probably assume that most of the money remains invested in the family firm (as is the case with the Bettencourt family with L'Oreal and the Walton family with Walmart in the United States."[132] The immense returns earned on these fortunes come from rents earned by business enterprises occupying the low end of supply curves in individual markets, loosely defined, just as Figure 3.6 depicts. L'Oréal and Walton heirs rake in surplus year after year, not because their companies are monopolies – there are lots of cosmetic companies out there, and Walmart's "everyday low prices" is hardly a monopolist's tagline – but because these companies either occupy a market niche that no other firms are able to challenge or simply have lower costs than their competitors, which is to say, in both cases: because of scarcity.

Investor Warren Buffett is another example. When he professes to look for firms with "moats" around them, he does not mean monopolies.[133] He means firms that control scarce resources, such as rail networks. Rail competes with trucking, marine, and air transport options. In those markets in which the competitive market price is in excess of rail costs, rail generates a profit. Until a cheaper technology emerges in

[127] *See id.* at 536–37.
[128] *See id.* at 597–746.
[129] *See id.* at 449.
[130] *See id.*
[131] *See id.*
[132] *See id.* at 559.
[133] *See* Tae Kim, *Warren Buffett Believes This Is "the Most Important Thing" to Find in a Business*, CNBC, https://perma.cc/M72H-XKH9 (last visited May 18, 2021).

those markets. Buffett, whose company Berkshire Hathaway purchased Burlington Northern Santa Fe railroad in 2010, will enjoy surpluses.[134]

But association of wealth with ownership of all the best stuff is also true for more middling fortunes, albeit for a slightly different reason. Piketty argues that "as we move down the list [of the largest fortunes] it is likely that many inherited fortunes are held in diversified portfolios . . . ."[135] But the diversified portfolios also tend to generate economic rents because, according to Piketty, they are large enough to enable their owners to afford superior investment advice – that is, to realize economies of scale in portfolio management – ensuring that the money is used to purchase the scarcest assets in the markets in which they are invested.[136]

The implication of Piketty's work is that antimonopolism misses the causes of contemporary inequality if it sticks to attacking true monopolies. Moreover, if antimonopolism shifts its focus and tries to use breakup to deal with scarcity in competitive markets, antimonopolism can only solve the problem in the way that Allied bombers did for Europe: by destroying enough capital so as to flatten the cost curve and drive down the rate of return on capital. Piketty therefore argues that the solution to inequality is taxation, rather than antimonopolism: Government must tax away scarcity rents and distribute them broadly to the public.[137]

III EXPLAINING CONTEMPORARY AMERICAN PROGRESSIVE INTEREST IN REDISTRIBUTION THROUGH THE ANTITRUST LAWS

A *The Long March around the Tax System in Legal Academia*

The fact that the progressives of a century ago a well as the intellectual godfather of contemporary interest in inequality both reject the notion that inequality is due to monopoly rents poses the question of why there is an antimonopoly movement in America today at all. The question is all the more interesting because the movement is not a product of the antitrust establishment, as was the mid-century push for a "no-fault" monopolization regime.[138] That old establishment, which pushed antimonopolism because it was its professional duty to do so, is long gone, replaced by enforcers and antitrust professors who have absorbed enough of the Chicago School critique that for decades they have been content to advocate only for incremental, centrist changes in enforcement.[139] There are, it appears, two causes

[134] *See* Patrick Morris, *The Truth behind Warren Buffett's Billion-Dollar Railroad Bet*, The Motley Fool, https://perma.cc/A539-J5UT (last visited May 18, 2021).

[135] Piketty, *supra* note 3, at 559.

[136] *See id.* at 571.

[137] *See id.* at 449.

[138] *See* Hovenkamp, *supra* note 105, at 1–2; Kovacic, *supra* note 64, at 1119–28, 1137–39.

[139] *See* Hofstadter, *supra* note 103 (discussing the institutionalization of antitrust); How the Chicago School Overshot the Mark (Robert Pitofsky ed., 2008) (collection of work reflecting the new center-left establishment); Jonathan B. Baker, *Economics and Politics:*

of the curious resurgence of antimonopolism, one a long-term cause and the other a recent triggering factor.

The long-term cause is the American tax revolt that started in the 1980s with cuts by the Reagan administration to the highest marginal income tax rates, and has continued more or less unabated to the present day, the rising tide of inequality, and bipartisan popular concern about it, notwithstanding.[140] Despite efforts by Democratic presidents to raise them, tax rates remain a fraction of what they were before Reagan.[141] Even the Biden administration, which proposed the most ambitious taxation and spending programs in decades, did not propose raising income tax rates back to where they once were.[142] Once it became clear in the 1980s that voters were no longer supportive of the use of the tax system to redistribute wealth, progressive scholars started to show interest in alternative redistributive schemes that had been considered, and eventually rejected, by the original progressives and which have now also been rejected again by Piketty.[143] Contemporary antimonopolism is an expression of this continuing urge to redistribute around the political barrier of tax policy.

Much of the literature that has emerged from this desire to avoid politically infeasible broad-based tax policy – a literature that continues to grow by leaps and bounds – focuses on rejecting an argument that developed, ironically, out of *progressive* fervor for redistribution through taxation and reached its highest form on the eve of the Reagan era tax revolt.[144] That was the argument against redistribution via manipulation of market prices and in favor of redistribution through the income tax.[145] As we shall see, the argument has since come to be associated with

Perspectives on the Goals and Future of Antitrust, 81 *Fordham L. Rev.* 2175, 2184 (2012) (articulating the contemporary center-left view of enforcement).

140 *See* Brownlee, *supra* note 7, at 182–83, 210–11, 228, 241, 272, 286; Piketty, *supra* note 3, at 499.

141 *See* Brownlee, *supra* note 7, at 178–249; *Historical Highest Marginal Income Tax Rates*, Tax Pol'y Center, https://perma.cc/686C-H4GG (last visited June 2, 2021) (showing that the highest marginal income tax rate, which was 92% in 1953, fell from 70% in 1980 to 50% in 1982, has not risen above 39.6% since, and is currently 37%).

142 *See* United States Department of the Treasury, *The Made in America Tax Plan*, Tax Pol'y Econ. (2021).

143 *See* Ramsi Woodcock, *Personalizing Prices to Redistribute Wealth in Antitrust and Public Utility Rate Regulation*, 2022 Wis. L. Rev. 1408 (2022).

144 *See, e.g.*, Anthony Atkinson & Joseph Stiglitz, *The Design of Tax Structure: Direct versus Indirect Taxation*, 6 *J. Pub. Econ.* 55, 602 (1976); Harold Hotelling, *The General Welfare in Relation to Problems of Taxation and of Railway and Utility Rates*, 6 *Econometrica* 242, 242 (1938).

145 *See* F. Y. Edgeworth, *The Pure Theory of Taxation III*, 7 *Econ. J.* 550, 568 & n.1 (1897) ("If a given amount ... is raised by taxing a few commodities ... there will in general occur under the head of those commodities a loss of 'consumers' rent' which does not occur when the amount is directly subtracted from income[.]"); Hotelling, *supra* note 144, at 242 (stating that "all taxes on commodities, including sales taxes, are more objectionable than taxes on incomes, inheritances, and the site value of land"); David Walker, *The Direct–Indirect Tax Problem: Fifteen Years of Controversy*, 10 *Pub. Fin. / Finances Publiques* 153 (1955); John Richard Hicks, Value and Capital: An Inquiry into Some Fundamental Principles of Economic Theory (2001) ("A tax on commodities lays a greater burden on consumers than

the work of Louis Kaplow and Steven Shavell, but it hardly originated with them. The argument started in earnest with Harold Hotelling in the 1930s and became the subject of a celebrated 1976 paper by two liberal lions of the economics world, Anthony Atkinson and Joseph Stiglitz.[146] These authors put forth the argument in an effort to defend, against attempts at suffocation through half-measures, the great insight of the original progressives that redistribution could best be implemented only through taxation.

For the original progressives the ideal way to tax scarcity rents was to narrowly tailor the tax to those inframarginal sellers that had lower production costs than the marginal sellers and so could appropriate a share of the surplus for themselves.[147] This may at first appear to involve taxing individual commodities – imposing a tax on oil, say, if oil companies seem to be earning large scarcity rents. But commodity taxation is in fact too blunt a tool, for it applies to all sellers, both inframarginal and marginal, low cost and high cost, with the result that such a tax would drive the marginal sellers from the market and effectively create artificial scarcity and hence inefficiency, rather than simply redistributing surplus as intended.[148] The sort of taxation that the original progressives therefore envisioned was much more narrowly targeted: It was meant to be personalized to each individual seller.[149] Those that earned scarcity rents were to be taxed and those that did not, were not.[150] In practice, of course, it is almost impossible for government to distinguish the inframarginal sellers from the marginal sellers, because economic cost is a subtle concept.[151] To tax away earnings above cost, one must decide what expenditures made by a seller really are necessary to keep the seller in the market and what expenditures are not, and should therefore count as taxable rents.[152]

Rather than give up, the original progressives turned to two workable proxies for scarcity rent. One was the taxation of some fraction of corporate profits net of interest payments – what has come to be known as the corporate tax.[153] The idea here was that marginal sellers probably only earn enough revenues to pay off their loans, plus

an income tax."); Atkinson & Stiglitz, *supra* note 144, at 74 ("If a general income tax function may be chosen by the government, we have shown that, where the utility function is separable between labor and all commodities, no indirect taxes need be employed."); A. B. Atkinson, *Optimal Taxation and the Direct versus Indirect Tax Controversy*, 10 *Can. J. Econ. / Revue canadienne d'Economique* 590, 602 (1977) ("We have not considered the administration of the two types of taxation, and the possibility that one may be more difficult to avoid or evade.").

[146] *See* Hotelling, *supra* note 144, at 242; Atkinson & Stiglitz, *supra* note 144, at 602; Atkinson, *supra* note 145, at 595. A somewhat different telling of the intellectual history that follows may be found in Woodcock, *Personalizing Prices to Redistribute Wealth*, *supra* note 143.

[147] *See* Fried, *supra* note 6, at 201–2.

[148] *See id.* at 202–3.

[149] *See id.* at 201–2.

[150] *See id.*

[151] *See id.* at 202 ("[T]he problems of isolating that portion of rents that reflect inframarginal tastes for current consumption or leisure seem . . . intractable.").

[152] *See* Woodcock, *The Antitrust Case for Consumer Primacy in Corporate Governance*, *supra* note 43, at 1412–26.

[153] *See* Avi-Yonah, *supra* note 6, at 1212–31.

whatever additional return is required to attract equity investment.[154] By allowing a deduction for interest, and also setting the corporate tax rate substantially below 100 percent, corporate taxation would avoid taxing returns that marginal firms need to satisfy lenders and investors. But corporate taxation would still take a substantial chunk of the scarcity rents earned by the inframarginal firms.[155] This one-size-fits-all approach would not get at all of the scarcity rents, but it would get at some. And the rest, it was argued, could be sopped up through an additional tax applied directly to the rich people to whom all scarcity rents were ultimately paid, either as dividends to shareholders or as salaries to superstar managers.[156] Such an income tax would necessarily be imperfect, because the government would not be able to say for sure what part of an individual's income was really surplus that could be taxed away without causing the employer or investment paying the income to alter its hiring or capital acquisition decisions, and what part would cause firms to do without more labor or investment.[157] But the hope was that by setting rates carefully, government could mostly avoid such distortions.[158]

But could it? Atkinson and Stiglitz argued that, whatever the level of distortion that income taxation might cause, it was at least less in amount than the distortion caused by the alternative of commodity taxation.[159] The controversy had more or less started out with an attempt by Harold Hotelling to answer the narrower question whether it is better to pay for infrastructure through general tax revenues drawn ultimately from "taxes on incomes, inheritances, and the site value of land," or through dedicated tolls.[160] Hotelling pointed out that tolls – on the use of a bridge, for example – create artificial scarcity and hence distortion; they push up the effective price of access to the infrastructure and thereby price some users out of the market, reducing usage.[161] The proceeds of what amounts to a use-based tax are in fact the monopoly rents created by this artificial scarcity.[162] It would be better, argued Hotelling, for the government to pay for infrastructure by taxing incomes.[163]

Hotelling himself pointed out that the argument could be generalized to apply to the choice between income and commodity taxation, not just tolls on infrastructure. Any tax directed at a specific commodity – not just the "use" commodity associated with infrastructure – would drive marginal buyers or sellers from the market,

[154] *See* Avi-Yonah, *supra* note 102, at 655–59.
[155] *See id.*; *cf.* Fried, *supra* note 6, at 203.
[156] *See* Fried, *supra* note 6, at 202–3.
[157] *See id.*
[158] *See id.*
[159] *See* Atkinson & Stiglitz, *supra* note 144, at 74.
[160] *See* Hotelling, *supra* note 144, at 242.
[161] *See id.* at 245–46.
[162] *See id.*
[163] *See id.* at 242.

creating artificial scarcity and hence inefficiency.[164] But Hotelling's argument begged the question whether there are any efficiency costs to the income tax: Does the income tax, too, create artificial scarcity – in this case, of labor?[165] Over the next few decades, the attempt to answer this question gave rise to what has come to be known as the double-distortion argument, which reached its highest level of mathematical formalization in Atkinson and Stiglitz's 1976 paper.[166] The argument was that the income tax would not create as much inefficiency – distortion – as the commodity tax, because the income tax would create artificial scarcity only in labor markets, whereas commodity taxation would create artificial scarcity both in commodity markets and, because the prices of goods affect consumer purchasing power and hence the effective value of wages, in the labor market, as well.[167]

In retrospect, it is rather difficult to see why scholars of the time took this argument to be a deathblow to commodity taxation, because it worked only by assuming away the second distortion for income taxation.[168] Atkinson and Stiglitz simply assumed that whereas increases in a specific product's prices caused by a commodity tax both make the product artificially scarce in relation to others and reduce hours worked as well, increases in wages paid by employers caused by an income tax make labor artificially scarce but somehow do not reduce consumption of some products relative to others.[169] In Atkinson and Stiglitz's 1976 paper, as in all earlier formulations of the double-distortion argument, there is no double distortion created by income taxation only because the link between commodity and labor market behavior used to reason from the distortion created by commodity taxation to distortion in the labor market is assumed away when the time comes to reason from the distortion created by the taxation of income to distortion in commodities markets.[170] And the assumption is obviously poor: The more income a person receives, the more the person buys of some goods (e.g., jewelry) relative to others (e.g., public transportation), and vice versa.[171]

[164] *See id.*

[165] *See* W. J. Corlett & D. C. Hague, *Complementarity and the Excess Burden of Taxation*, 21 *Rev. Econ. Stud.* 21, 21 (1953); I. M. D. Little, *Direct versus Indirect Taxes*, 61 *Econ. J.* 577, 580 (1951) ("[I]t was arbitrarily assumed that the supply of labour was constant; or, to put it in another way, that the consumption of one good, leisure, was unaffected by changes in its own or other prices. This is clearly an indefensible assumption which must be removed.").

[166] For early statements of the argument see Edgeworth, *supra* note 145, at 568 & n.1; Hicks, *supra* note 145, at 41. The "double-distortion" label is due to Chris William Sanchirico, *Taxes versus Legal Rules as Instruments for Equity: A More Equitable View Exchange: Should Legal Rules Be Used to Redistribute Wealth*, 29 *J. Legal Stud.* 797, 799 (2000).

[167] *See, e.g.*, Little, *supra* note 165, at 580.

[168] *Cf.* Atkinson, *supra* note 145, at 601 ("[O]ne can well imagine that even this limited separability requirement may not in practice be met: for example in the case of leisure goods.").

[169] *See* Atkinson & Stiglitz, *supra* note 144, at 68 ("If the utility function is weakly separable between labor and all consumption goods (taken together), then no commodity taxation need be employed[.]").

[170] *See* Atkinson, *supra* note 145, at 600–2.

[171] *See* Walker, *supra* note 145.

The great irony of Atkinson and Stiglitz's 1976 paper was that it seemed to strike a winning blow for progressive income taxation at almost the moment when the tax revolt made redistribution through the income tax politically impossible, forcing progressives to turn to some of the same alternatives that as an intellectual matter their progressive comrades Atkinson and Stiglitz had just apparently succeeded at undermining. In an example of intellectual blowback, the 1976 paper was transformed from a weapon into an obstacle, one that grew in power over time.[172]

Indeed, as matters stood in the early 1980s, Atkinson and Stiglitz's paper appeared to have only quite narrow implications. It appeared to establish only that actual commodity taxation – a tax on yachts, say – and its cousin, direct price or rate regulation (cousin because a government-mandated low price is like a tax paid to buyers) distort more than the income tax. This did not present much of a problem because neither commodity taxation nor rate regulation held great appeal for progressives in the 1970s and 1980s, who were not immune to the libertarianism that would soon inspire the tax revolt on the right.[173] Indeed, progressives were, at just that moment, working with conservatives to implement deregulation, which put an end to the price regulations that had once covered a quarter of the American economy by gross national product (GNP).[174] Commodity taxation also appeared excessively bureaucratic, centralized, and potentially tyrannical to the progressive mind of the time, which was only more likely than the conservative mind to recommended government intervention in markets when health and safety seemed to require it, as in the case of cigarette taxation.[175]

What progressives of this period wanted instead was to use changes to the remedies associated with breaking private law rules – the rules of contracts, property, and tort – to redistribute wealth in individual markets.[176] This appealed to

[172] *See* Woodcock, *Personalizing Prices to Redistribute Wealth*, *supra* note 143.

[173] Barbara Fried argues that progressives were also skeptical that rate regulation could effectively be applied to scarcity, as opposed to monopoly, rents, because of the difficulty of determining the costs of individual firms. *See* Fried, *supra* note 6, at 200–1. But this neglects that the use of price regulation to attack monopoly rents also requires identification of the costs of individual firms, because these are needed to determine the competitive market price that firms must charge in order not to earn monopoly rents. Moreover, rate regulation statutes, which require "reasonable" pricing, are generally interpreted to require pricing at economic cost, rather than competitive pricing, and so must be understood actually to attack scarcity rents in practice, even if rate regulation is generally imposed only in natural monopoly industries. *See* J. Stephen Henderson & Robert E. Burns, *An Economic and Legal Analysis of Undue Price Discrimination* 43 (1989) ("Traditionally, the zone of reasonableness has been understood to require cost-based rates.").

[174] *See* Thomas K. McCraw, Prophets of Regulation: Charles Francis Adams, Louis D. Brandeis, James M. Landis, Alfred E. Kahn 266–70, 293 (1984); Richard H. K. Vietor, Contrived Competition: Regulation and Deregulation in America 16 (1996); Joseph D. Kearney & Thomas W. Merrill, *The Great Transformation of Regulated Industries Law*, 98 *Colum. L. Rev.* 1323, 1330–40 (1998).

[175] *Cf.* Daniel A. Crane, *Harmful Output in the Antitrust Domain: Lessons from the Tobacco Industry*, 39 *Ga. L. Rev.* 321, 365–67 (2005).

[176] *See* Duncan Kennedy, *Law-and-Economics from the Perspective of Critical Legal Studies*, *in* The New Palgrave Dictionary of Economics and the Law 465, 472 (Peter Newman ed., 2002).

progressives' libertarian leanings because private law rules determine the ability of persons to engage redistribution on their own behalf either directly or through the filing of private lawsuits.[177] A liability rule for pollution with generous punitive damages could potentially enable average people to redistribute large amounts of wealth from big firms to themselves by taking matters into their own hands and filing lawsuits.[178] Similarly, reduced damages for those who trespass in search of food could potentially allow the hungry to feed themselves.[179] No administrative state – just the court system – would be required.[180] This libertarian outlook persisted for decades. Until the reappearance of antimonopolism over the past few years, antitrust played almost no role in progressive aspirations to redistribute around the tax system, perhaps because antitrust's combination of aspects that seemed to promote individual freedom (such as the protection of free market entry) with aspects that were deeply statist (such as the breakup of large private firms by government) offended progressives' libertarian mood.

Redistribution through private law seemed to escape the net of Atkinson and Stiglitz's 1976 paper until a duo of lawyer-economists made the inconvenient point that changing the damages associated with violations of private law legal rules is equivalent to imposing commodity taxes.[181] It represents a manipulation of market

[177] *See* Kennedy, *supra* note 13, at 30–33.

[178] *See id.*

[179] *See id.*

[180] *See id.*

[181] *See* Louis Kaplow & Steven Shavell, *Why the Legal System Is Less Efficient Than the Income Tax in Redistributing Income*, 23 *J. Legal Stud.* 667, 667, 680 (1994) ("[R]edistribution through legal rules offers no advantage over redistribution through the income tax system and typically is less efficient …. Our result is analogous to results on optimal taxation. In simple cases, specific commodity excises are inefficient in the presence of an optimal income tax."); Louis Kaplow & Steven Shavell, Should Legal Rules Favor the Poor – Clarifying the Role of Legal Rules and the Income Tax in Redistributing Income Exchange: Should Legal Rules Be Used to Redistribute Wealth, 29 *J. Legal Stud.* 821, 821 (2000)("[T]he income tax and transfer system is a superior instrument for redistributing income."). Kaplow and Shavell cite Joseph E. Stiglitz, *Chapter 15 Pareto Efficient and Optimal Taxation and the New New Welfare Economics*, 2 *Handbook Pub. Econ.* 991, 40 (1987) ("If the utility function is separable between consumption and leisure …, then all Pareto efficient tax structures entail no taxation of commodities."). The extension of the double-distortion argument to "government programs" was earlier made by Aanund Hylland & Richard Zeckhauser, *Distributional Objectives Should Affect Taxes but Not Program Choice or Design*, 81 *Scandinavian J. Econ.* 264, 265 (1979)("We have diverged from optimal income tax discussions in making government programs a major element of our model. To do so, we have assumed that benefits from such programs can be converted into an increased income equivalent."). That paper seems to have inspired an early contribution of Shavell's in this vein. *See* Steven Shavell, *A Note on Efficiency vs. Distributional Equity in Legal Rulemaking: Should Distributional Equity Matter Given Optimal Income Taxation?*, 71 *Am. Econ. Rev.* 414, 414 (1981)("[D]espite imperfect ability to redistribute income through taxation, everyone would strictly prefer that legal rules be chosen only on the basis of their efficiency."). I note, in connection with the reference to "lawyer-economists" in the text, that Shavell is technically an economist only; he does not hold a law degree.

prices. The generous liability rule for pollution is equivalent to a tax on whatever product the polluter makes, creating artificial scarcity and turning the resulting rents over to pollution victims.[182] Similarly, the reduction in damages for trespass creates artificial scarcity in food – not, to be sure, with respect to the hungry, but with respect to those who buy, for they cannot now buy as much and must pay more for it.[183] It followed, argued these scholars, that if income taxation is a better way to redistribute than is commodity taxation, then income taxation is also a better way to redistribute than is manipulation of damages for the violation of rules of private law.[184]

This bombshell exploded across the legal academy, spraying shrapnel not just at progressives seeking to make the long march through the common law but also at much of the non-economically inclined legal professoriate. For the implication of the work of Ronald Coase that the the availability of damages has distributive consequences had by now sunk in to the legal academy generally, and, as Kaplow and Shavell themselves delighted in pointing out, it was a small step from that realization to the realization that what really motivates most of the apparently non-economic, "fairness"-based arguments that law scholars make for particular choices of legal rules is in fact concern about the distribution of wealth.[185] Thus the legal academy generally was implicated in inadvertent participation in the long march to redistribute through the manipulation of private law rules and indeed in seeking to redistribute wealth in ways that did more harm to the economy than necessary. Kaplow and Shavell's intervention had the paradoxical result of making the double-distortion argument – itself a child of left scholarship – into a target of the left, which now vilified the argument as liberal centrism.[186] The intervention also made the double-distortion argument a target of the legal academy more generally, giving rise to a literature of

[182] *See* Kaplow & Shavell, *Why the Legal System Is Less Efficient Than the Income Tax in Redistributing Income*, *supra* note 181, at 680.

[183] *See id.*

[184] *See id.*

[185] *See* Louis Kaplow & Steven Shavell, Fairness versus Welfare 17, 43 (2009) ("In particular, it is our impression that most analysts of legal policy who attach importance to notions of fairness hold mixed normative views. That is, not only do they give weight to notions of fairness, but they also place weight, and perhaps significant weight, on how legal policies affect individuals' well-being – either because they understand individuals' well-being to be encompassed by some notions of fairness, or because they consider both fairness and individuals' well-being in reaching a final judgment."); Robert Cooter & Thomas Ulen, Law & Economics 98 (6th ed. 2012) ("If transaction costs equal zero and successful bargaining can cure inefficient laws, what difference does the law make? One answer is that the law affects the distribution of the cooperative product, which affects bargaining."); R. H. Coase, *The Problem of Social Cost*, 3 *J.L. & Econ.* 1, 7 (1960) ("Whether the $3 is a payment which the cattle-raiser has to make if he adds the third steer to his herd [which it would be if the cattle-raiser was liable to the farmer for damage caused to the crop] or whether it is a sum of money which he would have received if he did not keep a third steer [which it would be if the cattle-raiser was not liable to the farmer for damage caused to the crop] does not affect the final result").

[186] *See* Kennedy, *supra* note 176, at 468.

great size and longevity aimed at demolishing the argument from every possible angle.[187] The size of this literature is due in part to the fact that in implicating the

[187] *See, e.g.*, Richard L. Revesz, *Regulation and Distribution*, 93 *N.Y.U. L. Rev.* 1489, 1489 (2018) ("[T]ax policy is ill suited to provide compensation for significant environmental, health, and safety harms."); Zachary Liscow, *Is Efficiency Biased*, 85 *U. Chi. L. Rev.* 1649, 1666 (2018) ("[T]here is at minimum a plausible case that distributional consequences will not be fully offset."); David Blankfein-Tabachnick & Kevin A. Kordana, *Kaplow and Shavell and the Priority of Income Taxation and Transfer*, 69 *Hastings L.J.* 1, 8 (2017)("Kaplow and Shavell's purported efficiency advantage of tax and transfer is cast as a comparison of tax and transfer to individual rules of tort or contract, without attention to the selection of underlying property arrangements[.]"); Lee Anne Fennell & Richard H. McAdams, *The Distributive Deficit in Law and Economics*, 100 *Minn. L. Rev.* 1051, 1052–53 (2016)("[L]aw and economics has neglected a feature of reality that is no less foundational than that of positive transaction costs: the large and variable costs associated with the political impediments that must be surmounted to achieve welfare-maximizing distributive results."); Matthew Dimick, *Should the Law Do Anything about Economic Inequality*, 26 *Cornell J.L. & Pub. Pol'y* 1, 39–40 (2016)("[T]axation can increase social welfare by redistributing income and reducing inequality, according to the principle of diminishing marginal utility of money .... [H]igher inequality can [therefore] justify greater taxation – and hence a larger economic distortion."); David Gamage, *How Should Governments Promote Distributive Justice: A Framework for Analyzing the Optimal Choice of Tax Instruments*, 68 *Tax L. Rev.* 1, 9 (2014)("As compared to raising all revenues through a labor income tax, ... raising some revenues through excise taxes can reduce taxpayer incentives to engage in forms of tax gaming that operate like claiming artificial or inflated labor income tax deductions."); David Gamage, *On Double-Distortion Arguments, Distribution Policy, and the Optimal Choice of Tax Instruments*, No. ID 2489678, 7 (2014); Zachary Liscow, *Reducing Inequality on the Cheap: When Legal Rule Design Should Incorporate Equity as Well as Efficiency Note*, 123 *Yale L.J.* 2478, 2482 (2014)("[F]eatures other than income are often desirable bases for redistributing income, and legal rules may be institutionally better-equipped than taxes – or the only option – to redistribute based on such non-income features."); Brian Galle, *Is Local Consumer Protection Law a Better Retributive Mechanism Than the Tax System Tort Law in the Shadow of Agency Preemption*, 65 *N.Y.U. Ann. Surv. Am. L.* 525, 526 (2010)("While redistributive tort laws have costs that taxes do not, government cannot effectively satisfy a heterogeneous society's preferences for redistribution with a single national set of tax rules. Local tort rules can better capture a wide variety of preferences."); Richard S. Markovits, *Why Kaplow and Shavell's Double-Distortion Argument Articles Are Wrong*, 13 *Geo. Mason L. Rev.* 511, 519 (2005)("[E]ven if the relevant tax policies could [contrary to fact] be shown to be Pareto superior to the relevant legal rule adjustments, that demonstration would not guarantee the tax policy's greater moral desirability from all legitimate value-perspectives[.]"); Ronen Avraham et al., *Revisiting the Roles of Legal Rules and Tax Rules in Income Redistribution: A Response to Kaplow & (and) Shavell*, 89 *Iowa L. Rev.* 1125, 1130 (2004)("[I]n light of the heterogeneity of individuals and in light of their ex ante behavioral adjustments, Kaplow and Shavell's theoretical model of a tax-and-transfer alternative to redistributive legal rules is no longer simple. To the contrary, it is virtually impossible to implement."); Kyle Logue & Ronen Avraham, *Redistribution Optimally: Of Tax Rules, Legal Rules, and Insurance*, 56 *Tax L. Rev.* 157, 165 (2003)("[W]hereas one institution may have a comparative advantage at measuring the particular type of inequality at issue, another institution may have a comparative advantage at doing the actual redistributing."); Sanchirico, *supra* note 166, at 800 ("It is true that Kaplow and Shavell's formal modeling does indeed produce the result that damages should always be set efficiently. Yet a close inspection reveals that this result does not in fact follow from the logic of distortion counting. Rather, it follows from an implicit assumption that all agents are identical with respect to the tort system."); Christine Jolls, *Behavioral Economics Analysis of Redistributive Legal Rules Symposium: The Legal*

mainstream professoriate, as well as the left, Kaplow and Shavell's intervention, combined with percolation of Coasian thinking, pushed the mainstream to the left. It showed mainstream professors that they were actually progressive fellow travelers and forced them to defend their projects in explicitly distributive terms. Everyone, now, became interested in redistribution, even if, according to Kaplow and Shavell, they were going about it the wrong way.[188]

Progressives – and the legal academy more generally – need not have fretted as much as they did, at least about double distortion, because of the weakness of the "separability" assumption described above: Reductions in income do distort commodity purchase decisions.[189] But Kaplow added to double distortion a distinct objection that remains difficult to overcome even today: the objection that it is almost impossible to redistribute wealth accurately through intervention in individual markets because it is hard to determine the overall effects on individual income or wealth of a given rule change without considering the effects of the change on all markets.[190] Taxing yachts might not necessarily redistribute from rich to poor if yacht makers happen to pay their workers well.[191] By contrast, taxing individual income or wealth strikes directly at the variable of interest to redistributors: If you want to tax the rich, tax the rich directly, not particular products that may or may not serve as good proxies for wealth.[192] It is likely that this administrability argument will be the principal legacy of Kaplow and Shavell.

The administrability argument has shown no sign of actually stopping progressive interest in redistribution on a market-by-market basis. The persistence of this interest – there have been as many papers devoted to defending redistribution through private law rules published in recent years as there were when the attacks began in the late 1990s and early 2000s – reflects a continued progressive desire to make an end run around the political roadblock to taxation to achieve redistribution by other means.[193] Indeed, it seems more likely at this stage that the epochal realignments currently

Implications of Psychology: Human Behavior, Behavioral Economics, and the Law, 51 *Vand. L. Rev.* 1653, 1656 (1998)("Would an individual typically experience the same disincentive to work as a result of a more generous [to victims] tort regime as would be experienced as a result of a higher level of taxation? Behavioral law and economics suggests that the answer may be no [.]"). The author has also contributed to this literature. Woodcock, *Personalizing Prices to Redistribute Wealth*, *supra* note 143.

188 Well, not quite everyone. *See, e.g.*, Richard H. Fallon, *Should We All Be Welfare Economists?*, 101 *Mich. L. Rev.* 979, 1007 (2003)(accepting that, as far as pie maximization and division are concerned, pie maximization should be the main focus of legal rule choice, with pie division left to the tax system, but rejecting the notion that the purpose of the legal system, including tax policy, should be pie maximization and division, as opposed to achieving fairness in other normative senses).

189 *See* Atkinson & Stiglitz, *supra* note 144, at 69; Atkinson, *supra* note 145, at 601 ("[O]ne can well imagine that even this limited separability requirement may not in practice be met[.]").

190 *See* Louis Kaplow, The Theory of Taxation and Public Economics 21 (2011) ("It is usually best to use instruments that are most directly related to the matter in question.").

191 *Cf.* Crane, *supra* note 20, at 1208.

192 *See* Kaplow, *supra* note 190, at 21.

193 *See supra* note 188.

underway in American politics will remove the premise for the long march – the political impossibility of redistribution through income taxation – than that progressives will accept the realities of the administrability argument.

But on the eve of its possible demise, the impulse toward redistribution on a market-by-market basis rather than via the income tax has reached new heights in the form of the progressive antimonopolism of the past decade or so, which quite self-consciously wishes to use antitrust and competition policy as a kind of surrogate to direct price regulation, deploying antitrust breakup to push prices down at big companies and relaxation of antitrust enforcement to allow the prices charged by smaller, and presumptively poorer, businesses to rise.[194] Whether breaking big firms up really will bring prices down given the increase in production costs that breakup creates, and whether the increase in prices charged by small businesses will offset the lost wages to big firm employees, who typically earn more than employees at small firms, seems to play no more role in the contemporary antimonopolist's thinking than does the administrability problem of actually keeping track of the effects of all these price changes on the distribution of wealth.[195] Why progressives should have chosen antitrust – long ignored by progressives who push through changes to private law rules – as the latest locus for the march, and why they chose it now, is not at all clear from the project of redistributing around the tax system itself.

The answer lies outside of the academy, in the predicament of a unique political actor: the press.

B *The Press and Politicians*

It is generally a mark of lack of intellectual seriousness – indeed, of crackpot conspiracism – to treat the press as the cause of things. To do that is to blame the messenger, to fail to make a deeper inquiry, and indeed to throw one's lot in with authoritarians, who rail endlessly about bias in the media.[196] There is good reason to append to every razor, from Occam's to Napoleon's, this: never attribute to the press a result that can be explained by any other means.

The reason not to blame the press is that, in any country in which entry into the journalism market is free, the press tends to speak with one voice only when the facts support what the press says, in which case the facts, and not biased reporting, are the cause of whatever catastrophe one wishes to explain.[197] Absent some incontrovertible factual anchor, the press tends to splinter, each paper contradicting the others, each interpreting events in a different way, in which case even if one might

[194] *See* Longman, *supra* note 10.

[195] *See* Atkinson & Lind, *supra* note 9, at 64–67; Demsetz, *supra* note 65, at 2.

[196] *See* Juliane A. Lischka, *A Badge of Honor?*, 20 *Journalism Stud.* 287 (2019).

[197] *See* Ramsi Woodcock, Ramsi A. Woodcock, *Saving the News*, *in* Media and Society After Technological Disruption 261 (Kyle Langvardt & Justin (Gus) Hurwitz eds., Cambridge University Press 2024), https://perma.cc/MY48-WN5D (arguing that the only thing that unites an ideologically diverse readership is interest in the facts).

reasonably attribute a particular outcome to the biased reporting of a particular paper, one certainly cannot attribute any particular outcome to the control of the press as a whole over the minds of readers.[198]

The American press's promotion of contemporary antimonopolism is an exception, because, for possibly the first time ever in the United States, the existence of the entire news industry is threatened, and so the interests of every news organization are aligned to an unusual degree.[199] And they are aligned in a way that makes the promotion of antimonopolism deeply desirable for every reporter and every news outlet. For the past twenty years have seen the primary business model of the press – to use reporting to attract readers and to use readership to sell ads – all but wiped out by the Tech Giants – primarily Google, Facebook, and Amazon.[200] These companies offer e-commerce, search, and social media services that command far more attention than newspapers and so have competed successfully for advertising dollars that once flowed to newspapers, sending many papers to bankruptcy and creating a national crisis in newspaper funding.[201] Amazon has also put pressure on book

[198] *See* Wolfgang Donsbach, *Exposure to Political Content in Newspapers: The Impact of Cognitive Dissonance on Readers' Selectivity*, 6 *Eur. J. Commc'n* 155, 173, 179 (1991).

The author made the rather naive claims contained in this paragraph and the previous one before being reminded by mainstream reporting (or lack thereof) on America's genocide of Palestinians in Gaza via the State of Israel that the press is capable of lying with one voice and does so regularly, at least with respect to the colonization of Palestine.

[199] The last time the business model of the entire news industry was called into question was during the advent of radio, when it was thought that broadcast news would wipe out newspaper readership. *See* PAUL STARR, THE CREATION OF THE MEDIA: POLITICAL ORIGINS OF MODERN COMMUNICATIONS 376–77 (2006). That time, the "American Newspaper Publishers Association and major wire services, including the Associated Press," banded together and threatened to withhold news from the radio networks unless they agreed to limit the amount of news they put out over the air waves. As Paul Starr recounts,

> [t]he networks agreed to provide only two five-minute newscasts a day, one late enough in the morning and the other late enough in the evening so as not to undercut the sales of either morning or evening papers. All radio news would have to be at least twenty-four hours old, no single item could be longer than thirty words, a single combined wire service bureau would supply all items, and every broadcast would end with the words, "For further details, consult your local newspaper."

Id. at 377. Demand for broadcast news during World War II put an end to those limits. *See id.* at 376–78. But it turned out that they were not necessary to protect the news industry anyway, and broadcast was not the threat that it had appeared to be. The news industry remained immensely profitable for another half century, until the Internet came into its own two decades ago. *See* Robert G. Picard, *The Economics of the Daily Newspaper Industry*, *in* MEDIA ECONOMICS: THEORY AND PRACTICE 109, 109 (Alison Alexander et al. eds., 2003) ("The newspaper industry is the most profitable of all media industries and one of the most profitable of all manufacturing industries in the country."); Derek Thompson, *The Collapse of Print Advertising in 1 Graph*, THE ATLANTIC, https://perma.cc/A5EN-UYP7/ (last visited June 9, 2021); Fred Dews and Eric Bull, *The Decline of Newspapers, in Four Charts*, BROOKINGS (Oct. 23, 2014), https://perma.cc/8G8A-MM6L/.

[200] *See* Woodcock, Big Ink v. Bigger Tech, *supra* note 8.

[201] *See* Bull, *supra* note 199; Thompson, *supra* note 199; Michael Barthel, *Circulation, Revenue Fall for US Newspapers Overall despite Gains for Some*, PEW RESEARCH CENTER, https://perma.cc/55TA-LA73/; Elizabeth Greico, *Fast Facts about the Newspaper Industry's Financial*

publisher margins through its aggressive development of the e-book market, dealing a further blow to the writerly class.[202] In response, the news industry – each paper equally aggrieved by the rerouting of its advertising dollars to the Tech Giants – has, since around 2016 and peaking in 2020, engaged in a ferocious campaign to use its most powerful weapon – the bully pulpit that is the industry's reporting – to advance the cause of antimonopolism.[203] The industry appears to hope that antimonopolism will lead to the breakup of the Tech Giants and thence to the delivery of the press from the clutches of the firms that have outcompeted it for advertising dollars.[204]

There are no studies of press attitudes toward the Tech Giants – this is an area that badly needs further research – and there is no evidence of conspiracy. Whether the press has coordinated its promotion of antimonopolism or not, the interests of all news organizations and all journalists are sufficiently aligned to make it quite plausible that news organizations or journalists have acted independently to promote antimonopolism, pursuant to a diffuse anti-tech mood rooted in the competitive effects of technology on the industry.[205]

There is a great deal of anecdotal evidence that the press has in fact acted to advance antimonopolism in recent years, so far with great success.[206] To the

Struggles as McClatchy Files for Bankruptcy, Pew Research Center, https://perma.cc/WJQ4-TE5Z; Penelope Muse Abernathy, *The Loss of Local News: What It Means for Communities*, The Expanding News Desert, https://perma.cc/6D46-DSKT.

202 *See* Woodcock, Big Ink v. Bigger Tech, *supra* note 8.

203 *See id.*

204 *See id.*

205 This is particularly plausible for newspaper and print journalists, as opposed to broadcast news outlets and reporters, because newspaper and print journalists rely primarily upon news-based revenues for their daily bread. By contrast, broadcast news is usually an adjunct to a separate business – the sale of entertainment on a subscription basis through cable networking and, increasingly, streaming – that is immune to the Tech Giants' appeal to advertisers. Bloomberg News, which is an adjunct to Bloomberg's sale of finance and trading information, is another example of a news operation less threatened by the Tech Giants' advertising appeal. The author's subjective impression is that much of the antimonopolism in contemporary American journalism originates neither with broadcast outlets nor with Bloomberg.

206 The press's campaign has not gone unnoticed by other commentators, although its probable source in the competitive threat posed by the Tech Giants to newspapers has gone unremarked. Noted antitrust economist Carl Shapiro's bewilderment at the campaign is quite poignant:

> Until quite recently, few were claiming that there has been a substantial and widespread decline in competition in the United States since 1980 …. Yet, somehow, over the past two years, the notion that there has been a substantial and widespread decline in competition throughout the American economy has taken root in the popular press …. Since 2015, there has been a regular drumbeat in the press reporting on a supposed decline of competition in the United States. In October 2015, the Wall Street Journal, hardly an anti-business publication, wrote: "A growing number of industries in the U.S. are dominated by a shrinking number of companies". Later that month, the New York Times stated: "Markets work best when there is healthy competition among businesses. In too many industries, that competition just doesn't exist anymore." Eduardo Porter of the New York Times later connected increasing inequality with a decline of

antitrust scholar, the most striking manifestation of the press's antimonopolism was its embrace of the work of future FTC chair Lina Khan before she had even graduated from law school.[207] No piece of student scholarship in law may ever have received the attention from the press that Khan's student note received in 2017 and 2018. The New York Times, for example, published a glowing full-page profile of Khan, a separate column based on the note, as well as two op-eds authored by her.[208] The note was hardly news in antitrust circles; it does not appear to have changed the thinking of any antitrust scholar. But the appeal to a press that felt keenly that Amazon was part of a broader big tech problem that was destroying the press's livelihood is obvious.[209]

Khan's was not, however, the only nontraditional scholarly voice to receive an incongruous level of attention from the press. Just as no student note may ever have received the journalistic attention that Khan's piece received, perhaps no law review article published by a non-academic lawyer may ever have received the sort of approving profiles in both the New York Times and the Wall Street Journal that a paper by Dina Srinivasan received in 2018 and 2019.[210] But the appeal of a paper titled *The Antitrust Case against Facebook* to a press that had seen Facebook eat its advertising revenues is, again, obvious.[211]

> competition, under the title: "With Competition in Tatters, the Rip of Inequality Widens". The Economist, a highly respected publication regarding economic policy, has been especially sharp and persistent in asserting that there has been a substantial decline in competition in recent years .... The drumbeat continues. Business Week recently reported: "Market concentration in the U.S. has reached a three-decade high, while the government has opened fewer antitrust cases."

Carl Shapiro, *Antitrust in a Time of Populism*, 61 *Int'l J. Indus. Org.* 714, 717–18 (2018).

207 *See* Lina M. Khan, *Amazon's Antitrust Paradox*, 126 *Yale L.J.* 710 (2017).

208 *See* David Streitfeld, *Amazon's Antitrust Antagonist Has a Breakthrough Idea*, N.Y. Times (Sept. 7, 2018), www.nytimes.com/2018/09/07/technology/monopoly-antitrust-lina-khan-amazon.html; David Leonhardt, *Opinion | Amazon vs. Barnes & Noble*, N.Y. Times (May 7, 2018), www.nytimes.com/2018/05/07/opinion/amazon-barnes-noble.html; Lina M. Khan, *The Supreme Court Case That Could Give Tech Giants More Power*, N.Y. Times (Mar. 2, 2018), www.nytimes.com/2018/03/02/opinion/the-supreme-court-case-that-could-give-tech-giants-more-power.html; Lina M. Khan, *Amazon Bites Off Even More Monopoly Power*, N.Y. Times (June 21, 2017), www.nytimes.com/2017/06/21/opinion/amazon-whole-foods-jeff-bezos.html.

209 *See* Woodcock, Big Ink v. Bigger Tech, *supra* note 8.

210 *See* Dina Srinivasan, *The Antitrust Case against Facebook*, SSRN Scholarly Paper (Sept. 10, 2018), https://perma.cc/2LA7-FN9U; Jeff Horwitz, *She Argued Facebook Is a Monopoly: To Her Surprise, People Listened*, Wall St. J. (Dec. 10, 2019), www.wsj.com/articles/yale-law-grads-hipster-antitrust-argument-against-facebook-findsmainstream-support-11575987274; Daisuke Wakabayashi, *The Antitrust Case against Big Tech, Shaped by Tech Industry Exiles*, N.Y. Times (Dec. 20, 2020), www.nytimes.com/2020/12/20/technology/antitrust-case-google-facebook.html; Dina Srinivasan, *Why Privacy Is an Antitrust Issue*, N.Y. Times (May 28, 2019), www.nytimes.com/2019/05/28/opinion/privacy-antitrust-facebook.html.

211 *See* Srinivasan, *The Antitrust Case against Facebook*, *supra* note 210. In an interesting twist, the Wall Street Journal profile discloses that Srinivasan consults on the digital advertising market for Wall Street Journal parent company News Corp. *See* Horwitz, *supra* note 210.

The practice of using puff pieces to advance a news organization's pecuniary interests is a well-worn trick of the news trade. Here is Los Angeles Times reporter Michael Hiltzik reminiscing about how his former employer, the Buffalo Courier-Express, tried to fend off competition from Warren Buffett in the 1970s:

> The Conners family, which owned the Courier-Express, mounted an aggressive defense by hiring Frederick Furth, a renowned antitrust lawyer from San Francisco with a history of going after big corporate game. The newsroom did its part by running a series of puff pieces about local judges who might find the case on their dockets. One article, which described a jurist who was known as a martinet on the bench but a sweetheart in his family circle, was given an unfortunate but irresistible headline I remember vividly as: "Judge loses firmness when he doffs his robe."[212]

Hiltzik's experience at the Courier-Express bears a striking similarity to the press's campaign against the Tech Giants in that the campaign, too, involves an attempt to leverage reporting in service of antitrust intervention. Moreover, in both cases the press sought to stop competition from a rival offering consumers (in the case of the Tech Giants, advertisers; in the case of the Courier-Express, newspaper readers) a better product.[213] Buffett's paper was offering Sunday readers free Sunday delivery if they subscribed to the paper seven days a week, something that the Courier-Express, as a Sunday-only paper that was unable to recoup promotional costs by selling on the other six days of the week, could not match.[214] Where Hiltzik's experience differed from the press's campaign against the Tech Giants is that the campaign against the Tech Giants involves the *entire* press.[215] That has made the press's campaign particularly effective at influencing politicians, if not academics. Academics do not require bipartisan media coverage to make a career. But, for politicians, support from the entire press – left and right – is of the very highest value in elections. Indeed, although the puff pieces about academics have exerted a certain amount of influence over the minds of media-hungry scholars eager to share in the press's promotional largesse, there remains surprisingly little antimonopolism within the academy itself.[216] Not so among the surprising coalition of politicians on both the left and right who during the peak of the campaign against the Tech Giants were pushing for legislation on a par with the old no-fault monopolization legislation that was defeated in the 1970s.[217] As Ben Smith wrote while still at The New York Times:

[212] Michael Hiltzik, *Column: How Warren Buffett, Who Says the News Business Is 'Toast,' Tried to Kill My First Paper*, Los Angeles Times (June 4, 2019), https://perma.cc/2X9X-DDXE.

[213] *Id.*

[214] *Id.*

[215] *Id.*

[216] *See* Woodcock, Big Ink v. Bigger Tech, *supra* note 8.

[217] *See, e.g.*, Anti-Monopoly and Competition Restoration Act of ___ § 6(b)(4)(D) ("It shall be a presumptive abuse of market power under this section for a person with market power to engage or attempt to engage in the following conduct: … Serving as both a platform and a merchant that competes with third-party merchants.") (on file with author); Trust-Busting for the Twenty-First Century Act § 3(c)(2) (prohibiting acquisitions by any firm with a market

> [T]he power of the press, even nowadays, makes it a formidable political force. Rupert Murdoch's bare-knuckled News Corp. – born in Australia and broadly loathed by its more genteel and progressive global peers – has long led the fight to claw back revenue from the tech giants, and hostility to Google bleeds through the pages of The Times of London and Fox News's airwaves .... While much of the American media rejects the idea that it is crusading in its pages to support its publishers' business agenda, most news executives in this country share a viewpoint on the platforms, having seen them pull advertising dollars from the news business and spread misinformation at the expense of professional journalism. And even as the platforms employ armies of powerful lobbyists, politicians remain eager to please the press that covers them.[218]

This was a startling admission from a paper that had played a central role in creating contemporary antimonopolism.[219]

The major cases filed against Google and Facebook – not coincidentally the two Tech Giants most closely implicated in the demise of newspapers' ad-based business model – are another dividend paid on the press's campaign.[220] The haste of the Trump Administration to bring both of those cases before the 2020 presidential election – Attorney General Barr had to face down a revolt of Justice Department Antitrust Division staff to do so – suggests that the press's drumbeat of articles casting Google and Facebook as monopolies had managed to convince the Trump campaign that antitrust would be a winning electoral issue, despite the fact that polls have repeatedly shown that, however much the press may hate the Tech Giants, the public continues to adore these companies, which have revolutionized the way Americans live their lives.[221]

capitalization in excess of $100 billion), https://perma.cc/7RRZ-EJV9; Subcommittee on Antitrust, Commercial, and Administrative Law of the Committee on the Judiciary of the United States House of Representatives, *Investigation of Competition in Digital Markets: Majority Staff Report and Recommendations* 20 (2020) (calling for "[s]tructural separations and prohibitions of certain dominant platforms from operating in adjacent lines of business"); Shira Ovide, *How Klobuchar and Hawley See Things When It Comes to Technology*, N.Y. Times (May 13, 2021), www.nytimes.com/2021/05/13/books/amy-klobuchar-antitrust-josh-hawley-tyranny-big-tech.html.

[218] Ben Smith, *Big Tech Has Crushed the News Business: That's about to Change*, N.Y. Times (May 11, 2020), www.nytimes.com/2020/05/10/business/media/big-tech-has-crushed-the-news-business-thats-about-to-change.html.

[219] *See* Woodcock, Big Ink v. Bigger Tech, *supra* note 8.

[220] *See* Complaint, United States v. Google LLC, No. 1:20-cv-03010 (D.D.C. 2020); Complaint for Injunctive and other Relief, FTC v. Facebook, Inc., No. 1:20-cv-03590 (D.D.C. 2021). Antimonopolists in the Biden administration have brought cases against Amazon and Apple as well. Cecilia Kang & David McCabe, *After Google Antitrust Ruling, Here's Where Other Big Tech Cases Stand*, N.Y. Times (Aug. 5, 2024), www.nytimes.com/2024/08/05/technology/antitrust-google-amazon-apple-meta.html. The government's recent victory in the Google *case is another dividend. Steve Lohr, Google Makes History With Rapid-Fire Antitrust Losses*, N.Y. Times (Apr. 18, 2025), https://www.nytimes.com/2025/04/18/technology/google-antitrust-losses-history.html.

[221] *See* Katie Benner & Cecilia Kang, *Justice Dept. Plans to File Antitrust Charges Against Google in Coming Weeks*, N.Y. Times (Sept. 3, 2020), www.nytimes.com/2020/09/03/us/politics/google-

Although some of the antimonopolists that the press has promoted fervently believe that antimonopolism is a viable solution to the problem of inequality, the press itself may not much care whether antimonopolism works as intended.[222] Indeed, the broader appeal of antimonopolism as ideology or intellectual movement does not help the press except insofar as it serves to galvanize a coalition that will come to the press's aid by smashing the Tech Giants. It is the presence of this extraordinarily powerful institution promoting antimonopolism, not any new theoretical breakthrough regarding the usefulness of antitrust at fixing inequality, that created the immediate impetus for the rapid rise of antimonopolism starting in 2016.

C *Anti-Statism as Explanation*

Contemporary American antimonopolism is, in the final analysis, a peculiarly American phenomenon that reflects the powerful current of anti-statism that runs through American political culture on the left as well as the right.[223] It is unlikely that antimonopolism would enjoy its current appeal on the left if the anti-statist tax protest on the right had not taken place in the 1970s and persisted thereafter, causing progressives to give up – perhaps not altogether willingly, given their own anti-statist instincts – on redistribution through the income tax system and to open the door to embrace of alternatives, including, eventually, antitrust.[224] Anti-statism also surely plays a role in the enthusiasm with which progressives have sought to undermine the case for tax and transfer in favor of redistribution through private law, and thereby to transform the poor into masters of their own redistributive fate[225] Anti-statism can be found in equal measure in the resort of the press to appeals to antitrust, as opposed to the direct state subsidization of media found in many other Western democracies, to solve the crisis in media funding occasioned by the Tech Giants.[226] The press's appeal to antitrust is admittedly also a kind of appeal to the state, both because it calls upon the courts to reshape markets and because it is the government that brought antitrust cases against Google and Facebook, not the press itself. As a competitor that has lost out on technological grounds, the press could never win

antitrust-justice-department.html; Casey Newton, *This Is How Much Americans Trust Facebook, Google, Apple, and Other Big Tech Companies*, The Verge, https://perma.cc/BV65-9RJ8 (last visited May 18, 2021).

[222] *See* Longman, *supra* note 10.

[223] *See* David A. Moss, When All Else Fails: Government as the Ultimate Risk Manager 317 (2004) ("There can be no doubt that Americans have traditionally harbored deep anti-statist sentiments.").

[224] *See* Martin, *supra* note 7, at 2–15; Brownlee, *supra* note 7, at 182–83.

[225] *See* Kennedy, *supra* note 13, at 30–33.

[226] *See* Woodcock, Big Ink v. Bigger Tech, *supra* note 8; Ramsi Woodcock, *The Fourth Estate's Estate*, 26 U. Penn. J. Bus. L. 863, 866–883 (2024); Rasmus Kleis Nielsen, *"Frozen" Media Subsidies during a Time of Media Change: A Comparative Analysis of Media Policy Drift in Six Western Democracies*, 10 Glob. Media Commc'n 121, 125–30 (2014).

an antitrust case against these companies.[227] But the press's appeal to antitrust is also an appeal to smash firms and thus to bring greater anarchy to the market, which the press hopes it can exploit. In this sense, the press's appeal to antitrust is not a truly statist attempt to have government stabilize the press directly. Indeed, antitrust is a sort of middle ground between the pure anti-statism pursued by progressives in their long march to redistribute through private law regimes like property, tort, and contract, and the pure statism of tax and transfer.[228]

The peculiarly American circumstances in which antimonopolism has arisen suggest that other jurisdictions considering following antimonopolists' siren song should proceed with caution. Americans only became interested in market-based redistribution because American anti-statism took tax and transfer, which both the original American progressives and Piketty agree is the only way to solve the problem of inequality, off the table. In many other jurisdictions, however, tax and transfer is politically feasible, and, because it is also more effective at attacking inequality, ought to be pursued first.[229] The prominence of antimonopoly rhetoric in the American press, the profusion of cases against the Tech Giants, and any new antitrust legislation that may follow, should not be seen as the expression of a new American intellectual consensus that antitrust is a useful tool in the fight against inequality, but rather as the expression of an attempt by a uniquely powerful industry to find a solution to a funding crisis in newsgathering that most other countries would solve using government.

IV ANTIMONOPSONISM AND LABOR

Contemporary antimonopolism is as much concerned with monopoly – meaning seller power used to raise prices charged to consumers – as it is with its close cousin, monopsony, which is buyer power used to depress prices paid to input sellers below competitive levels.[230] Indeed, the movement's focus on protecting vulnerable sellers, understood to mean workers (who sell their labor) and small suppliers, against monopsonistic buyers has perhaps received more interest and support from academia than any other area of antimonopolism. Some have shown that employer power in labor markets depresses wages below competitive levels.[231] Others have argued that although current antitrust rules limiting the acquisition and

[227] *See* Herbert Hovenkamp, Federal Antitrust Policy, the Law of Competition and Its Practice 406 (6th ed. 2020); Ramsi A. Woodcock, *The Obsolescence of Advertising in the Information Age*, 127 *Yale L.J.* 2270, 2309–14 (2018).

[228] *See supra* Section III.A.

[229] *See supra* Section II.

[230] *See, e.g.*, Debbie Feinstein & Albert Teng, *Buyer Power: Is Monopsony the New Monopoly?*, https://perma.cc/QG7R-R6Z3.

[231] *See* Alan Manning, *Monopsony in Labor Markets: A Review*, 74 *ILR Rev.* 3, 6 (2021).

maintenance of seller power apply with equal force to buyer power, antitrust's nomenclature has been a barrier to enforcement of these rules against buyer power.[232] They have advocated renaming antitrust's "consumer welfare" standard the "trading partner" welfare standard, or a variant thereof, to emphasize that antitrust considers harms inflicted on workers or small suppliers by monopsonistic buyers of equal importance to harms inflicted on consumers by monopolistic sellers.[233] Some have called for treating harms inflicted by monopsonists, particularly those inflicted on workers, as more important than harms inflicted by monopolists on consumers. Accordingly, they argue that in cases in which breakup of a monopsonist would harm the firm's customers but benefit workers, antitrust would be required to carry out the breakup.[234]

Although antimonopsonists wish to protect all small sellers, including both workers and small suppliers, their primary focus has so far been the worker, understood broadly to include both those who count as employees as a legal matter and those who formally qualify as independent contractors and therefore as small suppliers, but who might in another age have been employees.[235] Antimonopsonists are primarily interested in the employee in the Amazon sorting facility, the Uber driver, and the church organist, but they would also like to help the local machine shop making tiny screws for an Apple assembly facility.[236] Such labor-focused antimonopsonism is even more clearly driven by concerns regarding wealth inequality than is antimonopolism generally because workers are more obviously poor than the mass of consumers that antimonopolism seeks to defend. Antimonopsonism seeks directly to increase the income of the masses, whereas antimonopolism seeks only to make products cheaper for everyone, including the idle rich. But, like antimonopolism, antimonopsonism, at least as applied to labor, is ultimately a poor method of attacking wealth inequality because its end goal – competition – again leaves scarcity rents more or less untouched.

The same scarcity rents that firms generate in competitive sell-side markets through their control over scarce resources appear in buy-side markets as firms' demand for labor and other production inputs. The firm that earns scarcity rents on the sale of some product in a competitive product market, because the firm happens to own a technology that no competitor can reproduce, naturally has more money available to spend on hiring workers and purchasing inputs from suppliers, and so

232 *See* C. Scott Hemphill & Nancy L. Rose, *Mergers that Harm Sellers*, 127 *Yale L.J.* 2090–92 (2018).

233 *See id.*

234 *See* Eugene K. Kim, *Labor's Antitrust Problem: A Case for Worker Welfare Note*, 130 *Yale L.J.* 428, 447 (2020) ("[A] firm cannot justify a merger simply because it reduces labor costs by creating monopsony power.").

235 *See* Longman, *supra* note 10 (giving, as examples of "small businesses" that antitrust should protect, ice skating instructors, animal breeders, music teachers, public defenders, doctors, dentists, home health aides, truck drivers, and Uber drivers).

236 *See id.*

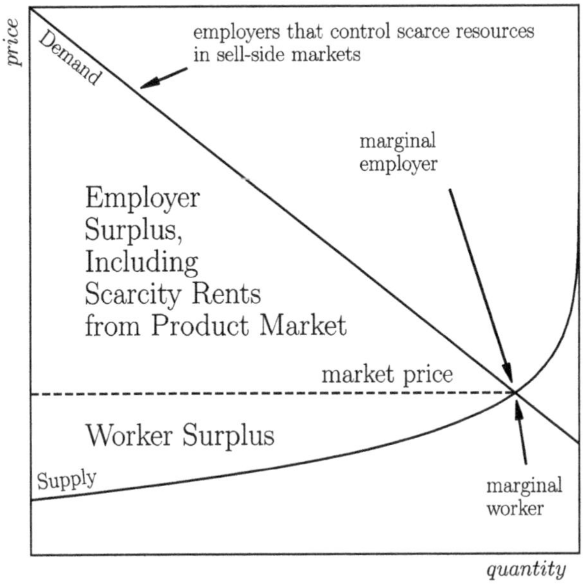

FIGURE 3.13 Employers enjoy most of the surplus in competitive labor markets

that firm will have a greater willingness to pay, and hence a higher demand, for workers and supplies. Scarcity, and the differing fortunes it creates for firms in sell-side markets, is one of the reasons for which demand for labor and other inputs can be depicted as downward sloping, as in the labor market depicted in Figure 3.13. The firms that control scarce resources and earn scarcity rents in sell-side markets occupy the highest portions of the demand line in that figure. The surplus they generate in buy-side markets, equal to the area in the figure above the price line and below the demand line, is in part a measure of the rents that they generate in sell-side markets. This suggests that policymakers should be able just as effectively to attack inequality by redistributing buyer surpluses in buy-side markets, including labor markets, as by redistributing seller rents in sell-side markets. The owner of scarce resources can be made to pay either by taxing him when he sells his product at a generous markup in competitive markets or when he buys his supplies and labor at prices far below the maximum that he is willing to pay given that markup. Moreover, antimonopsony can sometimes serve as the agent for redistribution of a firm's scarcity rents because an important characteristic of monopsony is that it increases the buyer's profits by enabling the buyer to dictate *infra*competitive prices – prices that are below those that would prevail in a competitive market. Because a firm's rents in sell-side markets are net of its costs, and a firm's costs are reduced when the firm exercises monopsony power to reduce the prices it pays in supply markets, it follows that attacking monopsony power and driving those supply prices back up to competitive levels enables workers and other suppliers to capture some of a firm's scarcity rents for themselves and so amounts to redistribution of scarcity rents. This stands in stark contrast to antimonopoly, which, as we have seen, cannot attack scarcity rents in sell-side markets because, by definition, antimonopoly attacks only rents generated by supracompetitive pricing in those markets, not the scarcity rents that exist even under competitive pricing.[237]

But whether antimonopsony is able fully to redistribute scarcity rents depends on whether the limit to its redistributive reach – the competitive price – is likely to allocate to workers and suppliers the lion's share of those scarcity rents. Here antimonopsony comes up short. The most that antimonopsony can do is to drive prices up from the infracompetitive levels to which they have been pushed by monopsony power to the higher levels consistent with competitive markets. But, just as we saw in the case of sell-side markets, whether competitive pricing is likely to redistribute a great deal of wealth or just a little depends on the relationship between inframarginal sellers and the marginal seller.[238] If sellers – in this buy-side context they are workers or suppliers – are highly differentiated in the quality of the products and services that they provide, or if some are able to provide those products or services at far lower cost than others, then the competitive price set by the marginal seller will be substantially above the costs of the inframarginal sellers and will leave inframarginal sellers with a large share of surplus.[239] Because that surplus in buy-side markets is ultimately traceable to scarcity rents in sell-side markets, the competitive price will therefore redistribute to sellers – workers and suppliers – a large share of scarcity rents. If, by contrast, sellers are not highly differentiated – workers do not tend to have unique talents or skills and suppliers do not tend to sell differentiated products or to have radical cost advantages relative to each other – then there will be little difference between the cost of the marginal seller and those of the inframarginal sellers. The competitive price will, therefore, leave sellers with a small share of the surplus and hence redistribute to them a small share of the scarcity rents earned by firms in competitive markets.

The trouble with contemporary antimonopsonism as applied to labor is that workers are not highly differentiated. The curse of labor is that it is not scarce. Celebrities and occupants of the relatively small number of highly skilled jobs aside, most work can be done by most people after a bit of training.[240] And most workers have about the same basic needs – the same production cost for their services – consisting of a bit of

[237] *See supra* Section II.B.1.b.

[238] *See supra* Section II.B.1.a.

[239] *See supra* Section II.B.1.a.

[240] *See* Elka Torpey & Audrey Watson, *Education Level and Jobs: Opportunities by State : Career Outlook: U.S. Bureau of Labor Statistics*, www.bls.gov/careeroutlook/2014/article/education-level-and-jobs.htm (last visited Nov. 14, 2021) (reporting that only 5 percent of jobs require an advanced degree).

food and shelter.[241] It follows that, celebrities and the highly educated aside, no worker appropriates much in the way of surplus when wages are priced competitively. The marginal worker is only slightly less able to carry out his job, or needs only to be slightly better fed, than the inframarginal worker, and so the price necessary to get the marginal worker into the market is not substantially higher than the price needed to get any other worker into the market. As a result, workers, unlike their employers selling in product markets, can hardly turn a profit under competition, and so an antimonopsony policy that seeks to secure the competitive wage rate for workers will not go far toward ending inequality.[242] In the context of our earlier discussion of sell-side markets, we are in Figure 3.4, which is reproduced in Figure 3.13 with the labels changed to reflect the buy-side, labor context. We are no longer in Figure 3.5, which depicts markets in which sellers earn hefty scarcity rents because they control scarce natural resources or technologies.

Given this reality, it is not surprising that antimonopsonism's most celebrated case to date was brought to protect multimillionaire bestselling authors against monopsonistic suppression of their royalties by book publishers.[243] The profits denied to average workers by monopsony, although too small significantly to move the needle on inequality, as we have seen, are substantial enough to fund major class action

[241] We think that we have greater needs – such as the ability to purchase a computer or television – only because our profits, despite being small in relation to those earned by employers, are large enough to allow most of us to afford these things, and so we have come to expect them. But were the wage to fall and squeeze these things out of our lives, we would still work to eat, and so these things are not strictly necessary to make us ready, willing, and able to work – which is the definition of cost in the economic sense. *See* Woodcock, *The Antitrust Case for Consumer Primacy in Corporate Governance*, *supra* note 43, at 1414. By contrast, we would not take a job that did not pay us enough to eat, for we are better off starving at our leisure than starving on the job.

[242] Antimonopsonists estimate, for example, that employer monopsony depresses wages by as much as 20 percent. *See* José Azar et al., *Labor Market Concentration*, 57 *J. Human Resources* S167, S167 (2020). If one were generously to interpret a return to competitive wages as increasing, in the long run, the share of wealth controlled by the bottom 90% of Americans by 20%, entirely at the expense of the richest 1%, that bottom 90% would control a mere 30% of wealth and the richest 1% would continue to control 35% of the nation's wealth. *See The Distribution of Wealth in the United States and Implications for a Net Worth Tax*, Equitable Growth (Mar. 21, 2019), www.equitablegrowth.org/the-distribution-of-wealth-in-the-united-states-and-implications-for-a-net-worth-tax/ (reporting that the bottom 90% control a quarter of national wealth and the top 1% control 40% of national wealth).

[243] *See* Memorandum, United States v. Bertelsmann et al., No. 21-2886-FYP (D.D.C. Oct. 31, 2022). Nor should we be surprised to find that the second-most-celebrated case was brought by mixed martial arts sports stars against their promotion company. *See* Kevin Draper, *Fighters Win Key Ruling in Case That Could Upend U.F.C.'s Business*, N.Y. Times (Dec. 10, 2020), www.nytimes.com/2020/12/10/sports/ufc-lawsuit.html; Kajan Johnson, et al. v. Zuffa, LLC, et al., No. 2:21-cv-01189 (D. Nev.); Cung Le, et al. v. Zuffa, LLC d/b/a Ultimate Fighting Championship and UFC, No. 2:15-cv-01045-RFB-BNW (D. Nev.).

lawsuits.[244] But it makes sense that the first labor antimonopsony lawsuits would be brought by distinctly non-average workers, for stars (and the well-educated) are alone scarce enough to generate substantial scarcity rents in the labor market and so they stand to gain the most from antimonopsonism. Indeed, stars and the well-educated occupy a position closer to that of business owners than to that of the average worker, for their scarcity makes them more likely to take the lion's share of the surplus in the markets in which they compete, and so they are more like to be on the happy side of the wealth gap.[245] It follows that monopsony does not deprive these special workers of equality so much as a spot in the 1 percent, and antimonopsony works to retore that spot to them. It is another irony of antimonopsonism as progressive cause that its major achievement thus far has been to make the rich richer.[246]

An important consequence of the fact that average workers are not scarce is that, tax and transfer and price regulation aside, only monopoly power for average workers and the monopoly pricing of wages can meaningfully reduce inequality. This stands in rather stark contrast to the situation on the sell side that we considered earlier, in which the scarcity of sellers meant that monopoly power and monopoly pricing could not have important distributive effects.[247] Because, on the buy side, the

[244] If, for example, a court were to conclude that Amazon had monopsonized labor markets and that hourly wages would be 20 percent higher were it not for Amazon's monopsony power, then, if all 950,000 Amazon employees were hourly workers, and given that Amazon pays a minimum wage of $15 per hour, the loss suffered by workers *for every hour worked* would be at least $28.5 million, and plaintiffs could recover three times that under antitrust's treble damages rule, for a total haul of $85.5 million per hour worked. *See* Azar et al., *supra* note 242, at 1218 (arguing that labor monopsony depresses wages by 20 percent); *1 in Every 169 U.S. Workers is Now Employed by Amazon*, NBC News, https://perma.cc/AQV2-LVKB; *Why Amazon Is Flooding the Country with $15 Minimum Wage Ads*, Vice, https://perma.cc/S2R7-T6YU. A lawsuit based on monopsonization over the course of a single 40-hour week of labor by the full company would, then, give rise to damages of $3.42 billion, far more than enough to bankroll a vigorous class action lawsuit.

[245] *See* Jonathan Rothwell, *Make Elites Compete: Why the 1% Earn so Much and What to Do about It*, Brookings (Mar. 25, 2016), https://perma.cc/W47K-6B94 (citing data showing that the groups with the largest representation in the top 1 percent of earners include the high-education professions of medicine, law, and accounting).

[246] This would also have been the outcome of the other major case celebrated by labor monopsonists if plaintiffs had prevailed at trial (in the event, they settled). The twelve hundred plaintiffs in the case argued that between 2010 and 2017 the defendant's monopsonization of their labor market cost them $1.6 billion in actual damages. *See* Draper, *supra* note 243. That averaged out to $190,000 per year each. Because they alleged that this loss represented 40 percent of what they should have earned over the period, the elimination of the monopsony in this market would have given the plaintiffs in the case average annual pay of $476,000, which was well above the cutoff of $357,552 for membership in the top 1 percent by income in 2021. *See id.*; *Who Are the Top One Percent by Income or Net Worth in 2021?*, DQYDJ (Sept. 30, 2021), https://perma.cc/FUC6-85DP.

[247] *See supra* Section II.B.1.b.

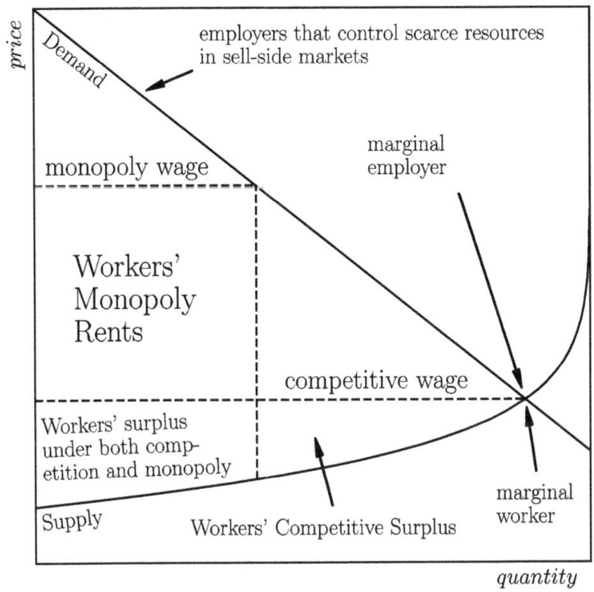

FIGURE 3.14 By charging monopoly wages, unionized workers can appropriate part of employers' share of the surplus in labor markets

surpluses that drive inequality are taken by buyers (i.e., employers), rather than sellers (i.e., workers), monopoly pricing enables the have-nots, which here are the sellers, to claw back the value that competitive pricing would otherwise confer on buyers. On the buy side, therefore, progressives ought to pine for the world depicted in Figure 3.14 in which workers are shown earning large monopoly rents by charging employers monopoly wages.

Workers charge monopoly wages by unionizing, so the fact that only monopoly pricing can take a bite out of inequality in labor markets has the important implication that only unionization, and not antimonopsonism, can meaningfully attack wealth inequality. Labor-oriented antimonopsonism – the breaking up of big employers to the end of promoting competitive pricing of wages – is, by contrast, a profoundly moderate, deradicalizing approach to inequality, because it does nothing that unionization cannot itself do, but caps the gains that can be had by workers at those consistent with the competitive wage rate, something that unionization does not do. Unionization can achieve whatever gains for workers that antimonopsonism can achieve because a union engaged in bilateral negotiations with a monopsony employer necessarily negotiates wages up to competitive levels in negotiating them up to even higher, labor-monopoly, levels. Thus unionization is already a complete solution to monoposony pricing, and embrace of antimonopsonism as an independent project serves only to restrict progressive horizons from monopoly profits to workers' meagre profits under competition. Progressives of a century ago understood that unionization, not antimonopsonism, held the greatest promise for workers, which is why, rather than fight to turn the antitrust laws against employers, progressives of that period fought instead to keep antitrust enforcers from targeting unions.[248]

Given the deradicalizing implications of antimonopsony, why has it become perhaps progressives' favorite flavor of antimonopolism? Antimonopsonism is, of course, just another part of the long march around the tax system, for workers could, like everyone else, be made equal through an aggressive tax and transfer regime even were their wages to remain at monopsony levels.[249] So progressive interest in antimonopsonism is plausibly driven by progressives' broader frustration at not being able to redistribute through taxation. What seems to have made antimonopsonism of particular interest to progressives is that it is also part of a second long march around a different political barrier: unionization, which went into serious decline at about the same time as the tax revolt made redistribution through the income tax system politically impossible.[250] Progressives have been unable to reverse workers' fortunes through new legislation making it easier to unionize, and price regulation – via increases in the minimum wage – has proven difficult to secure.[251] Progressives have therefore sought to leverage the press's love affair with antimonopolism to help workers by reconceptualizing the labor problem as a problem of strong employers rather than weak workers. In so doing, progressives have brought to the antimonopsonist branch of antimonopolism an additional and particularly vocal constituency. Political moderates, who perhaps appreciate the deradicalizing nature of antimonopsonism better than the long marchers, have been only too happy to oblige, which explains why academic uptake of antimonopsonism has been far more enthusiastic than academic uptake of antimonopolism as a whole.[252]

V CONCLUSION

The foundation of renewed interest in antitrust and inequality in a uniquely American anti-statism suggests that other jurisdictions considering using antitrust

[248] *See* Daniel R. Ernst, *The Labor Exemption, 1908–1914 Symposium: The Sherman Act's First Century: A Historical Perspective*, 74 *Iowa L. Rev.* 1151, 1162–72 (1988–1989).

[249] *See supra* Section III.A.

[250] *See* Danielle Kurtzleben, *The Decline of American Unions, in 7 Charts*, Vox, https://perma.cc/4QDK-NP86 (last visited Nov. 14, 2021).

[251] *See* Kate Andrias, *Labor Law Reform Is Essential*, Boston Review, https://www.bostonreview.net/forum_response/kate-andrias-fixing-law/ (last visited Nov. 14, 2021); Evan Soltas, *Everything You Need to Know about the Minimum Wage*, Vox, https://perma.cc/243H-VTT2 (last visited Nov. 14, 2021).

[252] Notable moderates who have made contributions to antimonopsony in recent years include Eric Posner, Herbert Hovenkamp, and Scott Hemphill. *See* Hemphill & Rose, *supra* note 232; Ioana Marinescu & Herbert Hovenkamp, *Anticompetitive Mergers in Labor Markets*, 94 *Ind. L.J.* 1031 (2019); Naidu et al., *supra* note 27; Suresh Naidu & Eric A. Posner, *Labor Monopsony and the Limits of the Law*, 57 *J. Human Resources* S284 (2021). For the academic reception of antimonopolism more broadly, see Woodcock, Big Ink v. Bigger Tech, *supra* note 8.

to address inequality should proceed with caution. As both the original American progressives, mainstream law and economics, and Thomas Piketty seem to agree, the tax system remains the most effective and radical tool for redistributing wealth. Any jurisdiction in which tax reform remains politically feasible ought to pursue tax reform first. Moreover, antitrust is not even a second-best solution (or, more aptly, not even a third-best solution given that the better option, taxation, is already a second-best solution due to its own inefficiencies). Antitrust's focus on eliminating only monopoly rents (and this only through the limited means of promotion of competition[253]) precludes antitrust from ever attacking the scarcity rents that are a major source of inequality.[254]

Moreover, other alternatives, such as the reform of remedies for violations of private law rules of property, contract, and tort originally espoused by progressives making the long march to redistribute around the tax system, would in fact be more effective at targeting inequality.[255] Unlike antitrust, private law rules can redistribute scarcity rents because private law rules are not required to quit the field once a competitive price has been achieved. The law can set damages for trespass by the poor below the competitive price for trespass. Antitrust cannot achieve the same result because its remit ends with competitive pricing. Of course, redistribution through private law rules is highly imperfect relative to income taxation. It is almost impossible for a judge to predict the ultimate distributive impact in all markets of changing a particular damages measure. Income tax incidence is far easier to estimate. But it says a lot about the peculiarity of contemporary American interest in antitrust as a redistributive vehicle that antitrust should present itself today as a solution to inequality before taxation or reform of the private law.

[253] *See* Woodcock, *The Antitrust Duty to Charge Low Prices*, *supra* note 96, at 1755–60 (arguing limiting antitrust to the promotion of competition prevents antitrust from carrying out its mission to maximize consumer welfare).

[254] *See supra* Section II.

[255] *See* Kennedy, *supra* note 13, at 30–33.

4

An Inframarginalist Argument for Mandating the Use of Pro-Consumer Boilerplate

Michael D. Guttentag[*]

CONTENTS

I INTRODUCTION

Much legal scholarship addresses the question of whether consumers should be bound by the terms included in the fine print of the contracts entered into when purchasing goods or services.[1] These contracts are almost always "contracts of

[*] This chapter has benefited from comments provided by John Coyle, James Gibson, Herbert Hovenkamp, Przemyslaw Palka, and Ramsi Woodcock.

[1] *See, e.g.*, MARGARET JANE RADIN, BOILERPLATE: THE FINE PRINT, VANISHING RIGHTS, AND THE RULE OF LAW (2012); Yehuda Adar & Shmuel I. Becher, *Taking Boilerplate Seriously: Tackling Exploitation in Consumer Contracts*, 62 B.C. L. REV. 2405 (2021); Douglas G. Baird, *The Boilerplate Puzzle*, 104 MICH. L. REV. 933 (2006); Randy E. Barnett, *A Consent Theory of Contract*, 86 COLUM. L. REV. 269 (1986); Omri Ben-Shahar, *Regulation through Boilerplate: An Apologia*, 112 MICH. L. REV. 883 (2014)(reviewing *supra* RADIN, BOILERPLATE); James Gibson, *Boilerplate's False Dichotomy*, 106 GEO. L. J. 249 (2018); Robin B. Kar & Margaret Jane Radin, *Pseudo-Contract & Shared Meaning Analysis*, 132 HARV. L. REV. 1135 (2019); Avery Katz, *Your Terms or Mine: The Duty to Read the Fine Print in Contracts*, 21 RAND J. ECON. 518 (1990); Friedrich Kessler, *Contracts of Adhesion-Some Thoughts about Freedom of Contract*, 431 COLUM. L. REV. 629 (1943); Karl N. Llewellyn, *What Price Contract? – An Essay in Perspective*, 40 YALE L.J. 704 (1931); Russell Korobkin, *Bounded Rationality, Standard Form Contracts, and Unconscionability*, 70 U. CHIC. L. REV. 1203 (2003); Vijay Raghavan, *Consumer Law's Equity*

adhesion"[2] and the fine print provisions are fairly characterized as "boilerplate."[3] Very few consumer purchasers understand this boilerplate, which is generally unreadable,[4] non-negotiable,[5] and one-sided in favor of the sellers.[6] The resulting lack of meaningful consent to these boilerplate terms leads many scholars to conclude that these provisions should not be enforced.[7]

Proponents of enforcement respond that even in the absence of meaningful consent there are reasons to enforce these provisions. One such argument is that contract provisions should be treated just as other product attributes are treated by a court even when the consumer is unaware of the particular product attribute.[8] According to this line of argument, judges should no more second-guess whether a particular boilerplate provision should be enforced than they should second-guess whether the memory board on a personal computer is fast enough.[9]

Those who argue for treating consumer boilerplate no differently than other product attributes acknowledge that evidence of a market failure could nevertheless

Gap, 2022 UTAH L. REV. 511; Todd D. Rakoff, *Contracts of Adhesion: An Essay in Reconstruction*, 96 HARV. L. REV. 1173 (1983); Laruen Henry Scholz, *Fiduciary Boilerplate*, 46 J. CORP. LAW. 143 (2020); Alan Schwartz & Louis L. Wilde, *Intervening in Markets on the Basis of Imperfect Information: A Legal and Economic Analysis*, 127 U. PA. L. REV. 630 (1979); Tess Wilkinson-Ryan, *The Perverse Consequences of Disclosing Standard Terms*, 103 CORNELL L. REV. 117 (2017).

2 *See, e.g.*, Rakoff, *supra* note 1.

3 For a discussion of the origins of the "boilerplate" terminology, see Michael I. Meyerson, *The Efficient Consumer Form Contract: Law and Economics Meets the Real World*, 24 GA. L. REV. 583, 595 (1990).

4 Yannis Bakos et al., *Does Anyone Read the Fine Print? Consumer Attention to Standard-Form Contracts*, 43 J. LEG. STUD. 1, 19 (2014)(reporting that customers visited the terms and conditions pages at rates around one-tenth of 1 percent). One reason is that the content is unreadable, Uri Benoliel & Shmuel I. Becher, *The Duty to Read the Unreadable*, 60 B.C. L. REV. 2255 (2019).

In fact, it would be illogical for a consumer to invest the time required to read the boilerplate. Wilkinson-Ryan, *supra* note 1 at 123 ("Most people should not read most terms, because the cost of reading is greater than its expected value.") (footnotes omitted); Gibson, *supra* note 1, at 255 ("Scholars agree that information processing costs routinely prohibit the reading of boilerplate no matter when consumers encounter it.") (footnote omitted).

5 *See, e.g.*, Rakoff, *supra* note 1.

6 Florencia Marotta-Wurgler, *Are "Pay Now, Terms Later" Contracts Worse for Buyers? Evidence from Software License Agreements*, 38 J. LEG. STUD. 309 (2009).

7 *See, e.g.*, RADIN, *supra* note 1; Gibson, *supra* note 1; Kar & Radin, *supra* note 1; Korobkin, *supra* note 1. *But see* Val Ricks, *Assent Is Not an Element of Contract Formation*, 61 U. KAN. L. REV. 591 (2013).

8 *See, e.g.*, Baird, *supra* note 1; Barnett, *supra* note 1; Ben-Shahar, *supra* note 1, at 885 ("Boilerplate apologists regard the fine print as merely a feature of mass-produced products, and a welfare-increasing feature at that – reducing transaction costs and prices and allowing firms to focus on improving product features that people actually care about."). *See also*, ProCD v. Zeidenberg, 86 F.3d 1447 (7th Cir. 1996) (holding that a clickwrap agreement is enforceable because the plaintiff could not purchase without seeing the link to the terms and conditions).

9 The example of the purchase of a personal computer is from Baird, *supra* note 1, at 936.

still justify legal intervention. For example, information asymmetry about the quality of a product can lead to a market where only transactions involving low-quality products take place, a "lemons" market failure.[10] Oren Bar-Gill and Elizabeth Warren draw a parallel between the need to regulate dangerous consumer products and dangerous financial products based on a concern about this kind of market failure.[11] However, proponents of enforcing consumer boilerplate provisions argue that the absence of consent to a particular provision in a consumer contract is not in and of itself sufficient evidence of a market failure to justify regulatory intervention.[12]

Missing from the arguments of both the proponents and opponents of enforcing consumer boilerplate provisions is recognition of the fundamentally inframarginal nature of the choice of whether to enforce these provisions.[13] Both the proponents and the opponents of enforcing consumer boilerplate provisions therefore fail to realize how crucial the distinctive role laws play in allocating inframarginal resources is to an analysis of whether to enforce consumer boilerplate provisions.

The first step in carrying out inframarginal analysis is the identification of situations where the main effect of a legal rule is on how inframarginal resources are allocated. For consumers, the effects of boilerplate provisions are largely inframarginal because the consequences of the ultimate impact of these provisions are almost always ignored when purchasing decisions are made.[14] For sellers of consumer goods, there is more of a possibility that whether consumer boilerplate provisions can be enforced will ultimately affect operations. Sellers might, for example, operate in such a competitive environment that they are immediately forced to pass any gains realized by enforcing pro-seller boilerplate provisions back to purchasers in the form of lower prices.[15] However, much evidence and economic theory suggest that in practice sellers can benefit from the enforcement of pro-seller boilerplate provisions without otherwise changing their business practices.[16]

The next step in carrying out inframarginal analysis is to consider how legal rules might lead to a fairer and more efficient allocation of these inframarginal resources than an unregulated allocation. Interestingly, as I have shown in detail elsewhere, the presumption that tax policy is more efficient than legal rules as a way to redistribute wealth does not apply when evaluating the gains from making the

[10] George A. Akerlof, *The Market for "Lemons": Quality Uncertainty and the Market*, 3 Q.J. Econ. 488 (1970)(explaining the lemons market failure is a species of the more general class of market failures associated with information asymmetries).

[11] Oren Bar-Gill & Elizabeth Warren, *Making Credit Safer*, 157 U. Penn. L. Rev. 1 (2008).

[12] *See, e.g.*, Oren Bar-Gill, *Algorithmic Price Discrimination When Demand Is a Function of Both Preferences and (Mis)perceptions*, 86 U. Chic. L. Rev. 217 (2019); Schwartz & Wilde, *supra* note 1.

[13] For limited exceptions, see *infra* notes 49 and 50 and accompanying text.

[14] See *supra* notes 4–6 and accompanying text.

[15] This possibility was treated as inevitable in the infamous Supreme Court decision in Carnival Cruise Lines, Inc. v. Shute. 499 U.S. 585 (1991). For a more detailed discussion, see *supra* note 48 and accompanying text.

[16] See *infra* notes 45–48 and accompanying text.

allocation of inframarginal resources more equitable.[17] In addition, while in some situations competition can improve outcomes, efficiency considerations in the context of allocating inframarginal resources generally point away from competition and toward cooperation, because competition involves investing resources in winning what is essentially a zero-sum game.[18]

Applying the tools of inframarginal analysis to the question of whether and how to regulate the enforcement of consumer boilerplate provisions generates two policy recommendations. First, inframarginal analysis suggests that pro-consumer boilerplate provisions should be preferred to pro-seller boilerplate provisions, because consumers are on average less well-off than sellers. Second, the enforcement of pro-consumer boilerplate provisions should be mandatory rather than default to discourage sellers from investing resources in what is essentially wasteful competition to shift the value of the resources controlled by boilerplate back to the seller. The rationales for these policy recommendations are illustrated graphically below.[19]

A specific example here in the Introduction can illustrate why the main effects of consumer boilerplate provisions are likely to be inframarginal and provide clarity about the benefits that can be realized by regulating these provisions. One term included in most consumer contracts is a choice-of-forum clause that dictates the forum in which legal disputes between the parties will be resolved.[20] Sellers of consumer goods and services predictably choose a venue for resolving legal disputes that is convenient for them, such as the jurisdiction in which their headquarters are based, even though this choice of forum can make it difficult or impossible for consumers to pursue even legitimate claims.[21]

[17] Michael Guttentag, *Law, Taxes, Inequality, and Surplus*, 102 B.U. L. REV. 1329 (2022) [hereinafter, Guttentag, *Law, Taxes, Inequality, and Surplus*]. For a more detailed discussion of this topic, see *infra* notes 26 and 27 and accompanying text.

[18] Michael Guttentag, *Evolutionary Psychology and Resource-Sharing Laws*, 44(3) EVOLUTION & HUM. BEHAV. 264 (May 2023) [hereinafter, Guttentag, *Resource-Sharing Laws*].

[19] See *infra* Section III.

[20] *See, e.g.*, Patrick J. Borchers, *Forum Selection Agreements in the Federal Courts after* Carnival Cruise: *A Proposal for Congressional Reform*, 67 WASH. L. REV. 55 (1992); John F. Coyle & Katherine C. Richardson, *Enforcing Outbound Forum Selection Clauses in State Court*, 96 IND. L.J. 1174 (2021); David Marcus, *The Perils of Contract Procedure: A Revised History of Forum Selection Clauses in the Federal Courts*, 82 TUL. L. REV. 973 (2008); Linda S. Mullenix, *Another Choice of Forum, Another Choice of Law: Consensual Adjudicatory Procedure in Federal Court*, 57 FORDHAM L. REV. 291 (1988); Linda S. Mullenix, *Another Easy Case, Some More Bad Law:* Carnival Cruise Lines *and Contractual Personal Jurisdiction*, 27 TEX. INT'L L.J. 323 (1992); Edward A. Purcell, Jr., *Geography as a Litigation Weapon: Consumers, Forum-Selection Clauses, and the Rehnquist Court*, 40 UCLA L. R. 423 (1992); Cara Reichard, *Keeping Litigation at Home: The Role of States in Preventing Unjust Choice of Forum*, 129 YALE L. J. 866 (2019).

[21] The choice-of-forum provision is "a prevalent feature of standard-form contracts [used to shuttle any] challenge into a forum that is, almost by definition, less convenient for the claimant and more convenient for the defendant [and] can serve as a significant obstacle to the claimant's chances of a favorable resolution." Reichard, *supra* note 20, at 869–70 (footnotes omitted).

Such a provision was the basis of a dispute between Eulala Shute and Carnival Cruise Lines that led to the infamous Supreme Court decision in *Carnival Cruise Lines, Inc. v. Shute.*[22] Shute had purchased a ticket for a cruise from Los Angeles to Puerto Vallarta, Mexico, in her home state of Washington. Shute alleged she slipped on a deck mat during a guided tour of the ship's galley and brought a lawsuit in the State of Washington. Carnival Cruise Lines argued the lawsuit should be heard in the State of Florida based on the choice-of-forum provision in the boilerplate of the ticket contract. The Supreme Court upheld the Florida choice-of-forum provision.

The *Carnival Cruise Lines* case provides a context in which to highlight the importance of inframarginal analysis as a tool to evaluate whether to enforce consumer boilerplate provisions. First, the facts of the case provide an example of a situation in which the effects of consumer boilerplate provisions are likely to be inframarginal, albeit for different reasons. For Shute, the purchase of her ticket would almost certainly have been unaffected by what the boilerplate on the back of the ticket said or whether its provisions were enforceable. In contrast, there are some scenarios in which Carnival Cruise Lines would have altered its behavior depending on how this litigation was resolved. Perhaps, the market for cruises between Los Angeles and Puerto Vallarta is so competitive that any cost saving from including a pro-seller choice-of-forum provision would immediately be passed on to consumers.[23] A decision enforcing this provision might also reduce the level of care Carnival Cruise Lines takes when giving galley tours, because Carnival Cruise Lines would need to worry less about the possibility of litigation. However, neither of these responses to a decision to enforce the choice-of-forum provision is inevitable. In fact, there is a significant amount of analytic and empirical work that suggests a decision to enforce this choice-of-forum provision would not lead a company like Carnival Cruise Lines to make any changes in pricing or operations.[24] The most likely scenario is that the effect of a decision of whether or not to enforce the choice-of-forum provision will be exclusively on whether Shute or Carnival Cruise Lines bears the costs of Shute's injury.

The facts in *Carnival Cruise Lines* also illustrate the advantages of implementing the policy recommendations that pro-consumer boilerplate should be mandatory. From a redistributive perspective, pro-consumer terms are probably of benefit in this case, because Shute is probably not as well-off as the owners of Carnival Cruise Lines. As for the benefits of a mandatory versus a default regime, anything less than making the pro-seller choice-of-forum provision mandatory would create a strong incentive for Carnival Cruise Lines to invest resource in finding a way to shift the forum for hearing the dispute back to the State of Florida. The intuition that Shute

[22] 499 U.S. 585 (1991). With respect to the infamy of this decision, see, e.g., Linda S Mullenix, Carnival Cruise Lines, Inc. v. Shute: *The Titanic of Worst Decisions*, 12 Nev. L.J. 549 (2012). For further discussion of this case, see *infra* Section IV.

[23] The Supreme Court in its opinion in *Carnival Cruise Lines* viewed this outcome as inevitable. 499 U.S. 585, 594 (1991). See *infra* note 69 and accompanying text.

[24] See *infra* notes 45–48 and accompanying text.

should not be required to go to Florida to pursue her claim proves to be grounded in sound economic analysis once the importance of inframarginal analysis is brought to the question.

The discussion proceeds as follows. Section II provides a brief overview of inframarginal analysis. Section III explains why the effects of consumer boilerplate provisions are largely inframarginal. Section IV uses a graph-based approach to explore the implications for policy of the fact that the effects of consumer boilerplate are largely inframarginal. Section V applies inframarginal analysis to the question of how choice-of-forum provisions should be regulated.

II INFRAMARGINAL ANALYSIS

Inframarginal analysis begins with the acknowledgment that there are many situations where the price at which a transaction takes place affects the behavior of both buyers and sellers. For example, if prices go down, then some current buyers may purchase additional units or new buyers may enter the market. Conversely, if prices go up, then current sellers may choose to sell more or new sellers may choose to enter the market. Low prices attract buyers and high prices attract sellers. This is the dynamic that explains why supply will tend to equal demand at some equilibrium price. What is true of price is also generally true of other product attributes. Changes in product quality can affect both the supply and demand of a good or service.

However, not every change in price or quality will affect the behavior of every buyer and seller. For many buyers and sellers a change in price or product quality over a limited range will not alter their behavior. If I am willing to pay $10 for an ice cream cone on a hot day, then whether the price is $2 or $5 will not affect my choice of whether to buy the ice cream cone. For buyers and sellers in this situation, changes in price or quality in a given range are inframarginal. More generally, in a market transaction where the willingness to pay ("WTP") of one party to the transaction exceeds the price at which the other party is willing to sell ("WTS") prices in the range between one party's WTP and the other party's WTS are inframarginal.

This does not mean that there will be no economic effects from changes in price or quality simply because the changes are within this inframarginal range. Changes in price or quality within this range can shift resources between buyers and sellers. Paying $5 rather than $2 for that ice cream cone means I will have $3 less and the seller will have $3 more than if I paid just $2, even if this change in price from $2 to $5 did not change behavior on the margin.

The inframarginal analysis of law investigates whether or how to regulate these kinds of inframarginal transactions.[25] Two general considerations inform this

[25] Michael D. Guttentag, *Law and Surplus: Opportunities Missed*, 2019 UTAH L. REV. 607 [hereinafter, Guttentag, *Opportunities Missed*].

investigation. First, the regulation of inframarginal transactions offers a unique opportunity to redistribute wealth. Other scholars have noted the potential for inframarginal transfers to serve a redistributional purpose, but are ambivalent about the significance of these transfers in light of the work of Louis Kaplow and Steven Shavell on what is commonly referred to as the "double distortion" justification for relying on tax policy as the first, best way to achieve redistributional objectives.[26] For example, Bar-Gill writes that the "overall welfare assessment depends on the relative weights of efficiency and distribution in the social objective function (unless the adverse distributional implications can be neutralized through an appropriate adjustment to the tax and transfer system)."[27]

However, it is a mistake to treat law as a second-best method to redistribute wealth when laws are used to regulate inframarginal transactions. The presumption that tax policy is more efficient than legal rules to redistribute wealth does not apply in the context of deciding how to allocate inframarginal resources.[28] As a result, laws that regulate inframarginal transactions are often superior to the tax-and-transfer system as a way to address inequality.

Second, the regulation of inframarginal transactions needs to address a significant risk inherent in these transactions. Competition for inframarginal resources is both hard to prevent and inherently wasteful because competition in this context involves the investment of resources in efforts to win a zero-sum game. The problem of the social costs of wasteful competition for inframarginal resources was first brought to prominence in the seminal work of Gordon Tullock on the social cost of what came to be known as "rent seeking."[29] In situations that invite wasteful competition, devising a mechanism to better align private incentives with social gains can be welfare-enhancing.

The law can address both the opportunities that arise in inframarginal transactions because resources can be distributed to those who are less well-off without creating inefficient incentives and the perils because unbridled competition can lead to resources being wasted in a value-destroying effort to gain for oneself at the expense of others. Property law provides examples. By granting one party a clear and

[26] *See, e.g.*, Louis Kaplow & Steven Shavell, *Why the Legal System Is Less Efficient than the Income Tax in Redistributing Income*, 23 J. Legal Stud. 667 (1994); Louis Kaplow & Steven Shavell, *Should Legal Rules Favor the Poor? Clarifying the Role of Legal Rules and the Income Tax in Redistributing Income*, 29 J. Legal Stud. 821, 825–26 (2000); Chris William Sanchirico, *Taxes versus Legal Rules as Instruments for Equity: A More Equitable View*, 29 J. Legal Stud. 797 (2000).

[27] Bar-Gill, *supra* note 12, at 220 (footnotes omitted).

[28] Guttentag, *Law, Taxes, Inequality, and Surplus*, *supra* note 17.

[29] Gordon Tullock, *The Welfare Costs of Tariffs, Monopolies, and Theft*, 5 Western Econ. J. 224 (1967). Anne Krueger coined the term "rent-seeking" to describe the wasteful efforts described by Tullock "aimed at obtaining special government privilege." Anne O. Krueger, *The Political Economy of the Rent-Seeking Society*, 64 Am. Econ. Rev. 291, 291 (1974). For a more detailed discussion of Tullock's insights and the limited way in which they have been applied in legal scholarship, see Guttentag, *Opportunities Missed*, *supra* note 25, at 617–22.

exclusive property right, the incentive to engage in wasteful competition for an inframarginal resource can be reduced. The finality and clarity of a property grant is likely to discourage efforts to abscond with property protected in this manner.[30]

Interestingly, in other settings the opposite approach, denying or reducing property rights, can also be a useful way to ensure that inframarginal resources are divvied up in ways that avoid wasteful competition. For example, the admiralty rule of salvage dictates that those who rescue goods lost at sea are not entitled to keep the full value of the goods rescued.[31] The effect of this law is to limit how much can be gained by engaging in a potentially wasteful competition to be the first to capture goods lost at sea. Richard Posner explains that limiting the property rights granted to the salvager helps to prevent "an expected gain [from being] translated into costs through competitive efforts."[32]

Examples of laws that address the opportunities and perils when regulating inframarginal transactions range widely from laws that prohibit polygyny[33] to laws that ban trading on inside information.[34] However, the study of law's role in divvying up inframarginal resources in ways that are both fair and efficient remains nascent with many exciting developments still to come. This chapter continues that exploration by showing not only that the effects of consumer boilerplate are primarily inframarginal, but also that a particular legal regime, mandated pro-consumer boilerplate, can produce a more equitable and efficient divvying up of the inframarginal resources involved than other policy choices.

III WHY CONSUMER BOILERPLATE IS INFRAMARGINAL

One of the policy debates where the inframarginal analysis of law can provide new insight is in considering whether or how the terms contained in consumer boilerplate should be enforced. The first step in justifying this claim is to show that the stakes in determining whether or how to enforce these provisions are largely inframarginal. The reasons why the effects of these provisions fall largely on inframarginal resources differ for purchasers as compared with sellers of consumer goods and services.

For consumers, the provisions contained in boilerplate are unlikely to affect their behavior because consumers predictably (and logically) ignore these

[30] For a consideration of the possibility that this legal solution builds an evolved predisposition, see Jeffrey Evans Stake, *The Property "Instinct,"* 359 PHIL. TRANSACTIONS ROYAL SOC'Y B: BIOLOGICAL SCI. 1763 (2004).

[31] 3A BENEDICT ON ADMIRALTY § 2, 1–3 (Martin J. Norris 7th ed., rev. 2005) (citations omitted). GRANT GILMORE & CHARLES L. BLACK, JR., THE LAW OF ADMIRALTY 566–70 (2d ed. 1975).

[32] RICHARD A. POSNER, ECONOMIC ANALYSIS OF LAW at 45 n.4. (8th ed. 2011). Posner concludes, "the denial of a property right can be as much an economizing device as the creation of one." *Id.*, at 47.

[33] Guttentag, *Evolutionary Psychology*, *supra* note 18.

[34] Michael D. Guttentag, *Avoiding Wasteful Competition: Why Trading on Inside Information Should Be Illegal*, 86 BROOKLYN L. REV. 895 (2021).

provisions.[35] There is, for example, survey evidence that consumers systematically underestimate the ultimate costs of boilerplate provisions.[36]

Moreover, other indirect mechanisms by which marginal efficiency might be achieved are likely to fail in this setting. For example, in some markets it may be true that there are enough buyers concerned about product attributes to effectively provide protection for all purchasers. However, there are unlikely to be enough buyers who pay attention to the content of boilerplate to provide this benefit.[37] It is also unlikely that there are strong enough reputational effects in consumer markets to push firms to adopt the kinds of boilerplate terms consumers would prefer absent any information or transaction costs.[38] As James Gibson presciently observes, "[t]he problem is that the market, even if competitive, exerts no discipline on [boilerplate] terms."[39]

The conclusion that consumers do not alter their behavior based on the content or enforceability of boilerplate provisions is consistent with research on consumer behavior more generally. For example, there is evidence that consumers often misperceive the ultimate price of the goods and services they purchase.[40] Sellers, moreover, use these predictable failings to their advantage by making goods and services appear less costly or more valuable than they really are.[41] As Bar-Gill observes, "when consumers are imperfectly rational, sellers compete by designing pricing schemes that create an appearance of a lower price."[42]

More specifically, Ian Ayres and Alan Schwartz explore the impact of what they describe as "'term optimism,' which exists when consumers expect a contract to

35 See *supra* notes 4–6 and accompanying text.

36 Aaron Perzanowski, *Consumer Perceptions of the Right to Repair*, 96 Ind. L. J. 361 (2021) (reporting on a survey that found that consumers systematically underestimate the cost of the boilerplate provisions that restrict the consumer's ability to have products repaired by a third party without voiding the product warranty).

37 *See, e.g.*, Korobkin, *supra* note 1, at 1234. For an article that acknowledges this problem and attempts to develop a method to address it, see Ian Ayres & Alan Schwartz, *The No-Reading Problem in Consumer Contract Law*, 66 Stan. L. Rev. 545 (2014).

38 *See, e.g.*, Yonathan A. Arbel, *Reputation Failure: The Limits of Market Failure in Consumer Markets*, 54 Wake Forest L. Rev 1239 (2019); *but see*, Lucian A. Bebchuk & Richard A. Posner, *One-Sided Contracts in Competitive Consumer Markets*, 104 Mich. L. Rev. 827 (2006).

39 Gibson, *supra* note 1, at 259.

40 *See, e.g.*, Peter R. Dickson & Alan G. Sawyer, *The Price Knowledge and Search of Supermarket Shoppers*, 54 J. Marketing 42 (1990).

41 *See, e.g.*, Botond Kőszegi, *Behavioral Contract Theory*, 52 J. Econ. Literature 1075, 1075 (2014) (summarizing research that "studies contracts designed primarily to take advantage of agent mistakes.").

42 Oren Bar-Gill, *Consumer Transactions*, *in* Behavioral Economics and the Law 469 (Eyal Zamir & Doron Teichman eds., 2014). *See generally*, Oren Bar-Gill, Seduction By Contract (2012). *See also*, Robert A. Hillman & Jeffrey J. Rachlinski, *Standard-Form Contracting in the Electronic Age*, 77 N.Y.U. L. Rev. 429, 433 (2002) ("Even as the electronic environment provides consumers with new tools to protect themselves from businesses, it also creates novel opportunities for businesses to take advantage of consumers .... Businesses still know more than consumers, and consumers still fail to read and understand standard terms.").

contain more favorable terms than it actually provides."[43] In the Ayres and Schwartz model, consumers do not have a systematic bias toward underestimating the costs of boilerplate, but only optimistic views remain uncorrected since firms will invest resources in correcting those whose views are unduly pessimistic.

The ubiquity of pro-seller provisions in boilerplate that consumers are unaware of does not fully resolve the issue of whether the content of these provisions is inframarginal. If these pro-seller provisions alter other aspects of the seller's business, then the effect of these pro-seller provisions may not be truly inframarginal. There are several ways that the enforceability of consumer boilerplate provisions might affect seller behavior. First, sellers may be operating in such a competitive environment that any gains from enforcing pro-seller boilerplate provisions are immediately passed back to purchasers. In fact, a belief that this would inevitably occur was part of the justification the Supreme Court offered for the decision in the *Carnival Cruise Lines* case.[44] Another possibility is that sellers will reduce the level of care they provide or the quality of the products they sell because the enforcement of pro-seller boilerplate provisions makes it less likely they will face liability for adverse consequences caused by the goods or services they sell.

There are, however, several reasons to expect that the benefits sellers realize by crafting and enforcing pro-seller boilerplate provisions do not affect their other business practices. Peter Diamond offers a canonical model in which the existence of buyer search costs allows sellers to charge prices above cost.[45] The insight driving the Diamond model is that search costs discourage buyers from shopping around endlessly to find the lowest price and sellers take advantage of the cost to the buyer to continue to search. In a related model, Glenn Ellison shows how profits generated from selling add-on products may not be competed away so long as add-on prices are not easily observed.[46] Xavier Gabaix and David Laibson model a situation where firms are not able to profitably debias consumers who do not realize they are being charged high add-on prices.[47] Taken together, these models identify several scenarios in which firms can profit by charging prices above cost for add-ons. To the extent that boilerplate provisions systematically work to the disadvantage of consumers, these analytic models suggest how such a practice can survive in equilibrium without sellers having to provide offsetting benefits to buyers.

43 Ayres & Schwartz, *supra* note 37, at 551 (footnote omitted).

44 499 U.S. 585, 594.

45 Peter A. Diamond, *A Model of Price Adjustment*, 3 J. ECON. THEORY 156 (1971).

46 Glenn Ellison, *A Model of Add-On Pricing Adjustment*, 120 Q.J. ECON. 585 (2005).

47 Xavier Gabaix & David Laibson, *Shrouded Attributes, Consumer Myopia, and Information Suppression in Competitive Markets*, 121 Q.J. ECON. 505 (2006). Rajiv Lal and Carmen Matutes model how stores can advertise prices below marginal cost to lure in consumers who will then pay above cost prices once they are in the store. Rajiv Lal & Carmen Matutes, *Retail Pricing and Advertising Strategies*, 67 J. BUS. 345 (1994). Unlike the models discussed above in the text, in the Lal and Matutes model the ability to charge prices in excess of cost once somebody has entered the store does not necessarily lead to a total purchase price in excess of cost.

A second area of research that suggests firms will not alter their business practices even if they profit from the enforcement of pro-seller boilerplate provisions is empirical research on the magnitude and sustainability of markups generally. There is evidence that companies in a wide variety of industries can sustain markups for long periods of time. If anything, the ability of firms to maintain above-cost pricing is growing. A study by Jan Loecker, Jan Eeckhout, and Gabriel Unger found that the magnitude of markups has increased steadily over the past forty years.[48] The assumption that firms can carry on a practice that benefits the seller at the expense of consumers without otherwise altering their business practices over a long period of time is reasonable both in theory and in practice.

The final possibility to consider in evaluating whether the effect of enforcing pro-seller boilerplate provisions is truly inframarginal is whether enforcing these provisions will invariably lead to a deterioration in product quality. While some change in the incentive to take care may depend on the enforceability of the boilerplate, it is unlikely that consumer boilerplate protections are the only or even an important mechanism that firms use to determine how much care to provide. Deterioration in product quality is by no means an inevitable outcome of enforcement of pro-seller boilerplate provisions.

As one final point of clarification, it is worth noting that others have previously suggested that boilerplate might have effects that I have described here as indicative of the inframarginal nature of these terms. Russell Korobkin observes that "[b]y seeding the 'fine print' with pro-seller terms and then refusing to negotiate those terms sellers capture more of the cooperative surplus created by the agreement than they would if the terms were negotiated."[49] With respect to the possibility of wasteful competition in this setting, Lee Goldman observes that if "a forum selection clause would cost the consumer ten dollars, but benefit the seller by only five dollars, societal wealth would be maximized by excluding the clause."[50] However, Korobkin, Goldman, and others have not offered the kind of systematic exploration of the policy ramifications of the inframarginal effects of consumer boilerplate provisions developed here.

The analytic and empirical work reviewed above suggests that enforcing pro-seller consumer boilerplate provisions will have little effect on marginal incentives. As a result, the effect of enforcing pro-seller consumer boilerplate will primarily be to facilitate inframarginal transfers from naïve consumers to sophisticated sellers.

[48] Jan De Loecker et al., *The Rise of Market Power and the Macroeconomics Implications* 135 Q.J. Econ. 561 (2020). *See also*, Rory Van Loo, *Helping Buyers Beware: The Need for Supervision of Big Retail*, 163 U. Pa. L. Rev. 1311, 1355 (2015)(observing that in the retail goods sector alone the leading study would imply overcharge for a family earning $50,000 annually is between $600 and $1,200 annually).

[49] Korobkin, *supra* note 1, at 1205.

[50] Lee Goldman, *My Way and the Highway: The Law and Economics of Choice of Forum Clauses in Consumer Form Contracts*, 86 Nw. U. L. Rev. 700, 718 (1991–92). *See also*, Meyerson, *supra* note 3, at 606.

Recognizing the largely inframarginal effects of enforcing pro-seller boilerplate provisions has clear policy implications as discussed next.

IV THE INFRAMARGINALIST ARGUMENT FOR MANDATING THE USE OF PRO-CONSUMER BOILERPLATE

Inframarginal analysis focuses attention on the ways legal rules can be used to distribute inframarginal resources in a manner that is fairer and more efficient than an unregulated outcome. In the context of deciding whether to enforce pro-seller boilerplate provisions, fairness concerns point toward preferring pro-consumer terms over pro-seller terms. Efficiency concerns point toward implementing a mandatory as compared to a default regime.

First, as a clarification before proceeding, it may be helpful to identify several policies regarding the issue of whether or when to enforce consumer boilerplate provisions that the analysis here will not disturb. First, both proponents and opponents of enforcing these provisions agree, as does the analysis here, that some form of the unconscionability doctrine should continue to apply to boilerplate as it would to other provisions in a contract.[51] Second, boilerplate provisions that materially alter the content of the expressly agreed-upon terms or are so "bizarre or oppressive" that it is unlikely assent would be forthcoming if the terms had been disclosed should remain unenforceable.[52] Third, statutory provisions that place restrictions on how certain terms contained in a contract can be interpreted should not be disturbed. For example, the Magnuson-Moss Warranty Act limits the ability of sellers to modify drastically what constitutes a warranty.[53] Finally, egregious boilerplate terms, such as provisions allowing for subsequent unilateral modification of material terms without negotiation, would remain unenforceable.[54] None of these general points of agreement between opponents and proponents of enforcing consumer boilerplate

[51] *See, e.g.*, Korobkin, *supra* note 1, at 1257–78. However, the unconscionability doctrine is unlikely to block enforcement of most boilerplate provisions. Under current doctrine, there must be both a procedural and a substantive failure for a contract provision to be deemed unconscionable and therefore unenforceable, and the process by which boilerplate terms are included in consumer contracts is designed to avoid the kind of procedural failure that would trigger the application of the unconscionability doctrine.

[52] The language "bizarre or oppressive" comes from RESTATEMENT (SECOND) OF CONTRACT § 211 cmt. F (1981). RESTATEMENT § 211 states: "Where the other party has reason to believe that the party manifesting such assent would not do so if he knew that the writing contained a particular term, the term is not part of the agreement." For a discussion of this rule, see Ayres & Schwartz, *supra* note 37, at 558–61; Gibson, *supra* note 1, at 258.

[53] Baird, *supra* note 1, at 949 (the Magnuson-Moss Warranty Act establishes that a "seller of consumer products that uses the word 'warranty' commits itself to a number of substantive promises, independent of anything that is said in the fine print.") (footnotes omitted).

[54] *See, e.g.*, Scholz, *supra* note 1, at 16 ("courts have found unilateral changes to the terms of service without notice to the consumer unenforceable, even where the contract terms give the firm the ability to do so, . . .").

provisions are disturbed by the questions addressed here as to the policy implications once it is recognized that the main effects of enforcing consumer boilerplate provisions are inframarginal.

Returning to the policy implications of recognizing that the impacts of consumer boilerplate provisions are largely inframarginal, two recommendations flow from applying inframarginal analysis to the question of whether to enforce these boilerplate provisions. First, fairness concerns point toward preferring pro-consumer terms over pro-seller terms. Second, efficiency concerns point toward implementing a mandatory as compared to a default regime.

A graph-based analysis supports these conclusions. This graph-based approach is helpful in two ways. First, a graph-based approach builds on foundational work such as that involving "Harberger's triangle" by providing a simple and powerful way to evaluate trade-offs, including inframarginal ones, when price or quantity deviate from an ideal equilibrium point.[55] Second, this graph-based approach has proven especially useful as a tool to evaluate the policy implications of insights about consumer behavior from behavioral economics. In this respect and particularly exemplary is Bar-Gill's use of a graph-based approach to analyze the trade-offs when firms price-discriminate and the demand for a good is a function of both preferences and misperceptions.[56]

The starting assumption to proceed with a graph-based analysis of pro-seller consumer boilerplate provisions is that consumers on average will not realize the added cost or burden that may result from the inclusion in the contract of these provisions. As a result, there are two ways to construct the demand curve for a consumer product that comes bundled with pro-seller boilerplate provisions. First, consumer demand can be graphed based on the value of the good or service as perceived by the consumer at the time of purchase ("demand based on perceived value"). Second, consumer demand can be graphed based on the value of the good or service as realized by the consumer once the effects of enforcing the pro-seller boilerplate are realized ("demand based on actual value").[57]

Figure 4.1 presents a graph of the economic effects of pro-seller consumer boilerplate showing demand based on both the perceived value of the good or service at the time of purchase and the actual value of the good or service realized by the consumer once the effects of pro-seller boilerplate provisions are considered. Based on Figure 4.1, the price at which this illustrative transaction will

[55] *See, e.g.*, Arnold C. Harberger, *Monopoly and Resource Allocation*, 44 AM. ECON. REV. 77 (1954); James R. Hines, Jr., *Three Sides of Harberger Triangles*, 13 J. ECON. PERSPECTIVES 167 (Spring, 1999).

[56] Bar-Gill, *supra* note 12.

[57] Analytically, the demand based on perceived value can be modeled as a claim that consumer boilerplate adds an unobserved markup (δ) where $\delta > 0$, so that the consumer pays $p + \delta$, while the consumer believes they are only paying p. *See, e.g.*, Ayres & Schwartz, *supra* note 37, at 564–65; Oren Bar-Gill, *Consumer Misperception in a Hotelling Model: With and Without Price Discrimination*, 176 J. INSTITUTIONAL & THEORETICAL ECON. 180, 184 (2020).

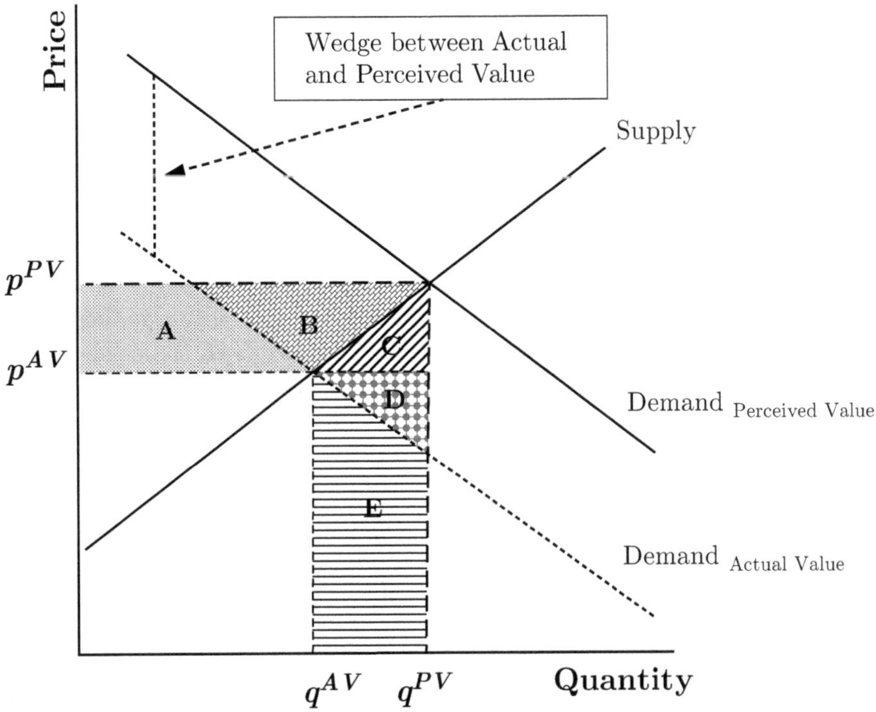

FIGURE 4.1 Effect of consumer underestimation of costs of boilerplate

take place is p^{PV}, and the quantity of the good sold at that price will be q^{PV}. However, this equilibrium price and quantity is based on a misperception of the actual value of the product when bundled with pro-seller boilerplate. If consumers had realized the costs imposed on them by the pro-seller boilerplate then the price in equilibrium at which supply equals demand would be p^{AV}, and the quantity of the good sold at that price would be q^{AV}.

To better understand the policy implications illuminated by Figure 4.1, it is helpful to consider the impact of the difference between perceived and actual demand along three different dimensions: (1) based on a traditional marginal efficiency analysis, (2) based on an analysis of the effects of this difference on the distribution of inframarginal resources, and (3) based on a consideration of how to minimize wasteful competition for inframarginal resources.

Traditional marginalist efficiency criteria are the first dimension along which to consider the policy effects of creating a wedge between actual and perceived demand by enforcing pro-seller provisions in consumer boilerplate. There are both short-term and long-term effects that need to be included when applying this traditional marginal efficiency analysis. The short-term component looks to see if there are transactions taking place where costs exceed benefits or if there are transactions that are not taking place even though the benefit of these potential transactions would exceed the cost. By way of example, this traditional short-term marginal efficiency analysis is the reason for concern about Harberger's triangle.[58] Harberger identified an area in a supply and demand diagram where both parties would benefit by carrying out a transaction, but where transactions would not occur when sellers use monopoly power to set a price above marginal cost.

There is a short-term inefficiency evident from Figure 4.1 caused by the failure of consumers to realize the adverse impact on them when pro-seller boilerplate provisions are enforced. In Figure 4.1, any transactions that take place in the range between q^{AV} and q^{PV} are short-term inefficient, because in this range the cost of producing the product exceeds the actual value the customer will ultimately realize by consuming the product. The magnitude of this short-term inefficiency is also illustrated by Figure 4.1 and is equal to the sum of the diagonal-shaded area **C** and the checker-shaded area **D**.

Another aspect of a traditional marginal efficiency analysis is a consideration of the deleterious effects on long-term investment that can result from a wedge between actual and perceived value. Ideally, firms only have an incentive to make investments in projects that are welfare-enhancing. Figure 4.1 shows that because of the wedge between actual and perceived value there is an incentive to invest in producing and selling products even when such production exceeds the socially optimal level of production. More specifically, this incentive to invest in production beyond a socially optimal level is evident in Figure 4.1 from the fact that the quantity produced is q^{PV} rather than the socially optimal quantity q^{AV}. There is not a simple way just by inspecting Figure 4.1 to determine the cost of this distortion in long-term investment incentive.

In summary, the existence of a wedge between actual and perceived value creates both short-term and long-term inefficiencies. This is a well-known finding.

Two additional considerations are worth noting. First, the magnitude of these inefficiencies depends to some degree on the elasticity of supply of the product. If, for example, as illustrated in Figure 4.2, the supply of the good or service is perfectly inelastic then there will be neither a short-term inefficiency nor a long-term incentive to over-produce when consumers misperceive the costs that may be imposed on them because their purchases come bundled with pro-seller provisions in the boilerplate. Thus, these traditional marginalist efficiency costs are lessened to the extent the supply of a product is more inelastic.

Second, while there are, as illustrated in Figure 4.1, clear inefficiencies when there is a wedge between actual and perceived value, these inefficiencies do not lead to an obvious regulatory mandate. Research has shown that there is much complexity and nuance necessary to reach a policy conclusion based solely on concerns about marginal inefficiencies created by this wedge between actual and perceived

[58] See *supra* note 55 and accompanying text.

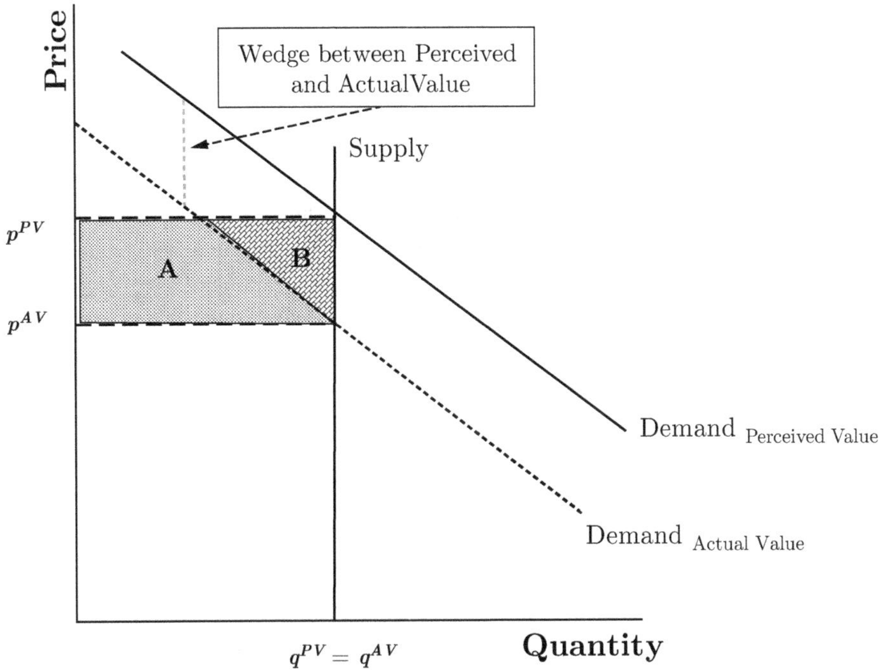

FIGURE 4.2 Effect of consumer underestimation of costs of boilerplate when supply is inelastic

value. At a minimum, the calculation of when regulatory intervention is justified needs to include the costs of regulation as well as a consideration of how the affected parties will react. There are many scholars whose work suggests that costs resulting from marginal inefficiencies do not provide an unambiguous and compelling reason to block the enforcement of consumer boilerplate provisions.[59]

Inframarginal analysis identifies two additional dimensions that need to be considered when evaluating the choice of whether to enforce consumer boilerplate. One additional dimension along which policy effects need to be considered is the redistributive effects of the choice of whether to enforce consumer boilerplate provisions. Inframarginal analysis posits that redistributive effects are a crucial consideration when using the law to regulate inframarginal transactions.[60]

The redistributive effects of the choice to enforce consumer boilerplate can be inferred from Figure 4.1, which shows that enforcing pro-seller consumer boilerplate provisions will transfer wealth from consumers to sellers. The amount of the transfer can be determined by, first, taking the difference between price p^{PV}, which is the

[59] *See, e.g.*, Bar-Gill, *supra* note 12; Schwartz & Wilde, *supra* note 1; Howard Beals et al., *The Efficient Regulation of Consumer Information*, 24 J. L. & ECON. 491 (1981).

[60] See *supra* note 17 and accompanying text.

price at which the transaction takes place and is based on the perceived value of the product to consumers, and the price p^{AV}, which is the price the consumer would have paid if she was aware of the actual value of the product with the costs of the pro-seller boilerplate netted out, multiplied by the quantity of the goods sold q^{PV}. In other words, algebraically the area $q^{PV} * (p^{PV} - p^{AV})$ is one component of the redistribution from consumers to sellers that results from the wedge between actual and perceived value. In terms of labeled sections in Figure 4.1, this redistribution is the combination of the dot-shaded area **A**, the brick-shaded area **B**, and the slant-shaded area **C**.

There is a second redistributive effect of the wedge between actual and perceived value. The second redistributive effect is caused by the fact that when demand is based on perceived value rather than actual value the amount of the good sold is likely to be more than the socially optimal level. This increase in quantity sold, $q^{PV} - q^{AV}$, provides marginal revenue to the seller equal to the price that would be paid if there was not a mismatch between actual and perceived value, p^{AV}, times the incremental quantity produced because of this misperception.[61] Algebraically the incremental revenue resulting from an increase in quantity sold that could lead to additional redistribution is equal to $p^{AV} * (q^{PV} - q^{AV})$. However, not all this incremental revenue represents a redistribution from the buyer to the seller, because buyers receive some value from the additional goods purchased as a result of the misperception. The amount of the redistribution resulting from those additional purchases is only the amount by which the purchase of additional goods exceeds the value realized by the purchasers. This difference is illustrated in Figure 4.1 by the checker-shaded area **D**.

Some amount of these redistributions from buyers to sellers is familiar and constitutes a redistribution of transaction surplus: the dot-shaded area **A**. However, other elements of this redistribution from the buyer to the seller are especially problematic because they represent payments by the consumer to the seller for which the purchaser is not receiving anything of value (the brick-shaded area **B**, the slant-shaded area **C**, and the checker-shaded area **D**). A redistribution for which the consumer receives nothing of value is normatively troubling as it constitutes a kind of taking. The consumer is spending more than they are receiving in value for the goods purchased.

These redistributive effects create a compelling prima facie case for preferring pro-consumer boilerplate to pro-seller boilerplate.[62] Presumably, consumers who

[61] The discussion in the text uses the price based on the actual value, p^{AV}, rather than the price based on the perceived value, p^{PV}, to avoid double counting. Recall that the revenue, $q^{PV} * (p^{PV} - p^{AV})$, was included in the calculation of redistribution above.

[62] To derive a more carefully specified policy recommendation with respect to the social welfare effects of these redistributions, we would need to know more about the relative wealth of buyers and sellers in consumer markets and then apply an agreed-upon social welfare function to estimate the welfare effects of the redistribution of wealth resulting when consumer boilerplate

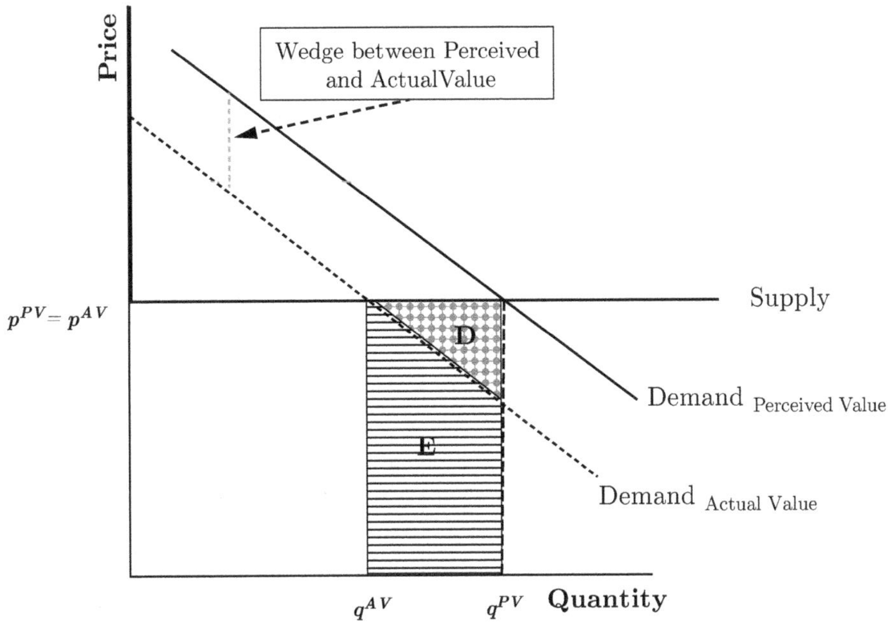

FIGURE 4.3 Effect of consumer underestimation of costs of boilerplate when supply is perfectly elastic

purchase goods are less well-off than those who sell to them. Allowing the enforcement of pro-seller consumer boilerplate provisions is undesirable not only because consumer misperceptions as to the effects of these provisions introduce short- and long-term inefficiencies, but also because these misperceptions lead to a marketplace where wealth is redistributed from those who are presumably less wealthy without those who are less wealthy receiving anything of value.

A final observation about the redistributive effects of enforcing consumer boilerplate provisions is that, as with the efficiency effects, the magnitude of the redistributive effects of enforcing pro-seller consumer boilerplate provisions is related to the elasticity of supply. Figure 4.3 shows that if the supply of a good is perfectly elastic, then enforcement of consumer boilerplate provisions will only have a limited effect on the wealth distribution that results from that enforcement. More specifically, only the redistribution that results from consumers purchasing additional units at a price above their actual WTP because of a misperception as to the ultimate value of the product (the checker-shaded area **D**) will redistribute wealth from buyers to sellers when supply of a good is perfect elasticity.

provisions are or are not enforced. *See, e.g.*, ANDREU MAS-COLELL ET AL., MICROECONOMICS THEORY 117 (1995); MATTHEW D. ADLER, WELL-BEING AND FAIR DISTRIBUTION: BEYOND COST-BENEFIT ANALYSIS (2012).

The third dimension along which to consider the policy effects of enforcing the pro-seller provisions in consumer boilerplate suggested by inframarginal analysis is a consideration of how to reduce wasteful competition.

Wasteful competition can occur when there is a mismatch between private incentives to engage in competitive activities and the social gains these activities might provide. At the extreme, when competitors are playing a zero-sum game, such as when they are competing for inframarginal resources, any resources invested in competition are wasted from an overall social welfare perspective unless there is no other less expensive way to allocate resources available.[63] Finding ways to avoid wasteful competition is central to the inframarginal analysis of law. The problem of wasteful competition can be addressed by the legal system in several ways.[64]

A first step in addressing a wasteful competition problem is to identify the magnitude of the problem. The size of the prize the parties are competing over provides a good first approximation of the size of the problem, because the size of the prize suggests a reasonable limit on the amount that might be logically invested to secure the prize.[65] Figure 4.1 provides an indication of the magnitude of the rewards that might be realized and therefore also resources that might be wasted because of a wedge between actual and perceived value. In Figure 4.1 (the dot-shaded area **A** and the brick-shaded area **B** represent gains available to sellers if they can successfully include and enforce pro-seller boilerplate provisions.

Figure 4.1 thus suggests that the incentives to engage in wasteful competition by means of enforcing consumer boilerplate provisions could be quite substantial. However, the identification of an incentive to engage in wasteful competition does not logically suggest any one policy solution. For example, above I noted that while in some situations an increase in the strength of property rights can help to reduce wasteful competition, in other situations putting limitations on property rights is the best way to reduce wasteful competition.[66]

One approach to reduce the incentive of sellers to include and then enforce pro-seller consumer boilerplate provisions would be to make the content of boilerplate

63 Jack Hirshleifer, *The Private and Social Value of Information and the Reward to Inventive Activity*, 61 Am. Econ. Rev. 561 (1971).

64 See *supra* notes 31–34 and accompanying text.

65 Of course, the amount of resources expended to capture a prize need not equal the value of the prize available for a number of reasons. *See, e.g.*, Kai A. Konrad, Strategy and Dynamics in Contests (2009); Luis C. Corchón, *The Theory of Contests: A Survey*, 11 Rev. Econ. Design 69, 81–84 (2007); Emmanuel D. Dechenaux et al., *A Survey of Experimental Research on Contests, All-Pay Auctions, and Tournaments*, 18 Experimental Econ. 609 (2015); Doron Klunover, *A Note on Rent Dissipation in Lottery Contests*, 168 Econ. Letters 90 (2018).

66 See *supra* notes 30–32 and accompanying text.

provisions mandatory. Of course, as is often true with efforts to avoid wasteful competition, the choice to use a mandatory regime might just shift the site at which the competition for inframarginal resources takes place from the courthouse to the State House. The degree to which this will happen in practice is an empirical question.

In addition, there are other costs of making the use of pro-consumer boilerplate mandatory. A mandatory regime does not allow parties to agree to terms other than those that are mandated for, even when both parties involved in the transaction would be better off if they were allowed to agree to different terms. A mandate might also reduce the sense of agency that parties might otherwise realize by entering into a transaction were they allowed to decide for themselves all of the terms of the agreement.

Even given these caveats, creating a mandated set of pro-consumer boilerplate provision would appear to be the most feasible way to reduce wasteful competition for the inframarginal resources controlled by boilerplate provisions.[67]

V AN APPLICATION: CHOICE-OF-FORUM CLAUSES

This section returns to the provision discussed in the Introduction, the choice-of-forum provision, to illustrate the usefulness of incorporating inframarginal analysis into the policy evaluation of whether to enforce a specific pro-seller consumer boilerplate provision.

A famous case concerning the issue of when to enforce choice-of-forum provisions is the *Carnival Cruise Lines* case discussed in the Introduction.[68] In the context of this case, we can see more concretely how both proponents and opponents of consumer boilerplate enforcement present incomplete arguments because they fail to incorporate inframarginal analysis into their policy analysis.

Starting with the proponents of enforcing the choice-of-forum provisions, part of the justification that the Supreme Court offers in support of its decision to enforce

[67] While the way I reach this conclusion is unique, the final recommendation is similar to the recommendations of others. For example, similar recommendations, but for different reasons, are offered by Adar & Becher, *supra* note 1; Gibson, *supra* note 1; and Korobkin, *supra* note 1, at 1247–52.

The recommendation is also similar to an approach that relies on a principle-based prohibition outlawing any consumer boilerplate provisions that might create a substantial wedge between the actual value and the perceived value. Such an approach is in place in Europe. For an overview of how the European Union consumer protection regime has attempted to protect consumers from pro-seller boilerplate provisions, see Marco Loos & Joasia Luzak, *Wanted: A Bigger Stick, on Unfair Terms in Consumer Contracts with Online Service Providers*, 39 J. Consum. Policy 63 (2016). Offering a method to deal with the enforcement challenges see Hans-W. Micklitz et al., *The Empire Strikes Back: Digital Control of Unfair Terms of Online Services*, 40 J. Consum. Policy 367 (2016) (suggesting how to "automate the process of abstract control of fairness of clauses in online consumer contracts").

[68] 499 U.S. 585 (1991). See *supra* note 15 and accompanying text.

the choice-of-forum provision in *Carnival Cruise Lines* is that cost savings from choosing a forum that is convenient for the seller, but not necessarily the buyer, will be passed on to the buyer. The majority opinion states that "it stands to reason that passengers who purchase tickets containing a forum clause like that at issue in this case benefit in the form of reduced fares reflecting the savings that the cruise line enjoys by limiting the fora in which it may be sued."[69] Following this logic, sellers have an incentive to include those provisions that provide the lowest net cost to the parties involved lest other competitors provide a more efficient bundle of rights and services at a lower cost. However, the conclusion that cost savings will pass through to consumers only holds in an industry where competitive pressures are sufficiently strong to prevent firms from retaining any benefits from lowered costs. The evidence, as discussed above, is that such industries are not the norm.[70]

However, there may be a deeper logic and more convincing argument that informed the Supreme Court's decision in *Carnival Cruise Lines*, namely the argument mentioned in the Introduction that consumer boilerplate is similar to other product features that consumers are not aware of at the time of purchase. The deeper logic would be that this lack of awareness of a product feature or contract term is not a sound basis on which to void a contract.[71] This "boilerplate as product feature" pro-enforcement argument is not contingent on the claim that all savings from selecting a pro-seller forum are passed back to consumers, because even if the seller could capture some of the incremental benefits the seller might still have an economic incentive to offer a socially optimal bundle of products and rights.

However, even this more robust formulation of the Supreme Court's policy argument in *Carnival Cruise Lines* fails once we recognize that the impact of these provisions is largely inframarginal. The application of inframarginal analysis for the reasons discussed above shows that welfare will be enhanced by mandating the use of pro-consumer boilerplate provisions, including a pro-consumer choice-of-forum clause.[72] The inframarginal nature of the effects of consumer boilerplate provides a policy reason for blocking enforcement of the choice-of-forum provision that the Supreme Court misses entirely, a justification, moreover, that can also address the implicit "boilerplate as product feature" pro-enforcement argument.

There are two related claims that those who criticize the holding in *Carnival Cruise Lines* and of enforcing pro-seller choice-of-forum provisions primarily rely on. First, critics reject the economic analysis that the majority opinion in *Carnival Cruise Lines* explicitly relies on. Linda Mullinex, for example, writes that the

69 499 U.S. 585, 594 (citation omitted).

70 See *supra* note 48 and accompanying text.

71 See *supra* notes 8–12 and accompanying text.

72 See *supra* Section III.

reduced fare rationale for enforcing pro-seller choice-of-forum offered by the majority in *Carnival Cruise Lines* "should make Econ. I students blush."[73]

On a superficial level Mullinex may be correct. The implicit assumption of near-perfect competition in the majority opinion in *Carnival Cruise Lines* is unrealistic. However, the true problems with the "boilerplate as product feature" argument implicitly relied upon by the in *Carnival Cruise Lines* majority require considerations that go well beyond the curriculum taught in any introductory economics class where marginalist analysis invariably rules supreme.[74] To treat the economic ideas underlying the Supreme Court's decision in *Carnival Cruise Lines* as obviously flawed is to miss the fact that there is deeper justification for their analysis that can only properly be rejected by applying the tools of inframarginal analysis.

The second line of argument offered by critics of enforcing choice-of-forum provisions in consumer contracts is that to enforce these provisions violates basic norms of fairness and is contrary to public policy. For example, John Coyle and Katherine Richardson note that it "is profoundly unfair to allow large companies to use such provisions to force consumers to consent to jurisdiction in the company's home jurisdiction."[75] This argument has a statutory foundation. There are many situations, as Coyle points out, where there is a statute that "clearly states that such provisions are void as against U.S. public policy and directs courts not to give them any effect."[76]

Addressing concerns about fairness and public policy is certainly appropriate in the context of consumer transactions. For example, such concerns justify prohibiting selling practices that are affirmatively deceptive. However, concerns about fairness and public policy are more difficult to apply to transactions solely based on concerns that the transaction is taking place between more and less sophisticated parties or between more and less economically powerful parties. The challenge in bringing in fairness and public policy concerns to address these kinds of situations is that it is difficult to delineate when and how these principles should be used to intervene in market transactions. As Coyle recognizes, "public policy and reasonableness are famously elastic concepts."[77]

The better normative explanation, also grounded in concerns of distributive justice, as to why choice-of-forum provisions should not be enforced, and the

[73] Mullenix, *supra* note 20, 323, 342 (footnotes omitted).

[74] One rare exception is in the textbook Austan Goolsbee et al., Microeconomics 521–24 (3rd ed. 2020).

[75] John Coyle & Katherine C. Richardson, *Enforcing Inbound Forum Selection Clauses in State Court*, 53 Ariz. St. L.J. 65, 119 (2021) (footnote omitted). Part of the reason to bring in concerns about fairness is, as Coyle observes, that "the modern enforcement regime for forum selection clauses strongly favors the interests of large corporations at the expense of natural persons." John Coyle, *Contractually Valid Forum Selection Clauses*, 108 Iowa L. Rev. 127, 167–68 (2022) (footnote omitted).

[76] John Coyle, *Cruise Contracts, Public Policy, and Foreign Forum Selection Clauses*, 75 U. Miami L. Rev., 1087, 1089 (2021) (footnote omitted).

[77] Coyle, *supra* note 75, 127, 131.

Supreme Court was wrong in deciding the *Carnival Cruise Lines* case as it did is provided by understanding the relevance of and then applying inframarginal analysis to the question of when or whether to enforce a pro-seller choice-of-forum consumer boilerplate provision.

The first step in carrying out the relevant inframarginal analysis is to ascertain whether the resources affected by the transaction are largely inframarginal. In the context of the facts of the *Carnival Cruise Lines* case, as discussed in the Introduction, we can reasonably speculate to what degree the choice of whether to allow Shute to pursue her claim in the State of Washington rather than the State of Florida would affect the behavior of either party.[78] From the perspective of Shute, the effects of enforcing the boilerplate choice-of-forum provision or not enforcing this provision are likely inframarginal. Shute would almost certainly have purchased the cruise ticket regardless of whether the boilerplate choice-of-forum provision ultimately proved to be enforceable.

While it is more difficult to ascertain whether Carnival Cruise Lines would change its business practices depending on whether the choice-of-forum clause would ultimately prove to be enforceable, the analytic and empirical research on how firms can maintain above-cost pricing reviewed above suggests that Carnival Cruise Lines could profit from including pro-seller choice-of-forum provisions in its consumer contracts without otherwise changing business practices.[79]

Once we have ascertained that the main effects of the decision of whether to enforce the choice-of-forum provision in consumer boilerplate are inframarginal, the problems with even the best characterization of the Supreme Court's reasoning in *Carnival Cruise Lines* become apparent. The Supreme Court's analysis ignores the redistributional opportunities and potential for wasteful competition that should be central to the analysis of provisions that largely have inframarginal effects.

Inframarginal analysis thus provides a nuanced justification to buttress and provide specificity to concerns about fairness and public policy in the context of choice-of-forum provisions and addresses the question as to why in certain circumstances a comparison of the relative wealth of the parties involved is not only appropriate but, in fact, of paramount importance.

VI CONCLUSION

There is a longstanding debate about whether to enforce the provisions contained in the boilerplate that comes bundled with most consumer purchases. This chapter shows that, despite this rich academic discourse, important trade-offs raised by this policy decision have been ignored entirely or, at best, underexplored.

[78] See *supra* notes 20–24 and accompanying text.

[79] See *supra* notes 35–48 and accompanying text.

Consumer boilerplate creates a wedge between the actual value and the perceived value of goods sold to consumers. One of the unusual aspects of this wedge is that the determination of whether consumers should be bound by these provisions has effects that are largely inframarginal. As a result, the correct analytic lens to address the policy choice of whether and how to enforce these provisions is inframarginal analysis. Inframarginal analysis, in turn, shows that the best policy response is to mandate that a standard set of pro-consumer boilerplate terms attach to all consumer transactions.

5

Inframarginalism and the Distributive Corollary of the Coase Theorem

Matthew Dimick

CONTENTS

I INTRODUCTION: REDISTRIBUTION THROUGH LEGAL ENTITLEMENTS?

Louis Kaplow and Steven Shavell's (1994) well-known paper, "Why the Legal System is Less Efficient than the Income Tax in Redistributing Income," remains the starting point for discussions within law and economics about using legal rules for redistributive purposes. Kaplow and Shavell's conclusion, sometimes called the double-distortion argument (Sanchirico 2000), is that using legal rules to redistribute income is a non-starter: Given the existence of the income tax, any redistribution through legal rules causes just as much economic waste as the tax system (because income redistribution of any kind has effects on labor-supply choices) while also generating distortions in the behaviors regulated by the legal rules. Any legal redistribution can be replicated by a distribution-equivalent change in the income tax schedule that saves resources and can make everyone, including the poor, better off. In that respect, redistribution through legal rules is said to be not only useless but also harmful.

Less commonly cited in debates about using legal rules to redistribute income – indeed, if cited at all in such debates[1] – is another famous paper in law and economics, Ronald Coase's (1960) "The Problem of Social Cost." Only a handful of writers have acknowledged what Stewart Schwab (1989) originally called the "Distributive Corollary of the Coase Theorem." This corollary says, "With zero transaction costs, initial entitlements cannot be justified on efficiency grounds, and so should be awarded on the basis of need or desert" (1195). Intuitively, if any distribution of legal entitlements leads to an efficient outcome, as the Coase theorem states, then criteria other than efficiency, such as the distribution of income or well-being, are the only remaining considerations when assigning or changing entitlements. This corollary would seem to have revolutionary implications – indeed, the exact opposite of Kaplow and Shavell's thesis – except for that pesky little problem of transaction costs. Thus, Schwab (1989) concedes, "The Distributive Corollary applies only when transaction costs are low" (1196). The substantial hurdle of transaction costs likewise leads Fennell and McAdams (2016) to dismiss the distributive corollary in a footnote, reporting, "If transaction costs were zero, legal rules could be selected based exclusively on distributive concern" (1052 n. 2). Liscow (2014) appears a little more sanguine about the distributive corollary, but also embraces the conclusion that it is relevant only in the atypical case when transaction costs are zero or negligible.

This chapter argues that the "Distributive Corollary" of the Coase theorem provides more support for legal-rule distribution than has been previously acknowledged. Contrary to received wisdom, it will be shown that transaction costs are largely independent of the distributive corollary: Changing legal entitlements can influence the distribution of income even when transaction costs are high enough to absolutely prohibit bargaining between parties. The only relevant issue is the one identified by Kaplow and Shavell (1994): Are the costs of shifting income with legal entitlements more or less than the costs of redistributing income with the tax system? This question cannot be answered by invoking transaction costs, but only by carrying out a proper, comparative evaluation of the effects of legal rules versus taxes in the Coasean context. To undertake this evaluation, this chapter builds on Ayres and Talley's (1995) model of Coasean bargaining with "divided entitlements." This analysis shows that redistributing through legal entitlements has an advantage over income taxes for inframarginal reasons. Liability rules encourage parties to reveal their heterogeneous, private valuations, which is information unobservable to the tax

[1] The literature barely acknowledges that Coase's "Theorem" has any implication for distributive questions. One way of stating the Coase theorem is that when transaction costs are zero, the distribution of entitlements is irrelevant to the efficient allocation of resources. Cooter and Ulen (2016, 81) interpret this as saying that "law is unnecessary and undesirable where bargaining succeeds, and that law is necessary and desirable where bargaining fails." Cooter and Ulen never pause to consider, even when transaction costs are negligible, whether the law might be useful or necessary to address questions of income distribution.

authorities. Shifting liability rules to favor the poor will, for that reason, cause less distortion in labor-supply responses than legal rules – to the extent that the distributional effects of entitlements and taxes are otherwise symmetric, a strong assumption that favors the double-distortion argument. As a result, the net economic cost of Coasean redistribution may well be smaller than that of income taxes.

Before proceeding, some remarks about this chapter's relationship to the existing literature are in order. With respect to Ayres and Talley (1995), two points are worth mentioning. First, although this chapter's central insight exploits the information-forcing function of Ayres and Talley's model of divided entitlements, it differs from their claim because the objective is to redistribute income rather than to maximize efficiency. This objective entails choosing liability rules with a different level of damages and justifies some sacrifice in efficiency in order to accomplish redistributive goals. Second, I want to forewarn the reader that the claim for the generality of the Coase's distributive corollary may be obscured by the reliance on Ayres and Talley. Ayres and Talley's model offers a tractable framework and has become a standard reference for analyzing the Coase theorem and legal entitlements (see, e.g., Segal and Whinston 2014, 2016). In other work, on which this chapter is based, Ayres and Talley's formal model is used to bring the distributive corollary into direct analytical conversation with the double-distortion argument. Ayres and Talley's model, which hinges on imperfect information, is perhaps not the only way to model transaction costs. However, imperfect information certainly is an enormously important source of transaction costs and for that reason, deserves some claim to generality. But as I hope should become clear, even by the end of Section III, little about the distributive corollary depends on any of the more particular assumptions of Ayres and Talley's model. Most simply, this is because the generality of Coases's insight revolves less around the particular source of transaction costs and more on the breadth of relationships it subsumes. Coase's theorem does not require transacting parties to be in market relationships, but encompasses transactions between "strangers," where the scope for legal redistribution is typically acknowledged to be greater.[2] In this respect, the more restrictive assumptions of Ayres and Talley's model, in addition to the assumptions most favorable to the double-distortion argument, allows us to push the distributive corollary to its limits, demonstrating that even on these assumptions legal rules can still redistribute more efficiently than taxes.

Kaplow and Shavell (1994) is of course the central reference for this chapter. Kaplow and Shavell never discuss the distributive corollary of the Coase theorem and its relevance (or irrelevance) to their double-distortion argument. We are therefore left to reconstruct their response.[3] They would probably cite labor-supply

[2] Recall Polinsky's (1989) remark that "legal rules often cannot redistribute income in contractual disputes, whereas legal rules always can redistribute income in disputes between strangers" (122). See also the general discussion in Schwab (1989).

[3] One reason Kaplow and Shavell might offer for the irrelevance is that parties in bargaining relationships are often in buyer–seller relationships, and so the so-called bargaining around the

effects as the most critical reason for the distributive corollary's irrelevance. After all, according to Kaplow and Shavell, the reason why redistributive taxation is at least as efficient as redistribution through legal rules is the latter are assumed to have *identical* labor-supply effects as a distribution-equivalent change in the income tax schedule. Discussions of the distributive corollary typically ignore labor-supply effects; once acknowledged, they raise the question of whether the absence of transaction costs is even a sufficient condition for the validity of the distributive corollary of the Coase theorem, let alone a necessary one.[4] Nevertheless, as this chapter will demonstrate, the existence of labor-supply effects does not defeat the distributive corollary of the Coase theorem. As the previous paragraph indicated, liability rules can elicit the revelation of information not available to the taxing authorities. Tailored to the marginal transacting parties in this way, the distributive incidence of legal rules is less than a distribution-equivalent change to the income tax schedule. In other words, the labor-supply effects of tailored liability rules are smaller – less inefficient – than the labor-supply effects of taxes. Moreover, one is certainly entitled to question the strong assumption that the distributional effects of legal rules and taxes are identical, even setting aside the role of inframarginal concerns. To the extent they are not, so much the worse for the presumptive superiority of taxes over redistributive legal rules.

Another closely related reference for this chapter is Sanchirico's (2000, 2001) emphasis on heterogeneity. As Sanchirico reveals, Kaplow and Shavell consider heterogeneity in individuals' productive abilities, but not in their precautionary abilities. Recognition of this latter possibility means that legal rules may be able to redistribute more efficiently than taxes. In this chapter, heterogeneity in individuals' valuations for a given entitlement also plays an important part in the analysis. However, what is more important, and different, in this chapter is how liability rules can elicit the revelation of private information about heterogeneous valuations. For reasons that will be addressed later on, the way legal rules work in this case means that we don't have to worry about the appropriate correlations of tastes or abilities in order for legal rules to have the most direct and efficient redistributive effects. Getting the appropriate correlations in tastes or abilities has been considered a weak point in Sanchirico's analysis (Gamage 2014; Kaplow and Shavell 2000). Those concerns are not an obstacle for efficient legal redistribution in this chapter's analysis.

argument against legal redistribution would seem to apply (Hamada 1976; Polinsky 1989). Obviously, however, not all bargaining relationships are buyer–seller ones – as the countless examples illustrating the Coase theorem indicate. So we need not fully entertain this objection here.

4 Neither Schwab (1989), Fennell and McAdams (2016), nor Liscow (2014) discusses labor-supply effects in connection with the distributive corollary. In his discussion of wealth effects, Schwab (1989) does acknowledge that wealth may not be redistributed when legal entitlements are changed between contracting parties, thus acknowledging, to some extent, the "bargaining around" objection to legal redistribution.

A final inspiration for this chapter, especially as it relates to the Coase theorem, is Calabresi (1991). Calabresi has probably carried the "Distributive Corollary" of the Coase theorem further than any other writer. Calabresi, in a nutshell, argues that once we fully acknowledge the existence and unavoidability of transaction costs, then society will already be on the (transaction-cost-adjusted) Pareto frontier. Being on that frontier, there are no more Pareto improvements to be had, and the only possible changes are movements *along* the Pareto frontier – that is, *distributional* changes.[5] At the least, Calabresi argues, this requires that the analyst fully acknowledge and address distributional concerns, rather than treating them as inconsequential. This more emphatic distributional interpretation of the Coase theorem provides direct inspiration for this chapter's claim. But because Calabresi's contribution appeared around three years prior to Kaplow and Shavell's article, it does not address the question of whether that distributional emphasis on legal-rule evaluation survives in light of the existence of the income tax. Certainly, Kaplow and Shavell would say it does not. The purpose of this chapter, therefore, is to respond to Kaplow and Shavell's argument that legal rules should be evaluated on the basis of efficiency, not distribution, even in light of the distributional reading of the Coase theorem that Calabresi advances.

The chapter is organized in the following order. Section 2 provides an overview of the Coase theorem. Readers already familiar with the Coase theorem are invited to skip to Section 3, where the "Distributive Corollary" of the Coase theorem is explained and its breadth illustrated. Section 4 explains the efficiency logic behind Ayres and Talley's (1995) argument for "divided entitlements" and then addresses the central issue of the paper: how "divided entitlements" used with a redistributive, rather than an efficiency, objective can redistribute income more efficiently than the income tax, by changing the identity of the inframarginal entitlement holder. Section 5 concludes with some reflections on the, in my view, odd receptions of the "Double-Distortion" argument and the Coase theorem.

II THE COASE THEOREM

This section will introduce the reader to the Coase theorem, which has a privileged and storied place within law and economics. Readers already familiar with the Coase theorem are invited to skip this section.

The Coase theorem can be summarized in two statements. First, when transaction costs are zero, an efficient use of resources results from private bargaining,

[5] Calabresi (1991): "For if where we are *is*, for the moment, Pareto optimal and, absent innovations, all improvements must, ex ante, entail some losers, then we can also do away with these other 'convenient' assumptions designed to negate the existence of losers. Distributional analysis becomes inevitable and hence essential, and economists must, at a minimum, become explicit about the distributional judgments (or guesses) that they are making" (1228, emphasis in original).

regardless of the legal assignment of property rights. Second, when transaction costs are high enough to prevent bargaining, the efficient use of resources will depend on how property rights are assigned.

We can illustrate the Coase theorem with a well-known example. Consider a rancher and a farmer, who engage in their economic pursuits on adjoining parcels of land. Initially, the boundary separating their land is unfenced. This creates a problem, because the rancher's cattle sometimes like to wander onto the farmer's land and, in the process, destroy the farmer's corn crops. There might be a number of possible responses to this dilemma, each of which is costly. For instance, the rancher could spend all of his time supervising the cattle or the farmer could grow less corn and confine her growing area to a far corner of her property. Alternatively, and more naturally, a fence could be built to prevent the cattle from wandering onto the farmer's land. Most importantly, the farmer and the rancher are always free to bargain, and make enforceable agreements, about how to manage their entangled affairs.

Legal rules also mediate the rancher and farmer's relationship. Should the rancher be liable for the damage his cattle cause to the farmer's crop? Consider two possible rules a court could adopt. The first would make the farmer responsible for protecting his own land and crops. Under this rule, which we will call the "open range" rule, the rancher is allowed to let his cattle roam freely. This means that the farmer has no legal cause against the rancher if and when the cattle wander and destroy her crops. If the farmer wants to avoid the destruction to her crops, she must build a fence or reduce the amount of crops grown. The second rule would make the rancher responsible for the damage that her cattle cause. Under this rule, which we can call the "closed range" rule, the rancher would be liable to the farmer for any damage which his cattle cause. This naturally implies that if the rancher wants to avoid paying damages to the farmer, he must erect a fence or continually watch his cattle.

We can say a little more about the costs involved. Suppose that crop destruction caused by the cattle amounts to $100. The farmer can also build a fence around her cornfields for $50, while the rancher could build a fence around his cattle range for $75 (say, because the area of land required to raise cattle is larger than that required to grow corn).

Which rule should the court adopt, the open-range rule or the closed-range rule? Part of Coase's answer is that this is not a fully formed question. To understand this, let's first establish what the *efficient* outcome is. We can do this by thinking of the farm and ranch as a joint enterprise, owned by a single entity. Or, as Cooter and Ulen (2016) put it, suppose that the farmer and the rancher got married. What would be the efficient, wealth-maximizing choice to prevent the cattle from destroying the corn? Certainly, we want to avoid corn destruction, which costs $100 and loses more money than either of the fencing options. Among the fencing options, building a fence around the cornfields is a clear winner, because it saves $25 over building a fence around the range. The efficient solution to the problem, one that maximizes the wealth of the joint enterprise, is to erect a fence around the cornfields.

We've established the efficient benchmark. Now let's see what happens when the farm and ranch, as originally conceived, operate as separate legal entities. Under the open-range rule, the farmer has no legal recourse against the rancher, and it would cost only $50 to build a fence, compared to losing $100 in crops. The farmer's choice is therefore an easy one: to erect a fence around the cornfields, which, as we just established, also happens to be the efficient outcome. Under the closed-range rule, the rancher is liable for the crop destruction, which would put him $100 in debt should he allow his cattle to wander. The rancher could also build a fence around his range for $75, which saves more money than paying the farmer damages. That may *seem* like what the outcome would be under the closed-range rule. And because building the fence around the cattle range is more costly than building a fence around the cornfields, that in turn *might* lead us to the conclusion that the open-range rule is actually the better rule, if we are judging rules on the basis of their efficiency consequences. But we have not yet considered the possibility of bargaining between the rancher and the farmer. Under the closed-range rule, building a fence around the cornfields is still cheaper than building a fence around the range. Knowing this, the rancher has every incentive to approach the farmer and offer to pay her $50 to build a fence around her cornfield, rather than spend $75 to fence the ranch. But the farmer is indifferent. If she rejects the deal, the rancher will fence his range, and the farmer is no worse off for it. Furthermore, if she takes the deal, the rancher only incurs costs of $50 rather than $75, leaving the rancher with all of the surplus from the bargain. The farmer might therefore counter by mentioning this information to the rancher, and proposing that they split the $25 savings the rancher will gain if the farmer fences her cornfield. The farmer's counteroffer would therefore have the rancher pay the farmer $62.50 to build a fence around the cornfields, making them both $12.50 richer than in the event of no deal, which would lead the rancher to build a fence around his property.

If the farmer and rancher can bargain, then under the closed-range rule, the outcome is the same, efficient outcome as under the open-range rule, which is to build a fence around the cornfield. That leads to Coase's conclusion that, with no transactions costs, it does not matter for efficiency which rule the court adopts – or, more generally, to whom the court assigns the legal entitlement. Thus, the tempting conclusion that the open-range rule was the more efficient rule was incorrect: Either rule leads to the same, efficient outcome. Put another way, this demonstrates the first version of the Coase theorem: When transaction costs are zero, an efficient use of resources results from private bargaining, regardless of the legal assignment of property rights.

The catch is that condition, "when transaction costs are zero." In our example, there is no additional cost to the time or other resources it takes to actually negotiate a deal between the farmer and the rancher. In general, transaction costs are typically broken down into three, more specific kinds of costs: (1) search costs, the time and resources spent in looking for an exchange partner; (2) bargaining costs, the time and resources spent in negotiating, drafting, recording, and reviewing an agreement; and (3) enforcement costs, the time and resources spent in monitoring performance and sanctioning or punishing violations of the agreement.

All exchanges have some transaction costs, but in some cases these may be small or negligible, so that Coase's insight about the irrelevance of legal rules for efficiency carries through. What happens, however, when transaction costs are large and prohibitive? Suppose that in our farmer–rancher example it costs \$35 to hire an attorney to draft and review the agreement. Because this \$35 eats up the entire surplus (\$25) from a deal between the rancher and farmer under the closed-range rule, neither has an incentive to bargain. Even if the rancher promises to pay all of the attorney's fees in exchange for giving the farmer \$50 to fence the cornfield, this would not make the farmer any better off than no deal, and it would make the rancher worse off than simply fencing the range. Any other distribution of the costs of the attorney would only make both worse off.

Positive, and significant, transactions costs then lead us to the second statement of the Coase theorem, that when transaction costs are high enough to prevent bargaining, the efficient use of resources will depend on how property rights are assigned. Under the closed-range rule, where transaction costs are high and there is no incentive for the parties to bargain, the outcome will be the rancher fencing the range, which is inefficient relative to the open-range rule. Under the open-range rule, the outcome will be the farmer fencing the cornfields, whether transaction costs are high or low, and it is the efficient outcome relative to the closed-range rule. It is now apparent that the choice of legal rules does matter for efficiency. Thus, when transactions were small or zero, it didn't matter (for efficiency) which legal rule the court adopted. Now, with significant transaction costs, the choice does matter and, in order to maximize wealth, the court should adopt the open-range rule.

III THE DISTRIBUTIVE COROLLARY TO THE COASE THEOREM

Usually, discussions of the Coase theorem end with the insight that, when transaction costs are zero, the choice of legal rules doesn't matter for efficiency. From that conclusion are drawn various policy prescriptions. That is, for example, because transaction costs are positive, legal rules should be chosen to promote efficiency or to minimize transaction costs. However, the Coase theorem does have more to say, in particular, about the distribution of economic resources. Other writers have recognized the "Distributive Corollary of the Coase Theorem," but assume that it is only relevant when transaction costs are zero (Fennell and McAdams 2016; Liscow 2014; Schwab 1989). This, too, is not a completely accurate statement of the relevance of Coase's insight into distribution. As we will see, legal entitlements determine the distribution of income, with or without the presence of transaction costs.

Cooter and Ulen (2016, 81) write, "It follows that law is unnecessary and undesirable where bargaining succeeds, and that law is necessary and desirable where bargaining fails." This is, in fact, a misleading, if not mistaken, statement. It implies that the only function or purpose of legal rules is to promote or enable efficiency. Of course, that Cooter and Ulen would draw this interpretation is hardly surprising. The notion that the law exists solely for purposes of efficiency is the deeply embedded conviction that this chapter interrogates. But as we will see, Cooter and Ulen's example itself demonstrates that efficiency hardly exhausts either the effects or necessity of law. It is the law itself that assigns the property entitlements that are the foundation of the economic system, whether or not transaction costs are negligible or prohibitive, whether or not the farmer and rancher strike a bargain. Because of this, legal entitlements, and therefore the law, always have distributive consequences.

This distributive import of legal rules can easily be seen in our farmer–rancher example. Let's first consider the case of zero transaction costs. Under the open-range rule, the rancher is not responsible for damage caused by his cattle. The farmer faces a choice of allowing the cattle to trample her cornfield, at a loss of $100, or erecting a fence, at a cost of $50. The private, and social, maximum is to build the fence. In this situation, recall, the rancher has no incentive to bargain. So, the cost of building the fence is born entirely by the farmer, even though building it on her own also saves her $50. Under the closed-range rule, as we know, the outcome is different. The rancher now has an incentive to bargain with the farmer about the efficient choice of building a fence around the cornfield – rather than one around the range. Because transaction costs are negligible, they make a deal, and the rancher pays the farmer $62.50 to build a fence around the cornfield.

While these outcomes are irrelevant as far as efficiency is concerned, the distributional contrast between the legal rules is significant. Under the open-range rule, the incomes of the farmer and the rancher are whatever they earn from market activities (e.g., selling corn or cattle) minus $50 for the farmer and nothing for the rancher. If the farmer's income is y_F and the rancher's is y_R, the open-range rule gives them $y_F - \$50$ and y_R. Under the closed-range rule, by contrast, the farmer gets her market income *plus* $62.50 minus $50 to build the fence, and the rancher is out $62.50: $y_F + \$12.50$ and $y_R - \$62.50$. The farmer is therefore $62.50 wealthier under the closed-range rule than under the open-range rule, and the rancher is poorer by the same amount. The adoption of the closed range rule has the same effects as a $62.50 transfer from the rancher to the farmer. If the farmer is poorer, in terms of market income, than the rancher, that is, $y_R > y_F$, then the adoption of the closed-range rule will increase social welfare, under any social welfare function. The choice of legal rules may be irrelevant for efficiency, but it matters quite a bit for welfare and distribution. Whereas, approached in terms of efficiency, we might say that the choice of rules is irrelevant or that law is "unnecessary and undesirable," we would have to reject the conclusion if we approached the matter in terms of welfare or distribution.

This observation is what Stewart Schwab (1989, 1195) has called the "Distributive Corollary of the Coase Theorem." He puts the corollary this way: "With zero transaction costs, initial entitlements cannot be justified on efficiency grounds, and so should be awarded on the basis of need or desert" (1195). This corollary applies perfectly to the farmer–rancher scenario. Because transaction costs are zero, there is no efficiency basis for choosing between the open-range or closed-range rules. However, income inequality is lower, and social welfare higher, under the closed-range rule than under the open-range rule. Distributive considerations – "need or desert" – direct us to adopt the closed-range rule. This distributive insight into the Coase theorem has also been recognized more recently by Zachary Liscow (2014). Liscow writes, "With costless bargaining, injunctive remedies or damages at any level will not cause distortions .... Thus, with costless bargaining, the scope for equity-informed legal rules expands significantly" (2500).

Both Schwab and Liscow appear to agree that Coase's distributive corollary applies only, or primarily, to the case of "zero transaction costs" or "costless bargaining." Schwab (1989) remarks, "The Distributive Corollary applies only when transaction costs are low" (1196). Fennell and McAdams (2016) concur, citing firstly Schwab, and then Liscow and others, for the proposition that "[i]f transaction costs were zero, legal rules could be selected based exclusively on distributive concerns" (1052 n. 2). The implication is that when transaction costs are positive or at least nonnegligible, the distributive implications of the Coase theorem are irrelevant.

Is this consensus true? Does the distributive corollary of the Coase theorem lose all force when bargaining is costly? It is at least not immediately obvious that that's true. If we assume, as before, that the transaction costs of bargaining between the rancher and the farmer amount to \$35, then any deal will not be worth that cost. The *efficiency* principle of the Coase theorem then becomes relevant, telling us that an open-range rule leads us to an outcome that maximizes social wealth. But the distributive implications do not thereby go away. Under the open-range rule, the distributive outcomes are the same as when transaction costs were zero: y_F–\$50 for the farmer and y_R for the rancher. But adopting the closed-range rules still changes the income distribution. Under the closed-range rule, without bargaining, the farmer gets her market income without any loss of income – either because the rancher is obligated to pay for damages or, more likely, decides to fence his range to prevent crop destruction. If the rancher does make the (privately) cost-minimizing choice, and fences his range, the rancher is \$75 poorer. Under the closed-range rule, the incomes are y_F and y_R–\$75. Adopting the closed-range rule therefore results in a transfer of \$50 from the rancher to the farmer, in addition to a loss of \$25, born entirely by the rancher.

At the risk of putting too fine a point on the matter, notice in this example that the \$25 loss from choosing the more redistributive, but less efficient, legal entitlement, is not the cost of transacting. They reflect, rather, the higher costs to the rancher of constructing a fence around his property. For that reason, the issue of transaction costs are independent of the underlying issue of the appropriateness of using entitlements to redistribute income. To be sure, transaction costs are not entirely irrelevant: If they are lower than the inefficiency created by the more equitable rule, parties can save on resources and entitlement redistribution becomes more efficient. But clearly the level and existence of transaction costs is not decisive. Rather, the issue is the one raised by Kaplow and Shavell: Do legal rules redistribute more or less efficiently than the income tax? In the context of our example, the sole issue is whether the loss of wealth caused by the closed-range rule, including the higher, $25 fencing cost to the rancher, is greater than or smaller than the loss of wealth induced by a change in that tax schedule that replicates the distributional effects of the closed-range rule.

This is an extremely crucial point and sets up the next section, so it is important to dwell on it for a little longer. The double-distortion argument would say that adopting the inefficient (because of transaction costs), closed-range rule would cause two distortions: (1) the loss of wealth caused by the distortion in the behaviors regulated by the legal rules, in this case the rancher's higher fencing cost; and (2) the distortion in farmers' and ranchers' labor supply that accompanies the legal rule's change to the distribution of income. As an alternative, Kaplow and Shavell would say that a change to the income tax schedule could yield the same distribution of income but only cause distortion (2). Moreover, this distortion to labor supply would be identical to the one caused by the closed-range rule, because the effects of income and its distribution are equivalent. That guarantees that distortion (1) will make the closed-range rule less efficient at redistributing income than the tax system.

But would the adoption of the closed-range rule have *identical* labor-supply effects as a change to the tax schedule? It is easy to question this assumption. For example, the rancher's increased fencing costs do not have any obvious connection to the amount of labor supply, or any other variable component of the rancher's economic activities. Instead, it seems more like a fixed cost, in which case it would have no, or minimal, effect on the rancher's output.[6] Alternatively, we could question Kaplow's (and Shavell's) familiar assumption that consumption and leisure are "weakly separable" (Kaplow, 2004, 165, 166, 166 n. 6). This assumption entails that the rancher's "willingness to pay" for each legal rule, measured in dollars, will have identical labor-supply effects. But suppose instead that the rancher likes to let his horses roam freely (rather than his cattle) because it enhances his leisure. In that case, although the closed range rule makes the rancher poorer, causing a reduction in labor supply, it would also increase labor supply, because it now makes leisure less valuable. If, on either assumption (because fixed costs do not change output or the positive and negative effects on labor supply cancel each other out), the closed-range

[6] One possibility, of course, is that if only some jurisdictions recognized the closed-range rule, and costless entry and exit between jurisdictions is possible, the rule will have long-term, negative effects on the supply of ranchers that adopt that rule.

rule has no other economic effects, then it is an open question whether that $25 loss in social wealth makes it, by itself, a loser compared to the income tax. For example, if an income tax scheme generated the same distributional outcomes for the farmer and the rancher as the closed-range rule (i.e., y_F and y_R–$75) but induced labor-supply distortions that exceeded the $25 greater cost of the rancher's fence, then the legal rule would be the more efficient choice to reduce income inequality.

The issue of labor-supply distortions raises another interesting possibility. Suppose instead that the costs of fencing were reversed and that transaction costs (again, $35) still make bargaining prohibitive. Now, it costs $75 to fence the farmer's fields and $50 to fence the rancher's range. Under the open-range rule, the farmer's welfare is y_F–$75 while the ranchers is y_R. Conversely, under the closed-range rule, we have y_F and y_R–$50. As long as ranchers are sufficiently richer than farmers, $y_R \gg y_F$, we might say the closed-range rule is a "win–win." Given transaction costs, the closed-range rule is both more equitable and efficient. But this conclusion is too hasty, because we have not yet considered labor-supply effects. Because the closed-range rule reduces income inequality it should, on Kaplow and Shavell's own assumptions, cause labor-supply distortions, just like an increase in marginal tax rates. Suppose that the closed-range rule's cost in labor-supply distortions is $50. Then the *net* effect of adopting the closed-range rule is still inefficient, and the closed-range rule still produces an overall loss in wealth: $25 – $50 = –$25. However, the closed-range rule now *obviously* redistributes income more efficiently than taxes. Because an adjustment to the income tax schedule that produced the same distribution of income as the closed-range rule would, again according to Kaplow and Shavell, produce the same labor-supply distortion, the cost of taxes is the full $50. Using legal rules to redistribute income saves $25 compared to taxes. Thus, even if the labor-supply effects of taxes and legal rules are identical, there is no a priori reason why Coasean redistribution should fail when stacked against taxes.[77]

77 Kaplow (2008) might also endorse the closed-range rule under these reversed cost assumptions because a distribution-neutral tax adjustment would, by neutralizing the labor-supply effects, show that the closed-range rule is "more efficient" than the open-range rule. For instance, a distribution-neutral tax adjustment would give, under the closed-range rule, y_R–$50–$\widehat{T}_R$ and y_F–$\widehat{T}_F$ to ranchers and farmers, respectively. The tax adjustments, $\widehat{T}_R$ and $\widehat{T}_F$, would be chosen so that the utility or well-being – and hence labor-supply decisions – under each legal rule would be the same. That choice would result in tax adjustments of $\widehat{T}_R$ = –$50 for the rancher (a negative tax, or subsidy) and $\widehat{T}_F$ = $75 for the farmer. Adopting the closed-range rule would in turn produce a budget surplus of $75 – $50 = $25 and therefore a Pareto *improvement*. In that respect, the closed-range rule looks efficient. But this is a somewhat arbitrary definition of efficiency, because it intentionally negates the effects of the closed-range rule on labor-supply decisions. We might concede Kaplow that definition. But it clearly fails to demonstrate the main issue, which is the relative redistributive efficiency of taxes versus legal rules. According to Kaplow and Shavell (1994), that comparison requires including labor-supply effects. Once labor-supply effects are included, it is clear, as shown in the text, that (1) the closed-range rule is inefficient and (2) redistributes income more efficiently (i.e., less inefficiently) than taxes.

In some ways, we have reached the most general insight of the distributive corollary. We can summarize the discussion thus far with two concluding observations. First, although the existence of transaction costs may make efficiency relevant to the evaluation of legal rules, they do not eliminate the distributive effects of legal rules. The validity of the distributive corollary therefore does not depend on the existence or level of transaction costs – as Schwab, Liscow, and Fennel and McAdams assume – but on whether the costs of redistributive legal rules are more than the costs of redistributive taxation – as Kaplow and Shavell identify. Second, there is no a priori relationship between the allocation of legal entitlements and labor-supply decisions, nor is there any a priori relationship between the costs of legal rules and their distributive effects. Once any of those assumptions are relaxed, the force of Kaplow and Shavell's argument against using legal rules to redistribute income loses much of its power.

Still, how far does the distributive corollary go? Can changing legal entitlements still redistribute income more efficiently than taxes even on assumptions more favorable for the double-distortion argument? We further investigate these questions by exploring Ayres and Talley's (1995) model of Coasean bargaining with divided entitlements in the following section.

In this model, choosing legal rules to redistribute income does cause some distortion in the behaviors regulated by the legal rules. I will also assume that legal rules and taxes will have identical effects on labor supply. Even with those concessions, we will also see that entitlements can redistribute more efficiently than taxes.

IV DIVIDED ENTITLEMENTS AND LEGAL REDISTRIBUTION

Ayres and Talley (1995) have advanced the argument that divided property entitlements can facilitate efficient bargaining and Coasean trade. This section develops the argument that similar legal interventions can redistribute income more efficiently than the tax system. The absence of bargaining is one of the assumptions in Kaplow and Shavell's double-distortion argument. Relaxing that assumption enlarges the scope for legal redistribution.

One of the unstated assumptions in Kaplow and Shavell's classic analysis is that bargaining is impossible unless parties are engaged in explicit market transactions.[8] In the tort scenario they imagine, this is of course a reasonable assumption: If you are uncertain who will injure you, there is no way beforehand you can negotiate a settlement to the injury.[9] More realistically, however, bargaining may well be

[8] In explicit and voluntary buyer–seller contractual relationships, redistribution through legal rules is generally thought not only to be less efficient than taxes, but impossible because of the ability of parties to "pass on" or "bargain around" these costs. For further discussion, see Hamada (1976) and Schwab (1989).

[9] It is probably only the strange kind of zero-transaction cost worlds that the Coase theorem generates that makes it possible to think about tort law as a case where transaction costs make bargaining impossible.

possible between parties outside of buyer–seller relationships, because they know very well the identity of the potential injurer. (Think of the ubiquitous Coasean example of the polluting factory, for instance.) Nevertheless, transaction costs certainly create obstacles to reaching efficient exchanges. I will argue that in these situations, divided property entitlements can not only facilitate bargaining, but increase the bargaining power of the poorer party to the transaction, and reduce income inequality and increase social welfare. In inframarginal terms, liability rules allow for a more appropriate tailoring of individuals' idiosyncratic valuations for the entitlement, which can both facilitate trade and redistribute income.

This argument that divided entitlements can redistribute income more efficiently than the income tax differs from that of Ayres and Talley because it does not assume that the social objective is to increase efficiency or maximize wealth. This means that courts, for example, should choose different liability rules or different divided property rights than suggested by Ayres and Talley. What the subsequent analysis demonstrates is that inefficient legal rules can nevertheless increase social welfare by, for example, reducing income inequality. This is not a conclusion that Ayres and Talley offer in their original analysis.

This argument also differs from those of Schwab, Liscow, and others because it does *not* assume that transaction costs are zero or that bargaining is costless. In fact, in what follows parties are assumed to have no better information about each other's valuations than does the government about either's valuation. As long as legal entitlements can be adjusted to facilitate bargaining, the government may wish to choose rules that do *not* maximize efficiency or wealth, but promote income equality and higher social welfare. This means that the scope for redistributive legal rules is even larger than Schwab, Liscow, or others have argued. Transaction costs are not necessarily a barrier to the use of redistributive legal rules.

A *Using Divided Entitlements to Facilitate Trade*

To understand the redistributive implications of divided entitlements, we first need to recapitulate briefly Ayres and Talley's argument. Ayres and Talley (1995) consider two different "axes" of divided property rights. The first refers to the "degree of protection" given to an entitlement, while the second refers to the "structure of ownership" itself. The first axis owes its genesis to Calabresi and Melamed's (1972) celebrated article, and their distinction between liability rules and property rules. Liability rules are a kind of divided entitlement, according to Ayres and Talley, because they give the "nonowner" of the entitlement the option of appropriating the entitlement nonconsensually, as long as they are willing to pay the damages associated with doing so. Property rules, by contrast, represent undivided entitlements, because they absolutely prohibit nonowners from taking legal entitlements without the consent of the owner. The second axis of divided property entitlements refers to the division of entitlements according to use, space, or time. For example, ownership in land might be "fractionally" divided such that Smith owns Greenacre in fee simple subject to an executory interest owned by Jones that becomes possessory should Smith ever use the property for some impermissible purpose.

Under either axis, divided property entitlements facilitate Coasean bargaining by serving an "information-forcing" function (Ayres and Talley 1995, 1032, 1034). I will focus on the liability-versus-property-rules axis, because this is the simplest and, in my opinion, the most policy-relevant application. Ayres and Talley's argument rests on a specific kind of transaction cost: the problem of private information. In all of our preceding examples, we have assumed that each party's valuation of the entitlement in question (e.g., the value for clean air, or the value attached to undisturbed land) is both fixed and commonly known. In reality, this is seldom the case, and negotiating partners do not know how the other values the entitlement. Some have a high value for the entitlement; others, a low value. Information uncertainty is a chief source of transaction costs, if surely not the only source. Uncertainty about other party's valuations may cause some exchanges never to take place. For example, we might say that Smith thinks that Jones values Greenacre highly, because he has lived there a long time. In fact, Jones is ready for a move and would take a relatively low offer for Greenacre to avoid the time and expense of placing it formally on the market. Private information about heterogeneous entitlement values makes bargaining more time-consuming and expensive, and parties may have to make efforts or act strategically (and wastefully) in order to discover the other party's valuation.

The problem of private information and the information-revealing function of divided property entitlements can also be easily translated into the language of inframarginalism. In this perspective, the assumption that preferences for land or other tradable assets are homogeneous, or that subjective preferences coincide seamlessly and inconsequentially with objective prices, is problematic – if not absurd. Also from this perspective, heterogeneous valuations are not just a source of transaction costs, but a fact about the social world that can be leveraged for redistributive ends. In the argument that follows, liability rules function not only to reveal private information about valuation, but also to shift the identity of the marginal entitlement holder in order to redistribute income in a more efficient and egalitarian direction.

Ayres and Talley's argument is that liability rules, but not property rules, give entitlement owners an incentive to reveal whether they are low- or high-value users. When an entitlement is protected by a liability rule, the owner has two different kinds of consensual transactions she could precipitate. She could "bribe" a potential taker not to take her entitlement, or she could "sell" the entitlement to the interested party, for less than she could get for damages. The insight that Ayres and Talley derive is that only a person who values the entitlement more highly than the damages amount will try to bribe the taker, in order to retain the entitlement, while the person who values it less will sell the entitlement. Which transaction the person expresses interest in provides valuable information to a person wanting to acquire the entitlement and, by so doing, facilitates trade. As Ayres and Talley demonstrate, parties are on average better off under a liability rule than under a property rule. This conclusion contrasts sharply with the thinking at the time about liability rules, property rules, and transaction costs. Prior to their "Solomonic Bargaining" article, the standard intuition was that in the presence of transaction costs, a property rule was superior to a liability rule, because it would force parties who desired an entitlement to bargain with the owning party.

To illustrate the Ayres-and-Talley insight, let us construct a slightly different version of the farmer–rancher entitlement problem. To simplify, let's remove the fence-building issues and focus on the underlying entitlement at hand: the choice between closed-range or open-range rule. As in Ayres and Talley, we can introduce transaction costs by supposing that the valuations that the rancher and farmer attach to this entitlement are private information. To make our problem as similar as possible to Ayres and Talley, say that the farmer values her undistributed tract of land in the amount v_F, which can vary anywhere between \$0 and \$100. Let us assume that these values are uniformly distributed so that, from the rancher's perspective, the expected valuation of the farmer is \$50. For instance, instead of cattle overrunning the farmer's cornfields causing a fixed amount of damage, let us instead say that the rancher does not know which use the farmer plans to employ for her land, that there could be many possible uses, and that each farmer has a different valuation, with at least some of them depending on her own subjective preferences, skill sets, experience, and so forth. Likewise, let us suppose that ranchers differ in the value they attach to the open-range rule. Some value highly the ability to have their cattle graze wherever they wish; others, less so. For example, some may prefer to use specific kinds of feed rather than let them graze. To again make our problem similar to Ayres and Talley, designate the value of the entitlement to the rancher as v_R, which can take one of two values, \$60 or \$40, with equal probability. Thus, the expected valuation of a rancher, from the farmer's perspective, is also \$50.

The problem now is that transaction costs, in the form of imperfect information, may prevent mutually beneficial exchanges from taking place. Because some ranchers value highly the ability to let their cattle roam freely (\$60) and some farmers value lowly the enjoyment of undisturbed land (on average only \$50), there are potential gains from trade. When the farmer values the entitlement less than the rancher, the farmer is willing to give up the right to undisturbed land in exchange for cash and allow the rancher to let his cattle roam free. On the other hand, some ranchers value the free-range option more modestly (\$40). If the farmer values the closed-range option more highly than the rancher does, it would be better (from an efficiency perspective) that no exchange takes place. First-best efficiency could be achieved if all of this information was common knowledge – that is, if every individual's private and idiosyncratic valuation was publicly known – and courts could deter inefficient transactions with damages that perfectly matched the valuations of the defendants. With perfect information and enforcement, whenever the valuation of the rancher exceeded that of the farmer, $v_R \geq v_F$, exchange would take place and both parties would be better off. Likewise, whenever the valuation of the farmer exceeded that of the rancher, $v_R < v_F$, no rancher would violate the farmer's entitlement because, taken to court, the rancher would have to pay in damages to the farmer more than the rancher valued the entitlement. In these circumstances, resources end up with their most highly valued users, and efficiency is achieved.

When information is private, circumstances are not so propitious. When the rancher and farmer do not know each other's valuation, time and resources are consumed in negotiating costs that seek to discover that information. More seriously, parties have an incentive to act strategically in order to extract a greater part of the surplus, and this may increase bargaining costs or derail wealth-enhancing exchanges. Nevertheless, not all is lost, and Ayres and Talley contend that liability rules, rather than property rules, can help facilitate exchanges when information is imperfect.

A property rule absolutely prohibits a nonconsensual taking of a defendant's entitlement. In particular, in light of Calabresi and Melamed's (1972) famous paper, we think of property rules in terms of the availability of equitable relief, which orders the defendant to stop the behavior that is interfering with plaintiff's property right, or return the property that is taken. Liability rules, in contrast, are thought of in terms of damages, where the plaintiff's relief is a monetary sum for the entitlement's interference or nonconsensual taking. Under a liability rule, courts try to set damages to fit with the plaintiff's valuation of the entitlement. But this is obviously difficult to do, because it may be impossible to verify the plaintiff's subjectively honest valuation. For instance, if the rancher "takes" the farmer's entitlement – allowing his cattle onto the farmer's land – the event is easily enough proved in court, but the plaintiff's valuation of the entitlement is difficult if not impossible to verify. Even if market value is readily determinable, for example, this will not necessarily equal the plaintiff's actual valuation. The problem is illustrated in the classic contracts case *Jacob & Youngs v. Kent*, where the court awarded the (de minimis) diminution in market value, rather than the much more exorbitant costs of repair. In cases like these, plaintiffs have a strong strategic incentive to overstate their true valuations.[10] In our problem, therefore, if a rancher "takes" the farmer's

[10] In *Jacob & Youngs v. Kent*, the plaintiff wanted the builders to install a very specific kind of pipe in his home. The builder installed a type of pipe of equivalent quality, but not the exact brand for which the plaintiff had contracted. It would have been very expensive for the builder to repair the fault, requiring the builder to tear out walls in order to replace the pipe with the desired brand. In this kind of situation, the plaintiff has the incentive *ex post* to insist that his valuation for this specific kind of pipe was very high. If failure to install the brand of pipe the contract called for is breach, the plaintiff stands to gain a windfall. Instead of granting plaintiff the cost of repairs, the court awarded only the diminution in market value which, because of the essentially equivalent pipe, was nominal. We therefore have good reasons for believing that court-awarded damages under a liability rule will not be perfectly tailored to the plaintiff's own valuation.

entitlement, the court, under a liability rule, will award some specified amount of damages, say *D*, which may depart from the farmer's subjective valuation.

Ayres and Talley show that one interesting way of seeing the relationship between the two kinds of rules is by thinking about property rules as a limit case of liability rules. Suppose, for example, that the court sets damages at $100 for an entitlement taking. Because $60 is the most that any potential rancher values the entitlement in our hypothetical, this effectively raises an absolute prohibition on nonconsensual takings. A liability rule, however, gives the rancher a "call option," an option to buy the farmer's entitlement in the amount specified by the damages. This, somewhat paradoxically, gives the rancher something to "sell" to the farmer, the one who otherwise holds the entitlement. This is not the case under a property rule. Because the property rule absolutely prohibits any taking, it deprives the rancher of his call option. If the rancher wants to bargain with the farmer about acquiring her entitlement, he must do so purely as a buyer. For Ayres and Talley, liability rules illustrate one way of dividing an entitlement, which gives both farmer and rancher something to sell.

When the farmer's entitlement is protected by a liability rule, two different kinds of transactions are made possible. In the first, which Ayres and Tally call Coasean bargain number 1, the farmer bribes the rancher not to take her entitlement. In this transaction, the farmer buys the rancher's call option, casting the farmer in the role as buyer and the rancher in the role of seller. In the second kind of transaction, Coasean bargain number 2, the rancher buys the farmer's entitlement, and each party assumes their more traditional roles. We can illustrate the first Coasean bargain, where the farmer buys the rancher's "call option," by using a simple example. Suppose the farmer values her undisturbed land at $90 and the rancher values the ability to let his cattle roam free at $60. Also suppose the court sets damages at $50 for taking the entitlement under this liability rule. Under these conditions, the farmer would be willing to pay the rancher $15 for the latter's call option. That is, in this bargain the farmer pays the rancher $15 not to take her entitlement (by running his cattle over the farmer's land). This deal is better than no bargain. If there is no bargain, the rancher would find it worthwhile to let his cattle run freely and pay the damages – in fact, $50 is less than the $60 the rancher would be willing to pay. If the rancher does this, the farmer receives $50 and the rancher has a net gain valued at $10. (The farmer does not get to enjoy her land undisturbed, which deprives her of the value of the entitlement, but she receives the $50 in damages awarded by the court; meanwhile, the rancher obtains the entitlement of letting his cattle roam free minus the damages paid, or $60 − $50 = $10.) However, if the farmer buys the rancher's call option, both are better off. If the farmer pays the rancher $15 not to take her entitlement, the farmer gets $75 (the value of entitlement less the contract price of the call option, or $90 − $15 = $75) while the rancher gets $15 (no entitlement but the price for selling the option).

In the second kind of Coasean bargain, the farmer sells her entitlement to the rancher. To illustrate this kind of transaction, suppose the farmer values undisturbed land at nothing more than $10, while the rancher values the ability to let his cattle run free at $40. With this allocation of preferences, the rancher would be willing to pay the farmer $25 for the right to let his cattle roam free. Likewise, the farmer would accept such an offer, because she values the $25 more than the right to undisturbed land. Without such an agreement, the rancher would not find it worth it to let his cattle roam free, because doing so would cost him $50, ten dollars more than his valuation of the entitlement. Without an agreement, the farmer has $10 and the rancher $0. With an agreement, each is better off: the farmer has $25 (no entitlement but $25 in cash) and the rancher has $15 (the value of the entitlement to the rancher less the contract price). (Note also that under this second kind of bargain the contract price will never exceed the damage amount. This is because the rancher can always take the entitlement nonconsensually and pay the damage award. Thus, even if the farmer knew that the rancher valued the entitlement at $60, the rancher would never be willing to pay such a price.)

While the possibility of entering into two different bargains generally does not constrain the rancher's incentives to misrepresent his valuations, it does constrain the farmer's.[11] Only high-value farmers, who value the entitlement more than the damages award, are willing to pay to purchase the rancher's call option (i.e., a Coasean bargain number 1). A farmer who values the entitlement less than the damages award has no reason to pay the rancher anything. Indeed, if the rancher takes the entitlement, the low-value farmer is in a position to make a windfall. Likewise, only low-value farmers have an incentive to express an interest in selling their entitlement (a Coasean bargain number 2). A farmer who values the entitlement more than the damages amount would never sell the entitlement for less than that amount ($50) and, moreover, would never be able to sell it for more than that – because a low-value rancher would never pay that much and because a high-value rancher can simply take the entitlement nonconsensually for that amount.

The result is that a liability rule reliably partitions the farmers into one of two groups: When damages are set at $50, high-value farmers will never offer to sell their entitlement for less than that amount, while low-value farmers will never be willing to pay the rancher not to take the entitlement. This is a case of self-selection: Farmers' own private incentives induce them to identify whether they are, relative to the damages amount, low- or high-value farmers. Ranchers can identify which kind of farmer they are negotiating with simply by asking the farmer which kind of transaction she prefers. This feature of liability rules gives them an "information-forcing" feature that is not shared by property rules (Ayres and Talley 1995). With a

[11] High-value ranchers, for instance, who would be willing to exercise their call option to pay the damages amount, would still be interested in paying less than that to acquire the entitlement. And low-value ranchers, who would not be willing to pay the damages amount, might represent themselves as having a high valuation in order to get plaintiffs to pay them to waive their (insincere) call option. Both high- and low-value ranchers therefore have an incentive to misrepresent their true valuations.

property rule – say, damages set at $100 – it is not possible for farmers to select themselves into either kind of Coasean bargain, because every farmer's valuation lies below the damages amount. It is precisely because there are some farmers that value the entitlement at more than, say, $50 that makes them interested in purchasing the rancher's call option; likewise, it is precisely because some farmers value the entitlement below $50 that makes them willing to sell their entitlement. The consequence is that liability rules do a better job at eliciting reliable information from farmers, and this, in turn, facilitates exchange. Exchanges are still possible under the property rule, but social welfare is not as high as under a liability rule. Likewise, a liability rule does not guarantee an exchange will occur, but it does improve the frequency of exchange.

We can report here some of the conclusions from Ayres and Talley's numerical model. As already indicated, any level of damages set above $60 or below $40 fails to elicit any self-selecting information from farmers. No rancher has an effective call option with damages greater than $60; and every rancher has an effective call option with damages below $40. Above or below this range, the expected welfare of the parties turns out to be the same: $59.75. Only damages in the intermediate range below $60 or above $40 facilitate trade. In fact, Ayres and Talley show that damages set at $50 maximizes the social surplus. Not surprisingly, this amount corresponds to the expected, or average, valuation of the farmers. Given the distribution of farmer types, damages higher than $50 result in too few of the first kind of Coasean bargain and damages lower than $50 result in too few of the second kind. The consequence is an expected social welfare of $59.875, higher than the $59.75 in either of the extreme damages scenarios.

The numerical results of Ayres and Talley's model are displayed in Figure 5.1. As the figure illustrates, as damages are increased (on the horizontal axis), total

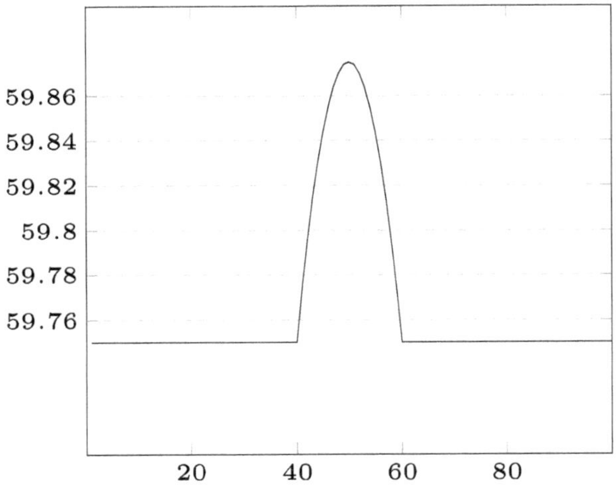

FIGURE 5.1 Efficiency effects of liability rules

welfare, farmer welfare plus rancher welfare, at first increases, and then decreases, in a single-peaked fashion. Total social welfare is maximized when damages reach $50. Any damages above or below $50 distort the information-forcing function of the rule (given the distribution of farmer types). Furthermore, any damages above $60 effectively act as a property rule. Thus, liability rules are more efficient than property rules.

This figure displays graphically the results of Ayres and Talley's (1995) numerical illustration of their model. The horizontal axis displays the damages level, ranging from $0 to $100. The vertical access displays total social welfare, the sum of the well-being of, in our version, the farmer and the rancher. The figure shows that total social welfare is single-peaked and reaches its maximum when damages are set at $50. Damages higher than $60 function effectively as a property rule, also showing that liability rules, by eliciting truthful information and facilitating trade, are more efficient than property rules.

B *Using Divided Entitlements to Redistribute Income*

Ayres and Talley show that liability rules, in place of property rules, can be adopted in order to facilitate trade. However, their objective is a wealth-maximizing one: efficiency. This section will show how liability rules can be used to further a different objective: income redistribution. Rather than showing that liability rules are more efficient than property rules in the context of transaction costs, because they facilitate trade, I will argue that courts can adjust damages away from the efficient level in order to strengthen the bargaining power of poorer parties. Using liability rules, instead of property rules (in order to facilitate trade) is still an important feature of this insight. But the difference is that some departure from efficiency can enhance welfare and promote a more equitable distribution of income.

To put this point in inframarginal terms, the marginal farmer, in our version of the Ayres and Talley model, is also the "average" farmer. This farmer's valuation is identical to the expected, or average, farmer valuation; this farmer is indifferent to sending a buy or sell signal. As we have seen, when damages are equal to this marginal farmer's valuation, efficiency is maximized. But if we also care about the distribution of wealth or welfare, we can change damages to shift the identity of the marginal farmer. This is of course possible because farmer valuations are heterogeneous; there *are* inframarginal farmers. Economic theory and policy-making too often forget to take advantage of such heterogeneity. Making this shift in damages can redistribute income, certainly at the cost of efficiency, but also less inefficiently than taxes.

To explore this claim, we will add a few more details to our farmer–rancher hypothetical. To begin, suppose that the ranchers are richer than the farmers: In addition to their (private, subjective) valuations of the entitlement, farmers and ranchers also receive income from their market activities, $y_R > y_F$. Let us also assume that the group of ranchers we are considering all earn the same amount of income; likewise, all farmers earn the same amount of income. Thus, for example, ranchers who value the entitlement differently ($v_{R,h} = \$60$, $v_{R,l} = \$40$) receive the same income: $y_R + v_{R,h}$ and $y_R + v_{R,l}$. These assumptions do two things. First, the income *differences* between farmers and ranchers ensure that we are dealing with a legitimately distributive concern. Second, the income *identities* among ranchers and farmers help ensure that the government has no better information about the farmers and ranchers than either has about the other. Thus, ex ante, ranchers, farmers, and the government each have the *same* information available to them: Only income is common knowledge, but not each person's private valuation of the entitlement.[12] Of course, the notion that all farmers and ranchers have, as a group, the same income is counterfactual. But the core observation this assumption captures – that an individual's private valuation cannot be determined by merely observing that person's income – is entirely valid. The persistence of private information is a key feature, both in Ayres and Talley's argument and in the distributive claim I will be making. As pointed out earlier, it is an accepted conclusion that the distributive corollary of the Coase theorem loses its force when transaction costs are positive or significant. And, because transaction costs are always present, the distributive corollary would appear to have little practical purchase. The purpose of this section is to challenge this conclusion and show that the distributive corollary is valid even in the presence of significant transaction costs. At the risk of overemphasizing this point, note the strength of the assumption of identical information sets between ranchers and farmers, on the one hand, and the government (or tax authority), on the other. It would seem quite plausible that neighbors would have *better*, not the same, information about each other than the government has about either. The stronger assumption is maintained, however, to show that, even here, legal redistributions can be more efficient than taxation.

1 Case without Labor-Supply Effects

What does the Ayres-and-Talley framework say about the redistributive value of legal rules? This subsection shows that the distributive corollary of the Coase theorem remains valid even in the Ayres-and-Talley framework. This claim can be illustrated most simply if, for now, we assume that changing liability damages (and therefore also prices in either type of Coasean transaction) has no effect on the labor-supply

[12] As will be shown, farmers' signals and ranchers' will reveal information to the tax authorities about their valuations, information that I will assume remains unknown to the tax authorities. Whether that assumption is valid is addressed in Section IV.B.3.

decisions of the ranchers or farmers. In this case we can simply choose the level of damages that maximizes social welfare for a given social welfare function. Without labor-supply distortions, the tradeoff is between the value of redistribution (as measured by a social-welfare function) and the wealth costs of choosing a less-than-efficient level of damages. In the presence of inequality, with farmers poorer than ranchers, this social-welfare-maximizing liability amount will in general be higher than the efficient level. Recall that when damages are at their "extreme" levels, less than or equal to $40 or greater than $60, expected social welfare is identical, at $59.75. That identity of outcomes at the social level, however, masks some significant distributive differences between farmers and ranchers. For instance, when the liability amount is set at $40, the farmer's expected welfare is $y_F + \$46.25$ while the rancher's is $y_R + \$13.50$. Conversely, when the liability amount is set at $60, the farmer's expected welfare is $y_F + \$56.25$ and the rancher's is $y_R + \$3.50$. Whether damages are set at $40 or $60, the sum of the expected welfare of the farmer and rancher is $59.75. But when the well-being of the farmer and rancher are taken separately, the difference in damages makes a significant difference in well-being.

In fact, in Ayres and Talley's numerical example, the distribution effects are far more dramatic than the efficiency effects. The amount that efficiency adds to total social welfare is twelve-and-a-half cents. By contrast, increasing damages can add $10.00 to the farmer's well-being and reduce the rancher's well-being also by $10.00. This is displayed graphically in Figure 5.4 where aggregate welfare is displayed alongside the farmer's and the rancher's expected welfare. The strong, parabolic shape of the efficiency effect in Figure 5.1 barely appears when compared to the changes in the farmer's and rancher's well-being in Figure 5.4: The graph of the efficiency effects is closer to a straight line. Of course, no strong quantitative conclusions can be drawn from these results of Ayres and Talley's arbitrarily chosen numerical illustration. But they do demonstrate the qualitative possibility that the distributional effects of legal rules can be more significant than their efficiency effects. This makes the value of redistribution quite large relative to its costs.

Clearly, a higher liability amount increases the farmer's expected welfare – at the expense of the rancher's and regardless of transaction costs. The reason is obvious: Higher liability amounts increase the farmer's bargaining power in either type of Coasean transaction. When damages are raised, farmers, knowing they are guaranteed that amount, can be more selective in accepting offers, requiring ranchers to increase their bids as damages increase. Farmers also know that the benefits that high-value ranchers' get from taking diminish as damages increase, meaning that farmers have to pay less for the rancher to sell his "take" option. Indeed, in our stylized model, it is easy to show that the rancher's optimal "buy" offer is increasing in the liability amount, while his optimal "sell" offer is decreasing in the liability amount, as intuition suggests. In sum, the distributive corollary of the Coase

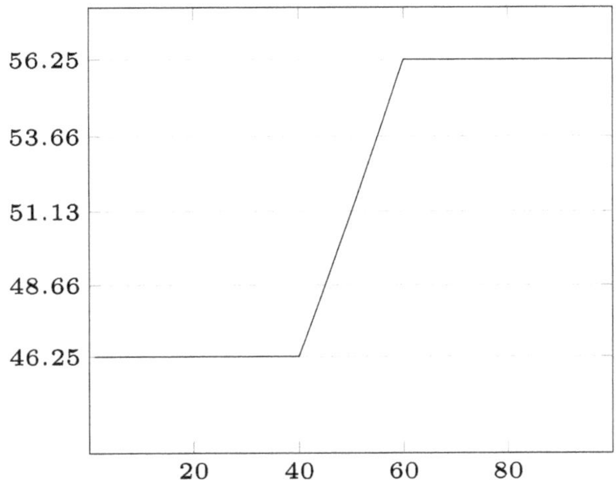

FIGURE 5.2 Distribution effects of liability rules: farmer's well-being

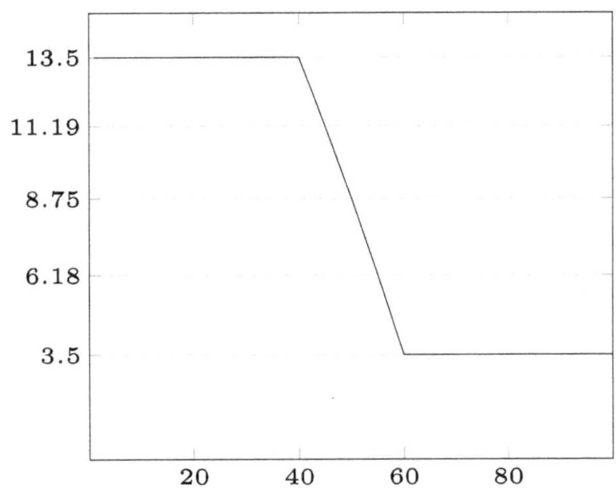

FIGURE 5.3 Distribution effects of liability rules: rancher's well-being

theorem applies even in the presence of transaction costs and in Ayres and Talley's version of the Coasean dilemma. When changes in liability damages do not affect labor supply and when the social welfare function is sensitive to the distribution of welfare or income, liability damages should be set at the amount that accounts for that distribution of income or welfare, not just its total amount, as in Ayres and Talley. Because there are no labor-supply effects, entitlement-based, Coasean redistribution is necessarily more efficient than the tax system in redistributing income.

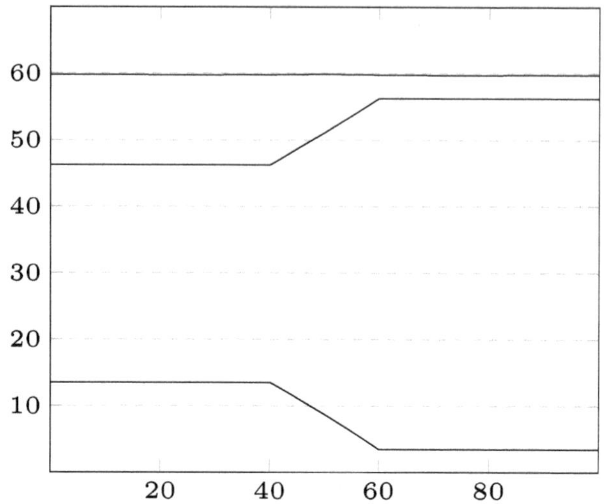

FIGURE 5.4 Comparison of distribution and efficiency

2 Case with Labor-Supply Effects

A more significant challenge is in showing that the distributive corollary of the Coase theorem extends to the case where changes in liability damages also affect labor-supply decisions. Bringing labor-supply effects into the model also allows us to engage directly with the double-distortion argument. This section will show that the distributive corollary to the Coase remains valid in this context, even when labor-supply effects are considered. This will be so for inframarginal reasons.

In accordance with Kaplow and Shavell (1994) and Kaplow (2008), we assume that the expected value of the entitlement has identical effects on labor supply as an equivalent amount of income. This means that changing the level of damages, for example, will have identical effects on labor supply as increasing taxes by the same expected dollar amount. For instance, we showed previously that raising liability damages from $40 to $60 reduces ranchers' expected utility by $10 and increases farmers' by the same amount. The assumption is that this change has the identical economic response as would increasing the income tax on ranchers by $10 (likewise, the same response as would lowering taxes on, or increasing subsidies to, farmers by $10). Finding cattle raising less profitable, for example, will cause ranchers to spend less time raising cattle (say, by reducing the number of cattle raised) and more time pursuing leisure. Likewise, farmers will respond to income changes by increasing or decreasing the time spent in growing crops. One can also think about a delimited legal jurisdiction, where ranchers or farmers are free to enter or exit, depending on the level of economic rewards. As taxes or damages increase, ranchers will leave the jurisdiction, reducing the number of cattle raised, and so forth.

These assumptions are strong, arguably counterfactual, and one should certainly question whether entitlement changes would have identical labor-supply decisions (or any other economically relevant margin of choice) as would changes in the income tax. There are more than plausible grounds to challenge this assumption. Most obviously, identical labor-supply decisions critically depends on Kaplow's (and Shavell's) controversial assumption that consumption preferences are weakly separable from leisure (Kaplow 2004). Other objections could be made. For example, Jolls (1998) makes the behavioral-economics point that probabilistic damages and certain taxes will induce different labor-supply responses, even if the expected amounts are identical. Given the uncertainty present in our farmer–rancher scenario, one could raise a similar objection to Kaplow and Shavell's identity assumption. To the extent that equivalence of labor-supply responses is weakened, so much the better for the distributive corollary of the Coase theorem. Nevertheless, I maintain these assumptions to facilitate comparison with the double-distortion arguments and show that the results do not depend on factors extraneous to the debate. Even in an environment where we assume equivalent labor-supply effects, changing legal entitlements can redistribute more efficiently than taxes.

Despite labor-supply effects, equity-adjusted liability rules redistribute income more efficiently (less inefficiently) than income taxes. The fundamental reason for this follows from the inframarginal, self-selection mechanism that was discussed in the previous subsection (Section IV.B.1). Liability rules take advantage of ranchers' and farmers' heterogeneous valuations – their "willingness to pay" so to speak – in a way that taxes cannot. Only high-value ranchers are willing either to exercise their call option or to pay for the farmers' entitlement; low-value ranchers are not. The distributive burden of the legal redistribution is, in this sense, distributed among those ranchers "most willing to pay" for the redistribution. Ranchers' labor-supply is therefore higher, on average, than if the same amount of revenue was collected from an income-tax increase whose incidence was uniform. The same sort of reasoning applies to farmers. By protecting high-value ranchers with damages, liability rules discriminate between high- and low-value farmers in a way that encourages greater overall labor supply than if all farmers were awarded with the same reduction in taxes (or increase in the tax subsidy).

These differences in labor-supply responses *should* dictate correspondingly different tax rates: not just different rates for (rich) ranchers and (poor) farmers, but different rates for high- and low-value ranchers and for farmers who send buy signals and those who send sell signals. But the tax authority, which sets taxes based on observed differences in income, does not have the relevant information about the various valuations among ranchers and farmers. It can only distinguish between ranchers and farmers – that is, by income – and not among ranchers or farmers – that is, by non-income factors. The legal system, in contrast, can exploit this unobserved information by eliciting inframarginal differences in individuals' valuations for the entitlement. The legal system receives information about individuals' differing valuations through the "signals" farmers send with their buy or sell offers and ranchers' "taking" behaviors. The legal system, therefore, can adjust damages, with redistributive objectives in mind, taking advantage of both observed taking behavior and incomes. By doing so, it shifts the identity of the marginal farmer, the one who is just indifferent between sending a "buy" signal (Coasean bargain number 1) and a "sell" signal (Coasean bargain number 2). Raising damages makes more farmers send sell signals but, more fundamentally, shifts bargaining power to farmers in an identical manner to the way illustrated in the case without labor-supply effects.

If the government had better information about ranchers' valuations, an optimal tax schedule would adjust tax rates for each type of rancher, setting higher rates on high-value ranchers (with the rate differential depending on the magnitude of the marginal social welfare differences and labor-supply elasticity differences). It could also do the same for farmers who send buy versus sell signals. However, with access only to information about income differences, and not entitlement valuations, this option is essentially foreclosed. In essence, because the tax authorities cannot discriminate between high- and low-value ranchers, for example, it sets a uniform tax on ranchers (more specifically, that level of income) in a way that taxes high-value ranchers "too little," causing them to supply "too much" labor (relative to the social-welfare optimum), and taxes low-value ranchers "too much," causing them to supply "too little" labor. For the legal system, on the other hand, farmers' transaction signals and defendants' takings actions reveal information about their type, and this can be used to adjust damages in a way that exploits marginal differences among ranchers and farmers to redistribute income more efficiently than, in this case, blunter tax rates.

We can summarize this conclusion by putting it in double-distortion terms. On the one hand, redistribution through the tax system has one form of economic cost: the distortion of labor supply incentives that accompanies the change in the distribution of income. On the other hand, redistribution through legal rules, by adjusting damages in a pro-plaintiff direction (or pro-farmer direction, in this example) does indeed have two forms of economic costs, rather than one. The first distortion is the economic loss that comes from moving the damages away from Ayres and Talley's efficient level. In their example, damages set at $50 maximizes efficiency. So, any increase from that level will cause a loss of total wealth. The second distortion is, just as with taxes, a distortion in labor-supply incentives that comes with changing the distribution of income. However, there is a crucial difference in this second, "tax-like" distortion. Because the increase in liability damages is better tailored to defendants' (ranchers') valuations of the entitlement, the labor-supply distortion is less than in the case of taxes for the same amount of redistribution. The double-distortion rests on these two labor-supply distortions being the same. When they are, we can automatically conclude that any second economic cost associated with the legal rule will make the total redistributive cost of the legal rule greater than taxes. But when, as in this case, the legal rule has a smaller labor-supply distortion than taxes, we cannot make that conclusion. The sum of redistributive costs by increasing damages may be less than the single redistributive costs of taxation.

To put this point a bit more formally, suppose that we can reduce income inequality by a certain amount by raising liability damages. This will cause some loss of wealth in Coasean trading by moving away from the Ayres and Talley benchmark. Say that the amount of loss is Δ. By reducing income inequality, the legal-rule adjustment will also distort labor-supply incentives. Suppose the amount of this specific loss is $\widehat{T}$. The total, "double" distortion caused by the legal rule is then $\Delta + \widehat{T}$. Now, assume as an alternative that we change the tax schedule to achieve the same, lower level of income inequality as the change to the liability rule. Say that the economic cost from doing this, again, in labor-supply distortions, is T. Because this is the only cost from using the tax system, T is also the total redistributive cost of taxes. Now, compare the two redistributive alternatives. Under Kaplow and Shavell's assumptions, T and $\widehat{T}$ are always equal: Changing the distribution of income by a given amount also causes equal distortions in labor supply. That would then make taxes more efficient than the legal rule at redistributing income. If $T = \widehat{T}$ then necessarily $\Delta + \widehat{T} > T$. But as I have argued, because liability rules don't affect all defendants (ranchers) equally, the labor-supply distortions caused by the legal rule will be less than taxes, for the same amount of redistribution. Thus, $\widehat{T} < T$. And if that is the case, the redistributive costs of legal rules may indeed be less than taxes, a condition that obtains when $\Delta + \widehat{T} < T$. Certainly, either outcome is possible. But that is the point: There is no reason to believe taxes will always redistribute more efficiently than legal rules.

Finally, a numerical example, reported in Table 5.1, will illustrate the conclusion a little more concretely. The population is divided into three groups, ranchers (R), farmers (F), and the "unemployed" or society's least well-off (0), who subsist entirely on transfers from the government. For simplicity, labor supply is captured on the extensive margin; that is, both farmers and ranchers decide whether to work in each of those occupations or stay unemployed. Utility is a function of income, y_i, taxes or transfers, T_i, and the results of the Ayres-and-Talley Coasean bargaining problem. This value is a complicated function of the players' buy offers, sell offers, individual valuations of the entitlement, and damages (if the rancher takes the entitlement) all weighted by the probabilities of each decision node of the game.[13] To ensure that

[13] For example, farmers who make a buy offer will get the amount of the rancher's offer, if the farmer accepts it. If the farmer rejects the offer, she gets her valuation of the entitlement if the rancher does not take it (because the rancher is a low-value rancher) or she gets the damages amount if the rancher takes it (because the rancher is a high-value rancher). And so forth for the other three categories: farmers who make a sell offer, high-value ranchers, and low-value ranchers. The reader is referred to Ayres and Talley (1995) for further details.

TABLE 5.1 *Efficiency of legal rule redistribution*

	D = \$50	D = \$55	D = \$50 + $\widehat{T}$
u_R	148.7500	146.1875	146.1875
u_F	59.1250	61.6563	61.6563
u_o	5.0000	5.0000	5.0000
$h_R \cdot u_R$	68.3777	67.1495	67.1501
$h_F \cdot u_F$	25.8946	27.0755	27.0745
$h_o \cdot u_o$	0.5185	0.5139	0.5138
W	94.7908	94.7389	94.7383

Notes: D = liability damages; u_i = utility for ranchers (R), farmers (F), and unemployed (o); $h_i \cdot u_i$ = per capita utility for $\sum h_i = 1$; $\widehat{T}$ = distribution-neutral income tax adjustment; W = total social welfare, or efficiency. As measured by total, social welfare, raising damages from \$50 to \$55 is inefficient (94.7908 > 94.7389). However, raising damages is a more efficient method of redistribution than the efficient legal rule plus an income tax adjustment that replicates the distribution of income generated by the redistributive (higher damages) legal rule (94.7389 > 94.7383).

the problem is genuinely redistributive, I suppose that rancher earned income is \$200, farmer earned income is \$10, and the unemployed is \$0. Tax rates are arbitrarily set at 30 percent for ranchers, 20 percent for farmers, and the unemployed receive a transfer of \$5. The first column of numbers gives the results when damages are set at their efficient level, as established by Ayres and Talley, $D = \$50$. The first three rows give individual level utility, u_i. The second three rows give per-capita utility, which is utility weighted by population shares *inclusive* of labor-supply effects, $h_i \cdot u_i$, where h_i is the population shares, $\sum h_i = 1$.

Finally, the bottom row is a sum of the per-capita utilities of the second three rows and gives total (per-capita) social welfare, W, or wealth (i.e., without regard to the distribution of welfare). The second number column gives the same results for a redistributive damage rule, which is higher than its efficient level, set at $D = \$55$, and redistributes income from ranchers to farmers. As expected, this change is both inefficient and redistributive. As reported in the bottom row, overall efficiency is higher with the efficient damages rule than with the redistributive one (94.7908 > 94.7389). And, as can be seen in the top three rows, the redistributive damages rule lowers ranchers' expected utility (from 148.7500 to 146.1875) and raises farmers' expected utility (from 59.1250 to 61.6563).

Can legal rules redistribute more efficiently than taxes? The third number column reports the results when damages are kept at their efficient level, but an adjustment is made to the tax schedule, labeled $\widehat{T}$, that gives the same distribution of utility as the redistributive legal rule. Comparing the second and third columns, we see that the utilities are identical between each group. However, the damages rule and the tax adjustment each affect labor supply differently, as can be seen in rows four through six in the last two columns. The reason for this is as explained before. Because the tax authorities only observe income, they cannot distinguish between the rancher's valuation of the entitlement. For example, under the efficient damages rule, the utility of high-value ranchers is 153.75 and that of low-value ranchers is 143.75. By contrast, under the redistributive damages rule, the utilities of high- and low-value ranchers are 149.19 and 143.19. The redistributive rule lowers the utilities of both kinds of ranchers, but it impacts high-value ranchers much more substantially. Between the two rules, the difference in utility of the high-value ranchers is 4.56, and that of low-value ranchers is only 0.56. Compare the effects of the change in the damages rule to the substitute method of distribution-preserving tax adjustment. Because the tax authorities cannot distinguish between high- and low-value ranchers, each type pays the same amount. This adjustment is determined by the difference of the *average* rancher utility and can be found by taking the difference of the second and first numbered columns. Or, taking into account the population weights (each type is half of the rancher population), $(0.5 \times 153.75 + 0.5 \times 143.75) - (0.5 \times 149.19 + 0.5 \times 143.19) = 2.5625$. Therefore, the utilities of both high- and low-value ranchers are reduced by the same amount under the tax adjustment, and in contrast to the redistributive legal rule. These utilities are, respectively, 151.19 and 141.19. Critically, this tax adjustment raises high-value rancher utility and lowers low-value rancher utility, compared to the redistributive rule. As we will discuss next, that shift among ranchers will mean that that tax adjustment causes more labor-supply distortion than the redistributive legal rule. The same sort of analysis applies to farmers as well.

Thus, the redistributive legal rule and the distribution-neutral tax adjustment have the same effect on the distribution of *average* rancher (and farmer) income. But they have different effects for labor supply – in contrast to Kaplow and Shavell's assumption that these labor-supply effects will be the same. The difference arises because taxes cannot take account of the heterogeneous valuations of the ranchers and farmers. The uniform tax hits the ranchers (or, *pari passu*, the farmers) indiscriminately and distorts labor-supply decisions more than the redistributive legal rule. All ranchers pay the same tax rate, but optimal tax theory requires that high-value ranchers should pay higher rates than low-value ranchers. Because only high-value ranchers are willing to pay the damages, the redistributive legal rule better approximates what optimal tax theory requires. The consequence is that the tax adjustment actually distorts labor-supply incentives more than the legal rule. And because of that, total welfare, or efficiency, is lower under the tax adjustment (in the final column) than under the redistributive legal rule. Welfare under the redistributive rule is 94.7389 and under the tax adjustment 94.7383. Because the legal rule redistributes more efficiently with the same amount of redistribution, a social-welfare function would evaluate the redistributive legal rule as "better" than the tax adjustment.

3 Responses to Objections

The remainder of this section will anticipate and address some challenges to the argument for entitlement-based, Coasean redistribution. There are at least three possible objections: (1) the inframarginalism point – how legal rules exploit differences in valuation among individuals – essentially boils down to the same argument that authors have already advanced in terms of "heterogeneity" (e.g., Avraham, Fortus, and Logue 2003; Sanchirico 2000, 2001); (2) as such, the argument is most vulnerable to Kaplow and Shavell's objections to the heterogeneity argument; and (3) the income tax system can exploit the information revealed by the legal system to overcome its inability to distinguish between individuals' heterogeneous valuations. I will address each objection in turn.

The first two objections concern the crucial presence of heterogeneous valuations among actors (farmers or ranchers in our example). One could object both that "heterogeneity" has already been introduced as a possible motivation for legal-rule redistribution (e.g., Avraham, Fortus, and Logue 2003; Sanchirico 2000, 2001) and that, more problematically, it is therefore vulnerable to the objections raised against that motivation (e.g., Kaplow and Shavell 2000).

With respect to the first objection, although the inframarginal argument presented in this chapter shares similar conceptual space with the "heterogeneity" argument, there are significant differences. To provide some background, the role of "heterogeneity" in using distribution-informed legal rules has been a point of debate in the law-and-economics literature.[14] For example, in their original contribution, Kaplow and Shavell (1994) acknowledged heterogeneity in income-earning ability, but not heterogeneity in what we might call "precautionary ability," that is, aptitude in reducing risky activities and avoiding harm. As Sanchirico (2000, 2001) showed, acknowledging heterogeneity in the latter could disturb Kaplow and Shavell's conclusion that, in their example, damages should not be adjusted to favor the poor and disfavor the rich. Nevertheless, Kaplow and Shavell (2000) responded that whether such heterogeneity favors adjusting legal rules to favor the poor is ambiguous. For instance, we might not want to raise damages on rich yacht owners who also happen to be "klutzy" compared to poor, well-coordinated fishing-boat owners. In fact, we would want to reverse the redistributive presumption and favor rich, klutzy yacht owners at

[14] See, for instance, the debate between Sanchirico (2000, 2001) and Kaplow and Shavell (2000).

the expense of the poor but deft fishing-boat owners. As Gamage (2014) puts it, "[A]lthough Sanchirico's framework prescribes that overall distortionary costs could be reduced by *either positively taxing or subsidizing* various luxury commodities (such as yachts), Sanchirico's framework does not prescribe whether yachts or other luxury commodities should be positively taxed or subsidized in order to reduce overall distortionary costs" (14, emphasis in original). In Sanchirico's framework, only if the correlation between precautionary ability and income-earning ability were reversed (so that we'd have adroit yacht owners and klutzy fisherman) would we want to adjust damages to favor the poor. The role of heterogeneity is therefore ambiguous.

The entitlement-based, Coasean approach to legal distribution presented in this chapter avoids Kaplow and Shavell's ambiguity objection because it works through parties' deliberate transactions and not the random coincidence of accidents. What is crucial is how liability rules, with distributive objectives, facilitate trade by revealing information when potential transactions exist between high-value ranchers and farmers, on the one hand, and low-value ranchers and farmers, on the other. It is therefore not essential to the results that ranchers' or farmers' valuations of the entitlement correlate in any particular direction with income-earning ability. All of the results obtain if entitlement valuations and income-earning ability are assumed to be independent of each other. Furthermore, nothing important hinges on assuming that farmers are poor and ranchers are rich. Assume instead the opposite, that farmers are rich and ranchers poor. The prescription would now be to lower, rather than raise, damages to favor the poor ranchers, but for precisely the same reasoning as before: Lowering the liability amount shifts bargaining power in favor of poorer ranchers. Once again, legal rules would be adjusted to favor the poor, in the conventional sense. Of course (returning to the case of poor farmers and rich ranchers), if farmers' valuations were systematically high and ranchers' systematically low, liability rules would be of no value. But this is because there is simply no gains from trade, which would take the problem not only out of the realm of redistributive interest, but outside of any economic interest whatsoever. There is therefore no ambiguity, as in the Sanchirico case, about whether damages should be adjusted to favor the poor: They should. Heterogeneity plays a different role than in Sanchirico's argument, and, for that reason, Kaplow and Shavell's objections to Sanchirico's argument do not apply to the case of Coasean redistribution.

Kaplow has another objection to the heterogeneity point, based on discussions about the value of differential commodity taxation, that may also potentially relate to this chapter's inframarginal claim. Double-distortion thinkers often object to heterogeneity arguments for using differential commodity taxation (on top of the income tax) as not "conventionally redistributive, that is, from rich to the poor" (Kaplow 2008, 141). Kaplow (2008) writes that using differential commodity taxation does not really redistribute from rich to poor but is actually a form of redistribution within income groups, because it is in fact the income tax system that handles redistribution from rich to poor. By exploiting the heterogeneity of tastes within particular income groups, commodity taxes and subsidies "allow the income tax to increase the extent of distribution by lowering the distortions from progressivity" (Weisbach 2015, 172).

A similar objection might be raised in the present context: Adjusting liability rules, upwards or downwards, exploits differences within the groups of ranchers (and likewise farmers) in a way that reduces the distortions of progressive taxation. To be sure, in our divided entitlements argument, increasing damages on high-value ranchers does allow an *effective* lower rate on the low-value ranchers when the income tax is set optimally (although both high- and low-value ranchers still pay the same "statutory" income tax rate). Nevertheless, it is still higher damages on the rich, and paid to the poor, that is the principle mechanism of redistribution. Indeed, when the income tax is set optimally, the damages adjustment *decreases* the amount of redistribution that takes place through the income tax system. More broadly, the fact that redistribution "really" takes place through the legal system when Coasean, entitlement-based redistribution is used, illustrates the empty formalism of the Kaplow and Weisbach objection to the claim that differential commodity taxation redistributes outside the income tax system. The key point, however, is that entitlement-based redistribution is not merely a disguised form of income-tax redistribution. This should be underscored by the fact that entitlement-based redistribution can take place even in the absence of an income-tax system.

One final objection to entitlement-based redistribution is that, with damages set at their Ayres-and-Talley efficient level, the tax authorities could use the information revealed by the legal system (farmers' "buy" and "sell" signals, and ranchers' taking behaviors) to adjust the income tax system optimally, and thereby distinguish between high- and low-value ranchers and farmers. This indeed would restore the superiority of the tax system as a more efficient redistributive instrument. Several responses to this specific objection can be made. First, the best response to this objection is to point out, once again, how totally it depends on the assumption that labor-supply responses to the distributive changes caused by legal rules versus taxes are *identical*. I have already pointed out reasons to be skeptical of that assumption and how it hinges on Kaplow's controversial supposition of a weak separability between consumption and leisure. That skepticism applies with greater force in the Coasean context, where individuals need not be involved in conventional buyer–seller, market relationships. For example, as mentioned earlier, it is not at all clear how or whether the rancher's extra fencing costs would influence their labor-supply or output decisions. Although the connection seems a little more obvious with respect to the rancher's taking behavior (allowing greater range for his cattle to roam may expand output), similar questions could be raised. As suggested earlier, perhaps the rancher also likes letting his horses (rather than his cattle) roam freely over the farmer's land, because this enhances his value for leisure. In that case, the value from taking the entitlement would not increase labor supply but decrease it. Thus, the idea that heterogeneous valuations for the entitlement can always be translated into equivalent earnings amounts seems doubtful. Even with better information and differentiated tax rates, the superiority of the tax system depends on that assumption. Second, one should recall that I have assumed for the sake of argument that individuals, the legal authorities, and the tax authorities all have, ex ante, the same information available to them. But, as also pointed out, it seems plausible that individuals have better information available to them than either, in which case even information elicited by the legal system and collected by the tax authorities may not be sufficient to give taxes a redistributive advantage. Third, and even more fundamentally, as also mentioned earlier, the distributive corollary of the Coase theorem that I have presented does not hinge on labor-supply effects at all, and indeed the case for it is strengthened when one drops the strong assumption that labor-supply responses are identical across taxes and legal rules. Finally, one could also invoke Fennell and McAdams's (2016) point that the income tax will not always be responsive and available as a corrective to inequality. In that case, the legal system is a practical alternative for redistribution when the tax system is unavailable.[15]

V CONCLUSION

The so-called Coase theorem and the double-distortion argument are two of the best known propositions in law and economics.[16] Interestingly, they stand for two, entirely *opposite* claims. The Coase theorem says that, in a world without transaction costs, the choice of legal rules is irrelevant for efficiency. What Schwab (1989, 1195) dubbed the "Distributive Corollary of the Coase Theorem" follows

[15] Kaplow supports the idea of using *observable* information so that the tax system can account for heterogeneity. For example, Kaplow (2008, 140–41) posits that the income tax can take into account preference heterogeneity when that heterogeneity is "wholly related to observable characteristics, such as age, geographic location, or family composition." However, Kaplow also appears to resist the idea of information gathering because it is costly. For example, he goes on to oppose differential commodity taxation on the grounds that it "adds to the administrative costs and presents opportunities for avoidance" (142). Kaplow and Shavell (2000, 832–34) are also skeptical of policy programs that require gathering information about indirectly observable characteristics, such as Sanchirico's (2000) proposal to empirically verify correlations between, for example, income-earning ability and precautionary skill. If there is one, the principle guiding when information should be acquired is not very clear. Is the line between directly and indirectly observable information? Should information gathering satisfy a cost–benefit test?

[16] "So-called" because none of the authors of either claim, Coase (1960) and Kaplow and Shavell (1994), respectively, use these terms to describe their propositions.

immediately and says that: "With zero transaction costs, initial entitlements cannot be justified on efficiency grounds, and so should be awarded on the basis of need or desert." In other words, *according to the Coase theorem, legal rules should be chosen on the basis of distribution, rather than efficiency*. According to Kaplow and Shavell (1994), the double-distortion argument says exactly the opposite: Legal rules should be chosen only on the basis of efficiency, not distribution. Redistributive legal rules distort economic activity (labor supply, investment, etc.) just like taxes, but also distort the activities regulated by those legal rules (precautionary activity in torts, performance in contracts, etc.). Consequently, taxes can accomplish whatever amount of redistribution legal rules can, but more efficiently, without the added – double – distortions. Thus, *according to the double-distortion argument, legal rules should be chosen on the basis of efficiency, rather than distribution*.

It is possible to reconcile these two propositions by recognizing that transaction costs are, in general, positive. When transaction costs are positive, then efficiency may indeed be relevant for the choice of legal rules (Cooter and Ulen 2016). Likewise, it is the existence of transaction costs – specifically, imperfect information – that at least raises a question about whether taxation is a more efficient redistributive tool than legal rules. For if the tax authorities had perfect information about individuals' abilities, the second fundamental theorem of welfare economics would apply, and taxation could be used to achieve *any* distribution of resources without sacrificing efficiency.

Does this mean that the double-distortion argument prevails against the distributive corollary of the Coase theorem in the end? The argument in this chapter has been: not necessarily. The question of whether legal rules should be used for redistributive purposes depends on the relative transaction costs between bargaining parties, on the one hand, and the tax authorities and citizens, on the other. If, for example, bargaining parties have better information about each other (i.e., close to zero transaction costs) than the tax authorities have about either, then it is at least quite likely that legal rules will beat taxes on redistributive grounds. Moreover, even if the information that the bargaining parties have about each other is no better than that of the tax authorities, this article has taken a redistributive twist on the argument that legal rules can be used to encourage parties in bargaining relationships to reveal information about themselves (Ayres and Talley 1995; Segal and Whinston 2014, 2016). That individuals value an entitlement differently not only generates transaction costs, as these authors have presumed. Shifting liability damages in a redistributive direction can also change the bargaining power of the marginal parties and reduce income inequality while also facilitating trade. Under these conditions, legal rules will again be more efficient than taxation at redistributing income. To put this in inframarginal terms, adjusting liability damages shifts the identity of the marginal bargaining parties, determining who is willing to entertain what kind of transaction. This has the effect, not just in facilitating trade as in Ayres and Talley (1995), but also of shifting bargaining power in a way that benefits the poorer party in the exchange.

The ultimate point is that the distributive corollary has greater scope than previously recognized. The absence of transaction costs are neither necessary nor sufficient for that corollary to apply. There is even warrant, I would suggest, for reversing the presumption that the double-distortion argument advances. Instead of that argument's presumption, perhaps we should return to the presumption of the Coase theorem: that adoption of legal rules be based primarily on distribution and secondarily on efficiency.

REFERENCES

Avraham, Ronen, David Fortus, and Kyle Logue. 2003. "Revisiting the Roles of Legal Rules and Tax Rules in Income Redistribution: A Response to Kaplow & Shavell." *Iowa Law Review* 89:1125.

Ayres, Ian, and Eric Talley. 1995. "Solomonic Bargaining: Dividing a Legal Entitlement to Facilitate Coasean Trade." *Yale Law Journal* 104 (5): 1027–117.

Calabresi, Guido. 1991. "The Pointlessness of Pareto: Carrying Coase Further." *Yale Law Journal* 100:1211–37.

Calabresi, Guido, and A Douglas Melamed. 1972. "Property Rules, Liability Rules, and Inalienability: One View of the Cathedral." *Harvard Law Review* 85 (6): 1089–128.

Coase, RH. 1960. "The Problem of Social Cost." *Journal of Law & Economics* 3:1–44.

Cooter, Robert, and Thomas Ulen. 2016. *Law and Economics*. 6th ed. Boston: Addison-Wesley.

Fennell, Lee Anne, and Richard H McAdams. 2016. "The Distributive Deficit in Law and Economics." *Minnesota Law Review* 100:1051–129.

Gamage, David. 2014. "How Should Governments Promote Distributive Justice?: A Framework for Analyzing the Optimal Choice of Tax Instruments." *Tax Law Review* 68:1–87.

Hamada, Koichi. 1976. "Liability Rules and Income Distribution in Product Liability." *American Economic Review* 66 (1):228–34.

Jolls, Christine. 1998. "Behavioral Economics Analysis of Redistributive Legal Rules." *Vanderbilt Law Review* 51:1653.

Kaplow, Louis. 2004. "On the (Ir)Relevance of Distribution and Labor Supply Distortion to Government Policy." *Journal of Economic Perspectives* 18(4):159–75.

2008. *The Theory of Taxation and Public Economics*. Princeton: Princeton University Press.

Kaplow, Louis, and Steven Shavell. 1994. "Why the Legal System Is Less Efficient Than the Income Tax in Redistributing Income." *Journal of Legal Studies* 23 (2):667–81.

2000. "Should Legal Rules Favor the Poor? Clarifying the Role of Legal Rules and the Income Tax in Redistributing Income." *Journal of Legal Studies* 29 (2): 821–35.

Liscow, Zachary. 2014. "Reducing Inequality on the Cheap: When Legal Rule Design Should Incorporate Equity as Well as Efficiency." *Yale Law Journal* 123 (7): 2478–510.

Polinsky, A Mitchell. 1989. *An Introduction to Law and Economics*. 2nd ed. New York: Aspen Publishers.

Sanchirico, Chris William. 2000. "Taxes versus Legal Rules as Instruments for Equity: A More Equitable View." *Journal of Legal Studies* 29 (2):797–820.

2001. "Deconstructing the New Efficiency Rationale." *Cornell Law Review* 86:1003–89.

Schwab, Stewart. 1989. "Coase Defends Coase: Why Lawyers Listen and Economists Do Not." *Michigan Law Review* 87 (6):1171–2459.

Segal, Ilya, and Michael D Whinston. 2014. "The Efficiency of Bargaining under Divided Entitlements." *University of Chicago Law Review* 81 (1): 273–89.

2016. "Property Rights and the Efficiency of Bargaining." *Journal of the European Economic Association* 14 (6): 1287–328.

Weisbach, David A. 2015. "Distributionally Weighted Cost–Benefit Analysis: Welfare Economics Meets Organizational Design." *Journal of Legal Analysis* 7 (1): 151–82.

6

Distributive Consequences of Regulating Boilerplate

Between Price Effects and Socialization of Risk

Przemysław Pałka[*]

CONTENTS

I INTRODUCTION

This chapter is about the distributive impact of boilerplate contracts.

Specifically, this chapter scrutinizes the role that consumer-unfriendly terms ("CUTs")[1] play in the distribution of wealth and risk in consumer society, including

[*] The research leading to these results has received funding from the Norwegian Financial Mechanism 2014–21, project no. 2020/37/K/HS5/02769, titled "Private Law of Data: Concepts, Practices, Principles & Politics." For helpful comments on the draft, I would like to thank Szymon Osmola, Maciej Próchnicki, and Ramsi Woodcock.

[1] "Consumer unfriendliness" is understood broadly to encompass all kinds of contractual clauses that render consumer's position precarious vis-a-vis the entrepreneur. In particular, the term

e-commerce. It nuances the view dominant in some sectors of legal scholarship, according to which it is the least affluent consumers who benefit from the lack of regulation of standard terms (as the prices are lower, and more people can afford the product).[2] The chapter argues that such an account ignores the fact that the poorest consumers – unlike the affluent middle class – often do not have the ability to internalize future damages, should an accident occur.[3]

Consequently, regulation of boilerplate contracts, guaranteeing consumers a right (and the factual ability) to seek damages (by, e.g., voiding clauses excluding liability for torts or class action waivers) could be seen as a mandatory, collective "insurance," where all consumers chip in a little for the benefit of the future injured party. The current situation in the American contract law, that is, the validity and enforceability of the CUTs, works in the opposite direction – we all pay a slightly lower price while accepting that once someone gets injured – and someone will get injured – their chances of taking a dispute to court and being compensated are lower than if the default rules were not contractually modified.[4] The problem is that, for some, this will be just a minor nuisance, while for others, it might be a life-ruining event.

The problem of the "CUTs" precedes the Internet and the growth of e-commerce in the last two decades.[5] Yet, the socio-technological changes intensify the CUTs' consequences while simultaneously offering a chance to combat them better. Large parts of our lives – from communication, travel, and shopping to dating and entertainment – are currently mediated by online platforms (whose boilerplate one needs to accept to use them).[6] Further, the ability to purchase goods and services from all over the country (and the world) has increased due to the

"CUTs" refers to clauses limiting consumers' remedies (exclusion of warranty or liability) and dispute settlement clauses (choice of law, choice of forum, mandatory arbitration, class action waivers). For a typology of such clauses regarding their legal status, see: Yehuda Adar & Shmuel Becher, *Ending the License to Exploit: Administrative Oversight of Consumer Contracts*, 62 B. C. L. Rev. 2405, 2415–20 (2021) (distinguishing between "legally invalid terms," "voidable unconscionable terms," and "unfair terms.").

2 *See infra*, Section II.A.

3 *See infra*, Section II.B.

4 *See* Margaret Jane Radin, Boilerplate: The Fine Print, Vanishing Rights, and the Rule of Law 16 (2013). (Writing: "Mass-market systems of form contracts that restructure the rights of users of products and services operate to undermine or cancel the rights of users granted by legislatures. In other words, these systems of contracts can delete rights that are granted through democratic processes, substituting for them the system that the firm wishes to impose.")

5 *See infra*, Section II.

6 This has been dubbed by some commentators as the "platform economy." See: Julie E. Cohen, *Law for the Platform Economy*, 51 U.C. Davies L. Rev. 133 (2017); Natali Helberger et al., *Governing Online Platforms: From Contested to Cooperative Responsibility*, 34 Info. Soc'y 1–14 (2018); Rory Van Loo, *Federal Rules of Platform Procedure*, 88 U. Chi. L. Rev. (2021); Nikolas Guggenberger, *Essential Platforms*, 24 Stan. Tech. L. Rev. (2021), https://papers.ssrn.com/abstract=3703361 (last accessed Nov. 17, 2020); Thomas Kadri, *Digital Gatekeepers*, 97 Texas L. Rev. (2021).

Internet assuming a central role in our lives. Hence, on the one hand, we are bound by many more contracts than we used to be in the twentieth century, with parties located much further from us than when the current legal doctrines were forged. On the other hand, the ability for firms to compete with one another (also on boilerplate clauses) has significantly increased.

The primary goal of this chapter is to get the idea across: Through unregulated boilerplate, lowering corporations' future costs and thereby retail prices, the poorest consumers subsidize the middle class risk-wise, on top of benefiting from short-term lower prices. This is contrary to the basic principle of social solidarity. Now, what the regulatory consequence of this idea should be – whether the government should intervene and in what way – is a political question. I survey the possible reactions – ranging from regulation, over the reinterpretation of common law doctrines, to market solutions – in Section IV. In Section III, II critique the mainstream distributive narrative surrounding the CUTs and offer an alternative. In Section I, I begin by looking at the philosophy of consumer law in the United States (US) and the European Union (EU), demonstrating how assumptions behind American contract law are neither necessary nor necessarily optimal.

II THE TRANSATLANTIC SPLIT: EFFICIENCY VS. SOCIALIZATION OF RISK

A *An Anecdote to Ponder*

The story of this chapter begins with a glass of beer and one question that shook my mind.[7]

In the fall of 2018, as a freshly minted Yale's Fellow in Private Law, I spent an evening chatting with an American contracts professor about the projects we worked on at the time. I was passionately describing a revolution in consumer protection that technological advances could bring – a subject of a book chapter I was struggling to finish writing.[8] For context: before coming to the US, I worked as a researcher at the European University Institute in Florence, Italy, where, with a team of lawyers and computer scientists, we have been trying to automate the

[7] One can only speculate how many (good and bad) ideas have not been born as the result the COVID-19 pandemic, which forced us into isolation and stripped us of the possibility of casually exchanging ideas in bars, as opposed to having each and every meeting planned and scheduled. For a theory of how unstructured interactions in non-work environments boost creativity, see: ANNIE MURPHY PAUL, THE EXTENDED MIND: THE POWER OF THINKING OUTSIDE THE BRAIN (2021).

[8] By now, fortunately, finished and published. See: Przemysław Pałka & Marco Lippi, *Big Data Analytics, Online Terms of Service and Privacy Policies*, *in* RESEARCH HANDBOOK ON BIG DATA LAW 115–34 (Roland Vogl ed., 2021).

evaluation of terms of service (ToS) of online platforms using machine learning.[9] Evaluation according to what standard?

According to European consumer law, a particular class of standard clauses (the so-called unfair terms)[10] – ranging from specific kinds of limitations of liability over companies' rights to unilaterally change the contract to choice of forum or class action waivers – are unlawful.[11] Not only does the law deem them non-binding should a dispute emerge, but it also empowers state administrative agencies to proactively seek out such clauses and order businesses to remove them from their boilerplate.[12] In the ideal world imagined by European lawmakers, if only standard consumer contracts were publicly available, those contracts would not contain unfair terms, as administrative agencies would have them removed. And yet, as our empirical analysis found out, essentially all ToS of online platforms were full of unfair terms.[13] How was this possible?

Our hypothesis, supported by anecdotal knowledge about the inner workings of consumer protection agencies, was that the problem was a lack of resources. Consumer protection bodies simply lacked the personnel necessary to go through thousands of documents and initiate the enforcement proceedings.[14] Such a task, quite dull and not very creative, while simultaneously laborsome, seemed like a

9 For the main output of the project, see: Marco Lippi et al., *CLAUDETTE: An Automated Detector of Potentially Unfair Clauses in Online Terms of Service*, 27 A. I. & LAW 117 (2019). For a "manifesto" paper, outlining the future possible research paths and ways to transform the technical experiments into usable tools, see: Marco Lippi et al., *The Force Awakens: Artificial Intelligence for Consumer Law*, 67 J. A. I. RES. 169 (2020).

10 *See infra*, Section 1.2.

11 *Id*. For a doctrinal and policy discussion of these regulations, see: Hans W. Micklitz & Norbert Reich, *The Court and Sleeping Beauty: The Revival of the Unfair Contract Terms Directive (UCTD)*, 51 COMMON MARKET L. REV. 771–808 (2014); Peter Rott, *Unfair Contract Terms*, *in* RESEARCH HANDBOOK ON EU CONSUMER AND CONTRACT LAW (2016); Marco Loos & Joasia Luzak, *Wanted: A Bigger Stick. On Unfair Terms in Consumer Contracts with Online Service Providers*, 39 J. CONSUM. POL'Y 63–90 (2016).

12 *See* Hans-W. Micklitz et al., *The Empire Strikes Back: Digital Control of Unfair Terms of Online Services*, 40 J. CONSUM. POL'Y 367–88 (2017); see also: Stephanie Law, *The Transformation of Consumer Law in Times of Crisis: The Ex Officio Control of Unfair Contract Terms*, *in* TRANSFORMATION OF CIVIL JUSTICE: UNITY AND DIVERSITY 283–307 (Alan Uzelac & Cornelis Hendrik (Remco) van Rhee eds., 2018).

13 *See* Lippi et al., *CLAUDETTE*, *supra* note 9 at 127.

14 For an overview of challenges to consumer law enforcement at the time, see: Hans-W. Micklitz & Geneviève Saumier, *Enforcement and Effectiveness of Consumer Law*, *in* ENFORCEMENT AND EFFECTIVENESS OF CONSUMER LAW 3–45 (Hans-W. Micklitz & Geneviève Saumier eds., 2018) (providing an overview of state-specific problems discussed throughout the book). Ever since, the EU has adopted a directive aimed at improving enforcement. See the Directive (EU) 2019/2161 of the European Parliament and of the Council of 27 November 2019 amending Council Directive 93/13/EEC and Directives 98/6/EC, 2005/29/EC, and 2011/83/EU of the European Parliament and of the Council as regards the better enforcement and modernization of Union consumer protection rules, December 18, 2019, OJ L 328/7. To what extent these changes will be sufficient remains to be seen.

perfect candidate to be automated. As we achieved initial success in the project,[15] I was describing a grand vision of bots crawling the net in search of unfair terms and sending businesses messages about the imminent legal action (which should be sufficient to have them modify the contracts to avoid the proceedings). "Soon," I was almost preaching, "there will be no unfair terms used in online boilerplate contracts, the law will be respected, and the consumers will finally be protected!"

My colleague looked puzzled. He took a sip of beer and said: "yeah, but what if these terms are efficient?"

This remark caught me off guard. I knew the typical (European) objections to the grand vision – that companies will reword the boilerplate in a way that makes unfair clauses harder to detect, that Europe's multilingualism would be a problem, in essence: that this won't work – but did not expect anyone to question the normative premise of the project. "What do you mean 'they are efficient,' they're illegal!" I answered. "Well, maybe they shouldn't be illegal," – my colleague responded – "maybe corporations value having these clauses included in boilerplate very highly, as they drive their future costs down, while consumers do not really care. If they cared, companies would compete on consumer-friendliness of their boilerplate; as they don't, it means that top-down regulation of boilerplate is inefficient." I had no idea what to say to that.

You might be surprised that I was surprised.[16] In the end, "efficiency" is a concept taught in torts or contracts 101.[17] Ever since the success of law and economics in American law and legal scholarship,[18] "efficiency" has been a part of the language we speak and the air we breathe. Of course, one might contest the weight that law or lawyers ascribe to "efficiency" as a guiding normative principle. However, one knows that it must be addressed, doesn't one?

Well, not in the EU. Believe it or not, in continental Europe (jurisdictions like Germany, France, Poland, etc.), one can graduate from law school, specialize in contract law and consumer law, and not stumble upon the concept of "efficiency" once. One can think of several possible explanations. First, a movement akin to legal realism (which paved the way for the success of law and economics in the US)[19] never

[15] *See* Lippi et al., *CLAUDETTE*, *supra* note 9 at 131–33. We achieved 80 percent overall effectiveness of the system, trained on a relatively small sample of contracts, suggesting that improvements can easily be made when increasing the size of the training set and using more sophisticated natural language processing (NLP) techniques. For certain kinds of unfair clauses (choice of law, choice of forum, and limitation of liability), the effectiveness was higher than 93 percent.

[16] If you are from the US. If you are from outside of the US, I might share my confusion from back then.

[17] *See*, e.g., Daniel Markovits, Contract Law and Legal Methods 19–512. (2012).

[18] For a discussion of how the economic analysis of law has become of the paradigms of American legal scholarship and practice, see: Guido Calabresi, The Future of Law and Economics: Essays in Reform and Recollection (2016).

[19] *See* Joseph William Singer, *Legal Realism Now*, 76 Cal. L. Rev. 465, 515 (1988), writing:

> Law and economics theory is very much an exercise in legal realism. … [E]fficiency theorists reject the idea that one can deduce the meaning of legal entitlements from

took place in the EU; we are still, essentially, formalists here. Second, European contract law has been expressed in civil codes for centuries now, and so when we study the general principles governing private law, we focus on those expressed in the codification and the doctrines built while interpreting the codes, and efficiency is not there.[20] We care about autonomy and interpersonal justice, not efficiency.

The reason why I wanted to begin with this story, and not just a dry statement to the effect of "efficiency has been a guiding principle in the US consumer contract law, but not in Europe," is to encourage the reader to ponder upon the collective mindset. Both the European and the American legal consciousness can be subjected to critical scrutiny. And, as it is the Americans I take to be the primary audience of this book, I want to invite you to imagine a contract law community that does not speak of "efficiency." It is perfectly possible to run a country – and one cannot accuse places like Germany, Norway, or France of not being affluent or having a starkly lower standard of living than the US – without giving one thought to the efficiency of its contract law system. It is not that the system necessarily ends up being inefficient (it might, through legislative amendments and judicial decisions, tacitly gravitate towards efficiency)[21] but that other values serve as the normative threshold.

B *Substance and Philosophies of Consumer Contract Law in the US and the EU*

The contents and structure of consumer laws in the US and the EU are similar. On both sides of the Atlantic, we have rules to combat unfair and deceptive commercial practices,[22] enact product safety regulations[23] and mandatory consumer

abstract concepts. Nor do they believe that one can understand how the legal system operates, as well as the kinds of considerations judges take into account in deciding cases, simply by reading judicial opinions.

20 For example, in Polish law, constituting an interesting mixture of rules and doctrines enshrined in French Code Civil and German Bürgerliches Gesetzbuch, one focuses on the principles of (1) will's autonomy, (2) primacy of subjective rights, (3) trust in commercial practices, and (4) social justice in legal relations. See: Marek Safjan, System Prawa Prywatnego, t. 1, Prawo cywilne – czesc ogólna (2012). In European civil law, these principles are: (1) framed autonomy, (2) protection of the weaker party, (3) non-discrimination, (4) effectiveness, (5) balancing, (6) proportionality, and (7) good faith. See: Norbert Reich, General Principles of EU Civil Law (2014).

21 As Richard Posner has been arguing since 1973, see: Richard Posner, Economic Analysis of Law (3rd ed. 1986).

22 For a recent analysis of the American doctrine, see: Lauren Willis, *Deception by Design*, 34 Harv. J. L. & Tech. 116 (2020) and; Luke Herrine, *The Folklore of Unfairness*, 96 N.Y.U. L. Rev. 431 (2021). For an overview of the European one, see: Willem van Boom & Amandine Garde, The European Unfair Commercial Practices Directive: Impact, Enforcement Strategies and National Legal Systems (2016) and Elisabet González Pons, *Addressing Aggressive Commercial Practices: Some Critical Aspects of Its Regime in the Unfair Commercial Practices Directive*, 6 Fin. Mkts. Valuation 27 (2020).

23 Luke Nottage, *Product Safety Regulation*, *in* Handbook of Research on International Consumer Law (Geraint Howells, Iain Ramsay, and Thomas Wilhelmsson eds., 2nd ed. 2018),

rights,[24] and heavily rely on mandated disclosures as means of consumer protection.[25] However, we differ in consumer contract law.

In the EU, the primary legislative instrument is Directive 93/13 on Unfair Terms in Consumer Contracts.[26] It defines "unfair terms" as follows:

> A contractual term that has not been individually negotiated shall be regarded as unfair if, contrary to the requirement of good faith, it causes a significant imbalance in the parties' rights and obligations arising under the contract, to the detriment of the consumer.[27]

This is a general clause, in principle, allowing courts to consider any kind of contractual term as "unfair." In addition, the Unfair Contract Terms Directive (UCTD) also contains an Annex listing an open catalogue of clauses presumed to be "unfair." These are, among others, terms excluding the company's liability for personal injury[28] or non-performance of the contract,[29] enabling businesses to unilaterally change the contract[30] or the service provided,[31] or limiting consumers' ability to take legal action or exercise legal remedy (including choice of law clauses, mandatory arbitration, or class action waivers).[32] As disputes emerge, the final say on what terms must be considered "unfair" throughout the Union is with the Court of Justice of the EU, which has already ruled on dozens of kinds of clauses.[33]

www.elgaronline.com/view/edcoll/9781785368202/9781785368202.00015.xml (last accessed Jan. 31, 2022); Duncan Fairgrieve & Geraint Howells, *General Product Safety: A Revolution through Reform?*, 69 Mod. L. Rev. 59 (2006); Eileen Flaherty, *Safety First: The Consumer Product Safety Improvement Act of 2008*, 21 Loy. Consumer L. Rev. 372 (2008); Jukka Ruohonen, *A Review of Product Safety Regulations in the European Union*, arXiv:2102.03679 [cs] (2021), http://arxiv.org/abs/2102.03679 (last accessed Apr. 2, 2022).

24 See, e.g., J. A. Luzak, *To Withdraw or Not to Withdraw? Evaluation of the Mandatory Right of Withdrawal in Consumer Distance Selling Contracts Taking into Account Its Behavioural Effects on Consumers*, 37 J. Consum. Pol'y 91 (2014); Sanford Shatz & Susan E. Chylik, *The California Consumer Privacy Act of 2018: A Sea Change in the Protection of California Consumers' Personal Information Survey – Consumer Financial Services*, 75 Bus. L. 1917 (2019).

25 In the EU called "information duties," see, e.g., Monika Namysłowska & Agnieszka Jabłonowska, *Information Obligations and Disinformation of Consumers: Polish Law Report*, *in* Information Obligations and Disinformation of Consumers 301 (Gert Straetmans ed., 2019), https://doi.org/10.1007/978-3-030-18054-6_8 (last accessed Sept. 7, 2020). For the classic analysis of how this works in the US, see: Omri Ben-Shahar & Carl E. Schneider, More Than You Wanted to Know: The Failure of Mandated Disclosure (2014).

26 Council Directive 93/13/EEC of 5 April 1993 on unfair terms in consumer contracts, Apr. 21, 1993, OJ L 95/29 [hereinafter "the UCTD"].

27 *See* the UCTD, Article 3.1.

28 *See* the UCTD, Annex, p. (a).

29 *Id.* p. (b).

30 *Id.* p. (j).

31 *Id.* p. (k).

32 *Id.* p. (q).

33 For an overview, see: Hans-W. Micklitz & Betül Kas, *Overview of Cases before the CJEU on European Consumer Contract Law (2008–2013) – Part I*, 10 Eur. Rev. Contract L. 1–63 (2014).

Unfair terms in a contract do not bind European consumers.[34] If a contract law dispute emerges, courts consider them null and void (this is the so-called individual control). In addition, various bodies (both administrative agencies and civil society organizations) have the competence to seek out unfair terms and order companies to remove them (or initiate proceedings to have them removed; this is the so-called abstract control).[35] This is supposed to prevent the use of the so-called *in terrorem* clauses, disincentivizing consumers from going to court.[36]

In short, the EU has substantive and procedural rules in place to ensure that no contractual terms "causing a significant imbalance of rights and duties to the detriment of the consumer" bind the latter.

The legal situation in the US is different. First, no general statute outlawing any kinds of contractual terms exists at the federal or state level. In common law, one can find the "unconscionability" doctrine;[37] however, the threshold for considering a clause unconscionable is much higher, and courts are reluctant to use it.[38] Second, the US Supreme Court has proactively deemed many consumer-unfriendly terms enforceable. These include choice-of-law and choice-of-forum clauses[39] or mandatory arbitration and class-action-waiver clauses.[40] Further, state and federal courts have generally enforced many other kinds of terms – like limitations of liability or unilateral alteration clauses.

Clearly, there are doctrinal reasons behind these decisions; the American contract law is simply different from the European one. However, there's also a difference in philosophy. Americans and Europeans hold divergent beliefs and assumptions about the overall purpose of consumer law.

The mainstream theory behind consumer law in the US is what Luke Herrine calls the "consumer sovereignty framework."[41] In his words, this framework:

> [T]reats the purpose of regulating consumer markets as trying to make them work as much as possible like a utopian market in which rational informed choices of consumers drive outcomes through the decentralized force of free competition.[42]

34 *See* the UCTD, Article 6.

35 See Law, *supra* note 12.

36 For an overview of the concept, see: Colin P. Marks, *Online Terms as in Terrorem Devices*, 78 MD. L. REV. 247 (2018).

37 See, e.g. Paul J. Morrow, *Cyberlaw: The Unconscionability/ Unenforceability of Contracts (Shrink-Wrap, Clickwrap, and Browse-Wrap) on the Internet: A Multijurisdictional Analysis Showing the Need for Oversight*, 11 PITT. J. TECH. L. & POL'Y [i] 1–29 (2011).

38 *Id.*

39 *See* Carnival Cruise Lines, Inc. v. Shute, 499 U.S. 585 (1991).

40 *See* AT&T Mobility LLC v. Concepcion, 563 U.S. 333 (2011); American Express v. Italian Colors, 570 U.S. 228 (2013).

41 *See* Luke Herrine, *What Is Consumer Protection For?*, 33 LOY. CONSUMER L. REV., 222 (2023), https://lawecommons.luc.edu/lclr/vol34/iss2/2.

42 *Id.*

Such a world would be the efficient one, with consumer products ending up in the hands of consumers who value them the most,[43] while the prices would be the lowest possible. Rory van Loo sees this latter quality, that is, lowering of prices, as the primary goal of the American consumer law (as it is now).[44] Ramsi Woodcock, albeit suggesting a radical idea of banning targeted online advertising as a policy means, reiterates the view that the goal of regulation is to facilitate informed decisions by consumers and lower prices.[45]

This view has profound consequences. First, note that the source of normative judgments about the value of particular products is the aggregate of individual consumers expressing their personal preferences. What matters in determining the prices and product allocation is not a collective, political decision of the community[46] but the normative choices of individuals acting in their own best interest. The mainstream philosophy behind American consumer law sees such a state of affairs as normatively superior to collective decisions, not just technically more efficient.[47] Second, the role of consumer law in this framework is not to replace any consumer choices with government decisions but rather to enable the former. If individual consumers choose boilerplate terms that favor the businesses, and one can expect

[43] *Id.*

[44] *See* Rory Van Loo, *Broadening Consumer Law: Competition, Protection, and Distribution*, 95 Notre Dame L. Rev. 211, 213 (2019) ("[M]any consumer protection and antitrust laws reduce the prices that people pay by removing overcharge . . . Although the field often focuses on goals other than lowering prices, many consumer laws nonetheless lower overcharge in diverse ways, including by addressing monopoly power, preventing deception, and removing entry barriers that get in the way of full competition.").

[45] *See* Ramsi A. Woodcock, *The Obsolescence of Advertising in the Information Age*, 127 Yale L.J. 2270, 2306 (2017).

> A ban on advertising outside of "add to cart" pages and firm websites would benefit consumers and improve efficiency in three ways. First, by eliminating the harmful effects of manipulative advertising on technological innovation, the prohibition would increase consumer welfare .... Second, the lower prices associated with a reduction in the anticompetitive effects of advertising would represent an efficiency gain because part of those lower prices would be made possible through the avoidance of wasteful advertising costs. Firms would no longer waste billions of dollars on seduction. Third, a ban would create an immediate efficiency gain by eliminating what economists call obtrusive advertising, advertising that is forced on consumers, preventing them from consuming product information at the times and places that they prefer.

[46] Herrine believes that this should be the goal of consumer law, proposing a "moral economy" theory. *See* Herrine, *supra* note 41 at 5–6.

> [M]oral economy view treats the purpose of consumer markets as ensuring that goods and services are provided in a way that comports with the values of those whom the political system represents. That is to say: A moral economy view treats consumer markets as contingent ways to solve problems of social provision, to ensure that the right goods and services get to the right people in accordance with principles of fairness.

[47] For an overview of normative and technical reasons to prefer markets over command economies, and the other way round, see: Przemysław Pałka, *Algorithmic Central Planning: Between Efficiency and Freedom*, 83 L. & Contemp. Probs. 125, 126–34 (2020).

that they do so due to the lower prices of such products (as lowering prices is the goal of consumer law), the government should think twice before meddling with these choices.

Within this philosophy, the legislature's choice to refrain from enacting something akin to the EU's UCTD, and courts' decisions to enforce consumer-unfriendly clauses in boilerplate, can be presented as pro-consumer measures. Absent decisive evidence of market failures or monopolies, stronger regulation of consumer contracts would make it harder for consumers to choose what they really want (as these choices would now be unlawful) and drive prices up (as the businesses' expected costs of future legal proceedings would increase and be shifted onto the consumers). Now, whether American consumers actually prefer marginally lower prices in exchange for unfavorable contract terms is beyond my ability to know. It is also not entirely clear to me what "actually preferring," in the world of cognitive bias and less-than-perfectly-competitive markets, means. However, even if we assume that all the descriptive assumptions here are correct – that is, a significant number of individual consumers consciously choose worse contract terms in exchange for lower prices – honoring that choice is not the only possibility for consumer law. The philosophy in the EU is different.

The mainstream theory behind the consumer contract law in the EU boils down to two propositions: protection of the weaker party and socialization of risk.[48] The former, mainly stressed by civil lawyers (so people who study civil codes, including rules of property, contract, and tort; this encompasses consumer contract law), has been succinctly phrased by Norbert Reich:

> EU civil law has emerged not so much as a body of rules with an objective of enabling citizens to use their autonomy for purposes (...) to be determined by themselves, but rather as a body of provisions that tries to protect the weaker party and to combat discrimination.[49]

One of the goals of private law in Europe has been to establish a society of equals, where every individual enjoys the same rights, duties, and the autonomy to shape their lives as they please.[50] This ideal – which needs to be judged against the

[48] As long as substantive principles are considered. There is a third goal, where consumer law has been used as one of the tools for constructing the internal market. Through harmonization and unification of consumer laws of various Member States, the EU has hoped to both remove barriers to trade and increase consumers' trust in transnational commerce. See: Geraint Howells et al., Rethinking EU Consumer Law 23 (1st ed. 2017).

[49] *See* Reich et al., *supra* note 20 at 38; see also; Stephen Weatherill et al., *Private Autonomy and Protection of the Weaker Party*, *in* General Principles of Law: European and Comparative Perspectives, 261 (Stephen Weatherill & Stefan Vogenauer eds., 2017) (writing: "There is no better example of the combination of legislative initiative and judicial interpretation in the protection of the weaker party than that which is provided by Directive 93/13 on unfair terms in consumer contracts.").

[50] This is what Franz Bohm has called "a private law society" (ger. Privatrechtsgesellschaft). For an exposition of this view in English, and comparison with Anglo-Saxon views, like, e.g., that of

preceding social structures of a formally enshrined class system, differentiating between the rights of aristocracy, clergy, and peasants[51] – has been embedded in the civil codes establishing the formal equality of persons. However, as the realities of the industrial revolution and the emergence of mass consumer markets made clear, formal equality does not translate into material equality.[52] On the contrary, given the structural differences in parties' bargaining positions, formal equality in the contract often leads to relations of domination.[53] Hence, the European legislatures, first on the state level and then on the Union level, decided to grant the structurally weaker parties, including consumers, more rights than businesses enjoy.[54] The goal of the private law in the EU is not formal equality; it is material equality, and the protection of the weaker party in contract relations is seen as a means to achieving this goal.

Notice how, within this mindset, the concept of "efficiency" never comes up. Of course, one could try to rephrase it in such terms by, for example, trying to claim that to express their true preferences, consumers need not only information but also legal recourse and certain decisions, clearly against their interests, taken off the table. However, the European legislatures do decide for their citizens on the minimum acceptable standards in a contract. Even if this choice is overall inefficient, the law sees material equality in transactions as a higher value.

The second proposition guiding the European consumer contract law is the socialization of risk. To understand it, one needs to remember that in the EU, consumer law, alongside with labor law, social security, nationalized healthcare, and so on, has always been treated as an integral part of the welfare state project.[55] This collective perspective, drawing not on the ideal of equality but social solidarity, can be well captured by the quote from some leading European scholars of consumer law:

> Things go wrong in the market either through incompetence, fraud or chance. Some risks consumers might have to accept as simple lessons to be learned, but

John Rawls, see STEFAN GRUNDMANN ET AL., NEW PRIVATE LAW THEORY: A PLURALIST APPROACH 131–55 (2021).

[51] See, e.g., Robert Millward, *The Early Stages of European Industrialization: Economic Organization under Serfdom*, 21 EXPL. ECON. HIST. 406 (1984).

[52] *See* HANS-W. MICKLITZ, THE POLITICS OF JUSTICE IN EUROPEAN PRIVATE LAW: SOCIAL JUSTICE, ACCESS JUSTICE, SOCIETAL JUSTICE 7–10 (2018).

[53] In the US, the landmark case supporting this proposition has been Lochner v. New York; for its recent rereading in the context of the current state of capitalism in the US, see: K. Sabeel Rahman, *Domination, Democracy, and Constitutional Political Economy in the New Gilded Age: Towards a Fourth Wave of Legal Realism*, 94 TEX. L. REV. 1329 (2015).

[54] For a detailed account of this process, see MICKLITZ, *supra* note 52 at 45–160. Also, notice how the UCTD outlaws standard terms, creating an imbalance of rights and duties of the parties "to the detriment of the consumer." However, there's nothing wrong with terms imbalanced to the detriment of businesses.

[55] *See, e.g.*, Iain Ramsay, *Consumer Credit Law, Distributive Justice and the Welfare State*, 15 OXFORD J. LEGAL STUD. 177 (1995).

> others need to be redressed either because of the harm caused or to clean up the market going forward. This socialisation of risk underpins many consumer rules. (…) All inalienable consumer rights could be viewed as enforced insurance as the potential liability has to be factored into the price of goods and services.[56]

Within this perspective, economic factors become much more salient. Indeed, we accept that prices might rise if the government regulates standard contracts to favor the consumers. And that is the point of regulation. What matters is, primarily, not the price but the fact that, when a consumer suffers injury as a result of market transactions, she has redress. As that consumer can be anyone, it is the role of society to "chip in" to ensure that redress is available when needed.

Is it possible that this market is inefficient? Absolutely yes. One can imagine a situation where a significant number of consumers prefer lower prices in exchange for a detrimental legal position in the future, should injury happen. In this sense, the EU consumer law makes it impossible for these consumers to act upon their actual preferences. However, the role of the EU consumer contract law is not to enable each individual to express their preferences to the fullest; it is to safeguard the rights of these least well-off.

Two caveats are in order. First, at this point, both the Europeans and the Americans could criticize the above characterization as omitting the concept central to both systems: democracy. The very point – one could say – of the "consumer sovereignty" (in the US) or of the "private law society" (in the EU) is to allow the consumers to "vote" with their money for the products and deals they like, just like – in their capacity of citizens – they vote in elections for the policies and policymakers they prefer.[57] The goal of consumer law, in this sense, is to enable the consumer choices.[58] I agree with this view, as both theoretically sound and normatively appealing. However, it is precisely because the goal of facilitating choices is common to both the US and the EU consumer law that I do not focus on it in this chapter. The question this chapter ponders could be rephrased as: As we agree that the overall goal of consumer markets is to allow the consumers to express their preferences, what should be the constraints we put on the choices the law will enforce? Here the difference becomes clear and is explained by the different philosophies.

[56] Howells et al., *supra* note 48 at 8. British spelling in original.

[57] For a succinct presentation and discussion of this view, see: Ramsi Woodcock, *Democracy as the Heart of Debates about Regulation*, https://zephyranth.pw/2022/08/02/democracy-as-the-heart-of-debates-about-regulation/ (Aug. 2, 2022); Ramsi Woodcock, *Libertarianism as Opposition to the Electoral Process*, https://zephyranth.pw/2021/10/26/libertarianism-as-opposition-to-the-electoral-process/ (Oct. 26, 2021).

[58] For the works exposing this view, see: Hanoch Dagan & Michael Heller, The Choice Theory of Contracts (2017); Szymon Osmola, *Reflective Choices: A Liberal Theory of Consumer Law*, 2022, https://cadmus.eui.eu/handle/1814/74986 (last accessed Dec. 2, 2022).

Second, the American consumer law also does a lot to socialize risk and protect the structurally weaker parties through, for example, extensive regulations of product liability[59] or the robust culture of class actions.[60] On paper, some of these protections might seem even stronger when compared to the European counterparts. However, the CUTs – containing caps on liability, exclusion of liability, or class action waivers – often defeat the real-world effects of these rights. This chapter limits its scope to the analysis of the CUTs' distributive consequences and attempts to explain their different treatment across the Atlantic by reconstructing the philosophies behind the laws.

Both philosophies – the American and the European – strike me as acceptable. It is possible that European and American citizens simply have different preferences regarding the (lack) of regulation of CUTs and choose to express them by (not) voting for political parties willing to change the *status quo*. In what follows, I provide some arguments for more socialization of risk, based on what I perceive to be the generally ignored distributive consequences of its adoption. However, the purpose of this section – and, as a matter of fact, of this chapter – is not to land an unhelpful and most probably false claim to the effect that "Europeans do consumer contract law better than the Americans." Far from it. My goal has been instead to show, by drawing attention to the differences, (1) what the implicit normative assumptions in American consumer contract law are and (2) that a completely different philosophy is possible not only in theory but also as a matter of practice of the second-largest economy in the world.[61]

III DISTRIBUTIVE CONSEQUENCES OF (NOT) REGULATING BOILERPLATE

Boilerplate contracts (or contracts of adhesion) have been a subject of legal scholarly interest for several decades.[62] Lately, given the rise of e-commerce and the platform

[59] For a presentation of the normative background, as well as discussions of its limitations online, see: Allison Zakon, *Optimized for Addiction: Extending Product Liability Concepts to Defectively Designed Social Media Algorithms and Overcoming the Communications Decency Act*, 2020 WIS. L. REV. 1107 (2020).

[60] *See* Deborah R. Hensler, *Third-Party Financing of Class Action Litigation in the United States: Will the Sky Fall*, 63 DEPAUL L. REV. 499 (2013).

[61] The GDP of the world's largest economy, the United States, was $20,893.75 billion in 2020, whereas the third economy, China, scored $14,866.74 billion. See *The 20 Countries with the Largest Gross Domestic Product (GDP) in 2020*, STATISTA (Oct. 2021), www.statista.com/statistics/268173/countries-with-the-largest-gross-domestic-product-gdp/. The combined GDP of the EU Member States, for the same year equaled $17,078.38 billion. See *European Union: Gross Domestic Product (GDP) from 2016 to 2026*, STATISTA (Oct. 2021), www.statista.com/statistics/527869/european-union-gross-domestic-product-forecast/.

[62] For inspiring and informative early contributions, see: Friedrich Kessler, *Contracts of Adhesion – Some Thoughts about Freedom of Contract*, 43 COLUM. L. REV. 629 (1943); Albert A. Ehrenzweig, *Adhesion Contracts in the Conflict of Laws*, 53 COLUM L. REV. 1072 (1953); Arthur Lenhoff, *Contracts of Adhesion and the Freedom of Contract: A Comparative Study in the Light of American and Foreign Law*, 36 TUL. L. REV. 481 (1961); Alfred W. Meyer,

economy, many tremendous doctrinal[63] and empirical[64] works have been published. In addition, scholars have been debating the normative question of how the American law should (or should not) be reformed to better address the problems of boilerplate.

On the one hand, scholars have marshalled many arguments for stricter legal control of boilerplate clauses. Probably the most well-known account has been offered by Margaret Jane Radin in her 2013 monograph.[65] Radin, having discussed the widespread use of consumer-unfriendly terms, argues against their enforcement, as they contribute to the normative degradation[66] (the meaninglessness of "consent" and "freedom of choice") and democratic degradation[67] (replacement of the Rule of Law with the rule of the corporations) in our society and political economy. Others

Contracts of Adhesion and the Doctrine of Fundamental Breach, 50 VA. L. REV. 1178 (1964); TODD D. RAKOFF, CONTRACTS OF ADHESION: AN ESSAY IN RECONSTRUCTION (1983). For a classic symposium on the matter, see the articles discussed in Omri Ben-Shahar, *Foreword to Boilerplate: Foundations of Market Contracts Symposium*, 104 MICH. L. REV. 821 (2006).

63 See Oren Bar-Gill & Kevin Davis, *Empty Promises*, 84 S. CAL. L. REV. 1 (2010); NANCY S. KIM, WRAP CONTRACTS: FOUNDATIONS AND RAMIFICATIONS (1st ed. 2013); Nathan B. Oman, *Reconsidering Contractual Consent: Why We Shouldn't Worry Too Much about Boilerplate and Other Puzzles*, 83 BROOK. L. REV. 215 (2017); Gregory Klass, *Boilerplate and Party Intent*, 82 L. & CONTEMP. PROBS. 105 (2019); Uri Benoliel & Shmuel I. Becher, *The Duty to Read the Unreadable*, 60 B.C. L. REV. 2255 (2019).

64 For empirical studies focusing on whether consumers read boilerplate (and showing that they do not), see: Yannis Bakos et al., *Does Anyone Read the Fine Print? Consumer Attention to Standard-Form Contracts*, 43 J. LEGAL STUD. 1–35 (2014); Jonathan A. Obar & Anne Oeldorf-Hirsch, *The Biggest Lie on the Internet: Ignoring the Privacy Policies and Terms of Service Policies of Social Networking Services*, 23 INFO. COMMC'N. & SOC'Y 128–47 (2018). For contributions discussing the effect of boilerplate on the socioeconomic reality, see: Tess Wilkinson-Ryan, *The Perverse Consequences of Disclosing Standard Terms*, 103 CORNELL L. REV. 117 (2017); David A. Hoffman, *Relational Contracts of Adhesion*, 85 U. CHI. L. REV. 1395 (2018); Shmuel I. Becher & Uri Benoliel, *Sneak in Contracts*, 55 GEO. L. REV. 657–730 (2021).

65 See RADIN, *supra* note 4.

66 *Id.* at 19–32, writing:

> Our legal system adheres to an ideal of private ordering and its importance to individual freedom. Within this system, freedom of contract is a core value, and 'involuntary' or 'unfree' contract is a contradiction in terms. . . . A system in which rights could be taken from people without their consent if they were paid the alleged market price for those rights would be a major departure from our own. If our system is tending in that direction because millions of people are without their consent being made subject to boilerplate that erases important legal rights, then surely our system of contract law, in which consent is essential, is being degraded.

67 *Id.* at 33, writing:

> When a firm's mass-market boilerplate withdraws a number of important recipients' rights – such as rights of redress granted by the state, or user rights that are free of owner control under intellectual property regimes – it is displacing the legal regime enacted by the state with a governance scheme that is more favorable to the firm. It is transporting recipients to a firm's own preferred legal universe. I am not referring here to all "contracts of adhesion." Rather I mean to focus on mass-market boilerplate rights deletion schemes: the deployment of boilerplate to rework a system of recipients' rights

have followed suit. Eric Encarnacion maintains that stripping consumers of their rights via boilerplate cannot be reconciled with their dignity.[68] Yehuda Adar and Shmuel Becher argue that enforcing boilerplate clauses leads to financial and non-financial costs to consumers.[69]

On the other hand, the proponents of enforcing boilerplate in its current form usually make the arguments from efficiency and price effects.[70] The idea here is simple: By including consumer-unfriendly clauses like limitations of liability, class action waivers, mandatory arbitration, and so on, corporations lower their expected future costs of legal proceedings and therefore are able to offer their services at a lower price.[71] Since lower prices are the goal of consumer law, any legal intervention countering the achievement of that goal should be seen as anti-consumer interest. Now, without a doubt, the ability to use the abovementioned boilerplate clauses drives the costs of running a business down. The question is: Who reaps the benefits?

On its face, the argument seems to boil down to one fundamental question: Are we willing, as a political community, to tolerate boilerplate contracts stripping consumers of their rights, as long as this translates into lower consumer prices? In other words, what do we care more about: lower prices or material equality in rights and duties? This is a political question where both sides have convincing arguments and where the American and European lawmakers went in different directions.

However, there is one deeper assumption in the "price effects" view, the one I'd like to attack in this chapter. This assumption is: Lower consumer prices, resulting from consumer-unfriendly boilerplate, favor the least affluent consumers, whereas it's mostly the lawyerly elite that cares about their rights. I don't think that is correct. So let us take a closer look at this narrative.

that are guaranteed by the polity in order to divest recipients of those rights, or of some substantial portion of them, for the benefit of a firm.

68 *See* Erik Encarnacion, *Boilerplate Indignity*, 94 Ind. L.J. 1305 (2019).

69 *See* Adar & Becher, *supra* note 1 at 2405, 2422, writing:

> For example, the inability to fully recover for an injury or an expense that was unjustly imposed on the consumer may lead to feelings of frustration, anger, alienation, bitterness, and other forms of mental distress or inconvenience. In some cases, it may even result in the consumer being unable to obtain compensation for a serious personal injury or a property loss that the seller or supplier inflicted.

70 See *supra* Section I. See also: Omri Ben-Shahar, *Regulation through Boilerplate: An Apologia*, 112 Mich. L. Rev. 883, 895 (2013) (writing: "one cannot evaluate whether boilerplate deletion of legal rights is good or bad for consumers without also looking at the price people are asked to pay for the 'product + boilerplate' package.").

71 This view is, sometimes, explicitly included in the text of the boilerplate itself. For example, Bumble, a popular dating app, states "THE LIMITATION OF LIABILITY HEREIN IS A FUNDAMENTAL ELEMENT OF THE BASIS OF THE BARGAIN AND REFLECTS A FAIR ALLOCATION OF RISK. THE APP AND SITE WOULD NOT BE PROVIDED WITHOUT SUCH LIMITATIONS"; see: Bumble's Terms and Conditions, updated on Nov. 19, 2021, https://bumble.com/en/terms (caps original).

A *Standard Narrative: Unregulated Boilerplate Favors the Less Affluent*

In his review of Radin's treatise on boilerplate, Omri Ben-Shahar – labeling himself a "boilerplate apologist"[72] – encapsulated the view widespread among the proponents of the CUTs toleration, namely that they distribute wealth from the more affluent consumers to the poorer ones. Or, at least, they do not distribute it the other way round.

Ben-Shahar concedes that certain rights deleted by boilerplate contracts – to sue in one's place of residence, to seek damages for breach of contract or tort, to have control over one's data usage, and so on – are important.[73] However, he observes that deletion of these rights comes with price consequences.[74] For example, a firm that does not fear litigation (due to mandatory arbitration or choice-of-forum clauses, as well as liability and warranty waivers) will have lower costs of business. Similarly, a firm that can benefit from using consumers' data and IP will enjoy higher revenue. Hence, the price that it directly charges its consumers can be lower.

Conversely, removing the CUTs (and thereby increasing the chance of litigation) will increase business costs. The firms will shift the costs onto the consumers by charging them higher prices. When the prices are higher, the least well-off consumers will no longer be able to afford the product. As a result, the affluent members of the society will spend more money (in exchange for better legal protections) while the poorer ones will not be able to afford the product in the first place.[75]

Ben-Shahar illustrates this view by pointing to the repeat customers of Apple. Despite knowing the ToS of iOS and other software (including the infamous "iTunes EULA"), they keep buying Apple products.[76] He argues that people purchasing the iPhones are happy to be charged a lower price in exchange for their rights' limitation. Further, in Ben-Shahar's words: "it is likely that the worst deal these Apple customers can make is to purchase better legal terms from Apple."[77] In the end, most iPhones won't malfunction, and most people will not suffer any damage. So, the chance that they will have to sue is so low that keeping a right to do

[72] *See* Ben-Shahar, *supra* note 70 at 900.

[73] *Id.* at 895.

[74] *Id.*

[75] *Id.* at 896, writing:

> But self-selection is not feasible when firms cannot price differentiate, or when transaction costs constrain firms to offer a uniform package. In this situation, a desirable solution, both efficient and consistent with democratic values, is for vendors to offer the bundles that match majoritarian preferences. Allowing a small minority to impose its preferences on the majority price of consumers, by enacting rules that mandate the quality bundle that this small subgroup prefers, would likely expel many who cannot afford this package out of the market.

[76] *Id.* at 897.

[77] *Id.* at 898.

so is not worth the necessary increase in the price – especially given that it would mean pricing some consumers out of the market.

The choice of example is very telling. Ben-Shahar further writes:

> There may be a minority of citizens – I would guess part of a sophisticated elite – for whom the boilerplate rights-deletion bargain is undesirable and even offensive. For them, the degradation of consent and of legal entitlements cannot be priced. They want the right to sue in courts, they want firm accountability measured by full consequential damages for their harms, they want personal data to remain personal, and they want access to information to be regulated by intellectual property law, not by license agreements. If they must, they are willing and able to pay more for this bundle of upgrades. Unfortunately, meeting the preferences of such groups would require the entire pool of consumers, including the vast majority indifferent to such privileges, to pay more as well. And so everyone would pay for benefits that some are disproportionately likely to enjoy.[78]

According to this view, rights to receive compensation for damages, to initiate a class action, or to sue in one's state are some luxury goods that only the "sophisticated elite" wants to retain. However, most iPhone users do not need such luxuries. Notably, within this particular example, Ben-Shahar is probably right. It might just as well be the case that, if given the option to get a cheaper iPhone with CUTs, or a more expensive iPhone with consumer-friendly ToS, many people would choose the former. The question is: why?

What this argument overlooks is that Apple customers are already more affluent than many members of society. Their ability to internalize the future loss is much higher than everyone else's.[79] Hence, they can afford to be risk-tolerant in their choices.

Indeed, understood in this way, the CUTs' presence in boilerplate functions exactly the other way round than purchasing insurance. With regular insurance, many people pay some premium so that the unfortunate (and supposedly random) individual who suffers damage (through an accident or other supposedly random event) can be compensated. The premium, obviously, needs to be lower than the loss expected from the accident. It makes more sense within the insurance logic to pay some premium and receive compensation for the future loss (even if the chance of it materializing is low) than to face the uncertainty stemming from a possible high

78 *Id.* at 900.

79 See Marianne Bertrand & Emir Kamenica, *Coming Apart? Cultural Distances in the United States over Time*, 20 (2018), www.nber.org/papers/w24771 (last accessed Mar. 17, 2022) (the authors empirically show the correlation between owning an iPhone and affluence. They write "Knowing whether someone owns an iPad in 2016 allows us to guess correctly whether the person is in the top or bottom income quartile 69 percent of the time. Across all years in our data, no individual brand is as predictive of being high-income as owning an Apple iPhone in 2016.").

loss. Yet, some people do not buy insurance, even health insurance.[80] Is it because they value the premium as not worthy? Some of them. Others, however, might simply not be able to afford it.[81]

With CUTs in the boilerplate, many people decide to pay a lower price – a "negative premium" – in exchange for accepting that once a (supposedly random) individual suffers a future loss, she will not be compensated (or at least have a much lower chance of receiving compensation). Notice that, by choosing to conclude a contract modifying the default rules, consumers do act to modify the price. In this sense, when the law tolerates the CUTs, and contracts containing them are concluded, the social outcome is different than simply having consumers not buy insurance. In the latter case, they would rely on the protections provided by the statutory law but simply refrain from purchasing additional protection. In the former, they opt for lower prices by choosing to forgo the legal protections. So, instead of everyone paying a higher price, and everyone retaining a right to a class action, we all accept that most of us will not suffer damage, but once one does, she will not be able to recover it.

However – and this is crucial – someone will suffer the loss. Someone's phone will malfunction. Someone will get addicted to an app using her data to personalize the experience.[82] Someone will realize that the actual price they are being charged is higher than what they expected.[83]

The affluent consumers are better equipped to tolerate the damage. You might want to call them "cheaper cost internalizers."[84] If their phone breaks down and they cannot get it replaced, they will get upset but ultimately buy a new one. If they realize that they misunderstood a contract and are being charged a higher price than expected – they will be angry but, eventually, pay the bill and move forward. If they develop a mental health problem by interacting with a service addictive by design,

80 In 2020, 31.6 million Americans were uninsured. See: Jenny Yang, *Number of People without Health Insurance in the United States from 1997 to June 2021*, Statista (Nov. 17, 2021), www.statista.com/statistics/200955/americans-without-health-insurance/.

81 For the discussion of when consumers' purchases (or lack thereof) signify their willingness to buy, and when their ability to buy, see: Michael J. Sandel, What Money Can't Buy: The Moral Limits of Markets (2012), writing:

> But this argument is unconvincing. Even if your goal is to maximize social utility, free markets may not do so more reliably than queues. The reason is that the willingness to pay for a good does not show who values it most highly. This is because market prices reflect the ability as well as the willingness to pay. Those who most want to see Shakespeare, or the Red Sox, may be unable to afford a ticket. And in some cases, those who pay the most for tickets may not value the experience very highly at all.

82 For evidence of social media addiction, see: Vikram R. Bhargava & Manuel Velasquez, *Ethics of the Attention Economy: The Problem of Social Media Addiction*, 31 Bus. Ethics Q. 321 (2021); for a legal analysis of the problem, see: Zakon, *supra* note 59 at 1107.

83 For a discussion of "overcharge" in consumer retail markets, see: Van Loo, *supra* note 44.

84 A variation of the "cheapest cost avoider" concept introduced by Guido Calabresi. See: Guido Calabresi, The Cost of Accidents: A Legal and Economic Analysis 35–95 (2008).

they will go see a therapist. However, someone who lives paycheck to paycheck will not see the lack of ability to sue for damages as a "missing luxury." Instead, they will – very personally – experience the pain stemming from the inability to join the class action.

Yes, the presence of CUTs has price consequences. However, the beneficiaries of these consequences are not (only) the least well-off members of society. Risk-wise, they are the primary victims, subsidizing the lower price with the future losses they will incur. These lower prices seem like a good deal to the affluent consumers who, should the future loss actually occur, will get upset but ultimately accept it and move on. The story we tell ourselves – that the CUTs benefit the poor – is based on an unrealistic view of how their livelihoods are funded – paycheck to paycheck and food stamps.[85]

B *Alternative Narrative: Boilerplate Transfers Wealth from the Poorer to the Wealthier*

Let me tell you another story. Imagine you are buying a laptop and the seller gives you the following choice. You can either pay $290, but the consequence will be that one family, somewhere in the US – a family you don't know and will never meet – will go bankrupt and be forced out of their home. Or you can pay $300, and that event will not take place. What would you choose? What is the morally right option to choose?

"Why would that happen?" – you might wonder – "what is the link between me buying the laptop and someone losing their livelihood?" The seller answers: "you know, these things sometimes malfunction. There is a very low but real chance that the laptop's charger will break, burning the electric installation in the household and ruining the computer. In our boilerplate, we exclude all liability linked to the damages stemming from your use of the laptop. We also stipulate that to sue us, you need to travel all across the country. If that event happens to a family who has insurance and can easily buy another laptop, good for them. However, statistically speaking, we know that at least one poor household will have that accident happen to them. This family needs a laptop to look for jobs and for children to study. They took a payday loan to buy the product. Yet, when the installation burns (making

[85] See Mark Robert Rank et al., Poorly Understood: What America Gets Wrong about Poverty 134 (2021), https://oxford.universitypressscholarship.com/10.1093/oso/9780190881382.001.0001/oso-9780190881382 (last accessed Mar. 26, 2022) writing,

> Median wages for full- time male employees are actually lower today than they were in 1973. Furthermore, the stability of jobs has become more precarious. Likewise, the social safety net has been weakened considerably over time. As a result, greater numbers of Americans are living one paycheck away from poverty. A recent study from the Federal Reserve found that 37 percent of Americans do not have enough savings put aside to protect them from a $400 emergency.

their fridge or AC unusable), as they don't have insurance, they'll spend all the little cash they have[86] on fixing it and foreclose on the payday loan. If not for the boilerplate, the legal aid office in their state would sue us and recover the damages. But that office does not have the resources to travel out of state and challenge our exculpatory clauses, so tough luck. But don't worry, you'll never meet them and will save ten bucks!"

Of course, there are many "ifs" in this story. And, admittedly, it is a bit unfair – appealing to emotions and vilifying consumers who simply look for the lowest prices. Yet, is it fair to claim that the right to sue for damages – according to some, the bedrock of American tort law rising up to the level of a constitutional principle[87] – is a luxury good appealing only to the "lawyerly elite?"[88] Who cares about lawyers and professors? They have money; they will be fine. Why would I spend a dime to help them? Yet, if it is about helping my high school friend, a good guy who had it tough, or a vet who fought for our freedom, I might happily show some solidarity. I don't have a preference to help the well-off. I might very much have a preference for social solidarity. You see, it's all about the narrative.

However, maybe the price effect of having the CUTs in boilerplate is not $10 but $100 on one laptop. Then, indeed, some people would be priced out of the market, and the problem becomes much more nuanced. This is an empirical question, an answer to which will depend on the specific circumstances. Yet, what is clear is that the more people chip in, the smaller the effect on the price will be. If everyone buys insurance, the premium goes down. Hence, it will be cheaper to help the unfortunate folks who suffer future damage if everybody pays the premium. Can we expect that of the individual consumers?

I think it is immoral to do so. Why should a consumer – often struggling herself – bear the weight of the moral choice of paying more to show solidarity or not? This is where the government should step in. If we mandate the "insurance" by making the CUTs unenforceable – as we already do with product-safety legislation – people won't need to decide whether they want to subsidize the future legal recourse of a

[86] Let us remember that more than one-third of Americans cannot afford more than $400 in emergency spending. *Id.*

[87] *See* John C. P. Goldberg & Benjamin C. Zipursky, Recognizing Wrongs 31 (2020), writing:

> The idea behind the principle of civil recourse is straightforward. Our legal system recognizes in various ways that each of us is entitled to be free of certain kinds of interferences [or to have certain things done for us]. The more serious government is about enjoining these interferences, and the more serious each of us is about complying with the relevant norms of conduct, the more powerful is the argument that rights are at stake. When a right of this sort is violated, the victim should be able to demand certain things from the wrongdoer. Yet a demand of this kind would be hollow if the wrongdoer were simply free to ignore it. Thus, the state renders the victim's demand legally enforceable, so long as it is authenticated through the judicial process. In opening courthouse doors, government gives victims an avenue of civil recourse.

[88] *See* Ben-Shahar, *supra* note 70 at 900.

poor household. They will simply have to do so when buying the product. Will this be contrary to the preferences of some individuals? Certainly yes. But should the law honor the preference for a marginally lower price if the consequence of meeting that preference is that someone will, without their fault, lose their livelihood? I am far from certain.

This is the logic of the European consumer contract law. This is what the "socialization of risk"[89] means in practice. And yes, some very affluent people would also benefit from it. A law professor will sue Apple if she wishes to, and all the iPhone users will have subsidized her right to do so. At the same time, a poor household whose livelihood depends on the legal aid office's ability to sue for damages will not go bankrupt. And all the consumers will have subsidized this ability as well.

IV POSSIBLE WAYS OUT

The primary aim of this chapter has been to get the idea across. My goal has been to demonstrate that the distributive consequences of enforcing the CUTs in boilerplate are such that the least-well-off consumers disproportionately bear the costs and subsidize those more affluent in the situations where injuries actually materialize. I believe that the stories we tell ourselves, and the paradigmatic examples we rely on, do influence the political process. For the CUTs to go, people need to want them to go. How exactly this goal is achieved concerns me less. Yet, it just so happens that in legal scholarship, one's expected to offer solutions to the problems one identifies. In the remainder of the chapter, I suggest some possible pathways. However, I'd like the reader to bear the distinction in mind – just because one might disagree with any of the means listed below, it should not yet translate into questioning the ultimate goal.

A *A Direct Challenge to CUTs in Boilerplate*

The first possibility is for the law to render the CUTs in the boilerplate void/illegal directly. One can conceive of two pathways: legislative intervention and common law. Let us look at each.

The most straightforward move would be to adopt legislation akin to the EU's Unfair Terms Directive.[90] Such an act could outlaw unfair terms as a matter of a general clause (like the EU does) or just focus on specific categories of CUTs. This is the classic "standards vs. rules" problem.[91] The latter approach could single out

89 *See* HOWELLS ET AL., *supra* note 48 at 8.

90 The idea has been discussed in American legal scholarship. See, e.g., RADIN, *supra* note 4 at 233–39; Adar & Becher, *supra* note 1 at 2431–32.

91 For the classic treatment of the subject, see Pierre Schlag, *Rules and Standards*, 33 UCLA L. REV. 379 (1985); see also: Louis Kaplow, *Rules versus Standards: An Economic Analysis*, 42 DUKE L.J. 557 (1992).

the most harmful clauses, like class action waivers or exclusion of tortious liability, without creating the legal uncertainty associated with newly adopted vague norms. It does risk, however, that businesses will try to game the system by creating new hurdles in their boilerplate.

Further, one could imagine both a federal statute outlawing the CUTs in the whole country and state legislatures experimenting with different approaches. The appeal of the former is that consumers would receive equal protection regardless of their place of domicile. The problem, on top of the difficulty of having such an act pass through Congress, is that, once passed (in a compromise version), further interventions on the state level could be preempted. The appeal of states acting in their own capacity, on the other hand, is the ability to observe the effects of such a law on prices and consumer disputes.[92] Maybe the "boilerplate apologists" are correct, and the effects on prices would be immense. Or perhaps, as the examples of countries having such legislation in place seem to suggest, the impact would be minimal. We do not know yet, though we could test this.

There is also the institutional choice to be made. Should we rely solely on courts to enforce such statutes, or are there reasons to engage in administrative oversight akin to the "abstract control" in the EU? The latter approach has been recently suggested by Yehuda Adar and Shmuel Becher.[93] Among several reasons to favor it, like speed or expertise, administrative oversight would also help eliminate the "in terrorem" clauses that, as of today, companies can include in the boilerplate without costs.[94]

However, legislative intervention is not the only path forward. Fortunately, one might say, given how difficult it would be to have it passed (at least on the federal level). Several suggestions on how common law could step up to combat the CUTs have been suggested in the literature.

Nancy Kim, writing specifically about online "wrap" contracts, suggested reconsidering the rules on assent to boilerplate.[95] As of today, courts look at boilerplate contracts as either assented to by consumers in toto or not assented to at all and thereby not binding.[96] To throw away an entire agreement, with all the consequences of doing so, is a difficult decision for a judge. Yet, if a court could find some clauses null and void because a consumer had no idea they were there, it could be more willing to step in. What would be the material ground to question some of the clauses?

[92] The "law as a product" approach. See Roberta Romano, *Law as a Product: Some Pieces of the Incorporation Puzzle*, 1 J. L. Econ. & Org. 225 (1985).

[93] See Adar & Becher, *supra* note 1 at 2441–60.

[94] Marks, *supra* note 36.

[95] Kim, *supra* note 63 at 193.

[96] *Id.* (writing "The problems created by contracts of adhesion in general, and wrap contracts in particular, stem from contract law's failure to provide a middle ground between assent and no assent").

Kim suggests reinvigorating the common law doctrine of unconscionability. As of today, the threshold for declaring a clause unconscionable is very high, as both procedural and substantive grounds need to be established. However, the courts (and the Restatement) have spelled out these requirements in a different socio-economic reality. The same high-level goals would possibly be better advanced by a different reading of the unconscionability doctrine.[97]

Margaret Jane Radin has advanced another interesting idea for common law, relying on tort rather than contract. Why would one do so when dealing with boilerplate? Radin writes:

> Receipt of boilerplate is often more like an accident than a bargain. What follows from this fact for legal oversight of boilerplate? Bargains come under contract law; accidents come under tort law.[98]

This, admittedly, is a bit of a stretch, but only a bit. As a matter of fact, consumers neither read the boilerplate nor know what's in there, not to mention that they often have no real choice. So you "bump into" your boilerplate as much as you accept it. Under Radin's conception, the courts should start recognizing the tort of "intentional deprivation of basic legal rights."[99] In her words:

> A firm that imposes severe remedy deletions of rights that are at least partially market-inalienable, under circumstances of nonconsent and mass-market distribution, could be liable in tort for intentional deprivation of basic legal rights (…) [P]reliminary suggestion is that a purported contract containing offending boilerplate should be declared invalid in toto, and recipients should instead be governed by the back-ground legal default rules.[100]

Relying on tort rather than contract common law comes with the same advantage as the "abstract control" under statutory law. One does not need to go to court to remove the CUTs from the boilerplate. Simply including such clauses, regardless of whether actual harm has materialized or not, is sufficient for the legal system to step in.

[97] *Id.* at 208, In Kim's words:

> I propose that the doctrine of unconscionability be looked at more holistically. Although consistent with the sliding-scale approach, it would not require an express finding of both procedural and substantive unconscionability. Unconscionability in many cases cannot be so easily divided. Courts are generally reluctant to assess the substance of terms. Furthermore, substantive unconscionability relies on norms which may be inappropriate in wrap contracting scenarios. Norms reflected in online terms may not evidence fairness or efficient business practices; rather they may be the product of anticompetitiveness. Standard terms that are adopted by all companies in a market segment result in de facto term fixing that, like price fixing, is suboptimal and eliminates consumer choice.

[98] Radin, *supra* note 4 at 197.

[99] *Id.* at 211.

[100] *Id.* at 211–13.

The last interesting proposal – aimed less at having the law remove the CUTs from the boilerplate but rather at facilitating market pressure – comes, again, from Nancy Kim. Noticing that courts impose the "duty to read" on consumers,[101] Kim believes that a corresponding duty – the duty to "draft reasonably" – should befall the businesses:

> The standard of reasonable drafting would require that businesses take specific measures to make their contracts noticeable. There are several aspects to this duty to draft reasonably. The first is visibility. The terms should be presented to attract the attention of the nondrafting party (. . .) The second aspect of reasonable drafting is that the drafting party should make reasonable efforts to present the terms in a way that makes it likely that the other party will *read* them, not simply *see* them (. . .) Another final aspect of the duty to draft reasonably is testing. There are many ways that companies can test the effectiveness of their contracts.[102]

With a reasonably drafted contract, consumers would be more aware of what exactly they assent to. This approach sees the market, not the law, as the primary vehicle for combatting the CUTs. Let us then look at that alternative.

B *Indirect Challenges: More Competition*

As already discussed, the EU has put in place a substantive regulation of consumer contracts, rendering the CUTs unenforceable and, sometimes, actively combating their continued use. Moreover, European consumers enjoy the "right to withdrawal," that is, a right to walk back from a contract, without any reason, for up to fourteen days after concluding it.[103] Further, consumers also enjoy sector-specific rights. For example, airline passengers have a right to compensation (ranging from 250 to 600 euro per person, depending on the distance) if their flight is delayed more than three hours.[104] All these measures clearly come with price effects, don't they?

Here's a puzzle: air travel in Europe is cheaper than in the US.[105] The last flight I took from Krakow PL to Bologna IT (600 miles) in March 2022 cost $20 each way. Cell phone contracts and data plans are cheaper as well.[106] My unlimited data, calls,

[101] For a discussion of the doctrinal arguments behind the duty to read, see: Benoliel & Becher, *supra* note 63 at 2260–66.

[102] Kim, *supra* note 63 at 186–89 (emphasis original).

[103] For an overview and discussion, see: Marco B. M. Loos, *The Modernization of European Consumer Law (Continued): More Meat on the Bone after All*, 28 Eur. Rev. Priv. L. (2020).

[104] See Jeremias Prassl, *Reforming Air Passenger Rights in the European Union*, 39 Air & Space L. (2014).

[105] *See* Rick Noack, *Why Are Flights So Much Cheaper in Europe than in the U.S.?*, Washington Post, www.washingtonpost.com/news/worldviews/wp/2017/10/12/why-are-flights-so-much-cheaper-in-europe-than-in-the-u-s/ (last accessed Mar. 30, 2022).

[106] *See* Sam Morris, *Are Your Country's Cellphone Plans a Rip-Off? – The Markup*, https://themarkup.org/2020/09/03/cost-speed-of-mobile-data-by-country (last accessed Mar. 30, 2022).

and texts cellphone plan in Poland costs $20 a month. Of course, some things – like fast food – are more expensive (not least because of the value-added tax in most EU countries), but life in Germany is generally cheaper than life in the US.[107] And this is the case despite the fact that European businesses cannot rely on the CUTs available to their American counterparts. How is that possible?

The answer is obviously complex, but one part of the explanation is competition. With its more fragmented market, paired with the European Commission's strict approach to antitrust enforcement and merger control, Europe's markets see many more companies fighting for a consumer than in America.[108] And the cost of compliance with strict consumer protection law is not high enough to render European consumer prices higher than in the US.

From this perspective, competition can be seen to fulfill two objectives: offsetting the costs of consumer rights' regulation or substituting this regulation in the first place. What could the latter look like? If we assume that people care about their rights not being taken away, and assume a competitive market, then we should observe corporations competing on their standard terms' consumer-friendliness. Both assumptions are bold, not to say counterfactual.

What would be needed for competition-in-pro-consumer-terms are (i) preferences and (ii) knowledge. Could we get people to care? Could we do something for consumers to develop a preference for fair boilerplate? The narrative presented in this chapter is one possible piece in the quest to do so. "By preferring a consumer-friendly boilerplate, you're doing your part!" a nicely done video about a family being able to recover after their home burned down could state.

As for knowledge – that is, consumers' understanding of the available boilerplates' contents – technology, discussed towards the very beginning of the chapter, could be helpful. Natural language processing-powered applications can be used not only to assess the fairness of boilerplate under some legal standards but could also (i) summarize them[109] or (ii) look at them purely from the consumers' interest point of view.[110] It is not at all clear that consumers should learn about the contents of boilerplate by reading them – why not learn it from a summary/evaluation prepared by a third party?

[107] *See* Cost of living in Germany compared to United States, www.mylifeelsewhere.com/cost-of-living/germany/united-states (last accessed Mar. 30, 2022).

[108] For a tremendous overview of data, as well as the analysis of legal and economic causes, see: Thomas Philippon, The Great Reversal: How America Gave Up on Free Markets (First Printing edition 2019).

[109] *See* Razieh Nokhbeh Zaeem et al., *PrivacyCheck: Automatic Summarization of Privacy Policies Using Data Mining*, 18 ACM Trans. Internet Technol. 53:1–53:18 (2018); Hamza Harkous et al., *Polisis: Automated Analysis and Presentation of Privacy Policies Using Deep Learning*, arXiv:1802.02561 [cs] (2018), http://arxiv.org/abs/1802.02561.

[110] *See* Yonathan Arbel & Shmuel Becher, *Contracts in the Age of Smart Readers*, 90 Geo. Wash. L. Rev. 84–146 (2022).

As for the competitiveness of markets, we're currently in an era that several commentators have dubbed the "new gilded age."[111] The Federal Trade Commission (FTC) allowed several controversial mergers to go through, and the market concentration is very high in some sectors. A revival of a more interventionist antitrust doctrine is one possible path to stopping or reversing this trend.[112] This, however, is a whole separate discussion to be had, beyond the argument of this chapter.

V CONCLUSION

"Maybe they shouldn't be illegal," – said my colleague in the Fall of 2018 about the terms considered "unfair" by the EU – "don't consumers prefer to have them in, in exchange for lower prices?"

Some do. The question is: Should the law, or should we as a society, honor this preference? In this chapter, I provided one argument for the negative answer: Unregulated boilerplate might lead to lower prices, but once an accident befalls a consumer unable to internalize the damage, me saving a couple of bucks seems irrelevant when someone else is losing their home. We should stop repeating the story according to which all "the consumers" benefit from the price effects of boilerplate, while the only losers are the "lawyerly elite" whose preference for having an ability to sue is not met. The real victims of boilerplate are the least affluent among us, who won't be able to shake off an accident as a small nuisance, and will suffer the consequences of the affluent consumers' preference for lower prices.

What exactly is the best way for the CUTs to go away is of secondary importance to me. I'm sure that technological advances can support the quest for market pressure. Personally, I believe that legal intervention – either legislative or by the courts – is necessary. Yet, I'm happy to be proven wrong. What matters, for now, is the realm of the mind: If we believe that the CUTs cannot be tolerated, the first step in the process is behind us. It's my hope that, with this chapter, I've convinced at least some readers to subscribe to this view.

[111] See Rahman, *supra* note 53; TIM WU, THE CURSE OF BIGNESS: ANTITRUST IN THE NEW GILDED AGE (Illustrated ed. 2018).

[112] For a paper widely seen as the first big splash, see: Lina Khan, Amazon's Antitrust Paradox, 126 Yale L.J. 712–802 (2016), https://digitalcommons.law.yale.edu/ylj/vol126/iss3/3; see also, Ramsi A. Woodcock, *Big Data, Price Discrimination, and Antitrust*, 68 HASTINGS L.J. 1371 (2016); Jonathan B. Baker et al., *Unlocking Antitrust Enforcement*, 127 YALE L.J. 1916 (2017); WU, *supra* note 111; HERBERT HOVENKAMP, *The Warren Campaign's Antitrust Proposals* (2019), https://papers.ssrn.com/abstract=3353716 (last accessed Feb. 1, 2021); Herbert Hovenkamp & Fiona Scott Morton, *Framing the Chicago School of Antitrust Analysis*, *in* FACULTY SCHOLARSHIP AT PENN LAW (2019), https://scholarship.law.upenn.edu/faculty_scholarship/2113.

7

(How) Does Competition Law Address Quality?

Adrian Kuenzler

CONTENTS

In the digital economy, quality is increasingly becoming the predominant variable of competition. Markets are expected to seek out that state of affairs in which product quality rather than efficiency is maximized. But an effective conceptual resolution of what constitutes product quality is more complex and elusive than previously thought, and there has been a widespread repudiation of the notion that dominant online platforms can be held accountable for failing to deliver something that a single descriptive standard would command them to produce. Furthermore, microeconomic theory provides little guidance for evaluating how adjustments in the level of competition in a market have a bearing on product quality. This chapter suggests that claims relating to product quality can best be resolved by underscoring loyalty. Product quality, viewed from this perspective, provides a framework for assessing the behavior of digital platforms while at the same time legitimizing the manner in which zero-price markets operate. The issue is most prominent with regard to search engine rankings, privacy, and the sale of goods in online marketplaces.

I INTRODUCTION

The emergence of big technology platforms that collect near-exclusive information about their users increasingly presents a puzzle to scholars of competition law. How can competition be maintained when much of today's technology sectors are governed by a few influential titans? The issue reaches deep into the origins of antitrust, when a consensus view materialized that the most analytically sound legal test for assessing antitrust liability was based on a perspicuous output/profitability method.[1] While output/profitability reasoning lies at the heart of maximizing Kaldor–Hicks efficiency,[2] the notion that a basic trade-off between positive and negative efficiencies exists in competition law was first recognized by Robert Bork and Oliver Williamson in the 1960s and was firmly established in its most administrable form by Richard Posner in the 1980s.[3] According to this view, the extent to which a restraint increases or decreases competition is assessed by looking at its consequences, rather than at the presence or absence of a particular type of rivalry. This method involves a simple determination of whether the restriction caused the firm's output to rise or fall: If the firm's output expands, the restriction must have made its product more appealing to consumers overall, permitting the firm to take business from its competitors. This equates to an increase in consumer welfare – the desired end result – given that the increase exceeds any net reduction in competition. Any reduction in competition, on its own, would increase the price to consumers and make the product less appealing. If, all in all, the product is more

1 For overview see A Kuenzler, *Restoring Consumer Sovereignty: How Markets Manipulate Us and What the Law Can Do about It* (New York: Oxford University Press, 2017) 221–63.

2 N Kaldor, "Welfare Propositions of Economics and Interpersonal Comparisons of Utility" (1939) 49 *Economic Journal*, 549; JR Hicks, "The Foundations of Welfare Economics" (1939) 49 *Economic Journal*, 696.

3 RH Bork, "The Rule of Reason and the Per Se Concept: Price Fixing and Market Division" (1965) 74 *Yale Law Journal*, 775; OE Williamson, "Economies as an Antitrust Defense: The Welfare Tradeoffs" (1968) 58 *American Economic Review*, 18; RA Posner, "The Next Step in the Antitrust Treatment of Restricted Distribution: Per Se Legality" (1981) 48 *University of Chicago Law Review*, 6; RA Posner, "The Rule of Reason and the Economic Approach: Reflections on the Sylvania Decision" (1977) 45 *University of Chicago Law Review*, 1. This chapter employs the term "competition law" rather than "antitrust," to incorporate insights and experiences gained from both US and European perspectives.

desirable to the firm's customers – as demonstrated by the fact that more of it is sold – the net effect of the restraint on competition must be positive.[4]

The method is based on three, albeit unstated, basic principles.[5] First, it is assumed that a consumer's maximization of utility is revealed by their own purchasing behavior;[6] second, consumer welfare rests on a neutral principle of promoting efficiency insofar as it ensures that the market itself caters faithfully and relevantly to consumers' tastes;[7] and third, competition provides a significant check on the exploitation of market power because of the ability of consumers to switch to different alternative offers.[8]

Though an overwhelming number of competition authorities and courts have endorsed output/profitability thinking, commentators have pointed out that its assumptions no longer hold, at least not unreservedly, in light of a growing degree of market concentration, product customization, personalization, and consumer segmentation.[9] Particularly in the digital economy where efficiencies of scale and scope, including network effects, are key, consumers are frequently better off when different product features are integrated in one single company rather than when they have to choose between distinct units.[10] Consumers tend to congregate around the biggest platforms, although they might be dissatisfied with (some of) their services.[11] As the platforms' underlying networks expand, the value consumers obtain in turn accretes because more users take advantage of the platform's offerings and the number of compatible ecosystem products grows.[12] Consumers understand the exceptional benefits they derive from the products offered by companies such as Facebook, Amazon, Apple, and Google; most of them are directly the result of the

4 Ibid.

5 Kuenzler (n 1), 3–22.

6 PA Samuelson, "A Note on the Pure Theory of Consumer's Behaviour" (1938) 5 *Economica*, 61.

7 DH Ginsburg, "Originalism and Economic Analysis: Two Case Studies of Consistency and Coherence in Supreme Court Decision Making" (2010) 33 *Harvard Journal of Law and Public Policy*, 217.

8 NW Averitt and RH Lande, "Consumer Choice: The Practical Reason for Both Antitrust and Consumer Protection Law" (1998) 10 *Loyola Consumer Law Review*, 44.

9 See most prominently JE Stiglitz, *People, Power, and Profits: Progressive Capitalism for an Age of Discontent* (New York: Allen Lane, 2019); T Wu, *The Curse of Bigness: Antitrust in the New Gilded Age* (New York: Columbia Global Reports, 2018); LM Khan, "Amazon's Antitrust Paradox" (2017) 126 *Yale Law Journal*, 710; Z Teachout and LM Khan, "Market Structure and Political Law: A Taxonomy of Power" (2014) 9 *Duke Journal of Constitutional Law and Public Policy*, 37.

10 F Jenny, "Competition Law and Digital Ecosystems: Learning to Walk before We Run" (2021) 30 *Industrial and Corporate Change*, 1143; GL Priest, "The Antitrust Attack on Big Tech" (2021) *Competition Policy International*, March 19, 2021, 1.

11 J Rochet and J Tirole, "Platform Competition in Two-Sided Markets" (2003) 1 *Journal of the European Economic Association*, 990; J Rochet and J Tirole, "Two-Sided Markets: A Progress Report" (2006) 37 *RAND Journal of Economics*, 645.

12 M Katz and C Shapiro, "Network Externalities, Competition, and Compatibility" (1985) 75 *American Economic Review*, 424.

platforms' magnitude. As other users join or utilize those platforms, the platforms become better at creating users' profiles and at offering personalized experiences.[13] In turn, however, there is a reduction in the ability of consumers – and/or indeed their willingness – to migrate to other offers and an increase in barriers to entry for new competitors, while the quantity and quality of the platforms' data bring about an even greater level of control for leading actors, along with a heightened risk of petrifying existing business models that depend – almost exclusively – on maximizing revenue from collecting and selling users' data.[14] Here, consumers' choices can no longer be equated with established output/profitability principles. In markets without a price, competition turns upon quality and innovation, but the perception of quality by consumers typically differs widely between them.[15] What is more, product manufacturers and sellers, through new technologies, are frequently in a position to sway consumers' choices and to limit their ability to meaningfully influence market supply.[16] Given the almost limitless ways in which an increase in output can be justified in these circumstances, big technology companies may rationalize almost any selling strategy under the revealed preferences approach.[17] In concentrated markets, there is thus a rift between consumer choices as we find them and the maximization of consumer welfare. Several recent competition investigations attest to this observation, particularly in relation to the limitations of the policies of big technology platforms when it comes to catering faithfully and relevantly to consumers' tastes, and in relation to the frequent lack of effective avenues of influence available to consumers, such as switching. At this point, competition law's primary task, to expand output, inexorably falls short of acting as a conclusive gauge for effective competition.

Certainly, some competition law commentary has been reluctant to depart from output/profitability reasoning based on Kaldor–Hicks efficiency. The argument is that most criticisms involving big technology platforms – relating, first and foremost, to their management of user privacy, their policies of giving preference to their own related services, or the spread of misinformation – do not concern competition law issues that would traditionally arise in an industrial or manufacturing scenario. In keeping with the existing standard of assessment, such criticisms arguably neglect the network character of the online industry where enhanced size affords apparent benefits to each participant.[18] While it is acknowledged that in theory there is some point at which the network benefits gained from adding additional parties will begin

[13] Ibid.

[14] P Belleflamme and M Peitz, *The Economics of Platforms: Concepts and Strategy* (New York: Cambridge University Press, 2021).

[15] A Hirschman, *Exit, Voice, and Loyalty: Responses to Decline in Firms, Organizations, and States* (Cambridge, MA: Harvard University Press, 1970).

[16] A Ezrachi and ME Stucke, *Virtual Competition: The Promise and Perils of the Algorithm-Driven Economy* (Cambridge, MA: Harvard University Press, 2016).

[17] Kuenzler (n 1).

[18] See sources quoted (n 11).

to diminish, it is evidently difficult, if not impossible in practice, to determine what that size actually is or at which point the benefits begin to taper.[19] The result of this indeterminacy is that the market authorizes big technology platforms such as Google, Amazon, Facebook, and Apple to engage in allegedly anticompetitive practices because the network benefits that these platforms generate are more significant than the disadvantages from scale, even if these practices entail a marginally higher cost for the economy overall than if they were condemned by a competition authority or a court (an issue that therefore would be better dealt with by other means than competition law).[20] Indeed, any application of competition law to big technology platforms would risk compromising the financial returns expected to be gained from the creation and maintenance of these platforms, and would reduce the incentive for companies to create new platforms in the future.[21]

These observations notwithstanding, competition authorities and courts are increasingly investigating – and have condemned – the platforms' most contested practices. Such authorities and courts ostensibly assume that there is a role for competition law to play in concentrated market settings despite the law's traditional emphasis on price and output.[22] By acting upon this assumption, the authorities and courts have proposed a shift, albeit implicitly, in legal doctrine from efficiency to wealth distribution.[23] In particular, the investigations have raised the issue of

[19] Ibid.

[20] See, for an overview, N Petit, *Big Tech and the Digital Economy: The Moligopoly Scenario* (New York: Oxford University Press, 2020); H Hovenkamp, "Is Antitrust's Consumer Welfare Principle Imperiled?" (2019) 45 *Journal of Corporation Law*, 65; JD Wright, E Dorsey, GA Manne, JM Rybnicek, and K Stout, "Consumer Welfare and the Rule of Law: The Case against the New Populist Antitrust Movement" (2020) 47 *Pepperdine Law Review*, 861.

[21] N Petit and DJ Teece, "Innovating Big Tech Firms and Competition Policy: Favoring Dynamic over Static Competition" (2021) 30 *Industrial and Corporate Change*, 1168.

[22] Bundeskartellamt, Decision of 6 February 2019, B6–22/16; OLG Düsseldorf, Order of 26 August 2019, VI-Kart 1/19 (V); Bundesgerichtshof (June 23, 2020) KVR 69/19 DE: BGH:2020:230620BKVR69.19.0; European Commission, Case AT.39740 Google Search (Shopping) [2017], paras. 378–398; Case T-612/17, Google and Alphabet v. Commission (Google Shopping), November 10, 2021, paras. 456–459; Federal Trade Commission, "FTC Sues Facebook for Illegal Monopolization" (2020) Press Release, December 9, 2020; Attorney General of Texas, "AG Paxton Files Antitrust Lawsuit against Facebook" (2020) Press Release, December 9, 2020; Attorney General of Texas, "AG Paxton Leads Multistate Coalition in Lawsuit against Google for Anticompetitive Practices and Deceptive Misrepresentations" (2020) Press Release, December 16, 2020; Second Amended Complaint, "In re: Google Digital Advertising Antitrust Litigation" (2021) Civil Action No.: 1:21-md-03010-PKC, October 22, 2021; Competition and Markets Authority, "CMA to Investigate Google's 'Privacy Sandbox' Browser Changes" (2021) Press Release, January 8, 2021; European Commission, "Commission Opens Investigation into Possible Anticompetitive Conduct by Google in the Online Advertising Technology Sector" (2021) Press Release, June 22, 2021; Thibault Larger and Laura Kayali, "Brussels Zeroes in on Google's AdTech Business" (2021) Politico, January 19, 2021; Sebastian Herrera, "Facebook to Counter Apple Privacy Update with Its Own Prompt" (2021) The Wall Street Journal, February 1, 2021, sec Tech.

[23] See, for a conceptual overview, RA Woodcock, "The Antitrust Duty to Charge Low Prices" (2018) 39 *Cardozo Law Review*, 1741; specifically A Kuenzler "Competition Law as a Catalyst

whether, and to what extent, competition law can help to ground the market's state of equilibrium on a notion that is characterized less by the business strategies of a small number of leading actors and more by the consumers' actual preferences, and whether competition law can simultaneously remain focused on the goal of preserving effective competition.[24]

This chapter explores that possibility. More precisely, it focuses on two main issues that expose a peculiar disjunct between conventional output/profitability thinking and the mechanisms that lie beneath concentrated markets with a zero price. The first issue concerns the observation that disagreement about what constitutes product quality regularly features prominently in the digital economy. Competition ordinarily is cast in terms of price and output, and much legal scholarship views digital markets in this way. Since the absence of prices is typically thought to be an issue to be cleared rather than as a facet to be acclaimed, ambiguity about what product quality entails lurks quietly in the background – although it essentially drives competition law analysis in these instances. But if the notion of product quality is ambiguous, how can quality guide competition authorities and courts in concrete cases? The second issue concerns the observation that in concentrated market settings, where consumer switching turns out to be ineffective or unattainable, an intensified extent of administrative action may serve the same or similar ends as those ordinarily represented by switching. Much legal scholarship is preoccupied with the idea that switching is the only disciplining mechanism on market actors' behavior, to the degree that leading platforms should permit consumers to relocate their data from one platform to another.[25] Most proposals

for Collective Market Governance: Gauging the Discursive Benefits of Intensified Administrative Action" (2022) 41 *Yearbook of European Law*, 252.

[24] H Hovenkamp, "Antitrust Harm and Causation" (2021) 99 *Washington University Law Review*, 787; JM Steinbaum and ME Stucke, "The Effective Competition Standard: A New Standard for Antitrust" (2019) 86 *University of Chicago Law Review*, 595; T Wu, "After Consumer Welfare, Now What? The 'Protection of Competition' Standard in Practice," *Competition Policy International*, October 7, 2018; D Wright and DH Ginsburg, "The Goals of Antitrust: Welfare Trumps Choice" (2013) 81 *Fordham Law Review*, 2405. Note that if consumer welfare is understood as the difference between price and quality, an increase in quality that is captured entirely by consumers is going to increase their share of the gains from trade.

[25] J Krämer, "Personal Data Portability in the Platform Economy: Economic Implications and Policy Recommendations" (2020) 17 *Journal of Competition Law and Economics*, 263; D Rubinfeld, "Data Portability" (2020) *Competition Policy International*, November 26, 2020; H Schweitzer and R Welker, "A Legal Framework for Access to Data – A Competition Policy Perspective" (2020); P de Hert et al., "The Right to Data Portability in the GDPR: Towards User-Centric Interoperability of Digital Services" (2018) 34 *Computer Law & Security Review*, 193; W Kerber, "Data Sharing in IoT Ecosystems and Competition Law: The Example of Connected Cars" (2019) 15 *Journal of Competition Law and Economics*, 381. Some major big technology companies have ardently supported this proposition, advancing their own industrial and partisan standards; M Zuckerberg, "The Internet Needs New Rules: Let's Start in These Four Areas," *Washington Post*, March 29, 2019; M Zuckerberg, "A Privacy-Focused Vision for Social Networking," Facebook, March 6, 2019; "13 Ways the Government Went after Google, Facebook and Other Tech Giants This Year," *The New York Times*, December 16, 2020. As a

naturally fit into two groups. One is about *entitlements*: Existing regulation should afford consumers a right to switch – to enable them to transfer data that they share to another platform, and, in so doing, animate rivalry by lowering barriers to entry, facilitating portability, and enabling new firms to compete.[26] The other is about *market structure*: Policymakers are concerned that the marketplace itself provides consumers with adequate opportunities to switch. The solutions they present almost inevitably involve forcing big technology companies to separate from (some of) their essential services and/or imposing mandatory interoperability.[27] Both approaches seek to reestablish competition, by rendering users' data portable and competing firms' services interoperable, and by pushing concentrated power out to the ends of the Internet, defying any consolidated arrangement around small groups of dominant undertakings, as if no alternative solutions existed. Portability provides consumers with an entitlement to switch; structural separation and/or interoperability affords consumers the ability to choose between different alternative offers by adjusting market structure. Both remedies are geared toward reinstating switching.[28] And switching is thought to be indispensable for maintaining product quality, facilitating privacy, and spurring new innovation.[29]

But entitlement-based and structural remedies are not the only possibilities – perhaps at times not even the most useful ones – that exist for consumers to exercise authority. In concentrated market settings, consumers can exercise control over product manufacturers and sellers by temporarily helping to administer them. Consumers' preferences can best be put into effect if users challenge, contest, and modify their favored segment – where no effective opportunity (or indeed willingness) to switch persists. The exercise of such authority, typically facilitated by means of an intensified extent of administrative action, constitutes an *institutional avenue*

consequence, switching is viewed as the main rejoinder to assuage policymakers' apprehensions about weakened competition in big technology markets.

26 Regulation (EU) 2016/679 of 27 April 2016 on the Protection of Natural Persons with Regard to the Processing of Personal Data and on the Free Movement of Such Data (General Data Protection Regulation), OJ L 119/1; Stigler Center for the Study of the Economy and the State, "Stigler Committee on Digital Platforms: Final Report" (Chicago, 2019), 16–18.

27 European Commission, "A European Strategy for Data" (Communication) COM(2020) 66 final, 11–20; G Parker, G Petropoulos, and M van Alstyne, "Digital Platforms, Market Power and Antitrust: A Proposal towards Efficient Information Sharing" (2020). Data portability commonly is referred to as the ability to transfer data without affecting its content while interoperability denotes the ability to integrate multiple datasets. The latter is bilateral and revolves around competitors aligning their products while the former is unilateral and is about consumers moving their data between platforms. Both significantly affect the use of data, with important implications for competition law; MS Gal and D Rubinfeld, "Data Standardization" (2019) 94 *New York University Law Review*, 737.

28 Both can be legislated or ordered by an authority or court.

29 For an overview, see UK Digital Competition Expert Panel, "Unlocking Digital Competition" (London, 2019); FTC, "Hearings on Competition and Consumer Protection in the 21st Century: Privacy, Big Data, and Competition" (Washington, DC, 2018).

of influence; it ensures that in concentrated marketplaces, consumers can determine market outcomes to a significant degree.

As policymaking aides, consumers can contest a segment from the inside rather than defy it from the outside. A competition authority or court can amend a dominant platform's terms and conditions of agreement that they find to be anticompetitive; they can modify portions of a platform's mode of operation to create incentives for rival actors to compete in relation to features that consumers truly value. Portability and structural separation are not the only paths of influence for consumers to pursue in concentrated market settings. Consumers can employ agency when they engage in their ongoing disagreement with the platform's offers through institutional channels of influence.[30]

The chapter is structured as follows. Sections II and III deal with the first issue; Sections IV and V elaborate upon the second one. The chapter first sets out the general instances in which the concept of product quality appears most prominently in digital marketplaces and demonstrates that employment of the term is essentially contestable and contested, allowing for a number of different kinds of possible use (Section II). It then sheds light on the concept from a novel perspective – that of loyalty and agency – describing the implications of this perspective for competition law in digital markets (Section III). Moving on, the chapter looks more closely at the notion of loyalty and considers why competition law has largely overlooked loyalty as an essential avenue of consumer influence (Section IV). The last part highlights the manner in which loyalty intersects with entitlement-based and structural remedies as an alternative channel of consumer influence in data-driven marketplaces (Section V). The chapter concludes with a brief summary of findings (Section VI).

II THE GENERAL PROBLEM

From a competition law perspective, the main issue with zero-price markets is that quality, unlike price, is predisposed to be contested for a variety of reasons. That is, there is typically no agreement between those who engage the concept and those who dispute its usefulness for application in competition law analysis as to whether quality is negatively affected by certain aspects of a firm's behavior. To pick an example, if an ordinary consumer good is offered at too high a price, a customer will refuse to pay for it because it lacks economic value, and there are usually no further quarrels as to the article's proper utility and function.[31] But if a *service* is said to be of low quality, the issue is apt to be contested, particularly if appreciation of the service differs widely among consumers, and if there is disagreement with respect to how it

[30] J Krämer, P Senellart, and A de Streel, "Making Data Portability More Effective for the Digital Economy" (Centre on Regulation in Europe, 2020); J Krämer, D Schnurr, and S Broughton Micova, "The Role of Data for Digital Markets Contestability" (Centre on Regulation in Europe, 2020).

[31] DM Kreps, *A Course in Microeconomic Theory* (Princeton: Princeton University Press, 1990).

is intended to be used.[32] Take social media websites such as Facebook, TikTok, or Twitter: Such platforms greatly benefit consumers by connecting them with friends and family, offering new content, and introducing tailor-made promotions. But the collection of more user data and the display of a growing amount of advertising may also lower the platform's value.[33] While personalized technologies typically enable firms to better satisfy consumers' preferences, such technologies also facilitate self-serving exploitation of user behavior through extensive profiling and sorting, nudging, or even manipulation.[34] More to the point, poor personalization might be perceived as a quality problem, as might poor data privacy, and these issues may even be mutually incompatible.[35] In the same way as one consumer's interpretation of quality of traditional products such as soap, food, drinks, or music will diverge broadly from that of another consumer, a particular variation in quality of a platform's service may produce distinct benefits and costs for different users.[36] So far as internet search, data privacy, and the sale of goods in online marketplaces are concerned, product quality is arguably multifaceted, convoluted, and complex, with each circumstance having different quality aspects. Given the intricacy of these issues, no unanimity about what constitutes product quality exists, and competition law sensibly refrains from endorsing any inflexible form of schematization that would establish a single application of the concept for the purpose of correcting market failures.[37] Such disagreement notwithstanding, quality is arguably the main variable of interest in concentrated markets without a price, and the concept is increasingly invoked in contemporary scholarship and practice. The following sections seek to provide some insight and clarification pertaining to its growing application.[38]

32 Ibid.

33 Australian Competition and Consumer Commission, "Digital Platforms Enquiry" (Canberra, 2019), 280; Stigler Center for the Study of the Economy and the State (n 26), 63.

34 N Richards and W Hartzog, "A Duty of Loyalty for Privacy Law" (2021) 99 *Washington University Law Review*, 961.

35 JT Llanos, "A Close Look on Privacy Protection as a Non-Price Parameter of Competition" (2019) 15 *European Competition Journal*, 225.

36 Hirschman (n 15).

37 G Day and A Stemler, "Are Dark Patterns Anticompetitive?" (2020) 72 *Alabama Law Review*, 1; JN Rosenquist, FM Scott Morton, and SN Weinstein, "Addictive Technology and Its Implications for Antitrust Enforcement" (2022) 100 *North Carolina Law Review*, 431; JM Newman, "Antitrust in Digital Markets" (2019) 72 *Vanderbilt Law Review*, 1497; some product quality attributes may be more certain, objective, and observable (such as the engine power of a car) while others are more subjective, unobserved, and contingent upon the perceptions of consumers (e.g., the prestige associated with a particular brand), OECD, "The Role and Measurement of Quality in Competition Analysis" (2013).

38 At the level of competition enforcement, quality is well established as a factor in defining boundaries of relevant markets as well as in assessing the legality of horizontal and vertical restraints. In contrast, the role of quality effects in merger control and, in particular, trading off between quality and price effects remains one of the most vexatious and unresolved issues, ibid.

A *Platforms as Intermediaries or Curators*

It is contentious in legal scholarship and practice whether the harms from deteriorating – or, indeed, inferior – product quality should be targeted at all, with one important issue turning upon whether innovation originates from competition that (in the short run) substitutes, complements, or recombines existing products, or from competition that (in the long run) renders obsolete entire industries by shifting markets to new technologies.[39] If the emphasis is on long-run innovation, forms of business conduct associated with self-favoring, excessive collection of users' data or bans on free distribution of third-party content in online marketplaces may not warrant scrutiny unless such conduct is capable of restricting the emergence of entirely new business sectors, new commodities, new sources of supply, new types of organizations, and so forth.[40] That is, if competition is meant, exclusively, to produce large-scale shifts in commerce – if it is geared primarily toward bringing about efficiency in terms of rivalry between copious ecosystems – the harms resulting from inferior quality are best thought of as temporary in nature and do not present a significant enough impact to be worthy of expending competition enforcement resources.[41] On the other hand, a multitude of recent government reports have pointed to significant ramifications that quality deteriorations in digital markets can produce.[42] Selective changes in a platform's business practices can reinforce or perpetuate a platform's dominant position and inhibit opportunities for other actors to reach efficient scale.[43] Some of the most sweeping risks include a dominant platform's power to constrict, amplify, or even manipulate information to influence or suppress the voices of other actors, including users and consumers.[44]

For the sake of illustration, consider the following instances in which authorities and courts investigated – and condemned – such practices, deviating from the existing narrative around the sole promotion of efficiency. First, in 2017, the European Commission (EC) condemned Google for skewing its search results to promote its own related services over those of rivals. The EC established that Google

[39] DJ Teece, "Reflections on 'Profiting from Innovation'" (2006) 35 *Research Policy*, 1131; J Ellig and D Lin, "A Taxonomy of Dynamic Competition Theories" in J Ellig (ed), *Dynamic Competition and Public Policy: Technology, Innovation, and Antitrust Issues* (New York: Cambridge University Press, 2001), 16–43; Petit (n 20).

[40] Petit and Teece (n 21); JA Schumpeter, *Capitalism, Socialism and Democracy* (New York: Routledge, 1976), 84.

[41] DJ Teece and H Kahwaty, "Rebooting Digital Market Power" (2020) *Competition Policy International*, December 14, 2020.

[42] J Crémer, Y de Montjoye, and H Schweitzer, "Competition Policy for the Digital Era" (Brussels, 2019); UK Competition and Markets Authority, "Online Platforms and Digital Advertising. Market Study Final Report" (London, 2020); UK Digital Competition Expert Panel (n 29); Stigler Center for the Study of the Economy and the State (n 26); Australian Competition and Consumer Commission (n 33).

[43] F Fukuyama et al., "Report of the Working Group on Platform Scale" (Stanford, 2020), 15–16.

[44] Ibid.

systematically demoted competitors' shopping websites to favor its own content.[45] Because leading search engines have the power to redirect, expose, and augment the information they bring into perspective, the platform's ranking mechanism was found to shape the course of rivals' businesses, the manner in which consumers made decisions, and the information consumers had considered previously.[46] Since users expected Google to list search results according to relevance, the EC worked toward ensuring that the platform displays its results on the basis of a benchmark that is applied in equal measure to the ranking of competitors' websites. Along these lines, one of the investigation's most central contributions was to enable users to make decisions in keeping with their expectations – an outcome that was not aimed at maximizing output but that sought to reinstate the ability of consumers to choose freely and in line with the putative quality of the platform's service.[47] Second, in 2016, the German Federal Cartel Office (FCO) condemned Facebook's collection, processing, and sale of user data from third-party websites and applications without users' knowledge and consent.[48] Facebook's conduct was found to be abusive because the network compelled users to unreservedly agree with the platform's data collection – to the extent that users lost control over their personal information, the manner in which their data were collected, and how they were processed.[49] Because the point of data-driven markets is to monetize consumers' information, the FCO did not rebuke the network's practice altogether but instead required Facebook to enable users to opt out of the platform's data tracking and to delete their collected data history. As in the EC's *Google Search (Shopping)* investigation, rather than requiring users who disagreed with Facebook's surveillance-driven business model to withdraw from the entire network, the authority enabled consumers to effectively disagree with the platform's policy, spurring competition for more privacy protective offers as opposed to simply giving way to the maximization of the leading platform's output.[50] Third, in investigations relating to some of the most prominent marketplaces and app stores, Amazon's growing use of customer data was challenged because the company allegedly exploited its position as a platform and a seller by appropriating the business information of third-party dealers to privilege its own private-label products and to ultimately supplant the products of competitors.[51]

45 Case AT.39740 Google Search (Shopping) [2017].

46 Ibid.; FM Scott Morton and DC Dinielli, "Roadmap for a Digital Advertising Monopolization Case against Google" (Omidyar, 2020).

47 See A Kuenzler, "Advancing Quality Competition in Big Data Markets" (2019) 15 *Journal of Competition Law and Economics*, 500.

48 Bundeskartellamt, Decision of 6 February 2019, B6–22/16; Bundesgerichtshof (June 23, 2020) KVR 69/19.

49 Ibid.; Scott Morton and Dinielli (n 46).

50 A Kuenzler, "Direct Consumer Influence – The Missing Strategy to Integrate Data Privacy Preferences into the Market" (2020) 39 *Yearbook of European Law*, 423.

51 European Commission, Case AT.40462 *Amazon Marketplace*; Competition and Markets Authority, "CMA Investigates Amazon over Suspected Anti-Competitive Practices" (2022) Press Release, July 6, 2022.

Equally, Apple was accused of requiring independent developers to sell exclusively through its App Store and to make use of Apple's payment system, taking big cuts off each transaction.[52] A predominant concern resulting from such behavior is that restraints on distribution may shape consumers' views of product quality because they direct consumer choices along one alternative or another.[53] More specifically, because distinct types of market settings can impact consumers' views of product quality, consumers' perceptions of quality will change depending on the market setting in which they are making their decisions.[54] For instance, market settings that allow free distribution of goods prompt consumers to be less inclined to indiscriminately agree with a platform's value proposition than do market settings that impose exclusive distribution.[55] Importantly, the available alternatives can effectively shift consumers' perceptions of a product's image and reputation: If consumers can evaluate two identical products side by side, they are inclined to see product quality as subjective – as relative or contingent; they might prefer a different option than the platform itself suggests and are predisposed to discover more about the good at issue, to arrive at a more accurate picture about its features, functions, and attributes.[56] However, if consumers are exposed, exclusively, to the platform's product proposition, they will likely find confirmation of their preconceived opinion about the proposed alternative and will have no interest in collecting additional information that might modify (or support) their initial views.[57] Here, consumers see product quality as objective – as absolute or unchanging – and are more likely to accept the platform's value proposition.[58] Exposure to one or another setting, including the platform's ranking and display of available alternatives, thus has an influence on quality in terms of image or reputation.[59] Consumers may either follow the platform's product proposition or be drawn to distinctive product features, functions, and attributes, evaluating arguments and rejecting weak ones but accepting those that are strong enough to be convincing.[60]

52 Apple Inc. v. Pepper, 139 S.Ct. 1514 (2019); Epic Games, Inc. v. Apple Inc., Case No. 4:20-cv-05640-YGR (N.D. Cal. September 10, 2021).

53 A Kuenzler, "Competition Law Enforcement on Digital Markets – Lessons from Recent EU Case Law" (2019) 7 *Journal of Antitrust Enforcement*, 249.

54 E Shafir, "Choosing versus Rejecting: Why Some Options Are Both Better and Worse Than Others" (1993) 21 *Memory & Cognition*, 546; E Shafir, I Simonson, and A Tversky, "Reason-Based Choice" (1993) 49 *Cognition*, 11.

55 Ibid.; B Nunez, "Developing Behavioural Economics as a Practical Tool for Market Authorities" (2016) 5 *Journal of Antitrust Enforcement*, 375.

56 J Andriessen and M Baker, "Arguing to Learn" in RK Sawyer (ed), *The Cambridge Handbook of the Learning Sciences* (3rd ed., New York: Cambridge University Press, 2022), 428–47; RS Wyer, "The Role of Procedural Knowledge in Consumer Judgement and Decision Making" in CV Jansson-Boyd and MJ Zawisza (eds), *Routledge International Handbook of Consumer Psychology* (New York: Routledge, 2017), 102–24.

57 Ibid.

58 Ibid.

59 Krämer, Schnurr, and Broughton Micova (n 30), 40–43.

60 Kuenzler (n 53).

Each example illustrates that quality features prominently in contemporary competition law disputes and that intensified administrative action taken by authorities and courts involves an underrated path of consumer influence. By investigating the platforms' policies, authorities and courts give permission to consumers to help modify (parts of) the manner in which the platforms operate, rendering those platforms trustworthy stewards of consumers' expectations. And modifying (parts of) a leading platform's policies works to readjust market incentives to invest and innovate in new products and services, and to align a dominant company's mode of doing business with consumer interests.[61]

Admittedly, authorities and courts are exercising some control when they work to reconfigure segments in this manner, and exercising control might seem particularly menacing when the advancement of new technologies is involved.[62] Precisely for this reason, legal treatment of quality deteriorations is contentious and is regularly in dispute. The following sections attempt to render the concept of quality more tractable, putting an emphasis on the perceived purpose and function of digital platforms:[63] At one end of the spectrum, this function is to perform all of a platform's vital operations such as procuring information, categorizing outcomes, and allocating content. As such, the platform operates as little more than a neutral conduit – as *intermediary*.[64] At the other end of the spectrum, a platform's essential function consists in ranking and classifying content based on its own set of rules, winnowing the desired from the undesired, bringing specific pieces of information to the attention of consumers, and submerging other content in the welter of material that is available through separate media and the World Wide Web. Here, the underlying platform operates more like a manager or overseer – as *curator*.[65] Either arrangement exhibits a tendency to accept or disapprove of deteriorations in product quality as a matter of competition law because the issue from this perspective is whether the platform unlawfully abuses or rightfully employs user data and attention.

[61] Ibid.; ME Stucke and A Ezrachi, *Competition Overdose: How Free Market Mythology Transformed Us from Citizen Kings to Market Servants* (New York: Harper Business, 2020).

[62] JB Baker, *The Antitrust Paradigm: Restoring a Competitive Economy* (Cambridge, MA: Harvard University Press, 2019); T Philippon, *The Great Reversal: How America Gave Up on Free Markets* (Cambridge, MA: Belknap Press, 2019); S Zuboff, *The Age of Surveillance Capitalism: The Fight for a Human Future at the New Frontier of Power* (London: Profile, 2019).

[63] J Grimmelmann, "Speech Engines" (2014) 98 *Minnesota Law Review*, 868; JM Balkin, "Information Fiduciaries and the First Amendment" (2016) 49 *UC Davis Law Review*, 1183; RA Woodcock, "How Antitrust Really Works: A Theory of Input Control and Discriminatory Supply" (2021); RA Woodcock, "To Produce Is to Self-Preference" (2021); RA Woodcock, "Antitrust and the Infinite, Circular Supply Chain" (2022) *Competition Policy International*, April 27, 2022.

[64] F Pasquale, "Dominant Search Engines: An Essential Cultural & Political Facility" in B Szoka and A Marcus (eds), *The Next Digital Decade: Essays on the Future of the Internet* (Washington, DC: TechFreedom, 2010), 401.

[65] E Goldman, "Search Engine Bias & the Demise of Search Engine Utopianism" in B Szoka and A Marcus (eds), *The Next Digital Decade: Essays on the Future of the Internet* (Washington, DC: TechFreedom, 2010), 461.

By highlighting data and attention rather than sheer size or market structure, the intermediary and curator theories of digital platforms address the central challenge of big technology markets: They remain firmly focused on promoting competition, but they take up the issue of whether privileged access to or self-serving employment of users' information affords leading actors undue advantages over rivals, causing detriment to consumers and the market as a whole.

B *Some Concrete Examples*

The intermediary and curator theories of platforms figure prominently in contemporary competition law analysis when different meanings of the term "quality" such as relevance, privacy, or reputation are considered. Disputes around *relevance* occur if the algorithms of a dominant search engine favor native content; concerns about *privacy* involve social media websites that get to know about how users reach their product page, the content that they access, whether they are using a particular application, if they click on advertisements from other actors, or which device they utilize when browsing; and arguments involving *image or reputation* concern the issue of whether leading app stores and online marketplaces are able to keep control over an item's presentation in order to define, independently, their product space, steering and redirecting parts of the customer's journey on the Internet.

Depending on the viewpoint taken, quality involves different aspects of these concepts and disagreement typically cannot easily be resolved even in the face of entirely reasonable evidence.[66] One standpoint views the platform as a passive and impartial intermediary that matches users with other actors and then recedes into the background. Another views the platform as an active and committed player that sorts through the existing content and employs knowledgeable expertise to curate the essential and imperative. Which theory we follow – the *intermediary* or the *curator* – has significant repercussions for the manner in which competition law contends with issues such as relevance, privacy, and reputation, and for what constitutes product quality overall.

1 Relevance

If product quality is about relevance, as has been the case in relation to self-preferencing claims around Google's dominant search engine, the notion of the platform as intermediary requires that third parties are enabled to effectively reach

[66] J Grimmelmann, "Some Skepticism about Search Neutrality" in B Szoka and A Marcus (eds), *The Next Digital Decade: Essays on the Future of the Internet* (Washington, DC: TechFreedom, 2010), 435; GA Manne, "The Problem of Search Engines as Essential Facilities: An Economic & Legal Assessment" in B Szoka and A Marcus (eds), *The Next Digital Decade: Essays on the Future of the Internet* (Washington, DC: TechFreedom, 2010), 419.

the public with the help of the dominant platform. The search engine, according to this view, is expected to meet principles of truthfulness and impartiality, just like a shipping company delivers goods from manufacturers to consumers.[67] Search engines that inflict their point of view on users inevitably fall short of this ideal. Underlying the intermediary theory is the presumption that search engines are designed in such a manner that they enable consumers to be exposed to the kind of content that is most pertinent to their interests because a number of distorting influences powerfully shape consumers' choices and behavior.[68] Owing primarily to the scarcity of attention,[69] the most prominent website ranking typically receives the highest consideration,[70] regardless of whether users ascribe a low value to a product's mere position.[71] Hence, where search engines are required to be neutral but fail to accurately map the content of the Internet, they are considered biased[72] – because they tilt results to prioritize commercial (or popular) subject matter,[73] and give precedence to their own for-profit interests.[74]

By contrast, the notion of the platform as curator requires the search engine to decide which content to disseminate and which subject matter to suppress. Search bias, from this perspective, is seen as a feature, not a bug, because search engines (are bound to) make their own editorial decisions about what (not) to highlight and what (not) to publish. Here, a website's rank as such amounts to relevance because it is precisely the search engine's professional judgment that consumers aspire to seek out when they choose between various alternative providers.[75] Because internet searches are very difficult to comprehend, any requirement to be neutral would

[67] O Bracha and F Pasquale, "Federal Search Commission?: Access, Fairness, and Accountability in the Law of Search" (2008) 93 *Cornell Law Review*, 1149; EB Laidlaw, "Private Power, Public Interest: An Examination of Search Engine Accountability" (2008) 17 *International Journal of Law and Information Technology*, 113.

[68] M Glick et al., "How Does Ranking Affect User Choice in Online Search?" (2014) 45 *Review of Industrial Organization*, 99.

[69] TH Davenport and JC Beck, *The Attention Economy: Understanding the New Currency of Business* (Boston, MA: Harvard Business Press, 2002).

[70] K Jerath et al., "A 'Position Paradox' in Sponsored Search Auctions" (2011) 30 *Marketing Science*, 612.

[71] MR Baye, B De los Santos, and MR Wildenbeest, "What's in a Name? Measuring Prominence and Its Impact on Organic Traffic from Search Engines" (2016) 34 *Information Economics and Policy*, 44.

[72] M Monmonier, *How to Lie with Maps* (3rd ed., Chicago: University of Chicago Press, 2018).

[73] J Kulshrestha et al., "Quantifying Search Bias: Investigating Sources of Bias for Political Searches in Social Media" (2017) *Proceedings of the 2017 ACM Conference on Computer Supported Cooperative Work and Social Computing*.

[74] B Friedman and H Nissenbaum, "Bias in Computer Systems" (1996) 14 *ACM Transactions on Information Systems*, 330.

[75] E Goldman, "Revisiting Search Engine Bias" (2011) 38 *William Mitchell Law Review*, 96; E Goldman, "Search Engine Bias and the Demise of Search Engine Utopianism" (2006) 8 *Yale Journal of Law and Technology*, 188; E Volokh and DM Falk, "Google First Amendment Protection for Search Engine Search Results" (2012) 8 *Journal of Law, Economics, and Policy*, 883.

be pointless and would require an external evaluation of an inscrutable number of websites, content, signals, algorithms, and results.[76] Beneath the curator theory lies the idea that consumers are comfortable with the manner in which search engines pick and choose from different sources of content, making up their own selection to control access to information.[77] Rather than placing too much emphasis on concerns about manipulation, the theory relies on a search engine's eminence, which acts as a reliable signal for the relevance of the search results that users get to see.[78]

The intermediary and curator theories of platforms differ in how they deal with relevance as part of a search engine's quality, and both theories focus on distinct aspects of a search engine's perceived purpose and function. Search engines as intermediaries bring websites' content to the attention of consumers in the way they find it. With the curator theory, search engines make their own selection as to what content to highlight; it is perfectly appropriate, according to this theory, to augment exposure of some content while diminishing coverage of other information in the eyes of consumers.[79]

2 Privacy

The intermediary and curator theories of platforms are equally applicable to privacy as a distinct aspect of product quality. On the intermediary theory, the platform is supposed to gather, analyze, and sell consumers' data only on the basis that users have control over the information they release. The platform as intermediary refrains from maximizing the audience's attention to its own benefit, goading users into sharing and following content that unwittingly works to bend their preferences.[80] As neutral conduits, platforms avoid employing algorithms that prompt users to release data they would not have released had they possessed viable alternatives.[81] Since social media platforms typically do not produce much of their own content and instead rely on material that third-party websites or users generate, the intermediary theory posits that such platforms empower even modestly technology-knowledgeable users to control the disclosure of their information.[82] Platforms as intermediaries

76 J Grimmelmann, "The Google Dilemma" (2009) 53 *New York Law School Law Review*, 939.

77 M Ammori and L Pelican, "Competitors' Proposed Remedies for Search Bias: Search 'Neutrality' and Other Proposals" (2012) 15 *Journal of Internet Law*, 1.

78 E Pariser, *The Filter Bubble: What the Internet Is Hiding from You* (London: Penguin, 2011), 206–8; Glick et al. (n 68), 100.

79 SP Crawford, "Network Rules" (2007) 70 *Law and Contemporary Problems*, 51; Ammori and Pelican (n 77), 10–11.

80 A Acquisti, L Brandimarte, and G Loewenstein, "Privacy and Human Behavior in the Age of Information" (2015) 347 *Science*, 509; AE Waldman, "Cognitive Biases, Dark Patterns, and the 'Privacy Paradox'" (2020) 31 *Current Opinion in Psychology*, 205; A Acquisti and J Grossklags, "Privacy and Rationality in Individual Decision-Making" (2005) 3 *IEEE Security & Privacy*, 26.

81 Pariser (n 78).

82 See JM Balkin, "The Fiduciary Model of Privacy" (2020) 134 *Harvard Law Review Forum*, 11, 27.

offer users content that pertains to their personal inclinations and they abstain from collecting data in a manner that is outside of the control and sphere of influence of those who supply it.[83]

The curator theory, however, submits that platforms are supposed to accumulate as much data as possible so as to best customize and personalize their services to users. The platform as curator seeks to identify who its users are, how they behave under what circumstances and why, and what consumers might prefer beyond what they already know. Based on this information, the platform as curator exercises editorial control over the material that it brings to the attention of consumers and tailors content and recommendations to consumers' elicited preferences. Culling tailored and bespoke choices, inferred from an individual's browsing habits and attendant information collected on third-party websites and applications, with the curator theory, platforms are at ease with the conventional bargain whereby consumers inadvertently disclose a possibly indefinite amount of personal data and in turn receive the platform's personalized services for free.[84]

3 Reputation

As with claims pertaining to relevance or privacy, if quality is about image or reputation, with the theory of the platform as intermediary, leading online marketplaces and app stores are supposed to open up their websites, entirely, to third-party sellers and applications. Platforms, in this way, communicate third-party sellers' offers as they find them, and enable consumers to make their own autonomous choices. Rather than selecting the kinds of products and applications consumers can buy or download onto their devices, anyone can list their offers on the platform, and the platform makes no attempt at sorting out what it considers to be better or worse alternatives.[85] The platform as intermediary, being the blank backdrop it is supposed to be, refrains from blocking sellers or putting some products at a disadvantage in relation to others, including the platform's own competing services. Rather, a platform's grip on certain product propositions inflicts a cost in the form of more expensive merchandize or less suitable replacements than consumers might

[83] TE Kadri, "Digital Gatekeepers" (2021) 99 *Texas Law Review*, 951.

[84] JC Cooper, "Lessons from Antitrust: The Path to a More Coherent Privacy Policy" (Washington, DC: US Chamber of Commerce Foundation Report, 2017); JC Cooper and JD Wright, "The Missing Role of Economics in FTC Privacy Policy" in J Polonetsky, E Selinger, and O Tene (eds), *The Cambridge Handbook of Consumer Privacy* (Cambridge: Cambridge University Press, 2017), 465.

[85] If a producer decides to sell not just some product with functionality, but an outlook, a community, or even an identity, vendors and third-party sellers, including online marketplaces, are equally supposed to impart the producer's view; F Wijckmans, "Coty Germany GmbH v. Parfümerie Akzente GmbH: Possibility in Selective Distribution System to Ban Sales via Third-Party Platforms" (2018) 9 *Journal of European Competition Law and Practice*, 373; R Winter, "Pierre Fabre, Coty and Restrictions on Internet Sales: An Economist's Perspective" (2018) 9 *Journal of European Competition Law and Practice*, 183.

otherwise have chosen. Consumers, by visiting the platform, are supposed to proceed to search the website, evaluate different products side by side, and encounter arguments, discarding unconvincing ones but endorsing those that are sufficiently strong to be persuasive. In this way, consumers consider, impartially, the market's offers and their contested esteem and values.[86] And in so doing, they arrive at a more accurate picture of the content that is available on the Internet than if they were only able to pick what is made available to them and within reach.[87]

By contrast, with the platform-as-curator theory, platforms act as unapologetic gatekeepers. The platform sorts through the array of available offers to unearth those products that the platform thinks consumers value most, alleviating their burden of doing so themselves. According to this theory, consumers choose a particular marketplace or app store because they appreciate the platform's own suggestions.[88] The platform is expected to discard those products that it considers to be in poor taste, that encourage improper behavior, or that overcharge consumers. There is thus tremendous value in a platform's vetting of third-party offers and its attendant efforts in trying to enlighten users about what is significant and what is not. Rather than eliminating consumers' choices and eroding their autonomy, platforms as curators act as arbiters on their behalf. They ensure that the product's features, functions, and attributes are those that appeal to consumers' preferences most.[89] In this regard, the benefit of curated marketplaces and app stores consists precisely in their function that requires them to refrain from offering everything to consumers that (and as it) is available on the Internet. Instead, platforms as curators are expected to make their own selections and to tailor their bargains to the inclinations of their customers.[90]

In sum, where concerns relate to image or reputation, both the intermediary and curator theories of platforms underscore the notion that the presentation of a platform's offers can effectively shift consumers' views of product quality. The two views are evidently centered on distinct notions of quality as image or reputation: One view holds that every attempt to catalog or classify third-party sellers' offers must be suspicious; according to the other view, platforms are encouraged to proffer, exclusively, their merchandize, to discriminate against inferior sellers, and to rule out compatibility with defective services. In this manner, the intermediary and

86 R Tushnet, "Gone in Sixty Milliseconds: Trademark Law and Cognitive Science" (2008) 86 *Texas Law Review*, 507; A Kuenzler, "Dilution Law, Vertical Agreements, and the Construction of Consumption" (2017) 37 *Oxford Journal of Legal Studies*, 75.

87 See B Orbach, "The Image Theory: RPM and the Allure of High Prices" (2010) 55 *Antitrust Bulletin*, 277; R Inderst and F Maier-Rigaud, "Vertical Restraints and the Forgotten Function of Prices in Brand Management" (2015) 5 *Antitrust Chronicle*, 1.

88 See RA Woodcock, "Yet Another Amazon Antitrust Paradox" (2021); Epic Games, Inc. v. Apple Inc., Case No. 4:20-cv-05640-YGR (N.D. Cal. September 10, 2021).

89 P Bordalo, N Gennaioli, and A Shleifer, "Salience and Consumer Choice" (2013) 121 *Journal of Political Economy*, 803.

90 See H Mercier and D Sperber, *The Enigma of Reason* (Cambridge, MA: Harvard University Press, 2017); Woodcock (n 88).

curator theories of platforms expose a fundamental split in how quality is construed: On the one hand, platforms create a set of background conditions through which third-party sellers involve themselves in the governance of markets so that consumers can choose freely from a variety of offers pertaining to differentiated goods; on the other, platforms impose restrictions on distribution with a view to segregating markets for distinct products and services, creating and maintaining separate segments in which uniform and consistent quality perceptions are maintained.

C *Repercussions for the Concept of Quality*

The intermediary and curator theories offer some refreshing insights into current legal disputes around big technology companies where quality rather than price competition dominates. The main difference between the intermediary and curator theories of platforms is based on the *locus* of a platform's content: platforms as intermediaries focus on disseminating what third parties offer; platforms as curators emphasize their own product propositions. Consequently, with the theory of the platform as intermediary, a dominant search engine's practice of self-preferencing presents a quality issue; with the theory of the platform as curator, concerns around quality and self-preferencing regularly lack merit. Similarly, with the intermediary theory, a dominant social media platform's collection, analysis, and sale of consumer data from third-party sources without users' actual knowledge and consent is viewed as a quality deterioration, while with the theory of the platform as curator, such activities achieve just the opposite. Lastly, with the theory of the platform as intermediary, a ban on free distribution of third-party products and applications or an undue demotion below the platform's private-label products in its ranking by a dominant marketplace or app store is to be condemned in terms of quality, whereas with the curator theory such practices are deemed legitimate. Just as there seems to be no general or agreed-upon arrangement to determine what constitutes quality in these cases, there are evidently no authoritative or given tenets of adjudication. Each theory has its own virtues because quality is either viewed as subjective or objective, as placed in the hands of third parties or leading platforms.[91] Ultimately, there is a continuous struggle between the intermediary or curator theories of platforms as to which theory is supposed to take priority, not only in terms of how platforms function but also in terms of acceptance of what each camp and its supporters take to be the proper criteria of competition on the merits.[92]

III PRODUCT QUALITY RECONSIDERED

The intermediary and curator theories of platforms expose the malleability of the concept of product quality and exemplify why competition law has long struggled to

[91] Grimmelmann (n 66).
[92] Pariser (n 78), 177–78.

adequately contend with quality deteriorations. Whenever scholars have tried to get a grasp of leading actors' alleged anticompetitive practices and have tried to explain why a quality deterioration might be unlawful, they have followed either the intermediary or curator theory of platforms and have embraced an ideal type of the concept as a heuristic device that allowed them to analyze the problem in view of its approximations or deviations from the ideal. In doing so, they have accepted the basic consequences that follow from traditional output/profitability reasoning as applied to each proposal: that competition law should either work to separate a platform's core functions – its role in sharing information from its role in editing information – or that competition law is incapable of dealing with quality deteriorations altogether because competition law only protects against impediments to large-scale (i.e., long-run) innovation (which amount to the creation of "artificial" as opposed to "natural" barriers to entry).[93] The platform-as-intermediary hypothesis accepts that leading operators such as Google, Facebook, Amazon, and Apple authorize third parties to share information with their users. At the same time, these platforms also have the ability to decide whether users will get to see a particular piece of information and how prominently, or whether they don't get to see it at all if the platform begs to differ. The first task does not entail any editing. The second task represents editing. What is more, the former involves network effects while the latter does not. From this it follows that if there is a role for competition law to play in disputes involving quality, this role consists in separating the sharing and the editorial function of big technology platforms. As concerns a platform's editorial activity without network effects, there should be competition. Search engines, social media platforms, online marketplaces, and app stores define their roles as editors so that consumers should be able to choose between a variety of alternative offers. As concerns the sharing activity, where there are typically strong network effects, including efficiencies of scale and scope, a platform is deemed to be something akin to a common carrier because everyone should be able to be represented on a dominant search engine's results page, to post on a leading social media website, to sell on the most important online marketplace, or to offer their products on dominant app stores.[94] The platform as curator hypothesis, for its part, assumes that the role of platforms consists *wholly* in curating information. In this view, platforms are shielded from competition law liability because a platform's editorial decisions are a natural result of the characteristics of the platform's market rather than of artificial anticompetitive conduct.[95] Consequently, this view suggests that search

[93] See, for an overview, LM Khan, "The Separation of Platforms and Commerce" (2019) 119 *Columbia Law Review*, 973; D Markovits, BD Richman, and R van Loo, "Law, Markets, and Distribution: Consumer Law as an Axis of Economic Inequality" (2022) 102 *Boston University Law Review*, 1169.

[94] Ibid.

[95] Note that there is a difference between liability for anticompetitive behavior and legal liability for content; JM Balkin, "To Reform Social Media, Reform Informational Capitalism" in L

bias, excessive data collection, or restraints on distribution, including undue demotions of third-party content in a platform's ranking, are not to be understood as arising from a lack of competition in the market but rather, if at all, from information asymmetries that cause consumers to accept unfavorable conditions. In the digital economy, consumers generally find themselves at a disadvantage relative to business corporations, regardless of whether these corporations have market power – that is, irrespective of whether there are active competitors in the market. After all, non-dominant companies typically collect and utilize the same amount of data as their dominant counterparts, often without consumers' knowledge and control. Dominant actors must thus not be found liable under competition law when they impose on users the same or similar terms of use that non-dominant firms can also impose on them. Particularly, if consumers have limited knowledge and understanding of how a platform's content or recommendations are selected, the provision of additional information is viewed as sufficient to remedy such market failures.[96] Equally, if a platform's editorial decision turns out to be subjectively dishonest or in violation of the law, contractual or extra-contractual liability, including tortious interference claims, is considered the most appropriate avenue to pursue. If competition law could be engaged for issues such as these, competition law would likely become an all-purpose enforcement mechanism for areas that are better dealt with by consumer and data protection regulations. Importantly, from a competition law perspective, if sufficiently informed consumers are dissatisfied, they are supposed to switch to alternative providers, each with their own editorial policy and discretion.

The postulated consequences of the two opposing views represent an almost mechanical application of traditional output/profitability thinking to market settings in which price and output are no longer (the most) pertinent variables of consumer interest. Such thinking only considers large-scale innovation that generates across-the-board (Kaldor–Hicks) efficiencies worthy of protection. The tension materializes when the two views attempt to resolve their positions in relation to the perceived purpose and function of leading platforms. The intermediary account presumes that *any* integration of intellectual, artistic, or editorial bias in a leading search engine's results is harmful, that *any* attempt to personalize and customize dominant social media platforms' services is reprehensible, and tends to *categorically* elevate the value propositions of third parties' offers on dominant marketplaces and app stores

Bollinger and GR Stone (eds), *Social Media, Freedom of Speech and the Future of Our Democracy* (New York: Oxford University Press, 2022), 101–36.

96 See, for an overview and an alternative approach, N Blickstein Shchory and MS Gal, "Voice Shoppers: From Information Gaps to Choice Gaps in Consumer Markets" (2022) 88 *Brooklyn Law Review*, 1; N Blickstein Shchory and MS Gal, "Market Power Parasites: Abusing the Power of Digital Intermediaries to Harm Competition" (2022) 35 *Harvard Journal of Law and Technology*, 73. If information is not easily obtainable or consumers' individual interests are too insignificant for them to become active, contractual liability is deemed appropriate.

over those envisaged by platform operators. However, the theory of the platform as curator is similarly incapable of producing more adequate results. It defers entirely to the platform, on the grounds that systematic bias that originates from a dominant search engine's economic interest in favoring its products vis-à-vis those of rivals may *never* divert consumers' attention, significantly hurt competitors, or cause substantial harm to innovation, that the unauthorized collection and utilization of consumers' data by leading social media platforms may *never* cause consumer detriment or undermine incentives to invest in more privacy-protective arrangements, and that the effects of a merchant's own projection of integrity and veracity of its products in dominant online marketplaces and app stores are *at all times undeserving* of affording protection.[97] Importantly, both theories fail to consider that relevance, privacy, and reputation are deeply ambiguous but pertinent variables of economic interest. Recent investigations into big technology platforms' practices fittingly exemplify this point. Here, the authorities did not ask those companies to be divided up, nor did they impose a blanket ban on their modes of doing business; rather, the authorities compelled those companies to *integrate* consumer preferences for relevance, privacy, and reputation into their segments while still enabling them to obtain the benefits from scale and scope, including network effects, from their technological underpinnings. Perhaps even more importantly, the authorities recognized that reliance on consumers' autonomous ability to switch between different segments would only have spurred those actors to vie for additional market shares rather than for consumer preferences – a difference that matters significantly in concentrated settings where advertising-driven business models prevail. However, even where consumers are mindful of a given quality deterioration, concentrated markets typically constrain their ability to turn to more satisfying alternatives, and constrain the ability of other actors to submit more gratifying offers. Affording consumers a path of influence through intensified administrative action, then, provides a far more adequate response to the consumer's disappointment than do pure entitlement-based or structural remedies:[98] Authorities and courts investigate – *and effectively readdress* – the policies of leading actors; they act to reinstate product quality when other remedies are unavailable or unworkable. Importantly, a more capable notion of quality acknowledges that leading actors may well disappoint the expectations of consumers but that there may simultaneously be significant economic benefits that these platforms generate.[99] By contrast, the intermediary and

[97] Grimmelmann (n 63); Goldman (n 65).

[98] A Kuenzler, "On (Some) Aspects of Social Privacy in the Social Media Space" (2022) 12 *International Data Privacy Law*, 63. Consumer and data protection laws, including some common carrier rules, also impose liability. None of them, however, is directed at modifying and adjusting terms and conditions of agreement, technical features of digital platforms, or predominant modes of doing business.

[99] The point is that consumers typically lack the time, knowledge, or ingenuity to choose the best components of a product. But in some instances, we cannot rely on the market to let the firm decide in the best interests of consumers either. Here, consumers ought to be allowed to use

curator theories either work to undercut big technology platforms' advantages gained from scale and scope, including network effects, or threaten to be inapposite to curb improper mechanisms of selection and propagation of leading actors' content that run counter to the expectations of consumers and simultaneously harm competitors, the market, and society at large.[100]

A *Platforms as Dependable Consultants*

So far, the concept of product quality has been considered from the perspective of the platform as intermediary or as curator, and this juxtaposition has revealed significant tensions between them. Both theories focus on the platform but the critical difference is the locus of the relevant information: The intermediary theory prioritizes *third parties' content* while the curator theory revolves around the *platform's subject matter*. From this perspective, dealing with issues of relevance, privacy, and reputation is highly antagonistic – it confronts authorities and courts with an almost irreconcilable choice between third parties' or platforms' vantage points. A more nuanced view refrains from emphasizing either third parties' or platforms' offers; in its stead, it turns on the *consumer* as the recipient of the content. Although both the intermediary and curator theories address consumers, neither of them fully appreciates their perspective. With the intermediary theory, platforms deliver third-party content to consumers – they connect websites and users; with the curator theory, platforms pull together, sift through, and identify information with a sharp eye for highly coveted subject matter. Both theories consider consumers to be passively absorbing some given material in front of them and neither contemplates them actively hunting for information, and becoming more cognizant and learned on a particular issue in this process. If this aspect is moved to the center, however, platforms are not seen as intermediaries or as curators but instead are better characterized as *dependable consultants*. They attend to the desires of consumers, accomplish tasks on their behalf, employ specialist opinion to comb through what

voice (as opposed to exit) to influence product design decisions. Typically, this encompasses some sort of social process that is not the market. That is, consumers will not make product design decisions by individually purchasing components themselves, for instance, and combining them with the firm's product. Rather, they usually do so by shouting at the firm until it changes its design decision. Where shouting at the firm turns out to be unfeasible or ineffective, however, voice may also take the form of institutional channels of communication for (groups of) customers to express their dissatisfaction when they otherwise experience difficulty in doing so. But this does not mean that judges or government agencies effectively make design decisions. Rather, this may result in remedies that require the firm to give consumers a choice regarding those variables of interest (relevance, privacy, reputation) they genuinely value. Put another way, government need not impose a product design decision of its own. Rather, it can require that firms give consumers a direct say over product design by requiring that firms offer a wider range of product options to consumers when they are unable to decide through the market.

[100] Fukuyama et al. (n 43).

they have gathered, and *listen* to their users to identify what they are expected to deliver and what to dispense with. This standpoint joins both the intermediary and curator theories together in that platforms relay content to consumers *and* exercise judgment in rendering their services. Rather than siding with third parties *or* platforms, the emphasis is on *counseling consumers*. Curation and intermediation must not be seen as antagonistic; rather they are to be viewed as complementary. Platforms connect content and users at the same time that they express their considered judgements. And since the emphasis is on consumers, the platform is obliged to act as a reliable, trustworthy guide. It attends to consumers' interests and refrains from swaying, converting, or manipulating content. It empowers consumers to acquire what they seek and yields to their desires in discovering what they want.[101] Rather than defining what is tantamount to product quality in the abstract,[102] the standpoint situates quality as a platform's duty to look out for the preferences of consumers – as a duty to be loyal to those customers whose loyalty platforms request.[103] The issue has profound implications for some of the most glaring problems lying beneath much of competition law's contemporary practice: recognizing that apart from price and output, aspects such as relevance, privacy, and reputation are meaningful variables of consumer interest.

B *Loyalty as a Distinct Avenue of Influence*

What does a fully-fledged concept of platforms as dependable consultants require us to consider? Since platforms frequently demonstrate superior skill and knowledge when searching for and posting content, the platform as dependable consultant primarily looks out for the aspirations of consumers when carrying out its functions.[104] By putting users first, the counselor theory underscores loyalty and retention of remaining members of the platform's segment rather than having these members leave in the case of dissatisfaction – that is, to switch to alternative offers. Most of the time, consumers benefit from the increased aggregation of supply and demand that big technology platforms offer, including the liquidity and lower search costs when activities are concentrated in a few large undertakings.[105] If a user wants to buy a

[101] This is also a way of adjusting content to the diversity of user interests. And catering to a diversity of user interests improves the quality of content that consumers receive; Grimmelmann (n 66), 899.

[102] RD Banker, I Khosla, and KK Sinha, "Quality and Competition" (1998) 44 *Management Science*, 1179; RD Blair and CP Durrance, "Restraints on Quality Competition" (2013) 10 *Journal of Competition Law and Economics*, 27.

[103] JM Balkin, "Free Speech in the Algorithmic Society: Big Data, Private Governance, and New School Speech Regulation" (2018) 51 *UC Davis Law Review*, 1149.

[104] Balkin (n 63); JE Cohen, *Between Truth and Power: The Legal Constructions of Informational Capitalism* (New York: Oxford University Press, 2019); RS Whitt, "Old School Goes Online: Exploring Fiduciary Obligations of Loyalty and Care in the Digital Platforms Era" (2019) 36 *Santa Clara High Technology Law Journal*, 75.

[105] Rochet and Tirole (n 11).

piece of rare memorabilia, for instance, they are better off if all potential sellers can congregate on a single marketplace. A similar logic applies if users are posting or sharing content on social media websites, or when they search for websites.[106] As such, big technology platforms' ecosystem advantages are crucial in data-driven, winner-takes-all markets.[107] And the loyalty of consumers is frequently encouraged and rewarded by big technology platforms when those platforms are working to make consumers feel engaged in their communities, their brands, and their outlooks.[108]

However, owing to their status as dependable consultants, competition law needs to step in to ensure the dominant platform's loyalty to its users when the platform ceases to cater to consumers' preferences, giving priority, instead, to its own profit-maximizing interests and significantly affecting other actors in the market.[109] Loyalty, in this way, gives rise not only to an enhanced degree of adherence to a dominant platform's ecosystem of products and services by consumers. It also gives consumers who are loyal to a dominant platform the opportunity to shift the platform's burden of inertia and to adjust terms and conditions of agreement when the platform fails to act in their best interests. Loyalty commands that a dominant search engine, operating on the assumption that users can expect an actual choice between a variety of options that reflect the benefits of commercial innovation, lists vertical search results on the basis of a measure that has been applied equally to the ranking of competitors' products.[110] Loyalty puts a limit on the use of consumers' personal information by leading social media platforms, to the platform's commercial advantage, unless consumers have given actual and voluntary consent for such employment.[111] And loyalty demands that prominent online marketplaces and app stores are required to abstain from appropriating competitors' private business data,

106 N Economides and E Katsamakas, "Two-Sided Competition of Proprietary vs. Open Source Technology Platforms and the Implications for the Software Industry" (2006) 52 *Management Science*, 1057.

107 J Cenamor, "Complementor Competitive Advantage: A Framework for Strategic Decisions" (2021) 122 *Journal of Business Research*, 335.

108 Ibid.

109 NM Richards and W Hartzog, "Taking Trust Seriously in Privacy Law" (2016) 19 *Stanford Technology Law Review*, 431; Balkin (n 82); Balkin (n 103).

110 Case AT.39740 Google Search (Shopping) [2017]; however, loyalty does not entail the sort of broad-scale prohibitions on self-preferencing in rankings proposed and/or adopted by various legislators in different jurisdictions. As has been pointed out, for instance, on platforms where monetization occurs through a commission on each sale, incentives for self-preferencing are significantly reduced, B Jiang, K Jerath, and K Srinivasan, "Firm Strategies in the 'Mid Tail' of Platform-Based Retailing" (2011) 30 *Marketing Science*, 757; A Hagiu and J Wright, "Marketplace or Reseller?" (2015) 61 *Management Science*, 184; F Etro, "Product Selection in Online Marketplaces" (2021) 30 *Journal of Economics and Management Strategy*, 614; F Etro, "Device-Funded vs Ad-Funded Platforms" (2021) 75 *International Journal of Industrial Organization*, 102711. In this sense, the findings in *Google Search (Shopping)* are likely limited to a specific constellation, Kuenzler (n 47).

111 Bundeskartellamt, Decision of 6 February 2019, B6–22/16; Bundesgerichtshof (June 23, 2020) KVR 69/19.

gathered in respect of consumers' observed purchasing behavior, in order to usurp competitors' products, and to apply equal treatment to all sellers when a particular way of ranking and displaying offers impairs, significantly, the expectations and independent judgment of consumers.[112]

Seen from this perspective, product quality attaches to a dominant platform's promises to users, made about its service's performance, and such promises are conveyed through explicit and implicit assertions of the platform's perceived purpose and function.[113] According to the intermediary and curator theories of platforms, product quality is framed in abstract terms and requires to either separate different lines of business or to presume that product quality is a variable of interest falling beneath the scope of competition law. However, in concentrated marketplaces with a zero price, there is regularly a strong interest in assuring quality – not in terms of imposing total bans on a platform's mode of doing business or as a result of mere contractual or extra-contractual liability – but in addressing the market-wide effects of product quality deteriorations because of their calamitous economic (and societal) repercussions.[114] Such accountability is not all-or-nothing but instead revolves around moderating and meeting consumers' expectations.[115] This necessitates affording space to the consumer's voice, intermediated by a competition authority or a court, when switching turns out to be ineffective or unattainable, compelling leading actors to modify their modes of doing business,[116] to adjust the technical architecture of their platforms,[117] or to reconfigure market incentives.[118]

Loyalty is thus best understood as a mechanism of participation in the organization of the market through which norms of reciprocity and trust are (re)established.[119] Nonetheless, as much as loyalty plays a part in the account of the platform as dependable consultant, a number of customary objections also highlight the contested role of loyalty in contemporary competition law analysis. Typically, loyalty is cast as a shortcoming on the part of locked-in customers who fail to switch to alternative providers rather than as an obligation on the part of dominant suppliers to act in the best interests of consumers. This notion of loyalty attempts to understand why users of digital platforms fail to switch, why consumers unswervingly embrace a segment (even in the presence of superior alternatives), and what substitutes exist to promote their welfare.[120]

[112] Commitments to the European Commission, Case AT.40462 and Case AT.40703 *Amazon Marketplace*.
[113] Balkin (n 103).
[114] Kuenzler (n 47).
[115] Ibid.; Balkin (n 63).
[116] Case AT.39740 Google Search (Shopping) [2017], paras. 593–597.
[117] Bundeskartellamt, Decision of 6 February 2019, B6–22/16.
[118] Autorité de la concurrence, Décision 21-D-11, June 7, 2021, *Google AdTech*.
[119] Kuenzler (n 47).
[120] P Klemperer, "Markets with Consumer Switching Costs" (1987) 102 *Quarterly Journal of Economics*, 375; P Klemperer, "The Competitiveness of Markets with Switching Costs" (1987) 18 *RAND Journal of Economics*, 138.

The basic notion of loyalty thus rests on the idea that switching is the main, perhaps the exclusive, mechanism for consumers to exert an influence on markets.[121] We can see this sort of reasoning on the policy side as well. In response to intensified scrutiny of big technology platforms by competition authorities and courts, policymakers have endorsed proposals that seek to reduce the platforms' size and reach, to restore the ability of consumers to migrate between multiple providers.[122] To alleviate the loss of scale and scope, including the network effects that big technology platforms generate, the proposals seek to render the platforms' services interoperable, personal data portable, and predominant facilities separable to enable other actors to compete and innovate in products that are currently controlled by a few undertakings.[123] A user's loyalty toward a single segment, as a consequence, is mostly seen as raising the costs of switching.[124] This chapter does not doubt the validity of these observations. But in data-driven marketplaces, loyalty may also be an avenue to facilitate consumer influence when switching turns out to be impracticable or ineffective.[125] With switching and separation, the essential mechanisms by which platforms operate – their incentive to sell more data to advertisers and third parties, and to maximize their proceeds from doing so – inevitably remain unaffected, since every single platform once more operates in line with the market's profit-driven precepts.[126] To make consumers' voices heard effectively, they must instead be given an opportunity to readjust their segments – to spur competition for relevance, privacy, and reputation. Such consumer influence, as opposed to switching, is geared toward restoring *quality* rather than to address mere issues of large-scale innovation or achieve sheer decentralization and diversity.[127]

[121] R O'Donoghue and J Padilla, *The Law and Economics of Article 102 TFEU* (3rd ed., Oxford: Hart, 2020) 755–62; H Hovenkamp, "Antitrust and the Design of Production" (2018) 103 *Cornell Law Review*, 1155; Statement of the FTC Regarding Google's Search Practices, *In the Matter of Google Inc.*, FTC File No. 111-0163, January 3, 2013, 3.

[122] See, e.g., Bill H.R.3825, to promote competition and economic opportunity in digital markets by eliminating the conflicts of interest that arise from dominant online platforms' concurrent ownership or control of an online platform and certain other businesses; Bill H.R.3849, to promote competition, lower entry barriers, and to reduce switching costs for consumers and businesses online; elaborate defenses are provided by Z Teachout, *Break'Em Up: Recovering Our Freedom from Big Ag, Big Tech, and Big Money* (New York: All Points, 2020); Rory van Loo, "In Defense of Breakups: Administering a 'Radical' Remedy" (2020) 105 *Cornell Law Review*, 1955; Wu (n 9).

[123] See, for an overview, M Kades and F Scott Morton, "Interoperability as a Competition Remedy for Digital Networks" (2020).

[124] SJ Liebowitz and SE Margolis, "Path Dependence, Lock- In, and History" (1995) 11 *Journal of Law, Economics, & Organization*, 205.

[125] Hirschman (n 15).

[126] A Kuenzler, "Intellectual Property on the Cusp of the Intangible Economy" (2021) 16 *Journal of Intellectual Property Law and Practice*, 692.

[127] See Parker et al. (n 27); Krämer (n 25); Schweitzer and Welker (n 25); M Burdon and T Mackie, "Australia's Consumer Data Right and the Uncertain Role of Information Privacy Law" (2020) 10 *International Data Privacy Law*, 222.

C *Loyalty as Agency*

The conventional notion of loyalty tends to neglect the fact that in concentrated marketplaces, big technology platforms' business models, crucially, are built on exploiting users' data and that separating lines of business will only reinforce incentives for other actors to engage in the same data-exploitative practices whose employment regularly results in consumer dissatisfaction.[128] To confront the guiding principles by which big technology platforms operate, consumers must effectively be able to express disagreement not by switching but by exercising agency. And opportunities for agency are brought about by authorities and courts that help to put into effect consumers' preferences and expectations. Agency, in this respect, affords consumers the ability to realign market incentives – to edit the market to a degree that consumer switching cannot authorize.

From a strict output/profitability point of view, competition law highlights switching as a way to bring about consumers' desired outcomes. Accordingly, diversity and choice (for the most part) dominate. Consumers can exert an influence on the market, for example, by choosing between a number of different social media platforms that exhibit different product features, affordances, conventions, and curation habits and by being part of distinct communities among which they can relocate. Diversity and choice, as opposed to agency, enable users to navigate between different alternative offers in the market to the effect that higher quality is found elsewhere. But in data-driven marketplaces, consumer switching is frequently incapable of shifting the basic incentive structure that determines the manner in which platforms monetize consumers' personal information. Where advertising-driven business models have resulted in a crowded ecosystem of digital companies that extract as much data as possible to maximize revenue, switching only creates additional opportunities for other companies to compete in collecting and selling personal information. Here, diversity and choice are bound to obstinately produce the same unwanted outcomes with respect to the most highly cherished variables of consumer interest.[129] And switching enables consumers to exercise authority only in that they can move to another segment. That is, consumers get to wield authority, but they are unlikely to get to wield it on behalf of their *preferred* product or service. Hence, with switching, consumers lack the ability to address the platform's underlying working logic of permanently customizing and tailoring content. In its place, consumers who exercise authority to target quality by way of intensified administrative action are in a position to modify terms and conditions of agreement, methods of doing business, and the design of their favored products –

[128] Kuenzler (n 126); ME Stucke and A Grunes, *Big Data and Competition Policy* (New York: Oxford University Press, 2016), 15–28; ME Stucke and A Ezrachi, "When Competition Fails to Optimize Quality: A Look at Search Engines" (2016) 18 *Yale Journal of Law and Technology*, 70.

[129] Ibid.

and along with it the way in which companies across the market monetize personal information.[130] More generally, if quality rather than price is at issue, consumers need to be able to administer (parts of) a market's segment rather than opting for different, perhaps equally disappointing, alternatives.[131] Here, loyalty as agency affords consumers the ability to exert an influence as inside decision-makers rather than as outside opponents of a segment.[132] Loyalty as agency is thus important precisely because it enables consumers to remain part of a segment. Where dominant platforms as dependable consultants act as trustworthy stewards of consumers' expectations, loyalty as agency affords consumers the weight and standing to dispute certain contested modes of doing business. Consumers can articulate disagreement from within the segment, back their claims up via an authority or a court's shared expertise and competence, and channel their arguments in a manner that is feasible for incumbent actors to consider. As a result of this sort of influence, they are in a better position to produce a pertinent reaction from, and adjustment of, the market than they could as outsiders of a segment.

IV WHY THE CHASM IN COMPETITION LAW? THE INTRICACIES OF LOYALTY

Once we recognize that loyalty represents a useful avenue of consumer influence, the issue is why it is frequently overlooked in contemporary legal scholarship. Competition law ordinarily seeks to maximize output by facilitating switching and avoids paying heed to loyalty. Consumers' revealed preferences are assumed to accurately reflect their own desires, and greater consumer choice is presumed to be procompetitive.[133] When consumers choose to join or use one leading platform rather than another, they are thought to know how particular product recommendations are created, what the decisional parameters provided to them are, and that the platform's offers reflect good value, at least in the aggregate, given there may

[130] G Roschke and A Zach, "Data to Go: The FTC's Workshop on Data Portability" (2020) *Competition Policy International*, November 26, 2020.

[131] See C Shapiro and H Varian, *Information Rules: A Strategic Guide to the Network Economy* (Cambridge, MA: Harvard Business School Press, 1998); such influence will ultimately cause other companies to pay heed to consumers' preferences, as is the case with Apple's decision to allow "do not track" on its phones; J Nicas and M Isaac, "Facebook Takes the Gloves Off in Feud with Apple," *The New York Times*, December 16, 2020, sec Digital Privacy; or Google's plan to stop selling advertisements based on individuals' browsing; S Schechner and K Hagey, "Google to Stop Selling Ads Based on Your Specific Web Browsing," *The Wall Street Journal*, March 3, 2021, sec Tech.

[132] For instance, in EU competition law, authorities can issue a so-called market notice engaging the commitment decision procedure according to Articles 9 and 27(4) Regulation (EU) 1/2003 of 16 September 2002, OJ 2003 L1/1.

[133] JD Wright, "The Antitrust/Consumer Protection Paradox: Two Policies at War with Each Other" (2012) 121 *Yale Law Journal*, 2216.

occasionally be deviations.[134] This is why competition law conceptualizes consumer disagreement from the outside and ignores opposition from the inside.[135] It has spent an enormous amount of effort contemplating the role consumers play in searching for the most affordable bargain as a result of switching but not their role in helping quality to prevail in concentrated settings.[136]

Seen from the conventional vantage point, an intensified extent of administrative action is thus often viewed as a deficit to be remedied rather than a feature to be emphasized. It is typically understood as an interference in the free interplay of market forces, not a mechanism that gives way to the articulation of consumers' preferences.[137] Competition law underscores the consumer's (autonomous) opposition but it lacks a depiction of loyal customers who nevertheless can put their views into effect. Yet loyalty and agency have long been integral to legal theory and practice. Scholars do account for agency in the administrative and corporate realm,[138] and work on social movements highlights loyalty in holding vendors accountable in enforcing the norms that govern markets.[139] Competition law, for its part, has grown so accustomed to the precepts of Kaldor–Hicks efficiency that it has failed to appreciate the benefits of the administrative arrangements illustrated in this chapter. When competition law refers to these arrangements, it typically associates them with "market shifting" or depicts their character as intrusive.[140] What is more, when consumers exercise agency to contest their preferred segments, concerns about lawlessness or intractability abound.[141] This vantage point ignores the fact that consumer influence assuming this form provides *loyal customers* with the decision-making control that ordinarily is associated with switching. Competition law overwhelmingly applauds consumers challenging a segment so long as disagreement takes the form of outside antagonism and validates sheer decentralization. Thus, much legal scholarship in competition law omits prior work on loyalty and agency, thereby failing to advance those issues that quality rather than price competition breeds.

[134] B Holzer, "Political Consumerism between Individual Choice and Collective Action: Social Movements, Role Mobilization and Signalling" (2006) 30 *International Journal of Consumer Studies*, 405.

[135] Liebowitz and Margolis (n 124).

[136] Hirschman (n 15).

[137] R Bork, "Legislative Intent and the Policy of the Sherman Act" (1966) 9 *Journal of Law and Economics*, 7, 10.

[138] R Kraakman et al., *The Anatomy of Corporate Law: A Comparative and Functional Approach* (3rd ed., New York: Oxford University Press, 2017); T Endicott, *Administrative Law* (5th ed., New York: Oxford University Press, 2021).

[139] See Holzer (n 134); YE Arbel and R Shapira, "Consumer Activism: From the Informed Minority to the Crusading Minority" (2020) 69 *DePaul Law Review*, 233.

[140] See, for an overview, KS Rahman, *Democracy against Domination* (New York: Oxford University Press, 2016); HS Richardson, *Democratic Autonomy: Public Reasoning about the Ends of Policy* (New York: Oxford University Press, 2002).

[141] Ibid.

Although most commentators would perhaps concede that some form of administrative action taken on behalf of consumers may be productive,[142] the notion that consumers can usurp parts of a leading platform's business strategy must conjure up a sense of *dis*loyalty. Consumers can disagree by switching segments; but they ought not to employ authority over a leading platform's mode of doing business. This view of agency is based on consonance and concurrence.[143] It suggests, sensibly, that leading market actors should accomplish their own visions and that consumers, if they disagree, need to look for alternatives. It regards consumer dissent that takes the form of loyalty as doubtful even when this may plausibly be the only avenue available to maintain quality. By doing so, competition law commentary tends to associate agency with disloyalty, and consumers are either assumed to accept what leading actors offer or to exert an influence on the market by moving back and forth between distinct segments. But in the digital economy, acts of agency – put in place as a result of intensified administrative action – are perhaps best understood as behavior by *loyal* customers: Rather than having recourse to entitlements or market structure, attention is paid to *institutional channels* of influence in which authorities and courts act on behalf of consumers.[144] Here, consumers can both contest an influential segment and work toward protecting leading actors' vested interests – they are in a position to challenge (parts of) an influential segment while simultaneously clinging to it.

Consumers who exercise agency in this way are behaving like loyal members of a segment. They share the commitments of the segment but are nonetheless at odds with the manner in which those commitments are achieved. That is, at the same time that consumers are contesting a particular segment, they are also endorsing it. In doing so, they help to reconfigure the segment and work to ensure that leading actors can nonetheless account for their own interests. It is precisely for this reason that the consumer's disagreement remains loyal; consumers seek to readjust the policies of their favored segments and put in place incentives that facilitate coherence with their preferences and expectations.

Consider as an example the FCO's Facebook investigation. The decision was drawn up with the intention and effect of reinforcing the platform's responsiveness to consumer interests, most notably, to authorize consumers to opt out of the platform's data collection and to delete their collected data history.[145] Once the FCO's measures were put in place, the force and effect of the decision had the

[142] See O'Donoghue and Padilla (n 121), 1046–64.

[143] See J Royce, *The Philosophy of Loyalty* (New York: MacMillan, 1908).

[144] Regulation (EU) 1/2003 of 16 September 2002, OJ 2003 L1/1; here, agency springs from the interests of a majority of customers, or, at a minimum, from a minority of users whose preferences are given effect in a manner that will not preordain the views of a majority of consumers.

[145] Bundeskartellamt, Decision of 6 February 2019, B6–22/16.

weight of a rule, or at least generated incentives for other firms to adapt.[146] In that manner, consumers' vantage points were given some space within a market where that space had been under challenge by an increasing tendency toward concentration and innovation-impeding power dynamics. Even this kind of agency is sometimes disdained as an act of disloyalty, however, not least because the FCO's proceedings had initially been depicted as involving a direct challenge to Facebook's underlying business venture.[147] But as a matter of fact, the FCO's investigation brought to bear the loyalty of Facebook's users. It served the identical purpose as that which switching ordinarily performs – affording consumers a choice with respect to their preferred level of privacy in the market – although it differed with regard to the manner in which this goal was attained.[148]

In this fashion, agency as loyalty involves the purposeful modification of a dominant platform's mode of doing business, carried out through institutional channels of consumer influence, and bringing the market's state of quality equilibrium in line with consumers' expectations. Agency, so understood, does not embrace, exclusively, disapproval and opposition. Rather, it encompasses acts of membership and affiliation.[149] Because agency as loyalty involves a formalized procedure of protest and contestation, consumers are not required to desert or to attempt to bring a business to a halt. Instead, they are given an opportunity to express concern *in relation to* their favored segment. When they oppose a segment in this manner, they simultaneously pledge allegiance to it, respecting and endorsing the dominant actor's value position but nevertheless requesting some modification. Note that the force of agency as loyalty essentially pivots on accomplishing cohesion, not disintegration. The decisions that authorities and courts issue in such cases are made in the best interests of *existing* segments, although they regularly deviate, at least in part, from the leading actor's policy. Rather than associating agency with disloyalty, then, agency seeks to integrate consumers' preferences into the dominant segment. Agency, so understood, authorizes at least partial disagreement and involves no less than partial loyalty. Consumers who are dissatisfied with (some aspects of) their favored segment exhibit divided loyalties toward that segment. They are neither entirely dedicated nor fully dissenting but are in some measure both. That is, they are affiliates *and* contenders, cultivating loyalty not simply to stay put but also to remonstrate and touch up.[150]

[146] Although the decision was appealed, it visibly led other leading platforms to position themselves as privacy advocates; E Johansson, "Google and Apple Seek to Position Themselves as Privacy Champions," *The Verdict*, July 29, 2021.

[147] See, for an overview, G Colangelo and M Maggiolino, "Antitrust über alles. Whither Competition Law after Facebook?" (2019) 42 *World Competition*, 355.

[148] See Section V.

[149] Most prominently J Rawls, *A Theory of Justice* (Cambridge, MA: Belknap Press, 1971), 363–67; G Sitaraman and A Alstott, *The Public Option. How to Expand Freedom, Increase Opportunity, and Promote Equality* (Cambridge, MA: Harvard University Press, 2019).

[150] See specifically A Kuenzler, "What Competition Law Can Do for Data Privacy (and Vice Versa)" (2022) 47 *Computer Law and Security Review*, 105757, 1.

V IS AGENCY IMPORTANT ENOUGH TO BE COMMENDED?

For all of the above, widespread reliance in competition law commentary on separating platforms and commerce, coupled with interoperability and/or data portability measures, raises the additional issue as to whether agency as loyalty is important enough to be commended.[151] If agency as loyalty can meaningfully correct for quality deteriorations, can entitlement-based and structural interventions achieve the same in digital marketplaces? This part works through some arguments that render agency as loyalty distinct from interoperability, portability, and structural separations.

A *Interoperability*

One of the most frequently endorsed remedies in competition law commentary is interoperability – compelled sharing of information, including data, productive assets, and operations – to address impediments to competition.[152] Devising effective interoperability remedies requires the identification of distinct behaviors or arrangements, including obstacles to successful implementation, that render markets less competitive than what they otherwise might be.[153] Such remedies are especially

[151] See TK McCraw, *Prophets of Regulation* (Cambridge, MA: Belknap Press, 1984); D Schoenbrod, *Power without Responsibility: How Congress Abuses the People through Delegation* (New Haven: Yale University Press, 1993); European Commission, "A European Strategy for Data" COM(2020) 66 final; Directive (EU) 2019/1024 of 20 June 2019 on Open Data and the Re-Use of Public Sector Information, OJ L 172/56; European Commission, "Towards a Common European Data Space" COM(2018) 232 final; Regulation (EU) 2018/1807 of 14 November 2018 on a Framework for the Free Flow of Non-Personal Data in the European Union, OJ L 303/59. Such measures may prove to be particularly important to stimulate competition and innovation and to empower consumers in secondary markets; S Vezzoso, "Competition Policy in Transition: Exploring Data Portability's Roles" (2021) 12 *Journal of European Competition Law and Practice*, 357. The basic policy considerations turn upon private control versus public open access approaches; European Commission, "A European Strategy for Data" COM(2020) 66 final. Specific data portability rights are enshrined in Regulation (EU) 2016/679 of 27 April 2016 on the Protection of Natural Persons with Regard to the Processing of Personal Data and on the Free Movement of Such Data (General Data Protection Regulation), OJ L 119/1, Article 20; Directive (EU) 2015/2366 of 25 November 2015 on Payment Services in the Internal Market, OJ L 337/35, Articles 66–67; Directive (EU) 2019/944 of 5 June 2019 on Common Rules for the Internal Market for Electricity, OJ L 158/125, Article 23. Regarding data access rights see Regulation (EU) 2017/1926 of 31 May 2017 on the Provision of EU-Wide Multimodal Travel Information Services, OJ L 272/1, Articles 4–5; Directive (EU) 2019/770 of 20 May 2019 on Certain Aspects Concerning Contracts for the Supply of Digital Content and Digital Services, OJ L 136/1, Article 5.

[152] For an overview, see H Hovenkamp, "Antitrust and Platform Monopoly" (2021) 130 *Yale Law Journal*, 1952.

[153] U.S. v. Trans-Missouri Freight Association, 166 U.S. 290 (1897); Associated Press v. U.S., 326 U.S. 1 (1945); U.S. v. AT&T Co. 552 F. Supp. 131 (D.D.C. 1982), aff'd sub nom Maryland v. U.S., 460 U.S. 1001 (1983); MCI Communications Corp. v. AT&T Co., 708 F.2d 1081 (7th Cir. 1983).

attractive in winner-takes-all markets with non-rivalrous goods and significant economies of scale and scope, including network effects, that give large undertakings considerable advantages over smaller ones.[154] Here, interoperability may decrease the costs of doing business, render a service more attractive to consumers, or both.[155] But interoperability may also bring about accidental costs. Forcing a dominant social media platform such as Facebook to make users' data portable to a different social network may alleviate the costs of switching but may also make it easier for users to transfer data from smaller actors to the dominant network's winner-takes-all market.[156] Another risk of imposing interoperability is that it may constrain product differentiation. In markets where consumers are given options that cater to their diverse interests – such as when they communicate with family and friends on Instagram or Snapchat but employ LinkedIn or Xing to maintain their professional relations – interoperability may have the effect of broadly introducing common standards and unduly removing or inflicting discrete or conjoint features such as instant messaging, or exposure of personal information. With interoperability, the market may then no longer reflect the variety of choices of distinct consumer segments.[157] Instead, it may constrain the emergence of diverse functionalities and unexpected aspects of innovation, removing the appeal of different products to separate audiences.[158]

[154] U.S. v. Microsoft Corp., 253 F.3d 34 (D.C. Cir. 2001); Rambus, Inc. v. FTC, 522 F.3d 456 (D.C. Cir. 2008).

[155] To enable effective competition, interoperability remedies must decentralize control over price and output, placing them in the hands of several firms that are unable to collude; Alaska Airlines, Inc. v. United Airlines, Inc., 948 F.2d 536 (9th Cir. 1991); see already U.S. v. Terminal Railroad Association of St. Louis, 224 U.S. 383 (1912).

[156] O Borgogno and G Colangelo, "Open Banking and the Ambiguous Competitive Effects of Data Portability" (2021) *Competition Policy International*, April 12, 2021. Or one may imagine that full data sharing in search engine markets will result in users flocking to Google search.

[157] S Bowman, "Why Data Interoperability Is Harder Than It Looks: The Open Banking Experience" (2021) *Competition Policy International*, April 12, 2021; D Awrey and J Macey, "Open Access, Interoperability, and the DTCC's Unexpected Path to Monopoly" (2021). Interoperability remedies must be limited to those aspects where they are required, leaving competition to work in the balance. This is not possible in all markets because the nature of data with strategic value varies from industry to industry and the same data may not be equally valuable to retail traders as to primary service providers.

[158] J Ezrielev and G Marquez, "Interoperability: The Wrong Prescription for Platform Competition" (2021) *Competition Policy International*, June 15, 2021; PR Dickson and JL Ginter, "Market Segmentation, Product Differentiation, and Marketing Strategy" (1987) 51 *Journal of Marketing*, 1; AK Dixit and J Stiglitz, "Monopolistic Competition and Optimum Product Diversity" (1977) 67 *American Economic Review*, 297. On the other hand, only "partial interoperability," whereby different platforms may continue offering differentiated features and exchange only "basic" information, may be of little benefit for users when the costs for multihoming are low; Kades and Scott Morton (n 123). In addition, with full interoperability, the benefits of investment in growing the size of the network, new advertising techniques, and new functionality may accrue in part to other platforms, which may lead to free-riding and diminished incentives to innovate. New rules for digital gatekeepers therefore classify interoperability-related obligations under a category that is susceptible of being further

Moreover, there are a number of technical obstacles to interoperability becoming a manageable solution to reinstating quality in digital markets. While in theory, the advantages of interoperability originate from the coordinated redistribution of otherwise high and hypothetically duplicative costs of developing and maintaining infrastructure-like facilities among multiple competing entities, these costs may not readily be divisible, nor actually divided, or may place a disproportionate burden on smaller actors.[159] Rendering data fully interoperable between different social media platforms can turn out to be problematic, for instance, when different websites employ different types of user information. Users of Facebook, Instagram, or TikTok each accumulate discrete records of messages, images, videos, and acquaintances, and making data fully interoperable will force smaller market actors to incur relatively high fixed costs of connecting to the comprehensive infrastructure of bigger platforms.[160] Compounding matters further, whenever users' collection of content and connections, and investment of effort in building each, grows with use of, and improvements to, a service, interoperability requirements leave smaller actors with no choice but to do so as well.[161] The more entrenched an interoperability standard becomes, the more likely it will keep a rein on the ability to innovate, and the more likely it will limit incentives of other actors to work out competing standards, dampening competition for the market.[162] Along these lines, interoperability may allow dominant actors to influence the pace of competitors' innovations and force rivals to make investments that they might otherwise not have made.[163] Interoperability standards may then represent unnecessary barriers to entry or stifle opportunities for other actors to compete.[164]

specified; European Commission, Regulation (EU) 2022/1925 of the European Parliament and of the Council of 14 September 2022 on contestable and fair markets in the digital sector and amending Directives (EU) 2019/1937 and (EU) 2020/1828 (Digital Markets Act) (DMA), Articles 6–7.

159 Awrey and Macey (n 157).

160 FTC v. Facebook, Inc., Case 1:20-cv-03590-JEB (D.D.C. January 11, 2022), 23; Bowman (n 157).

161 This may increase dependence between different companies and expose them to similar risks but the companies' different size may serve to reinforce big actors' advantages of scale; Awrey and Macey (n 157).

162 Crémer et al. (n 42), 59; but see Kades and Scott Morton (n 123), 15. Regarding the risk of manipulating standard setting to exclude rivals with different product characteristics or to entrench an incumbent's technology when there are no transparency and fair, reasonable, and non-discriminatory (FRAND) obligations, see OECD, "Data Portability, Interoperability, and Digital Platform Competition" (2021). On the other hand, interventions that seek to promote interoperability and data portability may disincentivize aggressive competition on the parameters covered by the standard and may be used as a cover for information exchange or otherwise facilitate collusion. Such interventions may also increase the risk of collusion due to a higher degree of transparency in a market as well as more multi-market contact; A Fletcher, "Digital Competition Policy: Are Ecosystems Different?" (2020).

163 Awrey and Macey (n 157).

164 R Feasey and A de Streel, "Data Sharing for Digital Markets Contestability. Towards a Governance Framework" (Centre on Regulation in Europe, 2020). Faced with an obligation to share data, a platform is likely to seek to minimize both its costs and disruption to existing

What is more, interoperability remedies must be designed to consider increased privacy and security risks. Greater third-party access to a platform's services will expose actors and consumers to compromised personal data or security breaches.[165] Smaller actors may likely fail to have the same resources as bigger market players to defend themselves against cyberattacks or hacking, and interoperability remedies that necessitate access to their services will create additional vulnerabilities. Depending on the size and characteristics of the market, the harm resulting from such hazards is exacerbated if a platform is required to permit access to several different competitors in a market.[166]

B *Data Portability*

There are similar concerns with data portability rights. Greater ease of data access (or opening up the free flow of data as a rule) through portability measures that facilitate data reuse may bring about a drop in economic value of the information that such data carry, may enable a greater extent of profiling, or may pose additional threats to privacy or cybersecurity, because competitor firms can get hold of the same or similar inferences from the same piece of information.[167] Moreover, access rights have turned out to be particularly difficult to design effectively.[168] Take the right to data portability enshrined in Article 20 of the General Data Protection

business practices by proposing that others adopt the proprietary standards in which it has already invested. The incumbent platform would, in doing so, become the standard setter for the rest of the industry. Alternatively, different standards may emerge in different contexts, which could create significant entry barriers for firms that seek to obtain access to data from several platforms and raise costs for all parties. Even with respect to commonly used technical formats, interoperability is not always achieved. Common formats may enable data transfers and decoding of data from one source system to another; however, they may not guarantee that the content of the data is understood by the recipient. More generally, data need to be discoverable, which requires them to be cataloged and/or searchable.

165 Bowman (n 157); I Graef and J Prüfer, "Governance of Data Sharing: A Law & Economics Proposal" (2021) 50 *Research Policy*, 104330; C Santesteban and S Longpre, "Effective Interoperability to Enhance Competition in Social Networking: Breaking Down Data-Driven Barriers to Entry" (2020) Antitrust: Antitrust Law & Policy.

166 Rubinfeld (n 25); Gal and Rubinfeld (n 27). Article 7(3) of the Digital Markets Act (DMA) requires with respect to the interoperability of number-independent interpersonal communication services that the level of security, including the end-to-end encryption, where applicable, that gatekeepers provide to their own end users shall be preserved across the interoperable services. This standard offers several privacy benefits for consumers but it also imposes demanding requirements on third-party services to comply with the DMA's interoperability provisions.

167 Rubinfeld (n 25); D Nguyen and M Paczos, "Measuring the Economic Value of Data and Cross-Border Data Flows: A Business Perspective" (2020) *OECD Digital Economy Papers*, 297.

168 G Nicholas and M Weinberg, "Data Portability and Platform Competition: Is User Data Exported from Facebook Actually Useful to Competitors?" (2019) *Engelberg Center on Innovation Law and Policy*; M Ananny and K Crawford, "Seeing without Knowing: Limitations of the Transparency Ideal and Its Application to Algorithmic Accountability" (2018) 20 *New Media and Society*, 973.

Regulation (GDPR) as an example. According to this provision, each data subject "shall have the right to receive the personal data concerning him or her … in a structured, commonly used and machine-readable format and have the right to transmit those data to another controller without hindrance from [it]."[169] The provision arguably seeks to facilitate consumer switching, lower barriers to entry, and increase contestability of a controller's or processor's market position. But it scarcely motivates large-scale data sharing between digital platforms. Without interoperable data formats and some minimum requirements of technical compatibility – including, in some instances, the provision of the necessary interface and infrastructure for data subjects to access that information – the provision's scope is far too narrow.[170] In addition, the GDPR's right to data portability fails to compel controllers or processors to grant consumers immediate and frequent access to their data to enable them to multi-home or try out different services.[171] Instead, Article 20 GDPR stipulates a right to all-or-nothing data transfers, which may increase transaction costs and create uncertainty in a competitor's ability to understand what specific data points connote. This will increase the cost of combining the available information into coherent datasets to achieve interoperability where some data are missing, and the data's value, significance, and worth are underrated as a result.[172] Similarly, the GDPR's right to data portability is non-waivable even in the face of a controller's high degree of market power. This can deter competitors from entering a market in which a dominant platform operates because the latter may entice

[169] Regulation (EU) 2016/679 of 27 April 2016 on the Protection of Natural Persons with Regard to the Processing of Personal Data and on the Free Movement of Such Data (General Data Protection Regulation), OJ L 119/1, Article 20.

[170] Directive (EU) 2015/2366 of 25 November 2015 on Payment Services in the Internal Market, OJ L 337/35, Articles 66–67 and Directive (EU) 2019/944 of 5 June 2019 on Common Rules for the Internal Market for Electricity, OJ L 158/125, Article 23 go further in this regard; see also Regulation (EU) 2018/858 of 30 May 2018 on the Approval and Market Surveillance of Motor Vehicles and Their Trailers, and of Systems, Components and Separate Technical Units Intended for Such Vehicles, OJ L 151/1, Articles 61–66; D Gill and W Kerber, "Data Portability Rights: Limits, Opportunities, and the Need for Going beyond the Portability of Personal Data" (2020) *Competition Policy International*, November 26, 2020.

[171] De Hert et al. (n 25); but see Article 6(1)(9) and (10) DMA, aiming to afford business users and end users of gatekeeper platforms continuous and real-time access, free of charge, European Commission, Regulation (EU) 2022/1925 of the European Parliament and of the Council of 14 September 2022 on contestable and fair markets in the digital sector and amending Directives (EU) 2019/1937 and (EU) 2020/1828 (Digital Markets Act) (DMA). This also applies to data generated by users, see recital 59 DMA; additional extensions are envisaged in Articles 3–5 Data Act, European Commission, "Proposal for a Regulation of the European Parliament and of the Council on Harmonized Rules on Fair Access to and Use of Data (Data Act)" COM (2022) 68 final (Data Act). These provisions contain data access rights that extend to non-personal data for users and third parties, except for gatekeepers covered by the DMA.

[172] E Giovannetti and P Siciliani, "The Impact of Data Portability on Platform Competition" (2020) *Competition Policy International*, November 26, 2020; for a reform proposal, see European Commission, "Data Protection as a Pillar of Citizens' Empowerment and the EU's Approach to the Digital Transition – Two Years of Application of the General Data Protection Regulation" COM(2020) 264 final.

consumers to its services, which exhibit greater network effects, economies of scale and scope, and better personalization.[173] Without the ability of entire groups of users to coordinate data transfers to a different platform all at once (or at least retaining access to multiple networks simultaneously), the right to data portability might even work to the detriment of other actors and favor the most data-rich providers.[174] Perhaps even more tellingly, the provision of a right to data portability may discourage market entrants from devising new services that minimize surveillance because data can be more easily transferred.[175] In turn, users will find themselves in an inferior position than if new entrants were compelled by market forces to vie more fiercely for new patrons in the absence of such a right.[176] And if users are more willing to share their data and can easily switch in case of disappointment in the presence of a right to data portability, their behavior may only reinforce the network effects of market leaders and further strengthen their dominant position.[177] Although, in theory, data portability aims to facilitate switching, in practice, it may bring about an additional consolidation of market power or raise barriers to entry, and may diminish the ability of consumers to meaningfully exert an influence on the market's state of quality equilibrium.[178]

C *Structural Separations and Divestitures*

There are related issues with structural separations, although such measures have in the past been applied successfully in networked industries such as energy, railroads, banking, television, and telecommunications.[179] The idea behind separations and

[173] Schweitzer and Welker (n 25).

[174] L Zingales and G Rolnik, "A Way to Own Your Social-Media Data," *The New York Times*, June 30, 2017, sec Opinion; G Nicholas, "Taking It with You: Platform Barriers to Entry and the Limits of Data Portability" (2021) 27 *Michigan Technology Law Review*, 263; see also P Swire and Y Lagos, "Why the Right to Data Portability Likely Reduces Consumer Welfare: Antitrust and Privacy Critique" (2013) 72 *Maryland Law Review*, 335.

[175] M Wohlfarth, "Data Portability on the Internet: An Economic Analysis" (2019) 61 *Business and Information Systems Engineering*, 551; see also Bowman (n 157).

[176] J Krämer and N Stüdlein, "Data Portability, Data Disclosure and Data-Induced Switching Costs: Some Unintended Consequences of the General Data Protection Regulation" (2019) 181 *Economic Letters*, 99.

[177] MS Gal and O Aviv, "The Competitive Effects of the GDPR" (2020) 16 *Journal of Competition Law and Economics*, 349; WMW Lam and X Liu, "Does Data Portability Facilitate Entry?" (2020) 69 *International Journal of Industrial Organization*, 102564; EF Ramos and K Blind, "Data Portability Effects on Data-Driven Innovation of Online Platforms: Analyzing Spotify" (2020) 44 *Telecommunications Policy*, 102026; on the other hand, if portability reduces the willingness of data subjects to allow their private data to be gathered, this may likely dampen data collection and innovation overall; Rubinfeld (n 25).

[178] Borgogno and Colangelo (n 156); Krämer (n 25), 15; acknowledging the hybrid nature of data portability I Graef, "The Opportunities and Limits of Data Portability for Stimulating Competition and Innovation" (2020) *Competition Policy International*, November 26, 2020.

[179] OECD, "Structural Separation in Regulated Industries. Report on Implementing the OECD Recommendation" (2016).

divestitures is to target anticompetitive behavior that flows inexorably from a firm's specific structure.[180] Where reliance on imposing entitlement-based rules and remedies is weak, breakups may be viewed as levelheaded – and sometimes even necessary – alternatives.[181] However, breakups usually require detailed orders laying down specific assets to be divested, execution of all aspects of a transaction, and detailed measures to oversee the process.[182] Accordingly, divesting dominant companies has turned out to be most feasible when it involves reversing previously approved mergers rather than breaking up firms that have expanded wholly through internal growth.[183] When anticompetitive effects concern a dominant firm's related operations (including separately organized subsidiaries, distinct business operations, or complementary goods and services), spinning them off is not nearly as disruptive and intrusive as separating a firm's integrated area of dominance.[184] But where data-driven platforms exhibit high economies of scale and scope and there is a propensity of markets to tip, separation of platforms into multiple smaller entities will not guarantee that the new companies will behave any better than the previous one did in the past. For instance, given the existing competitive pressure of digital platforms to observe stakeholders' (particularly advertisers') interests, how should a leading social media platform such as Facebook be broken up if the goal is to behave in a manner that takes notice of consumers' privacy? Separating platforms and commerce may result in a structurally more competitive market and more opportunities for consumers to switch. But such a market will likely lack the capacity to cure the most pertinent issues that quality deteriorations generate because more competition among multiple smaller actors for more advertising revenue also entails more data surveillance. To be sure, if a leading search engine such as Google were to be separated from its Android operating system, the company could no longer offer its operating system on commercial terms that depend on the use of its search engine.[185] Or if Google were vertically separated from its network of properties in

[180] European Commission, "Commission Notice on Remedies Acceptable Under Council Regulation (EC) No 139/2004 and under Commission Regulation (EC) No 802/2004," OJ [2008] C 267/1, N 17.

[181] See J Kwoka and T Valletti, "Scrambled Eggs and Paralyzed Policy: Breaking Up Consummated Mergers and Dominant Firms" (2020) *Competition Policy International*, December 17, 2020; UK Competition and Markets Authority (n 42). Divestitures do not always need to involve structural breakups but may instead focus on third-party platforms or involve internal data-separation policies.

[182] Ibid.

[183] Ibid.

[184] The literature on biased intermediation points out that where quality (not price) is key, separation might reduce consumer welfare; A de Cornière and G Taylor, "A Model of Biased Intermediation" (2019) 50 *RAND Journal of Economics*, 854; A Hagiu, TH The, and J Wright, "Should Amazon Be Allowed to Sell on Its Own Marketplace?" (2020); J Casanova, "Online Search Competition and the Risk of Unintended Consequences of Data Access" (2020) *Competition Policy International*, November 26, 2020; Giovannetti and Siciliani (n 172).

[185] Ibid.

advertisers', publishers', and exchange servers alike, it would need to refrain from operating simultaneously on all three levels of the digital AdTech stack to the detriment of rivals.[186] But such breakups are nevertheless unlikely to lead to predictable and reliable improvements when concerns around quality such as relevance, privacy, or reputation are meant to be meaningfully addressed.[187]

D *Agency as an Additional Opportunity for Disagreement*

Viewed against some of the most important functions of competition – enabling consumers to articulate, and put into effect, their preferences and expectations – agency has some considerable advantages over its entitlement-based and structural counterparts in concentrated market settings. It introduces sources of opposition and disagreement *within* leading segments. In particular, when consumers are unable – or indeed unwilling – to effectively express their dissatisfaction as a result of switching, agency embeds consumers' choices into the most contested segments and ensures that dominant actors attune the value of their policies to consumers' actual interests.[188]

The entire point of agency is thus to reinstate those qualities that concern consumers most and that are unable to be remedied by either entitlement-based or structural solutions: Where digital platforms rely on the revelation of free data passively collected from their users, abandoning a segment may set off a decline in a firm's capacity to offer content that consumers truly value.[189] This is the primary effect of the user's role as a data consumer *and* producer because most data-driven platforms rely on participation by consumers to generate relevant content, features, and information. Likewise, if users multi-home between different platforms, switching may fail to provide an effective feedback mechanism to the firm in relation to its shortcomings, and there will be few incentives for platforms to adjust.[190] Moreover, in concentrated marketplaces with network effects and ecosystem advantages, consumers usually *want* to satisfy their desires within distinct

[186] Ibid.

[187] Kuenzler (nn 23, 47, 50, 98, 126). To avoid ongoing court supervision, authorities and courts can proscribe concrete measures that permit the market rather than the government to determine post-relief competition.

[188] For example, in an ecosystem in which a leading actor offers multiple complementary products, consumers may exhibit a low tendency to switch or use third-party service providers. This may be due to a low interest in shopping around, inertia, status quo or default biases, or consumers favoring zero-priced products even if better-quality alternatives are available at low prices; Fletcher (n 162). But note that abuse of dominance is possible only if all of a firm's counterparties lack a say over the governance of the dominant firm. When all counterparties have an equal say over the governance of the firm, a balance of power will prevail according to which the firm will not exploit monopoly power that it may have; see RA Woodcock, "Antitrust by Interior Means" (2021).

[189] Kuenzler (n 47).

[190] Ibid.

segments, and most consumers continue to be users of at least some of the declining firm's products even if they switch (e.g., WhatsApp Messenger, which belongs to Facebook; Google's email services; or Amazon's speakers). Here, again, switching may turn out to be ineffective, because the platform will lose valuable data and information, or unattainable because users regularly cannot cease to be a member of a platform's tangled web of complementary products and services.[191] Furthermore, differences in product quality are typically less discernible to consumers than differences in price. Few consumers will, for instance, notice a platform's lowering of its privacy-protective safety measures or its accuracy of search results, and it might be arduous for rival platform operators to identify and convince consumers of those differences in quality that may encourage them to switch – although the consequences of such quality deteriorations may turn out to be significant.[192]

For all these reasons, entitlement-based and structural remedies can hardly preclude leading platform operators from lowering quality (while simultaneously increasing revenue). And because platforms crucially depend on collecting and selling users' data, smaller actors have every incentive to engage in the same surveillance-driven strategies to increase their profit.[193] While with switching, competition may become vibrant and productive in some dimensions, it may nevertheless fail to compel the market to pay heed to some of the consumer's most cherished variables of interest.[194] Recall again the point about product differentiation. Distinct messaging applications such as WhatsApp, Signal, Snapchat, and Instagram provide a variety of features that are not governed by common interoperability standards that apply to everyday short and multimedia messaging services (SMS and MMS). Compelling providers of such applications to adopt the identical standards to facilitate consumer switching would likely have forestalled their initial emergence, including a number of follow-on innovations such as new technologies for content-creation and moderation.[195] Assuming that consumers, overall, value a true variety of distinct offers, issues can be resolved not by reinstating switching, but when they are afforded a meaningful type of *agency*. This is why the FCO's *Facebook* decision mattered so much in terms of giving way to privacy in a market where competition for privacy coagulated due to behavioral surveillance strategies that brought about

[191] Ibid.; MG Jacobides and CJ Tae, "Kingpins, Bottlenecks and Value Dynamics along a Sector" (2015) 26 *Organization Science*, 889.

[192] MG Jacobides, C Cennamo, and A Gawer, "Towards a Theory of Ecosystems" (2018) 39 *Strategic Management Journal*, 2255.

[193] Philippon (n 62), 276–78; Stucke and Ezrachi (n 128).

[194] See "Facebookers Approve the New Policy, but Still Hate Redesign," *The New York Times*, April 24, 2009, sec Technology; "Facebook Tries to Become a Democracy," *The New York Times*, February 26, 2009, sec Technology.

[195] Legally mandated interoperability can even have anticompetitive effects if the costs of developing, maintaining, and governing common infrastructure cannot be effectively allocated across multiple firms, or might place disproportionate burdens on small competitors; Awrey and Macey (n 157).

exceptional degrees of profitability from snowballing returns to scale and scope. Ease of switching, achieved through interoperability, data portability, or structural separations, would only have raised additional privacy issues – more data would have been shared, more actors would have gotten hold of it, and more firms would have employed consumers' information for unrelated purposes without their knowledge and consent. In its place, the FCO leveraged the consumer's status as an agent embedded in a large ecosystem of data-driven services, bringing the platform's policy in line with user interests, proscribing the collection, utilization, and sale of personal information on third-party websites and applications without their consent. This diminished pressure on less data-rich market actors – many of whom in the past had been compelled to duck privacy issues in order to stay competitive – to exploit their supply of user information, putting them in a better position to meet their obligations as trustworthy stewards of consumers' expectations.

Agency, in this regard, permits consumers to express disagreement through institutional channels of influence so that consumers have *additional* leverage points over leading actors and can exert pressure over their objectives. Agency affords consumers the prospect of submitting a real-life example of their points of view, not an insulated act in defense of their private interests. Consumers are not merely given an opportunity to demonstrate that quality needs to adjust. They are also authorized to assert, collectively, that – and exactly how – quality can be maintained in relation to their chosen segment.

Agency also differs from new legislative provisions and/or proposals which contain a number of obligations that not only help to promote switching but also work to integrate consumers' preferences into the market.[196] Opportunities for disagreement, stipulated by the law, are cast in abstract terms, and the main dissenting actors are pressure groups, policymakers, and associations that express their views ex ante. The ongoing dialogue between leading actors and their constituency is distinct from that which consumers initiate ex post. Any dissent that occurs in retrospect is based on the reality of a given situation rather than on mere assumptions or abstract conjecture.[197] And it is certainly desirable for consumers to gain a more accurate perception of how a platform works in practice, particularly in light of the complexity and opacity of data-driven markets.[198] Consumers who act as agents of a segment are prone to have a better grasp of the circumstances of a given situation and may get hold of a broader variety of information. And consumer disagreement may come in

[196] European Commission, Regulation (EU) 2022/1925 of the European Parliament and of the Council of 14 September 2022 on contestable and fair markets in the digital sector and amending Directives (EU) 2019/1937 and (EU) 2020/1828 (Digital Markets Act) (DMA); see more specifically Kuenzler (n 150).

[197] F Flórez Duncan and G Shier, "A More Flexible, Effects Based Approach Is Required If the DMA Is to Foster Innovation and Protect the Value Platforms Offer" (2021) *Competition Policy International*, July 11, 2021.

[198] WE Kovacic and DA Hyman, "Regulating Big Tech: Lessons from the FTC's Do Not Call Rule" (2022).

repeated cycles, in response to concrete behavior and in reaction to new technological developments so that agency can approximate consumer interests more exhaustively than a one-off theoretical dispute.[199]

Admittedly, there are also disadvantages to exercising agency through intensified administrative action. Judged against new legislative proposals, consumers, helped by intensified administrative action, can disagree with a dominant actor's mode of operation without having to debate the issue on a public stage.[200] Investigations by authorities and courts can be lengthy, and authorities may have trouble tailoring remedies effectively.[201] By contrast, the establishment of new, particularly sector-specific legislation typically involves wholly different groups of actors and institutions, including agents of all categories of stakeholders, not only competition authorities and courts.[202] But where concerns around product quality include the interest of consumers in adjusting the course of business of dominant actors to calibrate market-wide incentives, agency sensibly takes the form of intensified administrative action. It seeks to give consumers control – the authority to assist in reconfiguring influential segments – rather than only to oppose or fall back on preexisting notions of what is ostensibly involved in disagreement. At the same time, agency, exercised through intensified administrative action, compels consumers to confine their criticism to a specific aspect of a segment; they cannot disagree across the board and cannot oppose an overly broad range of concerns that they encounter as constituents of the entire market. If agency and switching are put side by side, agency is sensibly viewed as an additional avenue for consumer influence to play a part in disputes involving quality. Nonetheless, switching is justifiably considered the predominant mechanism governing markets. Agency can complement this role, however, affording consumers some additional leverage points where switching is unavailable or turns out to be ineffective, fusing the consumer's position of outsider with the user's status as insider.[203]

VI CONCLUDING REMARKS

This chapter has shown that the issue of what constitutes product quality is best viewed as a function of what big technology platforms seek to accomplish. Any theoretical reconstruction of the concept, however, is inherently limited. From this it follows that the proposed grouping of the concept involves the manner in which

[199] Crémer et al. (n 42); for a more detailed treatment of these issues, see A Kuenzler, "Third-Generation Competition law" (2023) 11 *Journal of Antitrust Enforcement*, 133.

[200] Teece and Kahwaty (n 41); Petit (n 20).

[201] R Feasey and J Krämer, "Implementing Effective Remedies for Anti-Competitive Intermediation Bias on Vertically Integrated Platforms" (Centre on Regulation in Europe, 2019).

[202] CS Yoo, "Unpacking Data Portability" (2020) *Competition Policy International*, November 26, 2020.

[203] See Krämer (n 25); Rubinfeld (n 25); Gill and Kerber (n 170).

platforms as intermediaries or curators operate, joining both of them together and focusing on consumers' viewpoints by apprehending platforms as dependable consultants. This arrangement has largely been neglected in competition law debates in which quality rather than price and output dominate. This is due to the fact that competition law commentary has dedicated an overwhelming amount of vigor to the manner in which markets maximize efficiency and emphasize mostly large-scale innovation. An upshot of this thinking is that we have arrived at a fully fleshed-out account of switching as the main, perhaps the exclusive, avenue of consumer influence from both entitlement-based and structural points of view. In contrast, competition law commentary has devoted relatively little time and space to the issue of how consumers can influence leading segments, not just by moving back and forth between alternative offers, but also by exercising control more profitably from within them. Competition law, as a result, has largely overlooked the possibility that agency – put in place as a consequence of intensified administrative action – constitutes an additional path of influence for consumers in data-driven marketplaces.

Agency affords consumers an ability to wield control as members rather than as opponents of a segment. It gives consumers control over the market's state of quality equilibrium in circumstances where switching is impracticable or turns out to be ineffective. Affording agency to consumers by way of intensified administrative action therefore gives rise to at least two undertakings: Authorities and courts are called upon to ensure effective articulation of the consumer's point of view (agency as a channel of communication); and authorities and courts are supposed to enable leading actors to integrate consumers' views into their segments (agency as integration). Reinstating switching through interoperability, data portability, structural breakups, and agency all seek to advance these aims. However, they differ as to the manner in which they sensibly accomplish them.

Despite its emphasis on agency, this chapter does not submit that agency as a channel of consumer influence alone has benefits. But neither do switching nor portability. The fact that agency entails costs does not preclude us from considering its advantages. Although many commentators may believe that agency is, all things considered, incongruous with the free interplay of market forces, at a minimum, it is valuable to acknowledge its presence. What is most useful about agency is that it enables competition law to juxtapose switching with an additional path of consumer influence – one that can enrich our understanding of how quality rather than price competition functions.

8

Self-Colonization in American Law

The Internet and Personal Information Example

Daniel J. H. Greenwood

CONTENTS

I INTRODUCTION

The arc of American history, unfortunately, does not bend inevitably toward justice.[1] Instead, it reflects an ongoing struggle between proponents and opponents of justice and decency.

One view, in ideal type, could be called democratic partnership: shared governance with the goal of the common welfare. The other, often called conservative or in older forms, aristocratic, but which I'll call colonialist, sees the main function of government as preserving a preexisting hierarchy in which some govern and others are governed. I use this unconventional terminology to highlight particular aspects of the two views; the views themselves should be quite familiar.

The rise of the multinational corporations, and in particular the internet oligopolies, is not usually interpreted in terms borrowed from the anti-colonial movement. Yet the issues bear a close family resemblance.

Our current system can best be understood as a form of self-colonization. We have created institutions to govern us, including our major corporations. But we have not subjected these institutions to the norms of democratic partnership, in which the goal of the government is the good of the governed, and governing officers are understood to be servants rather than masters. Instead, our corporate law, intellectual property law, and internet regulation, taken as a whole, create institutions that treat us as subjects to be exploited.

Peculiarly, however, our system is not traditional colonial exploitation for the benefit of the metropole, or even the familiar class struggle of neo-Marxist or aristocratic theory, in which a dominant class uses a subordinate class for the former's purposes. While our system does create enormous wealth for a small group at the top resulting in levels of inequality that any classical theorist would have seen as incompatible with republican government, the legal structure that enables this upward redistribution of income and wealth is, ultimately, the product of quasi-democratic politics. Thus, theories that postulate one nation or one class forcibly exploiting another do not fit closely.

Better, instead, to think of our system as self-colonization. We, through our legal system, treat ourselves as subjects to be exploited instead of partners whose individual good is the collective goal. As a semi-sovereign people, we could choose otherwise, although the window of opportunity may be closing.

I proceed in three parts. Section II summarizes the conflict between democratic partnership and colonialism, offering some justification for using non-standard terminology to describe a well-known, even cliched, partial portrait of our history. Section III addresses the changes the Internet has wrought, concluding that it

[1] Made famous by Martin Luther King, the aphorism apparently dates back at least to 1918, based on a lengthier version from 1853. *The Arc of the Moral Universe Is Long, but It Bends toward Justice*, Quote Investigator (Nov. 15, 2012), available at https://quoteinvestigator.com/2012/11/15/arc-of-universe/.

changed everything and nothing at all, but currently reflects a victory of the forces of self-colonization. Section IV makes some small proposals to move us in the direction of self-rule and the common good.

In general, in our corporate law, we have not yet reached the stage of the eighteenth-century liberal revolutions. Basic principles of good government that have been accepted for two centuries – at least by those who support democratic partnership – are still unheard of in the corporate sector. That leaves plenty of room for half-familiar, half-radical, but in fact deeply conservative, changes. In particular, I suggest using the autonomy protections of property law to protect us against our corporate governors, instead of protecting them against our attempts to wrest back self-rule.

Section III discusses the rise of the internet megafauna, as a combination of market and legal failures to preserve the necessary conditions for a democratic, market-based, relatively open, innovative, and egalitarian politics and economy. Capitalist market systems, while far from nirvana, are a clear improvement over the feudal dependency relations that preceded them and to which they tend to return. But contract law ineluctably redistributes wealth upwards: Those with more money and power are always in a better position to demand more of the joint product. So, the struggle to prevent competition from collapsing into domination by the wealthy is never-ending.

In Section IV, I propose a few preliminary legal reforms we need to move toward an economy that better serves justice and prosperity. The basic reforms are relatively clear, even if the political path to reach them is not. As a first step, we need to rebalance the rules of markets to promote fairer competition, just as first-generation civil rights activists struggled to bring excluded groups into the market on a formally equal basis. Simply permitting African Americans and women to own and use property and spend money equally was a major step forward, even if equality of dollars is not nearly enough for equal citizenship or dignity. Similarly, creating the conditions for fair competition not entirely dominated by incumbent wealth will be a major step toward freedom and democratic equality.

II DEMOCRATIC PARTNERSHIP VS. COLONIAL EXPLOITATION

A *Democratic Partnership*

Modern representative democracies with market economies and broad spheres of personal autonomy free from governmental control aspire to democratic partnership. By this I mean that the people are, or should be, partners in creating and operating the mutual benefit society we call government.[2]

[2] The idea of government as a sort of mutual assistance association meant to improve the lot of all its members underpins social contract theories from Hobbes to Rousseau, to Rawls and even

On this view, the role of the state is to improve the lot of its inhabitants, who are simultaneously the ruled and the rulers. The preamble to the Constitution is illustrative: "We the people" institute it to "promote the general welfare." So, too, the Fourteenth Amendment: "we" and "the people" include all Americans; and all people born in the United States (US) are automatically Americans; and the general welfare must respect our fundamental liberties as equal citizens. The governed are to be the governors, and the governors are to govern on behalf of all the people, not just themselves or their party, faction, class, or race.[3]

Of course, the meaning of a common welfare, let alone how to pursue it, is fundamentally contested. We disagree on how to live our lives and what our goals are. Some social contract theorists tried to resolve this problem by postulating that everyone, regardless of whatever else they want, at least can agree on some basic rules: Life is good,[4] it is better to be rich than poor,[5] basic rights help everyone. Unfortunately, they are wrong. Antigone chooses honor; Juliet love; and religious martyrs and patriots loyalty to their faith or community, rather than life. Followers of Jesus's teaching in Matthew 19:24 believe that more wealth is a hindrance to the good life, not an aid. In any event, our egos conflict with superegos, our goals are self-contradictory, and the moral constraints we place on them are internally inconsistent.[6] We, individually and collectively as polities or nations, are large and contain

Nozick: The social contract is a rhetorical device meant to emphasize that each citizen ought to agree to government because it makes each citizen better off. See also, Declaration of Independence (1776) ("That to secure these rights [i.e., 'Life, Liberty and the pursuit of Happiness'] Governments are instituted among Men, deriving their just powers from the consent of the governed"); but *see*, Oliver W. Holmes, Jr., The Common Law 88 (contending that the state is not a "mutual insurance company").

[3] As Seyla Benhabib described this view:

> Ideally, democratic rule means that all members of a sovereign body are to be respected as bearers of human rights and that the consociates of this sovereign freely associate with one another to establish a regime of self-governance under which each is to be considered both author of the laws and subject to them. This ideal of the original contract, in the version formulated by Jean-Jacques Rousseau and adopted by Kant, is a heuristically useful device for capturing the logic of modern democracies.

Seyla Benhabib, Exile, Statelessness, and Migration 24 (2018). Leaving aside the mythical original contract, in this vision the subjects of the sovereign are also its members, who rule and are ruled, with limitations on that rule imposed by the rights of citizens and humans. Kant and Rousseau, however, underestimated the inevitability and importance of difference and disagreement, which underlie most postwar versions of democratic thought.

[4] E.g., Thomas Hobbes, Leviathan i. xiii. 9 (arguing that individuals agree to state to avoid the state of nature, where life is solitary, poor, nasty, brutish, and short).

[5] John Rawls contends that wealth is a "primary good," of which more is always better regardless of the holder's life plan. John Rawls, Theory of Justice 93 (1971).

[6] Yehuda Amichai, in his poem of his father giving him ten commandments, states:

ואמר: אני רוצה להוסיף שנים לעשרת הדיברות:
And he said: I want to add two more to the Ten Commandments:
"הדיבר האחד-עשר", לא תשתנה
The eleventh commandment, "Do not change."
"והדיבר השנים-עשר, השתנה תשתנה."

multitudes.[7] Even philosophers cannot reach reflective equilibrium, Rawls himself included.

Disagreement is fundamental to the human condition.[8] We – anyone who calls themselves "we" – inevitably will differ on both the ends and means of government.

One part of our tradition, classically associated with Plato or Augustine and in the modern era with authoritarians of all stripes, teaches that this disagreement is the chief threat to civilization. Government ought to do whatever it can to suppress it, whether through indoctrination or the sword.[9]

But our First Amendment is the product of a different understanding. Enforced conformity leads only to violence, but diversity and tolerance make us stronger. After centuries of wars of religion and nationalist fervor, the liberals of the Enlightenment concluded that instead of killing dissidents, we could agree to live together in peace without agreeing on our religions or history, which books to read, or even what language to speak.[10] America, the land of mobility, recapitulates this phylogeny in every generation. How many of us or our predecessors realized that we were unlikely to win any kulturkampf; having seen Paree,[11] refused the conformist hypocrisy of farm, Hawthorne's Massachusetts Bay,[12] Winesburg, Ohio,[13] or Peyton Place;[14] or fled the Old World or Jim Crow seeking a more just and peaceful alternative. The Yom Kippur service begins by the community authorizing itself to pray together with sinners and apostates.[15] Our Constitution extends this permission to all year round, and to living together not just praying together.

Rather than seeking to create national uniformity, liberal republican democrats instead seek to allow people to live together on a basis of equal respect and equal

And the twelfth commandment, "Surely you shall change." Yehuda Amichai, Open Closed Open (1998) (my translation).

7 Walt Whitman, Song of Myself, no. 51 (1892).

8 In biblical mythology, disagreement is the core of the human condition from Babel (Gen. 11:7), if not Adam and Eve eating the fruit of the tree of knowledge, until the return of Elijah, the prophet who will end history by reconciling children to their parents (Malachi 3:24), make peace in the world (Mishnah Eduyot 8:7), and even resolve the unresolvable disputes of the Talmud (Tosafot Yom Tov on Eduyot 8:7). *See*, Daniel J. H. Greenwood, *Beyond Dworkin's Dominions: Investments, Memberships, the Tree of Life and the Abortion Question (an Abortion Midrash)*, 72 Tex. L. Rev. 559, 612–19 (1994) at part 4B.

9 See also, Umberto Eco, *Ur-Fascism*, N.Y. Rev. Books (June 22, 1995) ("disagreement is a sign of diversity. Ur-Fascism grows up and seeks for consensus by exploiting and exacerbating the natural fear of difference .... Thus, Ur-Fascism is racist by definition.").

10 Indeed, the original Constitution sought to extend this principle beyond its breaking point, to allow both slave and free states to coexist in one union. That effort was doomed. It's not possible to coexist in peace with those who are committed to forceful oppression.

11 Joe Young & Sam M. Lewis (words), *How Ya Gonna Keep Them Down on the Farm (After They've Seen Paree)* (1919), sung by Sophie Tucker, Eddie Cantor, and soldiers in both World Wars.

12 Nathaniel Hawthorne, The Scarlet Letter (1850).

13 Sherwood Anderson, Winesburg, Ohio (1919).

14 Grace Metalious, Peyton Place (1956), later adapted into movies and a TV soap opera.

15 *Anu matirin lihitpalel im ha-avaryonim*. Yom Kippur liturgy.

citizenship.[16] A key liberal principle – epitomized in our First Amendment – is to take religion in particular, and personal matters of taste, opinion, and private behavior in general, out of the political sphere of collective decision. If we don't need to make collective decisions, we don't need to have culture wars. The best way to live together is to agree to disagree.

To be sure, the live and let live solution to politics is partial at best. Every reader of John Stuart Mill has noted that his strongest argument for liberty depends on a realm of actions that have no effect on others.[17] That realm is quite small. Perhaps non-existent.

Often, state neutrality and abstention are impossible. We must make a collective decision. Either we are all members of the polity or we are not. If the former, then neither slavery nor coverture can be permissible. A fertilized egg or a sacred sperm[18] either is a fellow citizen, or it is not. If the former, the state must intervene to coerce care for it, just as it would for a child. If the later, it is forbidden from doing so: Prohibition of drugs and procedures that might end a pregnancy violates the citizenship of anyone whose health or life-prospects are incompatible with being drafted into service caring for a conceptus or a child. There is no solution to these issues based on apolitical privatized individualism.

Collective decisions are unavoidable on smaller matters as well. Cigarette smoking and walking naked either are allowed in public or are not; driving on the counter-majoritarian side of the road or refusing to vaccinate imperil the health of all, not just the decision-maker;[19] schools in any given locale can only teach a limited number of versions of history, in only a few languages, and any curriculum will endorse or reject critical thought. Any school that purports to "protect" some parents by depriving children of access to classic works of art like Michelangelo's David, accurate accounts of American history, biological evolution or climate change, or opportunities to engage critical thought and controversy directly violates the rights of other parents – and all children – to learn about the world around them and prepare them to participate in the cultures to which they are heirs.[20]

16 This is not to deny the continued power of other traditions, notably neo-Confederate racism. A shockingly large number of actual Americans reject the basic American commitments expressed in the Civil War Amendments.

17 John Stuart Mill, On Liberty (1859).

18 Monty Python, *The Meaning of Life* (1983), lyrics available at https://genius.com/Monty-python-every-sperm-is-sacred-lyrics.

19 *See, e.g.*, Braidwood Mgmt., Inc. v. Becerra, ___ F. Supp. 3d ___, 2022 WL 4091215, at *19-20 (N.D. Tex. Sept. 7, 2022) (holding that plaintiff corporations have Religious Freedom Restoration Act (RFRA) right to deny employees HIV prevention and other public health coverage mandated by the Affordable Care Act (ACA)).

20 *See, e.g.*, Florida Parental Rights in Education Act (HB 1557) (2002) (banning most discussion of "sexual orientation" or "gender identity" in public schools, which, if taken seriously, would seem to ban most study of literature, biology, and social relations); González v. Douglas, 269 F. Supp. 3d 948, 950–64 (D. Ariz. 2017) (holding unconstitutional state statute banning "ethnic studies" and used to ban Mexican-American Studies program); Sarah Schwartz, *Map: Where*

In these cases and many others, it is a fantasy to imagine a liberal state that stands neutrally above the disagreements and debates of civil society.

When we must decide collectively, the democratic partnership view insists that we follow the majority, so long as the majority accepts the basic commitments of ongoing partnership. Only equal voting respects our equal membership in society and the reality of our varying views on how to live together.

However, mere majoritarianism does not make a partnership. In business law, by default ordinary partnership decisions are made by majority votes of the partners.[21] Recognizing, however, the potential for the majority to exploit a minority, rules important enough to be in the partnership agreement may be changed only by unanimous consent.[22] Politics is not precisely analogous, if only because we should not give beneficiaries of past injustice a right to bar all improvements (as a *liberum veto* would).[23] Nonetheless, incumbent winners have no defensible right, even if they have the power, to take more than their proportional share. In a partnership, all partners should benefit from the common good.[24] Losing a vote cannot justify exclusion from the common benefits of the commonwealth; a spoils system is always illegitimate.

Instead, equal partnership demands that we attempt to share the benefits of joint action. When benefits can be divided, the rule ought to be proportionality – log rolling – rather than winner-take-all, coercion, or minority oppression. Fairness suggests that a 4 percent or 40 percent minority ought to get 4 percent or 40 percent of the gains, not zero.[25]

Moreover, even when a single rule is necessary and spreading the wealth inapplicable, a liberal majority ought to tolerate and even to celebrate difference to the extent possible. Just because we decide to protect non-smokers from second-hand smells and carcinogens by banning smoking in public, or even to stigmatize cigarettes to protect the next generation from addiction, does not mean that we must ban smoking in private as well. We can tolerate things that the majority disapproves

Critical Race Theory Is Under Attack, Education Week (June 11, 2021) (describing statutes banning teaching of "divisive" subjects in public schools); James Finn, *Louisiana Republican Party Wants to Ban College Study of Diversity, Equity, Inclusion: Classes Examining "Inglorious Aspects" of U.S. History Too Divisive, Resolution Says*, New Orleans Times Picayune/NOLA.com (Apr. 15, 2023).

21 Unif. P'ship Act (Am. L. Inst., 1997) §§ 4.01(f), (j) [hereinafter UPA].

22 UPA § 4.01(j).

23 In addition, partners are legally guaranteed the right to exit the partnership at any time. UPA §§ 6.01, 6.02(a). *See also*, § 1.03(b)(6) (stating that right to exit is not waivable). Practically, this is often a realistic solution to deep differences. The political analogy would be emigration. Free countries ordinarily allow free emigration – but emigration is impossible for most people as a practical matter. On the one hand, people are enmeshed in particular communities, cultures, economies, and languages. On the other hand, emigration is impossible without a right to immigrate elsewhere, and few of us have that.

24 *See* UPA § 4.01(b) (providing default rule of equal distribution of profits).

25 This is the UPA rule by default, although partners may vary it by unanimous consent in the partnership agreement. *See* UPA § 4.01(b).

of, and we can celebrate tastes that many of us do not share. My city is richer for the many cuisines in its restaurants even if I have no interest in eating them.

In the liberal tradition, the most basic way to permit individual deviance even when public uniformity is required is to carve out spaces in which private, not public, norms prevail. This is the strongest defense of the institution of private property: This invention of liberal polities creates a space in which the property holder (the owner, or, more often, the lessee) may act with less attention to public norms. In your own home, you may smoke cigarettes, walk around naked, display execrable taste in decoration or amusement, practice widely despised religions, or none at all. You may even invidiously discriminate among your friends. Private property is not a pre-political natural right, but a supremely political attempt to limit politics itself, by creating a legal space in which the property holder is relatively free of (some of) the vicissitudes of public politics. We, the majority, voluntarily withdraw from this space to make room for a degree of individual deviance.

Contract serves a similar purpose, allowing parties to create private norms to partially replace public ones. The Little Red Hen is not a fable for our time. She harvests the wheat, mills the grain, bakes the bread, and keeps it for herself.[26] We, in contrast, do our small parts in a long supply chain leading to the bread and then pay to buy it from a legal entity that is no more able to cook without assistance than is a hen.

The foundation of liberal market economics is not the Lockean norm that the person who creates something owns it, but the agency law rule that every employee is presumed to have agreed by contract to reverse it. Contract allows those with bargaining power to set the terms of their relations with others, even if those terms deviate from the ones we, or our judges or legislatures, would impose were the decision collective.

Other constitutional rights serve a similar function. The rights to speech and religion create spaces for alternative norms in politics, worship, culture, and aesthetics.[27] The constitutional bars on quartering soldiers, warrantless searches, and takings, and their modern growth into the rights to privacy in the bedroom, create private spaces largely exempt from collective policing, where individuals or families (or, less appropriately, businesses) can follow the norms they view as binding.[28] The rules of criminal procedure should limit the ability of public officers to use their power for private, partisan, or partial purposes. The civil service and its ethos of professionalism help restrict winner-take-all or "spoils system" corruption, in which a party uses government power for its own benefit to the exclusion of other Americans.[29]

[26] *See The Little Red Hen*, Wikipedia (Feb. 18, 2023), https://en.wikipedia.org/wiki/The_Little_Red_Hen.

[27] U.S. Const. amend. I.

[28] U.S. Const. amend. III, IV, V; Griswold v. Conn., 381 US 479, 484 (1965) (finding zones of privacy in penumbra of Bill of Rights).

[29] Even federalism, if it is defensible at all, is defensible primarily on the ground that different levels may be more likely to respect diversity. As the original federalists argued, national decisions may reduce the likelihood of overbearing majorities, if only because majorities are more likely to be coalitions of potentially oppressed minorities. Conversely, pressing communal

Moreover, in a complex society, most issues are too complex for direct majoritarian decision-making. Few of us have the expertise, time, or interest to consider whether a given legal tool is appropriate for a given job, or how to balance conflicting goals and incompatible means in ways that both leave space for the losers on any particular issue and leave open the possibility that the losers now may be winners later.

Representative democracy, then, has a second major purpose beyond assuring all citizens of equal participation in governance. We bar aristocracy and permanent rulers, and we allow even uninformed majorities to "cashier" our leaders (as Burke put it),[30] to limit hubris. Powerful leaders may be incompetent, since the qualifications for clawing to the top (including a certain degree of antisocial personality traits)[31] are only loosely correlated with those necessary for performing the office (such as empathy, humility, or willingness to listen). Even those who do start off incompetent may become so, as they surround themselves with base flatterers, ambitious courtiers, and sycophants unable or unwilling to provide accurate assessments or information. Voting is a way of restraining the twin tendencies to corruption (preferring to be masters rather than public servants) and vanguardism (viewing themselves, rather than ordinary citizens, as the best determiners of what constitutes a better life).

In short, the liberal commitment to allowing dissent and criticism of the powers-that-be, as exemplified in the religion, speech, and petition clauses of the First Amendment, reflects a fundamental acceptance of disagreement itself. Liberalism learned from the bitter experience of religious and nationalist wars the cost of suppressing each other's religions, languages or cultural preferences. The only way to reach complete consensus is by actual or threatened murder.[32]

decision-making downward may allow for more people to live under law they'd approve, at least if people conveniently sort themselves into geographic areas by salient features of their public preferences or needs.

Of course, there is no guarantee that the reverse won't happen. Multiple jurisdictions may make pursuing the common welfare harder rather than easier. Coalitions may be unstable or manipulated by single-issue participants. Disciplined party politics may allow a radical vanguard within the party to multiply its influence well beyond its actual numbers. Illiberal factions may seek to make decisions at whichever level of government they expect to be able to prevail, arguing for states' rights only when they expect to lose nationally, but then limiting home rule when state governments are easier to dominate. Existentially, competitive pressures may invite particular jurisdictions to seize benefits while exporting costs elsewhere: promoting polluting industries at the expense of downwind, downstream, or coastal neighbors; permitting tax or consumer fraud while assuming that more responsible jurisdictions will maintain the high levels of trust necessary for a successful economy.

30 Edmund Burke, Reflections on the Revolution in France ¶25 (1790).

31 *See, e.g.*, Simon Croon, *12% of Corporate Leaders Are Psychopaths*, Fortune (June 6, 2021) (pointing out that lack of empathy is a common characteristic).

32 Rousseau suggested education as an alternative, but coercing all into a single formative education, as even Rousseau recognized, itself requires an extraordinary degree of violence.

Liberalism's partnership view suggests, that we should, instead, agree to disagree whenever that is compatible with the fundamental goal of promoting the common welfare. Or, given that living together in peace and comfort usually requires common norms, we should try to make spaces for those who disagree to, nonetheless, live according to their own views to the extent possible. Liberal societies permit family planning; they do not mandate it, even when the majority believes that a given would-be parent is not likely to be able to properly raise a child.

B *Colonialist Conservatism*

The alternative family of views is the illiberal right, disagreeing with liberals not just on goals but on the basic purpose of government. In this country, it is largely associated with the Confederacy and its modern friends. It has no single accepted name, perhaps because it comes in so many variants, sharing only a dedication to hierarchy, whether the petty despotism of the *paterfamilias*, the medieval metaphor of the great chain of being, laissez-faire apotheosis of the privileges of property, or political authoritarianism. The general principle is that government ought to guarantee the status of the incumbent hierarchs. Generally, this includes seeing the governors – both private bosses and government officials – not as servants but masters, in the manner of a pre-modern lord of the manor ruling his serfs. A place for everything, everything in its place; taxes are only for little people;[33] and any suggestion to close tax loopholes used by the richest is akin to the Holocaust.[34]

Usually, this rejection of the principles of equality and partnership is combined with hostility to disagreement, which it perceives as a threat to incumbent power holders or their political, economic, or cultural hegemony.

This is conservative reaction in all its forms: monarchy, aristocracy, oligarchy, authoritarianism, establishmentarianism, apartheid, sexism, and racism. It is exemplified by the holding of *Dred Scott v. Sanford*,[35] reasoning from the indisputable truth that race-based chattel slavery is incompatible with common citizenship not that slavery was a great wrong but that only some of us were "created equal"[36] or

This is the bitter lesson of nationalism. And it won't work anyway. Disagreement is fundamental to the post-Babel world.

[33] E.g., Robert W. Wood, *10 Notorious Tax Cheats: Queen of Mean Leona Helmsley Proved Little People Can Put You in Jail*, FORBES (Apr. 17, 2015) (quoting Leona Helmsley).

[34] Steven Schwartzman described closing the carried interest loophole, which allows a handful of extraordinarily overpaid hedge fund managers to treat their centi-million dollar pay as capital gains rather than salary, as "war ... like when Hitler invaded Poland in 1939." Andrew Clark, *Blackstone Billionaire Is Sorry for Nazi Jab against Obama's Tax Policies*, THE GUARDIAN (Aug. 17, 2010); *see also*, Lawrence Delevingne, *Hedge Fund Managers Stung by "Class Warfare" Rhetoric*, CNBC (May 23, 2015)," www.cnbc.com/2015/05/22/hedge-fund-managers-stung-by-class-warfare-rhetoric.html (quoting anonymous hedge fund manager comparing proposed tax to the Holocaust).

[35] 60 US 393 (1857).

[36] DECLARATION OF INDEPENDENCE para. 1 (U.S. 1776).

included in "We the People."[37] The same view reversed the commitments of the Fourteenth and Fifteenth Amendments, first by inventing the state action doctrine and then by repudiating equal citizenship wholesale in *Plessy v. Ferguson*,[38] *Shelby County v. Holder*,[39] *Dobbs v. Jackson Women's Health Organization*,[40] and similar cases permitting states to deny some of us the most fundamental rights of equal citizenship. The same spirit animates the extraordinary transmutation of equal protection into class warfare, upward wealth redistribution, and wage slavery in *Lochner v. New York*,[41] reinvigorated in "speech" cases building on *Virginia State Bd of Pharmacy v. Va. Citizens Consumer Council*[42] to weaken regulation designed to improve the fairness of markets;[43] the Borkian revolution in antitrust that allowed "malefactors of great wealth"[44] to consolidate their power; ongoing judicial burdening of unions in *Janus v. AFSCME*;[45] the manifold forms of discrimination against immigrant groups and their descendants epitomized by but hardly limited to the 1924 Johnson–Reed Act,[46] *Korematsu v. United States*,[47] and the second-class status of Americans living in Puerto Rico under the *Insular Cases*.[48]

More generally, this is the ideology driving modern exclusionary rhetoric of the far right, attacking those who dwell on the coasts or in cities, who don't go to the right church, have the wrong skin color or sexual orientation or kinds of families, who completed college or vote Democratic or believe in tolerance – that is, most of us – as not "real" Americans. All those who are uppity must be put in their proper place.

These cases and the political movements driving them bear a stark resemblance to colonialism and other forms of domination, including medieval aristocratic rule. In a colonial relationship, the colonizer uses the colonized for the metropole's purposes, not the colony's. Some colonizers employ the brutal exploitation of the Belgian Congo, the British famines in India and Ireland, or the Soviet Union's starvation of Ukraine. Other colonizers may decide that it is easier and more

37 U.S. Const. pmbl.
38 163 U.S. 537 (1896).
39 570 U.S. 529 (2013).
40 597 U.S. __ (2022).
41 198 U.S. 45 (1905).
42 425 U.S. 748 (1976).
43 *See*, Jedediah Purdy, *Beyond the Bosses' Constitution: The First Amendment and Class Entrenchment*, 118 Colum. L. Rev. 2161, 2174 (2018); Daniel J. H. Greenwood, *First Amendment Imperialism (A Response to Michael Walzer's Leary Lecture)*, 1999 Utah L. Rev. 659 (1999).
44 Theodore Roosevelt, *Address on the Occasion of the Laying of the Corner Stone of the Pilgrim Memorial Monument* (Aug. 20, 1907), available at www.theodorerooseveltcenter.org/Research/Digital-Library/Record.aspx?libID=o286435.
45 585 U.S. __ (2018) (barring union from charging for its services).
46 Including the Asian Exclusion Act and National Origins Act (Pub.L. 68–139, 43 Stat. 153) (imposing national origin quotas on immigration).
47 323 U.S. 214 (1944) (upholding wartime concentration camps).
48 *See, e.g.*, De Lima v. Bidwell, 182 U.S. 1 (1901).

profitable to extract surplus from the subject people by gentler means, as in Monty Python's view of the Roman Empire, or the white man's burden and the *mission civilisatrice*.[49] In each case, even if they sometimes claim otherwise,[50] colonial rulers act as if the ultimate purpose of government is not to improve the lives of the governed but, instead, to benefit someone else – the colonizing nation.

While colonialism strictly speaking refers to one nation dominating another, the term can usefully be extended metaphorically. The key characteristic of colonialism that I am concerned with is government of one group on behalf of another. Any benefits to the colonized – whether or not outweighed by the burdens – are not a goal but simply an accident of the dominating group's calculation of the best way to extract the most from the colonized at the lowest cost. Accordingly, colonialism is an appropriate metaphor even in situations where the dominant and subordinate groups are within the same state or identified by something other than nationality, geography, ethnicity, or even class.

Indeed, as a general metaphor, colonialism is a useful way to think about the commonalities between corporate law and many types of non-democratic, non-liberal ideologies and states. American corporate law gives corporate boards and top managers nearly complete power to govern the firm and the people associated with it; the Supreme Court's doctrine that those leaders may assert rights under the Constitution on behalf of the corporate entity[51] means that the Constitution protects their incumbent power. Corporate rights to property, speech, or privacy function precisely the opposite of similar sounding rights of citizens: They protect corporate governors from those they govern, increasing management's prerogatives and limiting the ability of others to use the standard political tools of disclosure, public opinion, regulation, or majoritarianism to restrain them. Indeed, corporate "speech" rights allow corporate leaders to use corporate funds regardless of the views of those

[49] Monty Python, *What Have the Romans Ever Done for Us* (2007), lyrics available at https://genius.com/Monty-python-what-have-the-romans-ever-done-for-us-annotated. *See also* Catherine Porter et al., *The Root of Haiti's Misery: Reparations to Enslavers*, N.Y. Times (May 20, 2022) (describing French colonial and post-colonial exploitation of Haiti for benefit of France).

[50] *See, e.g.*, Calhoun's claim that slavery is a "positive good" to the enslaved. John C. Calhoun, *Speech on Abolition Petitions* (Feb. 6, 1837), in John C. Calhoun, Speeches of John C. Calhoun: Delivered in the Congress of the United States from 1811 to the Present Time 222–26 (1843).

[51] Santa Clara County v. Southern Pacific Railroad Company, 118 U.S. 394 (1886) is usually cited as the foundation of this doctrine, but *Santa Clara* was preceded by a long series of cases giving corporate managers preferential access to the Federal courts. Later cases have consistently granted constitutional rights to corporate governors on behalf of the institution or its incumbent leaders. Thus, the same rights that protect us against our political leaders – for example, guaranteeing our right to dissent or to preserve spheres of privacy – disempower us against our corporate leaders. They have a right to speech, which means that we, in our roles as employees and customers, must fund and support their speech whether we will or not. They have rights to privacy and due process, which means that we, as employees or citizens, have fewer rights to learn what they are doing or reform how they do it.

who created them or have claims on them, in effect taxing customers and employees without representation.

Modern kleptocracies and traditional monarchies are similarly operated in the interests of ruling officials, not the ruled. Herrenvolk republics, like apartheid South Africa or Jim Crow America, and oligarchies like pre-modern Venice, rule in the interest of limited ruling classes or groups. Traditional feudal aristocracies treated the commoners as mere fodder for the enrichment of the nobility; some modern dictatorships take much the same view. Corporate, agency, and fiduciary law teach corporate managers that any benefit to employees and customers must be justified by extracting from them more value still: Corporate participants are in effect colonized by the firm. All reject the fundamental partnership ideal that government is of and for the (same) people.

The common element that warrants calling these systems "colonial" is that some people are subjects while others are citizens: Some of us are just tools for the projects of others.

C *Self-Colonization*

Colonial views are usually held by a dominant group that seeks to exclude another group – the colonial subjects – from full citizenship in order to exploit them. The British were willing to sacrifice innumerable Irish or Indian lives to preventable famine and Chinese lives to opium addiction, if that promoted the profits of British companies and officials or kept trade going to the advantage of the "home" country. The exploited group need not be overseas, of course. The British ruling class was equally willing to sacrifice their own compatriots to the demands of industrialization or land consolidation; American Jim Crow deprived one group of Americans of basic rights in order to force them to labor for the benefit of others. Today, our undocumented immigrants are exceptionally unlikely to protest unfair working conditions, because they rightly fear that protest will lead to exile from the country they've made their home.

Sometimes, in contrast, it simply reflects a desire to ignore the continued existence of people who the dominant group wishes had simply disappeared. So far as I know, the US does not exploit Native Americans in classic colonial fashion[52] nor profit heavily from the second-class status of Puerto Rico.[53] Still, denying the inhabitants of reservations or territories full citizenship makes malign neglect easier. This American pain, on the colonial view, is not "our" suffering.

52 Expelling the prior inhabitants from their land was manifestly unjust as are the continuing violation of treaty rights. But expulsions and land theft do not fit easily in the standard model of colonial exploitation.

53 However, I confess total ignorance of the economic significance of the Jones Act, for example.

Strangely, however, American legal culture also contains a powerful strain of *self-colonization* – in which governing majorities treat *themselves* as colonial subjects, mere tools to be exploited rather than citizens whose welfare is the state's goal and justification. In a form of idol worship, we create our own masters and bow down to them.

Unlike classical forms of class warfare or aristocracy, in which a ruling class dominates the general population, this American self-colonization is not based in explicit violence or control. Instead, it appears to have broad popular support or at least acquiescence, even among those seemingly excluded from public benefit.

Why we choose to exploit ourselves is a bit of a mystery.

To be sure, polls suggest that upward wealth redistribution and extreme inequality are deeply unpopular. Nonetheless, politicians promoting such policies routinely receive close to half the votes nationally, and more in the areas that have been especially hard-hit by the demise of the New Deal. Given the overrepresentation of rural areas and thinly populated states, gerrymandering, partisan packing of the judiciary, and the influence of campaign contributions, lobbying, and the revolving door, much of it driven by those who profit from regulatory arbitrage, governmental privileges, market distortions, and direct or indirect subsidy, this is quite enough to routinely win both national and state elections.

Pundits declare that politicians promoting unpopular policies retain their popularity because of the power of racism or cultural war, arguing that people vote against their economic interest because they are threatened by the existence of Americans who look or act different from themselves. Others point to unjustified optimism that the voter, too, will someday be in the upper class able to use these rules to exploit the rest of us. Many descry the power of money in our political system, pointing out that politicians – whatever their true beliefs, if any – are highly dependent on their ability to raise large sums of money from the beneficiaries of redistributive policies, and so our legislators respond to the views of donors rather than voters, while our governmental officials often hope to make their fortunes working for those they nominally regulate.

Perhaps the issue is that voters don't see themselves as full citizens of a common enterprise, but as collections of roles – consumers, future retirees with stock market investments, or taxpayers. What is good for us as consumers (low prices) or taxpayers (low taxes) is likely to be bad for us as employees (low wages, reduced unionization) or citizens (poor services). America's private wealth for a few and public poverty for all can look attractive if we focus only on our roles as consumers or taxpayers or future retirees dependent on stock market returns or ever-rising housing prices.[54] Weakening our wildly inadequate provisions for basic social services such as health care, unemployment insurance, low-cost housing, transit, or children's nutrition are

[54] John Kenneth Galbraith, The New Industrial State (1967) (noting the private affluence and public poverty of the US). Ironically, Galbraith wrote just as mass affluence was beginning its collapse into a shrinking and insecure few.

defended as helpful in our roles as taxpayers or as creating incentives for individuals to work in otherwise unattractive jobs.

But we are both employees and consumers, the subjects of profit taking and the recipients of dividends, debtors, and creditors. For most of us, the gains we make as consumers or in paying less taxes can't come close to the losses from not better working or living conditions. Focusing on particular roles may make it hard to see that virtually all of us would be better off if consumer goods cost a bit more because we were paid more to make them, if taxes were higher because they were financing the underpinnings of a growing middle class instead of undermining them, or if stock market prices were lower because more businesses were more tightly tied to producing useful products and good jobs and fewer were able to extract monopoly profits or externalize costs of the risks they impose on the rest of us.

More poignantly, too many people – voters and pundits alike – fail to see that if we changed the rules of competition to make more winners, it would matter less who wins. Affirmative action and its opponents focus on who should get into elite universities and thereby get the best jobs, or whether college is worth the cost when the number of graduates increases faster than the number of good jobs. Instead, we might ask why we don't provide equally good education for more people, or why we can't have more well-paying jobs that don't require degrees in the first place, or why Americans in the middle half of the income distribution no longer feel capable of attaining a secure and decent life. We subsidize failing rural economies and erect zoning rules to encourage middle-class housing or keep it out, but we could instead bring our mass transit up to international standards, thereby bringing more land (and people) within commuting distance of successful cities. Zero-sum competition would matter less if we rearranged our economy to allow more people to live satisfying, secure lives.

D *Corporate Law as Colonial Law*

One paradigmatic example of American self-colonization is corporate law. Every state has adopted the so-called internal affairs doctrine.[55] Under this doctrine, a corporation's rules of internal governance, including the powers and responsibilities of its top managers, are governed by the law of its state of incorporation, regardless of where it operates. Translated, this means that corporate officers may choose the corporate law they wish to govern them from among all available corporate laws of American states and foreign jurisdictions. Subject to formal approval by vote of the shares, they – not the citizenry – have the final say on the law which grants them authority and power to control the firm and limits their responsibility for doing so. Not surprisingly, they typically use this power to choose law that grants them broad control over firm resources, with limited answerability and little liability for errors or misdeeds.

[55] *See, e.g.*, McDermott, Inc. v. Lewis (Del. 1987) (stating that doctrine is fundamental to Delaware corporate law); Daniel J. H. Greenwood, *Democracy and Delaware: The Mysterious Race to the Bottom/Top*, 23 Yale L. & Pol'y Rev. 381 (2005).

So long as states accept the internal affairs doctrine, this structure keeps corporate law outside the purview of popular politics. Delaware has developed specialized structures to ensure that its corporate law tracks the desires of top corporate executives, and as a result the leaders of most national corporations incorporate there. Even those who do not, could. Most other states have responded by copying Delaware's substantive law, rather than by resisting. Any state has the option of rejecting the internal affairs doctrine and returning to the mid nineteenth century norm of requiring that corporations doing business in that state accept local corporate law or do business via a domestic corporation. Except in peripheral matters, no state has done so. Instead, for the last hundred years, no state has even tried to remind corporate officers that they too are servants, not masters, of the public.

Ordinarily, we think of a colonizer as having coerced the colonized into giving up their rights to self-rule. Here, however, we have colonized ourselves by the ordinary workings of our more-or-less democratic government. Few of us vote in Delaware. Yet we allow Delaware to legislate the governing rules of our largest corporations, the most important institutions of the American economy, and to tax them (and therefore us, as customers, employees, and investors) for the privilege.[56]

Colonization extends far beyond our having given up our votes or subsidizing Delaware's treasury. American corporate law is substantively colonial. Corporate officials set the organization's ends and means, strategy and tactics, protected by the business judgment rule, without answerability or regard to the values or interests of those they govern.

In recent decades, most corporate leaders have defined corporate interests to mean shareholder value maximization. Shareholder value maximization is a mysterious goal in many ways; finance should be a means not an end. But the colonial point is clear. If we are working for shareholder value maximization, we are working for a master that is not us.[57]

On the simplest level, no human being is just a shareholder.[58] Actual Americans have multifarious interests and values, many of which necessarily conflict with shareholder value maximization for any particular company.

[56] Delaware taxes corporations for the privilege of incorporating there. The incorporation tax is a major source of Delaware's budget. Since most Delaware corporations do most of their business elsewhere, Delaware is taxing us without representation, in classic colonial fashion. However, Delaware has not coerced the rest of us into this indefensible system. Instead, every state has adopted the internal affairs rule, the essential underpinning to Delaware's hegemony. Ending this taxation without representation would require no more than a state legislature standing up for its citizens. No revolution required.

[57] *See, e.g.*, Daniel J. H. Greenwood, *Fictional Shareholders: For Whom Are Corporate Managers Trustees, Revisited*, 69 S. Calif. L. Rev. 1021 (1996); Ramsi Woodcock, *Technology, Monopoly, and Antitrust*, SSRN (Dec. 13, 2022) https://papers.ssrn.com/abstract=4301486; Lynn Stout, The Shareholder Value Myth: How Putting Shareholders First Harms Investors, Corporations, and the Public (2012).

[58] Some shareholders, however, are not human beings at all. The Norwegian Government Pension Fund Global invests in part on behalf of unborn generations of Norwegians. www

First, few of us own much stock to start with, directly or indirectly. A large percentage of publicly traded shares is controlled by or for a tiny number of the international uber-wealthy – the modern robber barons, the descendants of the nineteenth-century ones, and sovereign wealth funds of oil-producing companies. To be sure, much of the remainder is held by institutional investors, which, in turn, indirectly work for many of us: although wealth is even more unequally distributed than income, about half of Americans have at least small retirement plans that own stock, and nearly all of us benefit from the work of a handful of important endowed research universities, hospitals, religious and arts institutions. And most of us would prefer our stock market investments, whether direct or indirect, to be worth more rather than less.

But all of us have something we value more than an extra dollar of potential retirement income. Even if few Americans accept the teaching that riches make entering heaven harder than camels passing through needles, human investors always have some set of morals or politics; care (or do not) about particular people, nations, or the survival of the species; have views about the things money just can't buy. For some it is "anti-wokeness," for others basic decency to our fellow Americans; nearly all of us oppose murder for hire, although we disagree on its statistical equivalents in the form of pollution or safety disregard.

Indeed, most narrowly, shareholder value maximization is rarely in the actual economic interests of the actual human beings who stand behind the shares. Few of us have material amounts invested in the stock market, even indirectly. Even if our retirement funds are invested in Microsoft or General Motors, most of us are more invested in their products, the people who make their products, the people who are dependent on those who make their products, or the communities – local and national – in which they operate and the influences they have on those communities and the surrounding ecosystems. Generally, most of us have far more of our wealth (and our children's wealth) tied to our roles as employees and customers than as shareholders; we'd be better off if successful corporations did not hoard the surplus they create or use it to pay dividends and astronomical executive pay, but instead used it to lower prices, improve employee pay or working conditions, or do less damage to our shared public spaces. "It may not be good for America but it's damn good for CBS"[59] does not reflect the actual interests of most CBS shareholders, employees, customers or other participants.

Moreover, nearly every stock market investor, human or institutional, is diversified, and those shareholders care less about the value of an individual stock than about the market as a whole. Portfolio investors are invested in a large part of the economy. It does them no good if one portfolio company makes more money by

.nbim.no/en/. Harvard's endowment states that its mission is to ensure the institution can "expand its leadership in education and research for future generations." www.hmc.harvard .edu/about/.

[59] Paul Bond, *Leslie Moonves on Donald Trump: "It May Not Be Good for America, but It's Damn Good for CBS"*, The Hollywood Reporter (Feb. 29, 2016) www.hollywoodreporter.com/ news/general-news/leslie-moonves-donald-trump-may-871464.

squeezing suppliers or customers, if the squeezed victims are also in the portfolios. Externalizing costs is often good for a particular company's bottom line, but the externalized costs have to be borne by someone, which may well be another portfolio company. Every company that saves by not using a safety or anti-pollution device costs another company a sale. Oil companies may make more money if they are allowed to heat the planet, but portfolio investors, even if they care about nothing but profit, will also hold investments in insurance companies, coastal real estate developers, food processors, and alternative energy source suppliers that are injured by carbon dioxide emissions.

Indeed, even squeezing employees or customers who are not part of the portfolio is unlikely to be in a diversified investors' narrow financial interests. Every employee is also a consumer, so when one company profits by paying employees less, another loses money from potential customers who can no longer buy.

Most importantly perhaps, every time a company deceives or defrauds a customer or mistreats an employee, or burns its reputation to increase short-term profits, it harms more than merely the sales of a more honest portfolio company. It also reduces the total amount of trust in the system, making it harder for companies and customers to do business with strangers, increasing the cost of credit, compliance, and long-term contracts, and slowing economic growth generally. Freeloading is often good for the bottom line of the freeloader, but it is never good for the rest of us. Diversified investors and citizens alike are far more invested in the success of the system as a whole than in the profits of any particular freeloading portfolio investment.

Delaware law declares that corporate managers have a fiduciary duty to act in the interest of the corporation.[60] But it does not define that interest.[61] Corporations, being human creations for limited human purposes, have no interests of their own, any more than any other tool does. We do not consider the interests of resistance coil electric stoves when deciding whether to switch to induction; when cars replaced horse-drawn carriages, no one thought that we had to consider the right to life of buggy-whip companies before abandoning horses.

60 Smith v. Van Gorkum, 488 A.2d 858 (Del. 1985).

61 *See, e.g.*, Kamin v. Am. Express, 383 N.Y.S.2d 807 (Sup. Ct. NY Cty 1976) (holding within board's authority to determine that corporation is best served by giving up multi-million dollar tax benefit in order to make underlying business loss less transparent to investors); Cheff v. Mathes, 199 A.2d 548 (Del. 1964) (holding that board could determine it is in company's interest to continue to use sales method that had led to massive fraud and fines); Paramount Communications, Inc. v. Time Inc., Fed. Sec. L. Rep. (CCH) ¶ 94,514 (Del. Ch. July 14, 1989), *aff'd*, 571 A.2d 1140 (Del. 1989) (holding that Time Inc board could determine that company's purpose was to publish magazine rather than maximize profits for shareholders). Dodge v. Ford Motor Co., 204 Mich. 459 (1919), the leading, and almost solitary, authority for the proposition that a business corporation may not be run as a semi-eleemosynary institution but must be run for the benefit of its shareholders, directly contradicts the rule set out in every corporation law that a corporation may be created for any legal purpose. E.g., Del. G. Corp. L. 101.

Corporate law gives corporate boards the discretion to determine the corporation's interests (and to change their minds at any time).[62] This unquestionably extends even to the point of deciding to destroy it; while we may deplore running up excessive debt, mismanagement, or merger because of their effects on the company's product, customers, employees, investors, or neighbors, no one thinks that the company itself has a right to life.

In American constitutional law, *Carolene Products* famously upheld that principle that courts ought to leave legislating to the legislature by deferring to legislative judgments of both ends and means except in the limited instances where legislatures are barred from treading.[63] Corporate law similarly protects managerial autonomy by refusing to second-guess managerial decisions (except in cases of extreme self-dealing) under the business judgment rule.[64]

Nonetheless, the structure and culture of the law encourage directors and top executives to treat all corporate participants as mere means to corporate ends. First, only shareholders are given the vote, suggesting that others are not "really" part of the firm. But even shareholders vote per share rather than per person: The shares, not their holders, are the actual citizens. Second, accounting conventions require that all expenditures on behalf of corporate participants, with the exception of dividends paid to shareholders, be recorded as expenses. Thus, on the books of the firm, improved welfare of consumers, employees, or the taxpaying public are all treated as losses to the firm. Third, in the last several decades, corporate boards have awarded top executives and themselves large grants of stock and stock options, thus giving the key decision-makers a direct financial interest in making undiversified shareholders better off.

Perhaps surprisingly, standard finance theory in effect treats even shareholders as an expense to the firm. The business schools teach that retaining earnings, borrowing or selling bonds, and selling stock are all means to the same goal – to get the firm as much funding as possible for as little as possible. But if this is the goal of corporate leadership, then they are treating shareholders just like every other corporate participant: as a tool to someone else's end.

In short, current law and business culture teach corporate directors and managers to attempt to give the least while taking the most from every corporate participant – consumers, taxpayers, neighbors, employees, managers, bondholders, other creditors, and shareholders alike. We are all colonial subjects. But to whose benefit? There is no metropole, no colonialist state seizing the ill-gotten gains. The system

62 Del. G. Corp. L. 144a (stating that business and affairs of a business corporation are to be managed by or under the direction of its board). The interests of the firm are not the same as the interests of its shareholders or even a controlling (majority) shareholder. Mendell v. Carroll, 651 A.2d 297, 306 (Del. Ch. 1994) (stating that board of directors could "deploy corporate power against the majority stockholders").

63 United States v. Carolene Products Co., 304 U.S. 144, 152 fn. 4 (1938).

64 E.g., Stone v. Ritter, 911 A.2d 362 (Del. 2006); Brehm v. Eisner, 746 A.2d 244 (Del. 2000).

encourages exploiting each participant's weaknesses, but the gains go only to cheaters, to those who violate its rules by taking more than they give.

E *Reaganomics as Self-Colonization*

Our law in the long Reagan-era seems committed to self-colonization in other areas as well. For two generations, our government has pursued policies of upward income redistribution. Middle-class Americans have seen stagnant wages for half a century, partially disguised by an extraordinary increase in the number of hours worked per household as women entered the paid workforce and by enormous increases in household debt. The dramatic gains from rising productivity due to computerization have gone almost exclusively to capital, top management, and a small slice of professionals. At the same time, the basics of middle-class life – housing, childcare, education, medical care and retirement – have soared in cost, leaving middle-class Americans with insufficient funds to support other industries.[65]

These failures are the result of specific legal choices which treat Americans as means rather than ends. Some are deeply embedded in our legal structure. Contract law automatically redistributes the surplus created by cooperation to the party that is better able to threaten to walk. Usually this will be the wealthier party. It is always harder to hold out for better terms when your rent or food is at stake.[66] Conversely, money is usually easier to redeploy than finding a new job. The problem has long been recognized – Leviticus, perhaps our oldest economic reform text, sets out an elaborate system of wage controls, poor relief, debt jubilees, and periodic land reform, to counterbalance the tendency of the rich to get richer while the poor get poorer.[67] American law, in contrast, weights its scales the other direction.

[65] That radical inequality can result in reduced growth was a core of Cobden's opposition to the nineteenth-century British Corn Laws, which kept the price of bread high:

> When provisions are high, the people have so much to pay for them that they have little or nothing left to buy clothes with; and when they have little to buy clothes with, there are few clothes sold; and when there are few clothes sold, there are too many to sell, they are very cheap; and when they are very cheap, there cannot be much paid for making them: and that, consequently, the manufacturing working man's wages are reduced, the mills are shut up, business is ruined, and general distress is spread through the country.

Richard Cobden, Speeches on Questions of Public Policy 129 (1870, 1995).

[66] An early recognition of this problem appears in the myth of Joseph in Egypt. Joseph stored grain in the abundant years and then sold it to its producers in the famine years, thus saving the lives of the Egyptians. *Genesis* 41:36, 41:56. But Genesis also notes that he used the economic power this gave him to "gather up all the money in Egypt," *Genesis* 47:14, and ultimately to force the Egyptians to agree to be "slaves to Pharaoh," *Genesis* 47:25. It is surely intentional poetic irony that the story immediately proceeds to Joseph's descendants becoming "slaves to Pharaoh," *Deuteronomy* 6:21. In the biblical view, one abuse of power must be balanced by another.

[67] *Leviticus* 25:10–13 (forgiveness of debts and cancellation of land sales in Jubilee year); 19:9–10 (corners of field must be left for poor); 19:13 (hired labor must be paid daily); *Deuteronomy*

American employment law was always weighted heavily against employees. Our corporate law makes it trivially easy for capital to bargain collectively; any would-be leader of united capital may create a corporation and the law will treat collective capital as an individual legal person.[68] In contrast, the process for creating a union is complicated and difficult, and the courts have reinterpreted the National Labor Relations Act to make it more difficult still. Most fundamentally, the Act usually requires employees to organize at the plant level[69] – but places few restrictions on a corporation simply abandoning the plant and the union together with it. Since the 1980s, corporations became increasingly aggressive in deunionizing, with regulators acquiescing where they were not actively supporting the campaign.

Other legal rules add to the effect of these deep organizing principles. Our stingy social insurance benefits heighten the disparity in bargaining power, while our peculiar decision to run health insurance, pensions, disability, and even unemployment insurance through employers means that quitting or being fired costs the employee not only a job but most social welfare benefits as well. The doctrine of employment at will means that managers and employers have near-total ability to dismiss critics or organizers who they deem a threat to incumbent power.

Similarly, free "speech" doctrine reoriented to protect the right of the wealthy to purchase advertisements, first in order to overturn New Deal-era restrictions meant to protect wages and professional income or limit producer promotion of items thought to be potentially dangerous,[70] then later to promote political positions or

15:1–3 (cancelling debt in the seventh year); 14:29 (requiring tithe for benefit of widows and orphans); 23:17 (barring return of fugitive slaves), 23:25–26 (permitting non-landowner to pick grapes or grain for personal use); 24:19–21 (gleanings must be left for foreigners, widows, and orphans); but *see*, Babylonian Talmud, *Gittin* 34b–37b (Hillel promulgated *prozbul* abrogating debt cancellation because it harmed peasants who needed to borrow in the sixth year). Similar provisions are found in other ancient law. *See, e.g.*, Aristotle, Constitution of Athens 6 (describing Solon's cancellation of debts); but *see*, U.S. Const., art. I, § 10 (barring states from "impairing" contracts, presumably to bar states from declaring a debt Jubilee).

68 *Infra*, Section III.B.1.

69 NLRA § 9(b), 19 USC § 159(b).

70 Thus, in Virginia State Bd of Pharmacy v. Virginia Citizens Consumer Council, Inc., 425 U.S. 748 (1976), the Supreme Court held that pharmaceutical price advertising is protected by the First Amendment. By overturning legislative restrictions on such advertising, the Court restructured the market to increase price competition. The result was the near demise of independent drug stores and reduced income for pharmacists, as well as a dramatic increase in incentives for pharmaceutical companies to focus research on products that can be advertised directly to consumers; *see also*, Bates v. State Bar of Arizona, 433 U.S. 350 (1977) (lawyers); 44 Liquormart, Inc. v. Rhode Island, 517 U.S. 484 (1996) (beer prices). Similarly, a long antitrust action ended the Ivy Overlap Group's prior practice of limiting price competition in admissions, thereby serving as a major step toward the near demise of need-based financial aid and transparent, uniform tuition in American higher education. United States v. Brown University, 5 F.3d 658 (3d Cir. 1993), settlement codified in somewhat modified form by the Improving America's Schools Act of 1994, 20 U.S.C. § 6301 (allowing common financial aid formula only for institutions committed to need-blind admissions).

antisocial behavior[71] and even to directly electioneer.[72] And so-called deregulation allowed companies to externalize their costs or walk away from the damage they did, while reduced regulatory enforcement budgets (except in the "war against (some kinds of) drugs") encouraged firms to compete by violating binding rules that others followed to their detriment.

Under the influence of Judge Bork's restatement of anti-trust theory, we allowed consolidation that created powerful corporations able to use their power to seize more profits. Large firms have more power, relative not only to individual employees but also to would-be regulators at the state or federal level. Similarly, the vast expansion of non-compete clauses and trade secret law threatens the bargaining power of employees even as individuals.[73] Our "free trade" regime, which places American workers (but not professionals) into direct competition with desperate people all over the world while protecting monopoly profits for owners of patents and copyrights, and our strong dollar policy, which weakens us by creating incentives for business to shift production overseas, hurt virtually every American, even those who – in the short term – profit from it.[74]

We re-regulated the financial sector and allowed it, too, to develop oligopolistic power and then bailed it out when the inevitable speculation backfired, with the consequence that finance has grown far faster than the economy with no associated benefits. In the medical sector, unlike finance, innovation has actually made life better. But we have encouraged monopoly profits in the pharmaceutical industry and privatized, anti-competitive consolidation of hospitals, increasing costs while leaving the country as a whole unable to afford care and unprepared for public health disasters like COVID.

Trickle-down theory argued that the social good is best promoted if government refrains from directly requiring companies to act in socially useful ways, and instead helps the wealthy to accumulate still more wealth. It sought to reduce the various social programs that make the middle class possible and life in the lower classes bearable: allowing the minimum wage to decline relative to rising productivity; eliminating "welfare as we know it"; reducing social security benefits (especially for those who work with their bodies) by raising the age of eligibility and using inflation

[71] *E.g.*, Central Hudson Gas and Electric Corp. v. Public Svc. Comm'n, 447 U.S. 557 (1980) (barring NY from attempting to reduce electrical consumption by means of restrictions on regulated industry using rate-payer funds to advertise); Rubin v. Coors Brewing Co., 514 U.S.476 (1995) (barring state from attempting to reduce harms from high-alcohol beverages by restricting advertising of alcohol content).

[72] *E.g.*, First National Bank of Boston v. Bellotti, 435 U.S. 765 (1978) (barring state from restricting corporation from funding advertising opposed to tax referendum); Citizens United v. Federal Election Commission, 558 U.S. 310 (2010) (overturning traditional bar on use of corporate funds to directly intervene in electoral campaigns).

[73] *See, e.g.*, Amy Kapczynski, *The Public History of Trade Secrets*, 55 U.C. Davis L. Rev. 1367 (2022).

[74] *See, e.g.*, Dean Baker, Rigged: How Globalization and the Rules of the Modern Economy Were Structured to Make the Rich Richer (2016).

measures designed to understate inflation for the elderly, while simultaneously shifting its cost downward by increasing tax rates but allowing the tax ceiling to trail rising inequality; refusing to create national health insurance or even adequately fund Medicare and Medicaid; reducing the once-important subsidies to middle-class and public housing; strategically shifting regulation to accommodate industrial consolidation and unfair competition; and far more.

Waves of tax cuts and privatization reduced public services from the Post Office to bridge maintenance, while security-state government funneled untold sums to militarized police, private prisons, wars, and arms. Rhetorically, deficit panic, a regular feature of our politics, urges politicians to reduce spending in order to reduce the burden on future generations and seeks to pressure the Federal Reserve to raise interest rates to cause higher unemployment and increase the cost of real economic investment, both of which reduce demand, in order to reduce inflation.[75] The Federal Reserve's persistent belief that rising wages are an inflationary danger that must be squelched regardless of the price paid by ordinary Americans just adds to the problem.[76]

But most Americans, present and future, would greatly benefit from more, not less, spending. It is hard to see who benefits when we underfund social security, Medicare, national health care, child care, adequate retirements, vacations, paid family leave, and, of course, adequately funded primary, secondary, and higher education, rapid transit, and low- and middle-income housing. Higher government spending (at least if it isn't entirely the crony capitalism of the military industrial complex), low unemployment, and controlled inflation would shift power and income from the incumbent elite to ordinary Americans.

Similarly, our governments' failure to take action to reduce the dangers of global climate change hurts us all. But it also slows economic growth. Our economy suffers from chronic lack of demand: Investors cannot find real productive activities that they expect to be profitable and so, instead, seek profit from leveraged buyouts or credit derivatives. The result is bubbles and crashes, instability instead of productivity. We could, instead, relearn the lesson of the Highway Trust Fund and the government subsidies that built the suburbs: A large government program can make us all better off. Instead of cutting taxes on the wealthy or bailing out financial

[75] The standard model predicts that in a fully competitive market at equilibrium, inflation results from an excess of demand, so reducing demand will reduce inflation. However, our markets are neither fully competitive nor at equilibrium, so the link between reducing demand and reducing inflation is not always clear. The post-COVID inflation, for example, seems to be the result of supply chain problems and insufficient building of residential housing. Increasing interest rates is a poor tool to solve those issues, since higher interest rates will make the necessary real investment more expensive and thus less likely to happen. We need more building, not less.

[76] *See, e.g.*, Joseph E. Stiglitz, *How Models Get the Economy Wrong*, THE AMERICAN PROSPECT (Apr. 3, 2023).

speculators, we could, for example, insulate our existing homes, offices, and schools; build out vast solar and wind generation capacity along with the infrastructure to move power to where we need it; bring our inter- and intra-city transit systems into the modern era; and reform our agricultural subsidy system to encourage sustainable practices instead of polluting, inefficient monoculture, and cheap, diabetes-inducing, grains. Tax cuts do not pay for themselves. Investments in our collective well-being do.

Similarly, annoying as inflation is, unemployment and weak labor markets are far worse. Nearly all of us depend on employment for our income; when unemployment is high, our bargaining power and ability to command better wages or working conditions is low. Moreover, most of us are net debtors; inflation makes that debt easier to repay. Perhaps deficit panic is just rhetoric disguising genuine exploitation of most of us by the small wealthy minority that would end up paying future taxes, but its advocates continue to win elections. Too many Americans, not just in Kansas, vote to exploit themselves.

While Americans once prided themselves on the openness of our economy, today we have less economic mobility than our rich peers in Europe. It is hard to break into an upper-middle class that increasingly depends on higher education, when the great free public universities of the past are today either expensive or not so great, and when the purpose of education has shifted from producing skills and increasing productivity to sifting and ranking the growing number of qualified candidates for the decreasing number of high-quality jobs. It is harder still to fall out of an upper class that is increasingly protected in its attempts to preserve and grow its wealth without the constraints of the rule against perpetuities; high income, wealth, or estate taxes; or the vicissitudes of a dynamic market economy.

Predictably, the broad middle class has seen setback after setback. But employees are also consumers. Without a strong middle class, the economy has suffered from an ongoing demand deficit leading to "secular stagnation." Consumers simply don't earn enough to drive the economy. Moreover, inequality has reached such extremes that the wealthy can fool themselves into ignorance of their dependence on government spending. If you fly a private plane and arbitrate private disputes, the lack of mass transit, public education, public justice, and public health – even impending climate disaster – may seem quite abstract, certainly not important enough to warrant taxes. But even the uber-rich ultimately depend on the stability of the American legal system, educated employees, and consumers with income to spend.

We are, that is, sacrificing the interests of the majority in order to benefit no one. As in classic models of class exploitation, a small elite has profited. But even they would probably be doing better, in absolute if not relative terms, if the wealth were spread more widely so that the economy could grow faster, with fewer crises and less destruction of both natural and social environments.

*

The long Reagan Revolution represents a major victory of the forces of colonialism over those of partnership. It transformed American law and political economy, leading to a decades-long upwards redistribution of income, wealth, and political power, accompanied by slower economic growth.[77] Beginning in the 1980s, the long decline in the number of hours worked by average Americans reversed, the share of income commanded by the top 1 percent increased, wealth inequality shifted from relatively egalitarian levels to equal or exceed the first Gilded Era,[78] and the middle class shifted from comfortable to precarious.[79] Worse still, rising inequality led to reduced health generally and an explosion in drug addiction and early death among less educated men.[80]

As is often the case in such redistributions, the process has accelerated over time as the most powerful players discover that taking is easier than making.[81] It takes a while to learn how to manipulate the new rules to overcome social and legal barriers to further wealth extraction. Then, as the wealthy get wealthier, they increasingly transform their concentrated wealth into political power, which, in turn, allows them to modify the rules of relevant markets to further enrich themselves. The result has been stagnant wages and income for most Americans while the lucky few have taken ever more for themselves.

III THE INTERNET: EVERYTHING NEW IS OLD AGAIN

The Internet changed everything and nothing at all. New technologies dislodged some incumbent businesses and opened new ecological niches to fierce competition for a short period. Sears Roebuck, which had run a home delivery shopping

77 *E.g.*, BAKER, *supra* note 74; ROBERT H. FRANK, THE WINNER-TAKE-ALL SOCIETY: WHY THE FEW AT THE TOP GET SO MUCH MORE THAN THE REST OF US (1996); JOSEPH E. STIGLITZ, THE PRICE OF INEQUALITY: HOW TODAY'S DIVIDED SOCIETY ENDANGERS OUR FUTURE (2012).

78 *E.g.*, THOMAS PIKETTY, CAPITAL IN THE TWENTY-FIRST CENTURY (2017); Jan Behringer et al., *Varieties of the Rat Race: Working Hours in the Age of Abundance*, SOCIO-ECON. REV. (2023), https://doi.org/10.1093/ser/mwac067 at figure 1(a), (b). Much of the increase in hours worked in the US was women entering the workforce: the one-income middle-class family of 1965 was replaced by a two-income family at the same status level. This process appears to have worked itself out by 2000. *See, id.* at figure 3(f).

79 *E.g.*, Edward Luce, *The Crisis of Middle-Class America*, FIN. TIMES (July 30, 2010).

80 *E.g.*, RICHARD WILKINSON, THE SPIRIT LEVEL: WHY GREATER EQUALITY MAKES SOCIETIES STRONGER (2011). The addiction catastrophe that struck young Black men four decades ago as factory jobs first started leaving northern cities has now spread to young men of every ethnicity with our massive export of formerly good jobs, eased by a strong dollar and open trade policies. On declining life expectancy, once something unheard of in wealthy countries absent war or events such as the collapse of the former USSR, *see, e.g.*, ANNE CASE AND ANGUS DEATON, DEATHS OF DESPAIR AND THE FUTURE OF CAPITALISM (2020); Shameek Rakshit, et al., *How Does U.S. Life Expectancy Compare to Other Countries?*, KAISER FAM. FOUND. (Dec. 6, 2022) www.healthsystemtracker.org/chart-collection/u-s-life-expectancy-compare-countries/#Life%20expectancy%20and%20healthcare%20spending%20per%20capita,%201980-2021.

81 *E.g.*, DARON ACEMOGLU & JAMES A. ROBINSON, WHY NATIONS FAIL: THE ORIGINS OF POWER, PROSPERITY, AND POVERTY (2012).

service for over a century but had been hollowed out by dysfunctional American corporate finance, seemingly made no attempt to stop Amazon from taking over its business. When mainframes were displaced by personal computers, IBM gave up its inherent advantages to Microsoft, even without an obvious intervention by predatory finance, and Microsoft, in turn, failed to dominate cloud-based services when they appeared. Stock market finance, in turn, pushed investment capital toward fast growth – which, of course, is inherently easier for a small company than for a large company with a small new division[82] – and away from companies with stranded costs from older technologies, well-developed middle management, unions, or generous pension and medical plans.

But fundamentally, the new success stories were the same as the old ones: Individuals and companies found ways to profit within the then-existing legal rules and then to convert that profit into economic and legal power, which they used to further change the rules to enhance their own ability to extract still more surplus.

A *Reorganizing*

The largest shifts predate the Internet or are extensions of processes already in place. Since the 1980s, multiple industries have reorganized to exploit law permitting redistribution from ordinary employees to investors and top executives. For example, the steel industry and large parts of the auto industry learned to avoid our plant-based unionization rules by declining to reinvest in older plants and instead shifting to smaller-scale, more mobile technology sited in low wage areas, with the implicit threat of further moves if employees pressed for better conditions. Unions, generally required to leave management to managers,[83] found – in this and many other industries – that they had few tools to resist disinvestment.

[82] From a tax perspective, this is surprising. An established company can use losses in a new division to reduce tax it would otherwise owe, while a start-up will not be able to make use of the tax subsidy until it makes profits at some later date. Similarly, one might imagine that established companies would have an advantage in attracting and assembling the appropriate teams for a new product (although incumbent firms may also be reluctant to take on new projects that potentially threaten established profitable lines).

The finance incentives, however, are different. Equity investors in start-ups generally expect to make their own returns by selling their stock rather than by waiting for the company to generate actual profits. The standard valuation techniques for stocks rely on discounted future earnings. Stock buyers are not very good at predictions, trapped in a one-way flow of time as we are. However, like all human beings, they are great at spotting patterns and extrapolating them. It is easier to imagine future earnings will be large (and the stock therefore worth more now) if they show a past pattern of rapid growth; early investors hoping to sell out soon thus strongly prefer to see rapid growth. Rapid growth, in turn, is always easier from a small base. Thus, finance pressures start-ups to be independent even if tax and experience might suggest the opposite.

[83] American collective bargaining agreements typically contain a broad "management rights" clause authorizing management to unilaterally determine many aspects of operating the company, including reinvestment policies.

Relatedly, after Carter-era deregulation allowed price competition in air service, it did not take long for start-up airlines to begin putting older ones out of business. Because American law makes pension and medical costs employer-based, a new firm with few retirees or middle-aged employees automatically has lower costs than an older competitor and can, therefore, charge lower prices. Older firms were under enormous competitive pressure to cut costs by eliminating benefits, pensions, and veteran employees.

The Walmart model – low pay and rapid turnover – became increasingly popular across the economy. Once firms learned how to make employees interchangeable and disposable, loyalty seemed an expensive luxury. Some firms found they could pay so little that even full-time employees required government assistance to survive. Turnover would be high, but for many firms that was either not a cost at all or one worth the price. In any event, constant turnover eliminates the threat of unionization and keeps the employer's medical insurance costs low. Or, in the case of Uber and other gig-economy jobs, they could shift costs to employees in ways that their supposed "independent contractors" found hard to calculate, and, again, drive real wages to desperation levels. Apparently, there are enough Americans without better options to keep the positions filled.

B *The Marginal Cost Problem*

Standard introductory economics courses usually start with a simple supply–demand model. The model assumes that when price increases, demand decreases. Conversely, as a producer produces more, it must bid for scarce resources, so its costs tend to increase. In competitive markets, any company that charges more than its competitors will lose customers to them. Competition, thus, tends to press prices down to the producer's cost. However, the relevant cost is marginal cost (its cost to produce the last unit) – not the average cost. A company makes more money selling than not selling at any price above its marginal cost. Accordingly, producers will keep producing (driving costs up and prices down) so long as prices remain above marginal cost. This leads to the familiar graph of upward sloping cost meeting downward sloping demand at an equilibrium point, in which price equals the marginal cost of the second-most efficient firm, and production equals demand.[84]

The model of price driven to marginal cost, increasing marginal costs, and a unique equilibrium where demand matches supply is the source of much of the ideological attractiveness of markets.[85] If the model held true, markets would assure

[84] Ronald H. Coase, *The Nature of the Firm*, 4(16) ECONOMICA 386 (1937). The most efficient firm has no reason to reduce prices to its own marginal cost, since it will have the same sales (but a larger margin) at a price slightly below the costs of its closest competitor.

[85] The basic model is mainly for introductory teaching purposes or ideological cover for otherwise indefensible upward redistribution of wealth; everything interesting happens when its assumptions are lifted. One example discussed below is the assumption of increasing marginal costs,

that products go to those who are able and willing to pay for them, that prices are fair in the sense that they reflect social costs, and that firm inputs – whether labor or capital – are paid no more than the minimum required to attract and retain them, and, in any event, less than they contribute to the firm.

Moreover, the model tends to justify nearly any unattractive economic reality as, instead, either necessity or a reward for virtue. Thus, the model suggests that if we see executives making shockingly high pay, it must be because that is the marginal cost of reproducing them and it must be that they contribute more to the firm. Even CEOs taking annual pay of tens of millions of dollars, or hedge fund managers taking hundreds of millions, must be contributing more than they are taking. Otherwise, the firm would replace them with someone offering better value, and if it did not, it would be unable to compete with firms with cheaper costs and, therefore, lower prices.

Conversely, if we see firms paying employees too little to live on – with major companies advising their employees how to apply for food stamps or other forms of poverty assistance – that too must be the result of competitive forces. The aggregate statistics show a sharp divergence between productivity and wages, which used to rise in tandem but stopped doing so at the beginning of the long Reagan era. But the model suggests that we shouldn't bother considering why. If companies were paying less than the most they can, employees would go elsewhere.

Marx, following Smith, Ricardo, and Malthus, contended that capitalist markets would tend to press wages down to the social cost of reproduction. The standard model argues that he was wrong. It treats wages as simply another price. Treating labor like any other commodity, it points out that markets tend to press prices to the marginal cost of continued use, regardless of social cost. Moreover, sunk costs earn no return in competitive markets. The cost of the employee's upbringing and education, both in dollars and effort, is a sunk cost, not a marginal cost. Accordingly, employees should be paid their marginal cost, not their cost of reproduction.

In this context, marginal cost means whatever is required to lead the employee to show up at work today – which may or may not be enough to compensate for investments the employee earlier made in education or other aspects of the cost of reproduction. Moreover, at equilibrium, assuming a rising marginal cost curve, marginal cost will equal marginal product, so each employee is paid precisely what the marginal employee produces. If they were paid any less, employers could profit by hiring more. If they were paid any more, the employer's costs would be higher

which is false in many important sectors of a modern economy. Many industries have economies of scale leading to rapidly dropping, not rising, marginal costs. The basic model suggests that diminishing marginal costs should result in market failure. More often, however, we see some combination of private consolidation and governmental action to restructure the market to limit "ruinous competition." *See, infra*, Section III.B.4.

than competitors', which, in a competitive market, would lead to its prices being higher than the market will bear.[86]

The standard model clearly is as wrong as Marx's. Since the 1980s, productivity gains have gone to capital and top management rather than employees.

The model's failing appears to be its oversimplification of the competitive dynamics of the job market. Specifically, for any actually existing individual of working age, a job is nearly always better than no job. One needs to eat and to pay the rent or mortgage now, not later. This is especially true in the US. Unlike most wealthy capitalist countries, we generally require individuals to fund necessities such as housing, health insurance, retirement, childcare out of their own earnings or from employment-dependent benefits, and we offer relatively modest unemployment benefits (and only to those recently employed). Moreover, in contrast to most other wealthy countries, we require young Americans to pay for higher education themselves by borrowing, rather than taxing successful members of the older generation to pay for the next. Consequently, few Americans have material savings. No current income causes crisis. It only takes a few missed paychecks to fall out of the middle class.

Given this deep insecurity, many employers find that they need not pay employees their marginal product, let alone enough to cover the actual social cost of reproducing the workforce. Most of the retail and fast-food sector consistently find Americans willing to work at wages that do not cover the cost of maintaining even a modest lifestyle with enough margin to cover the inevitable bouts of bad luck. Indeed, in much of the country, minimum wage employees, especially if they are unable to work full time, likely cannot even feed themselves or rent decent housing without enrolling in government poverty programs.

But the marginal cost issue strikes traditionally middle-class jobs as well. Entire industries, including publishing, social work, teaching, and even most of the legal profession, pay most of their professional employees too little to justify the cost of education yet have no trouble finding employees. Once you've got the degree, you are likely to be better off using it, even at a wage that wouldn't justify getting it in the first place.

Perhaps most importantly, the model suggests that excess profits result only from temporary mismatches of supply and demand. Therefore, profits that otherwise would look like profiteering are justified – extraordinary profits will induce extraordinary efforts to meet demand. And they are self-limiting – producers' attempts to capture excess profits will lead to increased production, driving prices back down to

[86] Even within the terms of the competitive model, the most efficient firm will have some surplus, since it can maintain its prices above its costs so long as they are at its competitor's costs. Managers of that firm can distribute the surplus as they like. They can reduce prices to try to increase market share. Or they can pay the surplus to firm participants in the form of innovation, quality control, better working conditions, fancier buildings, higher wages, executive bonuses, purchase of other companies, higher prices for suppliers, or higher interest, dividends, or tax payments.

marginal cost and eliminating the excess profit. Thus, the model suggests that profit is always deserved. If it is ordinary profit, it is the cost of attracting capital from its next best alternative; if it is extraordinary, it is temporary monopoly profit that we need to attract entrepreneurs to resolve lack of supply and it will go away as soon as the shortages do.[87]

Finally, the model suggests that the democracy deficit in American corporate law and the colonialist critique are not a large problem. American corporate law places nominal authority in the hands of the board, which delegates it to a CEO and his (or occasionally her) subordinates. In ordinary American practice, the CEO also chairs the board, setting its agenda, and the board has no staff of its own, so it is entirely dependent on the CEO and management for information and research. Board committees typically do hire outside experts in limited circumstances – auditors, compensation experts, and (after scandals or in connection with fundamental transformations) legal counsel – but even then, the recommendation of which expert to hire is likely to come from management. The firm itself, then, is run as a top-down, command and control, bureaucratic system.

The governance system lacks the basic eighteenth-century limits on tyranny or corruption. There are no checks and balances; the firm is operated, in effect, as a "unified executive" in which the CEO has full operational control. There is no independent judiciary or presumption that punishment be only in accord with written rules. Internal adjudicators have no independence; human resources, acting under hierarchal control by the CEO's subordinates, typically manages hiring, discipline, layoffs, firings, and adjudication, serving as prosecutor, judge, and jury.

Employees have no security of membership or right to due process; the firm may discipline or even fire them at any time for any reason or none at all. Necessarily, then, they are unlikely to criticize their superiors except in extremis. There is no fourth estate; the internal press, if any, is similarly controlled. The hierarchy maintains complete control over information; there is no equivalent to a public right to know, open meetings, or freedom of information acts. In short, there can be only the most limited discipline by public opinion.

Similarly, corporate governance lacks even the most limited democratic credentials. Boards in business corporations are elected by shares, which are usually freely saleable and typically vote on a one-share, one-vote basis. Other participants in the firm have no official voice. In other words, corporate elections are plutocratic rather than democratic – voting is on the basis of wealth rather than citizenship.

Moreover, the elections themselves are heavily weighted toward incumbents. Boards typically nominate a single candidate for each open position; it is difficult

87 This result, of course, stems from the model's assumption of perfect competition, not from any truth about markets. In real markets, as discussed infra, monopoly power is ubiquitous. *See, e.g.*, Ramsi Woodcock, *The Efficient Queue and the Case against Surge Pricing*, SocArXiv (2021), https://osf.io/preprints/socarxiv/g8tym/.

for potential dissenting voices to nominate a competing candidate. Moreover, the board is entitled to spend unlimited corporate funds to support its chosen candidates (providing that it can identify a policy difference with the opposition), while opponents must finance their own campaigns.[88] Not surprisingly, then, board elections typically resemble the plebiscites of Napoleon or Saddam Hussein more than any form of democracy, with overwhelming votes in favor of a single incumbent-endorsed candidate. With only rare exceptions, competitive elections happen only in connection with an attempted purchase or sale of the company or when a shareholder controlling a large number of votes seeks representation or fundamental change in opposition to the incumbents.

The model, however, suggests that this democratic deficit is no cause for concern. In the model's imaginary fully competitive marketplace, firms must maximize their productivity, lest a more efficient competitor undersell them, driving them out of business. Maximizing productivity is a task for experts with little role for shareholder or popular control; neither shareholders nor the population are likely to have the information necessary to correct expert error. Moreover, should the professional managers err, competitive markets are likely to discipline them faster and more effectively than any election could.

Additionally, were the model correct, there would be no room for distributional debates. The firm can earn no profits at equilibrium. Firms exist because they are able to generate a surplus by cooperative production. But they must use that surplus to lower prices, or they will lose their customers to a competitor. For the same reason, every firm is under intense competitive pressure to pay each employee (including top executives) and every other input (including capital) no more than the minimum to attract and retain them. If any firm participant were to take more than that minimum, the firm would have higher costs and therefore higher prices than the competition. If there is no surplus and no one has power to seize firm resources, we do not need elections to determine the appropriate distribution of communal wealth. The only possible stable distribution is already mandatory.

Finally, there would be no need for elections to determine company culture or goals. Within the model, a company, like Alice's White Queen, must run as fast as it can simply to stay in one place. Distractions doom it to competitive destruction. The goal is given, the means must be decided by experts, and corruption is policed by the market. The model vitiates the standard arguments for democracy.

Ideologically attractive as it is, the model rarely reflects reality. Indeed, in some ways the divergence is so extreme that the model can only be useful negatively: by demonstrating how much work its assumptions are doing and then examining the changes when we admit the complexity of the real world into our considerations. Paradoxically, perhaps, as a guide for decision-makers or value judgments, the most important lesson of the model is that in the real world, we absolutely must focus on

[88] *See, e.g.*, Rosenfeld v. Fairchild Engine & Airplane Corp., 309 N.Y. 168 (1955).

all the issues the model suggests would be unimportant in its imaginary perfect competition. For us, transaction costs, disparities of power, and information costs – none of which appear in the model – are critical. (This is especially true for professionals, including lawyers, academics, and managers. We are transaction costs hoping to make a living from information.) Our economy is not self-equilibrating but disastrously unstable. To prevent markets from collapsing into monopoly or failure requires careful structuring and policing of the rules of the game; laissez-faire leads only to bullying, anarchy, or abandonment. Corporate governance's democratic deficit is not peripheral but a core cause of the corruption that corrodes our economy and ecosphere. Upward wealth distribution must be restrained if contract or markets are to function. And corporate goals and culture are far too important to be left to the blind forces of the stock market, let alone the malign malefactors of great wealth that often guide them.

Taken on its own terms, the model is unrealistic to the point of absurdity. For example, the model says that a firm will pay its inputs – including employees and finance – no more than the minimum it must, because otherwise it will have higher costs (and higher prices) than competitors that do not give such gifts.

Yet we see firms paying tens and even hundreds of millions of dollars to their top executives, including exit bonuses when they no longer expect to receive services. Whatever these sums represent, the model's insistence that they are the minimum possible pay for professional services fails the laugh test. Managerial skills are not that arcane. Somewhere in this large world, there are competent individuals willing to lead these firms – or to quit when their leadership fails – for less than these astronomical sums.

Similarly, the model has no room for dividends or the profits that sustain them.[89] The only service shareholders provide to the firm is the original purchase price of the stock in the initial offering; they have no future services to withhold. Moreover, the firm has no obligation to pay for the capital it receives from stockholders and stockholders have no right to retrieve their capital at any fixed time (that is what distinguishes equity from a loan). Instead, shareholders expect to receive a dividend from time to time – in effect, rent for the use of their money, analogous to interest. However, one of the most basic rules of corporate law is that a corporation is never required to pay a dividend; its board may always choose to retain its earnings and pay the dividend later. Since they are being paid for services already rendered, shareholders are a pure sunk cost, unlike most other firm inputs. In a competitive market, sunk costs can earn no return.

Any firm that voluntarily pays a dividend is choosing to have higher costs, and therefore higher prices, than its competitors. In a fully competitive market, that is

[89] E.g., Daniel J. H. Greenwood, *The Dividend Puzzle: Are Shareholders Entitled to the Residual, or Faith Based Investing: Why Economics Can't Explain Shareholder Returns*, 32 J. Corp. L. 103 (2006).

not an option. Thus, if markets were as competitive as the model assumes, any corporation *permitted* to defer dividends would always defer payment to a tomorrow that will never arrive, because it will never have the luxury of increasing its costs (and prices) right now. The firm may promise to pay dividends in order to attract buyers in an initial offering. Later, managers may feel intense social pressure to pay dividends that they've implicitly or explicitly promised. Nonetheless, at any given time, in a fully competitive market, price competition will prevent them from doing so. Accordingly, if the model were correct, to be able to pay dividends for any extended period of time a company would have to be materially more efficient than its closest competitor.[90] Without dividends, there could be no public stock market, since the main thing that public investors buy is the potential for future dividends.[91] With no public stock markets, the initial public offering (IPO) market and most of angel investing would collapse as well. Each of those institutions depends on pricing power that the model denies.

1 Escaping "Ruinous Competition"

Dividends exist, as do over-paid founders and executives. So, something in the model is wrong.

Often, the problem is the model's assumption of perfect competition, which, like friction-free physics, exists only in introductory textbooks. In the real world, competition is often limited by law – as, for example, when patent or copyright creates monopolies. Indeed, a brand name, if sufficiently well established, may make a company's product unique and limit competition: there really is nothing like Coke.

Competition can also be limited by merger. Corporate law makes it trivially easy for a single manager to unite capital from manifold sources into a single bargaining unit, with the resulting possibility of bargaining power. No coordination is necessary among the capital sources themselves; under corporate law procedures, the firm is formed first and then invites investors to join while relieving them of any responsibility for collective actions. The law then treats the resulting union of capital – the corporation – as a single actor rather than, for example, a conspiracy in restraint of trade. Moreover, corporate law also allows multiple firms to be consolidated under a single leader, thus replacing competition with top-down central planning. Antitrust

90 *See*, Coase, *supra* note 84 (pointing out that most efficient producer can price at its competitor's marginal cost, not its own). Presumably, this monopoly or inframarginal pricing power is what Warren Buffett is referring to when he recommends investing only in firms that have a "franchise."

91 Franco Modigliani & Merton Miller, *The Cost of Capital, Corporation Finance and the Theory of Investment*, 48 (3) AM. ECON. REV. 261 (1958). Modigliani and Miller demonstrate that within the terms of the competitive model, investors should be indifferent between dividends now and dividends later. However, a firm in a competitive market will always chose dividends later. This implies that the dividends will never arrive; they will be deferred until the corporation has a run of bad luck or incompetence that destroys it. In a fully rational market, investors would notice this problem ex ante and refuse to play the game.

law places some limits on the consolidation itself, but enforcement has largely disappeared since the 1980s – and even at its peak, antitrust rarely reversed the general corporate law principle that any number of capital providers may limit competition among themselves by joining together as a single corporate actor subject to unified control.[92] The mismatch of power caused by easy consolidation under corporate law is amplified by the long-standing restrictions on employee joint action.[93]

The simplest supply–demand model also ignores the reality that incumbent economic wealth can be translated into political influence that, in turn, can be used to increase the wealth of incumbent economic elites. American economic history is largely the result of political support for particular industries: the slave trade, canals and railroads, and westward expansion (both dispossession of native Americans and resettlement) in the nineteenth century; automobiles, oil, electrification, western water, building the suburbs, and nuclear in the twentieth; and the Internet, social media, and (hopefully) renewable energy in the twenty-first each required both massive direct and indirect governmental subsidies and legal restructuring to favor the developing industries. As new industries establish themselves and wealth concentrates at the top, economic incumbents are both further empowered to dominate private negotiations – and more able to influence politicians and regulators to prefer their interests.[94]

Even aside from specific industries, the basic structure of American law redistributes upward, tending to concentrate wealth. As noted above,[95] "free" contract negotiations always tend to make the rich richer, because the party that is

[92] To be sure, employees could unite in a partnership or an employee-owned coop and then hire capital. Henry Hansmann has suggested understanding parts of the not-for-profit sector in this way, even when employee ownership is not explicit. HENRY HANSMANN, THE OWNERSHIP OF ENTERPRISE (2000); Henry Hansmann, *All Firms Are Cooperatives – and So Are Governments*, 2 J. ENTREPRENEURIAL & ORG. DIVERSITY 1 (2014). But such organizations are more difficult to form and fund. They deprive capital of political control, so they cannot access the equity markets, while the debt markets (which do not expect control absent insolvency) must charge high interest to risky firms, which, of course, increases the borrower's risk in a cycle that generally leaves risky firms unable to access debt. Even if the organization is created, if the organization accumulates capital or has pricing power, leadership may be tempted to find ways to privatize the communal resources for their own benefit or for current employees. This has been the pattern, for example, in the migrations of investment banks from partnership (formally controlled by the bankers) to corporations (allowing the converting generation to extract the present value of future returns as estimated by the equity markets); of hospitals from non-profits (largely operated for the benefit of doctors) to for-profits (operated by and for investors); and of limited-equity real estate coops converting to market (allowing incumbent owners to profit from the scarcity value of real estate).

[93] For a discussion of the platform economy exploiting the pattern of legally empowering capital over labor, *see, e.g.*, Sanjukta Paul, *Uber as For-Profit Hiring Hall: A Price-Fixing Paradox and Its Implications*, 38 BERKELEY J. EMPLOYMENT & LABOR L. 233 (2017).

[94] For one example of the resulting imbalances, see Ruth Berins Collier, et al., *Labor Platforms and Gig Work: The Failure to Regulate*, SSRN (Sept. 19, 2017), https://ssrn.com/abstract=3039742.

[95] See text after n. 57.

best able to walk away from a deal is best able to seize the surplus created by cooperation. Modern corporate law allows firms to grow to unlimited size and to shift operations with ease, placing them in an ideal position to seize surplus. Conversely, the bargaining power of the middle and working classes is minimized by the distinctively American lack of publicly provided social services – our privatized medical care, education, housing, pension, and child-care systems. Other market regulatory policies, intentionally or otherwise, similarly disempower the weaker: a disgracefully low minimum wage, employment at will rules, national banking policies that typically keep unemployment unnecessarily high, governmental and judicial hostility to unionization, and a tax system based on wage and sales taxes that allow the rich to pay less than a fair share.

Moreover, the rich consume a smaller proportion of their income than the middle class, so increasing inequality means that demand (and therefore economic growth) is likely to be weak.

To make up for weak private demand, the government often steps in. But the power of incumbent wealth means that government demand is often focused in ways that enhance preexisting inequalities: building roads to serve the automobile and oil industries and their suburban customers, building prisons to bring jobs to low-productivity rural areas and private incarceration entrepreneurs, fighting wars and military-industrial development to serve that already powerful industry. Legislatures are less likely to invest in industries that don't yet exist, such as renewable energy, skilled manufacturing, or the mass transit that makes moderate income housing possible; industries that do not yet exist always lack the pressure groups that could lobby for the market structures they need to thrive.

2 Variable Pricing, Gouging, and Gluts

Variable pricing – price gouging in times of shortage, individualized pricing to take advantage of weaknesses of particular counterparties, and discounts to powerful players – was clearly understood to violate market norms well before modern economics. Individualized pricing (and wage setting)[96] allows firms to take advantage of particular customers or employees who may be unable to jump to competitors, or of short-term fluctuations in supply and demand. Much of the political opposition to nineteenth-century railroads, eventually leading to regulation, centered around this particular abuse: Rather than reflecting marginal costs, as in the perfect competition model, prices reflected local monopolies and the railroads' ability to take advantage of farmers who needed to get crops to market promptly.

[96] *E.g.*, Zephyr Teachout, *Personalized Wages*, SSRN (Apr. 29, 2022) https://ssrn.com/abstract=4087698; Veena Dubal, *The Drive to Precarity: A Political History of Work, Regulation, & Labor Advocacy in San Francisco's Taxi & Uber Economies*, 38 Berkeley J. Empl. & Labor L. 73 (2017).

Modern medical pricing is similarly manipulative: Large insurance companies are able to pay less to providers than individual consumers who are not in a position to bargain, while hospital chains seek to be big enough to impose their will on the insurance companies.

Simple competitive market models *assume* a single price for all consumers. Real markets require *law* – like the regulated tariffs of the mid-twentieth-century transport industry, the stock market's best price rule, modern anti-race discrimination law – to make the world more like the model.

Similarly, the model assumes that shortages lead to price increases which, in turn, lead to increased production, rapidly driving prices back to equilibrium. Indeed, in the real world, shortages caused by war, drought, COVID or other disease, or, in the case of Uber or airlines, even rush hour, lead to rapid price increases. But adjustment may be slow. Building new factories or shipping lines – even changing food production from restaurant sizes to retail – takes time, even without the added complications of war or pandemic. Producers are likely to attempt to collude to maintain disequilibrium profits, as in Enron's famous manipulation of the California electric market or the oil producers' regular attempts to restrict production to keep prices high. And in oligopolistic markets, producers may find monopoly profits due to shortages more attractive than increasing production. Extensive regulation is the only way to make real markets approximate the model's imaginary ones.

Indeed, some sectors may not adjust at all. When peak demand is noticeably higher than ordinary demand, companies may conclude that the cost of dedicating resources to meet peak demand that will sit idle much of the rest of the time – taxis, power plants, airplanes, schools, theaters – is not worth the potential profits. Newcomers, recognizing that established companies with economies of scale could lower prices at any time, may decide that the game is not worth the candle.

Moreover, adjustment takes time. Accordingly, it is highly likely that companies will over- and underreact. High prices and shortages lead retailers to place large orders. If producers decide that the increase in demand is temporary, they may conclude that the profit-maximizing move is to ignore the invitation to increase production, thus extending the pain of the dislocation. On the other hand, if they expand to meet increased demand, but the demand was merely an artifact of hoarding, overproduction will lead to a classic nineteenth-century glut, price collapse, and depression.

As a result, sensible legislators have outlawed price gouging – sudden increases due to temporary or spot shortages – at least since Hammurabi.[97] During the

[97] The Code of Hammurabi includes several provisions fixing wages, rents, and hire of animals. Code of Hammurabi 228, 234, 241–43, 257–58, 261, 268–77, https://avalon.law.yale.edu/ancient/hamframe.asp. See also, JEAN-PHILIPPE LEVY, THE ECONOMIC LIFE OF THE ANCIENT WORLD 40 (1967) (describing price controls in Ptolemaic Egypt); ARISTOTLE, THE CONSTITUTION OF ATHENS 51, *supra* (describing role of grain commissioners to assure that wheat and barley were sold at fair prices); HUAN-CHANG CHEN, THE ECONOMIC PRINCIPLES OF CONFUCIUS AND HIS SCHOOL 488 (1911) (stating that law of the Chou dynasty required that merchants' price be set

shortage, this reduces consumer pain; in the medium term, while it may reduce incentives to rapidly increase production or find substitutes, dampening the price signal also reduces the likelihood of glut and rebound recession.

Today, computerization and "big data" make it far easier to rapidly change prices and give the appearance that it is easier to predict the resulting changes in demand and supply.[98] To the extent that computer models are correct, this should reduce the problem of the cycle of shortage followed by glut. On the other hand, as we saw during the housing bubble and crash, several financial crises, the COVID pandemic, and war-related disruptions of oil or grain trade, pricing models may fail dramatically during unusual times. Most pricing algorithms extrapolate past trends, but markets regularly act in unprecedented ways. Indeed, as the algorithms get better and computers get more powerful, we should expect the unprecedented to happen more often: trends that computerized traders can trade on will be competed away, leaving only the ones they don't identify.

Worse, predictive models are doomed to fail in any market in which the commodities are bought and sold not merely for consumption but also for investment or speculation. Consider the stock market. Regulation and computerization, together, ensure that buyers and sellers have more, and more timely, information than in any other market. Yet price fluctuations are severe, rapid, and common, and increased computerization appears to have increased rather than decreased volatility.[99]

The reason is not hard to see. When one reason people seek to buy is because they think others want to buy, price increases can make demand go up as well as down. The result is that predicting demand at any given price is not a matter of simple linear models. Instead, buyers and sellers look like herds of wildebeest simultaneously trying to find grass to eat and to avoid being eaten themselves. While it is clear that the herd will not stay in a place without grass indefinitely, for any individual striking out alone is far more dangerous than remaining with the crowd. The predictable result is stampedes, not tightly directed toward food or away from predators. But predicting when and where the stampede will go is extraordinarily difficult even with the largest supercomputer and dataset. Even the most careful investigator of the quantity and nutrition of grass or the speed and location of predators still won't have enough information to know whether a particular

according to cost and not allowed to rise during famine); BABYLONIAN TALMUD, BAVA BATRA 90b (barring hoarding to profit from shortages).

[98] *See*, Ramsi Woodcock, *Personalizing Prices to Redistribute Wealth*, 2002 WISC. L. REV. 1407 (2022).

[99] *See, e.g.*, Cheng Gao & Bruce Mizrach, *Market Quality Breakdowns in Equities*, 28 J. FIN. MARKETS 1 (2016) (finding that "flash crashes" and equivalent upward stock market instability are common); Arjun Kharpal, *Ethereum Briefly Crashed from $319 to 10 cents in Seconds on One Exchange after "Multimillion Dollar" Trade*, CNBC (June 22, 2017) (describing how single large trade led to computerized follow-up trades resulting in crash), available at www.cnbc.com/2017/06/22/ethereum-price-crash-10-cents-gdax-exchange-after-multimillion-dollar-trade.html.

individual's reevaluation of hunger and fear will lead it to gently nudge a neighbor or go viral.

The problem of volatile commodity markets seems to be as old as markets themselves.[100] The great Tulip Bubble did not require the Internet or computers any more than wildebeest stampedes do.[101] But cheap computers let more actors analyze what they think others are doing and how they ought to react. Modern social media allows rumors to spread more widely and more rapidly. Internet sales sites like eBay or Zillow make purchasing for resale rather than use far easier. The potential for bubbles, crashes, and crises is vastly increased.

At the same time, we've also abandoned rules that formerly restrained price volatility. Many modern industries have successfully eliminated the single price. Airlines and companies including Enron, Uber, and Amazon regularly generate prices well above marginal cost (and commensurate hostility) by surge pricing (formerly known as price gouging) during shortages (sometimes created, as in Enron's case, by the company itself).

3 Network Effects

The network effect is that many products become more useful as more people use them. ATT became the largest phone company and, eventually, a national monopoly, largely because it was the largest phone company at a time when the law did not require phone companies to interconnect. The point of a telephone was to be able to talk to other people. If you chose the largest company, you maximized your chance of reaching others. Why go anywhere else?

Market makers, in general, have powerful network effects. If you are seeking to sell something, you want to go to the market with the largest number of buyers; similarly, if you are seeking to buy. So, the largest automatically has an advantage over smaller competitors.

The network effect, then, explains a large part of Amazon's success, and why it has proven so hard for even well-funded potential competitors like Google, or cheaper intermediaries like Craigslist, to compete. Amazon has the most customers because it has the most sellers, and it has the most sellers because it has the most customers. Because it has the most buyers and sellers, it has the most funds to continue to improve its logistics, so it has not only network effects but greater efficiency – and if needed, it can also operate at a loss to destroy rising competitors. Airbnb, Facebook, and Linked-In's near monopolies benefit from a similar, if weaker, network effect: Sellers and self-promoters seeking a wide audience want to join the site with the

[100] Hyman P. Minsky, Stabilizing an Unstable Economy (2008).

[101] Charles Mackay, Extraordinary Popular Delusions and the Madness of Crowds (1852); Benoit Mandelbroit, The (Mis)behavior of Markets: A Fractal View of Risk, Ruin, and Reward (2004).

widest audience, which makes that site more attractive to the audience as well. Of course, sufficiently determined mismanagement can overcome even this advantage, as has been predicted for Twitter and, for very different reasons, Uber. Moreover, popularity can be fickle. Facebook must be dreading the oft-predicted day when the fashion leaders for the next generation decide, Yogi Berra style, that it is so crowded that no one goes there anymore.

But this is not an internet innovation. Famously if perhaps apocryphally, the QWERTY keyboard originally succeeded because it slowed down typists, thus reducing key jamming; it continues to dominate because typists want to learn the keyboard that most typists use.[102] I do not write in Word because I prefer it; even after all these years, I find it counterintuitive and intrusive. But students, readers, publishers, and editors are most likely to use it, while the user base (and therefore updating) on WordPerfect declines every year.

The network effect is often used to explain the rise of specialized cities: If you were making steel, Pittsburgh supplied not just nearby coal, but networks of parts manufacturers, subcontractors, and transportation, and a pool of skilled workers. Detroit did the same for cars, Houston for oil, and Hollywood for movies. Indeed, specialization isn't necessary.[103] A similar network story explains why New York continues to be our leading city long after the demise of the Erie Canal and the beaver trade that originally fueled its growth, and the obsolescence of the railroad lines and port that later made it so important in the sugar, tobacco, cotton, and slave trades. While other great American cities concentrated in single industries, New York diversified early. So, for people looking for jobs, or businesses looking to hire, outside of the specialty cities this was the place where the match was most likely.

Indeed, successful competition nearly always requires standards to make products or services interchangeable. If those standards are provided by governmental or quasi-governmental institutions – regulators or industry self-regulators like the old guilds, professional associations, or a "self-regulating" stock exchange – the resulting market may be relatively close to the commodity markets of the simplified model. If the market maker is itself motivated by its own profit, the market itself is likely to command excess profits (rents).

More broadly, success sometimes breeds success by transforming commodities into unique items able to charge monopoly rents: Corn flakes (1898), Cheerios (1941), Crest (1950), Coca-Cola (1886), Kraft Mac and Cheese (1937), and Skippy peanut butter (1932), all command enormous loyalty – allowing their manufacturers to charge more than marginal cost – largely because so many people grew up with them. While Coke seems to tap into some cross-cultural taste preference,

[102] W. Brian Arthur, *Competing Technologies, Increasing Returns and Lock-in by Historical Events*, 99 ECON. J. 116 (1989); Paul A. David, *Clio and the Economics of QWERTY*, 75 AM. ECON. REV. 332 (1985)

[103] MASAHISA FUJITA, PAUL KRUGMAN, & ANTHONY J. VENABLES, THE SPATIAL ECONOMY: CITIES, REGIONS, AND INTERNATIONAL TRADE (1999).

non-Americans often find the appeal of American breakfast cereals as incomprehensible as most Americans find Marmite or stinky tofu (chou dofu). Apparently, these are tastes that, if developed early, last a lifetime (I refuse to believe that any adult has ever developed a taste for Kraft without the heavy pull of childhood nostalgia).

4 Diminishing Marginal Cost

The diminishing marginal cost issue is, I think, even more important than network effects and the power of incumbency.

In successful internet-based industries, as in mass production generally, marginal cost is generally well below average cost. That is, it costs a great deal to develop a new computer program or to grow a marketplace or social media site to a scale that will attract users because it already has users. But once the product is designed or scale achieved, the cost to add another customer is quite low: It is almost cost-free to ship another copy of Windows, to add another user to Facebook or Twitter, or add a new product to Amazon's marketplace. Indeed, to a lesser extent, almost every mass-produced product has diminishing marginal costs – as the factory scales up, the cost to produce the last unit drops, allowing Chinese factories and mass marketers like Walmart and Amazon to reduce the prices of everyday items to astonishingly low levels. The dismal science's assumption of scarcity is falsified by disposable fashion.

Elementary standard market theory predicts that when marginal cost is below average cost, markets will fail. Indeed, this was clear long before marginal cost price theory was articulated. In industries, such as railroads, with high fixed costs (building the tracks) and low variable or marginal costs (an extra passenger adds almost nothing to the cost of operation), competition drives prices down to the point where investment is unprofitable.[104] That's why J. P. Morgan famously brokered a deal to end "ruinous competition" between the New York Central and the Pennsylvania Railroads.

The problem is well understood. In a competitive market, customers ordinarily will shift to the producer charging the least (quality adjusted) for the product. Any company maximizes sales by reducing prices below its competitors'; any company

[104] *See, e.g.*, Herbert J. Hovenkamp, *The First Great Law & Economics Movement*, 42 STANF. L. REV. 993, 999 (1990)(describing Henry Carter Adams' analysis of the issue in 1886); RICHARD T. ELY, ET AL., OUTLINES OF ECONOMICS 199 (3d ed. 1919). Indeed, the principle was understood long before the modern era. The Talmud requires regulating competition both to assure that the local merchants are able to make a minimum profit (some merchant will always be tempted to reduce prices below (average) cost simply to raise cash), as well as to prevent price gouging in times of scarcity. *E.g.*, BABYLONIAN TALMUD, BAVA BATRA 90b, 91a. Similarly, the U.S. Constitution, art. I § 8, permits Congress to grant temporary monopolies (patents and copyrights) for inventions and writings to "promote the progress of science and useful arts" because in competitive markets, prices would tend to drop to the marginal cost of reproduction, leaving no income for inventors or authors.

that refuses to match the decrease loses its customers. As long as prices are above marginal cost, a company can make more money by selling one more unit rather than not selling. So, competition drives prices down to marginal cost of the second cheapest producer (the cheapest producer does not need to go below that in order to maximize its customers).

But to make a profit over time, a company must cover its costs – not just at the margin, but the initial investment as well. If prices drop below average costs, producers are not charging enough to cover the reinvestment that is always necessary to stay in business. Sunk costs earn no return. That is, the market fails to pay for previous investments, to build railroad tracks, factories, or develop programs. Eventually, investors realize that they have no expectation of earning returns on their investments and stop financing the industry's fixed costs. When per-unit costs drop with increased volume, the end result of unrestrained competition is mutual destruction, as happened in the American passenger railroad industry.

In these conditions, competitive markets prevent the private sector from producing goods for which consumers would be happy to pay. Plenty of people would be happy to ride the rails with prices even at average cost. But investors anticipate that competition will drive prices below average cost. After all, once the train is running, each additional passenger is almost pure profit: The railroad pays barely more to move an occupied seat than an empty one. So, it will always be tempted to pick up another passenger from a competitor or who wouldn't have travelled at a higher price by reducing its price, until prices get so low that they only cover the cost of adding an additional passenger to an existing network. If that happens, investors will not receive any return on their investment. If they expect this to happen, they will refuse to invest in the first place.

Railroaders built even though they understood the problem of "ruinous competition." They were hoping to resolve the competition problem with monopoly or oligopoly, where the surviving firms would be able to charge prices well above marginal cost. Passenger railroads failed in that effort. In other industries, that is exactly what happened. Cable television, internet service, and pharmaceuticals share the passenger railroad economics of high start-up and average costs but far lower marginal cost. These industries survive because the government gave them legally enforceable monopolies.

Even without monopoly power, the most efficient firms will be able to keep their prices above their marginal cost. A larger factory usually produces at a lower per-unit cost. Most of the costs of an indexed mutual fund or a bank or developing a computer program are about the same for a small operation as a large one, so the large firm can produce for less per user. Often, then, the largest firm will be the lowest average and marginal cost firm. If it can charge prices that are below those of competitors, but still above its own (lower) average costs, it should be able to underprice competitors, allowing it to grow larger still while the others wither. Even if prices drop below its own average cost, if it has enough capital, it can simply ride out competition until its competitors are crippled by prices below their average costs.

Once the industry is down to one or a few firms, the survivors can then raise prices. By pricing above its own cost, it can extract huge and growing rents from consumers. This seems to be Amazon's business plan: It attracted huge amounts of capital, allowing it to operate at a loss for many years, thus putting intense pressure on its competition, and attracting still more capital to Amazon as investors predicted that once it dominates the retail world, it will be able to earn excess profits permanently.

Meanwhile, the largest firm's ability to cut prices at any time suppresses any potential competitors. Why try to build a better search engine if you know that Google can throw as many engineers as necessary into the task of reverse-engineering whatever you come up with, or cut its advertising rates below yours and make up lost margin on the volume? Why build a jet engine factory, if an existing larger factory has lower costs – you'll just end up out of business due to your higher costs. Even if you manage somehow to get up to scale, the net result will be that both you and the original firm will lose money, much as the N. Y. Central and Pennsylvania Railroads threatened to destroy each other before J. P. Morgan brokered his famous deal.

The same applies to every mass production product: The largest factory usually has the lowest costs. The way to get to scale is, like Tesla, to attract vast amounts of capital in an industry where the leaders are failing to make necessary changes. And even then, it requires the established businesses emulating IBM or Kodak by simply ignoring the threat to their old products. It is hard to see how Tesla will be able to outcompete the established car manufacturers when they decide to use their scale advantages to dominate electric car production, instead of simply lobbying to slow the transition from gas-powered vehicles.[105] Amazon could never have competed with Sears, which had a 100-year head start, had the latter not abandoned the game.

Market rules can be structured to accelerate this process or to dampen and even reverse it. In many industries, guilds or their modern replacements long set minimum quality and price standards, formally or informally, thus helping individual firms to avoid dropping prices to marginal costs.[106] In our largest industries, government subsidy has been a massive factor: for the railroads, massive land giveaways; for the auto, fuel and suburban housing industries, wars for oil, publicly financed roads, government mortgage finance, tax subsidies, and planning and zoning structured

[105] Paul Krugman, *Did the Tesla Story Ever Make Sense?*, N.Y. TIMES (Dec. 27, 2022), www.nytimes.com/2022/12/27/opinion/tesla-stock-elon-musk.html.

[106] Beginning with Va. Pharmacy Bd. v. Va. Consumer Council, 425 U.S. 748 (1976) (finding that restrictions on advertising discount pharmaceutical prices violated the First Amendment), the Supreme Court has repeatedly struck down various forms of New Deal-era protections that were intended to limit competition in order to preserve producer income and working conditions or product quality.

around cars; for aviation, military orders and airports; for pharmaceuticals, publicly financed basic research and public payments at monopoly prices for patented drugs; for private prisons, the war on drugs; and so on.

IV PROPERTY RIGHTS IN PERSONAL INFORMATION

The Reagan Revolution has used law, often in invisible ways, to facilitate upward redistribution. One clear example is property rights in personal information. To be sure, control over personal information is not of civilizational importance, unlike our failure to eliminate market subsidies for fossil fuels. Yet the unjustifiable peculiarities of our property rules serve to illustrate two basic points. First, markets generate determinate results only within a determinate set of rules; if we do not like the results (and we should not, in this case), we can change the rules. Second, our current information property rules create vast agglomerations of power which are incompatible with basic republican self-rule. Changing these rules will be an improvement in itself. But it will also, over the medium term, help us to regain the power of self-determination from the self-colonizing corporate powers we have placed above us.

A *All Your Information Is Mine: Mass Surveillance*

Current property law asserts that citizens have almost no rights in their own information about their shopping patterns, credit usage, internet searches, movements, legal records, or expressed opinions.[107] Credit card companies; internet shopping, search, and social media sites; insurance companies; owners of surveillance cameras and other mechanical witnesses of our activities; and information aggregators are free to gather information about us and analyze it to seek patterns without permission or even disclosure. Moreover, generally we have no rights to information we create as employees. Under standard agency principles, the product of an employee belongs to the employer, as does the equipment that an employee uses. So, employers are free to monitor how we do our jobs, our computer hard drives, email and keystrokes, to install video cameras, or to search an employee's desk or locker.[108]

In contrast, the corporations that surveil us and aggregate such information have full property rights – they may freely hold, use, manipulate, buy, and sell the information they gather from and about us. Advertisers may use our information to induce us to buy from them or sell it to others. Aggregators may analyze our data to look for patterns that they believe – accurately or otherwise – predict our creditworthiness, likelihood of making future insurance claims, or susceptibility to

[107] Even if a citizen's writing is protected by copyright, the information it discloses about the author is not.

[108] *See, infra*, Section IV.B.2.

particular appeals. Artificial intelligence (AI) producers use it to extract patterns to improve their search engines or for autocomplete or chatbots to imitate.[109] Employers may use it to transfer our skills to machines, computers, or processes, to place employees in competition with each other in a "speedup," or to suppress unionization, whistleblowing, or other forms of corporate dissent. As Brandeis noted well over a century ago, the resulting imbalance cries out for legal reform.[110]

Corporate law compounds the issue. Corporate managers have a fiduciary duty to act in the interest of the corporation, but they are not required to consider consumers or employees part of the corporation. Trained to seek maximum profits for the firm without regard to public costs, corporate managers are likely to gather and use information in the interests of profit alone, without consideration of the needs of citizens in a democratic republic. To add injury to insult, corporations exist indefinitely. Thus, once a property right is in the hands of a corporation, it can stay there, without limitations from the rule against perpetuities or estate taxes. So, too, can any profit from using or misusing it.

It is not news that website owners collect information about us as we use the Internet. Websites and advertisements on websites may be programmed to place cookies and related trackers on the user's hard drive. It may be less well known that trackers are often placed or read not by the website itself, but by intermediaries, such as Google and many other less well-known companies, which places advertisements for many companies on many sites.

When the user later visits the website, an affiliated one, or one using the same advertiser or advertising aggregator, the site's programming may commandeer the user's computer to read the cookie and identify the user. This allows the cookie placer – whether a website owner or an advertising intermediary – to track the user across webpages and through time, recording each time the user enters an address, views content, or puts an item into a "shopping cart."

Cookies are a physical invasion of the user's computer: They are actual code placed on the users' hard drive and they cannot be read without using the user's computing power. Nonetheless, the law does not treat placing a cookie as trespass to or expropriation of the user's personal property. Instead, cookies are placed without payment or, in many cases, even clear disclosure. The resulting information belongs to the cookie creator or information aggregator.

Tracking need not require physical invasion of the user's computer. Web browsers are programmed to routinely disclose various information to websites, including the browser's particular configurations and even unique codes associated

[109] E.g., Christopher Mims, *The Latest AI Tech Wouldn't Be Possible without a Key Contributor: You. Artificial-Intelligence Companies Are Using Content Created by Millions of People, without Their Consent or Any Compensation.* Wall St. J. (Apr. 29, 2023) (reporting that Twitter is attempting to charge for use of "its" data, meaning Twitter users' writing and reading).

[110] Samuel D. Warren & Louis D. Brandeis, *The Right to Privacy*, 4 Harvard L. Rev. 193 (1890).

with individual computers. Any advertiser or website programmer can use this identifying information to track viewers. Neither technology nor US law requires the advertiser or anyone else to disclose this action.

The extent to which we are subject to corporate surveillance can be seen by a few examples. Apparently, Tesla collects information that can be very useful in investigating crashes; the company releases it to researchers and other third parties only partially and with consent of individual owners (but uses it itself as it wishes).[111] Unrelatedly, Tesla employees have sometimes preferred their own prurient interests to company policy or customer privacy, sharing "invasive" images from car cameras.[112] Google takes it upon itself to police child porn. In one instance, the company flagged a father who sent his doctor a picture of his toddler's swollen penis, and then removed the father's access to all Google products including ten years of his own emails. The company provided its customer essentially no process before or after its unilateral action to discipline him.[113] In effect, Google stole its client's information and treated it as its own.

Information collection is by no means unique to the Internet. Shopkeepers have collected information about their customers for as long as shops have existed. Lenders long have routinely collected information about their clients' financial activities. So have insurance companies.

But computerization and the Internet have taken data collection and its interpretation to a new level, by making collection, processing, and monetizing the resulting data far easier. While in earlier decades, a shopkeeper or restaurateur might have known their best customers by name and preferences, today any retailer that convinces customers to open a frequent purchaser account can track every customer's purchases comprehensively. Similarly, website operators may easily design the website to track every click of identified users. Thus, an online store such as Amazon or an airline reservation system can collect not merely the customer's purchases, but searches, time spent viewing particular pages, items not purchased, and more. LexisNexis Risk Solutions allegedly collects, processes into searchable form, and then sells personal information – including non-public information such as correctional bookings, vehicle collision records, and license plate reader databases – to Immigration and Customs Enforcement (ICE) and other law enforcement agencies.[114]

[111] Cade Metz & Ella Koeze, *Can Tesla Data Help Us Understand Car Crashes?*, N. Y. Times (Aug. 18, 2022).

[112] Steve Stecklow, Waylon Cunningham, & Hyunjoo Jin, *Special Report: Tesla Workers Shared Sensitive Images Recorded by Customer Cars*, Reuters (Apr. 6, 2023), www.reuters.com/technology/tesla-workers-shared-sensitive-images-recorded-by-customer-cars-2023-04-06/.

[113] Kashmir Hill, *A Dad Took Photos of His Naked Toddler for the Doctor: Google Flagged Him as a Criminal*, N. Y. Times (Aug. 21, 2022).

[114] *LexisNexis Illegally Collected and Sold People's Personal Data*, Lawsuit Alleges, CBS (Aug. 16, 2022), www.cbsnews.com/news/lexisnexis-lawsuit-collected-sold-personal-data-immigration-advocates-allege; Maria Fernanda Castellanos Ramirez, et al. v. LexisNexis Risk Solutions, Circuit Court Chancery Dept. Cook County (Ill.), No. 2022CH07984.

Airlines have long changed their prices based on short-term shifts in demand and supply. Today, they can track those shifts minute to minute. But they can individualize prices even more by using customer information that they have appropriated without payment. An individual customer's searches and search history may suggest whether the customer is casually interested or committed to a particular flight, traveling for work or pleasure, more or less sensitive to price changes or trends, and so on. Make two searches for a given flight and you may find that the airline has increased the price, if it has concluded that you are committed or that in the past you've rushed to buy when prices increase. Alternatively, the price may decrease, if the airline's pricing algorithm interprets your patterns to suggest you are a bargain hunter. As in a Middle Eastern souk (or an university's "enrollment management" department), the price you pay depends on the seller's – or its computer's – assessment of how likely you are to walk away.

Or imagine a university with a large online program. Universities have long collected information about their students and faculty, but generally that information has been limited, since faculty do not record or report most interactions with students. Online programs, in contrast, often are programmed to automatically record every student and faculty action, including all their exams, papers, questions to teachers and advisors, and so on. The Family Educational Rights and Privacy Act (FERPA) restricts distribution of the information outside the university.[115] But it permits use of educational records within the institution for legitimate educational interests. Presumably, this would include programs designed to identify students who might drop out and ways to persuade them to continue paying tuition. Arguably, it might include creating a program to automate some aspects of education and/or advising.

To create the programs, the university's developers would have to use information provided by its students and faculty. Nonetheless, the program developed with that information would belong to the university, itself; neither the individuals who created it nor those whose information was used to make it work have any obvious claim to retain rights in the product. Once the advising programs are functioning, the university might seek to sell them to other schools, retaining sales proceeds for itself. FERPA appears not to apply, since no student's personal information is disclosed, even though such information was used to train the AI programs. Under current law, it appears that the university would hold all property rights to the program. The students and faculty whose information made it possible would own nothing, just as the donors of bodily parts used for medical research have been held to have no property rights in the resulting cell lines or processes.[116]

[115] *See generally*, Family Educational Rights and Privacy Act (FERPA), 20 U.S.C. § 1232g, and associated regulations, 34 CFR Part 99.

[116] *See, e.g.*, Moore v. Regents of the University of California, 51 Cal. 3d 120 (1988); JoAnne Belisle, *Note: Recognizing a Quasi-Property Right in Biomaterials*, 3 U.C. Irvine L. Rev. 767 (2015).

Off the Internet, employers may use Radio Frequency Identification (RFID) or Near Field Communication (NFC)-enabled identification and keycards to track employees' movements. Much like an old-fashioned watchman's punch, these enable the company to monitor when an employee passes particular checkpoints; with computerization, however, the quantity of information generated is vastly greater and may be easier to use. An electronic lock may simply exclude people lacking the correct identity card, but it can also record who uses the door and when. Video surveillance combined with facial recognition may (if the facial recognition is sophisticated enough) make it possible to monitor entire populations or particular individuals in real time, as China is alleged to be doing. Companies may also monitor employee keystrokes on their computers, keep records of email and other electronic communication, monitor phone calls for quality assurance or other purposes, or search electronic document libraries for sensitive words.

All this information can readily be added to large datasets, which may or may not be combined with data from business affiliates or third-party aggregators. Then, to whatever extent modern AI or marketing knowledge permits, customer, employee, or citizen information may be used to predict future behavior or, more lucratively, to influence it.[117]

If a company (or political party) can figure out what your interests are, it can sell you what you want; if it can identify your susceptibilities, perhaps it can change your desires, convincing you to buy stuff or vote for candidates you would otherwise never have considered. Advertising agencies and propaganda bureaus have been in this business at least since the early twentieth century. But the new deluge of information dwarfs the Stasi's file cabinets. A former employee claims that Cambridge Analytica was able to use internet-based information to generate directed ads (and misinformation) with enough success to affect the Brexit vote and the 2016 US presidential election.[118]

If you have made a political contribution in recent years, you may have noticed a deluge of emails from other candidates, each of whom appear to have obtained your contact information and, perhaps, additional data regarding the pitch that induced you to donate. The same is true of internet purchases, which seem to generate an immediate flurry of ads for related products. It can even affect the success of your job hunt, as a long-running LinkedIn study apparently did without disclosure to its subjects.[119] If a government can monitor your movements and combine them with

[117] *See, e.g.*, Frank Pasquale, The Black Box Society: The Secret Algorithms behind Money and Information (2015).

[118] Christopher Wylie, Mindf*ck: Cambridge Analytica and the Plot to Break America (2019).

[119] *See, e.g.*, Dashun Wang & Brian Uzzi, *Weak Ties, Failed Tries, and Success: A Large-Scale Study Provides a Causal Test for a Cornerstone of Social Science*, 377 Science 1256 (Sept. 15, 2022); Natasha Singer, *LinkedIn Ran Social Experiments on 20 Million Users over Five Years*, N.Y. Times (Sept. 23, 2022) (describing LinkedIn's view that users consent to research use of

others, it should be able to identify criminal or anti-trust conspiracies, political organizers and their associates, terror cells, and illicit lovers, or to verify alibis, with previously impossible speed, if not necessarily accuracy.

Credit bureaus do not ask for permission to surveil in even the pro forma manner of a website notifying you that its programmers intend to invade your computer with their cookies. Apparently, they also do not confirm the accuracy of their information, at least if anecdotal reports of false or misleading information in credit reports are representative.[120] Rather, they take the information they have obtained without permission, sell it to third parties that also do not necessarily have permission to view it, and use it as inputs into their own proprietary credit scores, which they then sell to prospective creditors, landlords, employers, and others to use, potentially to the detriment of the surveilled party.

All this is, of course, a complete reversal of Lockean property theory, which begins from the premise that property rights derive from individuals' right to the product of their own labor.[121] Instead, Google, Amazon, Facebook, and the credit bureaus sell my efforts and indeed my identity with no recompense to me. To be sure, I could opt to withdraw from the Internet and retreat from modern civilization, or I can try, to the extent that I have the requisite technical training, to break the information gathering capabilities of various websites. But realistically, I have no useful means to retain my information or sell it myself.

But we have not only given away our property rights. Even more importantly, we have given away our political rights. We have long struggled to restrain the state's ability to collect and use information about its citizens. Just as importantly, we have worked to create institutional limitations to assure that, at least ultimately, we have a say in how our information is used and to what ends. Notwithstanding the too real problems of voter suppression, gerrymandering, the anti-democratic allocation of senators, the absurd electoral college, massive paid electoral propaganda, and insecure voting technology, we still have the right to vote for legislatures and executives that, in turn, ultimately control the governments' collection and use of our information.

In the corporate sector, in contrast, we have made no attempt at all. We lack the basic fundamental rights of any liberal regime of law. We have neither search and seizure nor privacy rights against employers, shopkeepers, or suppliers.

We have no peer review, appeal, or double jeopardy rights preventing firms from imposing arbitrary or repetitive punishment for the same perceived errors, and no principle of proportionality preventing unjustly excessive punishment for, for

their data in its terms of service); The National Research Act of 1974 (Pub. L. 93-348, 88 Stat. 342, July 12, 1974).

120 Here is an anecdote to add to the pile: I was once locked out of a government database that uses private credit reports for identify verification, apparently because the report included an entirely erroneous prior address for me, and I was unable to correctly guess its error.

121 *See infra*, Section IV.B.2.

example, insolvency due to excessive medical fees, disability, or divorce, none of which are especially predictive of future credit risk.

When credit bureaus or internet sellers or other corporations use our information to rate us or change the price they offer us, or manipulate our psychological weaknesses, we have no due process or other rights to know where the information came from, how the algorithm generates the startlingly precise but ever-changing number it calls a credit score or the products or prices it offers us, or who else is using this accurate or inaccurate judgment.[122]

Arbitration agreements and limits on class actions mean that we have virtually no rights against arbitrary takings of property or person. Most fundamentally, we – except for wealthy individual stock investors – have no vote on retaining or discharging the incumbent corporate authorities.

Free countries throw off colonial and authoritarian governors, however benevolent, that view their subjects as tools for ends not their own. But we have created corporate law by which we command or allow corporate managers to govern us as if we were colonial subjects – mere means to the colonizers' end of profit maximization. It is time to fight to regain our freedom from our own idolatrous creations that we have placed above us.

B *A Small Reform: Property Rights in Personal Information*

Major reform might require restructuring the entire corporate sector. We could, for example, try to introduce the basic notion that corporate governors are servants of those they govern – and the governed are us, as citizens, employees, and customers, not the financial markets. Our Declaration of Independence stated this as self-evident about our governments; our task is to establish that our bosses, like our politicians, also work for us. Going further, we could bring the fundamental eighteenth-century political reforms into the part of the world where we spend our working lives.

The basic first step is ending the corporate equivalent of political exile, thus protecting those who disagree with incumbent officers. For employees, this means replacing the doctrine of employment at will with a presumption of continued employment on good behavior. For customers, it means generalizing the basic insight of first-generation civil rights acts: Anyone with money should have a right to be served on the same terms and at the same price as everyone else. That would

[122] Robert Shiller famously debunked a form of the efficient market capital hypothesis, which claimed that stock prices reflect all (and only) available information about the future dividends of the issuing firm, by showing that stock prices move far too much to be explained by changes in the available information about anything other than the stock prices themselves. ROBERT SHILLER, IRRATIONAL EXUBERANCE (2000, 2005, 2015). A similar analysis could be made of credit reports. Credit scores move far too much and too often to reflect the odds of crippling medical bills, let along divorce, disability, unemployment, or changes in character.

mean banning individualized pricing and the minute-by-minute changes of airline tickets to make real markets more like the imaginary ones of the simply competitive market model. It would also prevent corporate managers or business owners from using their economic power to harass perceived enemies by refusing service, as the controlling shareholder of the corporate owner of Madison Square Garden proudly does.[123]

We could also attempt to bring into the corporate sector the well-established principles of the eighteenth-century liberal revolutions and their nineteenth- and twentieth-century development. Thus, we might create due process rights, neutral adjudicators, checks and balances (perhaps in the form of an independent ombudsman position rather than a bicameral legislature or a parliamentary cabinet), and limits on officeholders' ability to use collective funds to promote their own candidacy or to lobby to change applicable law to promote managerial perceptions of corporate interests. We could, for example, effectively neuter *Citizens United* by requiring that any corporate decision to expend corporate funds to electioneer or lobby for changes in applicable law or regulation be preapproved by the entire corporation – shareholders, employees, and customers – voting on a democratic one-person, one-vote basis.[124] If collective money is going to be spent to influence outside authorities, especially on the critical issues of determining the limits of markets or the autonomy of managers, all the claimants on those funds should have a say. We could implement basic good government principles, limiting the revolving door by banning elected and appointed government officials from working in any industry they formerly regulated for five years after leaving government office, or by limiting nepotism in the corporate sector. And, of course, we could build on early capitalist hostility to inherited wealth and the dead hand of entailment by implementing a wealth tax and reforming trust law and the estate tax to limit the emergence of a new aristocracy of dynastic wealth.

These are heavy lifts, but just as our progress toward democracy, limited government, and an economy operated in the interests of all has been slow and partial, in the corporate sector as well small reforms can make a large difference. The existing structure (always) empowers the existing elites. They are not likely to give up their advantages easily, regardless of the merits of arguments for or against increased democracy.

Moreover, today, political democracy itself is generally under attack. In the corporate sector, this takes the form of arguments, well-articulated by Henry Hansmann, that stock voting works because shareholders share interests, while firms

[123] Kashmir Hill & Corey Kilgannon, *Madison Square Garden Uses Facial Recognition to Ban Its Owner's Enemies*, N.Y. Times (Dec. 22, 2022).

[124] Citizens United v. Federal Election Commission, 558 U.S. 310 (2010). Faced with such a requirement, few corporate managers would even consider lobbying or electioneering expenditures. Indeed, few managers would choose to seek approval for political expenditures even from shareholders alone. *See*, Daniel J. H. Greenwood, *After Citizens United: Extending the Liberal Revolution to Corporations*, SSRN 10.2139/ssrn.2647478 (2015).

run by vote of consumers or employees often fail since those groups do not share the same unity of interests.[125] This argument is wrong, on two levels.

First, it is simply false that shareholders share a narrow set of interests. Rather, current law creates an appearance of shared interest in profit alone by suppressing all other shareholder values or interests of human shareholders or beneficiaries of institutional shareholders. Most obviously, shares are bought and sold anonymously on the public markets, the underlying firms do not have real-time information about trades in their stock, and most trading is done by intermediaries that do not provide their own beneficiaries with real-time trading or holding data. In any event, institutional shareholders, by design and necessity, cannot perfectly represent their constituents. Indeed, our largest institutional shareholders are barred by law or market reality from reflecting the interests of their own investors: Their managers must manage to maximize the returns of the fund, not the welfare – let alone the values – of the fund's investors. Even union pension funds are barred by law from considering the reality that most of their investors have a far larger economic, let alone ideological, commitment to employee welfare than high stock prices.

Most shares are held by or for a small group of the ultra-wealthy international upper class. But about half of Americans own stock, usually in small amounts held indirectly through their pension or mutual funds. Thus, most American share*holder*s are ordinary Americans, in the top half of the American income and wealth distributions. For most of them, their economic interest is far stronger as employees and consumers and citizens than as shareholders. If the stock market crashed because our major corporations were focusing on providing good jobs, protecting the environment, and selling useful goods and services at reasonable prices – they would be better off, not worse off. That's even leaving aside the likelihood that increased equality would increase demand and thereby economic growth, or that reducing the probability of ecological disaster would make us all better off even in the narrowest economic measures.

Moreover, nearly all of us, shareholders included, have things we believe are worthwhile even if they are not wealth maximizing. For example, some of us might prefer to have more time away from work and less pressure to put in excessive hours to pay our bills or keep up with the perceived competition from our coworkers. Since half of us are direct or indirect shareholders, it is safe to assume that shareholders reflect our divisions in the "culture war." Some oppose forced birth and, presumably, think that companies ought to facilitate access to birth control and abortion even if (counterfactually) that increased costs. Others regularly vote for politicians who proclaim that corporations should abandon efforts to act respectfully toward our diverse population, even if anti-wokeism at this most symbolic level would mean alienating potential customers and employees: On this view, maintaining obsolete social hierarchies is more important than profit. Many shareholders,

[125] *See*, *supra*, note 92.

presumably, are patriots, and it is safe to assume that many take an old-fashioned view of patriotism as requiring pitching in for the common good. Others, clearly, agree with those of our leading politicians who proclaim that freeloading by not paying taxes is "smart" or itself a novel form of patriotism, or who would prefer to return to the norms of the *ancien regime*, when taxes were only for the little people.

In short, shareholders disagree as much as consumers and employees and citizens, because in large part that is who they are (or who their own investors are). Corporate law does not reflect these conflicts because the financial markets are arranged to suppress them, not because they don't exist.

It is often difficult to tell whether managers are doing a good job in any sense. But it is quite easy to see if they put "maximizing shareholder value" above all other values, including the long-term health of the firm or the economies, ecosystems, societies, and governments on which it depends. Any successful firm is worth more to the stock market if firm managers direct the surplus to the stock market than if they send it elsewhere. So, a buyer planning to place accounting profit first will always have an easy time raising funds to transform a firm with other values. Even conscientious shareholders are likely to have moments in which the prospect of simply selling for great wealth is tempting. Then the political, moral, and patriotic issues become someone else's.

Thus, the market creates a one-way ratchet. At a first approximation, every firm that is operated on behalf of any value other than stock-value-maximization could be worth more to the stock market if it abandoned that value. If even a few people care primarily about their personal wealth, a buyer will appear willing to pay a premium to move a firm toward private shareholder profit. The reverse is not true. Some shareholder must have and be willing to forego a large sum to redirect a profit-centered firm toward more diverse values.

Of course, this is an oversimplification. Greed is a low-quality motivator inside firms; successful firms depend on team spirit instead. Focus employees too much on stock prices, and they'll find it easier to cheat, as at Enron, than to cooperate in producing real profits.[126] Accordingly, it is in the long-run interests of every firm participant, even shareholders interested in nothing but profit, to restrain the malign influence of financial markets demanding a pure profit orientation. Profit, like happiness, often is best found by aiming elsewhere.

In any event, while our existing corporate system is hardly a model of stability, efficiency, or justice, it does produce sneakers and breakfast cereals effectively, and that is nothing to sneer at. A conservative respect for the difficulties of building functional institutions should suggest that we move slowly in modifying corporate law we've lived with for a century – and that we move, nonetheless, before the consequences of an approach designed to maximize exploitation of natural

[126] Daniel J. H. Greenwood, *Enronitis: Why Good Corporations Go Bad*, 2004 Colum. Bus. L. Rev. 773 (2004).

resources and ourselves does us in. Even more importantly for the prospects of quick reform, it produces massive wealth for a small group of economic incumbents that, predictably, uses those riches to influence our politics to accumulate more wealth still. Struggle against this process is always an uphill battle.

Today, there does not seem to be an immediate prospect of democratizing corporate law, although perhaps the nascent unionization movement will provide an opening. Thus, it makes sense to look for places where reform is possible without rousing the full resistance of economic incumbents dependent on the status quo.

One small reform would build on a different aspect of our own ideological heritage. Liberal freedoms began with the creation of property rights, creating a domain in which the powers-that-be could not simply take what they wanted, thereby creating a zone of protection for individual self-development. To be sure, property rights only protect the property holder, and the zone of property holder freedom can easily become a lawless zone of exploitation of non-property holders. Property rights are only a tool, not the goal. Still, property rights in our bodies ended serfdom and slavery and still provide a powerful justification for democratic self-rule. Taking self-ownership more seriously might end debt prison, pregnancy regulation, voter suppression, gerrymandering, and other oppressive limits to liberty.

Corporations, which are mainly groups of people working together, must not be viewed as property that can be owned – we fought a civil war to abolish property rights in other humans.[127] Instead, corporations are legal devices which, much like governments, allow a small group of managers to direct other people, control property, and negotiate on behalf of otherwise competing investors without running afoul of conspiracy in restraint of trade policies. Also like governments, they are our creatures, "instituted among men" to "secure" our rights to "life, liberty and happiness," and "deriving their just powers from the consent of the governed." In the spirit of self-rule, they should be entitled only to such privileges as we deem appropriate, subject to legislative change as the times change.[128] Today, corporations have property rights that they may use for and against us. We need more such rights against them.

One part of reasserting control over our corporate governors would be opening corporate management's decisions to public view. A corporate freedom of information act and open meetings law would be a first step to enable ordinary citizens and employees to understand what is happening behind closed corporate doors with what are ultimately our institutions. Of course, like any open government law or Freedom of Information Act, there would have to be many exceptions – but the guidelines should be set by legislatures and public regulatory agencies, not by

[127] In any event, under current corporate law in any corporation with multiple shareholders, no one has the basic bundle of rights we call ownership. *See, e.g.*, Daniel J. H. Greenwood, *Introduction to the Metaphors of Corporate Law*, 4 Seattle J. Soc. Justice 273 (2005).

[128] *See* Daniel J. H. Greenwood, *Person, State or Not: The Place of Business Corporations in Our Constitutional Order*, 87 Colo. L. Rev. 101 (2015).

unanswerable corporate managers or even by courts applying abstract constitutional principles that don't translate easily into the corporate realm.

Conversely, however, we should also assert control over our own personal information and its use by corporate managers. It is time to recognize a property right in our own information, designed to allow individuals a space in which they may act without corporate scrutiny or manipulation.

We've long known that knowledge is power. Early American criminal lawyers justified requiring religious oaths by (falsely) suggesting that the only restraint on lawlessness is fear of an all-knowing God, so that no one who refused to affirm belief in such a being could be trusted to testify truthfully. Bentham proposed total control over prisoners by the simple expedient of a Panopticon, in which a single central jailor could monitor every prisoner's movements at all times. Fordism shifted power from employees and increased productivity by monitoring and recording every movement of a skilled operator in order to allow managers to automate and impose a similar regime on all workers. Orwell's 1984, lightly fictionalizing the totalitarian surveillance states of fascism and communism, presented total control as beginning with total knowledge. Brandeis, annoyed at the interference of early paparazzi with the freedom of the upper class to ignore bourgeois sexual mores, argued for a right to privacy, to protect personal lives from public scrutiny.

The basic property principle should be that information about a human being belongs to the actor, including information about the individual's communications, buying or entertainment habits, location and contacts, as well as the associated metadata or patterns. Using another individual's information without explicit, purchased permission is a form of theft and should be treated as such in both civil and criminal contexts.

Moreover, for this property right to be meaningful, it must be alienable only under limited conditions. Blanket statements that users transfer their rights by using a program or website must be recognized as abusive and therefore unenforceable. Even full disclosure, let alone the hidden terms of a customer service "agreement," should be inadequate to alienate a citizen's rights. Certain rights are inalienable, and perhaps the right to wander without someone else receiving a detailed track of your location is one of them. Or perhaps not: maybe a fully transparent world is better. But in any event, anyone monetizing this information ought to owe its owner/creator royalties.[129]

Today, courts generally presume that employees, by the very fact of employment, have transferred property rights in their product to the employer along with control over the terms of employment and the workplace. To retain such rights, an employee must demonstrate a clear contract changing the presumed terms.

[129] See, e.g., Michael Kwet, *In Stores, Secret Surveillance Tracks Your Every Move As You Shop: "Beacons" Are Watching You, Using Hidden Technology in Your Phone*, N. Y. TIMES (June 14, 2019).

Instead, an equally strong presumption should run the other way: Citizens, whether customers or employees, should be presumed to retain their property rights in their information absent an actually negotiated agreement.

We do not allow employees to bargain away minimum wage or minimal safety standards. The same reasoning would apply here: We need the equivalent of a minimum wage for sale of information. Any entity using another person's data for profit should be required to pay a minimum, specified royalty, calculated as a percentage of the user-entity's revenues. Information buyers or users could offer more, but would be barred from offering less, just as employers may pay higher wages but must pay at least the minimum the law sets; or builders or car manufacturers may offer higher quality than the minimum set in the building code or safety standards, but not less.

The rationale is the same in each case: Unknowing or desperate customers or clients may be willing to accept exploitative terms.[130] Free societies, we long ago decided, cannot allow debt slavery, peonage, unlimited compound interest, or even non-dischargeable debt, even (or especially) if it means that some people will be barred from agreements they'd be willing to make (at least if "willingness" does not take into account how they came to be in such desperate straits).[131]

The law should include provisions to assure that payments, even if they are quite small, can easily be collected and distributed, perhaps modelled on radio-era royalties. Even a minimal minimum fee should be enough to prevent some of the worst abuses by increasing the costs of abusive information gathering.

1 Property and Liberalism

Liberal freedoms began by an expansion of property rights, limiting the powers-that-be from simply taking what they wanted. Property served as the castles of the new bourgeoisie, defining a space in which an overlord's reach, whether by law or fiat, was restrained. In the post-feudal era, property defined a space for individual self-development.

Today, tort law demands that I act reasonably in public. Fiduciary law insists that as an employee or officer, I look out for the interests of others. But I need not act reasonably with respect to my property: I am free to spindle, fold or mutilate my own cards, to remove the warning labels from my own pillows, to burn my own books, or to paint the walls of my house pink with purple polka dots, regardless of what others

[130] In the employment market, the author of the story of Joseph in Egypt noted long ago that starving people will voluntarily sell themselves or their children into bondage, perpetuating their poverty and powerlessness. *See supra*, note 59.

[131] But *see*, Robert Nozick, *Coercion*, in SIDNEY MORGENBESSER, ET AL. (eds.), PHILOSOPHY, SCIENCE, AND METHOD: ESSAYS IN HONOR OF ERNEST NAGEL 440 (1969) (presenting a narrow definition of coercion, in which "natural" background conditions don't count as coercion even, apparently, if alternative background conditions are perfectly feasible).

think. Importantly, I am free to ignore other people's standards and make what reasonable people might consider foolish investments, watch boring movies, or eat strange food.

Indeed, even more basic rights are often based in property. Contract law, following Locke, often suggests that the reason a person may make a contract, even if it looks unreasonable to an outside observer or a court, is we each own our own labor and its products. Patriarchal views of family law often implicitly or explicitly hold that the patriarch owns his children and spouse; authoritarian views see a woman's womb as public property subject to a draft if the state so wills. Freedom-enhancing views, in contrast, place ownership in each individual. As the slogan has it, "my body, my choice."

The autonomy of property holders, of course, has limits. Property use affects others, so property holders are restricted in how they use their property. Just because you own a pair of scissors doesn't mean you may stick them in your neighbor's back. If I own my home and have to answer to a homeowners' association or a zoning board, or if I rent and the landlord objects, I may not be allowed to freely choose my exterior paint colors; if I fail to paint at all, my insurance company and the municipality will have some objections. In any event, I will need to dispose of leftover paint or lead paint chips in accordance with local safety and pollution rules. Similarly, respect for personal autonomy and self-ownership is always limited by public health claims; a property interest in your own body or sewage disposal system does not justify spreading disease to others. Still, owners and lessees have a space in which they may act with relatively little concern for the opinions of others, whether private individuals or state officials.

To be sure, property rights only protect property holders. Much like the aristocratic autonomy on which it was based and which it limited, property's zone of protection for a property holder often becomes a zone of exploitation for others; property rights are only the beginning, not the middle or end, of a just society. A right to property in our own bodies ends serfdom and slavery;[132] it does not guarantee freedom.

2 The Limits of Freedom-Enhancing Property Law

Locke famously argued that the foundation of property rights is the natural law that an individual owns the product of his labor; when he mixes his labor with nature, he owns the product as well.[133] So, a craftsman owns what he makes, a farmer owns

[132] As discussed in the next section, this is only even partially true if property rights in oneself are accompanied by limits on alienation (as in agency law's "at will" provision or the Thirteenth Amendment's ban on slavery), by discharge of debts in bankruptcy or jubilee and by minimum employment standards and protections for the unemployable. Otherwise, most people will have to sell their persons in order to eat: Debt peonage is a form of respect for the right to autonomy.

[133] John Locke, Second Treatise of Government (1689).

what he grows, and a writer owns what he writes. Our law is quite to the contrary: What we create belongs to our employers and principals.

For most of us, the only way to make a living is to rent our bodily labor and mental efforts to an employer. Standard agency and employment law hold that the employer, as principal, has the right to direct employees during the working hours.[134] The employer decides when we come to work, what projects we work on and with whom, how we do our jobs, and what the working conditions will be.

Even more strikingly, agency law declares that employees owe their employer a duty of loyalty.[135] This duty requires employees, during the course of the relationship, to set aside their own interests and desires in order to work for the interests of the employer. There is no corresponding duty for employers;[136] this one-directional duty of loyalty does not create the mutual obligations of citizens, teams, or partners. Moreover, the duty is the exact reverse of the usual contract doctrine, often touted as the central foundation of a market economy, that each individual is entitled (or required) to look out for themself, within only the broad limits of anti-fraud or criminal law. Rather, agency law recreates, in effect, a pre-capitalist patron relationship as if between a lord and villein or master and a servant, in which the master gives orders and accepts fealty while the servant sacrifices out of loyalty. As Justice Cardozo famously wrote, "Many forms of conduct permissible in a workaday world for those acting at arm's length, are forbidden to those bound by fiduciary ties."[137] In case the point is not obvious, the older cases and the Second Restatement of Agency reinforce it by using this very language, referring to employers as "masters" and employees as "servants."[138]

Finally, standard agency law holds that anything an employee creates during the course of the agency relationship – whether working on a factory line or writing a brief, building a product, performing a service, or developing a relationship with a customer or supplier – belongs to the employer, in precise reversal of Locke's maxim.[139]

[134] Restatement (Third) of Agency §§ 1.01, 8.09.

[135] *Id.* at § 8.01. The rule also applies to independent contractors.

[136] *Id.* at § 1.01 comment e.

[137] Meinhard v. Salmon, 249 NY 248 (1928). Cardozo was describing the fiduciary relationship of partners, not employees. However, the duty of loyalty that partners or co-adventurers owe to each other is similar to the duty that employees or servants owe to their employer or master. The difference is that partners are required to be mutually loyal, while the employee–employer obligation is unilateral. Employers are free to treat employees according to "workaday" arms-length contract morality, with no regard for the interests of the employee.

[138] Restatement (Second) of Agency § 2 (1958).

[139] The rule is so basic that it is difficult to find it stated explicitly, except in circumstances where another doctrine might arguably override it. For example, copyright and patent statutes explicitly grant the monopoly right to the author or inventor, respectively, but the judicial "work for hire" doctrine holds that when an employee was hired to create a copyright-protected work or a patent-eligible invention, the copyright or patent belongs to the employer, not the creator.

The law, then, presumes that employees have transferred to the employer their property rights in their own autonomy and the creations of their mental and physical labor. In parts of our life, property rights (for those lucky enough to have them) create a zone of privacy in which the government, tort law, and our neighbors must defer, to differing extents, to the property holder's idiosyncrasies. But in the workplaces in which we spend much of our waking hours, agency law reverses this result. Here, property does not create a zone of personal protection against governmental or feudal overreach. Instead, it creates a zone in which employers assume the rights of feudal overlords to command and to appropriate the work of others.

To be sure, the master–servant relationship under modern agency law is a material improvement over actual feudalism. In particular, agency law guarantees each party the inalienable right to terminate the relationship at any time, regardless of any agreement to the contrary.[140] An employee may quit, and an employer may fire. This puts limits on the degree to which employers can demand loyalty or seize the products of their servants' labor.

The limits, however, are themselves somewhat limited. Most of us live under the regime of "those who do not work, do not eat." Few of us have capital sufficient to live on, and for Americans under Social Security retirement age, we provide few resources for the unemployed. Accordingly, for most employees, the right to quit is only a right to find a different master. Even that is meaningful only to the extent that market conditions (under the influence of Federal Reserve policies, antitrust enforcement, legal restraints on employer abuses, and employer norms) provide a reasonable expectation of finding a better position relatively quickly.

Agency law allows the employer broad discretion in creating the terms of employment and conditions of the workplace. American law's baseline rule is that the workplace belongs to the employer and only the employer has property rights in it. Employment contracts are assumed to leave this background rule in place unless the contract, or more often the employer's unilaterally promulgated policies, explicitly state otherwise. Similarly, the Supreme Court's state action doctrine means that we, as citizens, have no constitutional rights – such as rights against unreasonable searches or to express dissent – against even the largest corporations, regardless of how much governance power they exercise, so long as they remain nominally separate of the states that authorize, regulate, or grant privileges to them.[141]

A fortiori, we allow private-sector employers to monitor employees almost without limit. Thus, even if a condition of employment requires that a specific employee have exclusive rights to a desk, tools, locker, telephone, or other workspace, the courts do not view this as tenancy or any other property-like right.[142] The employer

[140] Restatement (Third) of Agency § 3.10(1).

[141] Edmonson v. Leesville Concrete Co., Inc., 500 U.S. 614 (1991); Civil Rights Cases, 109 U.S. 3 (1883).

[142] *See, e.g.*, Am. Fed. Teachers v. Kanawha Cty Bd of Ed., 592 F. Supp. 2d 883 (2009) ("Private employers are free to search their employees"); Acosta v. Scott Labor LLC, 377 F. Supp. 2d 647

retains the right to inspect, monitor, and reclaim these tools at its discretion; employees have little privacy interest in them because they have no property right in them.[143] An employer may monitor phone conversations and, even in states where wiretapping or recording is generally illegal, is free to deem employment to be consent to waive privacy rights.

Since the beginning of the computer era, the courts have consistently extended this arbitrary employer power to new technologies. Every company internal network and email system is designed to allow administrators to view individual users' accounts, usage, and to read their emails and the contents of their hard drives. There are good technical reasons for this: An individual user might download a virus, accidentally or otherwise; might have their account hacked or hijacked; might use it to violate copyright law; or might simply download enough cat videos or pornography to slow the system for everyone else. The law, however, does not require employers to monitor in a reasonable fashion designed to serve these limited purposes; management may monitor for any business purpose using any available means.

Thus, companies routinely use their ability to monitor to police and supervise employees. Administrators may set employer servers to monitor employee keystrokes or programs used or websites visited to determine if employees are slacking off from their assigned tasks to, for example, shop during business hours. Or they may install automated review of emails to search for key words that might suggest that an employee is breaching confidentiality or engaging in insider trading. Indeed, management may monitor to identify employees who complain about incumbent management or seek to organize a union: activities that, outside the workplace, would be protected by the core principles of self-government.

The First Amendment protects our right to speak out as part of the basis of representative democracy, but the First Amendment does not apply to private-sector employer censorship of employees. Notwithstanding the actual reality that email appears to be private and even when employees have been assigned specific, password-protected, accounts on a computer system, current law is that the employee has no property or privacy rights in the employee's own writing or other communication. Employers, the legal logic goes, own the premises and the computer system and may use them as they please. If employees place their work product

(ND Ill 2005) (finding no invasion of employee privacy where employer used concealed surveillance cameras); K-Mart Corp. Store No. 7441 v. Trotti, 677 S.W.2d 632 (1984) (because lockers were employer's property, even if locked, "jury could reasonably infer that those lockers were subject to legitimate, reasonable searches by employers" but search might be tortious invasion of privacy if "highly offensive to reasonable person").

143 Charles Reich's proposal that the law deem employees to have limited property rights in their jobs, of course, garnered many citations but little traction in the law. Charles Reich, *The New Property*, 73 Yale L.J. 733 (1964).

on the employer's system or create during business hours, they are deemed to have transferred ownership to the employer.

Workplace monitoring is as old as workplaces. It may even be the reason that the factory system appeared before the industrial revolution's centralized energy sources. However, new technologies are raising it to new levels.[144] Key stroke programs can log every key stroke an employee makes on their computer. Centralized email allows employers to scan every email for words that might indicate wrongdoing such as insider trading – or simple dissatisfaction with incumbent management. Cheap cameras, ubiquitous ID cards – some with RFID chips that allow monitoring by remote readers – and computerized data processing make it more practical for managers to record and monitor where every employee is in real time. Amazon recently patented a wristband designed to report and classify an employee's every hand movement,[145] while Three Square Markets convinced dozens of employees to have an RFID chip implanted under their skin, allowing the company to locate them any time they pass near a RFID reader.[146] Sometimes, control extends to the most intimate matters, as when employers regulate bathroom breaks or bar employees from getting pregnant, or even beyond the working day, as when airlines pay flight attendants only when the airplane door is closed, but nonetheless require them to help passengers load and unload in-cabin baggage, often the hardest part of the flight.[147]

Outside the workplace, the story is similar. Private eyes have existed for a long time, and the long-standing law is that we have no protection from their snooping in public places (including our trash), regardless of whom they are working for or why

[144] *E.g.*, Colin Lecher, *How Amazon Automatically Tracks and Fires Warehouse Workers for "Productivity,"* The Verge (Apr. 25, 2019), www.theverge.com/2019/4/25/18516004/amazon-warehouse-fulfillment-centers-productivity-firing-terminations (reporting on Amazon documents showing extent of Amazon's monitoring of its employees); Richard Vanderford, *Americans Wary of Big Brother AI Watching in the Workplace*, Wall St. J. (Apr. 20, 2023) (reporting on unpopularity of widely used AI surveillance technology).

[145] *See* Ceylan Yeginsu, *If Workers Slack Off, the Wristband Will Know. (And Amazon Has a Patent for It.)*, N.Y. Times (Feb. 1, 2018).

[146] Maggie Astor, *Microchip Implants for Employees? One Company Says Yes*, N.Y. Times (July 25, 2017).

[147] Occupational Safety and Health Administration (OSHA) regulation requires toilet facilities to be "reasonably" available during the workday. *Interpretation of 29 CFR 1910.141(c)(1)(i)*, U.S. Dep't. Labor (Apr. 6, 1998), www.osha.gov/laws-regs/standardinterpretations/1998-04-06-0. Details are left to the employer's discretion. Nonetheless, many companies limit bathroom breaks. *See, e.g., No relief: Denial of Bathroom Breaks in the Poultry Industry*, Oxfam Reports, https://s3.amazonaws.com/oxfam-us/www/static/media/files/No_Relief.pdf; Corilyn Shropshire, *6 Minutes a Day for Bathroom Breaks? Union Cries Foul*, Chi. Trib. (July 10, 2014) (stating that a company allegedly used identification cards to monitor employees' bathroom use and disciplined those who used more than 30 minutes per week). Many truck drivers report using bottles or cups due to employer restrictions on breaks. Michael Sainato, *14-hour Days and No Bathroom Breaks: Amazon's Overworked Delivery Drivers*, The Guardian (Mar. 11, 2021). On flight attendants' struggle to be paid for the work they do, *see, e.g.*, Jennifer Gonnerman, *Flight Attendants Fight Back*, The New Yorker (May 30, 2022).

they seek the information. (Of course some uses, such as blackmail, may be prohibited). But modern technology amounts to a qualitative transformation.

Today, cameras are ubiquitous. Storekeepers and governments have installed enough cameras that many public places are effectively under constant surveillance. Your neighbors' Ring not only may be picking up your visitors, but may be uploading its videos, where they are available for search by the subscriber, Ring itself, subpoena in a civil or criminal suit or government investigation, the NSA, or, if Ring's security is insufficient, hackers. The New York Times reports that every subway train in New York will soon have a camera recording passengers; stations already do.[148] But New York is not a leader here: London has far more publicly installed cameras.

Anyone with access, licit or otherwise, to these surveillance videos may also be using AI to identify persons or patterns of interest to them.[149] Indeed, one company is attempting to amass a database of every identified personal photo on the Internet, primarily in order to facilitate police identification of possible suspects in surveillance photographs.[150]

Similarly, your cellphone must track your general location in order to access local cell towers, and it contains a GPS device that determines your precise location. Most cell phones automatically disclose cell tower information to service providers, and many apps, including Google Maps and Apple's Find My service, routinely collect the GPS information. No rules prevent the firms that obtain such information from recording it, using it for their owner purposes, or disclosing it to advertisers or outside firms that specialize in finding patterns that might be useful to advertisers. Each such business presumably stores its findings somewhere that may be accessible to hackers. Moreover, each of the various businesses that have access to your location data may be required to disclose the data to government officials or civil litigants armed with subpoenas or warrants.[151]

In addition, the Federal government, local police departments, and even private companies may use dummy cell towers, known as international mobile subscriber identity (IMSI)-catchers, to identify cell phone users near a location of interest.[152] The dummy tower technology, sold by several private companies, mimics an actual cell phone tower and records the identification numbers of cell phones that access

[148] Ana Ley, *New York City Subway System to Install Security Cameras in Train Cars*, N.Y. Times (Sept. 20, 2022) (describing plan to install more cameras in NY's transit system).

[149] *See, e.g.*, Kashmir Hill, *Facial Recognition: What Happens When We Are Tracked Everywhere We Go? Your Face Is Not Your Own*, N.Y. Times Magazine (Mar. 18, 2021) (reporting on implications of facial recognition AI).

[150] *See, e.g.*, *Clearview AI, Used by Police to Find Criminals, Is Now in Public Defenders' Hands*, N.Y. Times (Sept. 21, 2022) (describing defense counsel's use of Clearview AI's data and facial recognition technology to identify a crucial witness who could provide an alibi).

[151] *See, e.g.*, Carpenter v. United States, 585 US _, 138 Sup. Ct. 2206 (2018).

[152] *See, e.g.*, ACLU v. United States Customs and Border Protection and United States Immigration and Customs Enforcement (SDNY 19-cv-11311), record and released documents available at www.aclu.org/cases/aclu-v-cbp-foia-case-cbp-and-ice-records-related-use-cell-site-simulator-technology.

it.[153] While the manufacturers generally require local law enforcement and private purchasers of the tracking equipment to sign non-disclosure agreements, the trackers do not obtain any consent from the individuals whose information they seize. National law regarding collection or use of this information is not entirely clear; some states have held, by legislation or judicial decision, that governmental agencies must obtain a search warrant under some circumstances.[154]

Use of tracking by law enforcement is routine, including in situations that may be less benign than tracking lost hikers, recovering stolen property, or identifying criminals. For example, the US government reportedly uses cell phone location data in tracking alleged terrorists it is targeting for assassination. The Customs and Border Control (CBC) used a Predator drone to surveil demonstrators in Minneapolis after the murder of George Floyd, despite the lack of any connection between those demonstrations and the CBC mission.[155] Some commentators have suggested that prosecutors in states that have criminalized abortion and related procedures might use cell phone location data to target people who have been in or near family planning clinics for investigation or prosecution.[156] Indeed, the Massachusetts attorney general settled a consumer protection lawsuit against an anti-abortion group that allegedly used phone data to target women whose phones were located in abortion clinics.[157]

As AI improves, the databases themselves will become even more clearly treasure troves for companies, investigators, and others searching for patterns or particular people.

C *The New Property Right to Information*

As others have pointed out, a property right to our own information – Brandeis' right to privacy expanded to match the capacities of modern computer data analysis; Orwell's reinterpretation of Bentham's Panopticon applied to our private-sector governors – could be a turning point from the new feudalism to a new democratic self-determination.[158]

[153] *See, e.g.*, Dell Cameron & Dhruv Mehrotra, *Cops Turn to Canadian Phone-Tracking Firm after Infamous "Stingrays" Become "Obsolete,"* GIZMODO (Oct. 23, 2020), https://gizmodo.com/american-cops-turns-to-canadian-phone-tracking-firm-aft-1845442778.

[154] E.g., Va. Code § 19.2-70.3; Ca. Penal Code § 1546 et seq.; Jones v. United States, 168 A.3d 703, 707 (D.C. 2017). *See also*, NYCLU, *Memorandum: Warrant Requirement for the Use of Stingrays in New York*, NYCLU (Aug. 2015), www.nyclu.org/sites/default/files/memo_stingrayuse_NY_201508_final.pdf.

[155] *See*, Kris Holt, *CBP Flew a Predator Drone over Minneapolis Amid George Floyd Protests*, FORBES (May 29, 2020).

[156] *See, e.g.*, Patience Haggin, *Phones Know Who Went to an Abortion Clinic: Whom Will They Tell?*, WALL ST. J. (Aug. 7, 2022).

[157] *Id.*

[158] E.g., Yochai Benkler, *Constitutional Bounds of Database Protection: The Role of Judicial Review in the Creation and Definition of Private Rights in Information*, 15 BERKELEY TECH. L. J. 535, 591 (2000).

Some reforms have been made in the direction of recognizing that we ought to be able to control our information. For example, California's Consumer Privacy Act[159] provides that certain information aggregators must give consumers the ability to opt out or restrict the resale of their information. But it does not require collectors or aggregators to obtain affirmative consent, thus rejecting the full implications of property rights in information. Nor does it have any provision to facilitate payments for use of citizen's information, which would be essential for a functioning market. Even more critically, it specifically exempts several of the most common and intrusive forms of information collection: information requested by a governmental agency, information used in a legal claim, aggregated and deidentified information, information subject to the Fair Credit Reporting Act related to creditworthiness or "reputation" collected by or for a "consumer reporting agency," and so on.[160]

Individually negotiated contracts to sell our information are obviously impractical. The market value of information is largely in aggregates, not individuals, so the sale price most likely would be extremely low. Moreover, the negotiation would be quite unbalanced: Those collecting information would have both the incentive and ability to produce one-sided form contracts, unlike citizens whose information is being collected.

Much as radio stations were required to pay a royalty each time they broadcast an artist's creation, and we are required to pay drug companies a royalty for every pill – so too, every firm should be required to pay us a royalty every time it uses or transmits our personal information. The fee could be collected and distributed by the Internal Revenue Service (IRS), which already aggregates similar information.

The result would be that more of the surplus created by aggregation and dissemination of information about citizens would go to the citizens themselves, and less to the monopoly holders of that data.

But more importantly, the fee would change market incentives. Boiler rooms have long contacted many people in the hope of finding a few who might be suitable targets for a sale or a scam. The Internet and computerization have made boiler rooms nearly free to operate: An operator can send out millions of emails or automatically call thousands of phones at almost zero marginal cost, so that the business remains profitable even if hitting a mark is no more likely than being hit by lightning. But the private cost to the boiler room does not reflect the social cost. For most of us, constant offers to extend our auto repair insurance, rescue relatives caught at the border, disclose our passwords to retrieve misdirected mail, or help displaced princes recover their fortunes are a significant annoyance, wasting our time and clogging our inboxes. For the victims of a scam, of course, the consequences may be far worse.

[159] Ca. Civil Code, Div. 3, Part 4, Title 1.81.5., California Consumer Privacy Act of 2018 [1798.100–1798.199.100].

[160] *Id.*, at 1798.145.

Even a small fee for using targets' personal information would leave most of the boiler rooms and those who supply their data insolvent. Neither sales nor scams are likely to be profitable enough to cover the even small charges for unsuccessful calls. Better still, any caller that failed to pay the required amount automatically would be in violation of a relatively easily enforced strict-liability law.[161] Today, ISPs and phone companies, and even Google probably could identify the misusers of their services, but they have little motive to crack down on mass mailers and junk callers, who may even be paying customers. If private actors were permitted to retain a portion of the fine in a *qui tam* action, these intermediaries would suddenly have a material incentive to identify the wrongdoers instead of accepting them as a cost of modernity. With the assistance of the companies that run the Internet, we might even purge these scourges from the Internet.

A larger fee might force even useful businesses to treat customers as purchasers of a service rather than raw materials to be exploited. Perhaps advertisers would pick up the extra cost. In that case, the basic business model would continue to be selling our eyeballs and attention – but we, as the sellers, would actually receive some of the financial proceeds, not merely addictive clickbait. Alternatively, Google, Facebook, and other content producers might have to produce something that people are actually willing to pay for, rather than pandering to weak wills and boredom. Either way would be a significant step toward autonomy, freedom, and markets to improve our lives instead of worsening them.

D *Further Implications*

Clarifying the law to ensure that citizens own their own information would have other benefits as well. Internet-based companies have arrogated enormous power, on matters large and small. A revised Lockean understanding, assuring citizens of their right to property, could be a basis for other, equally small and equally consequential, corrections to the law.

For example, cookies, under ordinary common law, should be viewed as trespass. Elementary principles state that no one has a right to use another's property or invade their private spaces. A cookie invades our private space, residing on our hard drives or private spaces in a virtual drive. Most of us own our hard drives and have property rights, by virtue of paying for them, to the virtual drives we use. Even if the drive is provided by an employer or by Google, it remains a private space – in the modern world, as private as a diary and far more private than a business's books and records.

161 Compare DEAN BAKER's proposal, *supra* note 74, for a small tax on stock market transactions, less to raise money than to drive out of business the most destructive front-running rapid traders, who extract value from the system while contributing nothing other than pointless marginal liquidity when the market is liquid and additional fuel when it panics upward or downward.

The First Amendment's freedom of speech, religion, conscience, and protest are each based on the idea that free individuals require a space in which they can think for themselves, or commit to a community other than the state, without undue interference from neighbors or government. In our legal system, the clearest way to instantiate that value into the law is to recognize that we each have a property right in our own hard drives (including virtual drives), just as we do in our writings, worship, and decorating choices. To avoid trespass liability, cookie users should be required to pay computer owners for the privilege of invading their space, perhaps including an automated royalty system. Anyone invading those drives for surveillance purposes should be subject to the same rules as would apply to a seizure of the contents of other private writings, such as a diary.

Similarly, credit bureaus, like advertisers, take our information, aggregate it, and use, or misuse, it against us. Advertisers seek to learn our desires and weaknesses, to convince us to buy their products or services whether or not they will actually serve our interests; information aggregators such as Facebook, Google, and Cambridge Analytica use our information to help those advertisers target those of us most susceptible to their messages.[162] Each of these should be recognized as invasions of the property rights of the person whose information is seized; credit bureaus and other information aggregators should be required to obtain explicit and affirmative permission from the subjects of their information and to pay for the information they use, with a minimum fee schedule set by regulation to prevent overreaching and deception.

Credit reports take our information and plug it into arcane and secret algorithms, which mysteriously claim to quantify our credit "worthiness." On its face, the credit report system seems deeply unlikely to be reliable. The leading causes of default continue to be, as they always have been, business losses for the wealthy, and unemployment, divorce, disease, and disability for the rest of us.[163] Credit reports have few tools for predicting any of these events.

[162] David Ingram, *Factbox: Who Is Cambridge Analytica and What Did It Do?*, REUTERS (Mar. 19, 2018), www.reuters.com/article/us-facebook-cambridge-analytica-factbox/factbox-who-is-cambridge-analytica-and-what-did-it-do-idUSKBN1GW07F.

[163] Most American consumer bankruptcies are precipitated by medical issues. *See, e.g.*, David U. Himmelstein, et al., *Medical Bankruptcy in the United States, 2007: Results of a National Study*, 122 (8) AM. J. MED. 741 (2009) (reporting that 62.1 percent of bankruptcies were medical in origin, including both medical bills and lost employment income), and that 54 percent of bankrupts in the sample stated that bankruptcy was caused by medical bills); but *see*, Carlos Dobkin, et al., *Myth and Measurement – The Case of Medical Bankruptcies*, 378 N. ENGL. J. MED. 1076 (2018) (concluding that hospital bills cause only 4 percent of bankruptcy filings); *response of Himmelstein et al.*, *id.* (reporting that over half of bankrupts reported medical bills as a cause, that medical bills are the bills most often sent to collection, and that over 80 percent of out-of-pocket medical expenses are not hospital bills); Carlos Dobkin, et al., *The Economic Consequences of Hospital Admissions*, 108 AM. ECON. REV. 308 (2018) (finding that hospital admissions have large and long-term correlation with reduced income).

Most Americans, of course, have little job security. But the credit agencies make little attempt to distinguish between those who have some security and the lucky few who have a lot. Similarly, most Americans have few liquid assets to draw on in times of financial stress, save little or nothing, and have little ability to quickly reduce their spending if their income drops. But credit bureaus apparently do not collect information about income or savings, so they have no way of distinguishing the majority who are living paycheck to paycheck from those who are saving, nor of determining whether a particular individual's level of debt is high or low relative to ability to pay from income or assets.[164] Indeed, credit reports do not even distinguish between people who run balances from those who do not – they track credit card debt by recording the amount due on a card as of the billing date. That is, they treat a person who charges large amounts and pays the entire bill each month as a bigger risk than someone who is forced to pay usurious interest on a small credit card balance due to lack of earnings sufficient to cover monthly expenses and emergencies. Instead, credit scores look at outstanding balances relative to credit limits, and to whether the debtor has had trouble paying in the past.

Since credit scores are not based on forward-looking information about the subject's medical insurance, health, job security, marital happiness, medical insurance, income or savings, housing expense relative to income, or even how much credit card interest the subject pays, their predictive value is minimal. To be sure, credit ratings will drop quickly after borrowers have trouble paying their debt. But this is purely retrospective, not prospective. The credit score, thus, functions less as prediction than as punishment.

Given these algorithmic flaws, it is not surprising that credit bureau predictions are routinely unreliable: Although banks routinely rely on credit scores in making loans, they equally routinely suffer large losses in recessions or real-estate market downturns. Credit scores, it appears, impose large costs on the citizens whose privacy is invaded without providing much protection to lenders or employers.

Regardless of whether credit reports provide useful information to their purchasers, one thing is clear: Credit bureaus, like other information aggregators, profit by taking our information and selling it to others. Ordinary property law suggests that information aggregators should be required to pay for the information they take to sell to others. Forcing the credit companies to pay for our information would have two beneficial effects. Most simply, your information is a part of you. A free person should be able to control their own presentation of self, at least in the first instance. No credit bureau ever asks our permission to collect, process, or disseminate

[164] Even the most basic measure of financial security – the ratio of fixed expenses to income – is nowhere to be found in credit reports. *See, generally*, ELIZABETH WARREN AND AMELIA WARREN TYAGI, THE TWO INCOME TRAP: WHY MIDDLE-CLASS PARENTS ARE GOING BROKE (2004).

information about us, and there does not seem to be any practical way to opt out of the system.

Second, these institutionalized gossips should be required to take responsibility for the consequences of their actions. A false credit report or a credit rating based on a faulty algorithm can have immediate and detrimental effects, making it harder or more expensive to get a loan or even a job. This meets the common law definition of libel per se. Yet I've been unable to find a case so holding.

On the contrary, the credit rating companies appear to act as investigator, judge, and jury, making their own determinations of both objective fact and evaluation. Even the minimal statutory remedies, allowing consumers to correct false information, appear to be honored mainly in the breach: In a recent check of credit bureau websites, none offered a simple way to challenge their routine misstatements of fact.

Recognizing that credit raters and other information aggregators begin by seizing property that is not theirs – our information – is a necessary first step to a proper regulatory regime, in which we would have remedies for the hassles and serious harm aggregators cause when they disseminate false or private information, use faulty algorithms to make unwarranted inferences from the information they have, or exploit our weaknesses to manipulate us into making purchases or supporting political candidates we wouldn't otherwise.

V CONCLUSION

The law should recognize that human beings have property rights in their information, including metadata and datasets based on that information. Designed properly, with limits on alienability to prevent unfair transfers, such property rights could be a material step toward a fairer distribution of power and wealth.

9

Taxing Imputed Land Rent

A Historical Perspective and a (Modest) Contemporary Proposal

Faisal Chaudhry[*]

CONTENTS

[*] Assistant Professor of Law & History, University of Massachusetts School of Law. I want to thank participants in the University of Buffalo's Baldy Center for Law and Social Policy's Law and Political Economy Workshop for providing feedback on early versions of the material that made its way into this chapter. I also want to thank the collection's editor, Ramsi Woodcock, for providing invaluable comments at all stages of the manuscript's progression.

I INTRODUCTION

In looking back on the epochal years of the first quarter of the twenty-first century, there will surely be no shortage of ways to frame the political-economic upheavals of the era from the Great Recession to the COVID-19 pandemic. Thinking specifically about the United States, among the ways of framing that most readily come to mind are ones that focus on two historic run-ups in the residential real estate market that bookended the period. Coinciding with the most pronounced interval within contemporary capitalism's post-millennial era of low interest rates, to be sure, there is much that distinguished the COVID-19 housing boom from the bubble of the early 2000s, the bursting of which precipitated the Great Recession.[1]

For starters, if the so-called subprime bubble was, like its jaundiced name suggests, most immediately driven by excessive lending on exploitative terms to down-market customers otherwise unable to secure traditional mortgage financing, that was clearly not the case for the COVID-era run up. Not only did lending restrictions put in place after 2007 remain tight throughout the pandemic years but the drivers of price escalation also proved more varied.[2] Likewise, as distinct from the early 2000s run-up, the COVID-era boom was more readily attributable to shifts in fundamentals, like the cost-push component of generalized inflation and, especially, the ceiling that was reached on housing inventory.[3]

[1] It is worth noting that I am using the term "bubble" advisedly. Of course, for most of the COVID era the sharp run-up in housing prices that took place was actively distinguished from the bubble in the real estate market between 2001 and 2006. However, by spring 2022, relevant authorities had started shifting their tunes, warning that prices were clearly outstripping "fundamentals." See Jarod Coulter et al., *Real-Time Market Monitoring Finds Signs of Brewing U.S. Housing Bubble*, Federal Reserve Bank of Dallas, Mar. 29, 2022, available at www.dallasfed.org/research/economics/2022/0329.

[2] The COVID-era run up witnessed a deepening of unaffordability both in already unaffordable markets like those of the coastal headline metros and areas like in the Sunbelt that started having visible problems with unaffordability only in the early 2000s. At the same time, the shift to remote work and other changes wrought by the pandemic meant a broadening of the unaffordability crisis as well, with a dramatic escalation in housing prices becoming more widely distributed across the American landscape via the northern Californians-invading-Boise, Idaho effect.

[3] Within the ongoing policy conversation about affordability that has been reignited by the COVID-era boom, the factor of inventory limitations has provided special fillip to those

Nonetheless, as different as these periods of ebb and flow in the residential real estate market can be understood as being, they also shared features that were fundamentally in keeping with one another. Most significantly, the twin bouts of house price inflation that bookended roughly the first quarter of the new millennium can be regarded as indicators of housing's ongoing transformation into a speculative asset in the United States during the second half of the postwar era. In parallel, the growing sense of a concomitant crisis of housing affordability clearly helped spur a renewal of discussion around policy interventions, ranging from relatively narrow measures aimed at eroding NIMBYism to more expansive calls to restructure the market for shelter around a regime of high-quality social housing.[4]

Somewhere in between are possible initiatives rooted in tax policy, which has generally featured less prominently than one might have expected in the resurgent discussion around affordability. Indeed, the relative neglect of taxation as a means of facilitating housing affordability seems to have persisted even despite the increasing visibility of the skewed nature of the tax system more generally[5] in an age of increasing concern about income and, especially, wealth inequality returning to gilded age levels in the United States since the 1970s, to say nothing of much of the rest of the world.[6]

In the present chapter, I access the question of affordable housing policy by focusing on one possible taxation-related measure, in particular. More specifically,

focused on zoning regulations as the key culprit in our national housing woes. Without denying the importance of this factor, it is worth seeing that the breathless way in which it is usually spotlighted is also liable to obscure as much as it reveals. This would seem to be not the least because of the appeal it carries for some as a way of castigating government for "interfering" in the economy in an age when its centrality to salvaging society from wreckage could not have been made more apparent, whether through forms of quantitative easing more dramatic than those put in place after 2007 (and already *before* the pandemic caused another "Lehman Brothers"-scale black swan event), the obvious yet all too rarely discussed role of the public fisc in subsidizing the development of the mRNA vaccines that were so central to fighting the pandemic, or the staving off of abject ruin for millions by (temporarily) strengthening the social safety net via measures like extended unemployment benefits and an expanded child tax credit. See, e.g., *How Did America Find the Answer to Its Child Poverty Problem – and Then Abandon It?*, The Economist, Checks and Balances Podcast, Apr. 1, 2022, available at www.economist.com/podcasts/2022/04/01/how-did-america-find-the-answer-to-its-child-poverty-problem-and-then-abandon-it.

4 Among the measures attacking NIMBY'ism have been California's SB9, which focused on enabling the splitting of single-family lots, the creation of accessory dwelling units, and the authorization to replace single-family houses with duplexes. See Shane Phillips et al., *Housing and Community Development in California: An In-Depth Analysis of the Facts, Origins and Trends of Housing and Community Development in California*, UCLA Lewis Center for Regional Policy Studies Report (2022), available at https://escholarship.org/uc/item/32m1g6xk. At the other end of the spectrum, on calls for social housing, see, e.g., Amna A. Akbar, Demands for a Democratic Political Economy, 134 Harv. L. Rev. 90 (2020).

5 Emmanuel Saez & Gabriel Zucman, The Triumph of Injustice: How the Rich Dodge Taxes and How to Make Them Pay (2019).

6 For the definitive accounting on inequality, see Thomas Piketty, Capital in the Twenty-First Century (2014).

the chapter considers a variation on the theme of taxing the imputed rent of owner-occupied housing. However, rather than exploring the taxation of overall rents imputable to individual housing units, I zero in on imputed ground rent,[7] in particular, as a purer variety of "unearned" return to the site value component of overall house price values. Here, in contrast to what the informed reader may be inclined to expect, it is worth making additionally explicit that the chapter does *not* thus focus on the long-standing idea of taxing land values but rather, as just noted, *imputed* returns to the land site component of housing price values. While I will discuss the concept of imputation further below, for now it suffices to say that imputing income/rent to assets involves attributing to them the notional amounts that others would have to pay their respective owners for their use. The imputed income of an asset can thus be thought of as its rental price. (Of course, determining what exactly represents a reasonable attribution of income to an asset that is already withdrawn from the market is a more involved matter, with there being two basic approaches to doing so – the so-called market value and opportunity cost methods, which I will discuss at greater length toward the end of the chapter.)[8]

To be sure, there are not only many reasons that recommend bringing imputed rent back onto the radar of tax/housing policy – and, more than that, doing so specifically in terms of imputed returns to site values – but also many that might seem to weigh against it. Therefore, even though the chapter clearly draws its thunder from the former, it is worth acknowledging up front that not the least among the latter is that even despite the fact that various countries do tax imputed rents, the prospect of doing so in the United States may be particularly fraught. In part, this is due to concerns about the political palatability of any such tax among the public in a society biased toward the ideal of home ownership, not to mention among legislators tied to homeowner vote banks. Likewise, it is also due to the significant challenges that exist in actually administering any such tax.[9] Lastly – and for the present purposes, most importantly – there is the fact that the very concerns that drive the chapter's proposal might be turned around to countenance against it. That is, in an age of rampant inequality that has overwhelmingly redounded to the very top of the income and wealth pyramid, one would have to be forgiven for wondering if taxing the personal use of shelter makes sense even were it to be possible to structure the incidence of doing so in a progressive manner;[10] in short,

7 In the paper, I generally use this term – of "ground" rent – interchangeably with "land," "land site," and "site" rent, despite the fact that most properly, if not always rhetorically as effectively, speaking of land site rent would be the best single choice.

8 Peter Saunders & Peter Siminski, *Home Ownership and Inequality: Imputed Rent and Income Distribution in Australia*, 24(4) ECON. PAPERS 346 (2005), 348–50.

9 See, e.g., Steve R. Johnson, *Imputed Rental Income: Reality Trumps Theory*, in ANTHONY C. INFANTI, ED., CONTROVERSIES IN TAX LAW: A MATTER OF PERSPECTIVE (2015), 65–92.

10 I owe special thanks to Martha McCluskey and Judy Fudge for pressing me to try to grapple with these reservations, to whatever extent I have imperfectly found space to do so. For a very different take on how income imputation and taxation align (or fail to), see Martha T.

why not instead focus on the ever more apparent financialized use of real estate by banks, investment trusts, and the like?

In the interest of moving forward, I will leave these vital points aside for now, returning to some of them in the third and final part of the chapter. As for the broader organization of the overall presentation into which Section IV fits, it is threefold. In Section II of the chapter, I start by providing a more thorough overview of the concept of imputed income, the underlying reasons for treating it *as* income for taxation purposes, and some of the major challenges it presents. In Section III, I turn to a historical discussion of economic rent and how it served as the basis for the central (and most lasting) insight of what is commonly known as the first law and economics movement. In this part of the chapter, I pay special attention to the relationship between rent theoretic analysis as pioneered by early twentieth-century thinkers in the Anglophone world after the neoclassical turn in economics and the analysis of ground rent as an "unearned increment" in pre-marginalist/classical political economy.

Of course, to the extent that the first law and economics movement of the early twentieth century has already long been an object of fascination, so too has its relationship to its antecedents. However, even though my discussion in Section III explores ground others have excavated to great effect in the past, it does not simply provide a summary of key aspects of the background to this volume's titular concern with "inframarginalism." To the contrary, as I explain further in a moment, my discussion in Section III focuses on how the neoclassical turn in economics arguably blunted the force of classical rent theory. This is not to say that there was something inherent within neoclassicism that made it necessarily de-radicalizing nor, in point of fact, that all of its strands were either equally so or even more so than its classical forebears. Obviously, the intellectual leitmotif of the first law and economics movement was formulated on the basis of trading mainstream neoclassicism's emphasis on the market as a generator of efficiency for the neglected implication of its own logic to the effect that returns beyond those made to cover costs were distributionally up for grabs. Yet if existing accounts of the first law and economics movement have thus concentrated on how the marginal revolution facilitated rent analysis in reaching its full theoretical potential, they have, invariably, concentrated much less on the ways the triumph of utility-based theories of value may have simultaneously clipped the wings of rent talk. Therefore, especially in a volume devoted to reinvigorating the insights of inframarginalism for the twenty-first century, Section III's development of the perspective it offers should serve either as a corrective to or, at the very least, thought-provoking departure from the most indispensable efforts of the recent past to intellectually situate the first law and economics movement.[11]

McCluskey, *Taxing the Family Work: Aid for Affluent Husband Care*, 21(1) Columbia J. Gender & L. 109 (2011), 168–71.

[11] See, e.g., Barbara Fried, The Progressive Assault on Laissez Faire: Robert Hale and the First Law and Economics Movement (1998); Herbert Hovenkamp, The Opening of American Law: Neoclassical Legal Thought, 1870–1970 (2014).

From the historical discussion of Section III, the chapter's third and final part turns in greater detail to its central policy proposal – of taxing income imputable to the land site component of owner-occupied housing. More specifically, in Section IV I discuss the growing importance of land site values in overall home price values in the second half of the postwar era, concentrating on how this rentierist component of returns only expanded in importance in the aftermath of the Great Recession. After going on to make the baseline case for the chapter's central policy proposal, in the final subsection of Section IV I briefly consider some other possible objections that might be raised against a tax of the kind I am proposing, even among those who are otherwise likely to be sympathetic to the concerns that motivate the chapter in the first place. Here, I focus not only on some relatively discrete objections – like about the supposed political infeasibility of any proposal geared toward increasing taxes, especially ones that could fall on individuals who can easily be painted as embodying the quintessence of the "middle class" Jane and Joe Homeowner demographic – but also more expansive bases for potential reticence as well. Particularly given the inframarginalist emphasis on the whole of the neoclassical surplus-cum-rent being distributionally up for grabs, for example, why shouldn't we regard any intensification of the social ethic and institutional fact of real estate rentierism simply as a virtue, all things considered? Why doesn't it represent the same unmitigated good of democracy-as-proprietary privateerism that the mythos of the United States has always been based upon and that was already reincarnated once before at the outset of the postwar age of mass consumption in the guise of the ideal of the homeownership society?

***

By way of picking up on these questions and better setting the stage for the main body of the chapter, it is worth pausing here before moving on to Section II in order to recount some of the potentially salutary effects of reframing discussion about housing affordability around the chapter's central policy proposal of taxing imputed ground rent. First, insofar as a focus on real estate rentierism doubles as a way of bringing attention to the structure of economic inequality, taxing imputed returns to the land site value component of owner-occupied housing necessitates consideration of a much more elaborate constellation of related policy questions – like about the growth of political polarization, the oft-lamented decline of the American middle class, and the treacherous effects of a political economy dominated by the proverbial one percent, along with those making up much of the residuum of the top 10–15 percent.[12] Indeed, it has long been to this roughly top quintile of the so-called postwar homeownership society – obscured as it has been by overextending

[12] See, e.g., Richard Reeves, Dream Hoarders: How the American Upper Middle Class Is Leaving Everyone Else in the Dust, Why That Is a Problem, and What to Do about It (2018).

the descriptor of the "middle class" – that the benefits of shielding housing assets from taxation has principally redounded, as through the notorious home mortgage interest deduction. This is even despite the fact that much the same social stratum has simultaneously benefited from using tax policy at the state and local levels to all but privatize well-off suburbs, stoking the shifting patterns of urban inequality that have characterized postwar American society and the de facto reality of post-*Brown v. Board of Education* segregation in residential life. Insofar as calling attention to the taxation of ground/land/site rents thus crystallizes the role of predation on socially determined scarcity in causing housing price inflation, it speaks to the rentierist character of the homeownership ideal itself.[13] Even if the legitimate unease that may be had with taxing the personal use of shelter is such that the specific policy proposal here contemplated proves ultimately unpalatable to the reader, the chapter should thus still help renew the need to reckon with the United States' fundamentally skewed economic geography.

As the last remark suggests, secondly, by helping to reframe how we think about the affordable housing crisis, the idea of taxing returns to the site value of owner-occupied housing also has the salutary potential to force a deeper understanding of the ways in which the ideal of the homeownership society has continued to mutate. Of particular importance here is how that ideal has increasingly licensed the transformation of residential real estate into a speculative asset. While this transformation has most dramatically taken place from the commanding heights of high finance – for example, as vast special purpose agglomerations of "structured" capital have evolved to purchase up housing through easy money or in order to repackage its revenue flows for sale to institutional investors as part of new kinds of securitized assets[14] – it is also visible from shorter distances as well.

[13] On the dark side of the ideal of the homeownership society, see, e.g., Kenneth T. Jackson, Crabgrass Frontier: The Suburbanization of the United States (1987); Lizabeth Cohen, A Consumers' Republic: The Politics of Mass Consumption in Postwar America (2004), 194–256; Lily Geismer, Don't Blame Us: Suburban Liberals and the Transformation of the Democratic Party (2015); and Camile Walsh, Racial Taxation: Schools, Segregation, and Taxpayer Citizenship, 1869–1973 (2018).

[14] In the years since the bursting of the so-called subprime bubble, the phenomenon of large-scale institutional investor entry into the market for single family houses has continued to grow in significance. Notwithstanding suggestions that the phenomenon is of only marginal importance (see, e.g., David Beckworth, *Emily Hamilton on the Current State of the U.S. Housing Market and Solutions for Reform*, Macro Musings Podcast, Feb. 28, 2022, available at www.mercatus.org/bridge/podcasts/02282022/emily-hamilton-current-state-us-housing-market-and-solutions-reform), at the high point of the COVID-era boom it was widely reported that some one in five homes sold in the United States were being purchased by institutional players like the Blackstone group. Contrary to claims that investor entry into the single-family housing market is as likely to be an unmitigated good (by creating economies of scale for high-quality rehabilitation of "flipped" units) as it is to be problematic, most information available to date suggests that a quite different conclusion is warranted. In a similar vein, on the way investors have sought to push beyond the traditional single-family housing sector, see Sheelah Kolhatkar, *What Happens When Investment Firms Acquire Trailer Parks*, New Yorker, Mar. 21, 2021,

Indeed, seen from the less commanding heights of the individual, housing's metamorphosis into a speculative asset has meant a creeping universalization of the aspiration to get by as a rentier. Consider, for example, the arresting annual figures reported by the real estate website Zillow for 2021, indicating that the typical home in the United States appreciated more year-over-year than the median annual salary (in twenty-five of the country's thirty-eight leading metro areas).[15] Indeed, it can be little surprise that the fixation on extracting value from real estate – by far still the largest asset class in the global economy at some $200-plus trillion[16] – has subsisted side by side with the ongoing erosion of labor's aggregate share of income generated in the economy, standing as it now does at barely above capital's.[17]

Finally, the chapter's central policy proposal should prove salutary for how we think about the housing affordability crisis in a third key way as well, which resonates both with long-standing concerns in legal theory as well as the titular historical perspective the chapter seeks to develop. This is because to highlight the problem of land site rentierism is to call to mind a long tradition of American policy thinking and polemic going back to the progressive era and, within the broader global history of legal and economic ideas, much further. While the name most likely to come to mind in this connection remains that of Henry George, a polarizing figure to be sure,[18] as Barbara Fried so well documents in her masterful study of the first law and economics movement, "rent theoretic" analysis was hardly the provenance of Georgist single taxers alone.[19] At the same time, especially for the chapter's historical purposes, George's polarizing reputation can serve as a feature as much as a bug. For insofar as he was regarded already in his own days by economists as a popularizer whose thought was neither novel – being largely derivative of David Ricardo's – nor

available at www.newyorker.com/magazine/2021/03/15/what-happens-when-investment-firms-acquire-trailer-parks.

15 *Skyrocketing Home Values Out-Earn Salaries*, ZILLOW RESEARCH, Mar. 18, 2022, available at www.zillow.com/research/home-value-appreciation-incomes-30862/.

16 SAMUEL STEIN, CAPITAL CITY: GENTRIFICATION AND THE REAL ESTATE STATE (2019), 2 (further noting that the value of the asset class comes to more than thirty-five times the value of all the gold ever mined).

17 As the share of capital income has steadily expanded since the 1970s, the share of labor income has declined from some 70 percent to around 55 percent. James Manyika et al., *A New Look at the Declining Labor Share of Income in the United States, McKinsey Global Institute* (2019), available at www.mckinsey.com/~/media/mckinsey/featured%20insights/employment%20and%20growth/a%20new%20look%20at%20the%20declining%20labor%20share%20of%20income%20in%20the%20united%20states/mgi-a-new-look-at-the-declining-labor-share-of-income-in-the-united-states.pdf.

18 George is best known for the sensation that became of his PROGRESS AND POVERTY (1879), despite the general lack of regard economists had for its merits. Likewise, even as a popularizer/polemicist, George's singular focus on land taxation as a panacea to all economic ills made him, in ways, less the antagonist of neoclassical orthodoxy than the antecedent of reactionary, anti-socialist, pro-property strains of a uniquely American libertarianism. See, e.g., Michael Hudson, *Henry George's Political Critics*, 67(1) AMER. J. ECON. & SOC. 1 (2008).

19 See, generally, Fried, *supra* note 11.

current – being largely indifferent to the marginal revolution in value theory – his identification with the Anglophone tradition of political economy raises questions about how we should think about the divide between classical and neoclassical economics. More specifically, it invites us to think more intently about the divide between classical and neoclassical rent theory and whether the former really is best thought of simply as a blinkered version of the latter.

As I have begun to suggest already, the answer most commonly given to this question tends, in effect, to cast classical theory's preoccupation with ground rent as the product of a failure of pre-marginalist thinkers, Ricardo included, to generalize the idea of differential returns to certain resources beyond the factor of land. On the whole, then, it tends to be rare to consider classical rent theory for the value – or, simply, integrity – of its own episteme. Indeed, not unlike other sympathetic accounts of the first law and economics movement,[20] even Fried's starts from emphasizing how the movement's central analytic – of what she calls rent theory Lockeanism[21] – was dependent on the greater insight the marginal revolution[22] bequeathed to the tradition of neoclassicism that her study is simultaneously devoted to showing was the principal object of that same analytic's critique. To be sure, Fried is too careful a thinker to fail to take stock of – much less, to understand – how the form of progressive rent theory articulated after the marginal revolution by the likes of Robert Hale had roots in the pre-marginalist political economy of John Stuart Mill or, for that matter, how it both resonated with and diverged from other strands of economic thought like Marxist

[20] See, e.g., Herbert Hovenkamp, *The First Great Law & Economics Movement*, 42 STANFORD L. REV. 992 (1990).

[21] Fried follows convention in reconstructing the normative basis of liberal property theory in terms of a "Lockean" idea of entitlement based on sacrifice/labor and a utilitarian counterpart. She also emphasizes how the exponents of the first law and economics movement accepted Lockean individualism as a premise, in part to contrast the animating spirit behind their politics and critique of the incipient orthodoxy in economics with the collectivist commitments of Marxist socialists. Fried, *supra* note 11, at 7. Against this backdrop, the notion of "rent theory Lockeanism" is meant to capture how these thinkers leveraged the inadequacy of trying to use Lockean grounds to justify producer claims to "property in exchange value" in an age when most production was no longer for personal use. If producer sacrifice corresponds at most to marginal cost – and for inframarginal producers, by definition, less than that – Lockean justifications for producers' claims on whatever values commodities happen to exchange at would appear to ring hollow. To the contrary, any claim on the portion of exchange value that exceeds cost simply becomes a claim by the producer – or, for that matter, anyone else who might procure it – on rent.

[22] See, e.g., *id.*, 122 (noting that "[t]he larger implications of rent theory … eluded" Ricardo, Malthus, and the others who first hit on the idea of differential rent), 126 (observing how it fell to marginalist thinkers like John Bates Clark and Knut Wicksell to "generalize Ricardian rent theory to all factors of production … under conditions of competition" in the course of developing marginal productivity theory and, thereby, "provid[ing] what classical supply-side explanations of distribution could not" via a unified theory of value and distribution).

exploitation theory, based as the latter was on a foundational idea of surplus (value) that differed in important ways from the neoclassical.[23]

At the same time, it would be hard to argue that the last series of points are any major preoccupation for Fried, or, for that matter, others who have recounted the achievements of the first law and economics movement. Indeed, even the repeated recognition that Mill was the key antecedent to early twentieth century progressive rent theory comes not by way of arguing that he was exemplary for the way he pursued classical analysis so much as for the way he exceeded its limitations.[24] Ultimately, then, in making a case for the taxation of imputed returns to owner-occupied housing on the more specific basis of the land site component of residential real estate assets, this chapter not only channels rent theory as it was brought to fruition by the first law and economics movement after the marginal revolution; it also asks whether after the neoclassical turn, notwithstanding the inframarginal critique of laissez faire orthodoxy, it is not possible that the concept of rent was denuded of much of what made it so forceful in the hands of classical thinkers, engaged as they more explicitly were in a kind of class analysis and trained as they had more specific reason to be on how (ground) rent could inexorably come to be confiscated by some particular stratum within the class matrix.

II INCOME IMPUTATION: GENERAL INTRODUCTION

A *The Standard Justifications*

The most commonly cited justification for imputing income to owner-held assets, housing chief among them, derives from equalizing the treatment of renters and non-renters. To understand how income imputation can contribute to achieving such a goal, consider the following simple scenario. A and B are neighbors who live

[23] *Id.*, 27 (noting that "[i]n its preoccupation with unearned surplus and its insistence that the market would allocate such surplus not by moral desert but in proportion to the relative bargaining power of the parties involved, progressive rent theory had strong and obvious ties to orthodox socialism. However, there were important analytical differences in the arguments, with important political implications. In Marxian economics, surplus value was created by the difference between the value of labor's input in the production of a given commodity, measured by the minimum wage that labor would demand to maintain some social minimum of existence, and the price paid for labor's output, the commodity itself. Since the former measure seemed to approximate Lockean sacrifice, at least as the progressives understood it, the case for labor's retaining the surplus above that measure was not strictly Lockean in the progressive sense. Rather, the case was based on the assumption that as between labor, which produced value, and capital, which produced none, labor had a greater entitlement to the surplus").

[24] *Id.*, 77–78, 114–23 (giving Fried's most sustained discussion of the classical tradition and drawing heavily on Mark Blaug, Economic Theory in Retrospect [4th ed. 1985]); for a generally contrasting take on the classical tradition, compare generally E. K. Hunt & Mark Lautzenheiser, History of Economic Thought: A Critical Perspective (3d ed. 2011).

in the state of State. Both A and B live in detached, single-family, three-bedroom houses (call them Houseacre A* and Houseacre C*) that are identical with respect to all relevant specifications. Say that A owns Houseacre A*, having procured it through investing $100,000 of their savings in its purchase five years earlier. As an owner-occupier, A eschews having to pay any third party the costs of (i.e., lease *rent* for) meeting their need for shelter. Equivalently, one can also say that A pays the rental value for shelter with Houseacre A*'s specifications – which, say, comes to an annual sum of $5,000 – to themselves.

Say, on the other hand, that B also had $100,000 of disposable savings five years earlier but that they opted to put that money into the stock market rather than the purchase of real estate, earning 5 percent annually, or $5,000 per year. Still in need of housing, further suppose that it was at that same point in time that B began leasing Houseacre C* from its owner, C, and that C, themselves, had procured Houseacre C* for $100,000 just prior to entering the tenancy arrangement with B. Under B's lease agreement, let us additionally imagine that B pays a little under $420 monthly in rent, making their yearly cost of shelter $5,000, the going rate for a dwelling place with the specifications of Houseacre C* (and, as we saw above, Houseacre A* as well). For the purposes of the example, we can assume B's rent has remained unchanged since the end of their initial annual lease term.

Being that Houseacres C* and A* are identical in this scenario, just as the former would do for C based on the value of its use as a dwelling place to B, as noted earlier we can also say that the latter, too, effectively returns $5,000 per year to A based on its use by A as a dwelling place. Imagine finally, however, that under State's tax law the $5,000 A gets from Houseacre A* in its capacity as their dwelling place – and, thus, the annual return A gets on their ongoing investment – does not count as taxable income whereas the $5,000 C gets as a return on their investment from the purchase of Houseacre C* (based on the annual price paid for its use as a dwelling place by B) is counted as taxable income. Here let us further assume that the $5,000 B earns annually from his own decision to invest $100,000 in the stock market five years earlier is also counted as part of C's taxable income under State's laws.

On the face of things, State's legal regime mandates an evident disparity between the treatment of owner-occupants like A and renters of dwelling places like B for the purposes of the jurisdiction's rules on income taxation. Indeed, to the extent that one might insist that at baseline residential real estate does not simply have value on the basis of its use as shelter but also as an investable asset, the same features of State's legal regime make for a corresponding disparity between A and B in their capacity as owners of different kinds of investable assets, not to mention as between A and C as owners of precisely the same kind of investable asset.

Insofar as State's tax law regime mirrors that of the contemporary United States with respect to the treatment of imputed returns to owner-occupied residential real estate, of course, there is more than what I have outlined above to the question of how disparate the treatment of owner-occupants versus renters or other kinds of investors really is in the end. A first potential complexity comes into view if we relax the assumption that a party like A's investment in Houseacre A* initially involves only the full sum devoted to its purchase. One might also, thus, demand that we take into account the real-world likelihood of the need for mortgage financing, whether to meet some portion of a total purchase price of $100,000 or whatever sum over and above a down payment of $100,000.[25] Another complexity derives from the possibility that the apparent tax advantage parties like A enjoy over those like B or C on the basis of their arbitrarily different respective choices about how to use the $100,000 each has to invest at time zero is not as much of an advantage as it first might seem. Rather than being arbitrarily different because ultimately involving the investment of $100,000 in all three cases, in other words, the cost of the different investment choices A, B, and C make at time zero might be meaningfully different. Say, for example, that the tax advantage A enjoys as an owner of residential real estate used for their own occupancy is only apparent, being depleted by the higher cost of entry it imposes on buyers of housing assets through inflating their prices within some relevant segment of the market for shelter at the point of their purchase.

While such complexities may be important in all sorts of ways, for the present purposes it turns out that we can do just as well to ignore them. With respect to the cost of mortgage financing, this is because nothing in the hypothetical scenario, much less our current law, prevents it from being accounted for under tax law. Indeed, beyond omitting the taxation of imputed rent, our fiscal regime distinguishes residential real estate through granting owner-occupants access to the notorious home mortgage interest deduction – a very direct way in which the costs of getting into the business of home owning are granted legal recognition. Likewise, with respect to the possibility that the tax advantages of being an owner-occupant will be (partly) eaten up by the disadvantages suffered when buying on the purchase price side of things, any such state of affairs would obtain, directly, only between A and B. As between A and C – another purchaser of/investor in residential real estate – it would not make any difference. In fact, it would make for another kind of disparity insofar as C's rental income from B for B's use of Houseacre C* would not only be taxed in a way that A's imputed return from Houseacre A* would not, but C, too, would be forced to suffer inflated prices at the point of purchasing an asset like Houseacre C* (or for that matter like Houseacre A*); indeed, this would be the case even without C being "responsible" for generating the inflated prices of such assets in the way that A more plausibly might be said to be. Finally, even as between A and

[25] Of course, if $100,000 represented only a down payment, say of the customary 20 percent, on a housing asset with a much greater total purchase price, the artificiality of assuming that A and C receive the same annual return from respectively investing in Houseacres A* and C* as B does from investing $100,000 in the stock market becomes more apparent. Be this as it may, it does not change anything fundamental about what the scenario illustrates insofar as the assumption of the same initial investment and same total return was made only for illustrative convenience.

B, it is just as likely to be the case as not that the price inflation taking a bite out of A at the point of purchasing Houseacre A* will do the same to B at the point of transacting with C for the use of Houseacre C* – namely, by inflating the cost of leasing as crowded out buyers are forced into the rental market. Given the countervailing nature of these factors, then, the possibility that the specification of the disparity between A, B, and C derives from an oversimplification becomes far less troubling than it might at first seem.

B *Legal/Constitutional Preconditions: What Counts as "Income" for Tax Purposes?*

Beyond the justifications typically given for imputing rent to owner-occupied housing, getting a handle on any proposal for taxing (any portion of) such returns in the United States necessitates at least some consideration of the constitutional complexities of doing so. As the informed reader may surmise based on an awareness of the Supreme Court's stunning historical obstinance toward permitting the federal taxation of income before the passage of the Sixteenth Amendment in 1909, these complexities are not insubstantial. At the same time, given that my principal aim in the chapter lies elsewhere, I will not attempt to provide any exhaustive discussion of this matter. Suffice to say, the main aspect that bears highlighting here revolves around the question of whether imputed rents can properly be classed as income subject to constitutionally mandated federal taxation in the first place.

To be sure, Congress' present power to tax derives not just from the Sixteenth Amendment in isolation but, rather, in combination with the several provisions (in sections 2, 8, and 9) of Article I of the Constitution, which allow the legislature to lay and collect taxes and to apportion direct taxes among the states.[26] As is often noted, if taken at face value the apportionment requirement would produce absurd and inequitable results, demanding – for example – that "if one state has twice the population of another, twice the amount of direct tax [would have to] be collected from within the more populous state."[27] Staving off such absurdity has generally entailed defining direct taxes narrowly enough to facilitate the wholesale bypassing of the apportionment requirement. Of course, in no small part, the Sixteenth Amendment was an exercise in codifying just such a maneuver, putting a tax exclusively on "income" outside of the apportionment requirement's ambit. As a result, the more broadly income is defined, the more likely any new potential object of taxation is to fall under that heading and, thus, the more likely is it to be freed from the practically fatal constraint of apportionment. With more specific regard to the taxation of imputed rent, this means it goes without saying that the question of

[26] *The Constitutionality of the Taxation of Imputed Income*, 9 VAL. U. L. REV. 221 (1974), 233–34.

[27] Calvin H. Johnson, *Apportionment of Direct Taxes: The Foul-Up in the Core of the Constitution*, 7 WILLIAM & MARY BILL RIGHTS J. 1 (1998), 3.

whether the return to owner-occupied housing qualifies as "income" is of great importance.[28]

For better or worse, the Sixteenth Amendment provides little direct guidance on this matter, providing no clear definition of income within its text. With the lacuna instead left to be filled by the judiciary, in the half century after 1909 the Supreme Court developed two key approaches to the issue – the so-called *Macomber* and *Glenshaw* tests. In essence, over this period – in the progression from the first to the second of the cases that gave these tests their respective names – the definition of what could be counted as taxable income expanded significantly. Dating from 1920, the first, *Eisner v. Macomber*, involved the Court holding that a pro rata stock dividend did not qualify as income. In *Macomber* the Court crafted a relatively narrow definition of income, equating it with a "gain derived from capital, from labor, or from both combined, provided it be understood to include the profit gained through a sale or conversion of capital assets, and ... a gain, a profit, something of exchangeable value proceeding from the property, severed from capital."[29] Here, as Alice Abreu and Richard Greenstein observe, it was the Court's emphasis on the need for *severance* of the return from the source from which it derived that imposed the narrowing effect.[30] Also known as the "realization" requirement, in *Macomber's* context severance must have carried an intuitive appeal to the Court given the focus on dividend payments that could arguably be cast as indistinct from the underlying stock from which they issued. Accordingly, in elaborating on the criterion, the Court maintained that gains were to be considered unrealized by the taxpayer if they failed to be sufficiently separated from the capital stock and, thus, held the dividends at hand in the case to constitute only an effective increase in the stock rather than a receipt of income from it.[31]

While *Macomber's* realization requirement has arguably been the case's most lasting legacy, whether it would be applicable to imputed returns from owner-used assets remains an open question among tax experts.[32] Regardless, the first criterion the case elaborated – on the need for the gain/profit to derive from (some combination of) capital/labor or for it to comprise something of exchangeable value – was considerably expanded some three decades later in 1955's *Commissioner v. Glenshaw Glass*. Here, focusing on section 61 of the Internal Revenue Code, the Court held that any "undeniable accession to wealth, clearly realized and over which the taxpayers have complete dominion" could qualify as income.[33] In the case, the

[28] *Id.*, 4.
[29] Eisner v. Macomber, 252 U.S. 189 (1920) at 207.
[30] Alice G. Abreu & Richard K. Greenstein, *Defining Income*, 11 FLA. TAX REV. 295 (2011), 301. See also Shreya Jain, *Taxation of Notional Income: A Comparison of Tax Regimes*, 6 NUJS L. REV 559 (2013).
[31] *Id.*, 564.
[32] *The Constitutionality*, *supra* note 26, at 235.
[33] Commissioner v. Glenshaw Glass, 348 U.S. 426, 431 (1955).

"accession" in question stemmed from punitive damages the defendant had won, which the Court did ultimately deem taxable income on this definition and, thus, which it ultimately saw as having wrongly gone unreported to the Internal Revenue Service (IRS).

On the traditional understanding of *Glenshaw Glass*, its approach to determining what qualifies as income proves overlapping with the so-called Haig–Simons definition of the same, which "is widely regarded as having provided the theoretical foundation for the income tax."[34] Conventional among public finance economists, Haig–Simons income is defined in terms of the sum of the monetary value of an agent's consumption and the change in their net wealth. Emerging from ideas formulated in the late 1890s by German legal scholar Georg van Schanz and two economists from the United States several decades later, Robert M. Haig and Henry Simons,[35] the measure focuses on potential rather than actual consumption and thus can be equivalently understood in terms of the monetary value of "the net increase in an individual's power to consumer" during a given period.[36]

At least in principle, then, apart from explicit statutory exclusions, the *Glenshaw Glass* approach gives the IRS wide latitude, with *any* realized accession within the taxpayer's so-called dominion capable of qualifying as income – thus, obviating the first part of the *Macomber* approach (and arguably its second as well).[37] Of course, in practice this latitude may have become more circumscribed, with some courts nonetheless having declined to allow particular accessions to be counted as income in subsequent years – as, for example, with employer-provided meals and lodging on the employer's premises – and the IRS, itself, sometimes declining to treat otherwise seemingly qualifying accessions as such.[38]

However, making too much of such deviations from *Glenshaw Glass* would be misleading, whether with respect to the breadth of its test for what counts as income in general or the question of whether imputed returns, in particular, fall within its ambit. As far as imputed income goes, this is because the case law is sparse and at the level of the Supreme Court essentially non-existent.[39] The closest case that is

[34] Abreu & Greenstein, *supra* note 30, at 296 (citing Henry C. Simons, Personal Income Tax 50 [1938] and noting that the *Glenshaw Glass* definition "differs from Haig–Simons" one mainly insofar as it "requires realization," although "its inclusion of all accessions" proves "otherwise just as broad").

[35] See, generally, Carl S. Shoup, *The Schanz Concept of Income and the United States Federal Income Tax*, 42 FinanzArchiv/Public Finance Analysis 433 (1984).

[36] Harvey S. Rosen, *Public Finance*, in Charles K. Rowley and Friedrich Schneider, eds., The Encyclopedia of Public Choice, Vol. 1 (1984), 252–62, 257.

[37] *The Constitutionality*, *supra* note 26, at 236 (arguing that the *Glenshaw Glass* approach eschews *Macomber's* concern both with severance and the source of the gain, instead focusing only on whether there is an increase in the taxpayer's wealth).

[38] Abreu & Greenstein, *supra* note 30, at 297–98 (citing Benaglia v. Comm'r, 36 B.T.A. 838 [1937]).

[39] The judgment should arguably be tempered, to the extent that, as Abreu & Greenstein note, "[e]very major tax casebook and treatise acknowledges that imputed income is not income for

typically touched on in this context is *Helvering v. Independent Life Insurance Co.*, which involved an office building occupied by the titular plaintiff corporation and an external tenant. In light of the plaintiff-corporation's seeking to take a deduction for its expenses on the building, the Court held that it would have to count the rental value of the part of the facility it was, itself, occupying as income. Where *Helvering* fell short of fully becoming an authoritative case on imputed rent was in the restriction of the Court's holding, with it counting the rental value from the owner-occupied part of the building as necessary only insofar as the plaintiff was simultaneously seeking to take a deduction for its ownership-related expenses. While the Court did go on to speculate that had the inclusion of the rental value been mandatory – rather than a condition of the deduction – its constitutionality as income would likely have become more doubtful, that the case took place in 1934 gives reason for additional pause in understanding its present-day implications. Indeed, *Helvering* was decided squarely in the period following *Macomber* but (some twenty years) before the latter's test for what counted as income was expanded in the way it came to be by the Court in *Glenshaw Glass*.[40]

III RENT AND ITS TAXATION: A DIVIDING LINE OR BRIDGE WITHIN THE HISTORY OF LEGAL AND ECONOMIC IDEAS?

As I suggested in the Introduction, any proposal to tax (the imputed) rent from land in the United States is likely to be hard-pressed to escape the shadow, for better or worse, of Henry George. Whether despite or because of the way he was so often reviled by economic experts in his day as no more than a polemicist, George was undoubtedly a figure who commanded great attention in the late nineteenth century. Indeed, as is often noted, across much of the globe his *Progress and Poverty* (1879) became a sensation – by 1900 selling nearly two million copies in the United States alone, second only to the Bible[41] – "in a sense," making him "to land"/"the land baron" what "Karl Marx was to labor"/"the capitalist." For if "[t]o Marx, the capitalist's extraction of wealth from the toils of the proletariat was the

tax purposes," *supra* note 30, note 9. Here, however, it seems necessary to recall that there is a plainly circular quality to the observation. That is, if tax casebooks have not found it fit to declare imputed income to count as taxable income by way of suggesting that so is what the law must be, as much can be inferred on the basis of an *absence* – or simple *dearth* – of law on this question as it can on the basis of an abundance. Moreover, as the various complexities that persist even around the question of how to legally define/conceptualize (taxable) "income" suggest, treating the category of "imputed income" monolithically for the purposes of making blanket declarations about the legality or lack thereof of "its" taxation seems less than completely sound.

40 *The Constitutionality*, *supra* note 26, at 237–38.

41 Tracy B. Strong, Learning One's Native Tongue: Citizenship, Contestation, and Conflict in America (2019), 151.

great injustice of capitalism," for George it was "the landlord's unearned wealth from rent . . . [that] was the key source of society's ills."[42]

Insofar as George reanimated the Ricardian theory of ground rent, his thought thus makes for a natural point of departure for any contemporary discussion about taxing imputed returns to the land site component of owner-occupied housing. At the same time – as to an obviously much greater degree with Marx – George also throws into relief the otherwise blurry line dividing classical political economy from neoclassical economics. Accordingly, any project of intellectual heterodoxy within the study of law and economics, especially one that seeks to re-embrace (aspects of) the first law and economics movement for the twenty-first century, stands to gain much needed perspective by invoking George.[43] For the present purposes, then, his name can be considered a signpost at the very crossroads between the classical and neoclassical traditions and, as such, a means of emblazoning the path trodden in this part of the chapter as it traces how the theoretical category of rent has fit into the disciplinary lives of economics, past and present.

A *(Dis-)Continuities? Rent in Classical Political Economy and in the Aftermath of the Marginal Revolution*

When George proposed his solution to the problem of the relative immiseration of labor at the hands of land barons and property speculators, he was building on a tradition of classical political economy going back, at least, to the pre-Smithian Physiocrats and their idea of *l'impôt unique*. Of course, distinguishing the tradition George punctuated by the name of classical political economy naturally carries the hazard of suggesting it had more uniformity than it actually did. At the same time, there can be no doubt that George's thought followed a clear line not only from the Physiocrats but also, even more notably, political economy's leading exponent, David Ricardo.

In Ricardo's thought, the conceptualization of rent was famously extended beyond any mere Physiocratic notion of the landed gentry as being among the "sterile" classes who contributed nothing to production such that their returns could be taxed away without affecting incentives. Ricardo also pushed well beyond the more piecemeal and inconsistent way Adam Smith characterized rent in *The Wealth of Nations*. There, Smith cast rent as a surplus over the necessary costs of

[42] Brian Czech, *The Neoclassical Production Function as a Relic of Anti-George Politics: Implications for Ecological Economics*, 68 ECOL. ECON. 2193 (2007), 2194.

[43] In addition to *id.*, see, e.g., Mason Gaffney, *Neo-classical Economics as a Stratagem against Henry George*, in his THE CORRUPTION OF ECONOMICS (1994), 29–39; Donald Stabile, *Henry George's Influence on John Bates Clark: The Concept of Rent Was Pivotal to Equating Wages with the Marginal Product of Labor*, 54(3) AMER. J. ECON. & SOC. 373 (1995); Ross B. Emmett, *Frank H. Knight's Criticism of Henry George*, 67(1) AMER. J. ECON. & SOC. 61 (2008); and John C. Medaille, *What Henry George Knew, What the Neoclassicists Forgot, and Why It Matters*, 36(4) INT. J. SOCIAL ECON. 447 (2009).

production, which – subject to demand – those who owned better quality land could command through charging a monopoly price.[44] (In this respect, as Smith put it, "[t]he landlords . . . love to reap where they never sowed," with laborers being required to "give up to the landlord a portion of what" they "collect[] or produce.")[45]

Likewise, Ricardo's so-called differential theory of rent was more systematically developed than the compatible idea of his friend and frequent intellectual adversary, Thomas Malthus.[46] It was Ricardo, thus, who envisioned rent as "the produce obtained" from employing "two equal quantities of capital and labour," whether on two *different* plots of land with varying fertilities or simply the same plot in two *different* successive doses/intervals.[47] Relatedly, it was also Ricardo who, in grappling with the long-term fate of a capitalist economy, put rent at the center of the dynamic precipitating the lurch toward the dreaded stationary state. Here, of course, was yet another way Ricardo's ideas would go on to underpin George's (if not, in fairness, a way in which the latter should be seen as having simply cribbed from the former). For as in George's conception of a relative immiseration of labor amidst overall growth – the titular "poverty" amidst "progress" in his magnum opus – the appropriation of land rent was the key motive force.

Indeed, for Ricardo, rent came into being only relative to some no rent point of contrast – whether at the so-called extensive margin constituted by the lowest quality, and thus highest cost of production, plot of land under cultivation or at the intensive margin constituted by the highest cost agricultural output that could be secured by the last dose of labor and/or capital it was worth anyone's while to apply to some self-same plot of land. As a result, the more the price-setting baseline of output produced from agricultural land was raised through extending the margin of cultivation, the wider the gulf became between production at that baseline and production on rent-commanding superior plots/at rent-commanding lower production cost intervals. The higher the price set for the whole market based on the greater cost at the margin of cultivation, then, the more rent would be diverted toward paying for non-marginal land. That is, as the margin of cultivation was extended, so too would the share of production absorbed as rent swell.

Assuming, moreover, that after competition among capitalist farmers equalized the rate of profit among them (as they all vied with each other for access to better quality land and thus bid up the rent going to landlords), the effects of this dynamic could not be contained simply within the agricultural sector. For if the (real,

44 Conway L. Lackman, *The Classical Base of Modern Rent Theory*, 35 (3) AMER. J. ECON. & SOC. 287 (1976), 287–89.

45 ADAM SMITH, AN INQUIRY INTO THE NATURE AND CAUSES OF THE WEALTH OF NATIONS (1937 [1776]), 49.

46 Alongside of Ricardo and Malthus, Sir Edward West and Robert Torrens are credited with having independently arrived at the idea of differential rent at the same time in 1815. See Fried, *supra* note 11, at 120.

47 DAVID RICARDO, ON THE PRINCIPLES OF POLITICAL ECONOMY AND TAXATION (1817), *reprinted in* PIERO SRAFFA, ED., THE WORKS AND CORRESPONDENCE OF DAVID RICARDO (2004), 57.

subsistence) cost of agricultural labor remained what it was – and if population grew[48] – as the increasing cost of cultivation at the margin pushed up the price of agricultural produce while simultaneously increasing the proportion of the total value of that produce ultimately going to the payment of ground rent, there would necessarily be less and less left over for profit on agricultural capital; and if the market at large was characterized by competition so as to equalize all rates of profit, it could not be long until the productivity of labor and capital on no-rent agricultural land, as the sole determinant of the rate of profit, would make its effect felt on the rate of profit in the manufacturing sector as well.[49] In short, as ground rent directly siphoned off ever more from the food-producing sector, so too would it more indirectly come to do the same from the rest of the economy, the inevitability of the stationary state thus becoming a fait accompli as the returns to the new capitalist bourgeoisie – whose interests Ricardo was ultimately an avatar for – were sapped.

For the time being, putting aside the influence of John Stuart Mill – whose political economy was, with respect to rent as well as various other matters,[50] true to its eclectic or, perhaps, mixed-up form,[51] borrowing as it did from the core of the classical tradition even as it foreshadowed key aspects of the neoclassical turn – Ricardo's approach remained the gold standard for the better part of the nineteenth century. Indeed, notwithstanding small additions and modifications of emphasis – as on the rent of urban land and urbanization more generally[52] – George's thought can clearly be situated according to a number of overlapping parameters that had come to clearly undergird rent theory by the time Ricardo was perfecting his own

[48] The two, of course, were not unrelated. Just because the so-called corn wage of agriculture might remain the same, this did not mean as the margin of cultivation was extended, the money cost also had to do so. Rather, as the money cost of agricultural wages increased, so too in Ricardo's model would population. See, e.g., Hunt & Lautzenheiser, *supra* note 24, at 95.

[49] *Id.* (noting that "[t]his view of profits has been called Ricardo's 'Corn Theory of Profit'" and that Ricardo "believed" it to be easily "expand[able] to include manufactured commodities. For if population increases decreased the rate of profit in agriculture, and if the rate of profit was determined solely by the productivity of labor and capital on the no-rent land, and if competition equalized all rates of profit, then it followed that the rate of profit in the manufacturing sector as well as in agriculture depended solely on productivity of the no-rent land").

[50] For Mill's more specific collection of views on rent, see Conway L. Lackman, *The Modern Development of Classical Rent Theory*, 36(1) Amer. J. Econ. & Soc. 51 (1977), 52–54 (characterizing Mill's views on rent variously as being transitional; as being in agreement with the essence of Ricardo's analysis but placing more emphasis on trying to distinguish payments that were really returns to agricultural capital that enhanced the soil's fertility; as emphasizing the importance of proximity to markets/location as a would-be source of rent even if all land was of equal quality; and as touching more generally on the importance of competing uses, including, for example, how non-agricultural land would be likely to have to pay as much rent as it would demand were it simply used for agriculture).

[51] See, e.g., Hunt & Lautzenheiser, *supra* note 24, at 185–87.

[52] Making the case for George as a mere borrower from Ricardo, see, John K. Whitaker, *Henry George and Classical Growth Theory: A Significant Contribution to Modeling Scale Economies*, 60(1) Amer. J. Econ. & Soc. 11 (2001).

elaboration. It is little wonder, then, that the classical approach to rent allowed for significant disagreement even as it appears, in retrospect, discernibly distinct from its counterpart enterprise in economics after the marginal revolution. Key among these parameters were those by which rent could be considered absolute versus differential, derivative of a kind of monopoly over land versus its naturally varying fertility, price-determining versus price-determined, a real cost versus a costless surplus, an earned versus unearned return (in the crucial sense of its reflecting a truly *productive* versus *non-productive* contribution),[53] and warranting of a laudatory versus condemnatory ideological valence to be attached to the landlord class.

As the last parameter can be understood to suggest, the way that rent was reduced in nineteenth-century political economy to ground rent – a position that George would popularize and extend as the basis for his own single tax proposal – was hardly just the mark of a failure to generalize Ricardo's lessons, whether on his own part or that of the classical tradition's other leading exponents. Of course, seeing the preoccupation with ground rent primarily in terms of classical theory's limited vision is not only common in contemporary accounts of the history of economic thought, as I noted in the Introduction; to the contrary, it has been a working premise among neoclassical thinkers going back to the origins of their enterprise, with the remapping of rent as a category within economic theory beginning in earnest already from the 1870s.

Therefore, it can be misleading to chart the course of economic discourse about rent based on ideas that the inframarginalist thinkers of the first law and economics movement, as heterodox practitioners of the tradition, developed on the basis of the category. In this respect, one can say that Alfred Marshall is likely a far better starting point than Hale – let alone, someone like Thorstein Veblen, who, even without advocating for a return to any sort of labor theory of value, was a much more vocal non-believer in marginalism's virtues, even if just for the heuristic purposes of perfecting a critique of it. This is because even though Marshall's analytic was not necessarily in conflict with Hale's, his way of retaining rent as a category was generally characterized by a greater ambivalence to the concept's normative implications.

Accordingly, Marshall's way of extending rent's conceptual reach can feel more deflationary than enlivening – as, for example, when noting how notwithstanding his classical predecessors' preoccupation with the topic, "the rent of land" made, in actuality, for "no unique fact, but simply the chief species of a large genus of

[53] At the risk of repetition, it is worth again highlighting that whatever way in which the present chapter distinguishes rent talk in the classical versus neoclassical tradition, it does not involve denying the applicability of the "earned" versus "unearned" descriptor for types of income to either tradition. What the chapter *does* argue is that there was a key difference in the way rent talk in classical political economy availed of that tradition's tendency to further develop the contrast between "earned" and "unearned" revenues by distinguishing activity that was productive (of value) from activity that was not.

economic phenomena." As if to put too fine a point on the matter, he continued, "the theory of the rent of land" was "no isolated economic doctrine, but merely one of the chief applications of a particular corollary from the general theory of demand and supply." According to Marshall, then, "there [was] a continuous gradation from the true Rent of those free gifts which have been appropriated by man" to various other kinds of returns.[54] It was in a similar vein that a compatible point was made by Marshall's contemporary, the American economist John Bates Clark – who is, often confusingly, associated both with logically perfecting the marginal productivity theory of distribution and transforming it into an allegedly *incoherent* apologia for class inequality that other marginalists thought just as well to disavow.[55] As Clark[56] thus put it:

> [g]round rent we shall study as the earnings of one kind of capital-goods – as merely a part of interest ... That is to say, the Ricardian formula, which describes what is earned by a piece of land, may be used to describe what is all wages earned by the whole fund of social capital: all interest may be made to take the form of a differential gain, or a surplus ... It is one of the most striking of economic facts that the income of all labor, on the one hand, and that of all capital, on the other, should be thus entirely akin to ground rent. They are the two generic rents, if by that term we mean differential products; and the earnings of land constitute a fraction of one of them.[57]

Notably, it was not just the effective necessity of attaching some kind of normative valence – whether positive or negative – to the landowning class that was obviated by

54 Alfred Marshall, Principles of Economics (Macmillan and Co., 3d ed. 1895), 705.

55 Compare the view of Clark developed in Hunt & Lautzenheiser, *supra* note 24, at 302–14 and Fried, *supra* note 11 (noting, e.g., that "Clark's arguments had considerable influence in their time" by offering "what many contemporaries took to be a powerful rights-based defense of economic laissez faire," *id.*, 2; that he "completed the work begun by Senior in extending the Lockean justification for property from labor to capital," *id.*, 132; and that he, like Marshall, was well aware "that the costs of marginal and inframarginal producers would diverge significantly," *id.*, 141; even while also, rather contradictorily, stating that Clark's was merely a "naïve apologetics" and thus "a source of embarrassment for most mainstream economists," notwithstanding its ability to "attract[] a significant following among economists and noneconomists alike," *id.*, 132).

56 By the lights of marginal productivity theory, of course, each factor of production was said to be paid its own marginal product/the marginal value that it contributed to production. At least some of Fried's emphasis on the logical incoherence of Clark's ideas – and hence, their character as an apologia – would seem to come from her starting point. That is, her study's point of departure is that Hale and other exponents of the first law and economics movement were fundamentally of the neoclassical orientation – in the sense of being fully *post*-marginalist with respect to how they thought about value – even as her study's topical focus demands treating the inframarginal critique of marginalism's blindness to questions of distribution under conditions of competitive equilibrium as, in effect, self-evident – or, at any rate, beyond reproach – as per how the inframarginalists themselves took things to be in virtue of otherwise granting marginalism its adverted conclusions about allocative efficiency under the same kind of equilibrium.

57 John Bates Clark, The Distribution of Income (1956), 191.

regrinding rent as a conceptual lens of such a kind. So too was that of choosing between many, if not most/all, of the other options within the decision space defined by the parameters giving classical rent theory its distinct identity. If Ricardian ground rent was nothing more than one species of the larger genus of supply and demand at work – or if all gains were differential in the sense of returning *more than* what a given resource should have been able to command just over and above the next best opportunity for its use – then there was no longer much point in disagreeing about whether rent was earned versus unearned (as noted earlier, in the crucial sense of its reflecting a truly productive versus non-productive contribution),[58] a real cost versus a costless surplus, or price determined versus price determining.

To be sure, this is not to say that along these various dimensions rent being viewed in one versus the other way did not matter. Rather, the point is that amidst the rise of neoclassicism in each case the theoretical decision space defined by the various parameters was narrowed, if not eventually closed, so that only one option among them any longer tended to make sense. In this respect, over time, one can say that the tendency of the neoclassical turn was to gradually dissolve the coherence of rent theory. Already with Marshall – to say nothing of Clark – as much as one could thus maintain that all returns were like ground rent, equally could one maintain that land was no different than the other factors of production. Indeed, as much is suggested by those who have observed that "neoclassical textbooks appearing in the 20th century increasingly ignored land and provided a production function … in which capital and labor were the only factors explicitly identified."[59]

Obviously, it is important not to get ahead of ourselves here, especially with regard to Marshall. For as in many aspects, born in London and ensconced for most of his life in Cambridge, he was more restrained in the degree to which he sought to break with the classical political economic past – in all of its supremely British esteem – than his effective role as a pioneer of neoclassicism might otherwise suggest. At the same time, true to form, what Marshall gave with one hand from classical rent theory he tended to take away with the other – transforming a categorical distinction into one of degree here, reframing a former point of emphasis there, and so on.

On the one hand, Marshall thus agrees with the idea that rent is an excess secured above (what he calls, "prime") cost.[60] In keeping with this aspect of his reasoning, the analogy through which he narrowed the difference between ground rent and other returns was offered not so much to the effect of sanitizing, so to speak, the reputation of the former, as sullying that of the latter. That is, for Marshall just as ground rent proper did not "enter into cost of production" nor, at least over some relevant short term, did remuneration for "other kinds of hire" of (some varieties of) capital. Here Marshall's point was that over such a short term, the supply of such

[58] See, *supra* note 53.
[59] Czech, *supra* note 42, at 2193.
[60] Alfred Marshall, *On Rent*, 3(9) ECON. J. 74 (1883), 76.

varieties of capital could not be freely increased – even in the face of growing demand. As he thus put it, "at any given time and place" there are various things that one might want to "hire" – like "a boat or a sewing machine, or a steam engine, or a horse or a cow" – for which "the owner charges . . . more than [one might think] they are worth" but that remain "as entirely out of the reach of multiplication by individual men as the acres of a farm."[61] Indeed, Marshall extends the same point to land itself, arguing that so is how one should think of returns to long-standing improvements that otherwise might be mistakenly attributed to "natural" advantages of fertility. Rather than "'isolat[ing]' the rent of land," then, according to what Marshall calls "modern analysis" (*viz.*, the early neoclassical analysis he was central in formulating), "what is true of the hire or net income earned by ponies for a short time, is true of the hire or net income earned by houses and permanent improvements in land for a long time."[62]

On the other hand, what Marshall subtracted out from classical rent theory was equally evident, while also likely/possibly being of greater magnitude and more lasting. Picking up from the last point, for example, a first and most obvious way this proved the case was through his simple insistence – as others like Mill had done before him – on drilling down into what Ricardo, himself, was content to attribute to nature alone through the idea that rent arose from the variability of land's fertility/ fecundity. As cogent as it may have been to interrogate this matter, however, it was also facile, given that Ricardo's own failure to do the same was unlikely to have been born from stubborn ignorance or oversight as much as the impossibility of clearly dividing where nature left off and long dead past investments of labor/capital began. Indeed, for his own part, Marshall, too, did little with the distinction beyond observing that it had to exist in principle, in the end deploying it mainly to the effect of making classical rent theory seem as if it was built on a category mistake.

Second, and even more important, to whatever extent Marshall concurred with the idea of ground rent as an unearned claim on the net social product, he also steadily wore away at its categorical distinction from profit – or, rather, as per another key neoclassical remapping of concepts, its categorical distinction from interest – on capital. While in one sense, therefore, Marshall was willing to sully the image of capital's remuneration by disaggregating parts of it into what he famously called quasi-rents, that term was suitably equivocal as to whether it entailed an emphasis on its prefix or base word. That is, if, as noted above, in some short term the type of payment commanded by livestock and steam engine capital was really a *rentierist* return that did not enter into the cost of production, judged from another perspective it was only seemingly ("*quasi-*") so. Thus, on Marshall's view, one might just as well say that even interest on "new investments of capital" – not to mention "interest

[61] *Id.*, 87.
[62] *Id.*, 88.

on 'free' or 'floating' capital" – was to be regarded as a "sort of rent"/quasi-rent.[63] The fate of terminological choice notwithstanding, Marshall was here hardly proposing to indict all such returns as parasitic diversions from the real cost of the social product.[64] It is, thus, little wonder that he should have hastened to add that "[t]here is no sharp line of division between floating capital and that which has been sunk for a special branch of production, nor between new and old investments of capital." Indeed, it was via this route that he eventually reached his earlier mentioned pronouncement about the "rent of land" being "not . . . a thing by itself, but as the leading species of a large genus."[65]

This brings us to a third way in which one can see Marshall as having dissipated the force of classical rent theory. For whatever ground rent's peculiarities, the larger genus to which Marshall assigned it alongside of capital was one he ultimately saw fit to rechristen "producer's surplus." This he more explicitly defined as "the excess of the gross receipts which a producer gets for any of his commodities over their prime cost; that is, over that extra cost which he incurs in order to produce those particular things, and which he could have escaped if he had not produced them." As far as the relationship between producer surplus and value went, then, to Marshall's eyes it was not any in which the former was best characterized as a diversion or drain upon the latter. In fact, their more precise relationship ultimately "depend[ed] not so much on the nature of the industry as on the period of time for which the calculation is made," since "a short period for one class of industry" might be "a long one for another; just as the age of youth for a dog is shorter than for an elephant."[66] Nor could the relationship be properly characterized in terms of the former's being unnecessary relative to the latter in any very coherent sense, whether in the short term or, assuming competition, because the entirety of the excess the producer captured "needed" instead to be eventually transferred away to consumers/ transformed into "consumer surplus."[67] In this respect, whether ground rent made for a necessary cost or not, one can say that for Marshall the larger genus of producer's surplus to which he assigned it – whomever exactly that surplus was ultimately distributed to – was more like the win–win of a pure value add.

[63] *Id.*, 76.

[64] See, *infra* note 67.

[65] Marshall, *supra* note 60, at 76.

[66] *Id.*, 76–77.

[67] As David Reisman puts it, for Marshall, "[i]n the short period the firm will have an incentive to produce so long as prime cost at least is covered." Anything above prime cost is, for that span of time, a surplus having "something of the nature of a rent," and yet this seems to be – paradoxical as it may sound – a surplus having something of the nature of a necessity; for, Marshall insisted, in Britain at any rate the "true marginal supply price for short periods . . . is nearly always above, and generally very much above the special or prime cost." Thus, whereas present-day economics teaches that the firm will not produce in the short run below the price which just covers average variable cost, the economics of Alfred Marshall teaches that the firm will not produce unless it receives not only *that* price but "a good deal" *more* as well.

David Reisman, The Economics of Alfred Marshall (1986), 54–55 (citations omitted).

Even notwithstanding all of the above, a fourth and final way Marshall can be seen as having partly taken back what credence he granted classical rent theory was by using the remainder left over from the analogy between ground rent and interest as a basis for highlighting their ultimate disanalogy. He thus did not shy away from emphasizing how, in the end, "the rent of land and the quasi-rents of most other things" were different; for unlike with the former, the "hire" of the latter "c[ould] never for any long time diverge much from normal profits on their cost of production." In fact, this claim was tied to an even deeper way that Marshall's thought can be understood to have helped dissipate classical rent theory – namely, in true neoclassical style, by elevating supply and demand to the status of the master norm of the whole economic system. Indeed, as he contended, just as "agents" of production like steam engines and ponies could be considered akin to land for a time, so too, for whatever other time, could land be seen as akin to them. This is because within whatever other such time frame, their hire would be "governed ... by the value of the services they w[ould] render," with that value, itself, being "determined by the relations in which the supply of ponies, &c., stands to the demand for such services." Consequently, "[i]f nothing unexpected" took place, "that supply [would come to be] so adjusted to the demand that an average (or normal) pony during a life of average length and activity w[ould] yield a hire giving normal profits on its cost of production." For Marshall, then, it was no less than "a rule" that when all was said and done quasi-rent commanding agents would "yield no surplus above normal profits to the producer."[68]

Of course, to some readers, the preceding discussion of Marshall will seem to suffer from a basic defect – namely, a failure to consider whether whatever way Marshall may have recast classical rent theory is more important for its possibly being correct than the bare fact of his having done so. Indeed, sympathy for such a view is as likely to be found among the readers of this volume as anywhere else given the likelihood of their sharing its basic aim of restoring the key insights of the first law and economics movement; for among the most central of those insights is one that can be made to partly overlap with the last point just recited about Marshall to close the previous paragraph. That is, if excessive rates of return on "quasi-rent"-commanding capital are *unlike* land, for Marshall this was only "if nothing unexpected took place" over some long-term before which the excess of demand relative to supply would wear off so as to equalize said quasi-rents back to normal profits. After all, those like Hale – so keen as they were in their now too often forgotten ambivalence to anti-monopolism and too rarely remembered insistence that scarcity profits would *still* persist even under properly idealized market conditions – would hardly be opposed to the idea that the long term was long enough to guarantee suppliers such above normal profits even when markets were competitive (or,

[68] Marshall, *supra* note 60, at 88.

equivalently, that "something unexpected *would* take place" under competition, in virtue of its very nature).[69]

Therefore, before leaving Marshall it is worth reminding the reader of the previously stated purpose of the foregoing discussion. For that purpose has not just been one scaled to the compass of intellectual history but also one that has been intended to offer a counterpoint to the existing reconstructions of the first law and economic movement. Lest the purposes of intellectual history be presumed strictly academic, however, one would be remiss here if one did not hasten to add that the point about Marshall dissipating the force of classical rent theory is not simply about Marshall. Accordingly, it does not stand or fall on whether the contents of his thought can just as well be exegeted in terms of their correctness, immunity from falsification, or the like. To the contrary, it stands or falls on whether, in point of historical fact, it is reasonable to see Marshall as one step along the way of the concept of rent's valence having come to be effectively reversed in much of the most prominent expert discourse surrounding it. It is, thus, in continued pursuit of tracing that reversal to which the next parts of this section turn.

* * *

Indeed, while talk of rent would obviously persist in the wake of the marginal revolution/neoclassical turn of the late nineteenth century, by the middle of the next it arguably had come to lose almost all of its earlier normative bite as economics became fully institutionalized and its new Neoclassical–Keynesian core became the substrate for the discipline's self-adverted transformation into a modelling science.[70] To be sure, by mid-century – already long past the prime of the first law and economics movement – most of the normative bite that rent theory would have even had to lose would have derived from the memory of its post-classical redeployment by inframarginalist thinkers like Hale rather than the recollection of its earlier incarnation among the classical political economists. All the same, it is unlikely that the first law and economics movement's affiliation with marginalism can plausibly

[69] As Ramsi Woodcock reminds us in his own entry in this volume, the key point of those like Hale was not so much that scarcity returns persist *even* under competition but due to its very defining criterion. As he thus notes,

> [t]he price line is kept uniform in competitive markets only because scarcity in a competitive market implies that there must be more willing buyers than willing sellers with respect to the low-cost production. Indeed, if the market is not competitive, and there is, for example, a single monopoly buyer, then the price line will sag: That buyer would insist on a price below the price at which the marginal seller would transact, and the inframarginal sellers would have to accept, because they could no longer be sure to find some other buyer willing to pay a price equal to the price at which the marginal seller would transact. Scarcity power derives from an excess of demand over supply that exists only when markets are fully competitive.

Ramsi A. Woodcock, *The Progressive Case against Antimonopolism*, *in* Toward an Inframarginal Revolution: Markets as Wealth Distributors 45, 60–61 (R. Woodcock, ed., 2025).

[70] See, e.g., MARY MORGAN, THE WORLD IN THE MODEL: HOW ECONOMISTS WORK AND THINK (2012).

be seen other than as a double-edged sword, being as capable of deadening the language of rent as sharpening it.

Indeed, by the 1970s, another two decades after the Neoclassical–Keynesian synthesis came to full flower under the influence of Paul Samuelson's canonization,[71] the blunting of rent's normative force that was arguably evident already in Marshall's thought had become even more complete. Under the influence of acolytes of the Austrian school, in fact, its thrust was totally reversed. Tellingly, the shortest route to effecting such a reversal proved that of simply pursuing a path Marshall, himself, had left open in arguing that returns to "kinds of hire" other than of land could be counted as quasi-rents only "relatively to short periods."[72] For example, it is essentially this same position – of Marshall's intellectual antagonist here, the Duke of Argyll[73] – that Murray Rothbard, the well-known American partisan of Austrian analysis, adopts by abandoning any emphasis on the short term (of production constraint) and instead declaring rent "the same as *hire*" and, as such, "*the unit price of the services of any good.*" According to Rothbard, therefore, the notion of rent "applies as well to prices of labor services (called 'wages') as it does to land or to any other factor ... whether durable or nondurable."[74] On such a logic, the "entire discussion of pricing," itself, simply reduces to a way of "deal[ing] with rental pricing."[75]

By insisting that it followed directly from the teaching of "marginal utility analysis ... that men value goods in *units* and not as wholes,"[76] Rothbard further demonstrates how his view is actually more proximal to Marshall's than one might otherwise assume. For when it came to explaining why "marginal production is not to be sought only in places and in businesses which have no differential advantages for production," Marshall, too, can be understood to have recast "Ricardo's theory of rent and his deductions from it" so as to sever any "depend[ence] on the existence of rentless land." Not unlike Rothbard, then, Marshall also insisted that it was not the margin of productive land that was important so much as the margin of the rational maximizer's subjective calculus: "[f]or every producer, whether well-placed or ill-

[71] It was Samuelson's textbook that finally/fully displaced Marshall's *Principles* as the definitive pedagogical on-ramp into the discipline. See, Paul A. Samuelson, Economics (1948). On the importance of Samuelson's text, see Mark Skousen, *The Perseverance of Paul Samuelson's Economics*, 11(2) J. Econ. Perspectives (1997), 137–52.

[72] That is, only during such short periods did such kinds of hire "not enter into the cost of production," according to Marshall. Marshall, *supra* note 60, at 86.

[73] As Marshall, himself, would note with regard to the Duke "I do not think there is a wide difference between us," *id.*, 78.

[74] Murray Rothbard, Man, Economy and State: A Treatise on Economic Principles with Power and Market: Government and Economy (2001 [1962]), 488 (emphasis in original; noting further that "[t]his concept of rent is based on the original contribution" of the economist Frank A. Fetter).

[75] *Id.*, 489.

[76] *Id.*

placed, whether cultivating rich land or rentless land, comes to some point at which he is on the margin of doubt whether to go further or not."[77]

A more scenic, if by now also more visible, Austrian-adjacent route to fully reversing the normative force of rent talk was carved out in public choice theory. As part of the latter discourse, beginning in the 1970s rent was conceptually redeployed in a way that continued to preserve the destigmatized equivalence it had achieved with profit/interest/producer surplus already within Marshallian thought by starting from its redefinition in the "standard textbooks of economic theory" of the day as "a receipt in excess of opportunity cost."[78] Simultaneously, however, in the hands of the exponents of the Virginia school of political economy and their allies in the wider world of public choice theory, through the notion of rent *seeking* the concept was fitted with new fangs, these being now sharpened for the sake of sinking into the corpus of government more than (landed) privateers.

As the leading light of the Virginia school, James Buchanan,[79] put it early on, in one sense, rent seeking was "simply another word for profit seeking," at least "so long as owners of resources prefer more to less." In this first sense, rent seeking simply "call[ed] to mind the familiar position that the behavior of persons in trying to maximize returns on their own capacities or opportunities [could] be socially beneficial,"[80] with rent, itself, thus "reflect[ing] the *creation* of added value in the economy" and emphatically not "the diversion of value that already exists."[81] (Clearly, for Buchanan, the question of whether rent was price determined versus price determining was not much of a question at all, this part of the decision space of classical theory having long since been narrowed to the point of being eliminated by the time he was writing.) However, for Buchanan, this only provided what he was willing to grant was an "ordered market structure."[82] As per the focus of his analysis, in contrast, things could be made to look very different in an "institutional" setting characterized, instead, by what he effectively portrayed as a bumbling or parasitic government plaguing the market by "entry restriction[s];" for in such a circumstance, the rent-seeking entrepreneur's "initial monopoly position" (without

77 Marshall, *supra* note 60, at 85.

78 James M. Buchanan, *Rent Seeking and Profit Seeking*, in James M. Buchanan, Robert D. Tollison, and Gordon Tullock, eds., Toward a Theory of the Rent-Seeking Society (1980), 3–15 at 3 (further proclaiming proximity to "the definition … found in standard textbooks of economic theory" as "that part of the payment to an owner of resources over and above that which those resources could command in any alternative use").

79 See, e.g., Nancy MacLean, Democracy in Chains: The Deep History of the Radical Right's Stealth Plan for America (2017). For a very different approach to the Virginia School/Buchanan, see Alain Marciano & Pete Boettke, The Soul of Classical Political Economy: James M. Buchanan from the Archives (2020).

80 Buchanan, *supra* note 78.

81 *Id.*, 7.

82 *Id.*, 5.

which there would be no entrepreneurs to begin with) would not be dissipated so as for the rent they created to ultimately redound to the benefit of consumers.[83]

Here, then, the key sense of "rent seeking" in public choice theory comes into proper view – namely, that according to which the term was "designed to describe behavior in institutional settings where individual efforts to maximize value [ultimately] generate social waste rather than social surplus." While at the level of the individual decision-maker, the behavior of the profit-cum-rent seeker remains the same, the generation of social waste comes not because the rent that is now sought suddenly becomes price determined rather than price determining but rather because of a "transform[ation]" of the "setting within which individual choices are made" as "institutions [move] away from ordered markets toward the near chaos of direct political allocation."[84]

* * *

Obviously, one need not read conspiratorial motives into the ongoing divergence of the mainstream of neoclassical rent theory from its classical forebear. As Conway Lackman notes, already in Mill's "conflicting conclusions regarding the rent–price relationship" a certain "problem" of "conflicting hypotheses" that has "plagued discussions of rent to the present day" was detectable. As is "ma[de] clear" in Mill's thought, according to Lackman, this is because

> [o]n the one hand, land is assumed to have no scarcity value; [but] on the other hand, it is assumed to have scarcity value. The first assumption is the classical position. If land has no scarcity value, the margin will be rentless and the classical postulates follow. If, however, land has scarcity value, the margins will yield rent. Therefore, rent is a cost of production and must be a part of price.[85]

At the same time, it should be even more obvious how misleading it would be to assume that the dissolution of classical rent theory was simply the product of the relentless march of intellectual progress, as if the ideological utility of shifting ideas can only be read backward from evidence of conscious and diabolical machination.[86]

Nor can the long-term fate of rent theory after the neoclassical turn be understood, as Lackman might be read to suggest, solely in terms of a change in some isolated prior. For saying that the possibility of a *rentless* margin assumes that land has no scarcity value is not necessarily the same as saying its possibility assumes the

83 *Id.*, 7.
84 *Id.*, 4.
85 Lackman, *supra* note 50, at 54.
86 If the point is liable to be read only as a paean to Marxian commonplaces about economics-as-ideology, it is worth noting that its truistic character is routinely demonstrated by any intellectual history worth its salt. In the present context, see e.g., Gaffney, *supra* note 43 and Czech, *supra* note 42.

availability of land for which no payment should, in principle, be necessary. Indeed, the propositions are only identical if one has already also traded in the classical emphasis on land's unproduced character – so central to rendering coherent the idea of its "costlessness" even notwithstanding its potential to command a fee – for the neoclassical idea of every factor being put into whatever particular employment it might be (including that of simply idling) through exchange. Insofar as the neoclassical stance was premised on little to no concern, even just in theory, with how those positioned to enter into "rational" and "voluntary" market exchanges over factors came to be endowed with control over them in the first place, this just brings us back to the way it made supply and demand the general law of economic behavior, most notably – as here – by universalizing scarcity.

Insisting on an equivalence between the notion that land – as an unproduced factor – should, in theory, have a margin with no real cost and the implicit assertion that it is devoid of scarcity value, thus, is predicated on much the same logic according to which any distinction between natural and market price – or, in some ways roughly equivalently, value and price – ended up being denied force.[87] It is likewise predicated on a logic according to which no real line can be drawn – or even entertained as needing to be drawn – between the more or less productive labor of putting a factor to work and the passive collection of returns from assets, especially already in-place ones, all due acknowledgment aside of the foundational role of "sacrifice" as the definitional criterion for ownership in the "Lockean" labor theory of property that Fried so strenuously identifies as the purported guiding light of the Anglo-common law tradition.[88]

87 The observation is compatible with what is spelled out at much greater length in MARIANA MAZZUCATO, THE VALUE OF EVERYTHING: MAKING AND TAKING IN THE GLOBAL ECONOMY (2018). As she puts it in an especially notable passage

> [f]or a long time the idea of value was at the heart of debates about the economy, production and the distribution of the resulting income, and there were healthy disagreements over what value actually resided in. For some economic schools of thought, the price of products resulted from supply and demand, but the value of those products derived from the amount of work that was needed to produce things, the ways in which technological and organizational changes were affecting work, and the relations between capital and labour. Later, this emphasis on "objective" conditions of production, technology and power relationships was replaced by concepts of scarcity and the "preferences" of economic actors: the amount of work supplied is determined by workers' preference for leisure over earning a higher amount of money. Value, in other words, became subjective. Until the mid-nineteenth century, too, almost all economists assumed that in order to understand the prices of goods and services it was first necessary to have an objective theory of value, a theory tied to the conditions in which those goods and services were produced, including the time needed to produce them, the quality of the labour employed; and the determinants of "value" actually shaped the price of goods and services. Then, this thinking began to go into reverse. Many economists came to believe that the value of things was determined by the price paid on the "market" – or, in other words, what the consumer was prepared to pay. All of a sudden, value was in the eye of the beholder. Any goods or services being sold at an agreed market price were by definition value-creating.

Id., 17.

88 See, generally, FRIED, *supra* note 11.

Indeed, after the marginal revolution, part of the way utility-based theories of value were able to do away with the idea that some returns represented remuneration for the production of value in a way that others did not simply follows from proffering/perfecting a new ontology of effort/exertion. This allowed the classical focus on labor to be displaced by an ultimately ethereal notion of sacrifice through "waiting"/the ability to defer consumptive exchange – even if one, in its own way, that has been as grave a source of difficulty for utility theories as the "objectivity" of their labor-based counterparts have usually been regarded as having been for them.[89] If the ability to "wait" for longer became the chief mark of capital, that of labor tended overall to become the opposite, given how that which it otherwise was seen as contributing to the social product generally terminated on a much shorter timescale, once subtracting for the exigency of the household to meet immediate needs by exchanging the lion's share of wages for day-to-day consumption goods, shelter, and the like.

It is little wonder, then, that yet another tendency of the neoclassical revolution was to jettison classical political economy's implicit sociological concern, as the connection it drew between the factors of production and the main classes among whom the social product was divided generally withered.[90] Indeed, in this connection, one can say that the triumph of "methodological individualism" that took place alongside of neoclassicism is best thought of as an anti-sociology, notwithstanding its obvious overlap with the *Methodenstreit* of the 1890s that took place between

89 My way of putting things here generalizes over how pre-marginal revolution utility theorists like Nassau William Senior (1790–1864) tried to understand capital and how it was understood, in essence, by marginalists, like Marshall or Eugen von Böhm-Bawerk (1851–1914), whatever their other differences. That is, it is sometimes said/suggested that Senior's thesis of capital as "abstinence" must be sharply differentiated from a focus on time preferences/the notion of capital as waiting that is associated with Bohm-Bawerk. See, e.g., James Buchanan, Cost and Choice: An Inquiry in Economic Theory in the Collected Works of James M. Buchanan, Vol. 6 (1999), 7–8, 12 (arguing that Senior's – and Marshall's – was, in essence, an idea of the cost to the capitalist as pain and, thus, a "real cost" theory in a way that the more properly "subjectivist" thrust of Böhm-Bawerk's – and other Austrians' – was not). While it is difficult to go into detail on the matter here, it hardly seems any foregone conclusion that the distinction indefeasibly holds. See, e.g., Hunt & Lautzenheiser, *supra* note 24, at 312–13, noting how

> [d]espite Böhm-Bawerk's insistence that his theory was completely different from that of Senior, it appears to be merely an extension and elaboration of the latter's theory. Böhm-Bawerk identified capitalist production with roundabout production. He thereby assumed that any production process that uses tools and intermediate products was a capitalist production process … [Thus], only a difference in mental and emotional attitudes differentiated laborers from capitalists. They had different time preferences. Laborers wanted their reward now, while capitalists had the moral character that permitted them to wait. But Böhm-Bawerk's notion of waiting, as well as Marshall's notion of waiting, was essentially identical to Senior's notion of abstaining. Like Marshall, Böhm-Bawerk was somewhat embarrassed by the use of the word abstinence, because he was uncomfortable with Marx's critique of Senior's claim that abstinence was a unique social cost of production.

90 See, generally, *id.*

exponents of the Austrian and historical schools of economics in the German-speaking world and that was tied into the official origins of sociology as a discipline.[91]

B *The Role of Rent Theoretic Analysis in Institutionalism 1.0 and Reviving the First Law and Economics Movement's Inframarginalist Critique of Neoclassicism Today*

While the classical theory of rent generally went into retreat after the marginal revolution, it clearly did not simply disappear. Even if inexplicitly and notwithstanding the important differences between Marx's ideas and the inframarginal critique touched on earlier,[92] aspects of classical rent theory can be seen as clearly having lived on in Marxist exploitation theory, where the formative idea of capitalist profit as being made possible by the unearned appropriation of surplus value generated by labor power (over and above its own cost of reproduction) bore some evident parallel to landlord rent as originating in the garnishment of the net produce that was left after deducting for necessary costs of agricultural production (and, more indirectly, accounting for the consequent effects on the profits of manufacture).[93]

[91] On the "method dispute" in the German-speaking world and its connections to marginalism more generally, see DIMITRIS MILONAKIS & BEN FINE, FROM POLITICAL ECONOMY TO ECONOMICS METHOD, THE SOCIAL AND THE HISTORICAL IN THE EVOLUTION OF ECONOMIC THEORY (2009). If it is accurate to understand the marginal revolution in terms of an anti-sociology, then it would be more fitting to see neoclassicism's true counterpart sociology as inhering in the new political economy of interest groups that went hand in hand with/that co-evolved with public choice theory. For a fuller diagnosis of the new political economy, see Biplab Dasgupta, *The New Political Economy – A Critical Analysis*, 32(4) ECON. POL. WKLY. 13 (1997).

[92] See, *supra* note 23.

[93] The statement here is meant to be taken literally – that is, as contending no more than that there is a rough parallel between Marx's idea of the capitalist's exploitation of labor (in the technical sense) and Ricardo's account of the landlord's rentierism. (For a fuller explication, see, e.g., Duncan Kennedy, *Law Distributes I: Ricardo Marx CLS* [Feb. 24, 2021], available at SSRN: https://ssrn.com/abstract=3813439 or http://dx.doi.org/10.2139/ssrn.3813439). As such, the present point is not to recapitulate – or even comment one way or another on – the oft-proclaimed charge that Marx was no more than a "minor post-Ricardian." For the original charge, see Paul Samuelson, *Economists and the History of Ideas*, 52(1) AMER. ECON. REV. 1 (1962); for a not untypical example of the many subsequent endorsements of Samuelson's view, to say nothing of earlier ones like it, see Anthony Brewer, *A Minor Post-Ricardian? Marx as an Economist*, 27(1) HIST. POL. ECON. 111 (1995). For a less insistently dismissive reading of the important differences between Marx and his predecessors' approach to labor theorizing, see HUNT & LAUTZENHEISER, *supra* note 24, at 202–46. Of course, outside of the neoclassical mainstream there have long been sympathetic attempts to fully appreciate as well as extend, clarify, and reconstruct Marx's economic ideas – from the basement ground of his approach to labor theorizing all the way up. For an historically noteworthy and fledgling, if lesser known, example, see early Soviet intellectual PAVEL V. MAKSAKOVSKY, THE CAPITALIST CYCLE: AN ESSAY ON THE MARXIST THEORY OF THE CYCLE (2009 [1929]).

As I have already described at some length in the Introduction, notwithstanding the issue of whether it was mainly through generalizing beyond classical economics' limitations, the pre-marginalist discourse of rent also obviously asserted its presence among the Fabian socialists in Britain and their counterpart exponents of the first law and economics movement in the United States, together with their institutionalist progenitors.[94] Of course, I will not here try to provide any much more detailed overview of early institutionalism. Indeed, even outside of the leading accounts of its connection to realism by legal scholars like Fried and Hovenkamp,[95] the obviously ample treatment of its place within the history of economics makes being exhaustive impossible in any case.[96]

At the same time, it is worth at least summarizing some key points. First, as will be known to many readers, it is likely best to dispense with starting from any connection one might be inclined to draw between the first generation of institutionalism and the post-1960s species that is associated, perhaps first and foremost, with Douglass North and rooted, in important ways, in Ronald Coase's work. As Ha-Joon Chang succinctly puts it, for example, in this New Institutional Economics (NIE), "institutions may be able to shape individual *behaviour*, but they are not able to change the motivation itself." As such, the view from NIE contrasts with the "constitutive role of institutions" in early institutionalism. For in the earlier tradition (and what Chang identifies as its more genuine inheritor today of institutional political economy) rather than being given, "motivations" are seen as, themselves, "being fundamentally shaped by the institutions surrounding the individuals," which "embody certain 'values'" that are, in turn, "inevitably internalize[d]" by those same individuals. The "hallmark of a truly institutionalist approach," this constitutive view makes for a categorical split between NIE's "neoliberal" commitment to seeing institutions as "products of maximizing behaviour by individuals with pre-formed preferences"[97] and the commitments manifest already within early twentieth-century work by the likes of Thorstein Veblen, Wesley Mitchell, Richard Ely, and John R. Commons.[98]

Of course, the work of most, if not all, of these figures started to achieve prominence already before the turn of the century. For example, Veblen's most

94 See, e.g., FRIED, *supra* note 11, at 4–7, 26–27, 72–73, 145–59.

95 See *supra* note 11.

96 See, e.g., MALCOLM RUTHERFORD, THE INSTITUTIONALIST MOVEMENT IN AMERICAN ECONOMICS, 1918–1947: SCIENCE AND SOCIAL CONTROL (2011). Also making any attempt at exhaustiveness futile is the inability to do justice to all the ways the bloom can be taken off the rose of "progressive era" American economics, which largely sympathetic accounts like Fried's – and, to an admittedly lesser extent, Hovenkamp's – tend mainly to leave aside. See, e.g., THOMAS C. LEONARD, ILLIBERAL REFORMERS: RACE, EUGENICS, AND AMERICAN ECONOMICS IN THE PROGRESSIVE ERA (2016).

97 Ha-Joon Chang, *Market, the State and Institutions in Economic Development*, in HA-JOON CHANG, ED., RETHINKING DEVELOPMENT ECONOMICS (2003), 41–60 at 54–55 (emphasis in original).

98 See, e.g., JOSEPH DORFMAN, INSTITUTIONAL ECONOMICS : VEBLEN, COMMONS, AND MITCHELL RECONSIDERED: A SERIES OF LECTURES (1963).

well-known/influential book, *The Theory of the Leisure Class*, appeared in 1899 while he was still a fellow at the University of Chicago, just a half decade before his *The Theory of the Business Enterprise* (1904). As Veblen's student, Mitchell had also come to be centered in Chicago by this point, before going on to spend the main part of his career at Columbia. Ely, known for being one of the founders of land economics, had come to settle at the University of Wisconsin already by 1892, where his own student, Commons, would arrive a little more than a decade later in 1904 as Madison fast established itself as, perhaps, institutionalism's leading center.

With all being critics of the disparities of the Gilded Age, the early institutionalists stood at more of a seeming distance from the emerging neoclassical mainstream than legal economists like Hale, even if still also askew from those more expressly informed by the politics of Marxian socialism. At the same time, it would be misleading to reduce the enterprise of the early institutionalists[99] – as is often suggested – to an offshoot of German historical economics or, even less sympathetically, a brand of anti-formalist philosophizing largely out of step with the changes to which "real" economics was concurrently subject. Indeed, as Michael Hudson observes, even among those who should know better, there has been an absence of "recognition ... that the institutionalists were the major school retaining the classical concept of economic rent as unearned income" and, thus, proposing that it be "tax[ed] ... away" and used to "keep natural monopolies in the public domain or at least to regulate the prices they charged so as to keep them in line with cost-value."[100] Commenting on the relative neglect of Veblen, as early institutionalism's greatest figure, Hudson's incisive way of spelling out the key achievement of its ranks is worth quoting at some length:

> [f]ocusing on technology and the rising productivity of labor and energy-driven capital, its members developed an alternative to Ricardian doctrine. Describing diminishing returns and British class antagonisms as a special case, they focused on increasing returns as the universal wave of the future ... From [Simon] Patten to Veblen, critics of rentiers were so diverse that it would be misleading to refer to

[99] As I will expand on further below, one should bear in mind the point touched on earlier about how the "early" institutionalists differed from the now better-known orientation associated with Douglass North and other late twentieth-century thinkers who are distinguished by the same name – of their belonging to the "institutional" school of contemporary economics. Of course, it is not that there are no connections between contemporary, post-Northian economists of this stripe and the early institutionalists, but the differences are likely as stark as any that render it untenable to see mainly continuity between the first law and economics movement and post-Coaseian "Law and Economics." On the new institutionalism (and its relation to the old), see also, e.g., John Harriss et al., *Introduction: Development and Significance of NIE*, in JOHN HARRISS, JANET HUNTER, AND COLIN M. LEWIS, EDS., THE NEW INSTITUTIONAL ECONOMICS AND THIRD WORD DEVELOPMENT (1995), 1–13 as well as Mushtaq Khan, *State Failure in Weak States: A Critique of New Institutionalist Explanations*, in *id*, 71–85.

[100] See, e.g., Michael Hudson, *Review of David Reisman*, The Social Economics of Thorstein Veblen, EH.NET (Oct. 2012) and Michael Hudson, *Veblen's Institutionalist Elaboration of Rent Theory*, Levy Econ. Institute of Bard College, Working Paper No. 729 (Aug. 2021), 11–12.

> them as a "school" as such. Their common denominator was a focus on unearned income and exploitation, which required government policy to reform . . . Nowhere was this more the case than in land rent, natural resource rent, and monopoly rent. Ricardo described land rent as stemming from diminishing returns widening the margin between high-cost producers (who set the price of food) and low-cost landowners who received the economic rent from rising crop prices. The American School cited progress in chemical fertilizers, mechanized farm production, and the development of transport infrastructure as increasing productivity in agriculture as well as industry. Instead of fertility being "original and indestructible" as Ricardo claimed, soil chemistry and capital investment in farm equipment and public support services were turning land into capital, yielding returns in the form of profit . . . Patten and Veblen anticipated [Joseph] Schumpeter in viewing rent as super-profit created by the increasing returns resulting from the advance of science and technology.[101]

To be sure, the above description is not out of keeping with how legal scholars sympathetic to the first law and economics movement have understood the importance of its institutionalist predecessors – from the initial strand of critical legal studies that was intent on recovering/using the legal realist mode of analysis illuminated by thinkers like Hale and Wesley Hohfeld,[102] to later works devoted to comprehensively reconstructing the intellectual history of the institutionalist-realist enterprise,[103] to the various more contemporary efforts at revitalizing its spark,[104] including the inframarginal orientation that gives this volume its name. At the same time, accentuating the continuity between the concerns of the so-called American school of economics and the focus in the classical tradition on distinguishing productively earned returns – together with the wider question of value with which it was tied up – puts institutionalism's development in a rather different light than that which has more typically been shone on it to illuminate its role as a progenitor of the first law and economics movement/legal realism. As I have already touched on in the Introduction, the contrast can be especially well brought out in relation to Fried's now canonical account, its great achievement notwithstanding. For in using

[101] *Id.*, 5–6.

[102] See, e.g., Duncan Kennedy & Frank Michelman, *Are Property and Contract Efficient*, 8 Hofstra L. Rev. 711 (1979–80); Duncan Kennedy, *The Role of Law in Economic Thought: Essays on the Fetishism of Commodities*, 34 Amer. Univ. L. Rev. 939 (1985), esp. at 952, fn 28; Joseph W. Singer, *Review Essay: Legal Realism Now*, 76 Cal. L. Rev. 465 (1988); and Neil Duxbury, *Robert Hale and the Economy of Legal Force*, 53 Modern L. Rev. 421 (1990).

[103] See *supra* note 11. See also, Hovenkamp, *supra* note 20 and Gregory S. Alexander, Commodity and Propriety: Competing Visions of Property in American Legal Thought, 1776–1970 (1997), 243–378.

[104] See, e.g., Frank Pasquale et al., *Eleven Things They Don't Tell You about Law & Economics: An Informal Introduction to Political Economy and Law*, 37 L. & Ineq. 97 (2019); Jedediah S. Purdy et al., *Building a Law-and-Political-Economy Framework: Beyond the Twentieth-Century Synthesis*, 129 Yale L.J. 1784 (2020); and Paulo Barrozo, *Critical Legal Thought: The Case for a Jurisprudence of Distribution*, 92 U. Colo. L. Rev. 1043 (2021).

Hale's work as a window into the ferment characterizing the period from the 1890s to the 1930s as progressive critics of laissez faire demonstrated the role of the state in determining the contours of the ostensibly unregulated free market via private law rules of property and contract, it is so-called rent theory Lockeanism as a fundamental improvement on the classical inheritance that Fried steadfastly keeps in focus as the North Star of her account.

Better situating institutionalism in relation to classical rent theory, thus, has the potential to enrich contemporary efforts at reinvigorating inframarginal analysis for the twenty-first century. By putting rent theory into more explicit dialogue with its pre-institutionalist past, including to the effect of suggesting that the founding preoccupation with ground rent was as prescient as it was limiting, we will be better poised to see both what the first law and economics movement gained and what it may have given up in granting neoclassicism its first principles, whether on grounds of fundamental agreement with them or merely in order to craft a more rigorous internal critique of their overarching logic.

Considered on its own terms, of course, the moniker of inframarginalism points its own way toward illuminating implications. For notwithstanding the first law and economics movement apparently finding little reason to engage with the question of value, capturing its essence in terms of a commitment to inframarginal analysis crystallizes the fact that its exponents were no ordinary neoclassicals. Whatever their personal intellectual convictions, then, their taking the marginal revolution in value theory for granted could not but have also been a way of paying the price of admission necessary for pioneering the kind of critique they were intent on. Viewed as a methodological conviction, in other words, the inframarginal orientation need not be thought of as being, in theory, any so categorical a rebuke of heterodox varieties of Marxian economics as one finds those sympathetic to the first law and economics movement often suggesting. This is so at least provided an intellectual open-mindedness enough to elicit an appreciation for Marxian perspectives beyond what can be immediately gleaned from the first volume of *Capital* alone, to resist any tendency to ignore or dismiss out of hand the attempts across the long twentieth century to "solve" the so-called transformation problem, and so on.[105]

Ultimately, therefore, it is from a more latitudinarian perspective that this chapter's historical excursus into rent theory suggests we re-approach inframarginalism. For such a perspective is only likely to enrich the view before us, even without doing anything to obscure the most central insights of the first law and economics movement as an intellectual tradition. As for the content of those insights, according to the first, it was emphasized that even if decision-making at the margin set the

[105] For an overview, see Hunt & Lautzenheiser, *supra* note 24, at 222–31, 522–24. For more comprehensive treatment see M. C. Howard & J. E. King, A History of Marxian Economics, Vol. I, 1883–1929 (1989), 21–38, 41–62 and M. C. Howard & J. E. King, A History of Marxian Economics, Vol. II, 1929–1990 (1992), 228–42, 265–84.

price/value of goods and services in neoclassical theory – and, hence, brought supply and demand into market clearing balance – by the lights of the same body of theory it had to be decision-making that took place before reaching the limit of the margin that determined how the fruits of market clearing (i.e. "efficient") balance were apportioned. That is, as Ramsi Woodcock clarifies in his own chapter in this volume, in a perfectly competitive market, not only does it have to be inframarginal buyers and sellers who generate the neoclassical surplus, but it also has to be the same agents who are ultimately responsible for how the price, which is set by decision-making at the margin, divides up that surplus; for by neoclassical theory's own lights, the division must depend on "how much more value the inframarginal buyers place on the good relative to the marginal buyer and how much lower sellers' costs on inframarginal units are relative to sellers' costs on marginal units."[106] Here, in other words, we arrive back to what Fried so effectively captures as Hale's most fundamental way of putting into doubt any supposed "Lockean" claim by producers to "property" in "the exchange value" their goods and services might generate in the market.[107]

From this first of inframarginalism's key insights, it is just a short step to a second: namely, that assuming a uniform price line for all sellers, even under competitive equilibrium – and, thus, outside of any situation characterized by monopoly power – some producers, meaning, those operating below the limit of the margin, will have an ineliminable scarcity power.[108] As a result, the producer surplus (*viz.*, the "rents")

[106] Woodcock, *supra* note 69, at 55. As a result, as Woodcock further notes,

> [w]hether the competitive price is fair in the sense that it divides the surplus equally between buyers and sellers, or fair in the sense that it minimizes the surplus enjoyed by sellers, or fair in any other distributive sense, depends on the values placed on the good by inframarginal buyers and sellers relative to the values placed on the good by the marginal buyer and seller; the fact that at the competitive price sellers are paid the marginal benefit they confer on consumers is just the starting point of the analysis and of no moral significance, at least insofar as distributive justice is concerned. All that competitive pricing guarantees is efficiency in the sense that it clears markets.

Id., 56.

[107] See, e.g., FRIED, *supra* note 11, at 145, noting that

> [a]lthough economists persisted for descriptive purposes in distinguishing among different forms of economic "rents" and in differentiating all such rents from monopoly profits, Hale's view that the distinctions were meaningless in justifying the (Lockean) right to market-generated incomes reflected the conventional wisdom of most socialist and progressive critics (economists and noneconomists alike) at the turn of the century. Sweeping all such deviations from cost into the broad category of "rent," such critics found in the newly constituted "rent theory" the natural replacement for the largely discredited Marxian critiques of the distributive effects of unregulated capitalism.

Compatible points can be found elsewhere among the contemporary inheritors of Hale (including as passing through the waystation of critical legal studies). See, e.g., DAVID KENNEDY, A WORLD OF STRUGGLE: HOW POWER, LAW, AND EXPERTISE SHAPE GLOBAL POLITICAL ECONOMY (2016), 193.

[108] This point is touched on earlier as well; see *supra* note 69.

that inframarginal sellers are able to garnish – based on the ability to charge a price equivalent to the higher-cost marginal seller's own, despite having lower costs – will necessarily derive from their superior access to cost-lowering inputs of one kind or another rather than any entrepreneurial know-how, remuneration necessary to incentivize their managerial sacrifice, and so on.[109] Indeed, as Woodcock again notes so instructively, it was precisely for this reason that the exponents of the first law and economics movement turned to "rate regulation and taxation" – rather than mere anti-monopolism – "as alternative means of addressing" what their analysis was meant to show as being the true source of "the problem of inequality."[110]

IV A MODEST PROPOSAL: TAXING THE IMPUTED RENT OF THE LAND SITE COMPONENT OF OWNER-OCCUPIED HOUSING

It should thus be plain that effectively calling for a redoubling of emphasis on ground rent is neither out of keeping with the key insights of inframarginalism nor an embrace of intellectual regression. Particularly judged against the backdrop of the last section's historical discussion, it is misleading – or, at any rate, far too limiting – to understand the course of post-classical rent theory simply as one of perfecting its logical completeness by shedding the needless preoccupations of old. Indeed, as I have sought to show in the last part, this is *even if* we cast the exponents of the first law and economics movement as unqualified partisans of the marginal revolution in value theory.

A *Returning to Land Site Returns: From the Great Recession to the COVID-19 Shock*

At the same time, turning attention to ground rent is also countenanced by world capitalism's political economy in the period since the advent of the second half of the postwar era, which in high-income countries like the United States, especially,

[109] Woodcock, *supra* note 69, at 20–21, further noting that

> [t]he power associated with scarcity is in an important sense indistinguishable from that associated with monopoly. Both are founded on an excess of demand relative to supply. In situations of scarcity, the reason the low-cost, inframarginal sellers are able to charge the same price as the high-cost, marginal sellers (and therefore to extract surplus for themselves) is that there are more buyers willing to pay the price necessary to cover the cost of the high-cost sellers than there are low-cost units available for sale. A low-cost seller can, therefore, refuse to sell to any buyer who insists on a lower price, secure in the knowledge that there is another buyer out there whose only option is to buy from a high-cost seller and who therefore would be just as willing to buy from the low-cost seller at the high-cost price ... Without this imbalance of demand and supply, which is baked into the concept of scarcity, there would be no reason for which inframarginal sellers could charge the same price as the price charged by the marginal sellers.

[110] *Id.*, 31.

has witnessed a consistent reversion to a world in which land rentierism has become ever more important. This, moreover, has not only been as part of the reality of the ostensibly quasi-feudal world that the increasing importance of rentierism has created,[111] but also the reawakened debate around inequality that followed from the events touching off the Great Recession in 2007.

In the particular strand of the debate spun out from Thomas Piketty's celebrated *Capital in the Twenty-First Century*, for example, returns to residential real estate figured with a particular salience. Consider Piketty's now famed R > G relationship, indicating that in all but the exceptional "golden age" period of modern capitalism between roughly 1945 and 1975 aggregate income going to capital has risen faster than the rate of growth. Among the lines of attack that quickly came to be mounted against Piketty's formulation,[112] which was meant especially to capture the historical experience of the United States since the early 1970s, likely the most visible emerged from then MIT doctoral student Matthew Rognile's suggestion that Piketty had failed to take stock of the fact that the trends he was documenting were driven "almost entirely by housing."[113] Of course, here, it is not possible to enter with any depth into the ensuing controversy around whether Rognile's work really had to be understood, in principle, to detract from the framing of the problem of wealth concentration coming out of *Capital in the Twenty-First Century* – around the 1 versus 99 percent dichotomy – by, in effect, dissolving the problem through instead suggesting that capital income was simply the other side of the rise of a proverbial "middle class" of Joe and Jane homeowners. Suffice to say, dismissing Piketty's work on the basis of refusing the price of entry by which it demands that real estate be treated as part of capital stock tends to assume the variety of critique now associated with Rognile more than directly establishing it.[114] Regardless, it is worth remembering that on no side of the controversy, evidently, was anyone disagreeing about

[111] It is worth emphasizing that it would seem rather pointless to become too contentious about how much is really attempting to be asserted by the term "reversion" here, or for that matter, "quasi-feudalized." In this respect, it would appear that criticisms of such a kind – or, at any rate, criticism that sum to being of such a kind – are off the mark. For an example that strikes this author as such, see, e.g., J. W. Mason, *Comments on Michael Hudson: Making Capitalism Great Again? A Critique of the "Rentier Takeover" Thesis*, 53(4) Rev. Radical Pol. Econ. 574 (2021).

[112] For other lines of attack, see, e.g., Gregory Mankiw, *Yes, r > g. So What?* 105 Amer. Econ. Rev. 43 (2015).

[113] Matthew Rognile, *A Note on Piketty and Diminishing Returns to Capital* (2014), available at http://mattrognlie.com/piketty_diminishing_returns.pdf. See also Matthew Rognile, *Deciphering the Fall and Rise in the Net Capital Share: Accumulation or Scarcity*, Brookings Papers on Economic Activity (Spring 2015).

[114] For a concise statement of this position, see, e.g., Marshall Steinbaum, *Is Piketty's Treatment of Housing an Excuse to Ignore Him?*, Washington Center for Equitable Growth, June 24, 2014, available at https://equitablegrowth.org/pikettys-treatment-housing-excuse-ignore/. See also Marshall Steinbaum, *Why Are Economists Giving Piketty the Cold Shoulder?*, Boston Review, May 12, 2017, available at www.bostonreview.net/articles/marshall-steinbaum-beyond-piketty/.

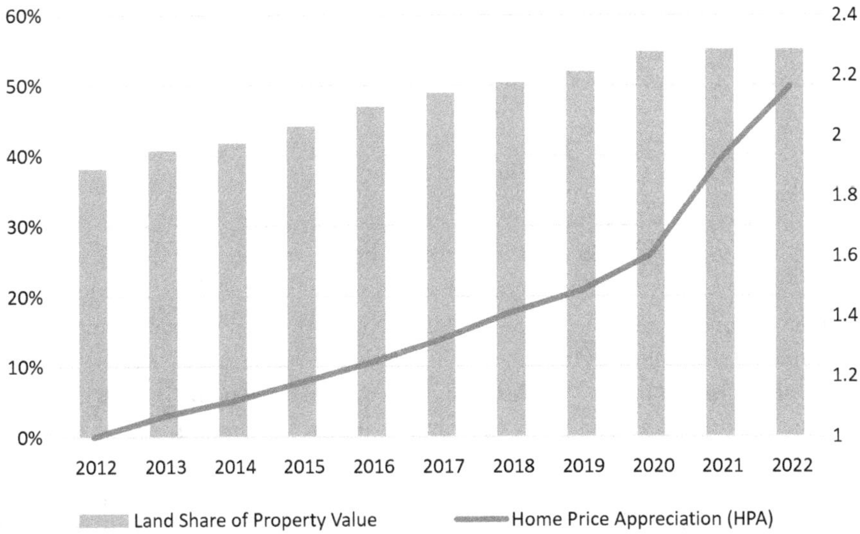

FIGURE 9.1 Land share of property value and home price appreciation (combination) for USA

whether a clear upward ascent was taking place in the level of returns to housing since the 1970s – indeed, most of all, Piketty himself, given his express insistence on treating housing as capital, in the first place.[115]

Elsewhere, I have sought to make my own contribution to ongoing discussion about these matters by emphasizing how much of the driving force behind aggregate home price value increases during this period has come through increases in aggregate land price values.[116] Indeed, updating for the subsequent period from the bursting of the last real estate bubble to the high point of the COVID-era housing craze in the United States, the trend becomes only more marked, with a dramatic new chapter becoming evident in the story. Drawing on data from the American Enterprise Institute,[117] Figure 9.1 shows a composite picture of the

[115] The consensus on this point becomes evident, for example, in the more expansive literature that has followed Piketty and his associates' thread other than by way of trying to deflate the significance of their findings. See, e.g., Gianni La Cava, *Housing Prices, Mortgage Interest Rates and the Rising Share of Capital Income in the United States*, BANK OF INTERNATIONAL SETTLEMENTS WORKING PAPERS, No 572 (July 2016), available at www.bis.org/publ/work572.pdf (arguing that the long-run increase in aggregate housing capital income is due to higher imputed rental income going to owner-occupants, with this itself being precipitated by factors like lower real interest rates and consumer price inflation as well as inventory constraints on new housing in large metro areas during the relevant period of concern); and, in a very different mode, Duncan Maclennan & Julie Miao, *Housing and Capital in the 21st Century*, 34(2) HOUS. THEORY & SOC'Y 127 (2017).

[116] Faisal Chaudhry, *Property as Rent*, 94 ST. JOHNS L. REV. 363 (2021), 41–23, esp. figures 1–3.

[117] American Enterprise Institute, *Land Price and Land Share Indicators*, available at www.aei.org/housing/land-price-indicators/.

lockstep rise of aggregate home price values and the aggregate share attributable to an appreciation of the land price component during the decade preceding the approximate "end" of the COVID-19 pandemic/public health crisis.[118]

B *What about the Property Tax?*

To be sure, from a policy perspective, the increasing role of aggregate land price values in driving up aggregate home price values – whether over the last decade or previously – is not wholly illegible to our current fiscal regime. Any proposal for taxing imputed income going to the land/site component of owner-occupied housing assets thus merits consideration of the property tax, given the way it at least partly serves as a tax on land values. Indeed, notwithstanding the acrimony the property tax is generally regarded as inspiring among the public, its partial convergence with a land value tax makes for an important factor behind its traditional bipartisan appeal among experts. Famously, for example, on the view of the doyen of Chicago economics, Milton Friedman, property taxation constituted "one of the least bad taxes, because it's levied on something that cannot be produced – that part that is levied on the land."[119]

And, certainly, despite the fact that the prospects of a modern levy on property at the federal level died in 1913 – after an earlier wave of criticism of state systems going back to Revolutionary times crested in 1907 – the local property tax remains an essential mechanism of public finance. Whereas even to state governments its relative importance was on a precipitous decline already well before World War II,[120] for local governments in various parts of the United States it has continued to make up some three-quarters of tax revenues and still over half of overall revenues; notoriously, relative to the level of school districts and townships the picture often looks even more dramatic, with property taxation having continued to constitute more than 90 percent of revenue intake in such areas where it has remained important,[121] like New England.[122] Indeed, even the acrimony that has surrounded

[118] *Id.*

[119] Adam Nash, *Q&A with Milton Friedman: Education, Health Care & Iraq*, Nov. 5, 2006, available at https://adamnash.blog/2006/11/05/qa-with-milton-friedman-education-health-care-iraq/.

[120] In 1902 the state-level property tax made for 52 and 45 percent of tax and general revenue, respectively, although it continuously declined for most of the period after – to the point that today, as Glenn Fisher puts it, it is entirely "insignificant" at the state level. See GLENN FISHER, THE WORST TAX: A HISTORY OF THE PROPERTY TAX IN AMERICA (1996), 200.

[121] As for the decline at the local level, as Fisher notes, in 1932 the property tax made up 97 and 85 percent of tax and general revenues, respectively. At the same time, its ongoing, contemporaneous importance at the local level is also testified to by the fact that even the seemingly significant gap in the property tax as a percentage of tax versus total local revenue is partly accounted for by the rise of a much more draconian regime of other fees and exactions that pad total local revenues. *Id.*

[122] Adam H. Langley & Joan Youngman, *Property Tax Relief for Homeowners: Policy Focus Report*, LINCOLN INSTITUTE OF LAND POLICY (2021), 18. Of course, the importance of the property tax

the property tax since the so-called tax revolt that started in the 1970s is rooted in illusion more than reality,[123] given the generally "weak evidence" for its overall regressivity and the questionable small-"d" democratic credentials of the agitation making for the proverbially "revolutionary" upsurge.[124]

As for the degree of convergence, in theory whereas a pure land value tax would fall on the unimproved value of land alone, property taxes fall on the value of both land and structures. To illustrate, consider the scenario Philip Bess spells out, comparing how it would look to elicit $5,000 of public revenue from two equal-sized and adjacent parcels – one consisting of vacant land assessed at $100,000 and the other with additional structures worth $300,000 – on the basis of taxing property versus land values. At a 1 percent *property* tax rate, $5,000 in tax revenue would accumulate from the neighboring parcel owners paying $1,000 and $4,000, respectively (with the owner of the non-vacant parcel paying an additional $3,000 on the $300,000 worth of structures over and above the same $1,000 they would owe on the value of their land). With a land value tax, on the other hand, $5,000 in public revenue could be elicited through a 2.5 percent levy on each of the two parcels (making for a return of $2,500 on each plot's $100,000 of land value).[125] While clearly to a lesser degree than a pure land value tax, then, property taxation does at least partly avail of a pure land value tax's chief justification from being free of negative incentive effects of the kind that would limit capital investment by dissuading land owners from spending on their own parcels.

Of course, as the attentive reader may know or have surmised already, looked at from a different angle this virtue of the property tax will appear just as much one of its main vices. Indeed, even beyond the only partial overlap between property and land value taxation in theory, caution is in order about assuming more congruence

even at the local level shows significant regional variation. As compared to New England, as the report notes, in Alabama or Arkansas, it provides for only 25 percent of local revenue – there being "a strong relationship … between revenue diversification and the level of local property taxes, with lower property taxes often accompanied by [reliance on] higher [and more regressive] local sales or income taxes," *id.*

[123] On the upward redistributive effects of the tax revolt, see, e.g., CLARENCE Y. H. LO, SMALL PROPERTY VERSUS BIG GOVERNMENT: SOCIAL ORIGINS OF THE PROPERTY TAX REVOLT (2015); and GEISMER, *supra* note 13.

[124] Richard F. Dye & Richard W. England, *Assessing the Theory and Practice of Land Value Taxation, Policy Focus Report*, LINCOLN INSTITUTE OF LAND POLICY (2010), 4, 9 (citing other relevant literature). See also Keith Ihlanfeldt & Luke P. Rodgers, *Homestead Exemptions, Heterogeneous Assessment, and Property Tax Progressivity*, 75 NAT. TAX. J. 7 (2022) (using data from 2018 for all single-family homes in Florida, arguing that the progressivity-promoting force of the homestead exemption dominates assessment practices that artificially lower the tax burden of wealthier homeowners). For more on assessment practices, see *infra* notes 126 and 134.

[125] Philip Bess, *Henry George's Land Value Tax: An Idea Whose Time Has Come?*, AMER. AFFAIRS, Feb 20, 2018, available at https://americanaffairsjournal.org/2018/02/henry-georges-land-value-tax-idea-whose-time-come/#:~:text=Both%20parcels%20(vacant%20and%2For,the%20assessed%20unimproved%20land%20value.

than there actually is in practice. First, whatever the extent of the overlap between the two, it is bound to be unstable and, over time, to likely diminish. This is because any given parcel subject to a land value tax will furnish a taxable base that will expand as the premia such parcels garner from improvements to surrounding parcels, area-wide public goods investment, and the like expand. In this respect, the degree to which a land value tax will acquit itself as a less blunt instrument than a property tax is likely to increase with time and, certainly, when most needed, amidst the bubble conditions of a seller's market. In other words, as areas become built up and the "location, location, location" factor increases in importance, so too will a greater share of property value be attributable to a swelling site value component of housing prices, which will remain insulated from the generally more substantial tax rate it would otherwise be subject to under a regime based purely on taxing land site values. Of course, this is wholly leaving aside the role of existing provisions – like, say, ones enabling fictitious depreciation – in artificially lowering property values and thereby even further cordoning off site values from administrative reach.

Second, notwithstanding what I earlier noted as seemingly being the overall case to the contrary, the property tax regime's alleged regressivity is a matter of considerable complexity, as can be surmised from how voluminous and long-standing debate about the matter has been. As per Keith Ihlanfeldt and Luke Rodgers' incisive summary, "[i]n essence, the debate has been about whether the property tax" is more like an "excise tax that disproportionately falls on lower-income households who spend a larger portion of their budgets on housing" (which would make for regressivity) or if it should instead "be considered a … tax on capital income that accrues largely to higher income households" (which would make for progressivity) or neither (based on seeing it, instead, as a kind of "fee[] for benefits and amenities" and, thus, the source of relevant kinds of sorting effects).[126] Even beyond the empirics that would be necessary to determine the ultimate veracity of these theories in any given context – and, hence, that would be needed to undermine any case for progressivity – there is also a question about whether the charge of regressivity is meant to apply based on comparing owners to renters on an economy-wide basis or wealthier to less wealthy homeowners in the ownership economy alone. Indeed, framed as a comparison of the second type, the notorious unreliability of assessment practices will impose a particularly long shadow over attempts to definitively answer the question of property taxation's progressivity versus regressivity.[127]

[126] Ihlanfeldt & Rodgers, *supra* note 124, at note 1.

[127] See, e.g., Mason Gaffney, *Tax Reform to Release Land*, in KENNETH C. WENZER, ED., LAND-VALUE TAXATION: THE EQUITABLE AND EFFICIENT SOURCE OF PUBLIC FINANCE (1999), 58, 67–68 (citing various studies) and Alanna Hartzok, *Pennsylvania Farmers and the Split-Rate Tax* in *id.*, 239, 241, 264 (pointing to the regressive weight of "farm owners with large amounts of land paying disproportionately less in taxes than those with less valuable holdings"); Joseph Hansel, *How Property Taxes Engender Regressive Taxation*, CHICAGO POLICY REVIEW ONLINE, Mar. 2018 (focusing on Chicago's Cook county and the practical roadblocks that owners of lower value property face in appealing appraisal decisions); and Natee Amornsiripanitch, *Why*

In ways, moreover, the length of this shadow makes for its own reason to remain cautious about the degree to which the current property tax regime really can be vindicated as a tool for getting at land site rentierism. For the problem is not simply one born from the inherent uncertainty of assessment or even ordinary divergences between assessed values and sales prices. Even with points of sales comparison of recent enough vintage, assessed values are liable to lag behind market values in the face of difficulties around how to determine when housing price inflation involves a fundamental reset of property values as opposed to merely putting froth on a bubble. Separately, there is also the systematic ways in which inequality – most dramatically, of the racial variety – distorts assessments, leading to overvaluation of properties owned by the disadvantaged for tax purposes simultaneously with their undervaluation for the purposes of lending and re-financing decisions.[128]

Finally, there is the tax revolt itself, which in its most visible form was a revolt against the property tax, in specific. Whether through the 1978 ballot initiative in California that added Proposition 13 to the state's constitution or its 1982 counterpart in Massachusetts that statutorily enacted Proposition 2.5 as part of state law, the express purpose of such measures has been to freeze rates irrespective of values. With such ceilings stymieing any increase in the property tax rate irrespective of what is happening with property values, the tax revolt has meant freezing out the very possibility of capturing any greater portion of increasing site values through the property tax regime.

C *The Baseline Case for Taxing Land Site Rents as Imputed Income*

In now coming more directly to the chapter's own proposal, it is worth making explicit that while one could take a page form the foregoing subsection to advocate for taxing land site value itself – whether through a land value tax proper or, as a second best, tweaks to the existing property tax system to make it better at targeting

Are Residential Property Tax Rates Regressive?, FEDERAL RESERVE BANK OF PHILADELPHIA WORKING PAPER 22-02 (Jan. 2022), available at www.philadelphiafed.org/-/media/frbp/assets/working-papers/2022/wp22-02.pdf. While Gaffney is hesitant about whether definitive evidence of racial discrimination in assessment is likely to be available, time has seemingly proved the hesitance unnecessary. See, *infra* note 135.

128 See, e.g., Jung Hyun Choi et al., *Three Differences between Black and White Homeownership that Add to the Housing Wealth Gap*, THE URBAN INSTITUTE: URBAN WIRE BLOG, Feb. 28, 2019, available at www.urban.org/urban-wire/three-differences-between-black-and-white-home ownership-add-housing-wealth-gap; *Racial and Ethnic Valuation Gaps in Home Purchase Appraisals*, FEDERAL HOME LOAN MORTGAGE CORPORATION ECONOMIC & HOUSING RESEARCH NOTE, Sept. 2021, available at www.freddiemac.com/research/insight/20210920-home-appraisals; and Julia Howell & Elizabeth Korver-Glenn, *The Increasing Effect of Neighborhood Racial Composition on Housing Values, 1980–2015*, 68 SOC. PROBS. 1051 (2021), 1051. See also, Debra Kamin, *Home Appraised with a Black Owner: $472,000. With a White Owner: $750,000*, N.Y. TIMES, Aug. 18, 2022, available at www.nytimes.com/2022/08/18/realestate/housing-discrimination-maryland.html.

land site values – such measures are destined to be difficult to enact for all the reasons already just rehearsed above. This is not to say, however, that we must throw the baby out with the bathwater and simply give up on taxing land site values. Indeed, the essence of the policy proposal I here lay out resides in its being an indirect means of doing so – namely, by taxing the returns that owner-occupants implicitly garnish from the land site component of their housing assets (or, if one likes, the rents that such owners would be able to charge for the use of their land if they were to rent it out to a third party). That is, taxing such imputed returns turns out to be economically the same as taxing land site values directly insofar as the value of a piece of land is no more than the flow of rents that can be charged for its use.

In fact, the various limits preventing a greater convergence between the existing regime of property taxation and one based more purely on land value taxation discussed in the previous section are not the only basis for bolstering the case for addressing land site rentierism through means other than just existing ones. Perhaps even more important is the way those limits also throw into relief the virtues of an *income* tax approach as a more politically palatable means of getting at the most quintessential of rentierist returns to site values. We need not shy away from the possibility that tapping into land site rent in its capacity as part of the imputed income attributable to owner-occupied housing could be free from many of the key features that have made tweaking the property tax in a less regressive direction an ever more fraught enterprise since the late 1970s. Among these features, there are at least six that are worth making explicit.

First, as I have already assumed for the purposes of Section II, a levy on imputed rental income would most naturally fall under the system of federal taxation. As such, it would have the advantage of being severed from the locality, which is well-known to be the nerve center of NIMBYism and the constellation of other forces immediately underlying the skewed economic geography of the postwar United States – and, hence, the tax revolt itself.[129] Indeed, notwithstanding the tax system's overall effective regressivity,[130] its federal income-based component has remained among the most committed/open to the ideal of progressivity. It is thus noteworthy, for example, that even the most significant recent effort to comprehensively assess the equitability of the tax system – by Gabriel Zucman and Emmanuel Saez – has been premised on demonstrating how it is state and local exactions that play the determining role in tipping the balance toward regressivity.[131]

[129] For one of the definitive statements of the case, demonstrating, in part, how the linkage of the property tax to school funding has allowed it to be used as an effective veto, both socially and juridically, over any changes to the localized structure of this skewed economic geography, see, generally, WALSH, *supra* note 13.

[130] See, generally, DAVID CAY JOHNSTON, PERFECTLY LEGAL: THE SECRET CAMPAIGN TO RIG OUR TAX SYSTEM TO BENEFIT THE SUPER RICH – AND CHEAT EVERYBODY ELSE (2005) and SAEZ & ZUCMAN, *supra* note 5.

[131] *Id.* While it did not affect the veracity of Zucman and Saez's picture of the determining importance of state and local taxation, their view elicited a notable pushback from a number of

Second, using the federal income tax as a vehicle for addressing land site rentierism would also likely make it easier to address the tendency of a property tax – and, for that matter, any would-be pure land value tax – to ensnare individuals who are "house-rich but income-poor," given the insensitivity of such measures to a homeowner's stage of life and source(s) of current income.[132] In the property (or land value) tax context, this lifecycle problem – alongside of other (at least, perceived) bases of regressivity – necessitate (or would necessitate) further bureaucratic engineering at the state and local level through an unwieldy array of so-called circuit breakers – from state aid, to tax deferrals, to homestead credits, to more diffuse aspirations toward better quality assessment practices. As a result, instantiating circuit breakers necessitates an intensification – not relaxation – of the ties that bind the politics of the locality to our (existing) means of partially recovering land rent. Even more worryingly, such circuit breakers cannot but be proposed by way of threading a needle whose eye has – for now several decades – already been clogged with tax-revolt style assessment and rate limits. To put it mildly, this would seem to run counter to whatever desired effect of increasing the appeal of the property (or, for that matter, a land value) tax, which constitutes the basic rationale for instituting such circuit breakers at the state and local level in the first place.[133]

Third, notwithstanding requisite caveats about the kind of unravelling to which the federal income tax's progressive rate structure has been subject in recent decades, providing relief to relevant strata of homeowners from a tax on imputed rental income would likely be administratively much simpler than it would be to create circuit breakers for a property (or, land value) tax. It would also be more automatic, in light of the way that the fate of such relief would be tied to the given taxpayer's more general profile of income – not to mention, the possibility of a wholesale reversal of the direction in which the rate schedule has been shifted in recent times were support for redoubled progressivity to be won at the public policy/legislative level.[134]

former officials within the Obama administration, including former Treasury Secretary Lawrence Summers. On the substance of controversy – or, ultimately, the lack thereof – see Annie Lowrey, *The Rich Are Different from You and Me: They Pay Less in Taxes*, The Atlantic, Jan. 23, 2020 (available at www.theatlantic.com/ideas/archive/2020/01/tax-code-regressive/605362/).

[132] Langley & Youngman, *supra* note 122, at 4.

[133] See *id.*, for a useful list.

[134] At the level of perceptions, especially for the income tax, the key shift is usually seen as beginning with Ronald Reagan 1981 Economic Recovery Tax Act (ERTA). For an account partly cautioning against mistaking perception for reality, albeit in a way that does not disturb the essential point made here, see W. Elliot Brownlee, *Tax Policy in the United States: Was There a "Neo-Liberal" Revolution in the 1970s and 1980s?* in Gisela Huerlimann, W. Elliot Brownlee and Eisaku Ide, eds., Worlds of Taxation: The Political Economy of Taxing, Spending, and Redistribution Since 1945 (2018), 155–86 (generally arguing that among the reasons why the perception is faulty is the consistency of the Reagan cuts with a policy mood that clearly began already in the Carter administration – if not, in ways, before –

Perhaps the most complex advantage of mechanizing a levy on rentierist returns to land through using the machinery of federal income taxation would be a fourth. For this involves the way that such machinery would be liable to help escape the myriad difficulties – both logistical and political – that house price value assessment of the kind that goes into the property tax has generally made for. (Most glaringly, there is the well-documented tendency to assess the homes of more wealthy homeowners proportionally much further below their actual fair market values than those of their less wealthy counterparts, both as a result of poor quality/unfair assessment practices and, now ever more, hard-wiring poor results into the system through tax revolt style assessment limits.[135]) Even allowing for the different methods there are for measuring imputed rents, they simply do not rely in the same way as the property tax does on such assessment decisions about the value of residential real estate (or, for that matter, on timely and proper reassessment decisions).

The so-called opportunity cost approach to calculating imputed rent, for example, is generally untethered from the vagaries and underestimating tendencies of assessment (by local officials or otherwise), whatever its other possible problems. This is because the approach is based on calculating the cash income foregone by homeowners considered as investors in "housing equity rather than financial assets through estimating the financial benefit of converting the equity in one's homes into an annuity."[136]

More to the point, the same remains the case even on the so-called market value approach to determining imputed rent, which, contrary to what the name might suggest, is not necessarily adequately formulated by simply taking data on market rents on the closest equivalent and projecting them, individually, onto owner-occupied units. While the market value approach thus generally does treat owner-occupants

but nonetheless conceding that policies like the ERTA and Tax Reform Act of 1986 "may have had a major impact on the distribution of income and wealth" – for example, through the former's taking the highest marginal rate down 27 percentage points from 77% to 50% – a 35% drop – and the latter by 22 percentage points, from 50% to 28%, making for an even larger 44% drop. *Id.*, 172).

135 For the best recent study of the disparity between assessed values of the homes of rich versus poor homeowners, see Christopher R. Berry, *Reassessing the Property Tax* (Mar. 9, 2021), available at SSRN: https://ssrn.com/abstract=3800536. For other aspects of the problem with assessment, within the voluminous literature, see Kenneth K. Baar, *Property Tax Assessment Discrimination against Low-Income Neighborhoods*, 13(3) URB. LAW. 333 (1981); Laura McCrystal, 165,000 *Philly Homeowners May Be Paying Too Much in in Property Taxes: Is the City Assessing Property Fairly*, PHILADELPHIA INQUIRER, Aug. 10, 2018, available at www.inquirer.com/philly/news/philadelphia-property-assessments-appeal-tax-market-value-20180810.html; Robert Ross, *The Impact of Property Tax Appeals on Vertical Equity in Cook County, IL*, UNIVERSITY OF CHICAGO, HARRIS SCHOOL OF PUBLIC POLICY WORKING PAPER (2017); Alan Dornfest et al., Taxable Value Increase Limits Revisited, 17(1) J. PROPERTY TAX ASSESSMENT & ADMIN. 3 (2020), retrieved from https://researchexchange.iaao.org/jptaa/vol17/iss1/3; and Carlos F. Avenancio León & Troup Howard, *The Assessment Gap: Racial Inequalities in Property Taxation*, 137(3) Q. J. ECON. (2022), 1383.

136 Saunders & Siminski, *supra* note 8, at 349.

as if they are renting their dwellings to themselves, it more specifically involves arriving at an estimate of a property's gross market rent – from which a subtraction can then be made for relevant expenses involved in earning that gross in order to arrive at the property's net imputed rent. One typical way the underlying estimate of gross market rent, itself, can be arrived at is by taking a fixed annual percentage of the value of the property. As for reaching this fixed annual percentage, this can be done on the basis of calculating the value of gross imputed owner-occupant rent as derived from a country's national accounts[137] and then dividing that figure by an estimate of the gross value of total owner-occupied housing stock – for example, as determined from estimates reported in a country's household expenditure-type survey (HES) or whatever i.[138] Of course, any determination of the gross value of owner-occupied housing stock in this chain of steps would not be without its own limitations – chief among them ones having to do with the reliability of self-reported values in a country's HES-equivalent. Granted, therefore, to the extent that the self-reporting of housing values in HES data is unreliable, it would add to the problem of the underestimation of gross imputed owner-occupant rent in a country's national accounts – including due to the way they might make an allowance for deducting (excessive) depreciation costs for built structures even as they might also make no allowance at all for land value appreciation. That said, there is good reason – and empirical data – to suggest that such self-reporting is not, in the final analysis, as unreliable as one might at first surmise. Accordingly, self-reported valuations as gathered from a source like an HES-type instrument are likely to be far less problematic than the assessment values that factor into the property tax in the United States, in all their infamy.[139]

A fifth basis favoring the use of a federal income tax approach to recovering rentierist returns to land site holdings is rooted only indirectly in any comparison to the property tax. More specifically, this has to do with correcting what I suggest we can profitably understand in terms of a problem of intra-sovereign regulatory arbitrage. Of course, the concept of regulatory arbitrage has typically been used to point to the way *firms* utilize loopholes in the rule regime to bypass unfavorable regulations, seeking out such "arbitrage opportunities" in contravention to government's seeming intentions. Therefore, through invoking the idea of *intra-sovereign* regulatory arbitrage I mean not simply to offer a play on well-established words; more substantively, rather, so too do I mean to highlight what we can see as a more general class of situations in which the state, itself, creates or exploits loopholes in its rule regime in a way that ultimately redounds to the benefit of dominant economic

[137] In the National Accounts of Australia, which is Saunders and Siminsky more specific main reference point, for example, this calculation of the gross is, itself, based on the market rents received for dwellings similar to the owner-occupied units. See *id.*, 349.

[138] *Id.* (further noting that the specific expenses deducted from the measure of gross imputed rent to arrive at the net figure include costs associated with mortgage interest repayments, repairs, maintenance, and insurance but not depreciation).

[139] *Id.*

interests by leaving them free to pursue lacunae in the rule system of precisely the kind gaps that a more internally consistent or complete regulatory approach would have eliminated.

As for the more specific version of the problem of intra-sovereign regulatory arbitrage that a federal income tax-based approach to land site rentierism would help address, it involves the clear disparity between how income imputable to housing is treated in tax law versus the rule regime beyond. As the economist Mariana Mazzucato has thoughtfully canvassed, returns to owner-occupied housing certainly are counted for the purposes of the National Income and Product Accounts (NIPAs) in the United States, to say nothing of national accounts in other countries. As a function of the rules relating to the keeping of national accounts, then, imputation is proactively used in the United States to recast real estate rentierism in laudatory terms as a source of addition to national income, even as the same rules block its use for the purposes of rendering other far more undeniably "value-generating" services like unpaid housework legible.[140] This contrasts with housing's value as capital, including that which derives from its land site constituent in specific, which is made legible *both* for the purposes of the rules relating to compiling national accounts[141] and, as we have discussed at some length already above, the rules of the taxation regime.

Against the backdrop of these multiple advantages of a federal income tax-based approach to recovering ground rent, there is a final overarching advantage as well. Amplifying all the others, this follows from the specificity of the proposal being advocated here, which, at the risk of becoming repetitive, is worth again noting is focused on applying any such tax to the income from the land site component of owner-occupied housing alone. Requiring that the taxable base of income imputable to owner-occupied housing be reduced to the proportion of the rent attributable to this land site component in specific means the chapter's proposal is even more modest than it otherwise would be given the various ways the federal income tax has remained the part of the tax system perhaps most connected to the ideal of progressivity.

[140] Mazzucato, *supra* note 87, at 91–93.

[141] The national accounts' approach is detailed in Odran Bonnet et al., *Does Housing Capital Contribute to Inequality? A Comment on Thomas Piketty's* Capital in the 21st Century, Sciences Po Economics Discussion Papers 2014-07, Sciences Po Department of Economics (2014). As the authors explain, typically, housing capital is the sum of buildings and land with constructs. In France, for example, to arrive at such a sum, a first step is undertaken by the French Institute of Statistics to estimate the total stock and value of housing in a reference year. The Institute then goes on to follow changes in the components of housing capital over time, with new buildings being evaluated at the price of existing housing units. The Institute thus tracks the evolution of buildings from aggregate housing investments – as deflated by the housing construction index; for the evolution of land with constructs, it tracks the evolution of the surface area covered by housing units as well as the development of the surface area covered by houses. Finally, the total volume of capital that is thus tabulated is multiplied by the price index of existing housing to arrive at a year-by-year value of housing capital stock. *Id.*, 4.

Indeed, even taking an exceedingly rough-hewn measure of the relevant proportion of the kind that can be gleaned from Figure 9.1, this would mean isolating from the overall income a pure ground/site rent, the taxing of which would be free of negative incentive effects. It would thus also mean that taxing any such return could avail of the key justification that is typically adduced to recommend a pure land value tax over a property tax. While the latter justification could not guarantcc that any such addition to the income tax would avoid political opprobrium, especially given the way imputed income from *any* source is bound to be intangible in a way money-in-the pocket is not, it obviously would make the addition more easily defensible. This, moreover, would be even apart from how, as mentioned above, any such tax's federal character would sever it from the locality-cum-nerve center of tax revolt politics. Of course, it is also probably worth looking past the exceedingly timid view of politics-as-pure optics that the last few remarks are premised on. For the greater defensibility of a tax on income attributable to the land site component of owner-occupied housing as compared to one linked to income attributable to owner-occupied housing in general could also prove catalyzing. That is, the less easily such a tax could be besmirched as a way of soaking Jane and Joe Average, the more easily could it be made to crystallize the vast differences within the obscurantist catch-all of "middle class" homeownerdom that may well put Jane and Joe, not to mention Abdullah and Fernanda, at considerable distance from one another, whether materially and/or ideologically.

D *Some Other Likely Concerns: A Closing Rundown of the Proposal's Further Cons and Pros*

As I indicated in the Introduction, even apart from arousing the opprobrium of the leading supporters of tax revolt-style policies or those who have otherwise used them to cement their political economic dominance, it would not be surprising if others who are generally sympathetic to concerns about the growth of inequality, the skewing of the tax regime, and the like were also to remain uneasy with the proposal I have offered in the chapter, notwithstanding its modesty. If such uneasiness does exist, it is likely based on a number of related intuitions. Therefore, in this final subsection of Section IV, I will briefly touch on several of these, in turn.

1 Tax the 1% not the 10 (or 20)%!

Picking up from the observation with which I closed the previous subsection, a first source of possible unease is likely to come from the sense that in the context of an ever more top-heavy pyramid of control over the fruits of economic prosperity in the United States it is beside the point to aim tax reform at the "upper middle class." In short, this basis of unease taps into the debate that has characterized much of the period since the end of the first decade of the new millennium around whether the real problem of inequality in the United States since the Reagan era has been one of the proverbial top 1 percent[142] or, instead, their "dream hoarding"[143] compatriots extending down into the remainder of the top 10 (to 20) percent.

To be sure, patterns of income and wealth disparity during the second half of the postwar era have been such that the gains of the so-called upper middle class/top quintile – as real as they have been – were bound to pale in comparison to those of the superrich within and at the high end of the top 1 percent.[144] Likewise, much of the telescoping out beyond the 1 percent undoubtedly has been facile, aimed at using the relative advantage of the top quintile to repackage hackneyed stories about the polarization separating red and blue America and the even more hackneyed apologia for Trumpism and the larger drift of American conservatism toward a kind of fascism,[145] autocratic legalism,[146] or what have you by laying the larger blame for these developments alone/primarily at the doorstep of "coastal elitism."[147] Suffice to say, the United States' gentry is hardly one that which is exclusively, nor even mainly, comprised of self-styled members of the creative class ensconced firmly within coastal cities and their affluent suburbs.[148]

142 See, e.g., TIM DI MUZIO, THE 1% AND THE REST OF US: A POLITICAL ECONOMY OF DOMINANT OWNERSHIP (2015); Jordan Weissmann, *Actually, the 1 Percent Are Still the Problem*, SLATE, May 18, 2018, available at https://slate.com/business/2018/05/forget-the-atlantics-9-9-percent-the-1-percent-are-still-the-problem.html; Matt Bruenig, *The Top 1 Percent Owns Nearly Everything in the US. We Need to Seize Their Wealth*, JACOBIN, Oct. 6, 2020, available at https://jacobin.com/2020/10/united-states-class-based-wealth-distribution.

143 The term comes from what is, perhaps, the best of the works in this vein. See REEVES, *supra* note 12. See also, Matthew Stewart, *The 9.9 Percent Is the New American Aristocracy*, THE ATLANTIC (June 2018), available at www.theatlantic.com/magazine/archive/2018/06/the-birth-of-a-new-american-aristocracy/559130/ and ELIZABETH CURRID-HALKETT, THE SUM OF SMALL THINGS: A THEORY OF THE ASPIRATIONAL CLASS (2019). For perhaps the earliest entry, albeit one that is also the intellectually most lackadaisical, see TYLER COWEN, THE COMPLACENT CLASS: THE SELF-DEFEATING QUEST FOR THE AMERICAN DREAM (2017).

144 See David Leonhardt, *Our Broken Economy, in One Simple Chart*, N.Y. TIMES, Aug. 7, 2018, available at www.nytimes.com/interactive/2017/08/07/opinion/leonhardt-income-inequality.html (providing an update to include the contrasting reality of the period of 1946–1980 on Piketty, Saez, and Zucman's striking hockey stick graph showing the near exclusive capturing by the top 1 percent of the gains of economic growth in the period from 1980 to 1914).

145 If one were to believe the tendency to dismiss invocations of fascism as overheated, it would suggest that there has been no meaningful effort to elaborate in reasoned fashion on why the invocation is warranted. Suffice to say, this is hardly the case. See, e.g., already in the early Trump era, the entry into these waters by JASON STANLEY, HOW FASCISM WORKS: THE POLITICS OF US AND THEM (2018).

146 On the concept of autocratic/authoritarian legalism, see, e.g., Kim L. Scheppele, *Autocratic Legalism*, 85(2) CHICAGO UNBOUND 545 (2018) 2 and Fabio de Sa e Silva, *Law and Illiberalism: A Sociolegal Review and Research Agenda*, 18 ANN. REV. LAW & SOCIAL SCIENCE (2022).

147 See, e.g., COWEN, *supra* note 143; David Brooks, *Who Is Driving Inequality? You Are*, N.Y. TIMES, Apr. 23, 2020, available at www.nytimes.com/2020/04/23/opinion/income-inequality.html/.

148 See, e.g., Patrick Wyman, *American Gentry*, THE ATLANTIC, Sept. 23, 2021, available at www.theatlantic.com/ideas/archive/2021/09/trump-american-gentry-wyman-elites/620151/.

Regardless, at least provided a less caricatured view of the geographic and cultural backdrop of advantage, it would be foolish to close one's eyes to the broader role of the top 10–20 percent in perpetuating the skewed political economy of the United States. This is especially when considering the more granular political economic mechanics of housing affordability. Indeed, even putting aside broader measures of the upper quintile's outsized material advantages – as through forms of cultural capital and network effects – there is a more serious question of politics that is underplayed by focusing mainly on economic indicators relating to the capture of growth, access to increasing capital income, and the like that tend to be used to justify narrowing concern to the compass of the 1 percent. Of course, this is not to say that the more serious question of politics – beyond apologetic or anodyne formulations about the aloof indifference of a so-called complacent class or the red versus blue state divide – has gone unnoticed.[149] However, it is to say that perhaps in no area of concern about social inequity is expanding focus beyond the superrich more imperative than that of its concrete grounding in the economic geography of residential living.

Indeed, not only should it be apparent that the dynamics of the residential real estate market underlie the forms of effective class and racial segregation that structure the most intimate and immediate experiences of inegalitarianism in everyday life, but also understanding as much has clearly been at the core of analytically grasping the barriers to achieving a more equal society long before the present/neoliberal era. For anyone concerned with such matters, it would thus require an active kind of forgetting of past lessons to mistake the rise of the 1 percent since the 1970s for reason to look past the pernicious effects of the homeownership ideal and its associated crabgrass frontier on our broader political economy,[150] whether writ large or more narrowly at the level of the crisis of affordable housing. With regard to formulating a politics more equipped to address the social and ideological, rather than just more discretely economic, basis of the structure of inegalitarianism in the United States, therefore, a reckoning is demanded with the

[149] See, e.g., Thomas Piketty, Capital and Ideology (2020) (diagramming the politics of the neoliberal era through a decline of class-based voting and the rise of a "merchant right" and, more importantly for the point at hand, "Brahmin left"). Of course, much the same idea can be gathered from a great deal of past political science and history work and, perhaps more notably, it is also implicit within concerns on the progressive to radical left about the professional managerial class, both as expressed already decades ago, and more recently, despite its largely derivative conceptualization, in a more posturing tone that virtually mimics facile laments on the post-Trumpism right about the corruption of politics by globalist cosmopolitan elites. Compare, e.g., Barbara Ehrenreich & John Ehrenreich, *The Professional-Managerial Class*, 11(2) Radical Am. 3 (1977); Alvin Gouldner, The Future of Intellectuals and the Rise of the New Class (1979); and Michael Albert & Robin Hahnel, The Political Economy of Participatory Economics (1991) (preferring the notion of a "coordinator class") with Catherine Liu, The Case against the Professional Managerial Class (2021).

[150] See *supra* at notes 13 and 123.

so-called merchant right and Brahmin left alike,[151] who jointly comprise the top quintile of the wealth and income distribution and whose social advantage derives, in no small part, from material and cultural capital tied to real estate.

2 The Path Dependency of Homeownership Equity-as-Personal Safety Net

A number of other bases of potential unease are, in one way or another, tied to the first. For example, one can imagine the first concern being rearticulated in terms of the path-dependent ramifications of having already tied our fates to the homeownership ideal (whatever, its concomitant effects of erecting a crabgrass frontier to cordon off the least well-off, notwithstanding). Any proposal, no matter how modest, to tax homeownership – even one that through the federal income tax could be graduated in on a progressive basis – might thus be said to stand against the whole weight of postwar suburban (and now exurban) modernism. On this view, the weight of the past looms only more heavily when it is buttressed by the more recent postwar backdrop of a neoliberal withdrawal of government from social provisioning and its redeployment toward the end of insulating the market, and the wealthy who dominate it, from popular democratic demands.[152]

Of course, here, as with the first – and all the other forms of the same – objection modesty is in order and demands that one not purport to attach more certainty to the wisdom of the chapter's proposal than is really possible. At the same time, a sense of proportion is equally necessary, as so too is it to guard against inadvertently lapsing into apparent timidity while giving relevant objections their due. As already made explicit at various points above – including in the Introduction and previous subsection – the chapter's proposal is calibrated to be modest and hardly structured to be indifferent to the obvious stratifications there are within the homeowning population. Indeed, the defining feature of the chapter's proposal to tax imputed returns by tying it specifically to the land site component of owner-occupied housing assets testifies to as much.

Even beyond the last instruction, common sense also warns against letting the idea that "we are all rentiers now" become ever more a self-fulfilling prophecy and, at that, an intensifying one. Doing so would not only be a form of giving up on a politics of reversing unchecked inegalitarianism, but it would also require blindness to various other crucial facts. Perhaps chief among these is that we really are not all rentiers in whatever sense the above sloganized version of the present objection suggests. In the housing market, renters very much are not. In this connection, it is necessary to remember that the affordability crisis that has increasingly gripped the

[151] The terms are borrowed from PIKETTY, *supra* note 149.

[152] See, generally, e.g., MELINDA COOPER, FAMILY VALUES: BETWEEN NEOLIBERALISM AND THE NEW SOCIAL CONSERVATISM (2017) and QUINN SLOBODIAN, THE END OF EMPIRE AND THE BIRTH OF NEOLIBERALISM (2018).

market for shelter in the United States since the turn of the millennium is a crisis not just of affordable stock for purchase but, even more dramatically, for rental.[153] By the time one further factors in the porousness of the line separating owners unable to access an unaffordable purchase market and renters facing escalating rents, little principled basis is left for distinguishing these ostensibly distinct types of individuals. Indeed, this is all the more once one tries to account for relevant shifts in the purchase market that have been wrought by housing's ongoing transformation into a speculative asset – like, for example, through the rise of the proverbial Wall Street landlord as vast pools of investment capital are directed toward hoovering up single family homes. In short, the idea that homeownership equity is our only remaining safety net in an age of neoliberal retrenchment is bound to be self-defeating.

3 The Banks Are the Real Rentiers

Yet another variation on the objection I have been exploring above could involve articulating unease with the chapter's proposal through highlighting how it is the banks and players in the broader financial sector that are the real rentiers given the ultimate capitalization of rent, including land rent, into mortgage and other kinds of interest on securities. To be sure, this is the most trenchant – or, at any rate, the most sophisticated – version of the objection. As such, it undoubtedly carries weight, reminding one of what Michael Hudson has so well described as the devil's bargain

[153] Of course, neither in theory nor in fact, must it be the case that rental rates increase in tandem with sales prices. And, indeed, even since the turn of the millennium the ebb and flow of market rents amid the booms and busts of the sales market had made the story of residential real estate a complex one. At the same time, it is at least equally true that there is hardly anything foreordained about market rents failing to keep pace with or even outpacing sales price rises in the way they so visibly did amid the COVID-era boom. Moreover, there is also the likelihood that the way in which the imputed rent of owner-occupied housing is counted for the purposes of the NIPAs may systematically underestimate the true dynamics of rental rates in the leasing market. Consider, for example, the run-up in market rents faced by lessees amid the COVID-era housing boom. As economist Jack Rasmus explains, official estimates of the inflation renters were facing on their leases were likely diluted by lowballing the rate at which owner-occupants were regarded as paying themselves increased rent based on the prevailing approach to calculating their imputed returns. In other words, had the rent imputed to owner-occupiers reflected more meaningful increases, the overall rate of rent inflation faced by ordinary leaseholders would have been more dramatic. See Jack Rasmus, ALTERNATIVE VISIONS PODCAST, Dec. 13, 2021 https://alternativevisions.podbean.com/e/alternative-visions-inflation-revisited-unpacking-the-cpi-report/ (last visited on Oct. 11, 2022). These points are especially worth keeping in mind when evaluating the corrective offered against PIKETTY'S CAPITAL IN THE TWENTY-FIRST CENTURY by Bonnet and co-authors, whatever its other merits or demerits. See Bonnet et al., *Does Housing Capital Contribute to Inequality* (arguing, centrally, that Piketty's measure of the value of housing capital in terms of the above-described national accounts method and based on housing prices – see *supra* note 141 – must be replaced with a method based on actualized values of rent if it is to be consistent with what Piketty, himself, seeks to establish about rising inequality).

by which mortgage banks were transformed into capitalism's main agents of central planning starting in the early twentieth century.[154]

However, in itself the objection does nothing to make policy intervention through the tax system – or, for that matter, whatever other mechanism – a zero sum game. Remaining aware of or even prioritizing attention to financial sector rentierism in public debate and policymaking, thus, is not mutually exclusive with directing effort along other paths as well. Indeed, it is unlikely that anyone would object on such grounds to, say, giving adequate attention to the notorious role of the home mortgage interest deduction in the upward redistribution of wealth and in making its own contribution to housing bubble dynamics.[155] Moreover, there is an obvious conjunction between upward redistribution policies and their myriad effects, asset inflationary and other, that would make highlighting the various destinations they reach complementary rather than conflicting.[156]

4 Beware of Zero Sum/Deficit Hawk Logic That Misframes the National Budget as Analogous to a Household Budget

A final objection worth considering derives from a possible unease one might feel with inadvertently reinforcing deficit hawk logic by countenancing the idea that directing tax policy at any segment of the rhetorical middle class is necessitated by our national budget being pressed to its limits. While laments about such "zero sum" thinking perpetuating the myth that the national budget is like a household budget have issued most audibly from those associated with modern monetary theory (MMT),[157] they are hardly copyrighted to its brand.[158] To the extent that this is likely to be a real objection – since, after all, even the exponents of MMT make

[154] See, generally, Michael Hudson, Killing the Host: How Financial Parasites and Debt Destroy the Global Economy (2015).

[155] Ironically, it was the first Trump administration that – in the name of its larger tax cutting policy – waged the most pronounced attack on the home mortgage interest deduction in recent memory, albeit in ways that still likely impacted lower tiers of the proverbial middle class most intensively. See Jim Tankersley & Ben Casselman, *As Mortgage-Interest Deduction Vanishes, Housing Market Offers a Shrug*, N.Y. Times, Aug. 4, 2019, available at www.nytimes.com/2019/08/04/business/economy/mortgage-interest-deduction-tax.html.

[156] See, e.g., Dean Baker, *Structuring the Economy to Give Money to the Rich Is Inflationary*, Center for Economic and Policy Research: Beat the Press Blog, July 18, 2022, available at https://cepr.net/structuring-the-economy-to-give-money-to-the-rich-is-inflationary/.

[157] See, e.g., Stephanie Kelton, The Deficit Myth: Modern Monetary Theory and the Birth of the People's Economy (2020).

[158] While the point hardly needs citation to any specific source given its truistic nature, for an example of the tone of bemused frustration with which it nonetheless must ubiquitously – even if probably futilely – be restated in the face of beliefs to the contrary in the halls of Congress and among the cable television punditry, see, e.g., Paul Krugman, *Nobody Understands Debt*, N.Y. Times, Jan. 1, 2012, available at www.nytimes.com/2012/01/02/opinion/krugman-nobody-understands-debt.html.

ample room for tax measures in any policy toolkit they imagine – it is also the easiest to set aside.

This is because the objection is ultimately one about the framing of questions of public policy or, as per the substance of the objection, their misframing. Yet as already noted in the Introduction and at various times since, one of the chief advantages of any proposal to tax imputed returns to the land site component of owner-occupied housing is likely to be found precisely in its salutary effect on how we think about the challenge of housing affordability. Not only is the chapter's central policy recommendation liable to broaden our view of the multiplicity of social forces bearing on the housing affordability crisis, but it is also likely to deepen our awareness of how sharp the edges of social stratification are that characterize the landscape of economic advantage and disadvantage upon which the residential real estate economy rests.

Furthermore, this is entirely leaving aside any number of other ways in which the chapter's policy recommendation would help shift our discourse around real estate and the broader political economy. Insofar as a tax on imputed ground rent could be offered as part of a solution to the boom and bust cycle of the housing economy, for example, it would open a vantage point from which to question the by-now fully normalized idea – and the underlying monetarist commitments it resonates with – that job one of the central bank should be fighting inflation, as need might be, through crashing the housing market or more generally visiting recession on ordinary consumers-cum-workers by precipitously raising interest rates. To take another example, the way the chapter's main policy recommendation highlights the disparity between how imputed rent is treated in the NIPAs and the federal income tax code, it helps shed light on the fundamentally distorting lens of the conventional private–public divide. After all, accounting for the imputed rent of owner-occupied housing in the NIPAs continuously suggests that the "private sector" is laudably generating positive flows of revenue even as omitting imputed returns from federal income taxation continuously denies government any fair share in the same.

V CONCLUSION

In the preceding pages I have sought to approach an old, and not terribly well-known topic – of taxing imputed rent – from new angles. Therefore, if nothing else, doing so should be a way of breathing additional life into what discussion there is of the topic, especially given the way it tends to fall into a familiar pattern of focusing on how politically feasible any such tax would be in a society thought to be so staunchly organized around the idea of the freedom of property as the United States.

Of course, for my own part, throughout the chapter, I too have gone to some lengths to highlight and make concession to an imagined interlocutor who, despite sharing a sympathy with the concerns that motivate the chapter, is still unlikely to be convinced of the merits of the new tax it is devoted to proposing. Now at the close of the chapter, therefore, it is worth reiterating that having done so should not be misconstrued as having intended to communicate that this author, at least, implicitly imagines the proposal to be more seismic than it actually is. Rather, as the titular reference to its "modesty" is meant to assert, at least on its surface a proposal to tax a circumscribed portion of income could not but be among the most technocratic – or, perhaps better put, dry and mundane – of instruments for creating a more egalitarian society imaginable.

All the more, however – not unlike the edited volume of which it is a part – the chapter is thus built on the hope that its ostensible sheepishness will double for an attire in which a wolfishness can be made to appear that is commensurate with attacking the crisis of economic maldistribution that characterizes the world of its writing. It is here that the importance of the other main – historical – perspective that preoccupies so much of the chapter should come further into focus. For by seeking to enrich our understanding of the original inframarginalist critique of neoclassicism, which this volume is intended to help reinvigorate, and by asking that we think more intensively about its exact relationship to the classical tradition of political economy, and to classical rent theory more specifically, new layers of the market's past and future lives as a wealth distributor – or, as the case may be, maldistributor – stand ready to be seen.

10

A Neo-Kantian Approach to Competition Law?

The Re-emergence of Fairness in Antitrust Law and Policy

Behrang Kianzad[*]

CONTENTS

I INTRODUCTION

Recent years have seen the dominance of neoclassical, marginalist and welfarist schools of law and economics being challenged more vigorously than ever. The

[*] This research has been supported by a grant by Johan and Jakob Söderberg Foundation.

classic tension between fairness and efficiency as object of law and policy is seemingly experiencing a paradigm shift[1] judging from policy statements[2] but also in types of cases being prioritized[3] and competition tools being introduced.[4]

This tension is nowhere more prevalent than the case of prohibition of undue wealth transfer as an object for antitrust law and policy. Why should the Sovereign intervene in functioning markets by attempting to control prices, when markets have an inherent ability to self-correct, and where high prices are signals to entry, thus ensuring lower prices and an efficient allocation of resources, as the main argument against excessive pricing and price gouging enforcement goes. Adam Smith, the founding father of modern political economy, on his part remarked:

> In ancient times too it was usual to attempt to regulate the profits of merchants . . . it may perhaps be proper [where monopoly exists] . . .. But where there is none, the competition will regulate it much better than any assize.[5]

The neoclassical forefathers such as Walras, Jevons and Menger, and later Arrow and Debreu,[6] all presupposed and developed different views on competition as part of the general theory on how markets function, placing great emphasis on this neutral arbiter.

Even Karl Marx presupposed existence of competition as a 'coercive force' and the main regulator of the process of circulation, although approaching it from a theory of labour and capital as opposing forces.[7] The concepts of perfect competition on the one hand and monopoly on the other, resting on neoclassical economics, are nevertheless essential for the mainstream understanding of the intricacies of competition law and antitrust, which ultimately aims to protect competition and hence directly or indirectly increase societal wealth.

It should be noted that although competition law invariably is intertwined with economic theory, there exists no 'conventional wisdom' nor any 'consensus' among

1 Herbert Hovenkamp, 'The Looming Crisis in Antitrust Economics', 30 January 2020, https://Papers.Ssrn.Com/Sol3/Papers.Cfm?Abstract_id = 3508832, 52.

2 Margarethe Vesterager, 'Fairness and Competition' (GCLC Annual Conference, Brussels, 25 January 2018); Lina Khan and Sandeep Vaheesan, 'Market Power and Inequality: The Antitrust Counterrevolution and Its Discontents', *Policy Review* 11 (2017): 60.

3 Sandra Marco Colino, 'The Antitrust F Word: Fairness Considerations in Competition Law', *Competition Policy International*, October 8, 2018, www.competitionpolicyinternational.com/the-antitrust-f-word-fairness-considerations-in-competition-law/.

4 European Commission, Impact Assessment for a Possible New Competition Tool, 8 September 2020, https://ec.europa.eu/competition/consultations/2020_new_comp_tool/index_en.html .

5 Adam Smith, 'The Wealth of Nations', 1776 bk. 1, cl. 10; cited in Edgar Watkins, 'The Law and the Profits', *The Yale Law Journal* 32, no. 1 (November 1922): 31.

6 Kenneth Arrow and Gerard Debreu, 'Existence of Equilibrium for a Competitive Economy', *Econometrica* 22 (1954): 265–90.

7 Giulio Palermo, 'Post-Walrasian Economics: A Marxist Critique', *Science & Society* 80, no. 3 (July 2016): 346–74, https://doi.org/10.1521/siso.2016.80.3.346.

economists, simply due to the existence of a vast and contrasting body of economics (and economists) in plural. As noted by Audretsch:

> In 1988, Audretsch wrote "discordance is alive and well in antitrust." Almost a quarter of a century later, little has changed. But few antitrust scholars or practitioners want to ground their work on the shifting sands of ideology. Rather, holders of different doctrines seek to claim sole universality and truth.[8]

Thus, the ontological point of departure regarding what competition is, or ought to be, affects the subsequent theories of harm, modelling and assessment. Broadly speaking, competition can be viewed as an idealized end-state (perfect competition), or rather as a process (dynamic competition). Where the former categorizes 'the most competitive market imaginable in which everybody is a price-taker', the latter rather describes competition as a 'complex and unpredictable dynamic process'.[9] As also noted by Stucke regarding the supposed 'consensus' in antitrust law and economics:

> Despite the push for a single economic antitrust goal, there is no consensus in the U.S. or worldwide on any well-defined goal. Four oft-cited economic goals (ensuring an effective competitive process, promoting consumer welfare, maximizing efficiency, and ensuring economic freedom) have failed to unify antitrust analysis. No consensus exists on what the four goals mean or how they are achieved.[10]

The Nobel Laureate in Economics, Joseph Stiglitz, in his call for new approaches to competition law and economics, noted that:

> Over the past third of a century ... the scope and effectiveness of competition policy has been narrowed, under the influence of certain ideas about the functioning of the market economy – ideas which have subsequently been widely discredited within the economics profession, but whose influence within antitrust law remains significant.[11]

As also demonstrated by behavioural and experimental research, both firms and consumers take fairness considerations seriously regarding fairness in pricing.[12]

8 Robert D. Atkinson and David B. Audretsch, 'Economic Doctrines and Approaches to Antitrust', *Indiana University-Bloomington: School of Public & Environmental Affairs Research Paper Series* No. 2011-01-02, 2011, p. 3.

9 Maurice E. Stucke, 'Reconsidering Competition', *Mississippi Law Journal* 81 (2011): 107–88.

10 Maurice E. Stucke, 'OECD Hearing on Competition and Behavioural Economics – The Implications of Behavioural Antitrust – DAF/COMP/WD(2012)12', 2012.

11 Joseph Stiglitz, 'Towards a Broader View of Competition Policy', in *Competition Policy for the New Era: Insights from the BRICS Countries*, ed. Tembinkosi Bonakele, Eleanor M. Fox and Liberty Mncube (Oxford University Press, 2017), 4–21.

12 Julio Rotemberg, 'Fair Pricing', *Journal of the European Economic Association* 9, no. 5 (2011): 952–81; Daniel Kahneman, Jack L. Knetsch and Richard H. Thaler, 'Fairness as a Constraint on Profit Seeking: Entitlements in the Market', in *Choices, Values, and Frames*, 1st ed. Daniel Kahneman and Amos Tversky (Cambridge University Press, 2000), 317–34; Holger Herz and Dmitry Taubinsky, 'What Makes a Price Fair? An Experimental Study of Transaction

We now have ample evidence that humans are hard-wired towards fairness in transactions, rather than prioritizing utility maximization.[13]

This further testifies to the universal character of the concept of fairness in pricing and social preferences, evolved during the human evolution, and codified in law as a prohibition of 'excessive pricing' and 'price gouging', especially so during crisis such as war, famine and pandemics.[14] This view of fairness, as being both universal as well as evolutionary, is in line with reasoning of Darwin, Smith, Kant, Rawls, Binmore et alia and further demonstrated by neuro-economic and neuro-psychological research.[15]

This legal-historical positioning by the Sovereign on 'fair pricing' is by some accounts mirrored in the articulation of Article 102a of the Treaty on the Functioning of the European Union (TFEU), as Barry Hawk notes:

> The emphasis on fairness in pricing is directly mirrored in European notions of competition law, as seen in Article 102a of the Treaty on the Functioning of the European Union's statutory ban on unfair trading conditions (including excessive prices) by dominant firms.[16]

The emphasis on 'fairness' can also partly be found in US law, namely in the Federal Trade Commission Act, 15 U.S. Code § 45, which prohibits 'unfair' methods of competition. Neither statues do define 'fairness', the reason for which is the fact that fairness is an evolving concept and an operational part of all aspects of law.

The Kantian philosophy of law departs from the proposition that the abstract concept (in this case fairness and justice) can and should be made 'real' by way of rational experience and by deference to the universality of the concepts, beyond individual tastes, cultures and so on.[17]

Experience and Endogenous Fairness Views', *Journal of the European Economic Association* 16, no. 2 (1 April 2018): 316–52.

13 Katherine McAuliffe, Peter R. Blake and Felix Warneken, 'Do Kids Have a Fundamental Sense of Fairness?', *Scientific American*, 23 August 2017; M. A. Nowak, 'Fairness versus Reason in the Ultimatum Game', *Science* 289, no. 5485 (8 September 2000): 1773–75; Stéphane Debove, Nicolas Baumard and Jean-Baptiste André, 'Models of the Evolution of Fairness in the Ultimatum Game: A Review and Classification', *Evolution and Human Behavior* 37, no. 3 (May 2016): 245–54.

14 Watkins, 'The Law and the Profits'; Nils Wahl, 'From Greek Olive Oil to Latvian Music: Is There Any Such Thing as Unfair Prices?', *Concurrences – Competition Law Review* 2 (2018): art. no. 86617.

15 A. W. Cappelen et al., 'Equity Theory and Fair Inequality: A Neuroeconomic Study', *Proceedings of the National Academy of Sciences* 111, no. 43 (28 October 2014): 15368–72, https://doi.org/10.1073/pnas.1414602111.

16 Barry E. Hawk, 'Antitrust in History', *The Antitrust Bulletin* 63, no. 3 (September 2018): 275–82; See also Michal S. Gal, 'Abuse of Dominance – Exploitative Abuses', in *Handbook on European Competition Law*, ed. Ioannis Lianos and Damien Geradin (Edward Elgar Publishing, 2013), p. 401; and in Watkins, 'The Law and Profits'.

17 Eric Watkins, 'Kant on the Distinction between Sensibility and Understanding', in *Kant's Critique of Pure Reason*, ed. James R. Oshea (Cambridge University Press, 2017), 9–27; For a practical application of this 'Kantian' approach in legal science, see Behrang Kianzad, 'Did the

As it is argued in this chapter, employing a legal-philosophical and political economy perspective, many of the clashes between the European and US approaches to the matter of monopolist pricing, at times taking the form of excessive pricing, find their roots in the rights-based versus utilitarian normative approaches to law, legality and desired outcomes.

The utilitarian approach being a common law construct is a stark contrast to the continental approaches in Europe. Fairness in and of itself as object of the law might present itself as unreconcilable with the strict utilitarian, neoclassical law and economics approaches, thereby giving rise to many decades-long debates on the object of competition law and the fairness versus efficiency discourse. Furthermore, an approach to the matter of legal substance by way of a Kantian, rights-based perspective and philosophy of laws runs counter to the strict legal-positivist as well as legal-realist traditions, prevalent on both sides of the Atlantic.

The outcomes produced by a competitive market and general equilibrium, however, 'sound' in a marginalist and neoclassical economic context are times and again counter-intuitive to a fairness discourse presupposed and expected from the legal codification and legal activity, thereby creating a seemingly unresolvable tension between law and economics disciplines.

It is argued that the classic tension between neoclassical economics with its singular focus on efficiency and 'total welfare' thus stands in bright contrast with the European discipline's focus on administration of fairness and justice.[18] This tension, highly observable in the divergent approaches to monopolist pricing,[19] is only to be understood through a soul-searching of the moral-philosophical foundation of the European Legal Corpus as opposed to the US antitrust approach, having its own distinct historical roots. The tension further finds it roots in what has been dubbed the 'adversarial institutions' of firms and markets, where although greed and profiteering is frowned upon on an individual level, firms have profit seeking as their main objective, which is why they should be granted a 'free pass' from the strict moralistic view on profit seeking, although within limits set by the Sovereign.[20]

Although competition law might not be intended, nor capable and suitable for solving all the grand problems of inequality if approached by way of redistribution, competition law remains the most important tool in regard to prevention of undue wealth transfer, reversal and correction of initial endowment (disgorgement) and

Danish Supreme Court Give the Fashion Industry the Kantian Boot?', *GRUR International* 70, no. 2 (February 2021): 159–63.

18 Michael Nance and Jeppe von Platz, 'From Justice to Fairness Does Kant's Doctrine of Right Imply a Theory of Distributive Justice', in *Kant on Freedom and Spontaneity*, ed. Kate A. Moran (Cambridge University Press, 2018), 250–68.

19 Michal S. Gal, 'Monopoly Pricing as an Antitrust Offense in the U.S. and the EC: Two Systems of Belief about Monopoly?', *The Antitrust Bulletin* 49, no. 1–2 (March 2004): 343–84.

20 Joseph Heath, 'The Moral Status of Profit', in *The Oxford Handbook of Ethics and Economics*, ed. Mark D. White, 1st ed. (Oxford University Press, 2019), 337–57.

thus the main checks-and-balances system in place regarding abuse of market power, which further contributes to inequality.

A *To Intervene or Not: Diverging Approaches to Antitrust Law and Policy*

Neoclassical-welfarist economic analysis of law, which has come to dominate much of antitrust debate during the past four decades, is in turn characterized by five core assumptions:

1. the assumption of scarcity of resources,
2. the belief in Homo Oeconomicus, presupposing that all economic agents are self-interested and act based on perfect and complete information and that the human good consists in nothing more than economic welfare,
3. the idea of Utilitarianism, meaning that human behaviour can be reduced to rational calculation and maximization of welfare,
4. that the value of any given thing originates from the value individuals consider it to have, and;
5. the belief in availability and readiness of multiple possibilities guiding the individuals in their search for the optimal choice.[21]

Looking at the implications for antitrust law and policy, as described by Atkinson and Audretsch:

> In fact, at least four separate schools of antitrust philosophy can be identified, each reflecting a different core economic doctrine … conservative neoclassical economics and in the context of antitrust, its analogue the Chicago school; liberal neoclassical economics and the post-Chicago school; liberal neo-Keynesian economics and the populist school of antitrust; and innovation economics and the 'innovation school'.[22]

Whereas the neoclassical economics finds its root in the utilitarian and welfarist perspectives, focusing on economic efficiency and total welfare, the Keynesian, neo-Keynesian or the 'populist' schools allow more room for other public policy rationales beyond economic efficiency.

Controlling prices and direct government intervention in the market to alter prices has always been a hotly debated issue depending on what economic theory and legal rationales one adheres to. Such rules can be found in the Old Testament

[21] Mariateresa Maggiolino, *Intellectual Property and Antitrust: A Comparative Economic Analysis of U.S. and EU Law, New Horizons in Competition Law and Economics* (Edward Elgar Publishing, 2011), footnote 11, p. 4; cited in Behrang Kianzad, Excessive prices and access to medicines – Compulsory licensing as an anticompetitive remedy under the TRIPS Agreement, http://lup.lub.lu.se/student-papers/record/5432497; the paragraph is an excerpt from said work by the author.

[22] Atkinson and Audretsch, 'Economic Doctrines and Approaches to Antitrust', p. 3.

prohibiting interest on loans to fellow Israelites; war-time governments price controls (such as the creation of the US Office of the Price Administration);[23] and more recent regulations of prices such as gasoline, wages or rents.[24]

Already back in 1780 BC, the Code of Hammurabi regulated prices and economic transactions.[25] Later during Roman times, the Diocletian's Edict on Maximum Prices (Edictum De Pretiis Rerum Venalium) sought to set maximum prices to combat inflation and excessive prices, built on the concept of 'laesio enormis', that is, great harm, or excessive harm.[26] There was further an equivalent to be found in the law of the Catholic Church, the Canon Law, where '... the sale of anything for more than its just price was considered turpe lucrum, or ill-gotten gain, and prohibited'.[27] This in turn built the basis of the Scholastic just price theory.[28]

The concept of prohibition of excessive/unfair prices and state-imposed price controls has indeed deep historical roots, from the time of Hammurabi, by way of Aristotle, through Jewish Halacha,[29] Christian[30] and Islamic[31] writings, and onwards to the Just Price framework developed by Albertus Magnus and his pupil, Thomas Aquinas, as well as other Scholastics.[32]

More recently, the ban on exacting excessive prices by Charles II in 1674 and the so-called Maximum Laws during the reign of Robespierre can be mentioned,[33] as well as laws prohibiting excessive prices on goods during times of war.[34] This further

[23] Office of the Price Administration, See records of OPA: www.archives.gov/research/guide-fed-records/groups/188.html#188.1.

[24] Rockoff, 'Price Controls', *The Concise Encyclopaedia of Economics*, Library of Economics and Liberty, available at: www.econlib.org/library/Enc/PriceControls.html.

[25] K. V. Nagarajan, 'The Code of Hammurabi: An Economic Interpretation', *International Journal of Business and Social Science* 2, no. 8 (2011): 108–17.

[26] Diocletian's edict on maximum prices, in AD 285, available at: www.forumancientcoins.com/NumisWiki/view.asp?key=Edict+of+Diocletian+Edict+on+Prices; Mark R. Reiff, *Exploitation and Economic Justice in the Liberal Capitalist State* (Oxford University Press, 2013).

[27] Reiff, *Exploitation and Economic Justice in the Liberal Capitalist State*.

[28] Daryl Koehn and Barry Wilbratte, 'A Defense of a Thomistic Concept of the Just Price', *Business Ethics Quarterly* 22, no. 3 (2012): 501–26.

[29] Itamar Warhaftig, 'Consumer Protection: Price and Wage Levels', in *Crossroads: Halacha & the Modern World*, ed. Ezra Rosenfeld and Rav Binyamin Tabory (Urim Pubns, 1999); Ephraim Kleinman, '"Just Price" in Talmudic Literature', *History of Political Economy* 19, no. 1 (1987): 23–45.

[30] Biblical writings include Leviticus 19:9, Ezekiel 18:13, Deuteronomy 23:19, Leviticus 25:37 and Proverbs 28:8, to name a few.

[31] Muhammad Bashar, 'Price Control in an Islamic Economy', *Journal of King Abdulaziz University-Islamic Economics* 9, no. 1 (1997): 29–52.

[32] John W. Baldwin, 'The Medieval Theories of the Just Price: Romanists, Canonists, and Theologians in the Twelfth and Thirteenth Centuries', *Transactions of the American Philosophical Society* 49, no. 4 (1959): 1–92.

[33] Hawk, 'Antitrust in History', 275–82.

[34] Watkins, 'The Law and the Profits'.

reconnects with the critique by Mestmäcker,[35] as some elements in the neoclassical legal-economic tradition do not have the necessary legal-historic perspective to understand how and why legal concepts are shaped and transformed and the 'values' uncovered by a structured doctrinal analysis.

Fundamentally speaking, the question of controlling prices concerns the reach of state authority, an issue fiercely debated within liberal economic theory. Economists such as Adam Smith regard most forms of government intervention as 'superfluous, useless and harmful'.[36] Instead, the built-in forces in the market such as demand, surplus and competition were supposed to form the 'invisible hand' that would serve as self-regulation of prices when high profit margins in turn would invite competition and innovation.

With Smith, then, 'just price' theory becomes 'price' theory, moving away from the normative domain to one that is purely descriptive.[37] In view of Smith and also John Stuart Mill, state-imposed price regulation was a futile and counter-productive exercise, to the detriment of 'industry and ingenuity'.[38]

To Nozick, who defined state interventions as morally wrong, this proposes a libertarian night-watchmen state. To Rawls, who emphasizes social justice, state intervention is instead deemed necessary,[39] same with Dworkin, causing the latter to criticize the Posnerian position of elevating 'wealth maximization' as the end result and an objective value to be pursued[40] – a matter that will be returned to more in depth in the next section.

The notion of the 'invisible hand' as the means to engage market regulation has thus invited two diverging approaches on intervention. One affirms the self-correcting capacity of excessive prices; the other maintains the necessary and beneficial aspects of intervention. The debate between non-interventionist and interventionist approaches to competition law unfolds in the tension between the two.[41]

The non-interventionist school dismisses the subjection of excessive prices to antitrust intervention. Since new actors will challenge dominant ones while entering the market, excessive prices are supposed not to be upheld on a long-term basis. Although intervention would lower prices and hence increase consumer welfare in the short run, the proponents of the non-interventionist school argue that

[35] Ernst-Joachim Mestmäcker, A *Legal Theory without Law*, Walter Eucken Institut, Beiträge zur Ordnungstheorie und Ordnungspolitik, 174 (Mohr-Siebeck, 2007).

[36] von Mieses 1923, http://mises.org/etexts/mises/critique/section5.asp.

[37] Reiff, *Exploitation and Economic Justice in the Liberal Capitalist State*.

[38] Watkins, 'The Law and the Profits'.

[39] Behrang Kianzad, 'Excessive Pharmaceutical Prices as an Anticompetitive Practice – Reviving Compulsory Licensing in Competition Law & Antitrust', in *New Developments in Competition Law and Economics*, ed. Klaus Mathis and Avishalom Tor (Springer, 2019).

[40] Ronald M. Dworkin, 'Is Wealth a Value?', *Journal of Legal Studies* 9, no. 2 (March 1980): 191–227.

[41] Liyang Hou, 'Excessive Prices within EU Competition Law', *European Competition Journal* 7, no. 1 (April 2011): 48.

new competitors would be less likely to enter the market, incentives and risk-taking would decrease, and dominant actors would be prevented from maximizing their efficiency in order to obtain a higher profit margin.

The non-interventionist school further objects to the capacity of a price–cost comparison to detect excessive prices, since audited financial data are not developed for the purpose of competition law and do not calculate investment in R&D, inflation, return on risk, and so on; this is not deemed viable.

Nor are comparisons to a competitive profit benchmark deemed 'economically sound', since this would require ex ante defining of what a competitive profit would be. Also, the experience and ability of authorities and courts to regulate prices and monitor markets are questioned, a problem escalated by the need for continued interventions and supervision of markets.[42] In sum, the non-interventionist school highlights the difficulties in assessing excessive prices and views enforcement as only one possible solution to the problem, while debating how lowered entry barriers can stimulate competition.

The interventionist school takes the opposite view, asserting that excessive prices must be included into the jurisdiction of competition law due to the manifest and inherent harm they pose to consumer welfare by undue rent transfer from consumers to the monopolist. They point both to the rather deep roots of the ban against 'unfair pricing' in legal history and to concomitant reasoning where a monopolist is able to extract undue profits for a prolonged period of time, be it due to in-elastic demand, barriers to entry or other reasons leading to a defunct competitive process.

B *Price, Value and Profit: Simply Different Names for the Same Concept?*

It is argued that as a normative starting point, there must be a distinction made between value, price and profit, a matter that has been the foundational cornerstone of political economy ever since its inception.

Where Smith, Ricardo, Marx and Sraffa advanced different notions of theory of value, the marginal utility school focused more on exchange and market value as such. Ricardo, in his Principles of Political Economy and Taxation, reconnected with Adam Smith and built a bridge to Marx and Sraffa, in that he espoused a 'labour-theory of value'. In Ricardian view, prices were a function of labour costs, however not measured in terms of monetary units (wages x labour hours) but in actual physical terms (labour hours alone).[43]

The subsequent marginalist revolution spearheaded by Walras, Jevons and Marshall did not engage with the inherent value of a good, in turn advancing the

[42] Massimo Motta and Alexandre de Streel, 'Excessive Pricing in Competition Law: Never Say Never?', in *The Pros and Cons of High Prices* (Kalmar: Swedish Competition Authority, 2007), p. 15 ff.

[43] The Classical School, available at: www.hetwebsite.net/het/schools/ricardian.htm.

theory of supply and demand coupled with a view of a perfectly competitive market; thus, the value dimension was not addressed beyond what it will fetch in a free and competitive market. Thus, the notions of value and profit became somewhat circular, with price being a function of competitive pressure, marginal cost and cost of fixed capital.

The main divide between classical (Smith, Ricardo et alia) and neoclassical and marginalist (Walras, Jevons et alia) theory of value is that the former put emphasis on value as a function of costs of production (material + labour), where the latter put the emphasis on the utility valuation by customers determining the value.

Regarding the matter of profit, however, profit is mainly a function not of fixed capital, but of variable capital, where the price reflects marginal cost plus profit as function of variable capital. This is the main reason why marginal and neoclassical economics are still today at odds with profits being a function of an inherent value reflecting cost of production, fixed and variable capital and associated opportunity costs, but instead attempt at de-coupling profit from value, and thus price, making it impossible for the theory to come to terms with an 'excessive profit', since no profit ever can be found excessive, as the profit is not a function of neither value nor price, but merely reflecting what the good can fetch in a (supposedly) free and competitive market.

The empirical evidence against this positing of 'free and competitive' market acting as an immaculate price arbiter is emerging at an alarming rate,[44] demonstrating rapidly growing mark-ups, market concentration and income inequality.[45]

It should be noted that the constraints on profit seeking enacted by the Sovereign by way of antitrust laws and other laws governing markets, pricing and related areas including regulatory areas fulfil this function of connecting the individual morality with market dynamics and firm organization.

According to the 'neoclassical' view, profits can thus rise dramatically without having any relation to 'economic value', something that is all but evident also in Tech and Digital Markets, where profits per stock shares are soaring, despite companies not producing corresponding profitable turnover, being valued after expectations of producing such value and turnover in the long term.

How 'economic value' is defined is thus foundational, and de-coupling this from any reasonable relation to costs incurred is not an optimal point of departure.

[44] Jan De Loecker, Jan Eeckhout and Gabriel Unger, 'The Rise of Market Power and the Macroeconomic Implications', *The Quarterly Journal of Economics* 135, no. 2 (May 1, 2020); Pauline Affeldt et al., 'Market Concentration in Europe: Evidence from Antitrust Markets', *Deutsches Institut Für Wirtschaftsforschung, DIW Berlin Discussion Paper* No. 1930, 2021.

[45] Ufuk Akcigit et al., 'Rising Corporate Market Power: Emerging Policy Issues', *International Monetary Fund (IMF) Staff Discussion Notes* 21, no. 1, 15 March 2021; Era Dabla-Norris et al., 'Causes and Consequences of Income Inequality: A Global Perspective', *International Monetary Fund (IMF) Staff Discussion Notes* 15, no. 13, 2015; General Secretariat OECD, 'Beyond Growth: Towards a New Economic Approach – Report of the Secretary General's Advisory Group on a New Growth Narrative', 12 September 2019.

It is important to note that for Aristotle, economic value contained both use and exchange value, which is why it might be worthwhile to quote him in full, not least due to his enduring influence:

> These names, both loss and gain, have come from voluntary exchange; for to have more than one's own is called gaining, and to have less than one's original share is called losing, e.g., in buying and selling and in all other matters in which the law has left people free to make their own terms; but when they get neither more nor less but just what belongs to themselves, they say that they have their own and that they neither lose nor gain. Therefore the just is intermediate between a sort of gain and a sort of loss, viz. those which are involuntary; it consists in having an equal amount before and after the transaction ... If, then, first there is proportionate equality of goods, and then reciprocal action takes place, the result we mention will be effected. If not, the bargain is not equal, and does not hold; for there is nothing to prevent the work of the one being better than that of the other; they must therefore be equated ... This is why all things that are exchanged must be somehow comparable. It is for this end that money has been introduced, and it becomes in a sense an intermediate; for it measures all things, and therefore the excess and the defect – how many shoes are equal to a house or to a given amount of food.[46]

Price determination has hence been the defining character of any respectable economic general theory, as the mathematical formulas depart from normative presumptions on the relationship and components of price relative to production, productive forces, exchange, demand and consumerism.[47]

The same normative assumptions enlighten the price-related concept of value and the price-value-related concept of profit. Profit is reachable by way of price and value components and subtraction of all relevant, calculable costs and risks involved. The equation of price with profit minus costs, or price with value, complicates many approaches on this theme.

Profit is determined not only by price component minus costs, but price must also be determined in relation to value, which in turn has since long been defined by monetary units. Nevertheless, the obvious risk of circularity in definition of price–value–profit will in the normative not be availed by its monetary unit definition. The monetary definition and fixation are normatively still conditioned towards the definition of the price–value concepts and their interrelation.

Value is thus the key, normative binding component between price and profit, enabling their interrelation and later fixation in monetary units. Unsurprisingly, all price and profit theory should assume to form subsidiary fields of theories of value, the latter historically attracting the greatest theoretical attention of political economy. As noted by Michal Gal:

46 Aristotle, *Nicomachean Ethics*, trans. W. D. Ross (Batoche Books, 1999), Book V, p. 79.

47 For an alternative account of 'price theory', see E. Glenn Weyl, 'Price Theory', *Journal of Economic Literature* 57, no. 2 (2019): 329–84.

> Alternatively, economic value can be measured objectively, as the value to *most consumers*. The market price can serve as a valuable tool for determining this benchmark. Yet in monopolistic settings without price discrimination it provides little guidance. Also, it requires determination of what weight should be given to specific circumstances, such as extreme changes in demand due to unforeseen events. Other options for determining economic value also exist. Yet they all suffer from the basic problem that we have no simple way of measuring value except by reference to the very price we consider.[48]

The matter of competition in the market between suppliers is a deciding factor when approaching the matter of what price would prevail in such a 'competitive' market, and this notion forms the basis of ratio legis of competition law and antitrust. Monopolies are able to raise prices beyond 'competitive' levels simply due to lack of competitive pressure, if one considers the dynamics on the supply side.

Nevertheless, the demand-side dynamics impact this competitive 'equilibrium' to a high degree, since if the customers are by one reason or another not price-sensitive, or have no other alternative product, this invariably affects the price the monopolist (or dominant actor) can charge without losing sales. This situation perfectly captures the COVID-19 pandemic, where there were both legal mandates regarding masks and hand sanitizers, as well as lockdowns, diminishing the mobility of consumers, enabling pricing above value.

Marginalist, neoclassical and, to some extent, welfarist schools of economics, being positivist and formalist in nature, tend to construct predictive theories rather than descriptive ones. In this, they are more capable of avoiding engagement with the value dimension in the normative, and thus being able to construct the value dimension alongside exchange-based, formalist fundamentals. This approach resolves, and refutes, the value dimension as incalculable in and of itself, also in legal terms.

The entrusting of definition of value on formalist approach to price and profit assumes some form of General Equilibrium, as well as coercive forces of supply, demand and competition to keep markets competitive and efficient.

Here lies a circularity, where the competitive price is the one that is 'efficient outcome', and it is the 'efficient outcome' because it is competitive. The market deficiencies, and the need for competition to correct deficiencies and enforce competitive market structure, should form part of any general theory of value, price and profit. Exception would be if one assumes monopolies preferable and assumes monopolies superior in delivering innovation, growth and allocation of productive resources.[49]

48 Gal, 'Abuse of Dominance – Exploitative Abuses', p. 401.

49 Richard Gilbert, 'Looking for Mr. Schumpeter: Where Are We in the Competition Innovation Debate?' in *Innovation Policy and the Economy*, vol. 6, ed. Adam B. Jaffe, Josh Lerner and Scott Stern (MIT Press, 2006), 159–215.

The normal competitive forces and concomitant economic analysis of price–value–profit dimension should be assumed to differ considerably in these cases. The result is the deep-rooted prohibition of the abusive and monopolistic practices that might be enabled by such market power and thus lead to welfare losses. Indeed, the European Ordo-liberal School demands this of the Sovereign and the soul of competition law. Same is true of neoclassical and marginalist theories, but also of Keynesian/rights-based approach to competition law.[50]

II FAIRNESS VERSUS EFFICIENCY: A TRADE-OFF?

At the outset, in regard to the 'fairness' versus 'efficiency' debate, one might observe that notions of fairness have had much better empirical successes[51] than notions of self-interest[52] and rationality.[53] On the normative side, as aptly summarized by Klaus Mathis 'In people's minds, justice – however it is defined – has an immanent value, which is very difficult to weigh up against an increase in economic efficiency.'[54]

The focus on 'wealth maximization' as well as 'efficiency' is more often than not at odds with other legal values such as 'fairness' and 'justice'. Indeed, nowhere are the normative tensions between law and economics disciplines as prevalent as regarding prevention of undue wealth transfer and profiteering, where the economic analysis of law with its singular focus on 'efficiency' and 'wealth maximization' faces off with a near universal legal prohibition against unfair, excessive pricing and its twin concept, price gouging.

This is not merely a philosophical note, but relevant in the positive analysis, a point seized upon by Glick and Lozada: 'economic efficiency is not about justice, but the law presumably is. Accordingly, Law and Economics' obsession with efficiency, whether real or contrived, has little place in the law.'[55]

Nevertheless, neoclassical and libertarian economists have more often than not rejected any other 'value' to be reckoned with beyond 'efficiency', with some casting equitable concerns with fairness and justice in economics 'a naive and basically

[50] See the next chapter on normative and theoretical foundations regarding theories of harm and their interrelation for an in-depth exposé.

[51] Joseph Henrich et al., 'In Search of Homo Economicus: Behavioral Experiments in 15 Small-Scale Societies', *American Economic Review* 91, no. 2 (1 May 2001): 73–78, https://doi.org/10.1257/aer.91.2.73.

[52] Daniel Kahneman, Jack L. Knetsch and Richard H. Thaler, 'Fairness and the Assumptions of Economics', *The Journal of Business* 59, no. S4 (January 1986): 285–300.

[53] Kahneman et al., 'Fairness as a Constraint on Profit Seeking'.

[54] Klaus Mathis, *Efficiency Instead of Justice?* (Springer, 2009), p. 48.

[55] Mark Glick and Gabriel A. Lozada, 'The Erroneous Foundations of Law and Economics', *Institute for New Economic Thinking Working Paper Series*, 15 February 2021, p. 91. Although they use the term 'Law and Economics', they are more commenting on the Chicagoan Economic Analysis of Law in the tradition of Aaron Director and Richard Posner than the tradition of Guido Calabresi.

infantile anthropomorphism'.[56] It is important to distinguish this 'normative' argument from the 'positive' argument against, for example, price gouging laws examined briefly in the previous section, as the latter targets the actual, empirical realities, or rather, it aims to do so.

In the words of Jenny, ' … the complementary concept of "fairness" is again a concept alien to economic analysis',[57] but this statement is only true given a narrow definition of 'economics', as one could also argue that economics might indeed contain conceptual basis for fairness,[58] as the law on its part indeed has shown to be able to accommodate economic reasoning.

The sheer number of economic papers on fairness in pricing and transactions as well as Nobel Prizes awarded to economists in one way or another addressing fairness-related issues also speaks for itself. Offering a contrary view, in the words of 2001 Nobel Laureate in Economics Joseph Stiglitz: 'This fallacious idea is that you can separate equity from efficiency. It's sometimes referred to as the Second Welfare Theorem. We now know that those two issues can't be neatly separated in that way.'[59]

This 'fallacious idea' of creating a strict dichotomy between total welfare and consumer welfare as regards the normative goals of intellectual property rights and competition law, respectively, needs indeed to be revisited and re-evaluated, as it affects both the holistic as well as the specific analysis of what these laws ought to be. On that normative note, as observed by Calabresi:

> Of Bentham, Mill said that he approached all ideas as a stranger and if they did not fit his test (the test of utility), he dismissed them as vague generalities. Mill then went on to say that what Bentham didn't realize was that "these generalities contained the whole unanalysed experience of the human race."[60]

The aforementioned evidence from behavioural and neuro-economics invariably demonstrates innate human morality and fairness preferences in transactions, and not a sense of 'utility maximization' or proneness to 'efficiency'.[61] The matter is not

[56] Harry G. Johnson, 'Some Micro-Economic Reflections on Income and Wealth Inequalities', *Annals of the American Academy of Political and Social Science*, 409 (September 1974), 54; cited in Arthur Okun, *Equality and Efficiency – The Big Tradeoff* (New York: The Brookings Institution, 1975), p. 5.

[57] Frédéric Jenny, 'Abuse of Dominance by Firms Charging Excessive or Unfair Prices: An Assessment', in *Excessive Pricing and Competition Law Enforcement*, ed. Yannis Katsoulacos and Frédéric Jenny (Cham: Springer International Publishing, 2018), 5–70, https://doi.org/10.1007/978-3-319-92831-9_2, pp. 56–57.

[58] Kahneman et al., 'Fairness as a Constraint on Profit Seeking', 1986; Kahneman et al., 'Fairness and the Assumptions of Economics'.

[59] 'Joseph Stiglitz: Competition Policy, the Need for a More Nuanced View', Interview, Concurrences, No. 2-2019, pp. 16–17.

[60] Guido Calabresi, 'Of Law and Economics and Economic Analysis of Law: The Role of the Lawyer', *Global Jurist* 19, no. 3 (2019): 2019–3001.

[61] Michael Koenigs et al., 'Damage to the Prefrontal Cortex Increases Utilitarian Moral Judgements', *Nature* 446, no. 7138 (April 2007): 908–11; Gregory S. Berns et a., 'The Price of Your Soul: Neural Evidence for the Non-Utilitarian Representation of Sacred Values',

so much of economic analysis of law preference for 'efficiency' to lack any empirical, neuronal backing, but more of a normative failure of the assertions regarding 'efficiency' being an optimal, even the optimal, goal to be pursued by legal rules.[62]

The efficiency paradigm in neoclassical law and economics, whether construed alongside Pareto, Kaldor–Hicks or consumer surplus,[63] is in inherent conflict with the legal discipline framing of, for example, excessive and unfair pricing, oftentimes alongside a winner–loser stratum.[64] This is a matter acknowledged by Calabresi, but ignored by Posner.

This focus on justice further underpins legal authority in the first place, if one subscribes to the Kantian and Rawlsian notions of legal and moral philosophy. Economic analysis of law in some of its most classical approaches by Bork, Posner, Kaplow and Shavell thus entails a near-insuperable conflict with the ratio legis of European competition law, but also with common law.[65]

The assertions and the economic analysis of law approach by Posner[66] as well as the welfarist approach by Shavell and Kaplow, which have been examined above, demonstrate this fundamental conflict. The inevitability of fairness considerations in law if viewed in its interconnection with a democratic order is also noted by Screpanti and Zamagni, who observe:

> But economic democracy and political democracy cannot diverge too much and for too long, otherwise the very foundations of the market system would be dangerously affected. Which is tantamount to saying that keeping the allocative

Philosophical Transactions: Biological Sciences 367, no. 1589 (2012): 754–62; Cappelen et al., 'Equity Theory and Fair Inequality'; Joshua D. Greene et al., 'The Neural Bases of Cognitive Conflict and Control in Moral Judgment', *Neuron* 44, no. 2 (October 2004): 389–400.

62 Eli Salzberger, 'Law and Economics – Limits of Analysis: The Case of Intellectual Property', in *Polish Yearbook of Law & Economics*, ed. Katarzyna Metelska-Szaniawska, vol. 2 (Wydawnictwo C. H. Beck, 2013).

63 Pareto efficiency, or Pareto optimality, concerns a situation where at least someone is made better off, an improvement without making someone else worse off. However, since this criterion might be difficult to achieve in reality, Kaldor–Hicks efficiency in turn categorizes a situation where the benefits exceed the costs of improvements and those who have benefited somehow compensate those who have been made worse off.

64 David Driesen and Robin Paul Malloy, *Critiques of Law and Economics*, ed. Francesco Parisi, vol. 1 (Oxford University Press, 2017); Cento G. Veljanovski, 'Wealth Maximization, Law and Ethics – On the Limits of Economic Efficiency', *International Review of Law and Economics* 1, no. 1 (June 1981); Dworkin, 'Is Wealth a Value?'.

65 Glick and Lozada, 'The Erroneous Foundations of Law and Economics'.

66 Richard A. Posner, 'The Ethical and Political Basis of the Efficiency Norm in Common Law Adjudication', *Hofstra Law Review* 8 (1980); Louis Kaplow and Steven Shavell, 'Fairness versus Welfare: Notes on the Pareto Principle, Preferences, and Distributive Justice', *Journal of Legal Studies* 32, no. 1 (January 2003): 331–62; Louis Kaplow and Steven Shavell, 'Fairness versus Welfare', *Harvard Law Review* 114, no. 4 (February 2001): 961–1388; Richard A. Posner, 'Utilitarianism, Economics, and Legal Theory', *The Journal of Legal Studies* 8, no. 1 (1979).

objective and the redistributive objective separate does not meet the criteria either of efficiency or of equity.[67]

The 'value-free' and 'objective' approach of an efficiency-oriented cost and benefit analysis is anything but 'value-free' and 'objective', and furthermore, as noted by Ernst-Joachim Mestmäcker:

> Cost-benefit analysis is end-neutral. It can be applied to any given purpose. Constitutions, statutes and precedents, however, are as a rule not end-neutral. The question then is how to accommodate the normative implications of economic analysis with diverse non-economic legal purposes.[68]

By mounting a powerful attack on the philosophical foundations of Posnerian position and contrasting it to Hayek's views but also drawing on Kant and Nietzsche, Mestmäcker seeks to reconnect the core function of the law (and law and economics) with legal and moral philosophy, which is and ought to be the DNA of the laws – although supplemented by sound economic analysis of laws where applicable. As noted by Mark Blaug on the matter of efficiency versus fairness:

> This notion of a neat divorce of efficiency from equity, of an objective value-free definition of efficiency, has haunted economics from its outset but it is, of course, a will-o'-the-wisp: there is in fact a different efficiency outcome for every different distribution of income, and vice versa. Efficiency is necessarily a value-laden term and welfare economics is necessarily normative, that is, a matter of good or bad and not true or false.[69]

As Kaplow and Shavell also partly concede, theirs is just another moral theory, albeit lacking all aspects of morality, defined in Kantian, Aristotelian terms or otherwise:

> In several different respects, the approach of welfare economics involves value judgments. First, value judgments underlie the assumptions that social welfare depends on individuals' well-being, that this dependence is positive, and that factors unrelated to individuals' well-being are irrelevant. In other words, to adopt welfare economics is to adopt the moral position that one should be concerned, positively and exclusively, with individuals' well-being.[70]

The trade-off envisioned by Kaldor–Hicks efficiency, with the winners in theory being able to compensate the losers, is a non-starter already in the normative, let alone its impractical, practical application. As noted by Kronman:

[67] Ernesto Screpanti and Stefano Zamagni, *An Outline of the History of Economic Thought* (Oxford: Oxford University Press, 2005).

[68] Mestmäcker, *A Legal Theory without Law*, p. 13.

[69] M. Blaug, 'Is Competition Such a Good Thing? Static Efficiency versus Dynamic Efficiency', *Review of Industrial Organization* 19 (2001): 47.

[70] Kaplow and Shavell, 'Fairness versus Welfare', 986.

> ... someone committed to the Kantian idea of individual autonomy would rightly feel that his moral principle had been violated, and it would not make any difference, from his point of view, that compensation could potentially be made even though it was not. For a Kantian, the Kaldor-Hicks test has no significance.[71]

Fairness becomes relevant in contexts such as price gouging and excessive pricing of essential items during a crisis simply because the core analytical structure of neoclassical and welfarist theories of harm does not neatly encompass such dynamics relative to the strongly held fairness perceptions that can be presumed to have influenced the creation of the legal prohibition against excessive pricing some 3000 years ago.

The main question thus for antitrust law and policy, or any other law governing economic activity, firms and markets, is how to strike a balance between the individual taste for fairness in pricing, and the firm obligation to pursue above marginal costs pricing in order to secure profits and at what levels. Without this boundary setting by the Sovereign, the general trust in markets and firms will erode among the general population, which will view the profit seeking by firms as illegitimate and 'greedy'. This will increase social tensions and decrease the overall support for a free market system. Using the Kantian approach as detailed in the next section can guide policymakers in this area.

III THE KANTIAN REQUIEM: AGAINST WEALTH MAXIMIZATION AND EFFICIENCY IN LAW AND ECONOMICS

The famous kidney problem perfectly illustrates the tension between fairness and efficiency approaches regarding the present theme of excessive pharmaceutical pricing. The not-so-hypothetical case concerns 'fair' division and allocation of an indivisible good,[72] such as a kidney, between two patients suffering from kidney failure.

Patient A will survive twenty-five years with a kidney transplant, whereas patient B will survive twenty years. One option would be to approach the matter from a strictly 'efficiency' perspective, awarding the kidney to patient A since there would be the most utilitarian and efficient outcome.

The second option would be to use a lottery, including or excluding strengths of the claims. The third, and the most 'fair' option held by some, would be to destroy the kidney altogether, respecting the sanctity of life and right to health of both patients as any other allocation would overrule the fairness paradigm.[73] This is many

[71] Anthony T. Kronman, 'Wealth Maximization as a Normative Principle', *The Journal of Legal Studies* 9, no. 2 (March 1980): 227–42, https://doi.org/10.1086/467637.

[72] Stefan Wintein and Conrad Heilmann, 'Dividing the Indivisible: Apportionment and Philosophical Theories of Fairness', *Politics, Philosophy & Economics* 17, no. 1 (February 2018): 51–74, https://doi.org/10.1177/1470594X17715248.

[73] For a detailed account of the different approaches to solving such puzzles, see: John Broome, 'Fairness', *Proceedings of the Aristotelian Society* 91 (1990): 87–101; James R. Kirkpatrick and Nick Eastwood, 'Broome's Theory of Fairness and the Problem of Quantifying the Strengths of

times the dilemma facing health and reimbursement systems, having a limited budget, and thus having to prioritize between different patient groups, and in so doing availing themselves a host of different metrics, economic cost-effectiveness being only one.

The goal of this chapter is not to solve this puzzle or reconcile law and economics, or fairness with efficiency, once and for all. Rather, the aim is to indicate the relevancy of fairness considerations as a matter of black-letter law, legislative history and sound economics related to certain goods[74] where fairness in the Kantian sense must be defined as equitable exchange on a competitive market when concerning laws governing economic activity.

Relative, subjective and abstract as the concept of fairness might present itself, the entirety of human history and experience is filled with in-depth inquiries on the matter of fairness and justice, alongside philosophical, legal, economic, psychological and even neurological studies in search of what constitutes fair and unfair, respectively.

The concept of fairness and the conceptual understanding of it has rarely been fixed in spatiotemporal terms, nor has it been a fully arbitrary and random process, owning to the fact that despite the manifest subjective character of the concept, there are both universal conceptual approaches and neurological and anthropological evidence for an innate human bias towards fairness, in various forms.[75]

Whether this innate bias is to be defined as a bias towards 'fairness', or rather a bias towards 'unfairness', is also a matter of contention. Further, what consequence, if any, this insight should bear upon the legal discipline in general, and the matter of unfair pricing, is another matter entirely.

Better explained, if the disclosed manifest human biases would rather expose humans as unfair, would this mean that the legal discipline and its rules should also reflect this human innate trait of 'unfairness', and thus, laws should be unfair to reflect human nature, if contrarily the laws should be fair and just to reflect the

Claims', *Utilitas* 27, no. 1 (March 2015): 82–91, https://doi.org/10.1017/S0953820814000259; Christian Piller, 'Treating Broome Fairly', *Utilitas* 29, no. 2 (June 2017): 214–38, https://doi.org/10.1017/S0953820816000303; Hugh Lazenby, 'Broome on Fairness and Lotteries', *Utilitas* 26, no. 4 (December 2014): 331–45, https://doi.org/10.1017/S0953820814000107; Gerard Vong, 'Fairness, Benefiting by Lottery and the Chancy Satisfaction of Moral Claims', *Utilitas* 27, no. 4 (December 2015): 470–86, https://doi.org/10.1017/S0953820815000357; Ben Saunders, 'Fairness between Competing Claims', *Res Publica* 16, no. 1 (February 2010): 41–55, https://doi.org/10.1007/s11158-010-9118-y; Patrick Tomlin, 'On Fairness and Claims', *Utilitas* 24, no. 2 (June 2012): 200–13, https://doi.org/10.1017/S0953820812000143; B. L. Curtis, 'To Be Fair', *Analysis* 74, no. 1 (1 January 2014): 47–57, https://doi.org/10.1093/analys/ant093.

74 Gary Chartier and Jere L. Fox, 'Incommensurable Goods', in *Research Handbook on Natural Law Theory*, ed. Jonathan Crowe and Constance Lee (Edward Elgar Publishing, 2019), 253–66.

75 Mario F. Mendez, 'The Neurobiology of Moral Behavior: Review and Neuropsychiatric Implications', *CNS Spectrums* 14, no. 11 (November 2009): 608–20; M. F. H. Schmidt and J. A. Sommerville, 'Fairness Expectations and Altruistic Sharing in 15-Month-Old Human Infants', *PLoS ONE* 6, no. 10 (2011): e23223.

disclosed human bias towards 'fairness' or the aversion towards 'unfairness'? And again, is it the outcome, or the process, that should be fair and just?

But, a certain progressive coherence in the conceptual framing of fairness and justice seems nonetheless evident, which is why Aristotle, Thomas Aquinas and Immanuel Kant still can be widely read and rediscovered in an age of algorithms-based economy having nothing in common with the features of their time, but for the eternal human ponderings on the matters of justice and fairness. Although, as mankind develops, so do the concepts of fairness and justice it seems, but certain connectivity is indeed discernible. Why is this the case?

One answer could be that the reason must be sought in an innate, deep structure of fairness in humans, holding constant over time and across space, however manifested in a myriad of variations, and even in counterfactuals such as 'unfairness' norms and rules.[76] Another answer could be the social element of humans and human society, with a high degree of 'acquired' sense of fairness reflecting the traditions, culture, religion and so on.[77]

The kidney example can thus serve to illustrate the tension between 'efficiency'-oriented economic analysis of law approaches on the one hand, against law and economics approaches on the other hand, when facing excessive pricing, which is also 'unfair' according to the chosen anchorage points, in that the price has no 'reasonable' relation to its 'economic value', which in turn builds the 'unfairness' element of the analysis.

Thus, one must first uncover what is meant by 'fairness', and alternatively, 'justice', in general, when discussing a general theory of law, or economics. In the words of Alf Ross:

> Like a harlot, natural law is at the disposal of everyone. There is no ideology that cannot be defended by invoking the law of nature. And indeed, how could it be otherwise when the ultimate basis for every natural law is to be found in a private (intra-subjective), direct insight, a self-evident contemplation, an intuition. Cannot my intuition be just as good as yours? Self-evidence as a criterion of truth explains the utterly arbitrary character of metaphysical assertions. It raises them above any form of inter-subjective control and opens the door wide to unbridled fantasy and dogmatism.[78]

Alf Ross defines justice ultimately as a claim for equality and moves on to characterize the different approaches to equality, these defined in turn as: (i) to each according to his merit; (ii) to each according to his contribution; (iii) to each

[76] Robert S. Taylor, *Reconstructing Rawls: The Kantian Foundations of Justice as Fairness* (University Park: Pennsylvania State University Press, 2011).

[77] Garrath Williams, 'Nietzsche's Response to Kant's Morality', *The Philosophical Forum* 30, no. 3 (September 1999): 201–16.

[78] Alf Ross, 'Analysis and Critique of the Philosophy of Natural Law', in *On Law and Justice*, ed. Alf Ross (Oxford University Press, 2019), p. 350.

according to his needs; (iv) from each according to his ability; and finally (v) to each according to rank and station. He then concludes that the formal demand for equality:

> By no means precludes making a difference between persons who are situated in different circumstances. The only requirement is that this difference be motivated by the individuals in question being placed in different classes, according to certain relevant criteria.[79]

Hence, not all should receive equal pay, but only those who do the same kind of work, and not all should receive the same social benefits, but each according to his need, and so on depending on the type of equality notions. Having defined justice as such, Ross concludes that 'the ideal of equality, as such, refers only to the correct application of a general rule', since 'In the very principle of equality, however, there is nothing that would tell us what criteria are the relevant criteria'.[80]

This approach to justice stands in direct opposition to the definition of justice and fairness by Kant, Rawls et alia, who indeed set up various relevant criteria for the general rule and its application, such as the Kantian Categorical Imperative, or the Rawlsian Veil of Ignorance and Original Position. Nonetheless, Ross admits the generality and universality of fairness and justice notions, noting 'Even small children appeal to justice if one child gets a thicker apple slice than the other. It has even been claimed that animals possess an incipient sense of justice. The power of justice is enormous.'[81]

But this begs the answer of how a universal notion, found even in small children not having any exposure to social context, can display such a consistent and 'general' notion of justice, which seems to denote 'to each its own fair share', which by Ross is translated to equal application of the general rule, even if the general rule does not lead to 'to each its own fair share'.

Against this positivist/realist account of justice, disconnecting law from morality, one can invoke the natural law tradition, which rejects such an approach and firmly connects law with morality, beyond matters of design of laws and rule of law. This is the inherent content in the Latin legal maxim of '*lex iniusta non est lex*', reconnecting to the body of Aristotelian thought, which was built upon by Thomas Aquinas, in that:

> Nothing other than an ordinance of reason for the common good, made by the person who has care of the community, and promulgated ... it can be taken to assert that law that is not in the service of the common good is defective as law.[82]

79 Ross, 'Analysis and Critique of the Philosophy of Natural Law', p. 361
80 Ross, 'Analysis and Critique of the Philosophy of Natural Law', pp. 361–62.
81 Ross, 'Analysis and Critique of the Philosophy of Natural Law', p. 348.
82 George Duke, 'The Common Good', in *The Cambridge Companion to Natural Law Jurisprudence*, ed. George Duke and Robert P. George, 1st ed. (Cambridge University Press, 2017), p. 375.

The above division is also relevant when discussing the obligation on the part of the citizens to obey the valid law, and what deviations alongside moral norms can be allowed and accepted in the normative against valid law adopted in a procedurally correct fashion by the competent Sovereign. What of unjust laws, laws that run counter to human rights and the universality of moral concepts? The legal positivist 'pure' answer is simple, in that:

> If the expression 'human rights' is meant to designate rights that human beings would possess and exercise independently of the state, or even against it, then from a strictly positivist point of view the question is easily resolved: there are no human rights.[83]

The positivist position can be contrasted to the concept phrased by Augustine of Hippo, known as St. Augustine, some 1500 years ago, noting that unjust laws are not laws at all.[84] In his approach to legal philosophy by way of semantic deduction of the Latin terms Legere (to read) and Elegere (to select), he concludes that 'lex' constitutes a selection of 'the just', where he distinguishes between the law of Man, which is temporal and might be just or unjust, and the eternal (natural) law, which is inherently just in and of itself.[85]

This view is further endorsed in the legal philosophy of Immanuel Kant as well as John Rawls,[86] and partly characterized in the debate between Ronald Dworkin and H. L. A. Hart, with the former offering a scathing criticism of the latter's positivist approach to law.[87]

Immanuel Kant can be said to have formulated the greatest treatise on the matter, complete with his formulation of the Categorical Imperative, a 'moral law' to be determined by reasoned experience, denoting that all actions should be such that they could be elevated to a universal law.[88]

The Categorical Imperative is the fundamental principle of ethical action in the philosophy of Immanuel Kant, where the criterion of whether an action is morally good is whether it follows a maxim whose validity would be acceptable to everyone,

83 Carlo Invernizzi-Accetti, 'Reconciling Legal Positivism and Human Rights: Hans Kelsen's Argument from Relativism', *Journal of Human Rights* 17, no. 2 (15 March 2018): 216.

84 John Stephens, 'Universal Human Rights and Their Justifiability', *Academia Letters*, 12 August 2021, p. 1.

85 Anton-Hermann Chroust, 'St. Augustine's Philosophical Theory of Law', *Notre Dame Law Review* 5, no. 2 (1950): 292 ff.

86 Immanuel Kant, *The Philosophy of Law: An Exposition of the Fundamental Principles of Jurisprudence as the Science of Right*; 1797, trans. W. Hastie (The Lawbook Exchange – Re-printed from Original by T & T Clark, Edinburgh, 1887, 2010); Taylor, *Reconstructing Rawls*.

87 Dennis Patterson, 'Dworkin's Criticisms of Hart's Positivism', *SSRN Electronic Journal*, 2019.

88 Immanuel Kant, *Grundlegung zur Metaphysik der Sitten* – 1785, 2, durchgesehene Auflage mit aktualisierter Einleitung und Bibliographie, Philosophische Bibliothek, Band 519 (Hamburg: Felix Meiner Verlag, 2016).

at any time and without exception, and whether all agents concerned are treated not as a mere means to an end, but as 'End in Itself' – Zweck an Sich.

The Kantian ethics further elevated the autonomy of will, moral duties and inherent human dignity, which would require ethical beings at times to act against their own preferences, in order to satisfy the moral principles adhered to, in direct opposition to the totality of the utilitarian approaches. Regarding the connection between Kantian ethics and legal philosophy and matters related to economics, as noted by Spector, quoting Valcke:

> Under the influence of natural lawyers, the law of contracts in civil law was shaped around the value of individual autonomy, which makes it recalcitrant to welfare maximization accounts. As Professor Catherine Valcke observes, "[t]he three foundational principles of civilian contract law-freedom of contract, binding force of contract, and consensualism – were directly derived from Kant's postulate of the autonomous will".[89]

The Kantian approach to the philosophy of science has been described as a Copernican turn in philosophy, with the major work being the Critique of Pure Reason.[90] The subjective manifestations of the objective, or 'the original position' in Rawlsian discourse, do not negate the universality of the innate bias towards fairness, nor its capability to be approached from a law and economics perspective. Nevertheless, the Kantian ethics relied on judgement, experience and balancing of obligations in a senseful way. As noted by White:

> This strong role for judgment in balancing duties, applying them to real-world circumstances with context, and choosing actions within the constraints of duty, makes his ethics far less demanding than perfectionist versions of utilitarianism, and closer to classical virtue ethics, with its emphasis on judgment and character.[91]

[89] Horacio Spector, 'Fairness and Welfare from a Comparative Law Perspective', *Chicago-Kent Law Review* 79, no. 2, Symposium: Law and Economics and Legal Scholarship (June 2004): 525.

[90] Immanuel Kant, 'Kritik der reinen Vernunft', zweite Auflage, 1787, §14; German Original of the entire passage:

> Es sind nur zwei Fälle möglich, unter denen synthetische Vorstellung und ihre Gegenstände zusammentreffen, sich aufeinander notwendigerweise beziehen, und gleichsam einander begegnen können. Entweder wenn der Gegenstand die Vorstellung, oder diese den Gegenstand allein möglich macht. Ist das erstere, so ist diese Beziehung nur empirisch, und die Vorstellung ist niemals a priori möglich. Und dies ist der Fall mit Erscheinung, in Ansehung dessen, was an ihnen zur Empfindung gehört. Ist aber das zweite, weil Vorstellung an sich selbst (denn von dessen Kausalität, vermittelst des Willens, ist hier gar nicht die Rede,) ihren Gegenstand dem Dasein nach nicht hervorbringt, so ist doch die Vorstellung in Ansehung des Gegenstandes alsdann a priori bestimmend, wenn durch sie allein es möglich ist, etwas als einen Gegenstand zu erkennen

[91] Mark D. White, 'With All Due Respect: A Kantian Approach to Economics', in *The Oxford Handbook of Ethics and Economics*, ed. Mark D. White, Oxford Handbooks (2019; online edn., Oxford Academic, 13 June 2019), http ://doi.org/10.1093/oxfordhb/9780198793991.013.6.

John Rawls on his part developed the concept of 'Original Position', denoting a situation where the actors were to choose between different theories of justice and fairness regarding the distribution of outcomes. However, the actors were to be curtailed by a 'veil of ignorance', deprived of all knowledge of their own personal characteristics and thus not aware in what position socially and politically they would end up after making the selection.

This would induce the actors towards the most 'rational' choice, which would be a society providing all actors regardless of their 'original position' with the same set of basic freedoms and liberties to be able to pursue the maximum good however conceived by the actors, and equality in education and employment opportunities.[92]

Virtue ethics on the other hand denote the discourse on the virtues of the agents, instead of the consequences of the action, or the volition and intent and duties regarding those actions, reconnecting the theory with Aristotelian ethics as briefly sketched above. As such, and in contrast with the previous approaches, virtue ethics have been described as:

> Whereas consequentialists will define virtues as traits that yield good consequences and deontologists will define them as traits possessed by those who reliably fulfil their duties, virtue ethicists will resist the attempt to define virtues in terms of some other concept that is taken to be more fundamental. Rather, virtues and vices will be foundational for virtue ethical theories and other normative notions will be grounded in them.[93]

Morality can thus be approached via both normative and descriptive routes, which in turn can be divided into group and individual levels, in defining the harm and good. As noted by Ernst-Joachim Mestmäcker in regard to the divide between Kantian[94] and Kelsenian[95] approach to the philosophy of laws:

> Positive law, according to Kant, is a matter of experience and is not necessarily in harmony with the principles of justice. But there are, according to Kant and contrary to Kelsen, principles of justice that are to guide legislation and adjudication. These principles follow from the inalienable rights of citizens against their sovereign to be respected in their dignity and liberty as self-governing individuals. The sovereign may not impose duties upon its subjects which the subjects would not impose upon themselves. This position is explicitly contrary to Hobbes, Bentham and their positivist followers, who find rights against the sovereign self-contradictory. In this respect, Kelsen is not a Kantian. Law, in his theory, is a

[92] John Rawls, *A Theory of Justice*, rev. ed. (Belknap Press of Harvard University Press, 1999).

[93] Glen Pettigrove and Edward N. Zalta, 'Virtue Ethics', *The Stanford Encyclopedia of Philosophy*, Winter Edition 2018, https://plato.stanford.edu/archives/win2018/entries/ethics-virtue/.

[94] Kant, *The Philosophy of Law*.

[95] Hans Kelsen, *Pure Theory of Law* (Lawbook Exchange, Ltd., 2009); German Original: Reine Rechtslehre – Einleitung in die rechtswissenschaftliche Problematik. Hrsg.: Matthias Jestaedt. Studienausgabe der 1. Auflage 1934.

> normative system backed by credible threats of using physical force against the violator of the norm. The norm is a legal norm not because of its content, but because it is created in a certain way, ultimately in a way determined by a presupposed basic norm.[96]

As also noted by Spector regarding the Kantian element of European legal tradition:

> One cannot understand German legal science, for example, without taking into consideration the influence of rationalist natural lawyers like Pufendorf and Kant. In fact, the most abstract part of Savigny's legal theorizing can be regarded as a philosophical theory of civil law. Though all this fascinating intellectual process was over-shadowed by codification, there is no doubt that the philosophical paradigm can be brought to bear on the explanation of civil law. In fact, the philosophical paradigm is inspired in the rationalistic natural law school, which was historically associated with civil law.[97]

Nevertheless, as noted by Saad in reviewing Finn's take on Aquinas, 'the natural law does not entail drawing moral conclusions from facts about human nature. Rather, it means basing moral conclusions on the requirements of practical reason, which process can yield facts about human nature.'[98]

This firmly connects the natural law tradition of St. Augustine and Thomas Aquinas to the Kantian approach (and criticism) of practical reason, deflecting the positivist and realist criticism against natural law as not being able to be approached objectively by way of a scientific falsification process.

The positivist criticism points to the fact that accepting the natural law approach would rule out all other approaches as standing against 'human nature' and 'divinity' or some other abstract deities such as 'morality' and 'universality', thus detracting from the 'rational', 'objective' and 'scientific' element of the theory. The Kantian approach rebuts this criticism, as the 'abstract' is being made 'real' by way of practical reason and universal experience, and thus no longer in the realm of 'divinity'.

Thus, the positivist criticism is not as strong when abstract matters such as fairness are made 'real' by way of practical reason and rational experience in the Kantian sense, making it able to be criticized and analysed in a rational way, where each concept invariably must rely on a validating and 'enabling' normative underpinning beyond the object of the study at hand.

Beyond the legal-philosophical perspective, there is support for this Kantian approach in the black-letter law of 'unfair pricing', not being defined further, and in the jurisprudence attempting to make the abstract 'real', by way of the United

[96] Mestmäcker, A *Legal Theory without Law*.

[97] Spector, 'Fairness and Welfare from a Comparative Law Perspective'.

[98] Toni C. Saad, 'The Cambridge Companion to Natural Law Jurisprudence', *The New Bioethics* 23, no. 3 (2 September 2017): 264.

Brands test targeting 'unfair in itself' and 'unfair when compared', offering some anchorage points for the fairness analysis to be undertaken, to remove it from the subjective realm and make it approachable, comparable and criticisable, by way of legal-dogmatic and teleological methods.

Hence in the Kantian discourse, it is the structured reasoning acting as a producer of experience, rather than merely a passive recipient of perception, which invariably must be organized. In so doing, Kant uses the legal discipline as an analogy, as one account of his analogy explains: 'Judges or legislators can be models for the critique because they can evaluate conflicting arguments or rulings and try to solve the dispute without being forced to choose between the claims of the parties.'[99]

This point reconnects also to the matter of vagueness in law as opposed to legal certainty, where a great body of thought in both philosophies of law and language has been devoted to the subjects, with some thinkers elevating the need, value and importance of 'vagueness in law', while others have castigated vagueness as being in direct conflict with the inherent value of legal certainty.

The division between Hart and Dworkin is apparent once more, in that the former elevated the importance of language philosophy in order to solve the problems created by 'vagueness' in law, while the latter forwards a theory of concepts and conceptions, where concepts denote the general terms of the debate, while conceptions translate to a competing understanding of the concepts. According to this view by Dworkin, judges would need to unlock the conception behind the concept which best explains it, while Hart disagrees and forwards discretion into the hand of judges.[100]

Fairness and justice may not be universally defined, nor so applied, but the notion of fairness and justice nevertheless forms the existential basis of all human societies throughout recorded history, if one approaches the legal science from a Kantian legal philosophy perspective. As noted by Baumard and Sperber:

> At first sight, moral judgments greatly differ across cultures, suggesting that human morality may be based on radically different systems of values. Evolutionary considerations on the bases of human cooperation suggest, however, that there must be evolved dispositions that make this cooperation sustainable. There are competing views regarding what these dispositions might be, an altruistic disposition to act for the benefit of the group even at an irredeemable cost to oneself, a mutualistic disposition to act and to expect others to act fairly, or some combination of both.[101]

Some may invoke, on the other hand, that the human nature and the innate nature of human societies are ones of self-interest, focusing on the immediate group

[99] Sofie C. Møller, 'The Court of Reason in Kant's Critique of Pure Reason', *Kant-Studien* 104, no. 3 (January 2013): 319.

[100] Timothy Endicott, 'Vagueness and Law', in *Vagueness: A Guide*, ed. Giuseppina Ronzitti (Dordrecht: Springer Netherlands, 2011), 182 ff.

[101] Nicolas Baumard and Dan Sperber, 'Evolutionary and Cognitive Anthropology', in *A Companion to Moral Anthropology*, ed. Didier Fassin (Chichester: John Wiley & Sons, Ltd, 2012), 611–27, https://doi.org/10.1002/9781118290620.ch34.

one belongs to, and ones of cruelty and injustices to the 'other', however defined. Much of this line of argument is construed, supposedly, on a 'Darwinian' notion of human evolution, where the process moves alongside 'value-free' and ' inexorable', almost automated meta-development, conditioned towards 'survival of the fittest'.

Indeed, the notion of Homo Oeconomicus, its implications for law and economics and the invocation of Darwin have been a matter of much heated debate, regarding individuals, 'markets' and political economy at large.[102] However, Darwin himself did not ascribe to such notions and indeed supported 'objective morality' alongside evolutionary ethics, and included in his theory of evolution the evolution of 'values' as such. Hence, Darwin noted that:

> There can be no doubt that a tribe including many members who, from possessing in a high degree the spirit of patriotism, fidelity, obedience, courage, and sympathy, were always ready to give aid to each other and to sacrifice themselves for the common good, would be victorious over most other tribes; and this would be natural selection.[103]

Adam Smith, being a moral philosopher, on his part did devote attention to moral philosophy in general, and the philosophy of laws, in particular, as developed in his Theory of Moral Sentiments.[104] For Smith, the basis of rights is a counterfactual account of injury, with Smith juxtaposing this against positive virtues, nevertheless adhering to the 'innate' and universal nature of justice, stating:

> The rules of justice are accurate in the highest degree, and admit of no exceptions or modifications but such as may be ascertained as accurately as the rules themselves, and which generally, indeed, flow from the very same principles with them.[105]

[102] Ryan Fortsont, 'Problems with Richard Posner's the Problematics of Moral and Legal Theory', *William Mitchell Law Review* 27, no. 4 (2001): 2345–74; Ronald Dworkin, 'Darwin's New Bulldog', *Harvard Law Review* 111, no. 7 (May 1998): 1718, https://doi.org/10.2307/1342478; Geoffrey M. Hodgson, 'Darwinism in Economics: From Analogy to Ontology', *Journal of Evolutionary Economics* 12, no. 3 (1 July 2002): 259–81, https://doi.org/10.1007/s00191-002-0118-8; Naomi Beck, 'Social Darwinism and Market Morality: A Modern-Day View', in *The Cambridge Handbook of Evolutionary Ethics*, ed. Michael Ruse and Robert J. Richards (Cambridge University Press, 2017), 58–71, https://doi.org/10.1017/9781316459409.005.

[103] Charles Darwin, 'The Descent of Man and Selection in Relation to Sex', *The Descent of Man and Selection in Relation to Sex*, 1847; Michael Ruse, 'Darwinian Evolutionary Ethics', in *The Cambridge Handbook of Evolutionary Ethics*, ed. Michael Ruse and Robert J. Richards (Cambridge University Press, 2017), 89–100, https://doi.org/10.1017/9781316459409.007; William J. FitzPatrick, 'Why Darwinism Does Not Debunk Objective Morality', in *The Cambridge Handbook of Evolutionary Ethics*, ed. Michael Ruse and Robert J. Richards (Cambridge University Press, 2017), 188–201, https://doi.org/10.1017/9781316459409.014.

[104] Adam Smith, 'The Theory of Moral Sentiments. To Which Is Added a Dissertation on the Origin of Languages', London: printed for A. Millar, A. Kincaid and J. Bell in Edinburgh; and sold by T. Cadell in the Strand, MDCCLXVII [1767], The third edition.

[105] Smith, 'Theory of Moral Sentiments', III, 6, § 10; cited in Knud Haakonssen, *The Science of a Legislator: The Natural Jurisprudence of David Hume and Adam Smith*, 1st ed. (Cambridge University Press, 1981), 86, https://doi.org/10.1017/CBO9780511628276.

Adam Smith worked partly in line with the virtue ethics of Plato and Aristotle but showed highly 'Kantian' tendencies in connecting the reason–experience–induction dots, which were later completed by Kant. As Smith explains:

> It is by reason that we discover those general rules of justice by which we ought to regulate our actions: and it is by the same faculty that we form those more vague and indeterminate ideas of what is prudent, of what is decent, of what is generous or noble, which we carry constantly about with us, and according to which we endeavour, as well as we can, to model the tenor of our conduct. The general maxims of morality are formed, like all other general maxims, from experience and induction.[106]

Thus, the grandfather of political economy seems to realize the inherent importance of fairness in relation to efficiency and its universal implication.[107] As such, both Smith and Darwin recognized not only the existence, but also the importance, of moral bonds and virtues in regard to human society. Nevertheless, Bentham broke with this tradition in forwarding utility as the only relevant and rational yardstick, dismissing philosophical notions of fairness and justice as superfluous. This utilitarian normative approach also dominates the economic analysis of law in the tradition of Posner et alia.[108] As noted by Joe Sery in regard to Posner:

> Posner situates his project as the most reasonable, the most useful, and the most efficient approach to law. In order to do so, Posner articulates a connection between economics and common sense, suggesting the former is simply a codified version of the latter. Good judgment requires common sense, which is economic judgment by his definition.[109]

One could here invoke the criticism mounted by Immanuel Kant in his seminal work Kritik der reinen Vernunft,[110] where he methodically dismantled the rationalist and positivist argument in regard to what can be known to man and how, exposing the biases and conditions for arguments in regard to rationality. Indeed, as noted by Kant regarding the legal principle and maxim of pacta sunt servanda:

> From what has been said, it is evident that all Duties, merely because they are duties, belong to Ethic; and yet the Legislation upon which they are founded is not

[106] Adam Smith, 'Part VII. Of Systems of Moral Philosophy', in *The Theory of Moral Sentiments; or, an Essay towards an Analysis of the Principles by Which Men Naturally Judge Concerning the Conduct and Character, First of Their Neighbors, and Afterwards of Themselves, to Which Is Added a Dissertation on the Origin of Languages (New Ed.)*, ed. Adam Smith (London: Henry G Bohn, 1861), 389–538, https://doi.org/10.1037/14198-007.

[107] Manfred J. Holler and Martin Leroch, 'Efficiency and Justice Revisited', *European Journal of Political Economy* 26, no. 3 (September 2010): 311–19, https://doi.org/10.1016/j.ejpoleco.2009.11.007.

[108] Posner, 'Utilitarianism, Economics, and Legal Theory'.

[109] Joe Sery, 'Richard Posner and the Rhetoric of (Economic) Common Sense', *Common Law Review* 16, no. 1 (2017): 3.

[110] Immanuel Kant, 'Kritik der reinen Vernunft', Riga, 1781, Johann Friedrich Hartknoch Verlag.

> on that account in all cases contained in Ethics. On the contrary, the Law of many of them lies outside of Ethics. Thus Ethics commands that I must fulfil a promise entered into by Contract, although the other party might not be able to compel me to do so. It adopts the Law 'pacta sunt servanda,' and the Duty corresponding to it, from Jurisprudence or the Science of Right, by which they are established. It is not in Ethics, therefore, but in Jurisprudence, that the principle of the Legislation lies, that 'promises made and accepted must be kept'.[111]

The fundamental difference in the normative approach to political economy between a utilitarian view and a Kantian view is thus equally manifest as irreconcilable. The Kantian approach is found essential for the purposes of the present inquiry on 'unfair pricing in European competition law', when determining the conditions for knowledge and the boundaries between what can objectively be known about things and concepts in and of themselves regardless of subjective conceptions of those matters and things (das Ding an sich v. das Ding als es erscheint).[112]

This fundamental separation of things as they 'appear' to us, on the one hand, and how things 'are in themselves', materially a distinction between 'sensibility' and 'understanding', differ not only in form, but in kind. The concept of 'thing in itself', or in the present inquiry, 'unfair in itself', amounts to something imaginable and researchable.[113] It is an 'abstract' made 'real'.

The reality of the concept nevertheless need not be theoretically demonstrable – what belongs to it can also be laid bare in practical sources of knowledge[114] and by way of accumulated experience along universal lines.[115] This also reconnects to the philosophy of Dworkin and the criticism of legal positivism of Hart et alia,[116] distinguishing between legal rules and legal principles. As noted by Bellamy:

[111] Immanuel Kant, Metaphysik der Sitten, 1797; German Original reads 'Hieraus ist zu ersehen, daß alle Pflichten bloß darum weil sie Pflichten sind, mit zur Ethik gehören; aber ihre Gesetzgebung ist darum nicht allemal in der Ethik enthalten, sondern von vielen derselben außerhalb derselben. So gebietet die Ethik, dass ich eine in einem Vertrage getane Anheischigmachung, wenn mich der andere Teil gleich nicht dazu zwingen könnte doch erfüllen müsse: sie nimmt das Gesetz (pacta sunt servanda) und die diesem korrespondierende Pflicht aus der Rechtslehre als gegeben an. Also nicht in der Ethik, sondern im Jus liegt die Gesetzgebung, das angenommene Versprechen gehalten werden müssen'; Translation from: The Philosophy of Law, an exposition of the Fundamental Principles of Jurisprudence as the Science of Right; Immanuel Kant, translation from German by W. Hastie and B. D. Edinburgh (T & T Clark, 1887), available at https://socialsciences.mcmaster.ca/econ/ugcm/3ll3/kant/sciencelaw.pdf.

[112] Immanuel Kant, Kritik der reinen Vernunft (Johann Friedrich Hartknoch Verlag, 1781); see also Rudolf Eisler, 'Das Ding an Sich', in Kant-Lexikon, available at: www.textlog.de/32917.html.

[113] Kianzad, 'Did the Danish Supreme Court Give the Fashion Industry the Kantian Boot?', 2020, 6.

[114] The paragraph is partly an excerpt from Behrang Kianzad, 'Did the Danish Supreme Court Give the Fashion Industry the Kantian Boot?' *GRUR International* 70, no. 2 (February 2021): 159–63.

[115] Watkins, 'Kant on the Distinction between Sensibility and Understanding'.

[116] Matthew H. Kramer, 'The Legal Positivism of H.L.A. Hart', *SSRN Electronic Journal*, 2019.

> Unlike rules, principles – such as 'no person may profit from his or her wrong' – do not simply apply or not apply. Rather, they operate as reasons that can be accorded different degrees of 'weight' according to both the case at hand and interplay with other principles.[117]

The (in)congruence of abstract and real and their interdependent possibility conditions lies at the heart of the analysis when approaching the law and economics theories. Thus, the wording of 'unfair in itself' regarding pricing by a dominant undertaking in United Brands has confounded those departing from the neoclassical-welfarist economic analysis of law. Nevertheless, the legal discipline is both capable of and obliged to work in line with such abstractions as a matter of tradition and principle, with Kant laying some of the foundations of the European philosophy of law, which came to exert an enduring influence on many European legal scholars and constitutions.[118]

The influence of Kantian and natural law tradition on European legal development and scholarship diminished due to the emergence of Legal Positivist and Legal Realist schools, but natural law had a tremendous impact on the ethical and philosophical roots of European codification of ancient legal and moral norms.[119]

The ratio legis of pacta sunt servanda is thus a moral one, not an economic one, although the concept entails immense relevance regarding economic efficiency.[120] That being said, the question remains how to integrate fairness considerations in pricing and constraints on profit making as evidenced by behavioural economics in competition law assessment when applied to the present context of 'unfair prices' as an exploitative abuse under Article 102a TFEU.

In so doing, one need not endorse the totality of the natural law approach to legal philosophy, morality and jurisprudence in order to recognize the limits of legal positivism concerning the relevancy of moral principles and collective preferences related to incommensurable goods (also called public goods, merit goods, etc.), beyond a 'mechanical jurisprudence'. Nonetheless, for example, the Scandinavian Legal Realism tradition has consistently resisted approaches by other social sciences, including economics, to form a more central role in the jurisprudence.[121]

[117] Richard Bellamy, 'Ronald Dworkin, Taking Rights Seriously', in *The Oxford Handbook of Classics in Contemporary Political Theory*, ed. Jacob T. Levy (Oxford University Press, 2015).

[118] G. Dietze, 'Natural Law in the Modern European Constitutions', *The American Journal of Jurisprudence* 1, no. 1 (1 January 1956): 73–91; The paragraph is an excerpt from Kianzad, 'Did the Danish Supreme Court Give the Fashion Industry the Kantian Boot?'

[119] Richard Tuck, 'The "Modern" Theory of Natural Law', in *The Languages of Political Theory in Early-Modern Europe*, ed. Anthony Pagden, 1st ed. (Cambridge University Press, 1987), 99–120; Antonio Padoa-Schioppa, *A History of Law in Europe: From the Early Middle Ages to the Twentieth Century*, trans. Caterina Fitzgerald, 1st ed. (Cambridge University Press, 2017); David Ibbetson, *Natural Law in Early Modern Legal Thought*, ed. Heikki Pihlajamäki, Markus D. Dubber and Mark Godfrey, vol. 1 (Oxford University Press, 2018).

[120] Mestmäcker, *A Legal Theory without Law*.

[121] Göran Skogh, 'Law and Economics in Sweden', *International Review of Law and Economics* 11, no. 3 (December 1991): 319–24.

Hence, granting a free pass to, for example, unfair pricing of, for example, incommensurable goods would contradict the totality of the philosophy of Thomas Aquinas and Scholastic thought, which was consequential in its pre-Kantian form, which by Kant came to be categorized as 'Metaphysik der Sitten'[122] and also formed the basis of the Kantian Legal Philosophy.[123]

Writings which equate the Scholastic just price theory with marginalist and neoclassical 'price obtainable in a free market' are a misreading of the just price tradition, and more espousing a Roman notion of the going market price under normal conditions.

Whether the only 'scientific' way to analyse the competitive process is neoclassical, marginalist and welfarist economics, or if there are other 'scientific' ways in economics to analyse the competitive process, or if the economic discipline can be said to adhere to 'scientific' principles in the same vein as physics or biology or even other social sciences[124] ties into the grand debate on the claims and assumptions of the said schools, which have garnered much criticism ever since the inception of the disciplines,[125] but is partly outside of the focus of the current inquiry.

Looking at experimental and behavioural economics science, there is ample evidence that both firms and people take fairness seriously also regarding economic decisions. The implication of fairness concerns for Game Theory and Equilibrium was already highlighted by Rabin in 1993, noting: 'People like to help those who are helping them, and to hurt those who are hurting them . . . one should care not solely about how concerns for fairness support or interfere with material efficiency, but also about how these concerns affect people's overall welfare.'[126]

Earlier still, the seminal work by Kahneman, Knetsch and Thaler in 1986,[127] which is of great importance in the context of the present work on excessive pricing, demonstrated that people are wary of pricing unfairness, where prior prices of the undertaking served as one benchmark for such fairness considerations. Just a year earlier in 1985, the non-maximizing tendencies (framed around non-rationality) and their implications for rationality and overall economic equilibrium were also investigated by Akerlof and Yellen.[128]

[122] Immanuel Kant, 'Metaphysische Anfangsgründe der Rechtslehre', as first part of 'Metaphysik der Sitten', 1797, Köningsberg, Nicolovious; this article has used Kant, *The Philosophy of Law*.

[123] Kant, *The Philosophy of Law*.

[124] Uskali Mäki, 'The Dismal Queen of the Social Sciences', in *Fact and Fiction in Economics*, ed. Uskali Mäki, 1st ed. (Cambridge University Press, 2002), 3–32, https://doi.org/10.1017/CBO9780511493317.002.

[125] Sery, 'Richard Posner and the Rhetoric of (Economic) Common Sense'.

[126] Matthew Rabin, 'Incorporating Fairness into Game Theory and Economics', *The American Economic Review* 83, no. 5 (December 1993): 1281–302.

[127] Kahneman et al., 'Fairness as a Constraint on Profit Seeking'.

[128] George A. Akerlof and Janet L. Yellen, 'Can Small Deviations from Rationality Make Significant Differences to Economic Equilibria?', *The American Economic Review* 75, no. 4 (1985): 708–20.

Building on prior work by Arthur Okun in 1981,[129] who had also observed that firms do not maximize prices despite facing excess demand (such as new models of automobiles or tickets for events, which ex ante are known to generate excess demand), Kahneman et alia investigated the fairness perceptions regarding (unfair) pricing.

The observed behaviour in the experimental games and the asserted human bias towards fairness and equity was by some labelled as altruism; however, the work by Fehr and Schmidt showed that this was not the case, as noted: 'Altruism is consistent with voluntary giving in dictator and public good games. It is, however, inconsistent with the rejection of offers in the ultimatum game, and it cannot explain the huge behavioural differences between public good games with and without punishment. It also seems difficult to reconcile the extreme outcomes in market games with altruism.'[130]

They further showed that the selfish behaviour could also be observed, alongside the fairness considerations, and it was the setting of the game or market overall, which also exercised a considerable impact, concluding:

> For example, in a market game with proposer or responder competition, it is very difficult, if not impossible, for fair players to achieve a 'fair' outcome. Likewise, in a simultaneous public good game with punishment, even a small minority of selfish players can trigger the unravelling of cooperation. Yet, we have also shown that a minority of fair-minded players can force a big majority of selfish players to cooperate fully in the public good game with punishment.[131]

In summary, as noted by Maurice Stucke, forwarding a behavioural approach to competition law and policy, ' ... antitrust policy is not divorced from subjective well-being. First, competition does not exist independently of legal and informal norms. Competition is defined in part by the prevailing legal and informal social, ethical, and moral norms',[132] thus underscoring the Kantian argument made in this paper that competition law must invariably rely on a ratio legis, preventing of undue wealth transfer, with fairness being a building block in both law and policy.

IV WEALTH MAXIMIZATION, PARETO AND KALDOR–HICKS: AN OPTIMAL ANTITRUST POLICY?

One of the main proponents of economic analysis of law, Richard Posner, did indeed attempt at framing wealth maximization as a value, which led to responses

129 Arthur Okun, *Prices and Quantities : A Macroeconomic Analysis* (Washington, DC: Brookings Institution, 1981).

130 Ernst Fehr and Klaus M. Schmidt, 'A Theory of Fairness, Competition, and Cooperation', *The Quarterly Journal of Economics* 114, no. 3 (1999): 817–68.

131 Fehr and Schmidt, 'A Theory of Fairness, Competition, and Cooperation'.

132 Stucke, 'OECD Hearing on Competition and Behavioural Economics'.

by Dworkin, Kronman et alia, a debate that still today is highly relevant, even more so when attempting at defining ratio legis of competition law in general, and prohibition of undue profiteering in particular.

The present article opts to recount this historic debate between Posner, and Dworkin/Kronman in-depth, as their debate frames much of the contentions that still are prevalent today.

Notably, and most relevant for the present work, Posner sought[133] to reconnect principle of Pareto optimality and personal autonomy to Kantian ethics, although, as will be demonstrated, this was as equally unsuccessful as misguided attempt. Kantian ethics, and most importantly, Kantian philosophy of law, run counter to the Posnerian ditto. This section will outline the Posner argument, before turning to the criticism and rebuttal by Dworkin,[134] Kronman[135] and Mestmäcker.[136]

Posner framed wealth maximization as the best approximation of justice, combining both utilitarian as well as Kantian approaches, though not having any of the weaknesses of both schools. Posner forwarded wealth maximization as an:

> ethically attractive objective to guide common law adjudication, rather than social choice generally ... wealth maximization, especially in the common law setting, derives support from the principle of consent that can also be regarded as underlying the otherwise quite different approach of Pareto ethics ... the political counterpart of consent-consensus-explains the role of wealth maximization in shaping the common law ... it is also possible to locate Pareto ethics in a different philosophical tradition from the utilitarian, in the tradition, broadly Kantian, which attaches a value over and above the utilitarian to individual autonomy. One ethical criterion of change that is highly congenial to the Kantian emphasis on autonomy is consent. And consent is the operational basis of the concept of Pareto superiority.[137]

Furthermore, in relation to his understanding of Kant, Posner noted:

> Suppose we consider consent an ethically attractive basis for permitting changes in the allocation of resources, on Kantian grounds unrelated to the fact that a consensual transaction is likely to increase the happiness at least of the immediate parties to it.[138]

To recapitulate regarding Pareto and Kaldor–Hicks efficiency mentioned by Posner:

> A 'Pareto optimal' situation is one where no one can be made better off without at least one person being made worse off ... Under Kaldor–Hicks efficiency (also

[133] Posner, 'The Ethical and Political Basis of the Efficiency Norm in Common Law Adjudication'.
[134] Dworkin, 'Is Wealth a Value?'
[135] Kronman, 'Wealth Maximization as a Normative Principle'.
[136] Mestmäcker, *A Legal Theory without Law*.
[137] Posner, 'The Ethical and Political Basis of the Efficiency Norm in Common Law Adjudication'.
[138] Posner, 'The Ethical and Political Basis of the Efficiency Norm in Common Law Adjudication'.

known as 'potential Pareto' efficiency), a move is Kaldor–Hicks superior if those who have benefited by some change could compensate those left worse off in a way that, after the (hypothetical) compensation, those worse off would now be at least indifferent, and those made better off would still be left better off.[139]

However, regarding the Kaldor–Hicks test, as noted by Kronman, there is no set guarantee that compensation will occur, and if this is the case, the principle runs counter to the Kantian approach, since the moral principle would have been violated, and thus 'for a Kantian, the Kaldor–Hicks has no significance'.[140]

Posner further presupposed voluntary exchange as one foundational criterion (manifestly different than in the present inquiry regarding life-saving, essential medicines, elevating matters of nullity of choice, indispensability, payer insensitivity, etc.). As explained by Kronman:

> Voluntary agreements have a special claim to recognition since the limit the actions of those who are parties to them in the only way that is consistent with their autonomy as persons. This idea is a familiar and important one and lies at the heart of contrarian tradition from Hobbes to Rawls.[141]

As noted by Kronman, while Posner seeks to frame wealth maximization as manifestly different than 'efficiency' regarding design of legal rules, they are indeed the one and same:

> But the voluntary transfers that Posner uses as illustrations also satisfy the Pareto principle and it could be argued that it is this which gives them their appeal. In fact, if one considered only Posner's examples, it might seem that wealth maximization and efficiency are different names for the same thing. Posner denies however, that these two principles are equivalent.[142]

Posner sought to frame wealth maximization as rather 'uncontroversial' as opposed to maximizing utility, as:

> (most of us prefer more to less of it for ourselves, and for our community), while wealth remains vastly easier than utility to measure, to compare, and to sum ... Economic approaches in general, and wealth maximization in particular, give the highest value to voluntary market transactions (as such transactions, almost by definition, make all parties to the transaction better off), and, in circumstances where voluntary transactions are not possible or practical, wealth maximization tries to determine what choices people would have made ('hypothetical consent').[143]

139 Brian H. Bix, 'Moral Philosophy and Law and Economics', in *The Oxford Handbook of Law and Economics: Volume 1: Methodology and Concepts*, ed. Francesco Parisi, vol. 1 (Oxford University Press, 2017), https://doi.org/10.1093/oxfordhb/9780199684267.013.022.

140 Kronman, 'Wealth Maximization as a Normative Principle'.

141 Kronman, 'Wealth Maximization as a Normative Principle'.

142 Kronman, 'Wealth Maximization as a Normative Principle'.

143 Bix, 'Moral Philosophy and Law and Economics'.

The choice of Pareto principle is the Posnerian rejection of unchecked utilitarianism, which does not accord any value to whose happiness has been increased and along what routes, thus building the moral element of Posnerian theory, where wealth maximization would act as a check on increasing utility. Posner further applied the theory to accident law, approached via negligence and liability routes, a matter that leads the present analysis a stray and has been addressed by others in other settings.

Starting with the framing the positing of wealth maximization as a value as opposed to egalitarian and equitable outcomes, Dworkin in his response noted:

> Wealth maximization, as defined, is achieved when goods and other re-sources are in the hands of those who value them most, and someone values a good more only if he is both willing and able to pay more in money (or in the equivalent of money) to have it. An individual maximizes his own wealth when he increases the value of the resources he owns; whenever he is able, for example, to purchase something he values for any sum less than the most he would be willing to pay for it.[144]

Indeed, as noted by Brain Bix:

> wealth maximization's analyses in terms of ability to pay create well-known paradoxical outcomes: for example, it seems that one would increase social wealth by giving the prized possessions of a poor person to her rich neighbour, even if the possessions meant everything to the poor person and almost nothing to the rich neighbour, simply because the rich person was able and willing to pay more to own those possessions than the poor person would be able to pay.[145]

As noted by Kronman in his response to Posner regarding positing of wealth as a normative value, thus lacking the drawbacks of utilitarian as well as Kantian (in Posner definition Pareto Superiority) approaches:

> Wealth maximization is not a happy compromise between utilitarianism and Pareto superiority, a compromise which somehow retains the best and eliminates the worst features of these other two principles. If anything, just the opposite is true: wealth maximization exhibits the vices of both and the virtues of neither.[146]

As Kronman explains, regarding Posner's approach to wealth maximization:

> the constraint imposed by the Pareto principle reflects a concern to protect the autonomy of individua persons; the principle of wealth maximization, on the other hand, constrains utilitarianism only because it defines wealth in terms of ability and willingness to pay . . . Wealth maximization is not utilitarianism limited by a respect for rights: if it is a species of utilitarianism at all, wealth maximization is

[144] Dworkin, 'Is Wealth a Value?'.

[145] Bix, 'Moral Philosophy and Law and Economics'.

[146] Kronman, 'Wealth Maximization as a Normative Principle'.

> utilitarianism constrained by a respect for something which is neither rights nor utility, something of uncertain and, as Ronald Dworkin has shown, dubious value.[147]

Most notably, as Posner frames Kaldor–Hicks approach to be the correct principle underpinning wealth maximization discourse in opposition to the Pareto Principle, as noted by Kronman:

> someone who believes that the Pareto principle moral ideal, but is unworkably demanding if applied to individual transactions, can never have a reason to soften it in the Kaldor-Hicks test, although he may wish to soften the expanding the notion of actual compensation, as Posner confuses this point in his ... article by first equating compensation with the Kaldor-Hicks test and then arguing that wealth maximisation can be defended by widening the idea of compensation. If wealth maximisation is equivalent to Kaldor-Hicks, Posner's argument about ex ante compensation is beside the point, since the Kaldor-Hicks test does not require that actual compensation be made. If, on the other hand, Posner believes, as his argument suggests, that wealth maximization requires actual as opposed to merely potential compensation, his concept of wealth understood as a normative ideal is indistinguishable from the Pareto principle.[148]

Indeed, many years have passed since the debate between Posner, Kronman and Dworkin, and even Posner today seems to have accepted some of the critique, although some scholars continue to 'argue that wealth maximization, or some other form of efficiency, is a worthy objective, they concede that it is merely one objective among many, and it may need to be traded off against fairness and justice and other objectives.'[149]

The proponents of this supposedly possible 'trade-off' between fairness and efficiency, as also addressed previously in the section on this matter, include Shavell and Kaplow. The famous assertion by welfare economists Louis Kaplow and Steven Shavell that 'any non-welfarist policy violates the Pareto-principle'[150] is only relevant if one adheres to and accepts the basic criterion set up by the Pareto principle, ignoring the fact that a Kantian, rights-based legal system does and cannot adhere to this core principle, but to principles of justice and fairness, in and of itself as the legitimizing basis of 'whole edifice'. The volition inherent in legal rules matters, not only their fair or unfair consequence, and as noted:

[147] Kronman, 'Wealth Maximization as a Normative Principle'; referring to Dworkin, 'Is Wealth a Value?'

[148] Kronman, 'Wealth Maximization as a Normative Principle'.

[149] Referring to Richard A. Posner, *Economic Analysis of Law*, 9th ed., Aspen Casebook Series (New York: Wolters Kluwer Law & Business, 2014).

[150] Kaplow and Shavell, 'Fairness versus Welfare: Notes on the Pareto Principle, Preferences, and Distributive Justice'.

> Pareto efficiency does not mean that a society is organized justly, however justice may be defined. This relates to the fact that a particular Pareto-efficient production combination can only be defined if the initial endowment of members of society with production factors or property rights is known.[151]

The Pareto principle forwarding 'welfare' in turn defined as the individual's utility is further conditioned on two limbs – the first centred on the truthfulness of the assumption, that is, individuals care most about their own utility; and secondly how 'welfare' is defined beyond 'utility'. As it has been demonstrated by Fleurbaey, Tungodden and Chang:

> Kaplow and Shavell ... base their crucial assumption on an "observation" that welfarism and the Pareto indifference condition are equivalent. This claim is surprising because it is well known among social choice theorists that no Pareto condition by itself entails welfarism.[152]

The argument that some policies grounded on fairness tend to make everyone worse off is only truthful and relevant if one agrees with the assumption of what being worse off means, on both individual and societal level. The focus being on individual well-being, and social welfare defined as the sum of the individual well-being, leads to a circular reasoning in regard to why legal rules do not emphasize the individual well-being as the sole object of the laws. Kaplow and Shavell reduce collective and societal fairness considerations to a matter of individual taste, stating '... individuals have a taste for a notion of fairness, just as they may have a taste for art, nature, or fine wine.'[153]

The problematic nature of such claim is rather self-evident, since most human beings can do without art, fine wine or hike in wonderous natural surroundings, but few would survive without a just and fair society based on inalienable rights regardless of physical power, gender, material wealth and so on. Although there is a myriad of individual, subjective 'tastes' regarding fine wine, art and hikes in the nature, we have substantial empirical, historical and normative findings pointing to an innate, universal and 'objective' sense of fairness in human beings.[154]

This might in certain situations lead to everyone being 'worse off' if defined per efficiency route, but is not in and of itself an argument against framing of fairness as the core underlying rationale in regard to codified laws.

[151] Mathis, *Efficiency Instead of Justice?*, p. 35.

[152] Marc Fleurbaey, Bertil Tungodden and Howard F. Chang, 'Any Non-welfarist Method of Policy Assessment Violates the Pareto Principle: A Comment', *Journal of Political Economy* 111, no. 6 (December 2003): 1382–85, https://doi.org/10.1086/378533.

[153] Kaplow and Shavell, 'Fairness versus Welfare', 982.

[154] M. Hsu, C. Anen and S. R. Quartz, 'The Right and the Good: Distributive Justice and Neural Encoding of Equity and Efficiency', *Science* 320, no. 5879 (23 May 2008): 1092–95, https://doi.org/10.1126/science.1153651.

To accept the assertion by Shavell and Kaplow would be akin to granting slavery a free pass if it would fit the 'individual tastes', where abolishing slavery would violate the cherished Pareto principle, since it most definitely would make the slave owners worse off. As stated by Amartya Sen, 'A state in which some people are starving and suffering from acute deprivation while others are tasting the good life can still be Parcto optimal.'[155]

This point reconnects with the next section, where surge pricing or excessive pricing of essential items during COVID-19 surely could be seen as Pareto optimal, but nevertheless against legislative intentions behind the prohibition, in turn reconnecting with strongly held preferences related to fairness in pricing, no less during such crisis.

V UNFAIR PRICING DURING COVID-19 AS A PROXY TO TEST FAIRNESS VERSUS EFFICIENCY THEOREM

Reports of dramatic price hikes for face masks, hand sanitizers, hospital gowns and so on emerged in virtually all countries affected by the COVID-19 pandemic. The responses in various jurisdictions to such instances of price gouging were rather divergent in nature, ranging from introducing price regulation, enforcing excessive pricing laws set against introduced maximum prices and using pre-crises prices as benchmark, to a more 'nudging' attitude adopted in European Union (EU).

An empirical inquiry was sent to all European competition authorities, following EU-wide reports of 'excessive pricing' and 'price gouging'.[156] The results of the inquiry will be compared with the responses in the United States (US) later in this section.

The empirical inquiry consisted of three questions sent to all European Competition Authorities addressed to the respective official email in June 2020, followed up in August and September, with a deadline for responses set in October 2020. The questions sent were as follows:

- How many excessive price complaints/cases have the Authority received connected to COVID-19 crisis?
- Has the Authority already opened any proceedings or does the Authority intend to do so?
- Other general comments in the context of excessive pricing and COVID-19 crisis.

155 Amartya Kumar Sen, *Resources, Values, and Development* (Harvard University Press, 1984), p. 95.

156 Behrang Kianzad, 'Excessive Pricing during the COVID-19 Crisis in the EU: An Empirical Inquiry', *Concurrences* 2021, no. 1 (15 February 2021): 250–59.

A *Unfair Pricing during COVID-19: EU*

Responses were received from twenty-three of the total twenty-seven Competition Authorities contacted, with Greece, Romania, Slovakia and Hungary abstaining. As the confidentiality rules regarding investigations, received complaints and system for registration of complaints differ considerably between the Member States, not all responding countries provided quantitative data, with some indicating complaints received/cases pursued, but not being able to specify further.

As some Member States organized Competition Authority and Consumer Protection Authority in one body, whereas some have a strict division between these bodies, any interpretation of the results must take account of this institutional divide, with excessive pricing/price gouging complaints in some instances thus not being reported to the Competition Authority.

The methodological challenges detailed above affect the data received considerably, cautioning against broad interpretations of the results, as the inquiry at best could offer a bird's-eye view and indicate some potential trends, convergences and divergences.

Competition Authorities around EU (such as Greece,[157] France,[158] Luxembourg,[159] Portugal,[160] Spain[161] and the United Kingdom (UK)[162]) at an early stage of the pandemic through public announcement made their intention known that they would closely monitor pricing behaviour regarding supply of some essential goods in high demand due to COVID-19.[163]

This was part of a joint effort by European Competition Network (ECN), which issued a joint statement in regard to applicability of competition rules during the pandemic, noting 'At the same time, it is of utmost importance to ensure that products considered essential to protect the health of consumers in the current situation (e.g. face masks and sanitising gel) remain available at competitive prices.

[157] Hellenic Competition Authority, www.epant.gr/enimerosi/deltia-typou/item/831-deltio-typou-antiantagonistikes-praktikes-se-eidikes-koinonikes-kai-oikonomikes-synthikes.html.

[158] French Competition Authority, www.lefigaro.fr/flash-eco/coronavirus-l-autorite-de-la-concurrence-surveille-les-eventuels-prix-abusifs-20200316.

[159] Luxemburg Competition Authority, https://concurrence.public.lu/fr/actualites/2020/coronavirus-responsabilite-entreprises.html.

[160] Portuguese Competition Authority, www.concorrencia.pt/vEN/News_Events/Comunicados/Pages/PressRelease_202003.aspx.

[161] Spanish Competition Authority, www.cnmc.es/sites/default/files/editor_contenidos/Notas%20de%20prensa/2020/20200312_NP_medidas_excepcionales_eng.pdf.

[162] UK Competition and Market Authority, 'CMA Approach to Business Cooperation in Response to Coronavirus (COVID-19)', www.gov.uk/government/publications/cma-approach-to-business-cooperation-in-response-to-covid-19.

[163] Christopher Thomas, Raphael Fleischer, Christian Ritz and Stefan Kirwitzke (Hogan Lovells), 'COVID-19 and Competition Law – Companies Must Not Quarantine Competition Law Compliance', 2 April 2020, Competition Policy International, www.competitionpolicyinternational.com/covid-19-and-competition-law-companies-must-not-quarantine-competition-law-compliance/.

The ECN will therefore not hesitate to take action against companies taking advantage of the current situation by cartelising or abusing their dominant position.'[164]

Some of the Member States opted to introduce price regulations, beyond issuing warnings at the onset of the crisis. This was the case in, for example, France, regulating the price of hydro-alcoholic sanitizers – 50 ml bottles are priced at € 2, 100 ml bottles are priced at € 3, 300 ml bottles are priced at € 5, and a litre of sanitizer costs € 15. It also fixed the price of surgical masks at € 0.95.[165]

This was the case also in Romania, where the Romanian competition authority announced that, should actions under its competences prove insufficient to limit price increases to acceptable levels, additional measures foreseen in statute – including introducing price caps – might be necessary.[166] Other countries such as Malta also introduced such pricing regulations, as during the peak of the crisis there were complaints regarding the prices of masks, particularly disposable masks, which from inspections carried out in retail pharmacies by Officers from the Consumer Affairs Office were being sold in the range of €1.25 to €2.25. A price order was issued establishing the maximum price at which these masks could be sold.[167] Similar measures were introduced in Croatia.

In Italy, facing numerous complaints in regard to price gouging, the Italian Competition Authority (ICA) commenced investigations into the pricing of a private health and laboratory group for serological tests to identify COVID-19 antibodies.[168] Italian Competition Authority also initiated proceedings against eBay and Amazon for misleading claims and price increases in the sale of masks, hand sanitizers and other pharmaceutical products.[169] There are further a range of investigations ongoing at ICA.

In Spain, the Spanish Market and Competition Authority (CNMC) as of 2 June 2020 had received more than 500 complaints during the two month the mailbox for complaints was set up, further announcing investigations into certain sectors such as funeral services, hydro-alcoholic gels and financial lending.[170]

164 European Competition Network, 'Antitrust: Joint Statement by the European Competition Network (ECN) on Application of Competition Law during the Corona Crisis'.

165 OECD, 'Exploitative Pricing in the Time of COVID', 2020, 15, www.oecd.org/competition/Exploitative-pricing-in-the-time-of-COVID-19.pdf.

166 OECD, 'Exploitative Pricing in the Time of COVID'; Romanian National News Agency, www.agerpres.ro/economic-intern/2020/03/25/chritoiu-daca-produsele-sanitare-nu-se-ieftinesc-vom-lua-masuri-de-urgenta-precum-rechizitionarea-sau-plafonarea-preturilor–473985.

167 Times of Malta, 'Price of Disposable Masks, Face Shields, Capped', 3 May 2020, https://timesofmalta.com/articles/view/price-of-disposable-masks-face-shields-capped.789815.

168 OECD, 2020, Box 3, www.agcm.it/media/comunicati-stampa/2020/4/DC9877.

169 OECD, 2020, Box 5, www.agcm.it/media/comunicati-stampa/2020/3/PS11716-PS11717.

170 Spanish Market and Competition Authority, CNMC, www.cnmc.es/novedades/2020-06-02-la-cnmc-recibe-mas-de-500-quejas-y-consultas-traves-del-buzon-habilitado.

In Greece, the Hellenic Competition Council (HCC) launched an inquiry into possible price increases and output restrictions of healthcare materials and other products, by way of requests for information to a large number of companies active in the production, import and marketing of healthcare products, in particular surgical masks and disposable gloves, as well as other products such as antiseptic wipes and antiseptic solutions.[171] Hellenic Competition Council employed an algorithmic approach in regard to analysis of the data, finding some prices as outliers.

Similarly in Sweden, the Swedish Competition Agency (SCA) upon receiving news of price hikes, although no formal complaints, sent requests to a range of providers. The news concerned a spike of 900 per cent[172] in pricing of filtering half masks, protective suits, certain protective goggles and visors as well as surface and hand sanitizers by one of the Government's major suppliers who cited force majeure as a reason for the price increase within the framework agreement. Both the Governmental Purchasing Center, which coordinates the government framework agreements, and SKL Kommentus Purchasing Center, which coordinates for Sweden's municipalities and regions, had approved the price increase.

The SCA conducted a study throughout the spring of 2020 regarding pricing of hand sanitization products due to media reports of significantly raised prices within a central framework agreement. The preliminary findings of the study showed an initial spike in demand, in combination with increased production costs, resulting in a significant but temporary rise in prices. Production of hand sanitization products increased throughout most of the month of April, after which the curve had flattened. Prices thus returned to a normal level within the framework agreement in May, and there were no indications of continued concerns regarding excessive pricing of such products either within the framework agreement or in a more general sense.[173]

Many other countries report complaints received (Estonia, Portugal, Malta, etc.) but could not provide further quantitative data.[174]

B *Unfair Pricing during COVID-19: US*

As excessive pricing in and out of itself does not constitute a federal antitrust liability, or so goes the dominant US interpretation by Federal Trade Commission and

[171] OECD 2020, Box 3, Hellenic Competition Council, 'Investigation in Healthcare Materials', Press Release, 21 March 2020, https://epant.gr/en/enimerosi/press-releases/item/840-press-release-investigation-in-healthcare-materials.html.

[172] Dagens Nyheter, 'Increases the Price of Vital Products by over 900 Percent', 3 April 2020, www.dn.se/nyheter/sverige/hojer-priset-pa-livsviktiga-produkter-med-914-procent/.

[173] Swedish Competition Agency, Communication to Author on file, dated 18 June 2020.

[174] See Annex 1 for the full results of the empirical inquiry.

Department of Justice (DOJ) (with others contesting this interpretation),[175] price gouging was the focal point for US policy.

As many states already had price gouging statutes in place,[176] most complaints were voiced to state attorneys general (AGs). State laws prohibit price gouging along the lines of sale of an 'essential commodity' at an 'unconscionable' price, some requiring a 'triggering event', such as war, pandemic, natural disaster and so on while others do not raise such requirement, some (like California, District of Colombia and New Jersey)[177] capping the price increase at 10 per cent during a pandemic or an emergency. Some states opted to introduce emergency legislation and executive orders, such as the case of Michigan introducing enhanced restrictions on price gouging.[178]

In a letter to all United States Attorneys as well as heads of departments and law enforcement agencies, Attorney General Barr voiced concerns about the possibility of price gouging and the need to be vigilant:

> We will not tolerate bad actors who treat the crisis as an opportunity to get rich quick. We are beginning to receive reports of individuals using the crisis to hoard vital medical items and then make inappropriate, windfall profits at the expense of public safety and the health and welfare of our fellow citizens. Hoarding and price gouging activities inhibit the government, health care professionals, and the public from implementing critical measures to save lives and mitigate the spread of the virus.[179]

The DOJ's National Center for Disaster Fraud (NCDF) complaint website offered the possibility of bringing instances of price gouging and hoarding to the attention of the authorities.[180]

The Secretary of Health and Human Services issued a notice designating some essential items as exempt from hoarding or being sold at exorbitant prices, including personal protective equipment (PPE), including masks, shields and gloves, respirators, ventilators, drug product with active ingredient chloroquine phosphate or

[175] Harry First, 'Excessive Drug Pricing as an Antitrust Violation', *Antritrust Law Journal* 82, no. 2 (2019): 59; Ramsi A. Woodcock, 'The Antitrust Duty to Charge Low Prices', *Cardozo Law Review* 39 (2018): 1741.

[176] The Food Industry Association, FMI, 'State Price Gouging Laws', www.fmi.org/docs/default-source/gr-state/price-gouging-state-law-chart.pdf?sfvrsn = 9058b75c_2.

[177] NBC News, 'States Push Price-Gouging Measures as Coronavirus Fuels Consumer Fears', 20 March 2020, www.nbcnews.com/politics/politics-news/states-push-price-gouging-measures-coronavirus-fuels-consumer-fears-n1163846..

[178] State of Michigan, Office of the Governor, Executive Order No. 2020-8, Enhanced Restrictions on Price Gouging, https://content.govdelivery.com/attachments/MIEOG/2020/03/15/file_attachments/1401335/EO%202020_8%20Emergency%20Order%20.pdf.

[179] Office of the Attorney General, 'Memorandum for All Heads of Department Components and Law Enforcement Agencies All United States Attorneys', 24 March, www.justice.gov/file/1262776/download.

[180] Department of Justice's National Center for Disaster Fraud (NCDF) Complaint Website, www.justice.gov/disaster-fraud/ncdf-disaster-complaint-form.

hydroxychloroquine, sterilization services, disinfecting devices and medical gowns or apparel.[181]

These actions relied on the Presidential Executive Order in regard to price gouging and hoarding, which was issued by President Donald J. Trump on 26 March 2020,[182] thus making hoarding or price gouging of some designated essential a misdemeanour punishable by up to one year in prison and a fine of up to USD 10,000.[183] The DOJ) further announced its commitment to pursue fraudulent activity and price gouging of items such as PPE and ventilators.[184]

Indeed, there were many thousand instances[185] of both hoarding and price gouging reported to the authorities already in March 2020, regarding both online and retail trade, where Amazon on its part issued a statement in regard to removing 500,000 items off its marketplace and banning 3,900 sellers for price gouging.[186]

Nevertheless, as per a recent report by Public Citizen, numerous examples of price increases were found on the e-commerce platform regarding essential products, some as much as 1,000 per cent over the expected price, as Amazon publicly blamed so-called third-party sellers for price increases while continuing to allow third-party sellers to increase their prices.[187] In New York, a retailer accused of hoarding and price gouging of essential protective equipment like masks and hand sanitizers settled a price gouging case brought against it by donating more than $450,000 worth of PPE.[188]

There are many reports of fines being awarded to some of those found liable of breaching state price gouging laws, such as in the case of New Jersey.[189] As there

[181] Department of Health and Human Services, Notice of Designation of Scarce Materials or Threatened Materials, Subject to COVID-19 Hoarding Prevention Measures under Executive Order 13910 and Section 102 of the Defense Production Act of 1950, www.justice.gov/file/1264276/download.

[182] Executive Order 13910 of March 23, 2020, Preventing Hoarding of Health and Medical Resources to Respond to the Spread of COVID-19, www.federalregister.gov/documents/2020/03/26/2020-06478/preventing-hoarding-of-health-and-medical-resources-to-respond-to-the-spread-of-covid-19.

[183] OECD, 2020, Box 5; 50 U.S.C. § 4513.

[184] OECD, 2020, Box 5, www.justice.gov/opa/pr/justice-department-cautions-business-community-against-violating-antitrust-laws-manufacturing.

[185] Politico, 'State AGs Join DOJ, FTC, Congress to Fight Price-Gouging', 26 March 2020, www.politico.com/newsletters/morning-tech/2020/03/26/state-ags-join-doj-ftc-congress-to-fight-price-gouging-786404.

[186] Amazon, 'Price Gouging Has No Place in Our Stores', 23 March 2020, https://blog.aboutamazon.com/company-news/price-gouging-has-no-place-in-our-stores.

[187] Alex Harman /Public Citizen, 'Prime Gouging – How Amazon Raised Prices to Profit from the Pandemic', 9 September 2020, www.citizen.org/article/prime-gouging/.

[188] Pix11.com, 'LI Retailer to Donate $450,000 Worth of PPE to Settle Price gouging Case: Officials', 26 September 2020, https://pix11.com/news/coronavirus/li-retailer-to-donate-450-000-worth-of-ppe-to-settle-price-gouging-case-officials/.

[189] South Jersey Times, 'N.J. Businesses Fined for Price Gouging during Coronavirus Pandemic and Lying about Antibody Tests', www.nj.com/coronavirus/2020/09/nj-businesses-fined-for-price-gouging-during-coronavirus-pandemic-and-lying-about-antibody-tests.html.

now exists a federal route by way of the Executive Order one might foresee cases being pursued at the federal level as well, depending on the willingness of the agencies to pursue such cases.

C *Analysis of the US and EU Responses to Price Gouging during COVID-19*

As a departing point of analysis of competition law dynamics in times of pandemic, a surge in demand combined with shortages in supply invariably causes the prices to rise, sometimes dramatically so.

Nevertheless, due to pandemic-specific conditions (lockdown nullifying mobility and choice of consumers, the necessity of face masks, hand sanitizers and disinfectants due to public orders and overall measures to combat pandemic), the legal 'fairness' rules are much more in focus of the attention of authorities, as opposed to normal times, where competitive market forces are presumed (at least in theory) to act as price arbiters.

Several European authorities could indeed make use of price regulation measures introduced by governments (and in the South African cases, the price regulations were also used in the competition law context); others used pre-emptive measures such as sending letters to different sector players urging them to abstain from profiteering.

Where investigations were opened in the EU, they assumed the character of investigating and monitoring price levels, and as price levels subsequently had decreased, the authorities opted not to pursue the cases further, for example, Sweden and UK, respectively, among others.

The institutional divide between competition authority on the one hand and consumer protection authority on the other hand complicates the analysis, as the kind of 'price gouging' in question in some jurisdictions is seen as 'unfair pricing practices' to be dealt with consumer protection authority, sometimes as a result of the governmental decrees issued in relation to the pandemic.

The results further indicate that Member States where the competition authorities in the past had pursued high-profile excessive pricing cases (notably UK and Italy) and early on in the set-up different reporting mechanism in regard to alleged excessive pricing practices, were also among those who had received the most complaints. This correlation of past, high-profile cases and increased reporting of such practices during the COVID-19 pandemic does not amount to a causal relationship based on the limited scope of the inquiry, but is one plausible explanation regarding the manifest divergence in number of complaints.

Generally, most competition authorities reaffirmed their commitment to pursue excessive pricing cases both during the pandemic and beyond. Nevertheless, one authority seemed to suggest that pricing levels were outside of the 'remit' of competition law, a position that, if interpreted broadly, might conflict with the letter of law as explicitly prohibiting 'unfair pricing' as an anti-competitive practice in and of itself. How the 'unfair' and 'excessive' price is to be determined does not affect the validity nor applicability of the law. Same holds true regarding competition authorities mandate and strict obligation to intervene, as the assessment is an entirely different, empirical matter, to be separated from the normative de lege lata of the prohibition.

The string of excessive pricing cases in the pharmaceutical sector is but one example of the increased activities on part of European Competition Authorities. The inter-twined regulation and competition law approach is also seen in the energy sector,[190] on both Commission and Member State level.[191]

Some European Competition Authorities raised the question of dominance, as per the letter of the law and settled jurisprudence of Court of Justice of the European Union (CJEU), where unfair and excessive pricing are attributable to a position of dominance. This is in line with some part of economic theory of harm[192] where high prices are not able to be maintained (at least in the long term) due to competitive market forces, and thus are only able to be maintained by way of a quasi-monopolist position, many times in markets protected by some barriers to entry, or other manifest market deficiencies.

The demand-side in-elasticity which captured consumer segments and indispensable products, especially during a pandemic, complicate this general analysis. The European Competition law approach to excessive pricing during a pandemic lacks the 'price gouging' tool available in US on the state level[193] (and on the federal level by way of presidential order during the COVID-19 crisis)[194] and as seen in the case of South Africa,[195] where the dominance is not required per se, and pre-crisis prices are

[190] See also the EU Commission Gazprom decision: European Commission, C(2018) 3106 final, Upstream gas supplies in Central and Eastern Europe, 24 May 2018, paras. 62–63, https://ec.europa.eu/competition/antitrust/cases/dec_docs/39816/39816_10148_3.pdf, 2020. Regarding enforcement on Member State level, see German Bundeskartellamt enforcement activities regarding water and energy prices, e.g.: www.bundeskartellamt.de/SharedDocs/Meldung/EN/Pressemitteilungen/2015/19_10_2015_WSW.html.

[191] Marco Botta and R. Karova, 'Sanctioning Excessive Energy Prices as Abuse of Dominance: Are the EU Commission and the National Competition Authorities on the Same Frequency?', in *Abuse of Dominance in EU Competition law*, ed. Pier Parcu and Giorgio Monti (Edward Elgar Publishing, 2017).

[192] Atkinson and Audretsch, 'Economic Doctrines and Approaches to Antitrust'.

[193] Price Gouging Laws per State, see: www.ncsl.org/research/financial-services-and-commerce/price-gouging-state-statutes.aspx.

[194] Executive Order 13910 of March 23, 2020, Preventing Hoarding of Health and Medical Resources to Respond to the Spread of COVID-19.

[195] South Africa Disaster Management Regulation of March 18 2020, published in Government Notice 318 of Government Gazette no 43107, where paragraph 10(6) authorized the minister of Trade and Industry to, inter alia, issue directions to protect consumers from excessive, unfair, unreasonable or unjust pricing of goods and services during the state of national emergency; The subsequent Consumer Protection Regulations issued by the Minister of Trade and Industry were published on 19 March 2020, The Consumer and Customer Protection and National Disaster Management Regulations and Directions GN R350 GG 43116, 19 March 2020 (consumer protection regulations).

used as comparative benchmark. This is also the case in some US states where a 10 per cent increase is seen as prima facie presumption creative liability.

Nevertheless, in the case of pandemic, even a local shop is able to exercise dominance, due to reasons above, let alone a main supplier to a governmental procurement central. Without a solid investigation alongside settled assessment metrics (cost-plus and pre-crisis prices being the preferred methods in this context), the risk that certain anti-competitive, exploitative pricing practices are given an ex post free pass is evident.

Pre-crisis prices were utilized as benchmark in both US[196] and in South Africa, although the two most recent South African COVID-19 cases[197] demonstrate diverging interpretations of how the metes and bounds of 'excessiveness' should be defined. South Africa introduced measures in regard to declaration of national emergency and its consequences for pricing in March 2020 as aforementioned. The regulations targeted material price increases, which did not correspond to increases in the costs of supplies, or increased the net margins or mark-ups above average margin or mark-up prevailing in the three-month period prior to 1 March 2020.

As seen from the global antitrust responses, the matter of price gouging and 'fairness' was squarely in focus for authorities, although their responses varied greatly, some opting to give a free pass to manifest instances of price increases as prices had subsequently fallen to normal levels, while other authorities took exception with even a local shop raising prices.

Apart from some ideologues, few would argue that the optimal policy would be to let prices rise to whatever levels market would bear in the midst of a global pandemic, famine, war or other similar crisis.

Although it can be argued from marginalist and welfarist positions[198] that the most efficient way to allocate resources would be free pricing even during such crisis, that price gouging laws perpetuate the empty shelves syndrome and so on, other values

[196] Executive Order 13910 of March 23, 2020, Preventing Hoarding of Health and Medical Resources to Respond to the Spread of COVID-19, www.federalregister.gov/documents/2020/03/26/2020-06478/preventing-hoarding-of-health-and-medical-resources-to-respond-to-the-spread-of-covid-19; Many states already had 'price gouging' laws in place, where an increase of 10 per cent of price during a crisis compared to pre-crisis prices is prohibited.

[197] South African Competition Tribunal, 'Babelegi Guilty of Excessive Pricing during COVID-19 Crisis, Fined R76K', 1 June 2020, www.comptrib.co.za/info-library/case-press-releases/babelegi-guilty-of-excessive-pricing-during-covid-19-crisis-fined-r76k; Case No: CR008Apr20, Competition Commission of South Africa v. Dis-Chem Pharmacies Limited, http://blogs.sun.ac.za/ccle/files/2020/07/Public-Reasons-CC-v-Dischem-CR008Apr20.pdf.

[198] Michael Giberson, 'The Problem with Price Gouging Laws', *Regulation – Cato Institute*, September 2011, www.cato.org/regulation/spring-2011/problem-price-gouging-laws; Rik Chakraborti and Gavin Roberts, 'How Price-Gouging Regulation Undermined COVID-19 Mitigation: Evidence of Unintended Consequences', *Working Paper – The Center for Growth and Opportunity at Utah State University*, March 2021, www.thecgo.org/wp-content/uploads/2021/03/How_Price_Gouging_Regulation_Undermined_COVID-19_Mitigation.pdf.

beyond efficiency make themselves known by way of law and logic during such crisis, which is why the legislature since time immemorial has opted to preserve the prerogative of price intervention.

VI MAKING MARKETS WORK FOR PEOPLE: A NEO-KANTIAN APPROACH TO ANTITRUST

As a normative starting point regarding the division between fairness and efficiency, prevention of undue wealth transfer sits at the core of competition policy, as noted:

> At the highest level, competition policy may indeed be theorised as an institution aimed at reconciling individual and collective rationality, i.e., each entrepreneur's efforts to maximise profits, on the one hand, and the welfare of society at large, on the other hand. To that extent, fair competition may entail that there are boundaries to profit maximisation strategies beyond which these are considered socially unacceptable by reference to certain standards of justice as articulated in anti-trust principles and applied by means of an array of legal tests and enforcement rules.[199]

Furthermore, the notions of fairness invariably affect not only the political sphere, but indeed the economic sphere, where ' . . . as a matter fact, widely held notions of fairness, that are identifiable at the micro level, have macro effects not only in the social and political systems, but even in the economy'.[200]

One practical example illuminating the normative tensions detailed above is the matter of excessive pharmaceutical pricing, which by way of COVID-19 crisis[201] have become yet more elevated on the global stage.[202] The COVID-19 crisis provided an apt example of revisiting centuries-old legal-economic debates such as the tension between efficiency and fairness.

Recent years had also before the COVID-19 crisis noted a surprising tide of competition law enforcement against unfair pricing and dramatic price hikes of mostly generic pharmaceutical products in EU.[203] This is partly surprising, given the

[199] Damien Gerard, 'Fairness in EU Competition Policy: Significance and Implications', *Journal of European Competition law & Practice* 9, no. 4 (1 April 2018): 211–12, https://doi.org/10.1093/jeclap/lpy027.

[200] Carl Davidson, Steve Matusz and Doug Nelson, 'Fairness and the Political Economy of Trade', *World Economy* 29, no. 8 (2006): 989–1004, https://doi.org/10.1111/j.1467-9701.2006.00832.x; see also Fehr and Schmidt, 'A Theory of Fairness, Competition, and Cooperation', 817–68; See also G. A. Akerlof and R. A. Shiller, *How Human Psychology Drives the Economy, and Why It Matters for Global Capitalism* (Princeton: Princeton University Press, 2009).

[201] Willem H. Boshoff, 'South African Competition Policy on Excessive Pricing and Its Relation to Price Gouging during the COVID-19 Disaster Period', *South African Journal of Economics*, 29 September 2020, https://doi.org/10.1111/saje.12268.

[202] Nature Editorial, 'A Patent Waiver on COVID Vaccines Is Right and Fair', 25 May 2021.

[203] David W. Hull and Michael J. Clancy, 'The Application of Competition Law to the Pharmaceutical Sector in the European Union', *Journal of European Competition Law & Practice* (22 January 2021): lpaa099, https://doi.org/10.1093/jeclap/lpaa099.

doctrinal adversity[204] in many works on the topic of unfair and excessive pricing in European competition law, relying on a marginalist and neoclassical approach to the goals of antitrust.

The enforcements have relied on the wording of Article 102a TFEU prohibition of 'unfair pricing' by a dominant undertaking. Such examples can be found in Italy, UK and Denmark[205] but also on the DG Competition level[206], as well as numerous investigations and bills being introduced in the US targeting drug prices, following a string of House and Senate hearings.

Pharmaceutical 'unfair' pricing seems indeed to occupy a unique position in this debate as many of the neoclassical core assumptions are not as suitable as they might be in other markets. The demand-side in-elasticity and the charging of prices to health systems rather than individual 'customers', in combination with the fog surrounding actual marginal costs and R&D spending compared to actual profits, complicate the matter further.

Add to this the competition through innovation[207] dimension and the Standard Equilibrium Model and static competition are all but fit for the purpose of analysing market dynamics and competition law rationales in this sector. There is further a regional as well as global push towards 'fair pricing' of medicines by EU, World Health Organization and the Organisation for Economic Co-operation and Development (OECD).[208]

At the same time, recent decades of behavioural, experimental and neuro-economics have cast doubt on the robustness of some of the core assumptions of the neoclassical school in regard to rationality, self-interest and whether or not economics should and could accommodate 'fairness' perspectives beyond the strict Walrasian, marginalist division.

As aforementioned, traditionally there has been a vigorous opposition to competition law enforcement against perceived unfair/excessive pricing, an opposition relying on marginalist, neoclassical economics models, arguing that market

[204] David S. Evans and A. Jorge Padilla, 'Excessive Prices: Using Economics to Define Administrable Legal Rules', *Journal of Competition Law & Economics* 1, no. 1 (1 January 2005): 97–122; Peter Davis and Vivek Mani, 'The Law and Economics of Excessive and Unfair Pricing: A Review and a Proposal', *The Antitrust Bulletin* 63, no. 4 (December 2018): 399–430

[205] B. Kianzad and T. Minssen, 'How Much Is Too Much? Defining the Metes and Bounds of Excessive Pricing in the Pharmaceutical Sector', *European Pharmaceutical Law Review* 2, no. 3 (2018): 133–48, https://doi.org/10.21552/eplr/2018/3/5.

[206] European Commission, 'European Commission – Press Release – Antitrust: Commission Opens Formal Investigation into Aspen Pharma's Pricing Practices for Cancer Medicines – IP/17/1323', 15 May 2017.

[207] Richard Schmalensee and David Evans, 'Some Economic Aspects of Antitrust Analysis in Dynamically Competitive Industries', *NBER Working Paper Series Working Paper* 8268 (2001).

[208] World Health Organization, 'Report on the Fair Pricing Forum' (Geneva, 2017).

dynamics are much more well-suited for the task of solving the problem of excessive pricing, if at all excessive pricing is perceived as a problem in and of itself.[209]

Furthermore, it has been argued that 'fairness is not an economic concept',[210] which is why both EU Commission and mainstream body of economists have been sceptical towards vigorous enforcement against unfair prices. It has also been asserted that the risk of Type I errors as well as harm to innovation and 'chilling innovation' supersedes the evils of excessive pricing in the form of monopolistic rents, at least in the short run, a claim that is empirically unsubstantiated, as the few studies point in the other direction.[211]

This opposition and reluctance seem now to have been cast aside by the highest appeal courts in Italy, UK and Denmark, as even European Commission has embarked on its first-ever excessive pricing case in the pharma sector, with Aspen offering commitments to lower prices throughout EU by 73 per cent,[212] an unthinkable approach just ten years ago as the 'more economic approach' was making headlines.[213] This trend, which never had any real success in EU jurisprudence,[214] now seems to have been abandoned even by the European Commission, which puts the emphasis on 'fairness' and 'making markets work for people', also in the realm of Big Tech, beyond Pharma.[215]

This new approach to the ability of markets translates to legal implications in the analysis, affecting everything from relevant market definition to the matter of dominance. As per OECD guidance on the matter, 'In some cases it may be preferable to look for direct evidence of exploitation of market power (for example, abnormally high prices or profits) rather than focus on market definition.'[216] Looking at the recent law and policy developments at both the EU Commission

[209] For a review of arguments for and against excessive pricing enforcement, see: Jenny, 'Abuse of Dominance by Firms Charging Excessive or Unfair Prices', 5–70.

[210] Jenny, 'Abuse of Dominance by Firms Charging Excessive or Unfair Prices'.

[211] Kiu Tay-Teo, André Ilbawi and Suzanne R. Hill, 'Comparison of Sales Income and Research and Development Costs for FDA-Approved Cancer Drugs Sold by Originator Drug Companies', *JAMA Network Open* 2, no. 1 (4 January 2019): e186875.

[212] European Commission, Press Release 'Commission Seeks Feedback on Commitments Offered by Aspen to Reduce Prices for Six Off-Patent Cancer Medicines by 73% to Address Commission's Concerns over Excessive Pricing', IP/20/1347, 14 July 2020, https://ec.europa.eu/commission/presscorner/detail/en/IP_20_1347.

[213] Pablo Ibáñez Colomo, 'Whatever Happened to the "More Economics-Based Approach"?', *Journal of European Competition Law & Practice* 11, no. 9 (11 December 2020): 473–74.

[214] Wouter P. J. Wils, 'The Judgment of the EU General Court in Intel and the So-Called "more Economic Approach" to Abuse of Dominance', *World Competition* 37, no. 4 (2014): 405–34.

[215] European Commission, 'Press-Release – Antitrust: Commission Consults Stakeholders on a Possible New Competition Tool – IP/20/977', 2 June 2020, https://ec.europa.eu/commission/presscorner/api/files/document/print/en/ip_20_977/IP_20_977_EN.pdf.

[216] R. Anderson et al., 'Abuse of Dominance', in R. S. Khemani et al., A Framework for the Design and Implementation of Competition Law and Policy (OECD, Paris), www.oecd.org/regreform/sectors/aframeworkforthedesignandimplementationofcompetitionlawandpolicy.htm; cited in Case No. CR008Apr20, Competition Commission of South Africa v. Dis-Chem Pharmacies Limited, para. 103.

level and the Member State level, one might note an overall trend regarding relaxing of the dominance test. One such example is the introduction of a new competition tool by the European Commission in regard to digital markets and the related activities at the Member State level.[217]

Another example is the update of some of Member State laws concerning the concept of 'economic dependence' informing the dominance test.[218] A further example is the German 'Anzapfverbot' regarding companies in relative market power exhausting the economic resources of dependent counterparts without any objective justification. This would describe a situation where an undertaking is economically dependent if in a vertical relationship realistic alternatives to the relatively dominant undertaking are lacking, where the dominant undertaking issues demands without objective justifications.[219]

Engaging with the core arguments against inclusion of 'fairness' in a coherent legal-economic discourse on competition law is not only warranted by the compounding weight of behavioural, experimental and neuro-economic evidence in regard to the human bias towards fairness – it is mainly motivated by the true nature of competition law and economics, if one is to take the 'law' as seriously as the latter part of 'economics'. As aptly noted by Mestmäcker, there is a manifest risk that without taking inherent legal values, informed by ethics, into account, the discipline risks translating into a 'legal theory without law'.[220]

Thus, the recent tide of excessive pricing cases in EU, after the concept's untimely death being proclaimed by the 'mainstream' law and economics in the past decades, is a testament to the vitality of the notion of 'fairness' when approaching political economy in general and 'unfair pricing' and undue profiteering in particular. This matter becomes yet more relevant in the present context where profiteering historically has been frowned upon, namely during crisis such as the COVID-19 pandemic. The ratio legis of the prohibition has little to do with 'hipster antitrust', if one by this labelling understands a radical use of competition law in regard to redistribution. The ratio legis is evident from the human bias towards fairness in pricing and transactions.[221]

[217] European Commission, Impact Assessment for a Possible New Competition Tool, https://ec.europa.eu/competition/consultations/2020_new_comp_tool/index_en.html.

[218] See Press Release by Belgian Competition Authority, 'Entry into Force of Abuses of Economic Dependence', 13 August 2020, www.abc-bma.be/sites/default/files/content/download/files/20200813_compresse_32_abc.pdf.

[219] Bundeskartellamt, Press Release, 'Federal Court of Justice Confirms Key Points of Bundeskartellamt's Landmark Decision concerning Unfair Trading Practices', 29 January 2018, www.bundeskartellamt.de/SharedDocs/Meldung/EN/Pressemitteilungen/2018/29_01_2018_EDEKA_BGH_Entscheidung.html; jsessionid = CCDD4796C0FFDCD9F88788B8D163F5B3.2_cid371?nn = 3591568.

[220] Mestmäcker, A *Legal Theory without Law*.

[221] Erik Eyster, Kristof Madarasz and Pascal Michaillat, 'Pricing under Fairness Concerns', *Journal of the European Economic Association* (29 August 2020), jvaa041.

The fact that core presumptions and assumptions of neoclassical economics are far from solid is hardly newsworthy in 2022; nevertheless, not even the famed prediction and explanation power of said theories stands serious scrutiny, demonstrated by dramatic rise of mark-ups,[222] market power and inequality.[223]

What is newsworthy is the fact that Nobel laurates such as Joseph Stiglitz describe ideas that have dominated competition law and policy of the last forty years as 'widely discredited within the economics profession, but whose influence within antitrust law remains significant'. Another Nobel Prize Laurate in Economics, Paul Krugman, have gone so far to liken engaging with the said discredited ideas 'arguing with zombies', referring to dead ideas pretending to be perfectly alive and well. A third Nobel Prize Laurate in Economics, Robert Solow, describes the idea of dynamic stochastic general equilibrium as not even passing a basic 'smell test', accusing its proponents to 'either have stopped sniffing or to have lost their sense of smell altogether'.[224]

The adherence by an economist, many economists or even all economists to this or that strand of economics is irrelevant for the legal discipline in the normative. This irrelevance has not so much to do with the manifestly erroneous assumptions and presumptions forwarded as 'conventional wisdom' or 'mainstream economics', but with the inherent tension between this 'mainstream economics' and 'mainstream law', the latter never having endorsed 'efficiency' as an overarching value over administration of fairness and justice. As noted by Joseph Stiglitz:

> This fallacious idea is that you can separate equity from efficiency. It's sometimes referred to as the Second Welfare Theorem. We now know that those two issues can't be neatly separated in that way.[225]

This 'fallacious idea' of creating a strict dichotomy between total welfare and consumer welfare as regards the normative goals of intellectual property rights and competition law, respectively, needs indeed to be revisited and re-evaluated, as it affects both the holistic as well as the specific analysis of what these laws ought to be.

Nevertheless, fairness is not only able to function as an economic concept, it is as noted by Adam Smith 'what holds the whole edifice together',[226] thus building the basis of the 'political' in political economy, the normative theory informing later formalistic and positivist approaches to the discipline. The claim that 'fairness is not

[222] De Loecker et al., 'The Rise of Market Power and the Macroeconomic Implications'.

[223] Dabla-Norris et al., 'Causes and Consequences of Income Inequality'; Sean F. Ennis, Pedro Gonzaga and Chris Pike, 'Inequality: A Hidden Cost of Market Power', *Oxford Review of Economic Policy* 35, no. 3 (11 July 2019): 518–49.

[224] Robert Solow, 'Prepared Statement – Building a Science of Economics for the Real World' (House Committee on Science and Technology Subcommittee on Investigations and Oversight, US House of Representatives, 20 July 2010).

[225] 'Joseph Stiglitz: Competition Policy, the Need for a More Nuanced View', Interview, Concurrences, No. 2-2019.

[226] Smith, 'The Theory of Moral Sentiments', p. 148.

an economic concept'[227] does simply not stand to 'serious scrutiny',[228] as it is a matter of choice and values inherent in rejecting fairness as being an incalculable externality,[229] to be dealt with by other disciplines. Indeed, an immense body of economics has concerned itself with different nuances of fairness and equity.[230]

If one would be inclined to provide a general principle regarding fairness in law and economics, highly related to the conceptual interpretation of 'fairness in pricing' norm, while mimicking the famous Pareto principle, such general principle could be postulated as:

> 'Any competitive outcome which is not fair is not efficient, and any fair outcome which is not efficient is not competitive.'

Posner could agree with the above, if fairness could be defined as meaning 'wealth maximization'. Also Rawls could agree with the above if 'fairness' would be defined as justice and equality in exchange. Thus, what definition one holds of fairness impacts the model, but no matter how fairness is defined, the claim that any 'fairness' notions would be alien to economics, or that any fairness notions would worsen welfare, does not hold up.[231]

As pointed by Eli Salzberger on the division between law and economics and the risk of irrelevance of the economic analysis of law in the Posnerian fashion:

> Mainstream Law and Economics ignores the deficiencies of the shift from assuming self-maximization of utility to assuming self-maximization of wealth, such as ignoring the decreasing marginal utility of wealth, or the endowment effect. The insistence of most scholars to continue the Chicago path in this realm too, therefore, makes their work of little contribution to the real world of law.[232]

The legal discipline not only has a mandate and obligation to work alongside abstract though administrable concepts (fair, reasonable, and non-discriminatory (FRAND) being one example), but also possesses an intellectual and historic capability to do so. The matter of what constitutes justice and fairness belongs to one of the most written-about topics in the legal philosophy since time immemorial,

227 Jenny, 'Abuse of Dominance by Firms Charging Excessive or Unfair Prices', 5–70.

228 Ioannis Lianos, 'Competition Law as a Form of Social Regulation', *The Antitrust Bulletin* 65, no. 1 (March 2020): 3–86.

229 Thomas S. Ulen, 'Law and Economics, the Moral Limits of the Market, and Threshold Deontology', in *Law and Economics: Philosophical Issues and Fundamental Questions*, ed. Aristides N. Hatzis and Nicholas Mercuro, 1st ed. (Routledge, 2015).

230 Lee Ann Fennell and Richard H McAdams, eds., *Fairness in Law and Economics*, Economic Approaches to Law Series (Edward Elgar Publishing, 2013).

231 Kaplow and Shavell, 'Fairness versus Welfare: Notes on the Pareto Principle, Preferences, and Distributive Justice'.

232 Eli M. Salzberger, 'The Economic Analysis of Law – The Dominant Methodology for Legal Research?!', *University of Haifa Faculty of Law Legal Studies Research Paper No. 1044382*, 2007, https://doi.org/10.2139/ssrn.1044382, p. 28.

and the legal discipline on a global scale has developed set guidelines and coherent approaches to this legal-philosophical eternal question.

Indeed, the aversion of some strands of law and economics disciplines towards issues of fairness, and their overt focus on over-formalism and parochialism as noted by Mattei have: ' … consumed much of its early capital of prestige, and that the decline phase of the economic approach in legal reasoning is well on its way'.[233] The neoclassical economists, nevertheless, continue to predict and profess the 'inevitable fall' of what they somewhat derogatorily label as 'Hipster Antitrust'.

Moses, Jesus and Thomas Aquinas in this context would probably serve as The First Hipsters, a fact unbeknownst to most hipsters and the neoclassical economists.[234] As also noted by Wouter Wils in regard to the risk of irrelevance of economic analysis of law for the legal discipline:

> The adherence by an economist to one or another approach or school, or the relative popularity of one or another approach or school in a certain group of economists or at a certain point in time is not the result of a process of falsification, the other approaches having been proved wrong. It rather reflects a preference for a way of looking at things that is found congenial or instrumentally useful for some tasks at hand, or, when the approach becomes conventional wisdom, loyalty to the tribe, possibly re-enforced through peer review and other mechanisms of professional discipline.[235]

The arguments against an overt reliance on neoclassical, welfarist antitrust school are plenty and forceful, on normative, empirical and behavioural levels. On the normative level, one can point to the inherent conflict indicated above between the subjects of legal and economic disciplines, that is, fairness and efficiency, respectively.

Furthermore, the empirical economic science is more often than not concerned with the 'is' questions, whereas the legal science first and foremost concern 'ought' questions. As noted by Viktor Vanberg in regard to welfare economics and what he labels constitutional economics:

> … as an empirical science economics can provide advice only in the form of hypothetical imperatives, and that in a democratic polity the citizens are the natural ultimate addressees of such advice. This implies the requirement to support whatever policy advice is given by arguments that appeal to the citizens' common interests, a requirement that is perfectly in line with the theoretical perspective of constitutional economics but that has not been recognized by traditional welfare economics.[236]

[233] Ugo Mattei, 'The Rise and Fall of Law and Economics: An Essay for Judge Guido Calabresi', *Maryland Law Review* 64 (2005): 220.

[234] Watkins, 'The Law and the Profits'.

[235] Wils, 'The Judgment of the EU General Court in Intel and the So-Called "more Economic Approach" to Abuse of Dominance' World Competition: Law and Economics Review 37, no. 4 (2014): 405–34.

[236] Viktor J. Vanberg, 'Consumer Welfare, Total Welfare and Economic Freedom – On the Normative Foundations of Competition Policy', in *Competition Policy and the Economic*

At the empirical level, the formalistic core assumptions of the neoclassical and welfarist schools, however useful as a predictive tool, are not matched by empirical reality. At the behavioural level, combining the normative and empirical elements, and perhaps the most persuading critique against the neoclassical and behavioural schools, one finds an inherent human bias towards fairness, and not maximization of utility.

There is also a normative aspect of what harm competition law should act against and along what rationales, as noted by Ioannis Lianos:

> Traditionally, the analysis of market power, and the corresponding trade-offs … focus on economic efficiency and do not explicitly deal with distributional issues. The case against monopoly is motivated by the desire to correct for the inefficiency caused by lost (marginal) transactions (or volume effect) – the deadweight loss – rather than the implicit wealth transfer from consumers to producers over (infra-marginal) transactions … However, it is possible to build a broader narrative for intervention, on the basis of some wider conception of 'consumer welfare' or 'consumer harm'.[237]

Where the neoclassical economic theory assumes humans to be rational, self-interested beings and having perfect willpower, the findings by behavioural and experimental economics show that human behaviour instead is best described by traits such as bounded rationality, bounded self-interest and bounded willpower.[238] Removing, or relaxing, the strict rationality assumption,[239] which does not hold up neither normatively nor empirically, does not mean removing economics from law and economic analysis of competition law. It merely entails a more balanced approach to the reality and human nature as it has shown itself to be when empirically and experimentally tested.[240]

Many of the textbook assertions in regard to how markets function and what the role of competition law ought to be in regard to excessive pricing are found not to pass a basic 'smell test', especially so during a pandemic. They stand in conflict with how the law is being administered around Europe and globally as the string of cases in the recent decade demonstrate and, most importantly for legal discipline, at odds with the legislative intent and the normative soul of competition law, in turn reflecting the aforementioned inherent values and human biases. Economic analysis of law, no matter how relevant and enlightening, is and will forever be an afterthought seen from the onset of legal tradition.

Approach: Foundations and Limitations, ed. Josef Drexl, Wolfgang Kerber and Rupprecht Podszun (Edward Elgar Publishing, 2011), https://doi.org/10.4337/9780857930330.00008, pp. 44–71.

[237] Lianos, 'Competition Law as a Form of Social Regulation', 49.

[238] Stucke, 'Reconsidering Competition'.

[239] Russel B. Korobokin and Thomas S. Ulen, 'Law and Behavioral Science: Removing the Rationality Assumption from Law and Economics', *California Law Review* 88, no. 4 (July 2000): 1053–144.

[240] Korobokin and Ulen, 'Law and Behavioural Science', 1051–144.

The synthesis of this normative framing of excessive pricing alongside fairness–welfare paradigm should inform the analytical framework in regard to the ratio legis and economic soundness of enforcement given certain screening conditions are fulfilled. Many previously held conceptions (markets will self-correct, excessive pricing enforcement would harm innovation, competition law should focus solely on economic efficiency, etc.) do not possess the theoretical and empirical vigour they profess to. Looking at the policy development at the European Commission level, one also notes a shift towards increased emphasis on 'fairness',[241] a clear step from the overt reliance on 'efficiency' as the sole legal and public policy objective to be pursued in regard to competition law and economics.

It suffices to summarize with the assertion that the economic analysis of law could and should never substitute the conclusive legal matter, concomitant legal analysis or coherent legal application of the black letter of the law and legislative intent inherent in legal statutes.

A matter that was already indicated in the seminal European case on excessive pricing, United Brands, with the court formulating what some five decades later still translates to more wishful thinking than scientific reality: 'Other ways may be devised – and economic theorists have not failed to think up several – of selecting the rules for determining whether the price of a product is unfair.'[242]

As it is evident from the progress of economic science during the past four decades, neither marginalist nor welfarist schools of neoclassical economics has had anything more to offer than what was offered by the likes of Jevons and Marshall some 100 years ago. Other strands of economics such as behavioural, experimental and neuro-economics have engaged more in depth with the matter of fairness in pricing and transactions, which is why these strands are more in line with the legislative aim and the legal history informing the prohibition against excessive pricing and price gouging during crisis.

It is by no way accidental nor anecdotal that in times of global crisis (financial crisis, health pandemic, etc.) we all become Kantian, and Keynesian, even antagonists such as Milton Friedman.[243]

[241] Johannes Laitenberger, 'EU Competition Law in Innovation and Digital Markets: Fairness and the Consumer Welfare Perspective' (Brussels, 10 October 2017), https://ec.europa.eu/competition/speeches/text/sp2017_15_en.pdf; Vesterager, 'Fairness and Competition'.

[242] Judgment of the Court of 14 February 1978 in Case 27/76, United Brands Company and United Brands Continentaal BV v. Commission of the European Communities, ECLI:EU:C:1978:22, para 253.

[243] Friedman, 'We Are All Keynesians Now'.

11

Is Commodity Private Property Inherently Regressive?

Zvikomborero Chadambuka

CONTENTS

I INTRODUCTION

The private property system's benefits have come to be much appreciated in the last few centuries, propelled by the system's association with the impressive economic growth during this period. Yet private property is not for all times and all places. The balance between the costs and benefits of deploying private property can change. Such changes can arise within the private property system itself over the long term. Changes can also arise when circumstances, especially relating to the value of the resources in issue, change. This chapter emphasizes those changes internal to the private property system. It focuses on how the balance between the costs – regressivity and some inefficiencies – and benefits of private property can change internally within the private property system over the long term.

The chapter makes four main points. First is that commodity private property is inherently regressive, inexorably pushing the bulk of the resources available in society into the hands of those who have more at the expense of those who have less. This arises because wealthier people have a higher willingness to pay (WTP) for normal goods, which constitute most goods and are most commonly in productive use. Regressivity also arises due to the monopoly power that ownership gives; wealthier people are better able to capture the gains from trade that come with this monopoly power. Second is that private property is allocatively inefficient. This is because the use of WTP as an allocational technology means that the allocation of property is partially driven by ability to pay (ATP) rather than a purchaser's greater productive efficiency or stronger innate preferences. Private property is also allocatively inefficient due to the monopoly power that it places in the hands of owners. The interaction between inefficiency and regressivity carries a feedback effect because the ATP component of WTP increases as inequality increases; this increasing ATP component, rather than actual productive use, increasingly drives the allocation of property and so property's increasingly regressive effects drive increasing inefficiency. Third, the regressivity of private property creates a powerful propertied class that can come to dominate the political system. That class can worsen both regressivity and inefficiency by further tilting the political and economic system in its own favor. Finally, both the regressivity and the inefficiency have become even more stark in the internet era because markets which already have strong network effects and are vulnerable to domination by monopolists exacerbate both regressivity and inefficiency. The internet age has introduced the additional challenge of even more direct political power in the hands of monopolistic internet giants. Such giants have the incentives and ability to choke off standard political avenues for political, economic, and social reform. A first step in adjusting to these realities is to abandon the idea that distributional issues ought to be confined to the tax and transfer system. Closely related to this is a need to move away from a commodity vision of private property to an alternative vision that emphasizes social and equitable considerations, for example, the social obligation norm of property. The internet age may also present a context in which there is need to curb the reflexive resort to rules based on private property as a primary regulatory option. Caution must be exhibited in using any unpaid-for WTP-based allocation of rights to the party who appears to value them the most as this approach exhibits extreme regressivity and often lacks meaningful efficiency benefits.

Following this introduction is Section II, which discusses the commodity vision of private property; this vision finds its modern roots in the work of Ronald Coase.[1]

[1] Ronald Coase, The Problem of Social Cost, 3 *Journal of Law and Economics* 1–44, 43–44 (1960). See also Harold Demsetz, Toward a Theory of Property Rights, 57(2) *The American*

Section II also presents wealth maximization and its WTP criterion – the WTP criterion is the premier driver of the economic analysis of law. Section III addresses the regressivity and inefficiency of commodity private property, each from the respective perspectives of WTP and monopoly power. Section IV then discusses commodity private property's reallocation of political power to the wealthy. In Section V, the impact of commodity property's regressivity and inefficiency in the context of the internet age is addressed. Section VI raises some approaches which may mitigate the negative effects discussed. It also offers a brief assessment of the implications of these negative effects for some areas of the law and how these implications may be mitigated. Section VII concludes.

II PRIVATE PROPERTY AND WEALTH MAXIMIZATION

A *Commodity Private Property*

Coase's epochal 1960 article "The Problem of Social Cost" prompted the rise to intellectual preeminence in the legal field – and more specifically, in property thought and scholarship – of law and economics.[2] Coase's famous theorem asserted that if property rights were well-defined and there were no transaction costs, then property would be moved to its most valuable use through the market mechanism.[3]

Economic Review 347–59 (1967); Yoram Barzel, *Economic Analysis of Property Rights*, 2nd ed., Political Economy of Institutions and Decisions (Cambridge University Press, 1997).

2 Ugo Mattei & Andrea Pradi, Property Rights: A Comparative Law and Economics Perspective in the Global Era, at 43–47, in Donatella Porrini & Giovanni Ramello (Eds), *Property Rights Dynamics: A Law and Economics Perspective* (Routledge, 2007), treating the Coase theorem as the paradigm in economic analysis of property law.

3 Coase at 1–8. The theorem has been subjected to various interpretations; for some of these, see the discussion in Hovenkamp, Marginal Utility and the Coase Theorem, 75 *Cornell Law Review* 782, 783–88 (1990). Property historically emphasized the *in rem* nature of property rights, that is, the idea that property gives an owner protection against a large and indefinite range of persons. Thomas Merrill & Henry Smith, What Happened to Property in Law and Economics? 111 *Yale Law Journal* 357, 360–62 (2001). *In rem* property protection is credited with saving on information costs by creating comprehensive rights with relatively standardized limitations, thus facilitating security and planning, and so investment in the property. Merrill & Smith (2001) at 362 and 386–87. The emergence of the alternative bundle of sticks idea of property in the early twentieth century facilitated the economic analysis of law; Merrill & Smith (2001) at 365–66 explain that the legal realists used Hohfeld's classifications of law to deconstruct property in order to provide intellectual support for state regulation and redistribution of property. This became evident from the idea's prominent role in Coase at 43–44, stating that "if the factors of production are thought of as rights, it becomes easier to understand that the right to do something which has a harmful effect (such as the creation of smoke, noise and smells, etc.) is also a factor of production." The bundle of sticks approach powers Coase's causal agnosticism, a key part of law and economics theorizing on property. Merrill & Smith (2001) at 394 note that causal agnosticism runs counter to long-established and pro-intuitive notions on the *in rem* nature of property rights and in doing so raises information costs for third parties. There is developing a more recent line of research which presents strenuous objections to the bundle of rights approach and engages in economic analysis of the

Commodification of interests in resources and their trading is thus presumed to be the route to efficiency. This chapter discusses economic analysis of property law as premised on the bundle of rights perspective, *à la* Coase.

Private property entails appointing one gatekeeper as an owner of a resource; the owner is legally empowered to exclude others from the resource and determine its use.[4] The conventional economic case for private property is that it ensures productive efficiency and allocative efficiency.[5] The productive efficiency claim is that private property's exclusion power leads to internalization of the costs and benefits of that resource by the owner as that owner uses the resource to its optimal point from their perspective, that is, up to the point where the marginal benefits of using the property equal the marginal costs of so doing.[6] This concentration of the risks and rewards of investment on an owner resolves the tragedy of the commons, thereby curbing overuse of the resource.[7] By ensuring that the benefits of any investment in the resource are reaped by the owner, private property also resolves the free-riding problem and so ensures maximal use of the resource.[8] Free alienation, particularly by sale, has been credited with ensuring allocative efficiency by allowing a resource to be moved from a current owner to a new owner if the latter values it more highly than the former.[9] This position is based on the assumption that it is the person who can use a resource most productively who will pay the highest price to successfully buy the resource from a current owner.[10] This assumption is highly questionable.

Law and economics scholarship accepts that there are general limits to the extent to which private property can be credited with generating productive and allocative

in rem notion of property; Merrill & Smith (2001) and Henry Smith, *The Economics of Property Law in the Oxford Handbook of Law and Economics* (Oxford University Press, 2017).

References to private property in this chapter relate to the Coasean commodity vision of private property unless the context otherwise indicates; this contextual exemption is in place in Section VI.B.

4 Thomas Merrill, Accession and Original Ownership, 1 *Journal of Legal Analysis* 459, 494 (2009) (Merrill (2009)).

5 Robert Cooter & Thomas Ulen, *Law and Economics*, 6th ed., at 114 (Prentice-Hall, 2012); Margaret Radin, *Reinterpreting Property*, at 7 (University of Chicago Press, 1993); Eric Posner & Glen Weyl, Property Is Only Another Name for Monopoly, 9 *Journal of Legal Analysis* 51, 61 (2017) (Posner & Weyl (2017)).

6 Cooter & Ulen at 114; Radin (1993) at 7.

7 Cooter & Ulen.

8 Cooter & Ulen.

9 Cooter & Ulen at 114; Richard Posner, *Economic Analysis of Law*, at 41, 9th ed. (Aspen Casebook, 2014). Demsetz at 349 says "all that is needed for internalization ... is ownership which includes a right of sale." It is sometimes stated that ownership does not imply alienability; in making this point, Posner at 42 nonetheless asserts that "from an economic standpoint, property rights should be at least presumptively alienable, so that the market can allocate them to the persons who can obtain the greatest value from them."

10 Posner & Weyl (2017) at 61. This chapter addresses the allocative concern only as understood within the law and economics framework. Libertarian arguments have been made justifying the market system on the basis of free choice. These non-consequentialist arguments are not addressed here.

efficiency. A failure of full internalization of the costs or benefits of a resource results in externalities as it leads to gaps between the privately optimal point in usage and the socially optimal point in usage.[11] Public regulation may be needed to limit resource usage where this produces negative externalities or to boost a resource's usage where it has positive externalities.[12]

Transaction costs can also interfere with private property's allocative mechanism. On the standard transaction cost view, property law should determine the extent of transaction costs and react accordingly. One principle is that when the information costs of finding out who values a right the most are lower than the transaction costs of moving the right to the user who values it the most through the market, then property law must seek to avoid transaction costs through directly allocating the right to the party who values it the most; this is an application of what Cooter and Ulen refer to as the normative Hobbes theorem.[13] Another principle is that the law should seek to remove impediments to private agreements; Cooter and Ulen refer to this as the normative Coase theorem.[14]

B *Wealth Maximization*

Most law and economics scholars assert some measure of utility as their ultimate goal, with few – if any – scholars still considering wealth maximization to be

[11] Mattei & Pradi, at 43 and 48, highlight that externalities are ubiquitous such that it is impossible for a market system to, alone, successfully dispense completely with externalities; regulation and other forms of social control must therefore exist although a regulatory system that, alone, dispenses with externalities is also impossible. They assert that the tragedy of the commons and the free rider problem convey only that scarce goods need regulation; they do not necessarily require property rights since the solution could as easily be property rights as communism.

[12] Mattei & Pradi at 45, noting that regulation is often justified as required to deal with externalities, but that this is associated with an "efficiency default" coupled with an onus – one that is very difficult due to the overwhelming idea of efficiency – to prove the need for regulation.

[13] Cooter & Ulen at 98–99; see also Posner at 299.

[14] Cooter & Ulen at 96–97; Mattei & Pradi at 40; see also Posner at 300. Another oft-discussed limit to private property's potential for efficiency lies in the possibility of the tragedy of the anti-commons. This is a scenario in which excessive physical or functional fragmentation of property results in multiple exclusion rights which holders may exercise without fully internalizing the costs of such exercise, leading to under-exploitation and inefficient use of a resource. Michael Heller, *Gridlock Economy: How Too Much Ownership Wrecks Markets, Stops Innovation, and Costs Lives* (Basic Books, 2010). See also Francesco Parisi, Entropy and the Asymmetric Coase Theorem, 54–76 at 54–57, in Porrini & Ramello (Eds), *Property Rights Dynamics: A Law and Economics Perspective* (Routledge, 2007), further explaining that because fragmentation involves one owner's decision whereas reunification features multiple nonconforming owners, reunification involves high transaction costs and the possibilities for strategic holdup. Jonathan Remy Nash, Packaging Property: The Effect of Paradigmatic Framing of Property Rights, 83 *Tulane Law Review* 691, 704 (2009) emphasizes that the bundle of rights view of property is complicit in the existence of the tragedy of the anti-commons and the failure to recognize the problems of disaggregation and fragmentation of property rights.

defensible as a normative theory.[15] Yet modern law and economics in practice almost invariably reverts to wealth maximization – specifically Kaldor–Hicks (K-H) efficiency as represented by WTP – rather than utility maximization.[16] K-H efficiency from a particular action exists when the gainers from that action could compensate the losers from that action and still have a net gain left; unlike Pareto efficiency, K-H efficiency does not require that the gainers actually effect the compensation.[17]

The motivating idea behind K-H efficiency was that an aggregate increase in wealth increased the economic pie and so made it possible for utility to be increased; whether or not utility was so increased became a distributive question beyond economics since interpersonal comparisons of utility were deemed to be normative so as to lie beyond empirical analysis.[18] From this arose the idea of wealth maximization as an ultimate goal in economics, thereby leaving to other fields even those distributive questions central to whether or not utility actually increased. The move to the K-H criterion was considered to be one that enabled scientifically grounded economic analysis by allowing scholars to eschew interpersonal comparisons of utility in favor of interpersonal wealth comparisons; wealth, unlike utility, was observable and so could be measured, cardinalized, and compared from one

[15] Jedediah S. Britton-Purdy, David Singh Grewal, Amy Kapczynski, & K. Sabeel Rahman, Building a Law and Political Economy Framework: Beyond the Twentieth-Century Synthesis, 129 *Yale Law Journal* 1784, 1797 (2020); Fennell & McAdams, The Distributive Deficit in Law and Economics, 100 *Minnesota Law Review* 1051, 1059 fn 22 (2016); Zachary Liscow, Is Efficiency Biased? 85(7) *University of Chicago Law Review* Article 4, at 1660, fn 41 (2018); Gregory Alexander, The Social-Obligation Norm in American Property Law, 94 *Cornell Law Review* 749 (2009), fn 8; all of these authors note that even Posner – initially an enthusiastic defender of wealth maximization as an appropriate end in itself – has now moved away from any suggestion that wealth maximization is appropriate as a theory of justice. See too Lee Anne Fennell, Remixing Resources, 38(2) *Yale Journal on Regulation* 589, 593 (2021) in which the author states that "to my knowledge, no law and economics scholar today views wealth maximization as the law's ultimate normative objective."

[16] Posner at 14–15; Liscow (2018) at 1652–53 and 1661–62; Noah Popp, Wealth versus Welfare: Correcting for the Marginal Utility of Wealth in Assigning Private Law Entitlements, 30 *Quinnipiac Law Review* 69, 75 (2011); Fennell & McAdams at 1059, fn 22; Britton-Purdy *et al* at 1797; Zachary Liscow & Daniel Giraldo Paez, Inequality Snowballing, 77 *International Review of Law & Economics* 1 (2024). The term utility maximization is here used to represent the various forms of welfare maximization in contradistinction to wealth maximization. While finer distinctions can be made within the welfare maximization paradigm, these are not necessary for purposes of this chapter.

[17] Margaret Radin, *Contested Commodities*, at 226, endnote 16 (Harvard University Press, 2001); Popp at 75. Liscow (2018) at 1660, noting that K-H efficiency is sometimes called "potential pareto efficiency"; see too Posner at 14. Liscow (2018) at 1658 further states that "K-H efficiency (also sometimes called 'cost-benefit analysis') measures the willingness to pay of the parties affected by various policy options and then chooses the policy that maximizes the sum of the willingness to pay of those parties." References to efficiency in this chapter relate to K-H efficiency unless the context otherwise indicates.

[18] Popp at 76, citing Kaldor. Ultimately, it became conceived of as a matter for welfare economics.

person to another.[19] Popp makes the point that Lionel Robbins and Karl Llewellyn – who both initially sought to divorce the "is" of positive economics which they sought to study as a science from the "ought" of welfare economics which they asserted to be a normative exercise – stressed that the distinction they sought to make was only being made for the purposes of temporary study.[20] During the time that Coase wrote "The Problem of Social Cost" – in the immediate aftermath of the intellectual battles which had given rise to K-H efficiency – the legal process theory of jurisprudence dominated the field with its institutional competence arguments.[21] Under this theory, courts were supposed to leave normative questions to the elected branches as "justice" considerations were deemed to lack academic or political consensus and so to introduce ambiguity into the judicial process.[22] Efficiency *à la* K-H appeared to give a non-normative standard indicating uncontroversial shared values that judges could pursue, apparently enabling them to avoid the criticism that they were injecting their own personal or political views into their decisions.[23] K-H efficiency thus found a ready home in the legal battlefields of the United States (US).

Predictably, an oft-made criticism of wealth maximization is that a wealth increase does not amount to a social improvement unless it furthers some other social goal such as utility or equity.[24] Two main arguments persist for why wealth maximization holds sway in practice in spite of its widely acknowledged normative indefensibility. First is the idea that legal rules ought only be designed to ensure efficiency and so the maximization of the economic pie, leaving distributional issues to the tax and transfer system; this notion has become the dominant view in

[19] Jonathan Klick & Francesco Parisi, Wealth, Utility and the Human Dimension, 1 *New York University Journal of Law & Liberty* 590, 596 and 600 (2005); Britton-Purdy *et al* at 1797; Hovenkamp at 805. The use of the term wealth maximization makes sense in an analysis of private law where monetary transactions actually occur or can, in principle, be meaningfully anticipated to occur. In discussing the public law context of cost–benefit analysis, Liscow (2018) at 1701–2 prefers to restrict his language to the notion of WTP since money is not in issue in that case; as he points out, in such cases, efficiency analysis merely maximizes "willingness to pay units" rather than actual dollars. In this chapter, both terminologies will be used interchangeably, save in contexts where there is no payment – as in the discussion of the normative Hobbes theorem – in which case the term WTP will be exclusively employed.

[20] Popp at 73 and 79; Robbins wrote from the economics perspective while Llewellyn wrote from the legal perspective.

[21] Popp at 79–82.

[22] Klick & Parisi at 593 citing Posner. The causal agnosticism of the Coase theorem fits well with the legal process theory of jurisprudence's call for judges to abandon issues of "justice" on the basis that these were subjective.

[23] Popp at 82; Posner at 301.

[24] Klick & Parisi at 600–1 citing Calabresi (1980) and Bentham. Oren Bar-Gill, Willingness to Pay: A Welfarist Reassessment, 38 *Yale Journal on Regulation* 503, 506 (2021) asserts that much of the criticism of the WTP criterion summarizes to the assertion that WTP is a poor proxy for utility, or that it contains limited information about preferences.

mainstream law and economics.[25] Although various scholars have made arguments along those lines, the most sophisticated argument in this respect comes from Kaplow and Shavell.[26] In comparing distributional measures effected through legal rules with those effected using the tax and spending mechanism, Kaplow and Shavell assert that while both sets of distributional measures generate some inefficiency by creating a labor–leisure distortion, distribution through legal rules produces an additional distortion by creating inefficient levels of activity in the specific domain to which the rule applies.[27] Their double distortion argument thus asserts that the tax and spending mechanism is a more efficient means by which to address distributional issues as it creates only the labor–leisure distortion.[28] This argument entails excluding from the distributive enterprise all mechanisms other than the tax and spending system, including court decisions, non-tax legislation, and administrative agency regulations.[29] Posner raises more general legitimacy concerns – somewhat in the spirit of the institutional competence concerns discussed above – against judicial involvement in distributive matters;[30] he thus accepts, in contrast to the implications of the double distortion argument, that general laws such as minimum-wage laws can be appropriate redistributive mechanisms.[31]

Liscow (2014) asserts that the double distortion argument can be avoided by using different standards of liability depending on the income of litigants who typically bring certain types of claims, rather than individualized award adjustments based on the relative incomes of the parties to a specific case.[32] De Geest notes that whereas

25 Liscow (2018) at 1661–63; Fennell & McAdams at 1062, fn 32; Popp at 85 and 91–92; see also Fennell at 590 making the same point, but noting that scholars are increasingly rejecting the double distortion argument and its division of labor.

26 Liscow (2018) at 1662–63; Fennell & McAdams at 1057, fn 15; Popp at 84.

27 Liscow (2018) at 1663; Popp at 85 and 89; both citing Louis Kaplow and Steven Shavell, Why the Legal System Is Less Efficient Than the Income Tax in Redistributing Income, 23 *Journal of Legal Studies* 667 (1994); Fennell & McAdams at 1054, fn 10, setting out the argument, and at 1057, fn 15, collecting various joint and solo works by Kaplow and Shavell developing their argument.

28 Fennell & McAdams at 1053, fn 7 and 1067; Liscow (2018) at 1656–57, fn 25.

29 Fennell & McAdams at 1053, fn 7 and 1067; Liscow (2018) at 1656–57, fn 25.

30 Posner at 301 and then at 730–31, where the legitimacy of judicial efforts at distribution is also questioned on the basis that judges are not subject to democratic control.

31 Posner at 730.

32 Zachary Liscow, Reducing Inequality on the Cheap: When Legal Rule Design Should Incorporate Equity as Well as Efficiency, 127 *Yale Law Journal* 2478, 2483–84 (2014). As an example, Liscow (2014) at 2490 elaborates that “to achieve this *costless* distribution of wealth, the legislature can see that, as a *group*, the polluters are wealthier than the pollutees and then alter the legal rule accordingly”; the effect of a switch such as that from negligence to strict liability is to change the distributive outcome of the case/s without actually changing the efficient course of action such that the (re)distribution of wealth this entails is costless. Liscow (2014) at 2500 notes that the Coase theorem itself could be an argument that such rules are effectively non-distorting since it asserts that, if there are no transaction costs, the initial entitlement only impacts the distribution of income and does not matter for efficiency as bargaining will produce an efficient allocation. The argument is that equity-informed legal rules of this nature can distribute more cost-efficiently than the tax and spending system.

the double distortion argument assumes perfect competition, markets often provide various rents to market participants;[33] further that ex ante legal rules are better at distinguishing between gains derived from rents and those arising due to talent and effort, and so at extinguishing the former at little cost in terms of the latter.[34] This advantage arises from the fact that ex ante measures require less information as they can function based on only estimations of aggregate rents whereas ex post measures require information on individual rents.[35] The tax system creates the labor–leisure distortion and also fails to deal with rents and so leaves unaffected the price distortion which rents introduce; by contrast, the legal system removes the rent ex ante and so avoids the labor–leisure distortion.[36] To this extent, there is an efficiency gain. De Geest also assumes that the recipient of rents[37] is wealthier than average and so asserts that rents create a regressive implicit commodity tax.[38] By eliminating this implicit commodity tax, legal rules do a better job at distribution than the tax and spending system.[39] The proposition's acknowledgement of the fictional nature of the perfect competition assumption provides significant support for the use of competition law as a distributive measure, perhaps by prioritizing enforcement in areas with desirable distributive impacts.[40] Legal rules are also credited with lower transaction costs as they distribute virtually whereas the tax and transfer system distributes through real transactions; real transactions entail additional administrative costs relating to the actual transactions themselves.[41] The very delay between the policy and its distributive correction also matters for fairness and well-being.

The second argument for why wealth maximization continues to hold sway in practice is the view that distributional consequences will generally even out across a large number of efficient policies as those disadvantaged by some policies will generally benefit from other policies such that almost everyone will be better off in the long-run.[42] Some responses to both this argument and the double distortion

[33] Gerrit De Geest, Removing Rents: Why the Legal System Is Superior to the Income Tax at Reducing Income Inequality, Washington University in St. Louis Legal Studies Research Paper No. 13-10-02 at 6 and 11 (2013), at 3 defining rents as "anything that exceeds the profits that would have been made in a perfectly competitive market" (De Geest (2013)).

[34] De Geest (2013) at 5.

[35] De Geest (2013) at 5 and 10.

[36] De Geest (2013) at 5.

[37] De Geest (2013) at 8, fn 23.

[38] De Geest (2013) at 6.

[39] De Geest (2013) at 31 thus states that "it seems obvious that correcting inequality caused by rents through creation of counter-balancing rents is an intrinsically inferior method compared to abolishing rents."

[40] De Geest (2013) at 32, where he limits his argument to scenarios where the income inequality in issue is caused by rents, somewhat highlights this point. The argument is therefore a corrective justice type of argument – in essence, it is about addressing the wrong done in markets.

[41] De Geest (2013) at 34–35.

[42] Liscow (2018) at 1661; Popp at 8; Lucian Bebchuk, The Pursuit of a Bigger Pie: Can Everyone Expect a Bigger Slice? 8 *Hofstra Law Review* 671 (1980).

argument are addressed in Section IV.[43] Briefly, the main points of those respective responses are thus: There is little reason to believe that the tax and transfer system will outperform legal rules in distribution given political difficulties in using the tax and transfer system in the real world, so the choice here is really between legal rules and no/little distribution; and the inherent regressivity of private property indicates that distributive outcomes get worse, not better, in the long run. The dominance of the arguments for confining legal rules to efficiency – in particular the double distortion argument – has led to a reflexive resort to efficiency in policymaking, allied with a tendency to retreat from systematic study of the distributional impacts of efficient policies, particularly by government bodies.[44]

III THE INHERENT REGRESSIVITY AND INEFFICIENCY OF PRIVATE PROPERTY

A *Regressivity: WTP*

Commodity private property is premised on wealth maximization and WTP. For a legal policymaker, what matters is what happens in the real world. People in the real world maximize their utility, not their wealth.[45] Given the nature of the debates around the wealth maximization criterion discussed above, it is worthwhile to assess the allocative implications of the reality of utility maximization in a private property world based on WTP. One may hypothesize a potential trade scenario between two idealized individuals, one wealthy and one poor.[46] In the initial case, there is a poor potential seller and a wealthy potential buyer of a good with a future income stream. The utility to the poor seller of the income from selling the good is likely to be relatively high as immediate consumptive needs are likely to provide great utility to such a seller. Even when it is likely to be wealth maximizing to retain that income

[43] There are other arguments sometimes presented in support of judicial withdrawal from distributive issues. It is occasionally argued that distributive effects are often minor; see Popp at 89, noting that Kaplow & Shavell asserted, in addition to their double distortion argument, that wealth maximization facilitates analytical simplification and that distributive effects are often minor. But this is not the case as courts establish precedent and so shape conduct and expectations beyond the courtroom. Fennell & McAdams at 1064. Utility maximization in a single case before a judge would serve to improve allocative efficiency in many future cases and in even more numerous circumstances which are ultimately never litigated. Popp at 100. Distributive injustices can also have effects that are individually highly significant to the parties before the courts; it is contrary to the nature of the judicial role as an individualized arbiter to ignore this. Posner at 731 also raises the idea that judicial changes should be slow as they are meant to be anticipated, and that a distributive function for the courts would undermine courts' ability to confine themselves to slow, incremental changes.

[44] Liscow (2018) at 1662.

[45] Hovenkamp at 788 and 801.

[46] This chapter references the "wealthy" and the "poor" as a shorthand with which to represent distributional consequences.

stream, it may not be utility maximizing due to immediate pressures. With more income at their disposal, the wealthy buyer is likely to be able to devote some of their income to purchasing the asset; the buyer may also decide which of the assets currently in their possession has lower value than the asset on the market and so release this to obtain the more profitable asset on the market. Profitable property will therefore move from the poor seller to the wealthy buyer. In the inverse scenario featuring a wealthy seller and a poor buyer, the utility to the wealthy seller of selling the property for income is relatively low due to the lower levels of consumptive pressures to which they are subject. For the poor buyer, the opportunity cost of devoting resources to buying the property from the wealthy seller is likely to be high due to a poor buyer's more immediate consumptive needs which must be covered.[47] A transaction moving property from the wealthy seller to the poor buyer is therefore less likely to take place than the inverse transaction. The less property one has, the higher is the utility from *exchanging it* for immediate consumptive value as opposed to keeping the property. The more property one has, the higher is the utility from *keeping such property* as opposed to exchanging it for immediate consumptive value. Private property is therefore inherently regressive even at the best of times. Only in the instance of perfect equality of resources would this effect not occur. Initial income inequality could result from any number of factors; indeed, it is inherent – and desirable within limits – in every society.

The effect is dynamic and systemic. Wealth inequality between buyer and seller shifts property from the poor to the wealthy; that induces an increase in inequality, which then shifts even greater property from the poor to the wealthy in a repeating cycle. Commodity private property is driven by WTP in the present and then drives WTP in the future.[48]

One reason for the outcome in the hypothesized trade scenario arises from the declining marginal utility of income. The intuitive idea that the marginal utility of income declines as income rises – that each dollar added to a person's wealth gives them a marginally lower level of utility than the preceding dollar – is a conventional economic assumption with a long history in economics and culture.[49] It is associated with the more general theory of the diminishing marginal utility of commodities.[50] The declining marginal utility of income implies that efficiency analysis

47 An indication of how realistic this range of concerns is can be found in Britton-Purdy *et al* at 1819, citing Jeff Larrimore *et al*, Report on the Economic Well-Being of U.S. Households in 2017, Board Governors Fed. Res. Sys. 21 (May 2018), where it is noted that "four in ten adults would need to sell property, borrow money, or not be able to pay at all if confronted with a four hundred dollar expense."

48 This mechanism is in part a private law variant of a general policy snowballing mechanism presented by Liscow & Paez at 23, stating that "more generally, what is needed is that (1) parties' WTP affects application of a legal rule, (2) the legal rule in turn affects WTP in the future, creating a feedback loop, and (3) compensation is incomplete." See also Bar-Gill at 513 and 530–31.

49 Popp at 92; Hovenkamp at 798; Liscow (2018) at 1660.

50 Popp at 93.

exhibits a systematic bias against people with lower wealth since they will have lower WTP.[51] A party's valuation of property depends on, *inter alia*, that party's wealth.[52] The increase in a party's wealth will decrease such party's marginal utility of income and therefore increase the party's monetary valuation of the property.[53] In other words, the diminishing marginal rate of substitution between the property and the composite good "money" means that an increase in a party's wealth will increase the number of dollars which that party is willing to substitute for the property.[54] While there is little question about these effects at the individual level, a systemic argument requires the additional assumption – a plausible and widely accepted one given that the shape and height of people's utility curves are unknown – that marginal utility curves are the same across income groups.[55] Wealthy people will thus generally have a higher WTP for property than poor people.[56] Because it connotes that each dollar added to the poor gives them more utility than the same dollar added to the wealthy, the declining marginal utility of income has been used to argue that utility gains can be made by distributing from the wealthy to the poor.[57]

A declining marginal utility of income will generally arise from systematic differences in the utility that different types of goods tend to provide, with a particular focus on goods that serve basic human needs.[58] This channels Maslow's hierarchy of needs in that basic consumptive goods are required by all, and the utility from these is quite high as they are immediately required for life. Willingness to pay increases as income increases for most goods.[59]

[51] Popp at 95.

[52] The general point is that utility is a broad measure including all elements of well-being such that, since wealth is only one of many ingredients in most people's utility functions, various things compete with wealth in a person's hierarchy of values. Hovenkamp at 806. The utility-maximizing output is therefore not the same as the wealth-maximizing output. Hovenkamp at 788 and 800; Klick & Parisi at 600–3.

[53] Bebchuk at 683. Liscow (2018) at 1682.

[54] Bebchuk at 682; Gregory Alexander and Eduardo Peñalver, *An Introduction to Property Theory* at 107 (Cambridge University Press, 2012) make this point thus: "the declining marginal utility of money would mean that the mere fact that a wealthy person is willing to pay $100 for a coat does not demonstrate that she will actually derive more utility from it than a very poor person only willing to pay $10."

[55] Posner at 640.

[56] Liscow (2018) at 1674–78 and 1682.

[57] Liscow (2018) at 1660; Fennell & McAdams at 1059; Fennell at 593; Popp at 96.

[58] Liscow (2018) at 1673; Popp at 94 where he refers to, among others, Maslow's hierarchy of needs. Posner at 13 notes that risk aversion is also a permutation of the declining marginal utility of income in that what one has is worth more to the risk-perverse person than an additional similar amount. The general belief is that many people are risk-averse most of the time. Some institutional responses to risk aversion, such as insurance and the corporation's limited liability, serve to make people risk-neutral in many situations.

[59] Liscow (2018) at 1674–78 and 1682. This can be seen in microeconomics' basic income and substitution effect analysis in respect of which the income effect generally tends toward higher WTP as income increases, a feature of what are called normal goods. Liscow (2018) at 1674 also points out that economists refer to these goods as "normal" goods because this is the standard manner in which goods operate. The occasional inferior good exists, which exhibits the

Beyond goods that serve basic human needs, each additional dollar can be spent on other goods. These other goods include additional consumptive goods as well as productive goods. That switch to the realm of productive goods is therefore determined by wealth. Long-term productive goods also tend to provide the highest returns; thus the less immediate one's financial demands are, the more ultimate wealth one can collect. The ability to invest in goods that are productive in the long term – and so to engage in actual wealth maximization – is therefore increasingly the privilege only of those who already have wealth. Differences in access to productive goods are a major source of private property's systemic regressive effects. Productive goods are essentially captured by the idea of capital; Pistor defines capital as "legal property that is assigned a pecuniary value in expectation of a likely future pecuniary income."[60] Pistor further describes law as serving the function of coding certain selected assets as capital and so as generating higher wealth for their owners. Such assets are provided with priority over other assets, durability, universality, and convertibility; an example of durability is the long-term protection from creditors provided by entails in the past and trusts up to today.[61] Assets are coded to have high value – that is, imbued with strong property rights – by lawyers.[62] Noting that, Pistor asserts that capital has regressive effects as only the best-paying clients can hire the best lawyers.[63] Thus, access to productive goods is also allied with control over the value-determining levers by which additional productive goods are structured and protected. Coding as capital protects the wealthy against loss of value through no fault of one's own, for example, due to volatility in commodities markets;[64] there is a reallocation of wealth through capital markets in that creditors receive protection

opposite effect, but this tends to be a subset of a broader set of normal goods – Liscow (2018) at 1678–79. With inferior goods, higher income leads to substituting away from the reference good toward "better" options within the broader set of goods and so higher (lower) income is associated with lower (higher) WTP for the reference good. Inferior goods tend to be basic consumption goods required for human survival with the substitution invariably into related higher-quality consumption goods. Thus, inferior goods are rare and generally a mere subset of some set of normal consumption goods. In the very rare case of Giffen goods – which have also been dubbed strongly inferior goods – this income effect overwhelms the substitution effect such that as the price of the good rises, WTP also rises. This occurs when the Giffen good is such a major part of the person's budget that the impact of a rise in its price on the person's income forces them to replace away all alternatives in their budgets with the reference good. This "basic consumptive good" rationale for Giffen goods emphasizes that the absorption of resources in basic consumption commodities entails their nonavailability for investment in alternative goods such as productive goods.

60 Katharina Pistor, *The Code of Capital: How the Law Creates Wealth and Inequality*, at 12 (Princeton University Press, 2019), taking Levy's definition. Pistor at 2, describes Piketty's explanation of inequality as follows: "a novel interpretation holds that in mature economies capital grows faster than the rest of the economy; whoever has amassed wealth in the past, therefore, will expand it further, relative to others."

61 Pistor at 13–15; see also Pistor at 24 for development of the trust form.

62 Pistor at 20.

63 Pistor at 20.

64 Pistor at 41.

from unanticipated loss of value whereas debtors are left to the vicissitudes of fortune.[65] The ability to weather the storm of bad economic conditions without falling into desperation is already a function of wealth. Coding of assets as capital enables the wealthy to then cash in on the poor's desperation in the wake of economic crisis.[66]

Even without considering the declining marginal utility of income, wealth maximization structurally prioritizes the interests of wealthier persons.[67] The use of WTP has systematic implications in an environment of initial income inequality. These effects exist even without the assumption – which assumption is required for the declining marginal utility of income – that marginal utility curves are the same across income groups. As noted above, the wealthier one is, the higher their ATP is.[68] That alone increases their access to productive goods, which increases inequality as they capture more of current resources as well as more of the resources produced by economic growth. An increasing component of ATP within the notion of WTP thus has regressive implications.[69] The greater ATP enables increased inequality by granting the wealthy relatively greater access to productive goods than the poor.

Perfect financial markets – in which people can always borrow against future income – would resolve the regressive effects of private property, but such markets do not exist. Collateral requirements to access finance directly implicate private wealth.[70] Information is often costly, especially when the information sought relates to concerns about the future, and so the wealthy – who can afford to purchase access to such information – will face far lower market risk and can more safely earn significant income.[71] Financial markets also tend to be a one-shot deal in a world

65 Pistor at 41.

66 Pistor at 41.

67 Britton-Purdy *et al* at 1790; Liscow (2018) at 1656.

68 Liscow (2018) at 1674–78 and 1682.

69 Posner at 47, in a discussion on broadcast frequencies, suggests that the implications of ATP are not greatly relevant; he argues that

> some of the objections to recognizing property rights in frequencies have an odd ring in an economist's ear. For example, it was said that if broadcasting rights could be bought and sold like other property, the broadcast media would come under the control of the wealthy. This confuses willingness to pay with ability to pay. The possession of money does not dictate the objects that will be purchased. The poor frequently bid goods away from the rich by being willing in the aggregate to pay more.

Posner's approach here treats WTP and ATP as completely separate in a manner that is wholly inconsistent with the entire point behind using wealth maximization rather than utility maximization. If the advantage of WTP is to be observability and measurability, then one must logically concede ATP as part of WTP. In addition, the coordination difficulties, especially in an environment where the wealthy can afford countermeasures to stymie such coordination, mean that Posner's suggestion is unrealistic at any genuinely competitive level. Each poor person could also remain unable to afford to pay whatever "small" share is required to purchase the broadcasting rights in the aggregate – this possibility rises with inequality.

70 Fennell at 602.

71 Posner at 4.

where entrepreneurship is not a one-shot immediate success game.[72] Even at their realistic best, financial markets do not give many big second chances in one lifetime, whereas private wealth gives multiple shots. Financial markets would not usually fund the poor's attempts to borrow for consumptive use; some level of private resources would still be required before financing can mitigate the regressive effects of commodity property.[73] Entrepreneurship itself is thus distributed regressively. Wealth, therefore, still makes a difference even in a business context with well-functioning financial markets. In fact, good financing in this case could, perversely, serve to widen the gulf between the wealthy and the poor by being available only to the wealthy.

Liscow (2018) notes that the use of WTP-based cost–benefit analysis in resource allocation entails an allocation of resources to the wealthy without their even having to pay for them on the basis that the wealthy's higher WTP suggests that they will benefit more significantly from the resources.[74] The result is a highly, unjustifiably regressive outcome as public resource allocation is heavily biased in favor of the wealthy. Private property in the hands of the wealthy then appears more productive than private property in the hands of the poor simply because the former is complemented by higher-quality public resources; for example, publicly funded improvements in transportation systems based on WTP make the wealthy disproportionately productive and raise land values in wealthy neighborhoods.[75] This justifies additional allocations of public resources to the wealthy on a WTP basis, thus sustaining a regressive feedback effect. These issues generally implicate any initial unpaid allocation of resources in the legal system. Thus, they arise in respect of the initial allocation of rights to resources in torts, property and in cost–benefit analyses more generally. Under the WTP premise, the judicial assignment of rights in terms of Cooter and Ulen's normative Hobbes theorem will similarly entail disproportionately allocating rights to the wealthy due to their higher WTP without their even having to pay for them.[76] Many estimates used in the context of the normative Hobbes theorem are based on WTP and are therefore clearly regressive. For example, estimates of the value of freedom from pollution are often made using property values; the wealthier have higher-valued properties, leading to the finding that they value freedom

[72] Entrepreneurs fail fairly often. Bureau of Labor statistics suggest that around 50 percent of new enterprises will have failed by their fifth year. www.bls.gov/bdm/entrepreneurship/entrepreneurship.htm.

[73] Fennell at 595.

[74] Liscow (2018) at 1656 and 1673; Bar-Gill at 511–12. Liscow (2018) at 1674 and 1689 notes that cost–benefit analyses based on WTP mean that rich-biased policies are ubiquitous in the public sphere.

[75] Liscow (2018) at 1691.

[76] Liscow (2018) at 1651 and 1673. Private property entails actual payment, which limits the worst of the criticisms in Liscow to cases such as the normative Hobbes theorem.

from pollution more highly.[77] Once the wealthy's property begins to benefit from higher-quality public resources, the regressive effects on the normative Hobbes theorem become self-enforcing, even if purportedly no longer premised on WTP.

B *Regressivity: Monopoly Power*

Private property is allocatively inefficient because it creates monopoly power in the property owner by allowing such owner to hold out for excessive prices.[78] Monopoly power arises due the fact that a property rule allows an owner a veto over transfer of their property.[79] The more unique or illiquid a property is, the more serious the monopoly problem becomes as holdout or holdup dynamics then come into play.[80] Some degree of monopoly power arises when there is private ownership of any asset other than homogenous goods.[81] Even those markets for relatively homogenous commodities tend to feature a few dominant firms or firms that collude, resulting in some monopoly power.[82]

The plight of the poor under private property is exacerbated when one considers this notion of the property owner as a monopolist. The increased pressure on the poor to sell means that the less property one has, the less ultimate monopoly power they have, and so the lower the proportion of the gains from trade they are able to capture. The more property one has, the higher the monopoly power they have and the greater the proportion of the gains from any trade they capture. The gains from trade are thus disproportionately divided in favor of the wealthy over the poor, increasing the regressivity of private property.[83] Matters are aggravated by the fact

77 Posner at 62, fn 1.

78 Posner & Weyl (2017) at 51–52 and 55, highlighting that this concern is not a new one, having been raised in some form or another by various past authors including Saint-Simon, Proudhon, Owen, Fourier, Marx, and Engels. Posner & Weyl (2017) at 57 further note that Myerson & Satterthwaite have identified the monopoly problem in a mathematically rigorous fashion that proved that private property was inconsistent with allocative efficiency; Roger B. Myerson and Mark A. Satterthwaite, Efficient Mechanisms for Bilateral Trading, 29(2) *Journal of Economic Theory* 265–81 (1983).

79 On property rules and liability rules, see Guido Calabresi & A. Douglas Melamed, Property Rules, Liability Rules and Inalienability: One View of the Cathedral, 85 *Harvard Law Review* 1089 (1972).

80 Posner & Weyl (2017) at 63; Fennell at 601 notes that this becomes an issue when actors seek to assemble valuable sets of complementary properties such as a highway or the intellectual property context where innovations covered by intellectual property often build on each other.

81 Eric Posner & Glen Weyl, *Radical Markets: Uprooting Capitalism and Democracy for a Just Society*, at 26–27 and 38 (Princeton University Press, 2018) (Posner & Weyl (2018)). Fennell at 601 asserts that the monopoly is sometimes meaningless, since there are sometimes very similar alternatives on the market.

82 Posner & Weyl (2018) at 27.

83 This also speaks to an inherent bias in favor of the wealthy in the distribution of gains from economic growth; see Liscow & Paez at 3 who note that increasing economic growth could induce a regressive "policy snowballing" mechanism by "increasing the absolute difference in income between rich and poor people."

that the shedding out of the poor means even less competition – and therefore greater monopoly – particularly in respect of productive goods.[84] Poor people may also be less likely to have relatively unique goods and so to have monopoly power. Posner and Weyl (2018) assert that economic profits – "profits above what would be expected under perfect competition, that is, profits attributable to monopoly power" – in the US have roughly quadrupled since the early 1980s and that this effect has been associated with a falling labor share and rising inequality.[85] Further that these monopoly profits have been overwhelmingly received by the extremely wealthy.[86]

Private property therefore produces an inherent movement of productive property from the poor to the wealthy. None of this movement is necessarily productively beneficial, a matter addressed below; at this point, it is only noted that it is inexorably regressive. This inherent regressivity of private property directly contradicts the claim that the distributional consequences of regressive efficient policies will generally even out in the long run.[87]

It is therefore clear that the regressive effect of private property is embedded in the very bargaining frameworks that typify the commodity vision of private property as advocated for in much of conventional law and economics.

C *Inefficiency*: WTP

Private property's claims to allocative efficiency operate on the premise that WTP is the marker of how much a person values a property and that those who are willing to pay the most for a resource are the ones who can most productively use that resource.[88] Yet the only circumstance in which such an assumption might hold is where the initial wealth distribution is relatively egalitarian.[89] This is because WTP includes an element that relates to ATP and a remaining part that relates to other determinants indicative of the ability to beneficially use the resources, that is, productive efficiency and/or some measure of innate preferences. The higher WTP of the wealthy, to the extent that it is driven by ATP, directs the flow of resources toward the wealthy without entailing any productive gain, that is, even when there is no basis to conclude that they are the ones who can most productively

[84] There are other related dynamics; one may consider the exclusive nature (limited to only those with a certain minimum amount of money or other social links) of highly productive funds, for example venture capital funds. While such exclusivity may be argued to be an attempt to lower transaction costs, the highly regressive implications are unmistakable.

[85] Posner & Weyl (2018) at 5–6 highlight that growing inequality is less about diverging skills and opportunities of the talented, which must be rewarded by rising income, and more about shift of national income away from labor to monopoly profit.

[86] Posner & Weyl (2018) at 6–7.

[87] Liscow (2018) at 1661; Popp at 8; Bebchuk at 671.

[88] Posner & Weyl (2017) at 61.

[89] Alexander & Peñalver at 107.

use a resource. As the wealth gap widens, allocation of property becomes increasingly driven by the wealth gap – that is, by the difference in ATP – and efficiency in the actual use of property increasingly becomes less important. Thus, from the perspective of analyzing the appropriateness of WTP as a proxy for utility, the informational content of WTP – with "informational content" defined as the amount of information contained about preferences in WTP – decreases as the wealth disparity increases.[90] Private property in this respect shows an allocative tendency to direct resources to other resources rather than to their most efficient use.

Given that private property increasingly drives up regressivity, the scenario is then that private property – left to its own devices – also becomes progressively less productively efficient. Thus, the assumption motivating the claim of allocative efficiency increasingly and inexorably fails, and with it fail too the claims of productive efficiency. Private property increasingly collects in the hands of those with more resources simply because it is possible, with little necessarily proffered in the way of productive gains in the use of those resources.

Inequalities generate a slew of other efficiency losses. Of particular importance in the human capital-centric internet age world of today is the fact that inequalities result in suboptimal human capital investments.[91] Fennell expresses this point, and the broader issue, as follows:[92]

"A current distribution that embeds unrectified past violations of principles of efficient allocation (as ours manifestly does) is especially likely to have continuing dampening effects on the production of new wealth going forward. For example, the inability of people to locate in places where their human capital can be put to its best use generates a large efficiency loss, one that finds roots in past injustices that continue to distort housing markets. The extent to which embedded past violations continue to produce inefficiencies is an empirical question, as is the question of how best to counter such effects at minimum cost. But these are matters at least as deserving of attention as any claim that the sowers of today must reap in full, or that currently entrenched interests must remain so for efficiency's sake."

One may argue that resources being directed to other resources increases investment incentives as persons seek to increase on their initial resource base. That argument accepts a (relatively egalitarian) point in time when there are high investment incentives, followed by a gradual but inexorable decline in such incentives as systemic inequality increases, ultimately creating an inefficient property scheme with little incentive for innovation as there is prevention of – or at least significant and increasing limiting of – any further movement up the economic ladder.[93] This suggests that a periodic distributive reset of private property allocations is necessary

90 Bar-Gill at 506 and 511.
91 Fennell at 598.
92 Fennell at 595–96.
93 This phenomenon is a particularly visibly stark feature of the internet age, as the discussion below will show.

in order to improve both the distributive outcomes and the efficiency of private property.[94] No doubt such a solution would need to address a raft of complications such as ensuring investment incentives, preventing rent-seeking and ensuring consistency with liberty and personhood interests. There may therefore be a premium on political institutions that can handle these episodes equitably and with minimal disruption to economic incentives and social stability.

Commodity private property therefore will tend to collapse into inefficiency. This ultimate collapse may entail cycles of sociopolitical discord and/or economic discord such as cycles of economic depression or recession. This may also occur through a political mechanism in which government policy becomes so pro-wealth biased that its inequities and inefficiencies create, solidify and/or sustain a range of political, social, and economic pathologies symptomatic of a failed polity.

Putting resources in the hands of those who often have no real use for – or will make much less meaningful use of – these resources may also lead to waste as society's resources are expended in production of things which provide little additional utility to the beneficiaries and little other social value.[95] There are principles in property law that are targeted at mitigating concerns relating to nonproductive ownership of resources;[96] for example, adverse possession laws are justified by the need to move property from those who do not make use of it to those who make actual use of it.[97] There is therefore every reason to give consideration to changes in property law that curb nonproductive use arising from inequality.[98]

94 See too Fennell at 607 in support of her argument on prior injustices quoted above, referencing Singer, Edges of the Field, as follows: "Property law has a tendency toward entrenchment that fosters stability but can have highly undesirable system-wide distributive effects over time. It acts as an accumulating machine that continually layers new accretions onto holdings shaped by a history of pervasive injustice. Carrying out a reset of some kind is essential to both distribution and efficiency."

95 Alexander & Peñalver at 16 note that differences in wealth can undermine a person's ability to express their utilitarian valuations through WTP; they illustrate the point with an example which shows the phenomenon's potential for wastefulness as follows: "Suppose Neruda is so poor that he cannot afford ice cream that costs more than $1. If he refuses to buy ice cream for $3, even though he wants it badly, is it accurate to conclude that he desires ice cream less intensely than Borges, who is rich and merely likes to buy ice cream to watch the patterns it makes when it melts?"

96 Posner at 35 highlights that in a world of scarce resources, waste is rightly regarded as immoral.

97 Francesco Parisi, The Fall and Rise of Functional Property, at 19–39, at 22 in Porrini & Ramello (Eds), *Property Rights Dynamics: A Law and Economics Perspective* (Routledge, 2007). The various property schemes which involve sharing of use rights in relatively small communities similarly show echoes of the concern with nonproductive ownership of resources, as does the fact that, in principle, economically optimal use of property can be attained through functional splitting of rights to allow multiple privately held use rights (although the anticommons concern and other coordination failures can, in practice, undermine this).

98 Posner & Weyl (2018) at 68–69 assert that monopoly can also lead to owner laziness, incompetence, and malice, stating that: "Private property allows lazy or misanthropic owners to hoard assets and to do so not for gain but out of sloth. This problem seems to have been prevalent under feudalism, when landowners were not accustomed to prudence thrift or hard work." They assert that their idea, which is based on an auction system, "disrupts the quiet life of a lazy

Liscow (2018) has also shown that WTP-based cost–benefit analysis leads to regressive allocation of public resources and makes resources in the hands of the wealthy seemingly more productive than resources in the hands of the poor.[99] This creates inefficiency by reducing the wealthy's private investment incentives. It also creates inefficient allocation of resources toward the wealthy as what are mistakenly deemed to be private property's outcomes are, in fact, merely a function of the disproportionate allocation of public goods.[100]

D *Inefficiency: Monopoly Power*

Private property gives rise to monopoly power and therefore inefficiency, leading Posner and Weyl (2017) to comment that "allocative efficiency and thus an efficient market economy is impossible in the presence of private ownership."[101] If you own property "which no one can take from you without your permission, you will be compensated for any investment you make by either your enjoyment of that [property] or the high price that you can charge a future buyer."[102] Monopoly's allocative inefficiency undermines productive efficiency since it is the sale rights that generate the price that is then employed in seeking to attain productive efficiency by equalizing marginal benefits and marginal costs. Thus, monopoly ultimately leads to a loss of both allocative and productive efficiency. This may explain the wastefulness sometimes associated with private property schemes; the high monopoly price may allow the use of, or investment in, resources even when it is inefficiently costly to so use or invest in such resources, giving rise to overuse and wastage. This provides another reason why private property can sometimes be conceived of as inconsistent with environmental and sustainable development considerations.

An owner's exclusive control exacerbates an additional variant of inefficiency. By guaranteeing an owner an increased return on their investment through enabling them to charge an increased price, private property provides incentives for the owner to invest in the asset.[103] However, such incentives are only available to the current owner. There are no investment incentives for other individuals, such as members of the surrounding community and the government, who can influence the property's value.[104] This highlights the argument that the ubiquity of externalities suggests that

monopolist by forcing her to generate the income to sustain a high valuation or turn her assets over to someone who can better use them."

[99] Liscow (2018) at 1656.

[100] In these cases where "WTP units" – rather than actual dollars – are being maximized, even the wealth maximization claim is patently invalid.

[101] Posner & Weyl (2017) at 51–52.

[102] Posner & Weyl (2018) at 35.

[103] Posner & Weyl (2017) at 64.

[104] Posner & Weyl (2017) at 64 note that there may also be cases where an owner cannot internalize all the benefits, leading to underinvestment in the property.

the market does not do a good job in efficient allocation of resources as externalities indicate that the price system transmits incorrect information on value.[105]

Commodity private property's premise of productive efficiency as an individualistic enterprise is therefore highly questionable and so would therefore be the idea of a property that gives an owner full monopolistic benefits.

The interaction between property's regressivity and monopoly goes both ways. Monopoly facilitates inequitable distributions while increasingly inequitable distributions facilitate further monopoly power and so further inefficiency. The result is the continual aggravation of both inequality and inefficiency. Commodity property alone is unable to arrest this downward spiral, it being responsible for it.

IV REALLOCATION OF POLITICAL POWER

Much of the debate raising issues of distribution in relation to private property takes place in the context of the institutional debates on whether courts ought to confine themselves to matters of efficiency or should also deal with distributive questions. Kaplow & Shavell's double distortion argument prescribes a two-step process where courts make determinations based on efficiency and relegate distributive questions to the political process. By increasing inequality, commodity private property's regressivity may, at the first step, create a powerful propertied class that can come to dominate the political system. This dominance raises the prospect of legal outcomes that are even more regressive and inefficient as such propertied class tilts the political and economic system in its own favor. Thus, by the time distributive processes are set to take place, the winners in the first step will have set matters up so that they emerge as winners yet again.

Indeed, substantial evidence suggests that, due to the nature of the political process, the distributional consequences of assertedly efficient decisions will tend to stick.[106] Legislative roadblocks – such as what Fennell and McAdams refer to as political action costs – stand in the way of the offsetting of distributional

[105] Mattei & Pradi at 43 and 48. Posner at 42 and 63 has acknowledged that the existence of substantial externalities and/or high transaction costs creates a scenario where exclusive rights may reduce efficiency.

[106] Fennell & McAdams and Liscow (2018) reference a variety of political frictions causing the distributional consequences of efficient policies to stick. There is some debate on the point, best made clear by Liscow & Paez at 8–9 as follows:

> Empirically, we are uncertain about the extent to which taxes and transfers compensate for legal rules' distributional impacts. There has been much recent attention to the lack of compensation to those harmed by trade (Autor *et al.*, 2013). Liscow (2018b) studies the universe of state school finance decisions and finds no taxes and transfers to compensate for those large distributional impacts, even decades after the fact. On the other hand, Boylan and Mocan (2013) find that there does appear to be rough compensation in the aftermath of court orders on prison spending, leading to a reduction in cash welfare expenditures. So it is not clear what reality is. Indeed, it could vary from context to context, depending upon the constellation of political actors, institutions, salience to voters, and a host of other factors.

impacts.[107] These costs include political inertia, since action is generally costlier than inaction, especially given many veto points.[108] Interest groups which would be negatively affected by the distribution can exploit veto points to block distribution.[109] Psychology's prospect theory consistently finds that people weight losses more heavily than gains; creating an inequitable judicial outcome and then waiting on tax and spending to resolve it therefore generate elevated disutility to the initial beneficiaries, thereby undermining utility maximization and creating increased political resistance to distributive measures.[110] It is notable that neither Congress nor the general public seem to think of taxation as properly serving distributive goals.[111] The experimental literature has also consistently found a strong aversion to any charges labeled as a tax.[112] Benefits and costs distributed across groups through legal rules tend to be implicit, while those distributed through the tax and spending mechanism are explicit.[113] The reduced visibility of the initial regressive policies relative to the distributive tax and spending policies makes the latter policies appear to be unfair and contrary to just deserts, increasing resistance to such measures.[114] Private property's privileged position in thought also dresses the results of judicial determinations on private property with an air of just inevitability which gives any second-stage distributive efforts an air of illegitimacy. In a socio-political world already beset by preexisting conflicts over various issues, including race and gender, distributive politics becomes extremely contentious.[115]

Law and economics features a non-transaction costs descriptive account of law; on this account, laws also result from the rent-seeking activities of politically

[107] Fennell & McAdams at 1053.

[108] Fennell & McAdams at 1082 and 1085; Liscow (2018) at 1665.

[109] Fennell & McAdams at 1087.

[110] Fennell & McAdams at 1094; Posner at 644.

[111] Fennell & McAdams at 1074, fn 69; Liscow (2018) at 1697.

[112] Fennell & McAdams at 1098. Constitutions, laws, and courts around the world, including in the US, place greater formal requirements on tax laws in many a context. One suggestion has been that distribution should avoid this hostility toward tax by focusing on the transfer element, that is, on fiscal policy; see Theodore Seto, A Challenge to Optimal Tax Orthodoxy, *JOTWELL* (July 30, 2018) (reviewing Liscow (2018)), attributing the suggestion to legal scholar Ed Kleinbard. But, as Liscow (2018) shows, spending policies are especially subject to a particularly pernicious form of pro-wealthy bias in which the wealthy receive more without even paying for it due to the predominance of cost–benefit analysis in public decision-making.

[113] De Geest (2013) at 7, fn 17 and fn 18. Public choice highlights that the benefits given to interest groups through the political system, more generally, are implicit. Posner at 734. Benefits and costs distributed across groups through legal rules also tend to be implicit. It thus appears that, in a world in which distributive questions are relegated to the tax and spending system, only distributional allocations to the poor – the one set of allocations meant to actually produce increased utility – end up being expected to be explicit, and so to bear the burden of resistance which such explicitness entails.

[114] Fennell & McAdams at 1099–101.

[115] Britton-Purdy *et al* at 1814.

powerful players.[116] This raises concerns with the double distortion argument's two-step process in that, in the first step, it further enriches the wealthy, thus affecting the political outcomes in the second step.[117] By taking such an approach, courts exacerbate socioeconomic inequality and class cleavages. This undermines the functionality of the very political system that courts would expect to resolve the problem created by their refusal to consider distributional issues or employ utility maximization. Given that private property's regressivity has already enriched one group through the courts' efficiency determination, the die is thus weighed against distribution. Pistor points out that efforts at distribution through taxes have become largely useless, with the tax system being used much more effectively in shielding the assets of the wealthy.[118] Awareness of the dynamic effects of wealth distribution as discussed above also increases WTP for the initial policy. The rise of intangibles as major holders of wealth, of which financial assets and data are the main examples, also means that control of the legal system has become even more important since intangibles exist only in the law.[119] Thus, contestation thereon is increased and between-groups differences in economic power and in knowledge on the political system become a major factor.[120] By increasing inequality, the idea that courts should not deal with distributive issues ultimately increases the costs imposed on society by rent-seeking activities – including damage to the political system – to a far higher degree than the ultimately less regressive outcomes from a judicial determination that considers distributive concerns.[121]

The political system itself thus becomes regressive in its allocations. Posner notes that one shortcoming of votes is that they do not reflect the intensity of preferences and then asserts that interest groups do reflect the intensity of preferences by using dollars to indicate their preferences.[122] This assertion of money as a marker of the alleged intensity of preferences is an acceptance of the political process as nakedly

[116] Christine Jolls, Cass Sunstein and Richard Thaler: A Behavioral Approach to Law and Economics, 50 *Stanford Law Review* 1471, 1508 (1998).

[117] Liscow & Paez at 8 note that "for example, it may be the case that a legal rule that benefits one group just improves its bargaining position for the next round of interest group politics."

[118] Pistor at 3 and at 20; see also Pistor at 8–9 and 71–72, noting that, by moving capital across different borders, the wealthy get to pick whatever law they want – and, using incorporation, whatever tax rate they desire – and so code their property any particular way they wish.

[119] Pistor at 8.

[120] These political power differences implicate many other parts of the legal system as well; for example, it has been argued that the criminal justice system, particularly in the sub-felony world of misdemeanors, "operates as a form of regressive taxation and wealth redistribution." Alexandra Natapoff, *Punishment without Crime: How Our Massive Misdemeanor System Traps the Innocent and Makes America More Unequal*, at 203–04 (Basic Books, 2018).

[121] Both judicial and political bodies will face rent-seeking, which will be influenced by inequality. However, there is no basis for a principle that specifically exacerbates inequality by excluding distributive considerations from either judicial bodies or political bodies. By prescribing exclusion of distributive outcomes from the judicial determination, the double distortion argument does just this.

[122] Posner at 15.

regressive. The judicially approved increased role for money in politics makes this concern particularly stark.[123] The WTP approach in public decision-making can affect the political system by exerting a regressive effect on the distribution of key democratic infrastructure; for example, the selection of voting locations might favor the wealthy.[124] With the ever-growing private power converted into public influence, it is folly to hope that commodity private property's beneficiaries would do anything other than change the meta-rules of the market to increase their accumulation of resources; in that increased rent-seeking lies the inevitability of further inefficiency. Britton-Purdy *et al* highlight that as private law became dominated by a wealth-maximizing approach in law and economics in the 1970s and 1980s – presumably duly leaving distributive issues to public law and the political branches – public law and the political branches moved away from distributive questions.[125] They attribute this to the US political system increasingly backing the interests of the wealthy as the wealthy get increasingly enriched by the private law system.[126] More generally, the US political system currently stands accused by various scholars of enacting the policy preferences of the wealthy rather than those of the majority,[127] with some evidence suggesting that only the preferences of higher-income groups matter for policymaking, with the preferences of lower-income groups being irrelevant.[128]

Given the various political action problems set out above, the two-step process that subjects only the distributive portion of the resource allocation inquiry to the political system – particularly to the political resistance of the tax and transfer system – is suboptimal from a welfare perspective as it prevents utility maximization.[129] If commodity private property is inherently regressive and results in increased resistance to an attempt to distribute and increase utility, then it seems that distributive matters should be an inherent part of the framework within which the structure of private property rights is determined so as to preclude the regressive effect from emerging; distributive questions should be determined together with efficiency questions.[130] As part of a response to Posner's consent justification for wealth

[123] Citizens United v. Federal Election Commission, 558 U.S. 310 (2010).

[124] Liscow (2018) at 1675 and 1677, fn 92.

[125] Britton-Purdy *et al* at 1789–90 and 1807–11. Other relevant measures by US courts that entail ceding ground on similar matters include those mentioned by Britton-Purdy *et al* at 1809; these are the judicial retreat from issues of structural inequality and the invalidation of laws that limit private spending or donations to electoral campaigns.

[126] Britton-Purdy *et al* at 1789–90 and 1807–11.

[127] Britton-Purdy *et al* at 1789 and at 1824 pointing out that the use of wealth maximization as an "orientating public value … has reinforced a very non-neutral drift toward elite control of government, increasingly described by political scientists as 'oligarchy.'"

[128] Britton-Purdy *et al* at 1789 and 1824; Liscow (2018) at 1665–66, fn 69 and 70. Olson's view that unitary groups with concentrated interests will generally prevail in the political market suggests that as inequality increases, the grip of the wealthy on the political system may also increase; this reinforces the dynamic instability of a commodity property framework.

[129] See also Fennell & McAdams at 1123.

[130] Fennell & McAdams at 1105–7.

maximization, Bebchuk points out that a wealth maximization criterion must carry a commitment to redistribution in order for it to be based on consent; as such, any wealth-maximization policy has to grant distribution as a matter of automatic right.[131] Bebchuk further notes that since the policy and redistribution are so closely attached to each other under a consent justification to a wealth-maximizing policy, a decision has to be made against such policy if the costs of distribution exceed the efficiency gains of the policy.[132] It seems counter to progress to insist that courts affirm a position that creates a one-way ratchet to inequity in the hope that another institution undo the damage done, especially when the judicial approach has already harmed the other institution's ability to undo such damage by creating economic imbalances that seriously undermine the asserted corrective measures.

Since private property is inherently regressive, ultimately inefficient, and vulnerable to manipulations of the political system, particularly by the economic beneficiaries of the private property system, the system is one that ultimately implodes if wealth maximization is its driving force. In order to get the best of the private property system, distributional questions ought to become part of the internal framework of property. Without this, commodity property is not a sustainable regulatory regime from both a theoretical and an institutional perspective.

V REGRESSIVE, INEFFICIENT COMMODITY PROPERTY IN THE INTERNET AGE

The inherent regressivity of private property and its inefficiencies have been highlighted particularly starkly since the advent of the internet age. Data-driven commerce increases monopoly power. Platform internet firms use data from sales to squeeze all gains from their interactions with sellers on their platform and ultimately to compete with them, eventually even excluding them altogether from the platform.[133] Personalized marketing enables commercial entities to use vast amounts of data to squeeze out much of the consumer surplus;[134] data themselves are for sale, facilitating the regressivity rush throughout the economy.[135] These measures take inequality to new heights. The internet age drives the regressivity and inefficiency further through reduced transaction costs and so increased transactions. Increased transactions could conceivably entail an increase in competition and so reduced monopoly power. But the dominance of platform entities and the capture of gains

[131] Bebchuk at 707.

[132] Bebchuk at 707. Fennell & McAdams at 1052–53 point out that, much like transaction costs are considered in determining the appropriate scope of law under law and economics, so should political action costs.

[133] Lina M. Khan, Amazon's Antitrust Paradox, 126 *Yale law Journal* 710 (2017).

[134] Gerrit De Geest, *Rents: How Marketing Causes Inequality* (Beccaria Books, 2018).

[135] Britton-Purdy *et al* at 1807, noting that, in what is possibly as much an indication of internet companies' political power as of their economic power, the sale of data has now received first amendment protection from regulation.

from trade using data undermine any such monopoly-reducing benefits that could have arisen.

Network effects in the internet age also create monopoly power and produce ever higher incentives on the part of property owners to increase their access to, and collect ever more, private data. De Geest has described network externalities, typical in the internet realm, as a source of rents creating income inequality which is best ameliorated through legal rules rather than the tax and spending system.[136] The Internet's network externalities suggest the existence of natural monopoly and concomitantly of regressivity. The long-standing understanding in legal and economic thought that natural monopoly justifies substantial regulatory activity highlights that this is therefore not a context for unrestricted commodity property.

The internet age is also an era associated with very high returns to talented and often initially poor entrepreneurs. This was initially a strength of the age, providing high returns to talent and innovation which created a unique entrepreneurship culture. As time has passed and early entrants have become entrenched, the wealth differential – rather than the level of talent and innovation – has become the main determinant of returns. From the perspective of the use of WTP, this is a case where increasing inefficiency has arisen in commodity property due to ATP increasingly becoming the major determinant of WTP. New innovations that threaten the established early entrants are acquired or forced out of the market as soon as their potential begins to show. Returns therefore accrue based on the mere fact of an initial resource advantage rather than higher creativity or productivity. Forced acquisition elbows out talented and innovative owners in an industry where talent and innovativeness are the source of a quality product. This scenario also undermines entrepreneurship incentives as many talented persons may find it unworthwhile to take the risk of expending time and effort on innovative activity. Those who nonetheless take the plunge risk being driven to penury and, even when they accede to a purchase, being deprived of control over a product that they may be best placed to develop. At the very least, their investment incentives are reduced by the reduction of their stake in the product. Some variant of property may have facilitated the internet age, but the current variant – which is probably the same, just further down the dynamic path – is choking it off. Relocation of resources under network effects means that first movers from that time have now become so empowered that they can block off the very channels that allowed them to rise; the age of the garage as an internet innovation incubator appears to be drawing to a (premature) end. At the societal level, this effect may block out already overlooked communities from enjoying the benefits of socioeconomic development in the internet age as members of such communities will tend to be underrepresented among first movers, particularly first movers of a bygone era.

[136] De Geest (2013) at 28.

Incentives for economic growth have become increasingly human capital related – especially since the onset of the internet age – and so require socio-economic mobility if they are to be sustained.[137] Posner asserts that much inequality arises from luck.[138] In this context, realigning property to emphasize talent and effort can accommodate, indeed requires, measures with an equitable bent. Even in the context of ensuring returns to talent and effort, the market system features a superstar phenomenon in which small differences in innate ability are magnified, with massive returns to the slightly more capable actor and minimal to the others. These massive returns to early entrants to the internet age and their consequent entrenchment entail present-bias as the benefits fall largely to the generations of these early entrants at a cost to future generations. Of note is that effect's interaction with luck in inheritance; the systemic implications are that the heirs of the superstars of yesteryear are able to retain a blockade on the potential superstars of today through limited social mobility. This constitutes a socioeconomic loss for society, one which has long existed with "old money" but is brought into sharper relief with the internet age's "new money." This present-bias also points to the fact that democracy's basic design neglects the interests of future generations. In addition to baking in current and past inequities, poor social mobility thus effectively leads to a loss of human capital and failure to maximize productivity, a major loss in what is rapidly becoming a knowledge economy.[139] Equity thus tends to converge with efficiency in respect of human capital.[140] More generally, evidence suggests that inequality reduces economic growth.[141] But even assuming the efficiency, or the wealth-creating effect, of scale due to network effects, there is a continuing regressive effect;[142] the empirical evidence suggests that benefits from any economic gains have not reached the poor in the last decades.[143]

The issue of systemic community effects bookmarks other concerns relating to political control. First-mover internet companies have become very politically powerful. There are risks that such companies may take control of other entities in cases where such a move is not economically efficient but is only profitable

[137] See Fennell at 595 highlighting that it is difficult to borrow, in financial markets, against one's human capital.

[138] Posner at 15, noting that

> much inequality of wealth reflects sheer luck – the luck of being born in a wealthy country, the luck of being a beneficiary or casualty of unpredictable shifts on consumer demands and labor markets, the luck of inheritance, the luck of the financial markets, the luck of whom you know, the luck of your parents' ability and willingness to invest in your human capital. The greater the role of luck in the distribution of wealth and economic opportunities, the more difficult it is to defend the existing distribution as just in a strong sense, though it may be just in the real sense that there is no practicable alternative.

[139] Posner at 647.

[140] Of course, prior inequities can result in misallocations in the *development* of human capital.

[141] Liscow (2018) at 1701.

[142] Bar-Gill at 506; Liscow (2018) at 1700.

[143] Liscow (2018) at 1701.

through the increased rent-seeking possibilities it provides. The data economy has featured the creation of echo chambers; these create political fragmentation and make political manipulation easy for any actors so inclined and especially easy for any internet monopoly that itself seeks to engage in such manipulation.[144] The monopolies in this internet age have the power to exacerbate inequalities through enabling and even promoting inter-group conflict in order to maintain political control and reap the resultant financial benefits. The internet age, as a function of its facilitation of increased elite control, can put a partial lid on vocal agitators for social and economic reform. This is because it ensures easier control over not just the actions and coordination of the populace, but also their views through the control of data. Britton-Purdy *et al* note that:[145]

"Even as public-law doctrine has skewed political influence toward corporations and the wealthy, the "private" economy has yielded a public sphere dominated by monopolies, from "old media" regional newspaper and television markets to Facebook, Twitter, and the other dominant digital platforms. Ironically, these developments have produced both concentration of ultimate control and fragmentation of political argument into ideologically homogeneous segments, whether in a city with only one newspaper or in the echo chambers of online argument."

There is therefore reason to question the choice to use commodity property as a primary regulatory option in the context of the internet age. Alternative regulatory schemes for the Internet – including forms of state ownership or regulation as well as adjustments to private property – ought to be considered as the internet age has introduced new challenges. These ideas also ought to be thought of in a transnational perspective given the reach of the Internet, which has effects that reach across jurisdictions in more extensive ways than have ever existed before. The ubiquity of cross-border implications in relation to the Internet means that the infusion of a public law aspect to the property scheme may be more difficult with internet-age products than it would be with standard-form physical goods.

VI REASSESSING PERSPECTIVES

A *Junking the WTP-Based Normative Hobbes Theorem*

The application of a WTP-based normative Hobbes theorem in a judicial context is well-nigh indefensible. As noted above, this approach entails allocating private rights to the wealthy without their even having to pay for them. It is therefore a particularly regressive element of commodity private property which does not come armed with

[144] A view consistent with the individual incentive premise of commodity property would suggest that there is little reason why the owners of these entities would not try to engage in manipulation if it benefits them.

[145] Britton-Purdy *et al* at 1807.

significant efficiency benefits.[146] The use of WTP in contexts where the allocated resources are not paid for by the recipients has been associated with massive failures to comport with utility maximization.[147] Courts should adjust for utility maximization and engage in a fairly standard consideration of distributive issues.

Given that the normative Hobbes theorem entails the allocation of property rights to the party who values them most when the information costs of finding out who values a right the most are lower than transaction costs, one could say that a WTP perspective features a highly regressive, inefficient, and unhelpful simplification by pretending that – through WTP – the costs of finding out the party who values a property right the most are lower than they really are. The WTP-based normative Hobbes theorem ought to be abandoned in most of its dimensions.

B *Possible Alternatives to Commodity Property*

Like private property, state ownership and government regulation can also seek to internalize externalities.[148] There are no doubt some complications, including loss of efficiency – particularly productive efficiency – and concerns about political control, in using the direct political system as implicated by these public alternatives, in seeking to counter commodity property's regressive effects. Mixed regimes dominate in the real world, with governments in modern market economies generally addressing the tension between allocative efficiency and productive efficiency by adopting a "mixed regime" of property featuring strong private property rights for most ordinary types of property and significant deviations in special cases.[149] Posner and Weyl operate on the premise that private property is productively efficient but allocatively inefficient while most deviations deploy systems that tend to be

[146] It is on this point that there is a key difference between accession and the normative Hobbes theorem. The efficiency advantages of accession are based on its ability to select fit owners, an ability which "depends on the existence of a close enough connection between the primary asset and the derivative asset that the owner of the primary asset can exercise effective control over the derivative asset." Merrill (2009) at 491. The normative Hobbes theorem features no such search for a link – if such a link happens to exist in any one case, it is incidental. There are therefore no efficiency advantages to the normative Hobbes theorem, yet there are high distributional costs.

[147] Bar-Gill at 509 states as follows:

> If Individual A's wealth is in the seventieth percentile and Individual B's wealth is in the thirtieth percentile (which means that Individual A's wealth is 14.7 times greater than Individual B's wealth), then a WTP-based assessment will support Individual A's preferred policy, Policy A, even when the benefit provided by Individual B's preferred policy, Policy B, is 14.29 to 200 times greater, depending on the scale of the policies considered.

[148] Thomas Merrill, The Demsetz Thesis and the Evolution of Property Rights, 31 (S2) *Journal of Legal Studies*, S331 at S333 (2002) (Merrill (2002)).

[149] Posner & Weyl (2017) at 53.

allocatively efficient but productively inefficient.[150] Mixed systems generally seek to use private property rights where productive efficiency is more important than allocative efficiency and the alternative systems where allocative efficiency is more important than productive efficiency.[151] On its own terms, the mixing approach is wasteful as it pushes every form of property into one of the extreme molds such that there is always extreme inefficiency along either the investment dimension or the allocative dimension, that is, either private property with high allocative inefficiency or alternatives which tend toward high productive inefficiency.[152] More generally, this chapter notes that private property suffers from both allocative and productive inefficiencies. The extent to which the alternatives to private property can resolve regressivity concerns is unclear. It is also unclear whether the alternative options, applied side by side with commodity property, have any particularly systematic effects that could undo commodity property's highly systematic bias. Given the scale and systematic nature of this bias, mixing alone may be mitigatory in some cases, but it may not be enough.

Another option is the relatively novel – but by no means wholly new – approach presented by Posner and Weyl (2017) as a counter to commodity private property's monopoly power.[153] Posner and Weyl (2017) suggest that the monopoly problem created by private property be dealt with by way of a tax on property which is based on an owner's self-assessed value at intervals, along with a requirement that the owner sell the property to anyone willing to pay a price equal to the self-assessed value.[154] What Posner and Weyl (2017) suggest is a version of the use of liability rules in order to overcome monopoly. There is reason to believe that this approach will increase allocative efficiency; this approach is likely to feature prohibitive administrative costs.[155] Its effects on equity are also less determinate.[156] Further, this approach is state-centric and features the associated afflictions.

A political system that fails to carry out distribution even within a static dimension can hardly be expected to successfully do so when the dynamic element associated

[150] Posner & Weyl (2017) at 53.
[151] Posner & Weyl (2018) at 51.
[152] Posner & Weyl (2018) at 51.
[153] Posner & Weyl (2017).
[154] Posner & Weyl (2017).
[155] Merrill (2009) at 487 notes that auctions of new resources have been suggested in contexts such as patents and been implemented in specific cases such as those of broadcast spectrum rights and that these are allocatively efficient. He asserts, however, that auctions seem to feature high administrative costs. One perspective could be that the transaction costs may be worth it when the gains from monopoly reduction are fully considered.
[156] Posner & Weyl's (2017) suggestion can serve distributive goals in that, much like the idea raised in picking the area of application for the alternative (to Kaplow & Shavell) legal rule in Liscow (2014) and suggested above in discussing ex ante legal rules qua De Geest (2013), the decision on when to apply or enforce a legal rule can be made with the specific goal of promoting equitable distribution. That decision does face a familiar challenge in that it is at risk of political takeover by those with political and/or economic power.

with commodity private property as set out above is introduced. Unlike the losses from isolated discrete policy decisions, here we have dynamic ongoing losses. The dynamic effect entails greater inequality such that much larger levels of compensation are required, but compensation for these dynamic effects is far less likely to be provided. Most tax and transfer type schemes do not effect an ongoing adjustment and so lack the dynamic element to keep up with private property's ongoing regressivity. The result is that, even in those cases where compensation can be found, under-compensation is endemic. An adjustment scheme that travels with commodity property's regressive mechanism is required. One possible source of such a schematic structure is a more socially sensitive notion of private property.

Another suggestion has therefore been an approach in which equitable and social considerations are factored into property's definition. This implicates the progressive account of property in which the role of property is viewed as being the facilitation of human flourishing.[157] One key idea here relates to the social obligation norm in property law.[158] It is the idea, one specifically presented as an alternative to the law and economics vision that has held sway for the last several decades, that social obligations inhere in all property rights.[159] The social obligation norm is associated with general limits on owners' power to use resources and the employment of limits on owners' rights to use their property and to exclude others from such property, as well as the use of liability rules in place of property rules to loosen the grip of property owners relative to the wider world.[160] Justifications for such measures include the fact that property holdings often arise from appropriations from others – there is no shortage of such appropriations in history – as well as the fact that public inputs often account for much of private property's value.[161] The latter point is made especially starkly by Liscow's (2018) exposition on the regressive implications of cost–benefit analysis. Another justification arises from the fact that property entitlements often draw from the public stock in ways that preclude others from being able to similarly exert effort on the same resources; this implicates the famous Lockean proviso that there must be "enough, and as good, left in common for others."[162]

It is clear that the use of a progressive vision of private property can at least mitigate some of the regressivity and inefficiencies associated with commodity property. The extent to which this can occur is debatable, especially given the novel challenges of governing in the internet age.

[157] Gregory S. Alexander, Eduardo M. Peñalver, Joseph William Singer, & Laura S. Underkuffler, A Statement of Progressive Property, 94 *Cornell Law Review* 743 (2009).

[158] Alexander at 745, 750.

[159] Alexander at 750.

[160] Alexander at 752; see also Calabresi & Melamed on property rules and liability rules.

[161] Fennell at 608.

[162] Fennell at 608.

C *Implications for Some Other Areas of the Law*

Private property's regressivity provides some justification for relatively strong social welfare systems. The role of different types of goods in generating the declining marginal utility of income suggests that private property is made more stable when the basics needed for daily life are more freely available and are less pressing on the citizenry. A stable property scheme therefore depends on a stable social safety net. This point might even provide some support to suggestions that there ought to be a universal basic income. Lower levels of inequality can also increase innovation by minimizing the costs of failure, a view fortified by the general consensus that most people are risk-averse in most settings. When one considers the regressive distribution of entrepreneurship, it seems that the provision of social welfare may increase innovation and enable innovation and its benefits to be more widely and fairly distributed.

The Maslow-based argument in respect of the declining marginal utility of income suggests that there is good reason to provide strong consumer law protection in respect of basic consumer goods. The inefficiency of commodity property, especially as raised by De Geest's arguments on rents, suggests a case for considering inequality in deciding upon enforcement priorities in competition law. The issue of commercial actors capturing all the consumer surplus as a driver of inequality has become especially important in our data-powered internet age.

Imperfect financial markets mean that the ability to invest in order to procure additional resources is driven by having resources and so is regressive. Baradaran's work highlights how long-term *en masse* systemic discrimination against minorities in financial markets has fostered lasting inequality.[163] Improving financial markets may, in principle, mitigate the regressive effects in issue. But a narrow focus on simply making financial markets more efficient is inadequate at best and very conceivably regressive. Otherwise, relatively efficient financial markets in a setting featuring other socioeconomic inequalities may merely serve as an engine that allows the wealthy to further outstrip others in capturing the gains of economic growth. A consciously equality-premised restructuring of financial markets – one that takes into account past and current socioeconomic inequalities – is therefore long overdue.

Private property shows a systemic present-bias in which efficiency is highest at an initial egalitarian point (often an immediate post-redistribution point) and then progressively declines in concert with reductions in equality. This suggests an inter-generational dynamic where current generations allocate high rewards to their

[163] Mehrsa Baradaran, *How the Other Half Banks: Exclusion, Exploitation and the Threat to Democracy* (Harvard University Press, 2015); Mehrsa Baradaran, *The Color of Money: Black Banks and the Racial Wealth Gap* (Belknap Press/Harvard University Press, 2017); Mehrsa Baradaran, Banking on Democracy, 98 *Washington University Law Review* 353 (2020).

own stars to maximize benefits for their generation, even if that comes at the expense of future generations and their stars.[164] This issue becomes highly visible when new realms such as the internet age are under consideration, in part because these circumstances initially often entail a relatively "egalitarian" new zone, much like Locke's plentiful land. This makes the consequent decline into inequality especially visible and exhibits that rising inequality at a stage where it has yet to take on the aura of inevitability. These concerns call for some discussion about the proper systemic role of succession law and private property. It may relate to a need to refashion the nature and role of estate taxes and to rethink the role of institutions such as the trust.[165] At a societal level is also suggested an inter-generational dynamic in which current generations hardwire current inequalities into the socioeconomic systems of the future. This range of inter-generational realities constitute a somewhat neglected, yet key, element of the overall sustainable development discourse.

VII CONCLUSION

A commodity vision of private property is inherently regressive. Further, it is often inefficient. Finally, it creates political incentives to make its effects even more regressive and inefficient. These failings reach fever pitch in the context of the internet age. There is now the need for a property that incentivizes usage of resources without necessarily incentivizing collection of more resources. Even though unjust and unsustainable patterns of resource usage have long been a concern, an internet age which facilitates access to ever wider swathes of resources, and is itself built on an accumulative bedrock that comes at high cost to democratic politics and subsequent entrepreneurship, has – together with other pressing demands of the age such as heightened environmental concerns[166] – now rendered this a matter of urgency. Perhaps a view which considers the social obligations of private property – and one which also looks beyond efficiency to consider other interests such as liberty, personhood and human flourishing[167] – provides a better range of options in dealing with these changes. Posner and Weyl (2017) note that "advances in technology and the design of institutions ... may shrink the zone in which private property is superior."[168]

[164] This is a generalization of the concern with patents, where excessive current patenting can undermine future innovative activity. This concern afflicts private property in general, in ways that may require significant adjustment or resolution.

[165] Note the detailed discussion of the trust in Pistor at 42–45.

[166] Britton-Purdy *et al* at 1788 assert that "the model of economic growth and resource extraction at the heart of today's capitalism is on a collision course with human existence as we have known it."

[167] Alexander & Peñalver at 17.

[168] Posner & Weyls (2017) at 58.

Failures in the political market suggest that there is reason to worry that policy may not be taken on a principled basis.[169] Those failures also indicate that this critique of private property is no claim that government regulation of some sort can prove itself a panacea. Indeed, the case for market orientation (and so commodity property) included not just the market fundamentalist notion that markets were efficient and ideal, but also a market tragedy idea from public choice theory – which gives us the rent-seeking descriptive account of law discussed above – in terms of which governments were not to be trusted to make judgements about value and distribution.[170] Yet if the market tragedy idea stands, then the consensus view in law and economics that courts ought to decide based on efficiency and leave distribution to the political market is akin to an abandonment of distributive issues. A property vision that ignores vast swathes of the measure of human well-being surely disserves its own asserted *raison d'être*. Even ideas of private property as a force for democracy, important as they are, may require rethinking. For private property may well proceed to undermine democracy if pressed into service in areas where it is no longer a good fit. The value of private property as providing for decentralization of power is now highly questionable in the context of the internet age where worldwide monopoly and oligopoly reign supreme.

If it be shown that a commodity idea of private property is inherently regressive, generally inefficient, and given to an undermining of political, economic, and social systems, then the idea of commodity property as the natural order of things – or of such property as being appropriate in any sustainable long-run sense – is open to serious question. And the internet age has begun to raise those serious questions particularly starkly; it is on the shores of the internet age that the regressivity and inefficiency of commodity property may ultimately lead to its ruin.

[169] Klick & Parisi at 591.
[170] Britton-Purdy *et al* at 1801.

12

The EU Regulatory Patchwork for Dark Patterns

An Illustration of an Inframarginal Revolution in European Law?

Inge Graef

CONTENTS

I INTRODUCTION[1]

In January 2023, the European Commission and a range of national consumer authorities in Europe announced that 148 out of 399 online shopping websites they had investigated as part of a screening exercise employed some form of dark

[1] Please note that this chapter was finalized in May 2023 and is based on sources available at that time. References to the AI Act and the Data Act were updated in January 2025 to reflect the adopted text, but other sources could not be updated or added.

patterns.[2] Dark patterns are 'tricks used in websites and apps that make you do things that you didn't mean to, like buying or signing up for something'.[3] They concern manipulative practices that exploit consumer vulnerabilities or lead consumers to making choices that are not in their best interests.[4]

The announcement is only one instance of the current regulatory wave against dark patterns in the European Union (EU). Beyond the EU consumer rules,[5] the General Data Protection Regulation (GDPR)[6] can be relied upon to protect individuals against dark patterns in some circumstances. And scholarly literature has started to discuss the role of competition enforcement in this area as well.[7] Beyond this, provisions targeting dark patterns have been included in the Digital Services Act,[8] the Digital Markets Act,[9] the Artificial Intelligence (AI) Act[10] and the Data Act.[11] Each of these frameworks has its own substantive scope and enforcement mechanisms.

2 Press Release European Commission, 'Consumer protection: Manipulative online practices found on 148 out of 399 online shops screened', 30 January 2023, available at https://ec.europa.eu/commission/presscorner/detail/en/ip_23_418.

3 The term 'dark patterns' was first used by Harry Brignull in 2010, available at www.deceptive.design/#:~:text=Deceptive%20design%20patterns%20(also%20known,companies%20that%20use%20these%20patterns.

4 For a discussion of the definition of 'dark patterns', see OECD, 'Dark Commercial Patterns', OECD Digital Economy Papers October 2022 No. 336, pp. 8–9, available at www.oecd-ilibrary.org/docserver/44f5e846-en.pdf?expires=1678448863&id=id&accname=guest&checksum=6283E62D95CBE1A7A9E7A2A046E1B797.

5 Council Directive 93/13/EEC of 5 April 1993 on unfair terms in consumer contracts (Unfair Contract Terms Directive) [1993] OJ L 95/29; Directive 2005/29/EC of the European Parliament and of the Council of 11 May 2005 concerning unfair business-to-consumer commercial practices in the internal market (Unfair Commercial Practices Directive) [2005] OJ L 149/22; Directive 2011/83/EU of the European Parliament and of the Council of 25 October 2011 on consumer rights (Consumer Rights Directive) [2011] OJ L 304/64.

6 Regulation (EU) 2016/679 of the European Parliament and of the Council of 27 April 2016 on the protection of natural persons with regard to the processing of personal data and on the free movement of such data, and repealing Directive 95/46/EC (General Data Protection Regulation) [2016] OJ L 119/1.

7 See, for instance, Gregory Day & Abbey Stemler, 'Are dark patterns anticompetitive', *Alabama Law Review* 2020, Vol. 72 No. 1, pp. 1–45.

8 Regulation (EU) 2022/2065 of the European Parliament and of the Council of 19 October 2022 on a Single Market for Digital Services (Digital Services Act) [2022] OJ L 277/1.

9 Regulation (EU) 2022/1925 of the European Parliament and of the Council of 14 September 2022 on contestable and fair markets in the digital sector (Digital Markets Act) [2022] OJ L 265/1.

10 Regulation (EU) 2024/1689 of the European Parliament and of the Council of 13 June 2024 laying down harmonised rules on artificial intelligence and amending Regulations (EC) No 300/2008, (EU) No 167/2013, (EU) No 168/2013, (EU) 2018/858, (EU) 2018/1139 and (EU) 2019/2144 and Directives 2014/90/EU, (EU) 2016/797 and (EU) 2020/1828 (Artificial Intelligence (AI) Act) [2024] OJ L 2024/1689.

11 Regulation (EU) 2023/2854 of the European Parliament and of the Council of 13 December 2023 on harmonised rules on fair access to and use of data and amending Regulation (EU) 2017/2394 and Directive (EU) 2020/1828 (Data Act) [2023] OJ L 2023/2854.

The increasing attention for the issue of dark patterns may be seen as an illustration of an inframarginal revolution in European law and policy. The use of dark patterns is typically an attempt by businesses to increase their revenue at the expense of consumers who purchase products they may not need, spend more time or give up more personal data than they would otherwise do. Furthermore, there is evidence that less educated consumers are more prone to be affected by dark patterns than more educated consumers.[12] Dark patterns thus raise distributive issues that are worth considering from an inframarginal perspective. The elimination of dark patterns has the simultaneous effect of redistributing wealth from firms to consumers and addressing inefficiencies that result from the distortions in demand. Dark patterns therefore implicate the part of inframarginalism involving redistribution of wealth that is efficient in character.

Instead of focusing on the more normative issue of when dark patterns should be considered harmful, the chapter compares the different legal frameworks applicable to these practices and asks to what extent the increasingly fragmented EU regulatory landscape can offer effective overall protection against dark patterns. The objective is to draw lessons for improving the enforcement against dark patterns based on the current EU regulatory framework and for informing possible future inframarginal revolutions against other practices in European law.

Section II gives some background to the issue of dark patterns. Section III analyses the different forms of legal protection available to address dark patterns by focusing on two features, namely the main triggers for protection (for instance, type of behaviour, processing of personal data, existence of market power) and the method of enforcement. Section IV evaluates the current state of affairs and offers some suggestions to improve the coordination between the different legal frameworks and enforcers involved. Section V concludes.

II DARK PATTERNS AND THEIR IMPACT

The term 'dark patterns' brings together a wide range of practices relating to the use of choice architectures or user interfaces to trick users into making decisions desired by the designer. Dark patterns can take different shapes and may, for instance, consist of pop-up boxes or the use of colours or persuasive language to give prominence to certain options. They can emerge in all sorts of services, such as apps, e-commerce platforms, cookie consent notices, online games, and so on.[13] Beyond the variety in which they appear, what dark patterns have in common is that they often involve the exploitation of consumers' behavioural biases.[14] This includes

[12] Jamie Luguri & Lior Jacob Strahilevitz, 'Shining a light on dark patterns', *Journal of Legal Analysis* 2021, Vol. 13 No. 1, p. 47.

[13] OECD, 'Dark Commercial Patterns', OECD Digital Economy Papers October 2022 No. 336, p. 9.

[14] Luguri & Strahilevitz, 'Shining a light on dark patterns', p. 44.

biases like default or status quo bias (the tendency to remain with the default choice), framing effects (bias towards choosing options that are presented as a gain rather than a loss) and social proof bias (the tendency to make choices that align with those of others). Dark patterns trigger 'System 1 thinking' to induce individuals to respond more quickly and unconsciously without activating the more slow and rational 'System 2 thinking'.[15] Several categories of dark patterns are distinguished, namely:[16]

- forced action: consumers being tricked into thinking registration is necessary or sharing more personal data about themselves and others than intended
- interface interference: hidden information, emotionally manipulative framing, preselection of options
- nagging: repeated requests to act favourably to the business, exploiting consumers' limited willpower
- obstruction: making it difficult for users to reject or opt out of a service
- sneaking: hidden costs or unanticipated automatic renewal of subscriptions
- social proof: false or misleading testimonials or activity messages of other consumers
- urgency or scarcity: messages about low stock, high demand or the use of a countdown timer

The ultimate goal behind a business's decision to use dark patterns is to increase one's revenue by tricking consumers into buying products or services they may not need, buying more than they need, or, in case of advertising-based business models, spending more time and attention or giving up more personal data than they would otherwise do. Commercial pressure and market forces may sometimes lead businesses to use dark patterns if everyone else does and give rise to a 'race to the bottom' when consumers can or do not discipline the use of dark patterns by switching to businesses who do not employ such practices.[17] The inability of the market to self-correct against dark patterns pleads for regulatory intervention.

Dark patterns can cause economic as well as non-economic harm for individuals. Economic harm consists of financial losses when consumers purchase products or services they would not have bought otherwise or spend more money than they

[15] Daniel Kahneman, *Thinking, Fast and Slow* (Penguin Books, 2011).

[16] See consolidated versions of existing dark pattern taxonomies in OECD, 'Dark Commercial Patterns', OECD Digital Economy Papers October 2022, No. 336, p. 53 (Annex B) and Luguri & Strahilevitz, 'Shining a light on dark patterns', p. 53 (table 1).

[17] M. R. Leiser, 'Dark patterns: The case for regulatory pluralism between the European Union's consumer and data protection regimes', in E. Kosta, R. Leenes & I. Kamara (eds.), *Research Handbook on EU Data Protection Law* (Edward Elgar, 2022), p. 242 and Stigler Committee on Digital Platforms, Final Report 2019, p. 87.

intended. Non-economic harm concerns the impact on the individual's privacy and independent decision-making as well as emotional distress in situations where dark patterns induce impulsive and addictive behaviour.[18] When a dark pattern causes a consumer to spend unnecessary time, attention or energy, the non-economic harm can also take the form of an increased cognitive burden.[19] Beyond harm at the level of individual consumers and citizens, dark patterns can also have a collective impact. While the impact of dark patterns on individual welfare has dominated the literature so far, their effect on collective welfare can also be pronounced in the form of weaker competition and less consumer trust.[20] Dark patterns can reduce price transparency, limit the ability of consumers to choose offerings that truly match their preferences, and make them lose faith in market forces and disengage.[21] As a result of these effects, the mechanism of supply and demand may no longer deliver proper market outcomes.[22]

Commercial practices, including in a brick-and-mortar context, often have a persuasive element, and distinguishing persuasion from manipulation can be difficult.[23] However, dark patterns are more effective and therefore potentially more harmful than equivalent practices in a brick-and-mortar setting because of their larger scale and more intrusive character.[24] While the increasing regulatory attentions shows a strong consensus that dark patterns are harmful, establishing the boundaries of legal protection remains a challenge. The determination of what is and what is not allowed under the current EU legal framework mainly stems from inherent restrictions in the scope of the different legal domains and not so much from a normative assessment of the risks of dark patterns – as we will see in the next section.

III PATCHWORK OF EU REGULATORY RESPONSES AGAINST DARK PATTERNS

The nature of dark patterns brings together several policy concerns, both at the level of individual and collective welfare – as indicated in Section II. These concerns

18 Arunesh Mathur, 'Dark patterns at scale: Findings from a crawl of 11K shopping websites', *Proceedings of the ACM on Human–Computer Interaction*, Vol. 3/CSCW, pp. 3–4.

19 Arunesh Mathur, Jonathan Mayer & Mihir Kshirsagar, 'What makes a dark pattern … dark? Design attributes, normative considerations, and measurement methods', *Proceedings of the 2021 CHI Conference on Human Factors in Computing Systems*, p. 10.

20 Mathur et al., 'What makes a dark pattern … dark?', p. 11.

21 OECD, 'Dark Commercial Patterns', OECD Digital Economy Papers October 2022 No. 336, pp. 26–28. On consumer disengagement, see Luguri & Strahilevitz, 'Shining a light on dark patterns', p. 69.

22 See also George A. Akerlof & Robert J. Shiller, *Phishing for Phools* (Princeton University Press, 2016).

23 In the context of advertising, see Ramsi Woodcock, 'The obsolescence of advertising in the information age', *The Yale Law Journal* 2018, Vol. 127 No. 8, pp. 2204–585.

24 Mathur et al., 'What makes a dark pattern … dark?, p. 9.

relate to values like privacy, autonomy and competition as well as to interests regarding the protection of our society and democracy against the steering of choices by commercial players. It is thus logical that the use of dark patterns can trigger the application of several legal regime in parallel. This section analyses the different forms of legal protection in the current EU regulatory framework against dark patterns along two features: the main triggers for protection and the method of enforcement.

A *Triggers for Protection against Dark Patterns*

1 EU Consumer Law

The EU consumer law framework can be used to target dark patterns, both through broad principle-based protections as well as specific provisions. As this section will show, the notion of 'fairness' is at the heart of protection under EU consumer law. Beyond broad provisions prohibiting 'unfair practices' and 'unfair contract terms', the more specific protections applicable to dark patterns in the EU consumer law framework can be seen as concrete interpretations of the more general concept of 'fairness' as well.

Most relevant is the Unfair Commercial Practices Directive,[25] which prohibits a commercial practice as unfair if it is contrary to the requirements of professional diligence and 'materially distorts or is likely to materially distort the economic behaviour' of the average consumer.[26] The latter is at issue when the use of a commercial practice appreciably impairs 'the consumer's ability to make an informed decision, thereby causing the consumer to take a transactional decision that he would not have taken otherwise'.[27] In its December 2021 Guidance on the Unfair Commercial Practices Directive, the European Commission interpreted the requirement of professional diligence as including a general principle for traders to 'take appropriate measures to ensure that the design of their interface does not distort the transactional decisions of consumers'.[28] One could regard this as a duty for

[25] For a discussion of the application of the Unfair Commercial Practices Directive to dark patterns, see also M. R. Leiser & Mireille M. Caruana, 'Dark patterns: Light to be found in Europe's consumer protection regime', *Journal of European Consumer and Market Law* 2021, Vol. 10 No. 6, pp. 245–48.

[26] Article 5(2) of Directive 2005/29/EC of the European Parliament and of the Council of 11 May 2005 concerning unfair business-to-consumer commercial practices in the internal market (Unfair Commercial Practices Directive) [2005] OJ L 149/22.

[27] Article 2(e) of the Unfair Commercial Practices Directive. This is known as the 'transaction test'.

[28] Commission Notice – Guidance on the interpretation and application of Directive 2005/29/EC of the European Parliament and of the Council concerning unfair business-to-consumer commercial practices in the internal market OJ C 526/1, p. 101.

traders to do 'fairness by design' by avoiding that interfaces give rise to dark patterns and instead ensuring that the design of the online environment enables people to make choices in a fair way.[29] According to the Commission, international standards and codes of conduct for ethical design may inform what the standard of professional diligence entails in the area of interface design and no intention is required for a dark pattern to be captured by the prohibition of unfair commercial practices.[30] Because of the open-ended nature of the requirement of professional diligence, many manipulative practices distorting the consumers' decision-making could potentially qualify as an unfair commercial practice. Annex I to the Unfair Commercial Practices Directive blacklists practices that are to be regarded as unfair in all circumstances. This includes practices that can be labelled as dark patterns, for instance the use of false statements referring to the limited time period in which the product or service will be available.[31]

Apart from laying down a general definition of 'unfairness', the Unfair Commercial Practices Directive distinguishes between two main categories of unfair practices: misleading and aggressive ones.[32] Again, a key element in the assessment is whether the misleading or aggressive commercial practice 'causes or is likely to cause the average consumer to take a transactional decision that he would not have taken otherwise'.[33] Beyond this, a commercial practice is regarded as misleading if 'it omits material information that the average consumer needs' or contains false information, including overall presentation, and therefore 'deceives or is likely to deceive the average consumer' even if the information is factually correct.[34] The inclusion of the overall presentation of information as a possible factor is especially relevant for dark patterns involving hidden information or pre-selection and more prominent display of certain options.[35] The use of ambiguous language or trick questions may also qualify as a misleading practice or omission when it can deceive consumers.[36]

[29] See also Netherlands Authority for Consumers and Markets (ACM), 'Guidelines on the protection of the online consumer', version of 15 March 2023, available at www.acm.nl/sites/default/files/documents/2020-02/acm-guidelines-on-the-protection-of-the-online-consumer.pdf.

[30] Commission Notice – Guidance on the interpretation and application of Directive 2005/29/EC of the European Parliament and of the Council concerning unfair business-to-consumer commercial practices in the internal market OJ C 526/1, p. 101.

[31] No. 7 of Annex I to the Unfair Commercial Practices Directive.

[32] Article 5(4) of the Unfair Commercial Practices Directive.

[33] Article 6(1), 7(1) and 8 of the Unfair Commercial Practices Directive.

[34] Article 6(1) (on misleading actions) and 7(1) (on misleading omissions) of the Unfair Commercial Practices Directive.

[35] BEUC, '"Dark patterns" and the EU consumer law acquis – Recommendations for better enforcement and reform', February 2022, p. 7, available at –www.beuc.eu/sites/default/files/publications/beuc-x-2022-013_dark_patters_paper.pdf.

[36] Commission Notice – Guidance on the interpretation and application of Directive 2005/29/EC of the European Parliament and of the Council concerning unfair business-to-consumer commercial practices in the internal market OJ C 526/1, p. 101.

A commercial practice is aggressive if 'by harassment, coercion, including the use of physical force, or undue influence, it significantly impairs or is likely to significantly impair the average consumer's freedom of choice or conduct with regard to the product'.[37] Examples in the context of dark patterns are the use of emotions, for instance to make consumers feel guilty about not opting in to a service, or obstruction techniques whereby a consumer has to click through multiple steps in order to cancel a service.[38] Regarding the latter practices, the Commission required traders in its 2021 Guidance to adhere to the principle that unsubscribing from a service should be as easy as subscribing to the service.[39]

Beyond the Unfair Commercial Practices Directive, the Consumer Rights Directive[40] and the Unfair Contract Terms Directive[41] can offer protection against dark patterns in some circumstances. The Consumer Rights Directive contains a specific provision entitling consumers to reimbursement of payment for additional services outside of the main contractual obligation when the consent of the consumer has been obtained by the use of default options.[42] In addition, the Consumer Rights Directive requires online marketplaces to provide the consumer with 'general information, made available in a specific section of the online interface that is directly and easily accessible from the page where the offers are presented, on the main parameters determining ranking'.[43] More generally, the Consumer Rights Directive lays down information obligations that are applicable before the conclusion of a contract,[44] whereas the Unfair Contract Terms Directive focuses on the contract terms themselves and requires them to 'be drafted in plain, intelligible language'.[45] As such, dark patterns relating to the lack of transparency or clarity in contract terms or information may fall foul of these two legislative frameworks. However, as many types of dark patterns occur beyond contracts, the Unfair

[37] Article 8 of the Unfair Commercial Practices Directive.

[38] Regarding obstruction techniques, see, for instance, the work of the Norwegian Consumer Council that led Amazon to make it easier for consumers to cancel their Prime subscription. See Press Release Norwegian Consumer Council, 'Amazon makes it easier to cancel Prime following complaints from European consumer organisations', 1 July 2022, available at www.forbrukerradet.no/side/amazon-makes-it-easier-to-cancel-prime-following-complaints-from-european-consumer-organisations/.

[39] Commission Notice – Guidance on the interpretation and application of Directive 2005/29/EC of the European Parliament and of the Council concerning unfair business-to-consumer commercial practices in the internal market OJ C 526/1, p. 102.

[40] Directive 2011/83/EU of the European Parliament and of the Council of 25 October 2011 on consumer rights (Consumer Rights Directive) OJ L 304/64.

[41] Council Directive 93/13/EEC of 5 April 1993 on unfair terms in consumer contracts (Unfair Contract Terms Directive) OJ L 95/29.

[42] Article 22 of the Consumer Rights Directive.

[43] Article 6a of the Consumer Rights Directive, as amended by Directive (EU) 2019/2161 of the European Parliament and of the Council of 27 November 2019 [2019] OJ L 328/7.

[44] Articles 5 and 6 of the Consumer Rights Directive.

[45] Article 5 of the Unfair Contract Terms Directive.

Commercial Practices Directive is the most relevant instrument in the current EU consumer protection framework.

What can be concluded from this overview is that the regulatory approach against dark patterns in EU consumer law consists of a continuum from open-ended provisions protecting against unfairness of commercial practices and contract terms, to more narrow prohibitions of misleading and aggressive commercial practices, and to very targeted prohibitions banning specific practices deemed unfair in all circumstances (including the Annex to the Unfair Commercial Practices containing blacklisted practices and the prohibition to use default options for additional payments in the Consumer Rights Directive). This combination of techniques strikes a balance between the effectiveness of targeted bans and the flexibility of open-ended protections to capture new concerns or practices that the legislator has not considered yet. However, only a limited range of dark patterns falls within the scope of the specific bans, so that in practice a case-by-case analysis is often required to assess whether a particular manipulative practice is to be considered as unfair under the more general provisions of the Unfair Commercial Practices Directive.

2 EU Data Protection Law

As the main instrument of EU data protection law, the GDPR[46] can offer protection against dark patterns if they involve the processing of personal data.[47] In February 2023, the European Data Protection Board (EDPB) published Guidelines on 'deceptive design patterns in social media platform interfaces', in which specific examples of dark patterns are described throughout the life cycle of a social media account and reference is made to data protection principles as they apply to dark patterns more generally.[48] There are several ways in which dark patterns may violate the GDPR. Compared to the EU consumer law framework, the protections available for dark patterns in the GDPR are not as targeted as, for instance, the specific bans on certain practices in the Unfair Commercial Practices Directive and the Consumer Rights Directive. Dark patterns relating to pre-ticked boxes will not meet the conditions for a valid consent in the GDPR and the ePrivacy Directive,

[46] Regulation (EU) 2016/679 of the European Parliament and of the Council of 27 April 2016 on the protection of natural persons with regard to the processing of personal data and on the free movement of such data (General Data Protection Regulation) [2016] OJ L 119/1.

[47] Article 4(1) of the GDPR defines personal data as: 'any information relating to an identified or identifiable natural person ("data subject"); an identifiable natural person is one who can be identified, directly or indirectly, in particular by reference to an identifier such as a name, an identification number, location data, an online identifier or to one or more factors specific to the physical, physiological, genetic, mental, economic, cultural or social identity of that natural person'.

[48] European Data Protection Board, 'Guidelines 03/2022 on Deceptive design patterns in social media platform interfaces: How to recognise and avoid them', 14 February 2023.

requiring an affirmative action from the data subject.[49] Similarly, dark patterns may involve the use of personal data for purposes incompatible with the original purposes of data collection (GDPR principle of purpose limitation) or go beyond what is necessary for the purposes for which the data are processed (GDPR principle of data minimization).[50] As a result, dark patterns may violate the regular EU data protection rules that are not specifically targeted at manipulative practices but aim to regulate the processing of personal data more generally. A similarity between the EU consumer and data protection frameworks is the role of the notion of 'fairness' as an underlying standard of protection.[51]

The principle of fair processing is key to the GDPR[52] and requires personal data not to 'be processed in a way that is unjustifiably detrimental, unlawfully discriminatory, unexpected or misleading to the data subject'.[53] According to the EDPB, the fairness principle acts as an umbrella that protects against 'deceptive design patterns' irrespective of whether other data protection principles are complied with.[54] The EDPB defines deceptive design patterns as: 'interfaces and user journeys implemented on social media platforms that aim to influence users into making unintended, respectively unwilling, and/or potentially harmful decisions, often toward an option that is against the users' best interests and in favour of the social media platforms interest, with regard to their personal data'.[55] Due to this broad definition, many dark patterns distinguished in Section II will fall foul of the GDPR's principle of fair processing in the view of the EDPB as long as they involve the processing of personal data.

Other more general data protection principles relevant in the context of dark patterns are accountability, transparency and data protection by design.[56]

[49] Article 4(11) of the GDPR and Articles 5 and 13 of Directive 2002/58/EC of the European Parliament and of the Council of 12 July 2002 concerning the processing of personal data and the protection of privacy in the electronic communications sector (ePrivacy Directive) [2002] OJ L 201/37. For a discussion of consent banners, see Colin Gray, Cristiana Santos, Nataliia Bielova, Michael Toth & Damian Clifford, 'Dark patterns and the legal requirements of consent banners: An interaction criticism perspective', *Proceedings of the 2021 CHI Conference on Human Factors in Computing Systems*, May 2021, available at https://doi.org/10.1145/3411764.3445779.

[50] Respectively, Articles 5(1)(b) and (c) of the GDPR.

[51] For an in-depth discussion of the role of fairness in EU data protection law, see Damian Clifford & Jef Ausloos, 'Data protection and the role of fairness', *Yearbook of European Law* 2018, Vol. 37, pp. 130–187.

[52] Article 5(1)(a) of the GDPR.

[53] European Data Protection Board, Guidelines 4/2019 on Article 25 Data Protection by Design and by Default, 20 October 2020, par. 69.

[54] European Data Protection Board, 'Guidelines 03/2022 on Deceptive design patterns in social media platform interfaces: How to recognise and avoid them', 14 February 2023, par. 3.

[55] European Data Protection Board, 'Guidelines 03/2022 on Deceptive design patterns in social media platform interfaces: How to recognise and avoid them', 14 February 2023, par. 9.

[56] European Data Protection Board, 'Guidelines 03/2022 on Deceptive design patterns in social media platform interfaces: How to recognise and avoid them', 14 February 2023, par. 10–19.

Accountability entails a responsibility of the data controller to ensure and demonstrate compliance with the GDPR, which can include tests or experiments showing how the design of the interface facilitates fair and informed choices relating to the processing of personal data.[57] The principle of transparency requires information relating to personal data processing to be provided to the data subject 'in a concise, transparent, intelligible and easily accessible form, using clear and plain language'.[58] Similar to the transparency and information requirements in EU consumer law, the GDPR thus has provisions protecting data subjects against a lack of clarity. Data protection by design concerns the implementation of 'appropriate technical and organisational measures ... designed to implement data-protection principles ... in an effective manner and to integrate the necessary safeguards into the processing' to meet the requirements of the GDPR and protect the rights of data subjects.[59] According to the EDPB, compliance with the principle of data protection by design would result in avoiding dark patterns in the first place as any problematic elements are to be identified before launching the service.[60]

With its guidelines, the EDPB thus gives a strong signal that dark patterns violate the GDPR once they involve the processing of personal data and deceive data subjects. However, unless a dark pattern breaches a particular GDPR provision (for instance, the validity of consent in case of default options), a case-by-case assessment is required to determine whether the practice indeed manipulates the data subject's decision-making. Effective protection against dark patterns under the GDPR therefore also depends on adequate implementation and enforcement of the relevant data protection principles.

3 Digital Services Act

The Digital Services Act, adopted in October 2022, includes a provision requiring providers of online platforms not to 'design, organise or operate their online interfaces in a way that deceives or manipulates the recipients of their service or in a way that otherwise materially distorts or impairs the ability of the recipients of their service to make free and informed decisions'.[61] While the provision is to be welcomed as a specific and clear prohibition on the use of dark patterns, it does have several limitations.

[57] Article 5(2) of the GDPR.

[58] Articles 5(1)(a) and 12(1) of the GDPR.

[59] Article 25(1) of the GDPR.

[60] European Data Protection Board, 'Guidelines 03/2022 on Deceptive design patterns in social media platform interfaces: How to recognise and avoid them', 14 February 2023, par. 19. For a discussion of how to apply the requirement of data protection by design to dark patterns, see Leiser, 'Dark patterns: The case for regulatory pluralism between the European Union's consumer and data protection regimes', pp. 246–248.

[61] Article 25(1) of the Digital Services Act. See also recital 67.

First, the ban only applies to providers of an online platform defined as 'a hosting service that, at the request of a recipient of the service, stores and disseminates information to the public'.[62] While the Digital Services Act applies some of its other obligations to the broader category of intermediary services, including, for instance, internet service providers and web-hosting services,[63] these latter services are not affected by the ban on dark patterns.

Second, the Digital Services Act entitles the Commission with the competence to issue guidelines on how the ban on dark patterns applies to specific practices and mentions three of them: (a) giving more prominence to certain choices when asking the recipient of the service for a decision; (b) repeatedly requesting that the recipient of the service make a choice where that choice has already been made, especially by presenting pop-ups that interfere with the user experience; and (c) making the procedure for terminating a service more difficult than subscribing to it.[64] While these are indeed common dark patterns, other dark patterns also exist that seem equally problematic. If it is the wish of the EU legislator to prioritize these forms of manipulative practices, one wonders why it has not laid down stricter rules or even targeted bans against these practices instead of leaving it up to the Commission to issue guidelines.

Third, the ban on dark patterns contained in the Digital Services Act does not apply to practices covered by the Unfair Commercial Practices Directive or the GDPR.[65] As discussed in the previous sections, these two instruments can indeed target dark patterns but often require a case-by-case analysis, and because of the broad, principle-based protections, their scope is not clear-cut. Although the assumption of the exclusion in the Digital Services Act seems to be that effective protection is already available under the Unfair Commercial Practices Directive and the GDPR, this is thus not necessarily the case.

Compared to the more general fairness-related triggers for protection under EU consumer and data protection law, the Digital Services Act is more explicit by including a specific ban on dark patterns targeted at online platforms. However, as discussed, the scope of the ban is narrow so that the Unfair Commercial Practices Directive and the GDPR are likely to remain more relevant as instruments in protecting against dark patterns. At the same time, a welcome aspect of the ban on dark patterns contained in the Digital Services Act is that it goes beyond the individual relationship between a trader or data controller and the consumer or data subject that forms the heart of the assessment in EU consumer and data protection law. Even if dark patterns do not have clearly distinguishable harm at the level of individual consumers or data subjects due to lack of proof of financial loss or

[62] Article 3(i) of the Digital Services Act.
[63] Article 3(g) of the Digital Services Act.
[64] Article 25(3) of the Digital Services Act.
[65] Article 25(2) of the Digital Services Act.

psychological detriment, they can still negatively impact the collective welfare by weakening competition and lowering consumer trust and engagement in markets.[66]

The stronger focus on the more collective impact is also clear from another provision in the Digital Services Act, which requires providers of very large online platforms and search engines to assess systemic risks 'stemming from the design or functioning of their service and its related systems' including 'the design of their recommender systems and any other relevant algorithmic system including algorithmic systems'.[67] Considering the references to the design of services, the risk assessments may relate to practices involving dark patterns as well.

4 AI Act

The AI Act was adopted in June 2024 with the aim of laying down harmonized rules across the EU for AI systems.[68] A number of AI practices are prohibited, including: 'the placing on the market, the putting into service or the use of an AI system' that:

(a) 'deploys subliminal techniques beyond a person's consciousness' or
(b) 'exploits any of the vulnerabilities of a natural person or a specific group of persons due to their age, disability or a specific social or economic situation'

with the objective or the effect of materially distorting the behaviour of a person or a group of persons in a manner that causes or is reasonably likely to cause that person, another person or group of persons significant harm.[69] It is clear that these prohibitions target dark patterns as part of AI systems. The AI Act defines an AI system as 'a machine-based system that . . . infers, from the input it receives, how to generate outputs such as predictions, content, recommendations, or decisions that can influence physical or virtual environments'.[70]

Beyond the AI system as constituting the material scope of the prohibitions, the main trigger for protection against dark patterns is similar to the Digital Services Act and the Unfair Commercial Practices Directive that both also require some form of material distortion of an individual's decision-making. While the Digital Services Act also targets the collective impact of dark patterns, the AI Act focuses on harm at the level of the individual or a group of individuals only and therefore takes a step backwards to the approach of the Unfair Commercial Practices Directive and GDPR again. Beyond this, the final text of Article 5 of the AI Act refers to 'significant harm' – whereas the proposal for the AI Act specifically referred to 'physical or

66 OECD, 'Dark Commercial Patterns', OECD Digital Economy Papers October 2022 No. 336, pp. 26–28.
67 Article 34(1) and (2) of the Digital Services Act.
68 Article 1 of AI Act.
69 Article 5(1)(a) and (b) of the AI Act.
70 Article 3(1) of the AI Act.

psychological harm'.[71] The recitals do clarify that significant harms are understood as 'in particular having sufficiently important adverse impacts on physical, psychological health or financial interests'.[72] The reference to physical and psychological health is welcome (despite being moved to the recitals), because it indicates that the protections in the AI Act go beyond the more economic harm or financial interests relating to an individual's decision-making that is at the heart of the relevant provisions in the Unfair Commercial Practices Directive and, to some extent, the Digital Services Act as well. However, because of the requirement of individual harm at the level of a person or a group of persons, the AI Act's prohibitions of dark patterns seem to contribute little to capturing practices that are not already within the scope of the Unfair Commercial Practices Directive.[73]

5 Data Act

Another relevant EU legislative instrument is the Data Act, which was adopted in December 2023. The Data Act aims at facilitating access to and use of data, with a particular focus on Internet of Things devices.[74] Within that context, the Data Act contains a specific provision requiring third parties that receive data at request of a user to refrain from making the exercise of choices or rights regarding data access 'unduly difficult, including by offering choices to the user in a non-neutral manner, or by coercing, deceiving or manipulating the user, or by subverting or impairing the autonomy, decision-making or choices of the user, including by means of a user digital interface or a part thereof'.[75] Explicit references are made to dark patterns in the recitals, indicating in particular that it 'should be as easy for the user to refuse or discontinue access by the third party to the data as it is for the user to authorize access' and that users should not be nudged 'into decisions on data disclosure transactions'.[76] Compared to the different legal frameworks discussed so far, the provision regarding dark patterns contained in the Data Act is narrow in scope. It only applies in cases where data are transferred using the data access rights of the Data Act. The practices to which the Data Act refers can already be captured under other regimes that similarly focus on the impact of dark patterns on the individual, namely the Unfair Commercial Practices Directive and the GDPR. While the Data

[71] Article 5(1)(a) and (b) of the proposal for a Regulation of the European Parliament and of the Council on laying down harmonised rules on Artificial Intelligence (Artificial Intelligence Act), 21 April 2021, COM(2021) 206 final.

[72] Recital 29 of the AI Act.

[73] Michael Veale & Frederik Zuiderveen Borgesius, 'Demystifying the Draft EU Artificial Intelligence Act Analysing the good, the bad, and the unclear elements of the proposed approach', *Computer Law Review International: A Journal of Information Law and Technology* 2021, Vol. 22 No. 4, pp. 98–100.

[74] Article 1(1) of the Data Act.

[75] Article 6(2)(a) of the Data Act.

[76] Recital 38 of the Data Act.

Act does not expand the scope of existing bans of dark patterns, it forms a welcome reminder for data holders to design their interfaces in relation to data access in a fair manner as well.

6 EU Competition Law

The relevance of EU competition law in targeting dark patterns mainly lies in its ability to capture the competitive impact of such practices, which goes beyond the effects at the level of the individual consumer or data subject on which the EU consumer and data protection frameworks focus. Scholarship has already started to discuss the extent to which competition law can address dark patterns.[77] As already noted above in the context of the Digital Services Act, dark patterns may cause harm to collective welfare even if individuals do not perceive any harm to them personally.[78] Where the harm to collective welfare takes the form of harm to competition, there may be a role for competition law to step in. Consumer sovereignty and consumers' freedom of choice are relevant values deserving protection under competition law as well. By manipulating consumer decision-making, market players can shape consumer choices and control competition by steering demand in directions that further their own commercial interests. This may not only result in consumers being exploited, but also in competition being weakened.[79]

From the perspective of EU competition law, dark patterns could be a form of abuse of dominance under Article 102 of the Treaty on the Functioning of the European Union (TFEU). A distinction is made between exclusionary and exploitative abuses. Exclusionary abuse concerns behaviour foreclosing competitors from the market and indirectly harming consumers because the reduced level of competition will lead to higher prices, lower quality or less choice of products and services. Exploitative abuse involves conduct that directly harms consumers through the imposition of excessive prices or unfair conditions. While competition authorities in Europe have so far prioritized exclusionary conduct, cases against exploitative abuses seem to be on the rise. The most prominent example is the case against Facebook (now Meta) by the German competition authority in which it held Facebook liable for abusing its dominance in the market for social networks by

[77] See Day & Stemler, 'Are dark patterns anticompetitive', pp. 1–45 and Lirio Barros, Timo Klein, Anastasia Shchepetova & Tim Hogg, 'The rise of dark patterns: Does competition law make it any brighter?', *Competition Law Journal* 2022, Vol. 21 No. 3, pp. 136–44.

[78] OECD, 'Dark Commercial Patterns', OECD Digital Economy Papers October 2022 No. 336, pp. 26–28.

[79] See Inge Graef, 'Consumer sovereignty and competition law: from personalization to diversity', *Common Market Law Review* 2021, Vol. 58 No. 2, pp. 479–80.

imposing unfair conditions on users.[80] Beyond this, concerns relating to excessive data extraction and personalized pricing are discussed in the literature as possible forms of exploitative abuse.[81] These are categories of behaviour that could also be applied to determine if certain dark patterns violate Article 102 TFEU as an exploitative abuse. Where dark patterns as employed by a dominant firm have the effect of lowering competition and foreclosing competitors from the market, they may also qualify as an exclusionary abuse.[82] The German *Facebook* case provides an illustration of this, as the German competition authority argued that the unfair conditions Facebook imposed did not only exploit users but also gave Facebook an unfair advantage over competitors who did not engage in such behaviour.[83] There is thus room to enforce against dark patterns under EU competition law as well. Beyond establishing abuse and anticompetitive effects, the main trigger for taking action is the existence of a dominant position. This is a difference with the other legal domains discussed so far, which all target market players irrespective of whether they are dominant.[84] In this regard, EU competition law can complement the other legal regimes by targeting behaviour that has a competitive impact on consumers and markets overall.

7 Digital Markets Act

The Digital Markets Act was adopted in September 2022 and lays down a set of obligations for so-called gatekeepers that offer core platform services.[85] The

80 Case B6–22/16, *Facebook – exploitative business terms*, 6 February 2019. The Court of Justice endorsed the approach of the German competition authority to rely on the GDPR to establish an exploitative abuse under competition law; see Case C-252/21 *Meta Platforms v Bundeskartellamt*, ECLI:EU:C:2023:537.

81 See Viktoria H. S. E. Robertson, 'Excessive data collection: Privacy considerations and abuse of dominance in the era of big data', *Common Market Law Review* 2020, Vol. 57 No. 1, pp. 161–90 and Marco Botta & Klaus Wiedemann, 'To discriminate or not to discriminate? Personalised pricing in online markets as exploitative abuse of dominance', *European Journal of Law and Economics* 2020, Vol. 20 No. 3, pp. 381–404.

82 Barros et al., 'The rise of dark patterns: Does competition law make it any brighter?', p. 141.

83 Case B6–22/16, *Facebook – exploitative business terms*, 6 February 2019.

84 However, note that some have proposed to incorporate a market power analysis in the interpretation of the Unfair Commercial Practices Directive in EU consumer law as well. See Johann Laux, Sandra Wachter & Brent Mittelstadt, 'Neutralizing online behavioural advertising: Algorithmic targeting with market power as an unfair commercial practice', *Common Market Law Review* 2021, Vol. 58 No. 3, pp. 719–50.

85 Article 3(1) of the Digital Markets Act defines a gatekeeper as an undertaking that: (a) has a significant impact on the internal market; (b) provides a core platform service which is an important gateway for business users to reach end users; and (c) enjoys an entrenched and durable position, in its operations, or it is foreseeable that it will enjoy such a position in the near future. Once the quantitative thresholds laid down in Article 3(2) of the Digital Markets Act are met, there is a presumption that the undertaking qualifies as a gatekeeper. In accordance with Article 2(2) of the Digital Markets Act, the following services are core platform services: online intermediation services, online search engines, online social

obligations aim to ensure the fairness and contestability of the digital sector[86] and include prohibitions of self-preferencing, restrictions on the combination of personal data as well as duties regarding portability and interoperability.[87] Once an undertaking qualifies as a gatekeeper, it will have to comply with the list of obligations regardless of whether any harm can be established. This is a difference from the abuse of dominance framework of Article 102 TFEU, where action against dominant firms (which is a lower threshold than gatekeeper) can only be taken after anticompetitive effects of conduct have been established.

There are no obligations in the Digital Markets Act directly targeting dark patterns. However, dark patterns are addressed in the context of the anti-circumvention measures of the obligations imposed on gatekeepers. Gatekeepers cannot engage in behaviour undermining effective compliance with the obligations of the Digital Markets Act, 'regardless of whether that behaviour is of a contractual, commercial or technical nature, or of any other nature, or consists in the use of behavioural techniques or interface design'.[88] This means that dark patterns can be addressed under the Digital Markets Act when they are linked to behaviour regulated by the other obligations. The scope of application of the Digital Markets Act towards dark patterns is thus limited. The focus is more towards collective welfare, considering the objectives of fairness and contestability that the Digital Markets Act pursues.

B *Method of Enforcement*

The previous subsection has illustrated that the different regulatory frameworks analysed can each be applied to target dark patterns. Nevertheless, compared to what is possible on the basis of the legal rules, enforcement actions have so far been limited. Together with the substantive scope of the regulatory frameworks, the method of enforcement matters to ensure effective protection.

The EU consumer and data protection law frameworks are enforced at the national level.[89] Both regimes rely on a one-stop-shop system, where the outcome reached in a case with cross-border relevance investigated at the national level

networking services, video-sharing platform services, number-independent interpersonal communications services, operating systems, web browsers, virtual assistants, cloud computing services and online advertising services.

86 Article 1(1) of the Digital Markets Act.

87 Articles 5–7 of the Digital Markets Act.

88 Article 13(4) of the Digital Markets Act.

89 Article 68(5) of the GDPR and Article 1 of Regulation (EU) 2017/2394 of the European Parliament and of the Council of 12 December 2017 on cooperation between national authorities responsible for the enforcement of consumer protection laws (CPC Regulation) [2017] OJ L 345/1.

applies across the entire EU. Under the GDPR, the national data protection authority of the main establishment of the company under investigation is automatically competent to act as the lead authority.[90] In its two-year review of the GDPR, the European Commission pointed at the problems the latter system has created due to the largest tech companies being established in countries like Ireland and Luxembourg that do not have strong data protection authorities with enough resources to investigate important cross-border cases.[91] The enforcement system in consumer protection where the national consumer authorities collaborate in the Consumer Protection Cooperation Network and assign one authority as best placed to coordinate the case can therefore be seen as more effective.[92] The Consumer Protection Cooperation Network already took action against dark patterns under EU consumer law.[93]

EU competition law relies on parallel enforcement at the EU and national level.[94] Decisions of the European Commission are binding across the EU, while actions of national competition authorities only have an effect in their respective territories. There is thus no one-stop-shop system applicable to enforcement actions of national competition authorities, unlike in consumer and data protection law.

The Digital Markets Act centralizes enforcement at the European Commission,[95] while the Digital Services Act relies on a dual enforcement model. Very large online platforms and search engines are subject to enforcement by the European Commission, and enforcement against other providers takes place at the national level.[96] And finally, both the AI and Data Acts foresee enforcement to happen at the level of the EU Member States.[97]

What one can conclude from this overview is that the legal frameworks targeting especially powerful undertakings are enforced at the EU level (namely the Digital Services Act and the Digital Markets Act, and to some extent the EU competition rules as well – although they can also be enforced at the national level), whereas the legal frameworks with a general scope of application rely on enforcement at the national level. Market players active EU-wide are often the more powerful players,

[90] Article 56(1) of the GDPR.

[91] Communication from the Commission to the European Parliament and the Council: Data protection as a pillar of citizens' empowerment and the EU's approach to the digital transition – two years of application of the General Data Protection Regulation, 24 June 2020, COM(2020) 264 final, p. 6.

[92] Article 17(2) of the CPC Regulation.

[93] Press Release European Commission, 'Consumer protection'.

[94] Articles 4 and 5 of Council Regulation (EC) No 1/2003 of 16 December 2002 on the implementation of the rules on competition laid down in Articles 81 and 82 of the Treaty [2002] OJ L 1/1.

[95] Articles 20–31 of the Digital Markets Act.

[96] Articles 49 and 65 of the Digital Services Act.

[97] Article 70 of the AI Act and Article 37 of the Data Act.

so that enforcement at the EU level is especially relevant. For the legal frameworks enforced at the national level, an effective one-stop-shop mechanism is key to ensure that national authorities do not need to duplicate efforts, and divergences across Member States are minimized.

Beyond the issue of the level at which enforcement takes place, the ex ante or ex post nature of the regulatory instrument is an important factor impacting enforcement. Ex ante interventions prescribe future behaviour, while ex post interventions look back at past behaviour. Enforcement of EU consumer, data protection and competition law takes place in an ex post manner. The relevant authorities or courts take up cases and investigate whether behaviour that is or has been taking place violates the rules. Even if enforcement happens ex post, the interventions can also have an impact ex ante on the future strategy of market players through the setting of precedents. In practice, the difference may sometimes be a matter of degree and also depend on the specificity of the legal obligation. The notions of fairness in the consumer and data protection frameworks as well as the abuse of dominance prohibition in competition law are broad and open-ended. The advantage of open-ended provisions is that this offers flexibility to apply the provisions to new circumstances not yet foreseen by the legislator. The disadvantage of open-ended provisions is that it takes time to investigate and reinterpret the rules for new circumstances.

The other legal frameworks considered in this chapter, namely the Digital Services Act, the AI Act, the Data Act, the Digital Markets Act, all have more specific provisions in place targeting dark patterns and banning certain behaviour in a more ex ante manner. Although these provisions still contain open notions in need of application or interpretation, like whether a practice deceives users or materially distorts their behaviour, they are much more prescriptive than the EU consumer, data protection and competition law frameworks and aim to steer behaviour of market players upfront. The advantage of specific, ex ante obligations is that they can allow for more timely intervention because of their targeted nature. The disadvantage of specific, ex ante obligations is that their scope needs to be set upfront and can therefore at some point become outdated when concerns move towards other issues or areas.

One can argue that the combination of more open-ended regulation with more specific legislative obligations strikes a good balance between, on the one hand, having regulation that is flexible and future-proof because it can be applied to new circumstances and, on the other hand, having ex ante obligations that are specific and allow for timely intervention against practices for which there is consensus that they are harmful. The question is whether the substantive rules and enforcement mechanisms indeed complement each other and can offer effective overall protection against dark patterns (see the comparison in Table 12.1). The next section will reflect on this.

TABLE 12.1 *Comparison of how different EU regulatory frameworks apply to dark patterns*

	Main scope and triggers for protection	Focus on individual or collective harm	Type of enforcement
EU consumer law	Fairness of commercial practices and contract terms applicable to consumers	Individual harm	Ex post National level
EU data protection law	Processing of personal data Fair processing	Individual harm	Ex post National level
Digital Services Act	Online platforms Design, organise or operate online interfaces: • in a way that deceives or manipulates the recipients of platform services, or • in a way that otherwise materially distorts or impairs the ability of the recipients to make free and informed decisions	More towards collective harm	Ex ante EU level for very large online platforms and search engines National level for other online platforms
AI Act	Placing on the market, putting into service or use of an AI system Deployment of subliminal techniques or exploitation of vulnerabilities Material distortion of a person's behaviour Causing significant harm	Individual harm	Ex ante National level
Data Act	Third parties receiving data from a user under the data access right Making the exercise of choices or rights regarding the data access right unduly difficult	Individual harm	Ex ante National level
EU competition law	Dominance Abuse and anticompetitive effects	Collective harm	Ex post EU and national level
Digital Markets Act	Gatekeeper Core platform service Anti-circumvention of the obligations	Collective harm	Ex ante EU level

IV THREE NEEDS RESULTING FROM THE CURRENT STATE OF PLAY

The overview of main triggers and methods of enforcement in the previous section illustrates the current piecemeal nature of the EU regulatory framework against dark patterns. While useful complementarities may arise when parallel sets of rules target different concerns or protect different values, there are also risks of inconsistencies that may lead to either under- or over-enforcement due to the fragmentation of the overall regulatory framework. This section submits that three needs result from the state of play and offers suggestions to improve the enforcement against dark patterns based on the current EU regulatory framework. The recommendations can also inform the use of regulatory techniques more generally for other practices or areas where inframarginal revolutions are or will be occurring.

A *Need for Clarity on the Relationship between Legal Norms*

It is not uncommon for several legal regimes to apply in parallel to a particular situation. Legal systems have approaches in place to address conflicts of norms. Several doctrines of interpretation exist to decide which legal norm prevails in case several legal norms apply to the same matter, including: the *lex specialis* doctrine, according to which a law governing a specific matter takes precedence over a law governing general matters; the *lex superior* doctrine, according to which the hierarchically superior law overrides the hierarchically inferior one; and the *lex posterior* doctrine, according to which more recent law prevails over older law.

In the case of dark patterns, conflicts of norms mainly exist in the fact that some legal frameworks impose stricter or more specific obligations than others. Emotionally manipulative framing may, for instance, trigger the application of the Unfair Commercial Practices Directive, the GDPR, as well as the AI Act. How can one determine which rules and which legal regime apply?

These legal frameworks are all part of EU secondary law, so that there is no difference in their hierarchy. It is also hard to claim that the AI Act as the most recent regime applicable to dark patterns automatically takes precedence over the other, older relevant legal frameworks, because each of them has a different focus and underlying objective. Even though they all apply to emotionally manipulative framing, they do not aim at regulating the same subject matter or concern. And for the same reason applying the *lex specialis* doctrine is also not intuitive, considering that one could possibly regard each of the three regimes as the most specific one depending on the perspective one takes. Because of its focus on AI systems, the AI Act could be seen as the one having the most specific material scope of application. However, the Unfair Commercial Practices Directive aims at protecting the consumer against unfair commercial practices, which is a more specific concern compared to the more general range of obligations under the AI Act. In turn, the GDPR could be seen as the most specific one from the perspective of its focus on the processing of personal data. As a result, application of the traditional doctrines of conflicts of norms does not give clarity on which legal framework to apply.

Looking at the recitals to the AI Act, they explicitly mention that the rules laid down in the AI Act 'should be without prejudice to existing Union law, in particular on data protection, consumer protection, fundamental rights . . .'.[98]

Such use of 'without prejudice' clauses does not indicate how the legislator intended different regimes to interact. More upfront clarity would therefore be welcome to understand the relationship between legal regimes that apply in parallel to practices like dark patterns. Without additional guidance, it is up to regulators and courts to decide on this, which takes time and could undermine the effectiveness of the overall regulatory framework. The Digital Services Act does clearly outline that its ban on dark patterns does not apply to practices covered by the Unfair Commercial Practices Directive or the GDPR.[99] However, because these regimes rely on broad principle-based protections, it is not so apparent which dark patterns fall within their reach. By making the scope of the ban in the Digital Services Act dependent on these two other regimes with unclear boundaries, the EU legislator therefore in the end still leaves it up to regulators and courts to decide which dark patterns the Digital Services Act covers.

B *Need for Triggers for Protection Aligning with the Harm*

A concern stemming from the fragmented regulatory framework is whether the different triggers for protection can still capture the core of the harm resulting from dark patterns. The analysis in Section III illustrates that the triggers for protection are not determined by the type or nature of the harm, but rather by the inherent scope of the relevant legal framework. For instance, the extent to which the GDPR can target dark patterns is dependent on whether a practice involves personal data and meets the principle of fair processing, and EU competition law is only relevant in targeting dark patterns when a dominant firm is involved whose practices give rise to anticompetitive effects. The same is happening in the newly adopted legal regimes, with the Digital Services Act addressing dark patterns on online platforms, the Digital Markets Act targeting dark patterns relating to compliance with its other obligations, the AI Act focusing on dark patterns in AI systems, and the Data Act addressing dark patterns in case users give third parties access to data in the context of Internet of Things devices. This approach assigns protection based on the legal definitions of services, whereas the harm is agnostic to these definitions and does not stop at their outer boundaries.

While the fact that several legal frameworks apply in parallel can also lead to over-enforcement, the concern regarding dark patterns is so far rather one of

98 Recital 9 of the AI Act.

99 Article 25(2) of the Digital Services Act.

under-enforcement. Different mechanisms of protection apply that each have a regulator competent to act, but the fragmented nature of the overall regulatory framework may leave some dark patterns unaddressed that slip through the cracks between legal regimes. If there is consensus that certain practices are so problematic that they should be banned, it seems vital to ensure that the triggers for protection align with the harm. In the case of dark patterns, the harm consists of different aspects covering both individual and collective welfare. One can even wonder if it would not be more effective in such situations to have a specific regime in place with dark patterns as the regulatory target, rather than spreading protection across a range of legal domains that each protect against part of the harm resulting from dark patterns.

To do so, one would need to overcome the scepticism expressed by Easterbrook in 1996 in his 'Cyberspace and the Law of the Horse' that still impacts the field of technology regulation today in determining how to regulate new technologies or practices that do not neatly fit within the categories of existing legal frameworks.[100] Easterbrook argues that there is no need for specialized legal rules to regulate cyberspace just as it would make no sense to create a separate body of law for regulating all activities relating to horses. In his view, 'the best way to learn the law applicable to specialized endeavors is to study general rules' and any effort to collect separate sets of rules into a 'Law of the Horse' 'is doomed to be shallow and to miss unifying principles'.[101] However, the regulatory framework regarding dark patterns is so fragmented that even unifying principles are lacking, despite the fact that protection stems from regimes with a general scope of application. If Easterbrook's arguments regarding the 'Law of the Horse' no longer hold up, should one create some sort of 'Law of Dark Patterns'?[102] The Digital Services Act could have been the framework to put in place rules specifically targeting dark patterns, but the EU legislator decided to defer to the Unfair Commercial Practices Directive and the GDPR instead of banning certain dark patterns more widely.

C *Need for Integrated Enforcement*

With substantive rules regarding dark patterns now being included in various EU legislative instruments, the question is how to make enforcement most effective considering the fragmented regulatory landscape. The creation of more integrated modes of enforcement will be key in this regard. Coordination networks already exist to enable cooperation between the EU and the national levels in each of the different legal regimes in the form of the EDPB, the Consumer Protection

[100] For a discussion, see Ronald Leenes, 'Of Horses and Other Animals of Cyberspace', Technology and Regulation 2019, pp. 2–3.

[101] Frank H. Easterbrook, 'Cyberspace and the law of the horse', *University of Chicago Legal Forum* 1996, Vol. 1996, p. 207.

[102] In the context of a 'Law of Data', see Inge Graef, 'Paving the way forward for data governance: A story of checks and balances', *TechReg* 2020, Vol. 2020, pp. 27–28.

Cooperation Network and the European Competition Network. Similarly, the new Acts also create such bodies, namely the European Board for Digital Services, the European Artificial Intelligence Board, the European Data Innovation Board and the high-level group for the Digital Markets Act. The latter one includes other coordination networks, including the EDPB, the European Competition Network and the Consumer Protection Cooperation Network,[103] which is a welcome development considering that the other bodies only bring together enforcers within the respective Act.

The challenge is how to create coordination across these bodies and the different legal domains they represent. At the minimum, joint priority setting is desirable to clarify responsibility and better target enforcement resources. For instance, if data protection authorities focus on e-commerce or dark patterns involving social proof, consumer authorities could prioritize social media or dark patterns involving obstruction. By jointly setting priorities, both under-enforcement can be prevented as well as duplication of resources and battles among enforcers about who will take up a case.

Beyond this, there could be joint policymaking to clarify the scope of the legal rules and their interaction to address the concern discussed in Section IV.A. An illustration showing that it is feasible to do this is the 2021 joint statement by the Competition & Markets Authority and the Information Commissioner's Office in the UK on competition and data protection law.[104] A more recent example is the joint work of the European Commission and the EDPB to create guidance on the interplay between the DMA and GDPR.[105]

A next level of integration would be joint cases. While this may seem complex to achieve, the international networks in the areas of consumer protection, the International Consumer Protection and Enforcement Network (ICPEN), and data protection, the Global Privacy Enforcement Network (GPEN), have already successfully collaborated. Following intervention by consumer authorities within ICPEN, Google announced in May 2021 that app providers will have to indicate on the Google Play Store what personal data each app keeps and potentially shares about its users. GPEN endorsed this joint action.[106] This is a first inter-network collaboration in the domains of data protection and consumer law.

[103] Article 40(2) of the Digital Markets Act.

[104] Competition and data protection in digital markets: a joint statement between the CMA and the ICO, 19 May 2021, available at https://assets.publishing.service.gov.uk/government/uploads/system/uploads/attachment_data/file/987358/Joint_CMA_ICO_Public_statement_-_final_V2_180521.pdf.

[105] Press Release European Commission, 'Commission services and EDPB will start joint work on guidance on the interplay between DMA and GDPR', 10 September 2024, available at https://digital-markets-act.ec.europa.eu/commission-services-and-edpb-will-start-joint-work-guidance-interplay-between-dma-and-gdpr-2024-09-10_en.

[106] Press Release ICPEN and GPEN, 'Google Play Store to require app providers to provide consumers with detailed information regarding data collection and use following growing international pressure', 27 May 2021, available at www.pcpd.org.hk/english/whatsnew/files/google_play2021.pdf.

The enforcers across the different legal regimes in the EU could take inspiration from these examples, even though they are still scarce, to integrate enforcement and maximize the benefits of the current fragmented EU regulatory framework by dividing responsibilities and teaming up.

V CONCLUSION

Dark patterns are in the midst of a regulatory wave in the EU. Beyond existing regimes in the areas of consumer, data protection and competition law, many of the new Acts include a provision regarding dark patterns. On the one hand, this serves as a welcome reminder to market players about the harm associated with dark patterns. On the other hand, it creates fragmentation by spreading protection as well as responsibility for enforcement across a range of legal regimes and regulators. While parallel application of different legal regimes can be helpful if it creates synergies across areas, in the case of dark patterns the risk is so far rather one of under-enforcement.

To make enforcement as effective as possible, there is a need to integrate enforcement and assign responsibility across enforcers. This could happen through joint priority setting, joint policymaking and joint cases. At least, joint priority setting is needed so as to spread enforcement resources effectively and enhance each other's scope of action. Joint policymaking is welcome to clarify the relationship between the different legal regimes and their scope, which is often interdependent – as the ban on dark patterns in the Digital Services Act illustrates. Joint cases are the most advanced level of integration, where enforcers could exchange expertise and issue a common decision where concerns overlap.

As a lesson for future lawmaking and inframarginal revolutions against other practices, the increasing regulatory attention for dark patterns in the EU shows that it may not necessarily be effective to add protections across many legal regimes. The risk of such an approach is that despite the many applicable legal rules, some practices remain unaddressed because the protection becomes too piecemeal. Every legal regime has its own legal definitions and material scope of application that determine its range of action, while the harms cross the boundaries between legal regimes and lead to broader, overarching concerns. Effective lawmaking would require aligning the triggers of protection with the harm, which may sometimes call for the adoption of a specific regime for the targeted practices that prevails over existing regulation.

13

Inframarginalism and Economism

Vijay Raghavan

CONTENTS

In many ways, the recent turn in legal scholarship toward "progressive rent theory" or what this book terms "inframarginalism" is a welcome one.[1] Early-twentieth-century attempts to apply inframarginal analysis to public policy lost favor, in part, because of their potential regressive distributive implications.[2] As Barbara Fried

[1] Examples in this turn include the scholarship of Ramsi Woodcock; see Ramsi A. Woodcock, *Personalizing Prices to Redistribute Wealth in Antitrust and Public Utility Rate Regulation*, 2022 Wis. L. Rev. 1407 (2022); and Michael Guttentag, see Michael D. Guttentag, *Law and Surplus: Opportunities Missed*, 2019 Utah L. Rev. 607 (2019). Inframarginal themes appear in my work as well, see Vijay Raghavan, *Consumer Law's Equity Gap*, 2022 Utah L. Rev. 511 (2022). A related strand of scholarship comes from Eric Posner and Glen Weyl's attempt to revive the ideas of nineteenth-century political economist Henry George. Eric A. Posner & E. Glen Weyl, Radical Markets: Uprooting Capitalism and Democracy for a Just Society (2018). George argued that the gains from technological and social progress inured to the benefit property owners in the form of economic rents. Henry George, Progress and Poverty (1879). George sought to redistribute these gains in the form of a progressive land tax. Posner and Weyl build on George's framework and set out to extend his logic to a wide set of modern problems that have a Georgian shape. The modern turn toward inframarginalism reflects the same impulse, but instead of economic rents and Henry George, inframarginalists like Woodcock look to economic surplus and the early-twentieth-century institutional economist and legal scholar, Robert Hale.

[2] To be sure, the early inframarginalist movement suffered from other problems, which Barbara Fried contends included the fungibility of capital in response to an inframarginal tax on investments; the regulatory costs of identifying and isolating rents; and potential disincentives

explained, the incidence of a legal rule redistributing producer surplus could be borne disproportionately by labor as opposed to capital.[3] And, as such, if one seeks to redistribute wealth, one is better off focusing on redistributing wealth through a labor income tax and designing legal rules to minimize economic distortions outside the tax system.[4]

But it is no longer obvious that this is correct. Scholars have shown that there are important political constraints to redistribution through tax-and-transfer,[5] and that efficient legal rules carry their own allocative bias.[6] Moreover, there are reasons to think that redistributing producer surplus is no longer necessarily regressive or that the initial objections to inframarginalism were overstated. For example, Ramsi Woodcock argues technological innovations that allow producers to engage in price discrimination can also ensure that the distributive implications of inframarginal redistribution are progressive.[7] Similarly, Michael Guttentag argues that where there is economic surplus in a transaction, it is not clear that redistribution through tax and transfer is superior to redistribution through a legal rule.[8]

One area that might immediately benefit from the renewed attention to inframarginal returns is the regulation of consumer financial markets. Consumer

of private investment. BARBARA H. FRIED, THE PROGRESSIVE ASSAULT ON LAISSEZ FAIRE ROBERT HALE AND THE FIRST LAW AND ECONOMICS MOVEMENT 201–3 (2001).

3 Fried illustrated this point with the following example:

> [Inframarginalism] replicates the distributive embarrassments of Ramsey taxation, when (for example) it taxes the $1 surplus value accruing to the worker paid $3/hour, who (being destitute) would work for $2 if necessary, but leaves untouched the $1,000 an hour paid to a millionaire, who (little valuing additional money) would not work for a penny less.

FRIED, *supra* note 2, at 204. Ramsey taxation is a theoretical framework for optimal taxation that was developed by the economist Frank Ramsey in the early twentieth century. F. P. Ramsey, *A Contribution to the Theory of Taxation*, 37 ECON. J. 47 (1927). Ramsey argued that a tax system could maximize revenues and minimize economic distortions through a wide range of small taxes "on different commodities inversely proportional to the elasticity of demand for a good." FRIED, *supra* note 2, at 203. But there was a central flaw to the Ramseyian approach: By tying rates to elasticity, Ramsey taxation was arguably regressive. This suggested "tax rates ought to be highest on the necessities of life like food and shelter, and lowest on discretionary luxury purchases like yachts." *Id.* ("[T]he less price-sensitive one's desire is for a given good, the less likely one is to be deterred from purchasing it if the price is raised by a tax"). For Fried, inframarginal redistribution "is, in effect, a Ramsey tax placed on producer (worker's or saver's) surplus rather than on consumer surplus." *Id.* at 204.

4 *Id.* at 203. This approach, commonly referred to as the double distortion argument, reflected the consensus on wealth redistribution in the late and early twentieth century. See Louis Kaplow & Steven Shavell, *Why the Legal System Is Less Efficient Than the Income Tax in Redistributing Income*, 23(2) J. LEGAL STUD. 667 (1994). As discussed in Section IV, there are good reasons to think this is no longer the consensus view.

5 See Lee Anne Fennell & Richard H. McAdams, *The Distributive Deficit in Law and Economics*, 100 MINN. L. REV. 1051 (2016); Richard L. Revesz, *Regulation and Distribution*, 93 N.Y.U. L. REV. 1489 (2018).

6 See Zachary Liscow, *Is Efficiency Biased?*, 85 UNIV. CHI. L. REV. 1649 (2018).

7 Woodcock, *supra* note 1.

8 Guttentag, *supra* note 1.

financial markets feature large imbalances between financial institutions and consumers.[9] Financial institutions can leverage these imbalances to extract large amounts from consumers.[10] And there is at least some evidence that financial institutions regressively redistribute this surplus in order to cross-subsidize cheaper services for wealthier consumers.[11] Thus, the case for examining and redistributing surplus in consumer financial markets seems particularly strong.

This chapter, however, offers a critical take on the recent inframarginal turn in legal scholarship. In important respects, inframarginalism is less about the specific contours of policy and more about the ways we justify a particular policy. For example, public utility rate restrictions predated the development of inframarginalism, and their maintenance did not turn on inframarginalism's continued viability.[12] Inframarginalism was merely one of many ways to design and defend rate restrictions. Similarly, many of the specific reforms that neo-inframarginalists such as Woodcock and Guttentag endorse have been justified by scholars on other grounds.[13] The important question then is not whether we ought to pursue policies such as rate restrictions or mandates but whether we ought to defend these moves on inframarginalist grounds.

In this chapter, I suggest that there are serious limitations to inframarginalism as a defense to progressive public policy. The modern turn toward inframarginalism tends to give short shrift to the broader legal and institutional context out of which the original inframarginal movement arose and the ways it differs from the present. Inframarginalism grew out of a critique of a particular mode of economic and legal reasoning that was then dominant. Robert Hale and his contemporaries set out to deconstruct the intellectual framework that justified laissez faire. From this critique, Hale and others turned to inframarginal analysis as an alternative way to shape public policy. But they pivoted toward inframarginalism in an institutional setting that accommodated plural approaches to economics and public policy.

[9] See, e.g., Kathleen C. Engel & Patricia A. McCoy, *A Tale of Three Markets: The Law and Economics of Predatory Lending*, 80 TEX. L. REV. 1255 (2002) (on imbalances in mortgage markets); Will Dobbie & Paige Marta Skiba, *Information Asymmetries in Consumer Credit Markets: Evidence from Payday Lending*, 5 AM. ECON. J. 256, 258 (2013) (on imbalances in fringe financial markets). For older accounts of imbalances in consumer markets, see, e.g., Friedrich Kessler, *The Contracts of Adhesion – Some Thoughts about Freedom of Contract Role of Compulsion in Economic Transactions*, 43 COLUM. L. REV. 629 (1943); Karl N. Llewellyn, *What Price Contract? – An Essay in Perspective*, 40 YALE L.J. 704 (1931).

[10] See Raghavan, *supra* note 1.

[11] See Natasha Sarin, *Making Consumer Finance Work*, 119 COLUM. L. REV. 1519 (2019) (on regressive cross-subsidies in overdraft market).

[12] See William Boyd, *Just Price, Public Utility, and the Long History of Economic Regulation in America*, 35 YALE J. ON REG. 721 (2018).

[13] See Vijay Raghavan, *Shifting Burdens at the Fringe*, 102 B.U. L. REV. 1301 (2022); Luke Herrine, *What Is Consumer Protection For?*, 34 LOY. CONSUMER L. REV. 240 (2022); Sanjukta Paul, *Recovering the Moral Economy Foundations of the Sherman Act*, 131 YALE L.J. 175 (2021).

In the intervening years, much has changed. The particular mode of economic and legal reasoning that Hale and his contemporaries fought to extinguish is back. This mode, which has recently been referred to as "economism"[14] or the "economic style of reasoning,"[15] is not only back but is fully internalized in federal administrative policy.[16] And it creates a strong default presumption in favor of market ordering[17] and against rules that change market-ordered outcomes.

Neo-inframarginalism dislodges Hale's prescription from his underlying critique of market ordering. In doing so, it appears to largely concede that market ordering is normatively desirable except in limited cases. The specific approach of conceding economism's basic descriptive and normative claims but offering cases where these claims may not hold, and intervention is warranted, has been tried before. Over the last twenty years, scholars have attempted to justify interventions on behavioralist grounds by largely conceding that markets are good and desirable but need to be fixed where consumer decision-making is biased. But these efforts have largely failed to materially alter public policy.

The failure of behavioral law and economics should serve as a cautionary tale for neo-inframarginalists. Because of the strong default presumption in favor of market ordering, any attempt to supplant economism by largely conceding its main premises is destined to be subservient to it. You simply cannot dislodge Hale's prescription from his critique. And any attempt to transform public policy must begin where Hale and his contemporaries began: with a critique of the intellectual framework that justifies the status quo.

I INSTITUTIONALISM AND THE ORIGINAL INFRAMARGINAL TURN

In the late nineteenth and early twentieth centuries, laissez-faire economics was dominant in political discourse and constitutional jurisprudence.[18] The intellectual justification for laissez-faire largely rested on two ideas: (1) that individual liberty and property rights ought to be protected from the coercive powers of the state; and (2) that the market allocated resources in a way that was natural and just.[19] These two arguments provided what Barbara Fried calls a "powerful rights-based defense of

[14] See James Kwak, Economism: Bad Economics and the Rise of Inequality (2017).

[15] See Elizabeth Popp Berman, Thinking Like an Economist: How Efficiency Replaced Equality in U.S. Public Policy (2022).

[16] See *id.* at 1–24.

[17] By market ordering, I do not mean an autonomously functioning market. Instead, I mean rules that set out to encase the distributional outcomes that follow from simple microeconomic models. See Quinn Slobodian, Globalists: The End of Empire and the Birth of Neoliberalism 7 (2018) (describing neoliberalism as the "idea that markets are not natural but are products of the political construction of institutions to encase them"); see also Katharina Pistor, The Code of Capital: How the Law Creates Wealth and Inequality (2019).

[18] Fried, *supra* note 2, at 31.

[19] See *id.* at 1–2.

laissez faire."[20] And Hale and his contemporaries set out to reveal the hollowness of this defense.

Hale's critique had two components. First, Hale contested the notion that the state held a monopoly over coercive power. For Hale, the state's coercive power did not turn on its ability to limit an individual's "free" choice with the threat of violence. Instead, the state's coercive power operated "as background constraints on the universe of socially available choices from which an individual might 'freely' choose."[21] By reconceptualizing coercion as a background constraint on socially available choices, Hale revealed that coercion was not limited to what was then understood as state action.

As an example, consider a simple transaction between a landlord and tenant renegotiating the terms of a lease. The landlord can withhold the right to their property to coerce more favorable lease terms. Conversely, the tenant could withhold future payments to "coerce" the landlord to accede to terms more favorable to the tenant. As Hale argued, this kind of mutual coercion was a common feature of all market exchanges and markets are best understood as networks of mutual coercion.[22]

The coercive power that each party wields in a transaction stems from legal rights each party has. In the example above, these rights are likely delineated by property law, contract law, fair housing law, and landlord–tenant law. Importantly, the coercive power these legal rights generate is contingent on the existence of state machinery to protect those rights. And in this sense, market exchanges were best understood as public and coercive as opposed to private and voluntary.

Second, Hale contested the notion that the market allocated resources in a natural and just fashion. This concept had roots in Lockean ideas about property and natural rights. Proponents of this view tended to believe that ownership rights were naturally derived and predated the state, that "the market would reward labor and capital in proportion to the value each had generated," and that the distribution of wealth in society "was the inevitable result of natural economic forces beyond human control."[23] Hale's attack on the naturalness and justness of market exchanges built on his work on coercion.

For Hale, the distribution of wealth in society did not reflect the natural and just results of a market economy but instead reflected the distribution of coercive power in market exchanges. But the distribution of coercive power in market exchanges did not derive from natural rights that predated the state. Instead, the distribution of coercive power derived from legal rights that were created by the state. In other words, the distribution of wealth in society reflected the particular way the state allocated coercive power to various market participants.

[20] *Id.* at 2.

[21] *Id.* at 48.

[22] See *id.* at 49–59.

[23] See *id.* at 76.

The radical implication of Hale's critique and reconceptualization was that the state could reallocate coercive power by manipulating legal rights to achieve a fundamentally different distribution of wealth. The important question then was how the state should allocate coercive power in market exchanges. Hale devoted the latter half of his career to this question. And his answer helps form the basis of the main themes of this book.

In determining how the state ought to allocate coercive power, Hale drew inspiration from progressive rent theory of the early twentieth century. Progressive rent theory was an extension of late-nineteenth-century rent theory. Rent theorists argued that the surplus landowners were able to extract over cost was "an economic 'rent' that the [landowner] was able to extract from buyers merely because fortuities of natural and social circumstances had produced a market price in excess of the seller's costs."[24] For rent theorists, economic rents did not belong to the landowner "but the community at large"[25] and rent theorists sought to find ways to redistribute these economic rents.[26]

Rent theory was largely built on a classical understanding of the economy.[27] Progressive rent theorists set out to update rent theory to incorporate insights of neoclassical economics and the marginal revolution of the late nineteenth century. Marginal analysis "asserted that in a competitive market, the prices of products and services would be determined not by the cost of factors that go into their production (as classical economists believed), but rather by their value to the marginal consumer."[28] This meant that commercial transactions may generate land-like rents in the form of economic surplus to inframarginal producers and consumers. And thus, one could extend rent theory principles to redistribute surplus in commercial transactions.

Hale became a proponent of this approach and attempted to apply inframarginal analysis to a wide range of legal issues including the regulation of public utilities. But in some ways, Hale's turn toward progressive rent theory or inframarginalism is a curious one. A core component of Hale's assault on laissez-faire economics was his critique of the normativity of market ordering. Yet Hale's turn toward progressive rent theory seemed to suggest that market ordering was generally normatively desirable.

Though progressive rent theory held that market-generated surplus ought to be redistributed, it did not fundamentally challenge the way we understand how markets price and distribute goods and resources. Instead, it largely accepted the normative desirability of a market-based allocation. In his critique of laissez-faire,

[24] *Id.* at 74. As described in *supra* note 1, Henry George argued that the gains from technological and social progress inured to the benefit property owners in the form of economic rents. George, *supra* note 1.

[25] Fried, *supra* note 2, at 74.

[26] The most famous example being Henry George's land tax.

[27] See *id.* at 125 (noting that George's analysis "was wholly within the Ricardian tradition, which – with the notable exception of land – left unquestioned the claim of pre-Ricardian classical economics that the competitive market would automatically achieve distributive justice").

[28] *Id.* at 125–26.

Hale contested the notion that market ordering was independent of the law. Yet in his embrace of the implications of marginalism, Hale seemed to shy away from the implications of his critique. Why?

It is not entirely obvious why Hale built an affirmative agenda out of rent theory and marginalism. Other institutional economists were quite critical of marginalism. For example, Thorstein Veblen charged that marginal analysis "omitted virtually all that was of interest in economic life" including "the way in which preferences came to be created" and "the influence of cultural phenomena ... on all facets of the economy."[29] And Hale himself incorporated some of the institutionalist critiques in his work, all of which makes his turn toward marginalism more perplexing.

Fried suggests that Hale may have embraced progressive rent theory "as a means to enlist the individualistic impulse behind laissez-faire economics in a program that he found more palatable on strictly utilitarian or (less likely) idealist grounds."[30] And Hale may have thought that by grounding his affirmative agenda in this manner he might avoid charges of socialism.[31] What does seem clear is that Hale did not view this choice as a particularly fraught one. And that is likely because Hale developed his ideas in a methodologically pluralistic setting.

Hale produced most of his scholarship during the heyday of institutional economics. Institutional economics developed as a rejection of the deductive formalism of neoclassical economics and its ideological conservatism.[32] Institutional economists favored an inductive approach that sought to understand how institutions shaped economic behavior in specific contexts,[33] drew from a variety of sources, and generally favored an interventionist state.[34] Though Hale's adoption of progressive rent theory is in some tension with institutional methodology, it is consistent with the generally progressive ends of institutionalism. Moreover, because of institutionalism's pluralistic approach to economics, Hale's embrace of progressive rent theory did not necessarily imply that Hale believed that some measure of market ordering was normatively desirable. Instead, it was merely one of many viable ways to approach problems of regulatory design and wealth distribution.

II THE RISE OF THE ECONOMIC STYLE

Much has changed in the intervening years. The particular mode of economic and legal reasoning that Hale and his contemporaries fought to extinguish is back. Unlike nineteenth-century proponents of laissez-faire, modern proponents of laissez-faire do not ground their views in moral claims about what is natural and

[29] *Id.* at 128.

[30] *Id.* at 75.

[31] *Id.* at 33.

[32] See Berman, *supra* note 15, at 27; Fried, *supra* note 2, at 11.

[33] See Berman, *supra* note 15, at 27.

[34] See *id.*

just. Instead, modern proponents ground their views in what James Kwak has referred to as "economism" and Elizabeth Popp Berman has referred to as "the economic style of reasoning." As Berman explains:

> The economic style of reasoning is a loose approach [to] policymaking [that] starts with basic microeconomic concepts like incentives, various forms of efficiency, and externalities[;] takes a distinctive approach to policy problems that includes using models to simplify, quantifying, weighing costs and benefits, and thinking at the margin. It also includes causal policy stories linked to economic theories – that, for example, investing in education will increase human capital and raise income.[35]

Berman argues that though "the economic style is a loose and flexible approach to analyzing policy problems . . . it does reflect two core stances": "a deep appreciation of markets as efficient allocators of resources" and "a very high value on efficiency as the measure of good policy."[36]

There is vast disagreement about what caused the shift from institutionalism to economism. For some scholars, the shift was a function of the political conditions in the mid to late twentieth century. The political fallout from the "red scare" created natural conditions for the rise of the economic style.[37] And the set of "overlapping crises of the 1970s and the rebalancing of political conditions to manage them" helped displace conflicting approaches to policy and governance.[38] Other scholars emphasize the intellectual origins of the economic style. For these scholars, the economic style was an ideological project developed in response to the social and political revolutions of the early twentieth century.[39] Berman, herself, offers a different account: Rather than locating the shift as an exogenous phenomenon, Berman sees the shift as endogenous to the efforts by New Deal-era policymakers and scholars to solve policy problems.[40]

Though scholars disagree about what caused the shift, few disagree about the dominance of the economic style and its costs. The economic style of reasoning is the primary way we justify public policy today and is firmly embedded in American

35 BERMAN, *supra* note 15, at 5.

36 *Id.* at 6.

37 See LANDON R. Y. STORRS, THE SECOND RED SCARE AND THE UNMAKING OF THE NEW DEAL LEFT (2012); Landon Storrs, The "Economic Style" as Red Scare Legacy, The Law & Political Economy Project Blog (Sept. 13, 2022), https://lpeproject.org/blog/the-economic-style-as-red-scare-legacy/.

38 Luke Herrine, Politics and Expertise: On Elizabeth Popp Berman's Thinking Like an Economist and Paul Sabin's Public Citizens, Phenomenal World (Sept. 2, 2022), phenomenal-world.org/reviews/politicizing-expertise/.

39 See, e.g., KIM PHILLIPS-FEIN, INVISIBLE HANDS: THE MAKING OF THE CONSERVATIVE MOVEMENT FROM THE NEW DEAL TO REAGAN (2009); SLOBODIAN, *supra* note 17; STEVEN M. TELES, THE RISE OF THE CONSERVATIVE LEGAL MOVEMENT: THE BATTLE FOR CONTROL OF THE LAW (2008).

40 See BERMAN, *supra* note 15; see also Herrine, *supra* note 38 (describing the various histories of the late-twentieth shift to the economic style).

administrative governance.[41] In various domains, the style and its efficiency maxim operate as simple tests that constrain decision-making. For example, much of modern antitrust turns on the application of the consumer welfare standard.[42] This standard, which is found nowhere in the text of the Sherman Act, limits the application of antitrust law to "inefficient" monopoly harms. Similarly, much of federal regulation turns on the application of cost–benefit analysis.[43]

Cost–benefit analysis is embedded in the federal regulatory process through legislation, executive orders, administrative guidance, and regulation.[44] Though the test is, in theory, a neutral technology, it has non-neutral effects. As Zachary Liscow has shown, cost–benefit analysis tends to have a bias toward the rich where the government is evaluating how it should allocate finite resources.[45] Efficiency analysis measures willingness to pay. Because of the declining marginal utility of income, allocative decisions like determining how to allocate Department of Transportation funds tend to be biased toward those who are more willing to pay for things. In most cases, that means policy is tilted toward the provisions of services that primarily benefit the rich.

Conversely, as I have argued, cost–benefit analysis can also have a deregulatory bias against the poor where an intervention would primarily affect the availability of a product used by poor consumers.[46] For a class of goods known as inferior goods (or products or services with similar features), demand is primarily concentrated at the lower end of the income distribution. Thus, although poor people have less dollars to spend and value each marginal dollar more, they can outvote rich consumers who value these products at close to zero. And that means interventions that attempt to constrain the supply of inferior goods or similar products are presumptively welfare-diminishing and ought to be avoided under an efficiency analysis.[47]

The net effect of efficiency's allocative bias toward the rich and deregulatory bias against the poor is that the economic style tends to sharpen rather than diminish inequality. And this generally implies that though proponents of the economic style do not explicitly adopt the moral claims of laissez-faire, the style tends to encase the same set of hierarchical social arrangements and wealth distribution that laissez-faire proponents sought to encase.

[41] See BERMAN, *supra* note 15.

[42] See Marshall Steinbaum, *When It Comes to the History of Economics, Don't Think Like an Economist*, THE LAW & POLITICAL ECONOMY PROJECT BLOG (Sept. 6, 2022), https://lpeproject.org/blog/when-it-comes-to-the-history-of-economics-dont-think-like-an-economist/.

[43] CASS R. SUNSTEIN, THE COST-BENEFIT REVOLUTION (2019). Cost–benefit analysis attempts to approximate the results that would obtain from a rigorous determination of whether an intervention is a Kaldor–Hicks improvement the intervention results in an increase of aggregate welfare. See Liscow, *supra* note 6, at 1658. Cost–benefit analysis generally holds that one should not intervene in markets if the cost of a regulation outweighs its benefits.

[44] See Berman, *supra* note 15; Liscow, *supra* note 6, at 1688–91.

[45] *Id.*

[46] Raghavan, *supra* note 1, at 22–27.

[47] See Raghavan, *supra* note 1, at 532–36.

As the economic style rose to prominence, a central challenge for progressives was how to respond to this methodological shift. In particular, how should progressives justify regulatory interventions in the era of economism? For most of the late twentieth century and early twenty first century, progressives answered this question in a modest way. Rather than attempting to fully dislodge the economic style, progressives instead sought to work within its boundaries.

Progressives conceded the basic premises of economism[48] but argued that the set of inefficient market outcomes was larger than proponents of the economic style assumed. Markets occasionally fail, and when they do, government ought to intervene on efficiency grounds. The progressive project was directed at developing a robust account of market failure that justified regulatory interventions.

Early steps in this effort focused on negative externalities and information symmetries.[49] In economic regulation, progressives eventually settled on bounded rationality as the trump card against the prescriptions of economism.[50] For the past two decades, progressives have tried to use the concept of bounded rationality and other insights from behavioral finance to unwind the deregulatory settlements of economism. These efforts have largely failed, and analyzing this failure is instructive for the project of this book.

Behavioral law and economics set out to contest one of the central assumptions of efficiency analysis: rational choice. Efficiency, as it is defined in the economic style of reasoning, generally refers to Kaldor–Hicks efficiency. An intervention is Kaldor–Hicks efficient if it results in more aggregate welfare than the status quo with welfare tied to the price a consumer is willing to pay for a product. The Kaldor–Hicks efficient option among a set of policy options is "the policy that maximizes the sum of the willingness to pay of [the parties affected by various policy options]."[51]

Behavioral law and economics' primary move was to contest whether price was a useful proxy for willingness to pay. Building on decades of research in experimental psychology, behavioral law and economics argued that consumers decision-making was bounded in ways that suggest consumers' revealed preferences did not match their true preferences.[52] For example, a poor consumer might be present-biased and value immediate consumption more than future consumption. A business that recognizes this fact might sell the consumer a product at a price above what the consumer is "truly" willing to pay. As a result, welfare analysis that uses price as a

48 That the market efficiently allocated resources, that the government should only intervene in markets if the interventions were efficient, and that non-efficient redistribution of resources should only take place through the tax-and-transfer system.

49 See Raghavan, *supra* note 13, at 1310.

50 Behavioral law and economics influence was perhaps greatest in the regulation of insurance markets and consumer markets. By contrast, behavioral law and economics had a very little impact in other areas such as environmental regulation.

51 Liscow, *supra* note 6.

52 Ryan Bubb & Richard H. Pildes, *How Behavioral Economics Trims Its Sails and Why*, 127 Harv. L. Rev. 1593, 1603 (2014).

proxy for willingness to pay may favor an inefficient and welfare-diminishing outcome over an efficient and welfare-maximizing outcome.

Behavioral law and economics seized on this concern as a reason to reconsider the allocative and regulatory defaults of the economic style. Behavioral law and economics proposed a menu of interventions to "fix" market inefficiencies caused by bounded decision-making. These interventions were famously described by Cass Sunstein and Richard Thaler as a form of "libertarian paternalism" – interventions that preserve choice and autonomy but try to "nudge" consumers and debias market transactions.[53]

The interventions proposed by behavioral law and economics scholars proved "remarkably" ineffective at curbing market abuse. As Lauren Willis demonstrated, motivated firms could easily unwind "nudges" in ways that fundamentally undermined the intervention.[54] For example, a default that required consumers to affirmatively opt into a program like bank overdraft could become a default opt-in through aggressive firm marketing around the benefits of overdraft. Conversely, as Ryan Bubb and Richard Pildes argued, because behavioralists did "not properly evaluate, at times, how its own regulatory tools function," suboptimally set defaults can effectively function as mandates.[55]

Behavioral law and economics extended beyond regulatory design. Arguments grounded in behavioral law and economics were also offered as a justification for classic regulatory interventions such as mandates and price controls. Though these classic interventions did not preserve choice, price controls or mandates might still be justified, the argument went, if market prices or market defaults reflected biased demand. Because of the strong efficiency presumptions formally and informally embedded in administrative procedure, behavioralist justifications proved just as ineffective as behavioralist interventions at supporting and sustaining more classic interventions.

Inframarginalism is, in my view, best understood as a justification for classic interventions such as price controls or mandates as opposed to a new approach to economic regulation. As such, examining behavioral law and economics' failure to justify policy interventions can help illustrate the limits of the neo-inframarginal turn. In the next section, I explore these themes in the context of the regulation of fringe finance.

III A COMPACT HISTORY OF FRINGE FINANCIAL REGULATION

A *The Rise and Fall of Fringe Financial Regulation*

For well over a century, consumer scholars and advocates have struggled to reign in fringe finance: the set of marginal credit products sold to poor people. Known at

[53] *Id.* at 1604.

[54] See Lauren E. Willis, *When Nudges Fail: Slippery Defaults*, 80 U. Chi. L. Rev. 1155, 1186–87 (2013).

[55] Bubb & Pildes, *supra* note 52, at 1599.

various times as salary loans, chattel loans, credit sales, payday loans, title loans, and installment loans, these high-cost, short-term products tend to impose significant social and economic costs with arguably little social or economic benefit.[56] And creating a coherent legal framework for these loans has been a central challenge in consumer financial law.

Problems with fringe financial products first surfaced in the early twentieth century. Prior to that point, fringe financial products were generally outlawed by historic usury laws: usury laws in place during the first half of the twentieth century in almost all states. These state laws often had an ancient pedigree dating to the founding of the state and, in some cases, the founding of the Republic.[57] Unlike modern consumer financial laws, which seek to strike a balance between harmful and beneficial credit, historic usury laws reflected a general contempt for consumer lending,[58] and usury limits were set to make most consumer lending unprofitable.[59]

Historic usury laws began to unravel in the early twentieth century under a number of economic and political pressures.[60] American cities saw rapid economic and population growth, which led to increased demand for consumer credit. The usury laws in place made it difficult for mainstream commercial lenders to satisfy this demand. At the turn of the twentieth century, New York's general usury limit was 6 percent per year,[61] and Illinois' usury limit was 5 percent per year.[62] Other states had similarly restrictive usury limits.[63]

Commercial banks did not meet the needs of low-income wage earners at the time.[64] That demand was instead satisfied by a new class of fringe financiers who operated outside the boundaries of restrictive usury laws.[65] In her history of twentieth-century fringe finance, Anne Fleming details the techniques these lenders used to overcome usury restrictions and state efforts to regulate these practices.

56 This is, of course, debatable. See Andrew T. Hayashi, *Myopic Consumer Law*, 106 VA. L. REV. 689 (2020).

57 See Christopher L. Peterson, *Usury Law, Payday Loans, and Statutory Sleight of Hand: Salience Distortion in American Credit Pricing Limits*, 92 MINN. L. REV. 1110, 1118 (2008) (table listing usury limits in all thirteen colonies at independence).

58 See *id.* at 1119 (noting that "deep American skepticism of consumer lending encouraged a legal commitment to limited interest rates that continued largely unabated through the end of the nineteenth century").

59 See ANNE FLEMING, CITY OF DEBTORS: A CENTURY OF FRINGE FINANCE 13 (2018) (noting that nineteenth-century usury laws "made it nearly impossible for lenders of small sums to turn a profit" because the authorized interest was generally insufficient to cover the marginal cost of originating a new loan).

60 See *id.* at 14.

61 See *id.* at 13.

62 See Illinois Interest Act of 1891, available at https://archive.org/details/lawsofstateofill1891illi.

63 See Peterson, *supra* note 57, at 1116–19.

64 See FLEMING, *supra* note 59, at 13.

65 See *id.* at 23.

Fleming's history is focused on New York City, but the practices she documents were common in other cities at the time.[66]

As Fleming explains, one of the earliest forms of high-cost credit available to wage earners was a salary loan. A salary loan was a cash loan secured by a borrower's pledge of their future salary.[67] If the borrower defaulted on their obligation, the salary lender would serve a garnishment notice on the borrower's employer to satisfy the borrower's debt. Salary lenders avoided New York's usury limit through complex contract provisions that took advantage of a consumer's general ignorance of the law.[68]

Consumers who sought a loan from a salary lender assumed they were executing a promissory note to obtain credit in New York when in fact they were granting a power of attorney to an undisclosed person to take out a loan in the borrower's name in another state.[69] The other state was typically a state with a more generous usury limit.[70] Although the consumer's transaction took place entirely in New York, as a formal matter, the consumer was obtaining credit from a financial institution in another state not subject to New York's usury limit.

Exploitative practices by salary lenders led to calls by progressive-era reformers for regulation of the industry. As Fleming explains, these early efforts sought to loosen the noose imposed by strict usury laws to create a space for lenders to legally and profitably operate.[71] An early leader in this effort was the Russell Sage Foundation, and an early example of the kind of reform these progressive-era organizations pushed for is the Uniform Small Sum Law.[72] The Uniform Small Sum Law provided an exemption from general state usury laws for licensed personal finance companies. These companies would be allowed to charge annual rates of interest between 24 percent and 46 percent.[73]

The Uniform Small Sum Law was adopted in a number of states and established the basic framework for future consumer financial regulation: licensure, price controls, structural limits, and oversight.[74] This infrastructure-like framework created a narrow and tightly regulated channel for prudent consumer lending and banned lending outside this channel. This early twentieth-century framework came under pressure in the mid twentieth century as a result of several forces. The first was competition from mainstream financial institutions, which began offering revolving consumer loans to White and middle-class borrowers. The second was a product of

[66] See ROBERT MAYER, QUICK CASH: THE STORY OF THE LOAN SHARK (2010) (chronicling early "loan sharking" in Chicago).

[67] See *id.*

[68] See FLEMING, *supra* note 59, at 25.

[69] See *id.* at 26–27.

[70] See *id.*

[71] See *id.* at 36–38.

[72] See Peterson, *supra* note 57, at 1120.

[73] See *id.*

[74] See *id.*

urban poverty and segregation, which led to expansion of extractive credit products known as credit sales targeting primarily Black and poor borrowers.

Credit sales allowed consumers to purchase goods on credit from a seller and had long been outside the scope of consumer financial law due to a long-standing legal distinction between sales for cash and sales on credit known as the "time-price" doctrine.[75] Under the "time-price" doctrine, credit sales were not subject to state usury laws because these transactions did not involve lending money. The interest rate was not viewed by courts as a finance charge but rather the additional price of purchasing the goods at a later time.[76] The time-price doctrine was a legal fiction and failed to account for the fact that credit sales and cash loans were economically indistinguishable. Cash loans secured by collateral could be restructured as a credit sale to evade usury limits. Consumer advocates had long fought for the elimination of the time-price doctrine and the regulation of credit sales.

In the middle of the twentieth century, these efforts became entangled with broader fights over civil rights and against racial discrimination. The Great Migration fundamentally changed the demographic makeup of many northern cities. Black people who left formal and explicit state-sanctioned segregation in the South moved to northern cities and encountered informal and state-subsidized segregation through private intermediaries. This segregation is most famously associated with "redlining" in home sales but was also a central feature of consumer credit markets. As Anne Fleming explains:

> [Black and poor consumers] shopped and borrowed in a consumer landscape strikingly different from that of [their] white, middle-class, suburban counterparts. Poor consumers continued to finance new purchases through installment credit, which required regular payments at scheduled intervals. In contrast, many retailers to the middle-class offered their customers "revolving" credit, loans for goods purchased that were repayable in irregular amounts over time with no set payment schedule or end date. Revolving borrowers paid interest on their outstanding debt but had greater flexibility in deciding when and how much to pay each month, and their purchases were not subject to repossession by the seller .... In the two-tiered credit economy, [Black and poor consumers] were trapped at the bottom.[77]

These dynamics are on display in the famous twentieth-century unconscionability case *Williams v. Walker-Thomas Furniture*.[78]

Williams v. Walker-Thomas Furniture concerned Ora Lee Williams, a single-mother of seven on public assistance, who purchased various goods on credit from Walker-Thomas Furniture over the course of five years.[79] Williams' payments were

75 See Fleming, *supra* note 59, at 113.
76 See *id.*
77 See Anne Fleming, *The Rise and Fall of Unconscionability as the "Law of the Poor"*, 102 Geo. L. J. 1383, 1394–95 (2014).
78 350 F.2d 445 (D.C. Cir. 1965).
79 See *id.* at 448; Fleming, *supra* note 77, at 1385.

allocated using pro rata accounting whereby payments were distributed in equal portion to each debt Williams owed.[80] At the time Williams' defaulted, she owed very little on most of her purchases and had paid Walker-Thomas $1,065 on $1,500 of charges.[81] After she defaulted in late 1962, federal officials acting on behalf of Walker-Thomas entered Williams' home and seized "a bed and chest purchased in 1958, along with a more recently acquired washing machine and stereo."[82]

Williams is famous for establishing the contract defense of unconscionability. And discussion about the case has often centered on Williams' lack of sophistication and Walker-Thomas' abuse of standard-form contracts. Yet, as Anne Fleming shows, the transaction was fundamentally shaped by the legal and social context in which it arose. Ora Lee Williams moved to the District of Columbia from the South in the 1940s or 1950s as part of the Great Migration. As Fleming notes, "[b]etween 1940 and 1960 . . . the black population of [DC] more than doubled." DC, like most northern cities, was very segregated.[83]

Williams settled in Northeast DC, which was then majority Black. Walker-Thomas was located on Seventh Street in the U Street Neighborhood, a historically Black neighborhood. The stretch on Seventh Street where the Walker-Thomas store was located was known as "easy-credit corridor."[84] The following two maps show the demographic makeup of DC in 1960 and the locations of Ora Lee Williams and Walker-Thomas Furniture (Figures 13.1 and 13.2).

Thus, the transaction was fundamentally bound up in the racial dynamics of that era and not solely about bargaining asymmetry and contractual boilerplate.

Consumer scholars and advocates responded to the problem of credit sales and discrimination in credit markets in several ways. First, they pushed for state sales financing and retail installment sales act laws, which brought sales finance within the ambit of sate consumer financial law.[85] Second, and more importantly, they pushed for the passage of federal laws that created a national framework to both standardize and support state consumer credit regulation. Two of the most important laws passed during the consumer credit "revolution" of the late 1960s and early 1970s were the Equal Credit Opportunity Act of 1974, which banned discrimination in consumer credit transactions, and the Truth in Lending Act of 1968, which standardized the definition of credit and interest across the country.[86]

These federal laws were core components of the mid-twentieth century settlement in consumer finance. That settlement reflected a compromise position that

[80] See *id.* at 1396.

[81] See *id.*

[82] See *id.*

[83] See FLEMING, *supra* note 59.

[84] See *id.*

[85] See *id.* 107–76 (as Fleming explains, the historic distinction between cash and credit sales made the effort to regulate credit sellers much more complicated than salary lenders, but these efforts eventually led to state laws with disclosure requirements and rate caps).

[86] See Anne Fleming, *The Long History of "Truth in Lending"*, 30 J. POL'Y HIST. 236–71 (2018).

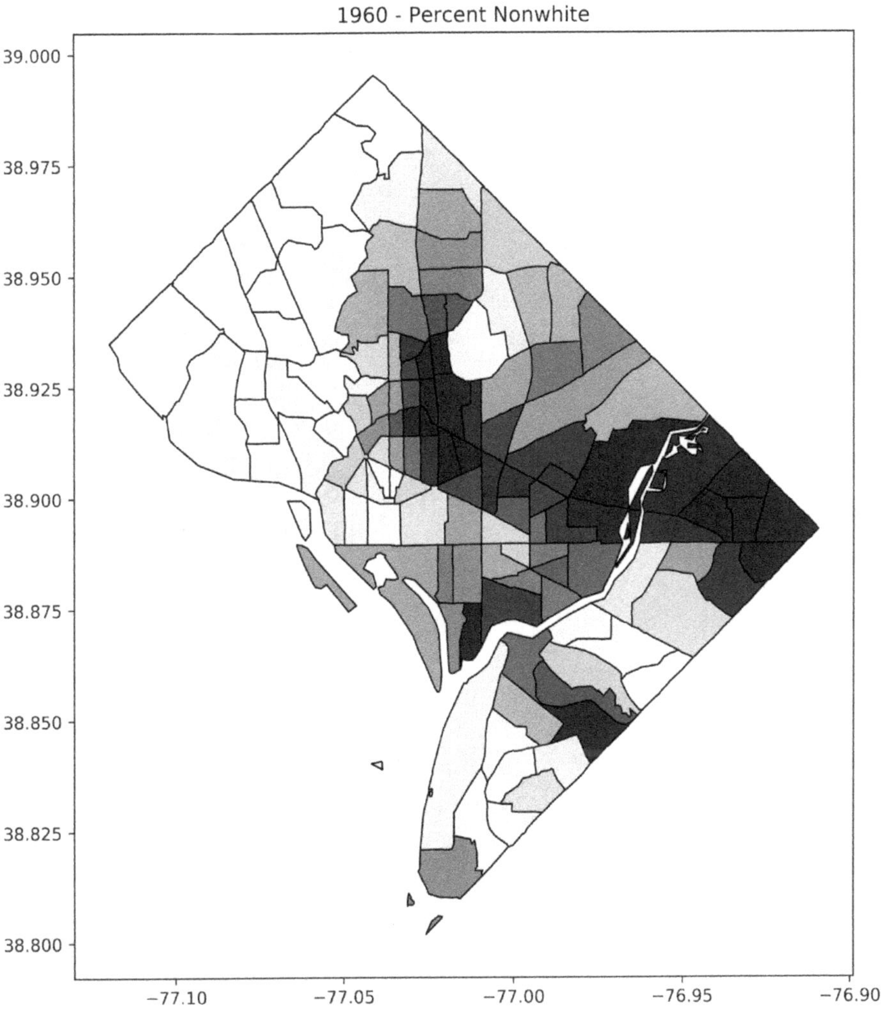

FIGURE 13.1 The demographic makeup of Washington, DC, in 1960

allowed marginal credit but subjected it to tight regulation. The normative aims of mid-twentieth-century consumer financial regulation were grounded in concerns about fairness and distribution as opposed to a narrow conception of efficiency. That is not to suggest that mid-twentieth-century consumer financial regulation was a perfect enterprise[87] but that it was a pluralistic enterprise, which provided some measure of protection for consumers.

[87] See, e.g., Dylan C. Penningroth, *Race in Contract Law*, 170 U. PA. L. REV. 1129, 1163–70 (2022) (on racist tropes in the "law of the poor"); Anne Fleming, *The Public Interest in the Private Law of the Poor*, 14 HARV. L. POL'Y REV. 159 (2019) (on tropes about dependence in early-twentieth-century consumer reform movements); GUNNAR TRUMBULL, CONSUMER LENDING IN FRANCE

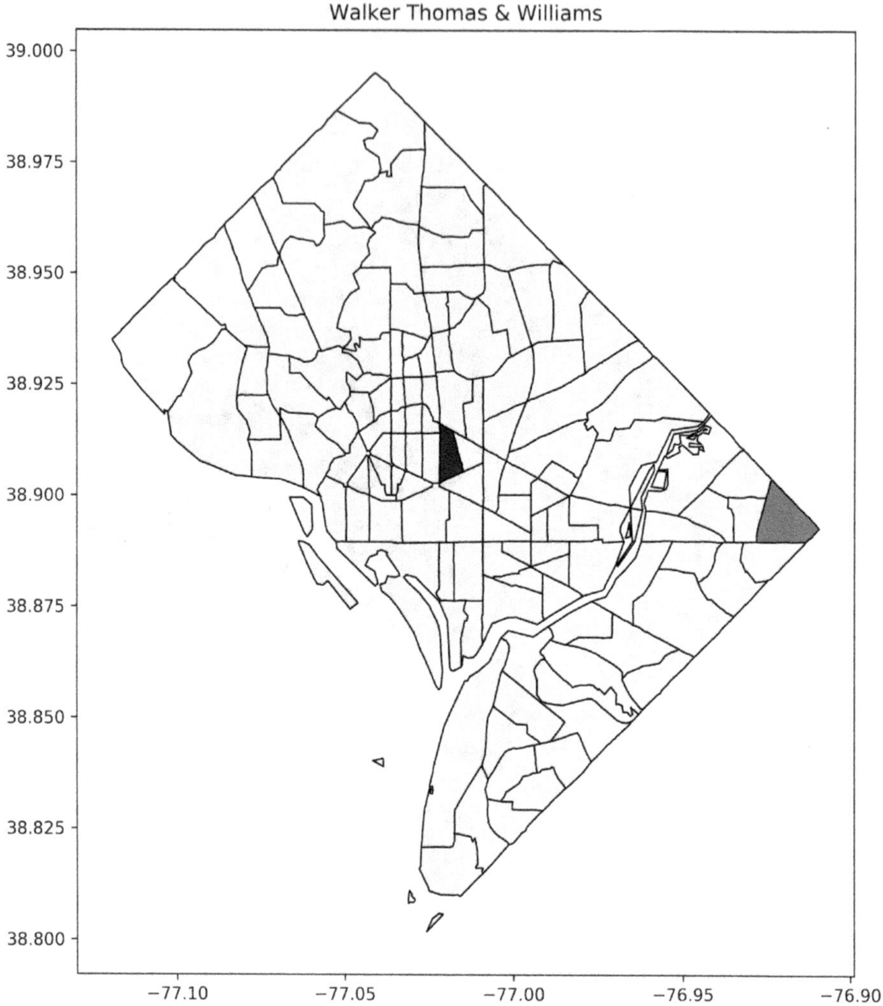

FIGURE 13.2 The locations of Ora Lee Williams and Walker-Thomas Furniture

This framework would unravel in the late twentieth century under deregulatory measures and a conservative assault against economic regulation. Perhaps the most important deregulatory measure was the effective elimination of state interest rate caps, which began with the Supreme Court's 1978 decision in *Marquette National Bank of Minneapolis v. First Omaha Service Corp.*[88] In *Marquette*, the Court held that federal law preempted state laws that restricted the interest rate federally

AND AMERICA: CREDIT AND WELFARE 13 (2014) (on the third-way politics of the consumer reform movement).

[88] See Marquette National Bank of Minneapolis v. First Omaha Service Corp., 439 U.S. 299, 309–13 (1978).

chartered banks could charge outside the bank's home state. *Marquette* allowed national banks to export high interest rates into jurisdictions with restrictive usury caps and gave national banks a significant competitive advantage over state-chartered banks. In order to address this competitive imbalance, Congress passed the Depository Institutions Deregulation and Monetary Control Act (DIDMCA) of 1980,[89] which gave state-chartered banks the same interest rate importation privileges as national banks. DIDMCA was followed by similar efforts at the state level to allow banks incorporated in states with restrictive usury laws to compete with other depository institutions.[90]

These deregulatory moves occurred in conjunction with a conservative assault against what was characterized as a heavy-handed and paternalistic state regulation[91] and the eventual contraction of the welfare state.[92] Together, these pressures contributed to the emergence of a new class of fringe products for low-income consumers, which included payday loans, title loans, installment loans, and products from more mainstream financial institutions such as overdraft and credit cards that operated on a "sweatbox" model of lending.[93] Surveying the consumer financial landscape in 2007, Chris Peterson found the conditions in consumer financial markets resembled the conditions that existed at the turn of the twentieth century.[94] This state of affairs is perhaps best reflected in narratives such as the following one:

One borrower, Oscar Wellito, testified that he took out a signature loan from Defendants after he went bankrupt. He was supporting school-aged children while trying to service debt obligations with two other small loan companies. He earned about $9 an hour at a Safeway grocery store, which was not enough money to make ends meet, yet too much money to qualify for public assistance. "That's why," he testified, "I had no choice of getting these loans, to feed my kids, to live from one paycheck to another paycheck." He needed money for groceries, gas, laundry soap, and "whatever we need to survive from one payday to another payday." Mr. Wellito borrowed $100 from Defendants. His loan carried a 1,147.14 APR and required repayment in twenty-six biweekly installments of $40.16 with a final payment of $55.34. Thus, the $100 loan carried a total finance charge of $999.71.[95]

89 See Public Law 96-221, 94 Stat. 132.

90 See Peterson, *supra* note 57 at 1122.

91 See Luke Herrine, *The Folklore of Unfairness*, 96 N.Y.U. L. Rev. 431 (2021)

92 See Vijay Raghavan, *The Case against the Debt Tax*, 91 Fordham L. Rev. 1849, 1867–70 (2023).

93 Ronald J. Mann, *Bankruptcy Reform and the "Sweat Box" of Credit Card Debt*, 2007 U. Ill. L. Rev. 375, 384 (2007).

94 Peterson, *supra* note 57, at 1140.

95 King ex rel. v. B&B Inv. Group, Inc., 329 P.3d 658, 664 (N.M. 2014) (finding the products at issue in the case were longer-term loans the defendants offered to evade state payday lending restrictions).

B *The False Promise of the 2010 Reforms*

The financial crisis of 2008 created an opportunity for a course correction. That course correction eventually came in the form of a new federal agency, the Consumer Financial Protection Bureau (CFPB), to police the consumer financial marketplace. The blueprint for the agency was set out by Elizabeth Warren in academic and popular work. For Warren, there were at least two reasons why we ought to have a new agency to regulate the national market for consumer finance.

The first reason was a lack of parity between the regulation of consumer goods and consumer financial products.[96] Consumers could purchase consumer goods such as toasters with relative confidence that they would not explode but could not take out a loan with the same confidence. The second reason was the regulatory authority that existed over consumer finance was spread across many different federal and state entities.[97] For Warren, the way to solve this regulatory gap was to create a new federal agency with consolidated regulatory power over consumer financial markets.[98]

In co-authored academic work, Warren sketched out another justification for the new agency that was tethered, in many ways, to behavioralist arguments about market failures.[99] As Warren and her co-author Oren Bar-Gill argued:

> The problem, of course, is that consumers are not always perfectly informed, and very few consumers are perfectly rational. When the ideals of perfect information and perfect rationality are replaced by their real-world counterparts, imperfect information and imperfect rationality, the rosy picture of optimally designed products and welfare- maximizing transactions must be redrawn.[100]

In other words, the primary case for a new agency with regulatory authority over consumer financial markets was to correct market imperfections and support market transactions as opposed to, say, redistribute power in financial markets.[101] Indeed, Warren and Bar-Gill were clear that their proposed solution would benefit "a booming market" and encourage welfare-enhancing competition.[102]

96 See Elizabeth Warren, *Unsafe at Any Rate*, 5 DEMOCRACY 8 (Summer 2007).

97 See *id.*

98 See *id.*

99 Oren Bar-Gill & Elizabeth Warren, *Making Credit Safer*, 157 U. PA. L. REV. 1 (2008). Indeed, the first half of the paper is largely devoted to applying the insights of behavioral law and economics to consumer financial markets.

100 See *id.* at 8.

101 To be sure, Warren and Bar-Gill did point to distribution as a basis for intervention, but even here, they grounded their normative claims in the economic literature on information asymmetries and bounded rationality. *Id.* at 64, 98–100 (explaining that disparate impact due to differences in information and rationality may warrant intervention in consumer financial markets).

102 See *id.* at 4.

These ideas were embedded in Title X of Dodd-Frank, which created the CFPB.[103] Perhaps the most notable way is through the CFPB's authority over "abusive" acts and practices:

> The Bureau shall have no authority under this section to declare an act or practice abusive in connection with the provision of a consumer financial product or service, unless the act or practice-
> (1) materially interferes with the ability of a consumer to understand a term or condition of a consumer financial product or service; or
> (2) takes unreasonable advantage of-
> (A) a lack of understanding on the part of the consumer of the material risks, costs, or conditions of the product or service;
> (B) the inability of the consumer to protect the interests of the consumer in selecting or using a consumer financial product or service; or
> (C) the reasonable reliance by the consumer on a covered person to act in the interests of the consumer.[104]

As Patrick Corrigan has argued, the statutory language of this provision "rejects traditional neoclassical economic logic [and instead] directs the CFPB to regulate problems articulated by the burgeoning literature of behavioral law and economics, particularly problems of imperfect rationality."[105] The decision to tie the CFPB's regulatory authority to behavioral law and economics would prove fatal to the Bureau's effort to regulate fringe finance.

Shortly after the CFPB was created, it set out to create a federal framework for fringe finance.[106] Over the course of five years, from 2011–2016, the Bureau held countless meetings with stakeholders and the public over a national framework. The Bureau also gathered a wealth of industry and survey data, which it used to meticulously make the case for reform. In 2016, the Bureau unveiled its proposed Payday Lending Rule, which set out to replicate the framework for salary loans established a century earlier. Under the Bureau's framework, high-cost, small-dollar loans would be presumptively legal if they conformed to certain price and structural limits. Nonconforming loans would not be banned but subject to an underwriting standard that would have likely been very difficult to meet.

[103] To be fair, Adam Tooze suggests that the various compromises embedded in Dodd-Frank might have less to do with Warren and more to do with Ben Bernanke and Timothy Geithner. Adam Tooze, Crashed: How a Decade of Financial Crisis Changed the World 304–7 (2018) (describing how, in negotiating the language of Dodd-Frank, Ben Bernanke and Timothy Geithner used the CFPB "as a pawn sacrifice" to neuter the "'populist fury' of the 'atonement agenda,'" which included the push to nationalize banks: "[the creation of the CFPB] allowed the reform campaign to claim a major win" but "was largely irrelevant to the vision of systemic stabilization that Geithner and Bernanke were pursuing").

[104] 12 U.S.C. § 5531(d).

[105] Patrick M. Corrigan, *"Abusive" Acts and Practices: Dodd-Frank's Behaviorally Informed Authority over Consumer Credit Markets and Its Application to Teaser Rates*, 18 Legis. Pub. Pol'y 125 (2015).

[106] I chronicled this saga in prior scholarship. Raghavan, *supra* note 1, at 547–52.

In 2017, the Bureau promulgated a final Payday Lending Rule that was narrower in scope. In both the proposed rule and the final rule, the Bureau tied the normative and legal case for the rule to survey data that showed payday borrowers did not understand the true costs of the loan.[107] As I detailed at length in prior scholarship, the implications of the payday survey data were the subject of deep scholarly disagreement.[108] That dissensus was then used by Trump administration officials as a justification for repealing virtually all of the Payday Rule except for modest provisions related to payments.[109] As I explained:

> The analytic linchpin of the [Trump] CFPB's rescission of the Payday Rule was the ... CFPB's purported failure to give adequate weight to ... survey data. In particular, [Trump appointed officials] argued that the ... CFPB cherry-picked [survey data] to support its argument that borrowers did not understand the risks associated with payday loans. As [Trump appointed officials] explained: "[T]he [survey] data overall indicates that payday borrowers in general – i.e., including consumers who engage in short sequences of payday loans – are able to predict the length of their loan sequences with reasonable accuracy." The new CFPB concluded that the thin evidence the old CFPB relied on was insufficient to fundamentally reshape the payday industry.[110]

IV INFRAMARGINALISM AS ECONOMISM

In some ways, it seems unfair to draw hard lessons from the failure of behavioral law and economics. Inframarginalism does not set out to unsettle any of neoclassical law and economics' core assumptions. Instead, it merely sets out to suggest that there are ways to redistribute surplus without any loss of efficiency. Moreover, the CFPB's failure to create a national framework for payday loans had more to do with politics and less to do with the claims of behavioral law and economics.

But that is precisely why inframarginalism's third-way politics are unlikely to succeed.[111] Redistributing wealth through legal rules is fundamentally a political and moral decision. The defaults of law and economics that are embedded in regulatory policy do not reflect neutral and empirically derived principles subject to change and contestation. Instead, these are political choices that create strong

107 See *id.*

108 See *id.*

109 Which, in a perverse twist of fate, is the rule that set up the present constitutional challenge to the CFPB's funding structure. Community Financial Services Association of America v. CFPB, No. 21-50826 (5th Cir. Oct. 19, 2022).

110 See Raghavan, *supra* note 1, at 550.

111 See Bubb & Pildes, *supra* note 52, at 1595 ("[a]s politics, BLE offers the promise of a possible political consensus – built around minimalist forms of government action that preserve freedom of choice, such as default rules and 'smart disclosure' – that cuts through today's hyperpolarized, partisan conflicts and offers a tantalizing third way between conventional ideologies of right and left").

allocative and regulatory defaults, which favor a regressive distribution of wealth. You simply cannot unsettle these assumptions within the analytic framework of law and economics.

And there is a deeper problem with both behavioral law and economics and inframarginalism in its original and current form. Both center elite expertise in regulatory design.[112] At a time when many scholars and activists are contemplating how we might repurpose our institutions to reallocate governing power over markets,[113] inframarginalism's expert-led tinkering seems like a step backwards.

In the last five years, policymakers and advocates have slowly chipped away at the empire of economism. For example, in Illinois, the state legislature passed a universal rate cap of 36 percent in 2021 on racial equity grounds.[114] This spurred similar action in other states and reignited a national conversation over a federal rate cap.[115] At the federal level, the Federal Trade Commission and the CFPB have been busy promulgating rules to ban noncompete clauses in employment contracts,[116] mandating easy opt-outs in membership contracts,[117] to collect data on small-business lending,[118] and issuing reports shedding light on dark patterns[119] and algorithmic discrimination.[120] These gains are often not grounded in technocratic arguments about inefficiency and surplus. Instead, they are grounded in a deep critique of the economic style and its dominating tendencies.

112 Zachary Liscow & Daniel Markovits, *Democratizing Behavioral Economics*, 39 Yale J. on Reg. 1217 (2022).

113 See, e.g., Sabeel Rahman, Democracy against Domination (2016).

114 See Jenny Whidden, Gov. J.B. Pritzker Signs Illinois Legislative Black Caucus' Economic Reform Package, Chicago Tribune (Mar. 23, 2021), www.chicagotribune.com/politics/ct-black-legislative-caucus-economics-20210323-pwgm7expr5cinppbtkn4sf4lne-story.html. The rate cap legislation was one of four bills passed by the Illinois legislature, which were part of "the economic reform pillar of the Illinois Legislative Black Caucus' agenda." *Id.* As the Tribune explained: "The Black Caucus' agenda aims to address systemic racism in criminal justice, education, the economy and health care. It was crafted over the summer amid the unrest that followed the police killings of George Floyd, Breonna Taylor and other African Americans." *Id.*

115 See NCLC Advocates Applaud 36% National Rate Cap Bill to Curb High-Cost, Predatory Loans across the Nation, NCLC (July 21, 2021), www.nclc.org/nclc-advocates-applaud-36-national-rate-cap-bill-to-curb-high-cost-predatory-loans-across-the-nation/.

116 See FTC Proposes Rule to Ban Noncompete Clauses, Which Hurt Workers and Harm Competition (Jan. 5, 2023), www.ftc.gov/news-events/news/press-releases/2023/01/ftc-proposes-rule-ban-noncompete-clauses-which-hurt-workers-harm-competition.

117 See Adi Robertson, The FTC Wants to Ban Those Tough-to-Cancel Gym and Cable Subscriptions (Mar. 23, 2023), www.theverge.com/2023/3/23/23652373/ftc-click-to-cancel-subscription-service-dark-patterns-ban.

118 See Small Business Lending under the Equal Credit Opportunity Act (Regulation B) (final rule), https://files.consumerfinance.gov/f/documents/cfpb_1071-final-rule.pdf.

119 See Bringing Dark Patterns to Light (Sept. 14, 2022), www.ftc.gov/system/files/ftc_gov/pdf/P214800%20Dark%20Patterns%20Report%209.14.2022%20-%20FINAL.pdf.

120 See CFPB Acts to Protect the Public from Black-Box Credit Models Using Complex Algorithms (May 26, 2022), www.consumerfinance.gov/about-us/newsroom/cfpb-acts-to-protect-the-public-from-black-box-credit-models-using-complex-algorithms/.

The stakes of this debate are not merely theoretical. Consider the recent intra-left debate over the merits of the Biden administration's proposed overhaul of the regulatory review process. As noted above, the federal regulatory review process turns on a narrow application of cost–benefit analysis to final agency rulemaking. Early in his administration, Biden called for modernizing the regulatory review process[121] and brought in critics of cost–benefit analysis to aid with this overhaul.

On April 6, 2023, the Office of Management and Budget released its proposed revisions to the regulatory review process.[122] The proposed revisions propose important changes to the evaluation of a regulation's costs and benefits. These changes include using less punitive discount rates, considering macroeconomic factors such as business cycles in measuring a regulation's impact, adding distributional weights to the cost–benefit calculation, and incorporating modern insights from econometrics and behavioral economics in the evaluation of costs and benefits.[123]

Proponents of the overhaul cast it as "a revolution in cost–benefit rules," which is "reversing several decades of pseudo-technical right-wing mischief."[124] And Sabeel Rahman, a leader of the overhaul effort, describes the proposed changes as an "important front-line in the broader effort to create an inclusive political economy."[125]

Some on the left, however, find less to celebrate in the proposed revisions. Instead, they see the revisions as "a recalibration, rather than a rejection or rethinking," which preserves the logic of the regulatory review process as "one that commensurates costs and benefits in terms of additive individual willingness to pay, that holds up market competition between capitalist firms as the presumptively optimal form of social organization, and that treats regulation as a presumptively unwarranted intrusion into the freedom of the market."[126] The approach still centers on market failures as the primary justification for regulatory intervention, largely ignores insights from heterodox approaches to economics, and suggests that some forms of regulation, such as price controls, will likely fail regulatory impact analysis.[127]

[121] www.whitehouse.gov/briefing-room/presidentialactions/2021/01/20/modernizing-regulatory-review/.

[122] www.whitehouse.gov/wp-content/uploads/2023/04/DraftCircularA-4.pdf.

[123] *Id.*

[124] Robert Kuttner, *A Revolution in Cost-Benefit Rules*, The American Prospect (Apr. 11, 2023), https://prospect.org/day-one-agenda/2023-04-11-revolution-cost-benefit-rules-oira/.

[125] K. Sabeel Rahman, *Rewiring Regulatory Review*, The Law and Political Economy Project (May 1, 2023), https://lpeproject.org/blog/rewiring-regulatory-review/.

[126] Luke Herrine, *Some Short Circuits in the Rewiring of Regulatory Review*, The Law and Political Economy Project (May 8, 2023), https://lpeproject.org/blog/some-short-circuits-in-the-rewiring-of-regulatory-review/; see also Daniel Deacon, *Identifying Alternatives: Some Old, a Little New*, Yale Journal on Regulation Notice & Comment (May 25, 2023), www.yalejreg.com/nc/identifying-alternatives-some-old-a-little-new-by-daniel-deacon/.

[127] Herrine, *supra* note 126.

At the center of this chapter's critique is a similar concern about the virtues of inframarginalism. By tethering its approach to an orthodox understanding of economic surplus, inframarginalism may serve as a mere recalibration rather than a rejection of economism's basic precepts. There may be pragmatic reasons why recalibration efforts are more sensible than radical reimaginings that draw from heterodox approaches to economics. But, as this chapter argues, there are important costs to this kind of pragmatism. None of this is to argue against the instrumental ends of inframarginalism nor to suggest there is no room for empiricism in regulatory design. It is instead to question whether markets as presently conceptualized and configured can ever meaningfully serve as sites for wealth redistribution.

14

Hipster Antiplagiarism

Brian L. Frye[*]

What religion do you profess, preacher?
The religion the Almighty and me worked out betwixt us.[1]

CONTENTS

Everything old is new again. Even after decades of consumer welfare theory, the dream of the 1890s is alive in antitrust. While the Chicago School still dominates antitrust policy like a velvet glove cast in iron, the New Brandeis School has begun to get the upper hand. Suddenly, low prices aren't enough, if they mean fewer competitors. While Chicago squares just want to see a chicken in every pot, New Brandeis hipsters want to see a thousand florists bloom.

[*] Many thanks to Ramsi Woodcock for his thoughtful comments and suggestions on a draft of this essay. Special thanks to Diana Liebenau for introducing me to the Matthew Principle.

[1] *Night of the Hunter* (Charles Laughton 1955).

Personally, I'm agnostic about which theory is right. Both the Chicago School and the New Brandeis School theories of antitrust have their merits, as does their oft-forgotten Harvard School predecessor. Increasing consumer welfare sounds great, but so does reducing market concentration. The real question is what antitrust policy is supposed to achieve, and which policies are most likely to achieve it. Maybe focusing on consumer welfare is good, because it makes markets more efficient, but maybe it's bad, because it ignores other important values. Maybe focusing on market concentration is good, because it increases competition, but maybe it's bad, because it makes everyone worse off. Who knows? Either way, it's a gamble that reflects the priorities of the person making the choice. I just hope policymakers adopt flexible policies and pay attention to results.

In any case, I'm a plagiarism scholar, so I care about what antitrust theory has to say about plagiarism norms, if anything. And I suspect it has a lot more to say than you'd think. I think plagiarism poses an antitrust problem. What's more, I think the Chicago School and the New Brandeis School theories imply different answers to the problem.

For better or worse, we take plagiarism norms for granted. It's elementary that plagiarism is wrong, so punishment is obviously justified. But why? Who knows. Plagiarism norms are so widely observed that no one even bothers to defend them on the merits. That's a problem. Plagiarism is a serious charge with serious consequences. We shouldn't punish people for plagiarism unless we can explain why it's wrong and who it harms.[2]

Good luck. The plagiarism police don't even try. They just assume plagiarism harms both authors and readers, without substantiating either claim. But neither is compelling. Authors aren't harmed by plagiarism, which rarely reduces their sales or stature, and can even increase them. And readers aren't harmed by plagiarism at all; they just consider it a moral wrong deserving of punishment.

Why do plagiarism norms exist and why do we punish plagiarism? The answer is simple. Authors want to own things that copyright doesn't protect, but plagiarism norms do. Copyright is fundamentally an economic right. It protects the right to sell copies of a work, but encourages others to create and sell similar works by excluding ideas from protection. But authors hate competition. They don't want anyone to create similar works and steal their audience. So they created plagiarism norms, which do protect ideas and enable authors to collectively police the production of works and reduce competition. In other words, plagiarism norms are the means by which authors manage their cartel.

The antitrust problem should be obvious. But what remedy does antitrust policy provide? It depends on your theory of antitrust. Under the prevailing Chicago

[2] See generally Brian L. Frye, *Plagiarism Is Not a Crime*, 54 Duquesne L. Rev. 133 (2016) and Brian L. Frye, *Plagiarize This Paper*, 60 IDEA 294 (2020). See also Steve Fuller, *Against Academic Rentiership: A Radical Critique of the Knowledge Economy*, 1 Postdigit. Sci. Educ. 335–56 (2019).

School theory, the answer may be nothing. After all, it's unclear whether plagiarism norms affect consumer welfare. They may even increase it, by increasing the quality and diversity of works created. However, the iconoclastic New Brandeis School theory is more promising, or at least more likely to recommend antitrust enforcement. Plagiarism norms benefit successful authors at the expense of unsuccessful authors, precisely the kind of harm the New Brandeis School finds most troubling.

What does it all mean? Well, if you accept the New Brandeis School theory of antitrust, maybe you should object to plagiarism norms. If the Chicago School supports the plagiarism police, surely the New Brandeis School should defund them. Plagiarism has always been hip, ask any artist. We've punished plagiarism for too long. Maybe we should legalize it (Figure 14.1).

I A POTTED HISTORY OF UNITED STATES ANTITRUST LAW

Plagiarism isn't obviously an antitrust problem. If it were, other people would have noticed. But antitrust scholars have ignored plagiarism norms, just like everyone else. We take plagiarism norms for granted and find it distasteful to question their legitimacy.

In order to understand why plagiarism is an antitrust problem, it's helpful to understand a little something about the history of antitrust law and policy.[3] While competition law has existed since time immemorial, antitrust is a modern phenomenon, and federal antitrust law has existed only since 1890.[4] While pre-modern societies used competition law to benefit the state and maintain social order, modern societies use antitrust law to benefit consumers by preventing unfair competition. But policymakers have always disagreed about not only the goals of antitrust law, but also how to achieve them.

As is so often the case, how you tell the story of antitrust law depends on where you begin. If antitrust is simply a synonym for competition law, then it has always existed, albeit often in service of suppressing competition, rather than promoting it. While the common law prohibited anticompetitive combinations in restraint of trade, it was often observed in the breach.

In any case, convention holds that United States antitrust law begins with the Sherman Act of 1890, and who am I to buck convention? In the late nineteenth century, United States companies began to coalesce into large conglomerates or "trusts." Many people opposed this consolidation and proposed state and federal antitrust legislation to prohibit or break up those trusts, which culminated in the Sherman Act.

[3] See generally Laura Phillips Sawyer, *US Antitrust Law and Policy in Historical Perspective*, Harvard Business School Working Paper 19–110 (2019).

[4] See generally Ramsi Woodcock, *Technology, Monopoly, and Antitrust from a Historical Perspective* in RESEARCH HANDBOOK ON LAW AND TECHNOLOGY 142 (Edward Elgar 2023).

FIGURE 14.1 "I Like a Little Competition" – J. P. Morgan by Art Young

The premise of the Sherman Act was that cartels and monopolies harm consumers and society by reducing competition, so it prohibited combinations in restraint of trade, in order to promote competition.[5] The Sherman Act was intended to empower the federal government to enforce common law rules prohibiting anticompetitive conduct.[6] While the text of the Sherman Act prohibits all restraints of trade, the Supreme Court soon adopted the narrowing "rule of reason," holding that the Sherman Act only prohibits "unreasonable" restraints of trade.[7]

Initially, the Sherman Act produced mixed results. In theory, it was supposed to empower the federal government to prohibit the concentration of economic power in dominant firms or monopolies. But in practice, it may have actually hastened consolidation, by making it harder for small firms to compete and encouraging them to merge into larger firms.

The Supreme Court didn't help, adopting a tortured interpretation of the Sherman Act that made it difficult to use and even more difficult to use effectively. For example, in the *Sugar Trust Case*, the Court held that the American Sugar Refining Company didn't necessarily violate the Sherman Act, even though it controlled 98 percent of sugar refining in the United States, and required the government to show specific actions in restraint of trade.[8] In *Trans-Missouri Freight Association*, it held that an agreement among railroads to regulate prices was illegal, even if the agreement was intended to reduce prices.[9] And in *Workingmen's Amalgamated Council of New Orleans*, it held that the Sherman Act prohibited unions from organizing strikes and boycotts.[10] It's hard to believe that's how Congress envisioned the purpose of the Sherman Act.

Subsequent federal antitrust laws expanded the scope of the government's regulatory authority. The Federal Trade Commission Act of 1914 created the Federal Trade Commission (FTC) and empowered it to enforce the Sherman Act.[11] And the Clayton Act of 1914 not only prohibited anticompetitive mergers and acquisition, but also created a private cause of action for parties harmed by anticompetitive conduct in violation of the Sherman Act or Clayton Act to sue for treble damages or injunctive relief.[12]

While the Progressive Era saw considerable antitrust enforcement, overseen by reformers like Louis D. Brandeis, it petered out in the Roaring Twenties. The Hoover

[5] The Sherman Act provides, "Every contract, combination in the form of trust or otherwise, or conspiracy, in restraint of trade or commerce among the several States, or with foreign nations, is declared to be illegal." 15 U.S.C. § 1.

[6] John B. Kirkwood & Robert H. Lande, *The Fundamental Goal of Antitrust: Protecting Consumers, Not Increasing Efficiency*, 84 Notre Dame L. Rev. 191 (2008).

[7] Standard Oil Co. of New Jersey v. United States, 221 U.S. 1, 87 (1911).

[8] United States v. E. C. Knight Co., 156 U.S. 1 (1895).

[9] United States v. Trans-Missouri Freight Association, 166 U.S. 290 (1897).

[10] United States v. Workingmen's Amalgamated Council of New Orleans, 54 F. 995 (1893).

[11] 15 U.S.C. §§ 41–58.

[12] 15 U.S.C. § 12.

administration was "pro-business," which often meant pro-monopoly and pro-cartel. Companies once again started to consolidate, and competition was largely managed by trade associations. The first wave of antitrust enforcement was over.

A *The New Deal*

Then came the stock market crash of 1929 and the onset of the Great Depression. Hoover's efforts to spur economic growth were ineffectual, and FDR was elected in 1932 because he promised a "new deal" that would end the depression. Among other things, the New Deal meant a wholesale rethinking of economic regulation, including antitrust enforcement.

At least initially, the FDR administration abandoned Progressive Era efforts to prevent collusion and promote competition, in favor of cartelization and regulation. For example, the National Industrial Recovery Act (NIRA) of 1933 encouraged monopolization and the Robinson–Patman Act of 1936 prevented price discrimination by prohibiting manufacturers from giving retailers volume discounts.[13] While the Supreme Court resisted these policy changes, among other things invalidating the NIRA as unconstitutional, it eventually caved and gave Congress extensive authority to regulate the national economy.[14]

However, when the FDR administration realized cartelization wasn't working, it revived Progressive Era antitrust policy. In 1938, FDR appointed Thurman W. Arnold to lead the Antitrust Division of the Department of Justice, with a mandate to pursue vigorous antitrust enforcement. And Arnold delivered, bringing successful actions against many different companies and organizations, including the American Medical Association. While the FDR administration put the brakes on antitrust enforcement during WWII, in order to focus on the war effort, it still occasionally asserted its authority to regulate competition and use antitrust law to prevent monopolization.[15] But antitrust enforcement took a back seat to ensuring the United States could meet wartime production goals.

B *The Harvard School*

The end of the war was the beginning of a new era in antitrust theory and enforcement. A consensus antitrust theory gradually emerged, which held that the primary

[13] See National Industrial Recovery Act, 48 Stat. 195 (June 16, 1933) and Robinson-Patman Act, 49 Stat. 1526 (1936).

[14] Compare A.L.A. Schechter Poultry Corp. v. United States, 295 U.S. 495 (1935) (holding the NIRA unconstitutional) with National Labor Relations Board v Jones & Laughlin Steel Corporation, 301 U.S. 1 (1937) (holding the National Labor Relations Act of 1935 constitutional).

[15] See, e.g., United States v. Alcoa, 148 F.2d 416 (2d Cir. 1945) (Hand, J.) (holding that monopolies are effectively *per se* illegal).

purpose of antitrust law is to promote competition by preventing market concentration. It became known as the "Harvard School" of antitrust theory, because it was based on the work of Harvard economists like Edward Chamberlain, Joe Bain, and Edward Mason, who argued that the structure of an industry determines its efficiency: the more concentrated, the less efficient.[16]

Following their lead, Harvard School antitrust scholars argued that antitrust law should focus on reducing market concentration in order to increase efficiency. They observed that market concentration tends to encourage anticompetitive conduct and decrease efficiency. It follows that reducing market concentration should discourage anticompetitive conduct and thereby increase efficiency.

The Harvard School focused on market concentration, because it's hard to prevent anticompetitive conduct directly. As a great philosopher once observed, "People of the same trade seldom meet together, even for merriment and diversion, but the conversation ends in a conspiracy against the public, or in some contrivance to raise prices."[17] It's even harder when collusion is tacit, rather than explicit.

The Harvard School argued that market concentration encourages anticompetitive conduct by facilitating tacit collusion. In a concentrated market, coordination is easy, all it takes is a wink and a nod between similarly situated rivals. But the more firms you have to coordinate, the harder implicit collusion becomes. Accordingly, the Harvard School saw reducing market concentration as the easiest and most reliable way of discouraging anticompetitive conduct, by making tacit collusion more difficult. While it's hard to regulate tacit collusion directly, antitrust can reduce it by prohibiting the market concentration that makes it possible. And if tacit collusion is impossible, then coordination requires explicit collusion, which is far easier to catch and prosecute.

Accordingly, the Harvard School opposed market concentration even when it benefited consumers by reducing prices or improving service, because market concentration would inevitably lead to anticompetitive conduct.[18] The short-term benefit of efficient concentration isn't worth the long-term cost.

But the Harvard School's focus on market concentration had its own costs and benefits. For one thing, it was clear and predictable, but imprecise. After all, market concentration is at best an imperfect proxy for competition. Reducing market concentration often increases competition and efficiency, but not always. Hopefully, the net effect was positive, but it was hard to be sure.

16 See, e.g., Edward Chamberlain, The Theory of Monopolistic Competition (1935); Joe S. Bain, Barriers to New Competition: Their Character and Consequences in Manufacturing Industries (1956); and Edward S. Mason, Economic Concentration and the Oligopoly Problem (1964).

17 Adam Smith, An Inquiry into the Nature and Causes of the Wealth of Nations, bk. 1, ch. 10, pt. 2 (1776).

18 See, e.g., Donald F. Turner, *The Definition of Agreement under the Sherman Act: Conscious Parallelism and Refusals to Deal*, 75 Harv. L. Rev. 655, 663–73 (1962).

Ironically, the Harvard School approach to antitrust enforcement probably discouraged some of the most aggressive forms of competition. After all, why would firms push to lower prices or outcompete their rivals, if their reward was an antitrust enforcement action for increasing market concentration? Better to play it safe and rely on your nominal competitors to do the same. Over time, the Harvard School approach came to look as a recipe for conformity and stagnation, not competition and efficiency.

C *The Chicago School*

Enter the Chicago School of antitrust theory and its relentless focus on efficiency, in the form of consumer welfare. According to the Chicago School, the only legitimate purpose of antitrust policy is to increase net social welfare by making markets more efficient. Unlike the Harvard School, which focused on protecting and promoting competition as its primary policy goal, the Chicago School saw competition as a means to an end, not an end in itself.

And the end is consumer welfare. According to the Chicago School theory, antitrust enforcement is justified only if it will increase net consumer welfare by making the market more efficient. This "consumer welfare standard" is the defining feature of the Chicago School theory. Unlike the Harvard School, which sought to protect competitors in order to promote competition, the Chicago School sought to promote competition only in order to increase consumer welfare.[19]

In practice, the premises of the Chicago School made it considerably more skeptical of antitrust enforcement than the Harvard School. Chicago School scholars tend to assume that free and open markets are usually efficient, so antitrust enforcement is generally unnecessary and may even be harmful. Accordingly, the Chicago School argues that antitrust enforcement is appropriate only when regulators are certain that a market failure exists and know how to solve it.

While the Chicago School theory gradually came to dominate antitrust scholarship in the 1970s and 1980s, some scholars trace its ascendence to the 1974 Airlie Conference, in which Chicago School scholars like Robert Bork challenged the premises of Harvard School scholars. In any case, the Chicago School theory was largely adopted by both antitrust regulators and the federal courts, and the consumer welfare standard effectively became the basis for showing an antitrust harm.

[19] Ironically, the Chicago School's adoption of the consumer welfare standard is actually inconsistent with its original focus on net social welfare. Under the consumer welfare standard, regulators and courts must maximize consumer welfare, even if doing so reduces net social welfare. As a result, rigorously applying the consumer welfare standard should result in a wealth transfer from firms to consumers. See, e.g., Ramsi A. Woodcock, *The Antitrust Case for Consumer Primacy in Corporate Governance*, 10 U.C. IRVINE L. REV. 1395 (2020) and Ramsi A. Woodcock, *The Antitrust Duty to Charge Low Prices*, 39 CARDOZO L. REV. 1741 (2018).

D *The New Brandeis School*

Recently, a group of economists and lawyers has challenged the Chicago School of antitrust theory and advocated a return to more aggressive antitrust enforcement, paired with a refocus on broader social goals. The members of this group generally call it the "New Brandeis School" of antitrust theory, reflecting their goal of returning to the aggressive antitrust enforcement advocated by Louis Brandeis in the early twentieth century, but the movement is popularly known as "hipster antitrust."[20]

The New Brandeis School is a diverse movement and its ideas come in many different flavors. The members of the New Brandeis School emphasize different problems and different solutions for different reasons. But they are united by some core principles, primarily their rejection of the consumer welfare standard as the basis for antitrust enforcement and their focus on reducing the concentration of market power. As a consequence, members of the New Brandeis School generally favor antitrust enforcement whenever market power is concentrated, regardless of the effect on consumer welfare.

While the New Brandeis School embraces many different approaches to antitrust reform, its core principles are summarized in the "Utah Statement." In 2019, three prominent members of the New Brandeis School – Lina Khan, Marshall Steinbaum, and Tim Wu – drafted a list of principles and proposed reforms, which they presented at the "A New Future for Antitrust" conference, hosted by the University of Utah.[21] Of course, the authors of the Utah Statement don't speak for everyone associated with the New Brandeis School, or necessarily even agree with each other on all points, and presumably their own views have evolved over time. But the Utah Statement still represents the best and most comprehensive description of the New Brandeis School's core ideas and goals. I'll focus primarily on the ideas, because they are most relevant to applying a New Brandeis School analysis in a novel context.

According to the Utah Statement:

1. Subjecting concentrated private power to democratic checks is a matter of constitutional importance;
2. The protection of fair competition is a means to a thriving and democratic society and an instrument for both the creation of opportunity and the distribution of wealth and power;
3. Excessive concentration of private economic power breeds antidemocratic political pressures and undermines liberties; and

[20] The members of the New Brandeis School understandably object to the term "hipster antitrust" as condescending and dismissive. But it's also distinctive and makes them sound cool. From a branding perspective, they might want to consider embracing the label, even if they find it distasteful. At the very least, it's considerably more distinctive and memorable than their preferred alternative.

[21] Tim Wu, *The Utah Statement: Reviving Antimonopoly Traditions for the Era of Big Tech*, OneZero, Nov. 18, 2019, at https://onezero.medium.com/the-utah-statement-reviving-antimonopoly-traditions-for-the-era-of-big-tech-e6be198012d7. The Utah Statement was a response to Daniel Crane's challenge to articulate the goals of the New Brandeis School in concrete terms.

4. While antitrust is not an answer to every economic distress, it is a democratically enacted and necessary element in achieving these aims.[22]

The Utah Statement's policy proposals follow from these core principles. Among other things, it rejects the consumer welfare standard for antitrust enforcement, holds that offsetting benefits can never justify anticompetitive harms, observes that false negatives and false positives in antitrust enforcement are at least equally undesirable, and argues that clear and convincing evidence of anticompetitive intent should be seen as presumptive evidence of harm.[23]

The defining principle of the New Brandeis School is probably its rejection of the Chicago School's focus on the consumer welfare standard, in favor of a focus on preventing market concentration. The Chicago School is famously indifferent to market concentration, so long as it benefits consumers by reducing prices. By contrast, the New Brandeis School opposes market concentration, even if it increases consumer welfare by reducing prices.

While the rationale for the New Brandeis School's rejection of the consumer welfare standard is unclear, and different scholars may reject it for different reasons, the consensus position seems to be that the consumer welfare standard focuses on short-term outcomes, at the expense of long-term outcomes. In other words, while focusing on consumer welfare may reduce prices tomorrow, focusing on reducing market concentration and encouraging competition will eventually reduce consumer prices and will ultimately produce better results.

Of course, this is an empirical proposition that may or may not actually be true. It will be interesting to see whether members of the New Brandeis School update their premises if it turns out that reducing market concentration does not in fact increase long-term consumer welfare.

What's more, some antitrust scholars associated with the New Brandeis School seem to have taken an even harder line against the consumer welfare standard, arguing that consumer welfare should always be subordinate to distributive justice. For example, adherents of the New Brandeis School tend to be especially solicitous of the interests of the creative class, especially journalists. Some of them go so far as to suggest that antitrust enforcement should prioritize increasing the welfare of journalists and other creatives, even if doing so has a net negative impact on consumer welfare.

In any case, the New Brandeis School has made a significant impact on antitrust policy, especially since Lina Khan was appointed chair of the FTC. As a consequence, New Brandeis School ideas are likely to influence antitrust enforcement priorities in the near future.[24]

22 Wu, *The Utah Statement*.

23 *Id.*

24 This essay was written in 2002, during the Biden administration. The New Brandeis School will probably be less influential under the Trump administration, all the more reason for it to identify projects it can pursue outside of government.

E *The Squares v. the Hipsters*

Obviously, the principles and goals of the New Brandeis School are a sea change from those of the Chicago School. Where the Chicago School looks exclusively to consumer welfare, primarily as reflected in the price of consumer goods, the New Brandeis School looks to the economy as a whole, including the interests of both competitors and stakeholders. Where the Chicago School is cautious, advocating antitrust enforcement only if and when it will clearly benefit consumers, the New Brandeis School is bold, advocating antitrust enforcement whenever consolidation threatens competition. Where the Chicago School is at least nominally apolitical, disavowing any normative values other than maximizing consumer welfare, the New Brandeis School is explicitly political, championing democratic values and the ability of antitrust policy to promote those values.

One fundamental difference between the Chicago School and the New Brandeis School is their perspective on error risk. The Chicago School worries about "Type I" errors or "false positives," while the New Brandeis School worries about "Type II" errors or "false negatives." Or to put it another way, the Chicago School opposes antitrust enforcement unless it's certain to increase consumer welfare, even if that means permitting some anticompetitive conduct. By contrast, the New Brandeis School supports antitrust enforcement unless it can't reduce market concentration, even if that means prohibiting some procompetitive conduct.[25]

Unsurprisingly, adherents of the Chicago School and the New Brandeis School are critical of each other, often bitterly so. The New Brandeis School tends to characterize the Chicago School as apologists for big business, especially "Big Tech," at the expense of consumers. They often characterize Chicago School analysis as designed to make antitrust enforcement effectively impossible. After all, it's never absolutely certain that antitrust enforcement will increase competition and improve long-term outcomes. The Chicago School responds that the New Brandeis School is simply indifferent to evidence and economics, pushing antitrust enforcement against companies and industries it dislikes, with no concern for actual outcomes.[26]

II WHAT IS PLAGIARISM?

Plagiarism is the ultimate academic crime, the scholar's mark of Cain, indelible and inexcusable. The plagiarist is the *homo sacer* of academia, cast out of the academic

[25] See Darren Bush, *Consumer Welfare Theory as an Ethical Consideration: An Essay on Hipsters, Invisible Feet, and the "Science" of Economics*, 63 ANTITRUST BULL. 509 (2018). See also Blake E. Reid, *The Antitrust Concern Troll Bar Association's Playbook for Not Solving Problems*, June 17, 2020, at https://blakereid.org/the-antitrust-concern-troll-bar-associations-playbook-for-not-solving-problems/.

[26] See generally Joshua D. Wright et al., *Requiem for a Paradox: The Dubious Rise and Inevitable Fall of Hipster Antitrust*, ARIZ. ST. L.J. (2019).

fold for transgressing its most sacred principle, and disappeared from its roll, leaving only a palimpsest.[27] Plagiarism demands corruption of the blood. Not only the plagiarist is repudiated, but also their literary offspring. Humiliation passes with time, but retraction is forever.

Everybody hates a plagiarist. Indeed, it seems that everyone has always hated plagiarists. Ancient Greek philosophers objected when someone stole their ideas, and Roman orators objected when someone stole their words. The word "plagiarism" itself is an anglicization of the Latin word *plagiarium* or "kidnapper," used by the poet Martial to satirize a patron who appropriated a poem without paying for it.[28] Even saints refused to turn the other cheek to a plagiarist.[29]

Today, plagiarism is the basest literary offense, perhaps the only one left. In the cleansing sunlight of postmodernism, do what thou wilt is the whole of the literary law, with the sole exception of plagiarism, which remains as unforgivable and unpardonable as ever, perhaps even more so. We deplore scholars who stoop to copying themselves. We admonish our students never to plagiarize, and convene a star chamber at the barest accusation. And we shun ghostwriters, who allow themselves to be plagiarized for pay.

And yet, plagiarism is perfectly legal. It isn't a crime.[30] It isn't even a trespass, unless it also infringes a valid copyright. There's no cause of action for plagiarism. And the Supreme Court has even explicitly endorsed plagiarism as a perfectly legitimate business practice.[31] You can plagiarize all you like, and there's nothing the government can do about it. But the plagiarism police will ensure you suffer, irrespective of the government.

So, what is plagiarism anyway? Ask a stupid question, get a stupid answer. Everyone knows what plagiarism is, but everyone has a different definition. Typically, they know it when they see it. Or rather, people tend to internalize plagiarism norms and then take them for granted. In a sense, plagiarism is in the eye of the beholder. Or rather, plagiarism is as plagiarism norms do. Different social groups have adopted different plagiarism norms for different reasons, and they all enforce their own norms in their own ways.

It turns out, plagiarism norms are contextual and depend on the discursive community creating, interpreting, and enforcing those norms.[32] Lawyers, publicists, journalists, novelists, and academics have all adopted different plagiarism norms, which they enforce in different ways for different reasons. Academics would say

[27] See generally GIORGIO AGAMBEN, HOMO SACER: SOVEREIGN POWER AND BARE LIFE (1998).

[28] See generally SCOTT MCGILL, PLAGIARISM IN LATIN LITERATURE (2012).

[29] See, e.g., BRIAN L. FRYE, THE STOLEN POEM OF ST. MOLING, IN FORGOTTEN INTELLECTUAL PROPERTY LORE (Shubha Ghosh ed. Edward Elgar 2019).

[30] Frye, *supra* note 2 at 133.

[31] See Dastar Corp. v. Twentieth Century Fox Film Corp., 539 U.S. 23 (2003).

[32] See generally CAROL PETERSEN HAVILAND & JOAN A. MULLIN, WHO OWNS THIS TEXT?: PLAGIARISM, AUTHORSHIP, AND DISCIPLINARY CULTURES (2009).

lawyers plagiarize all the time, but lawyers would disagree, or at least claim their plagiarism is unobjectionable, because it's permitted by the rules of their profession.[33]

Plagiarism norms are both unusually stringent and surprisingly permissive, depending on the context. At least in theory, academic plagiarism norms require the attribution of all expressions and ideas copied from another work.[34] Seems simple enough, if rather expansive. After all, what counts as an expression or idea, and what counts as copying? Literary theory tells us that every expression is informed by the entirety of its social context.[35] It seems a little daunting to cite everything, not to mention potentially unhelpful.

Of course, in practice, academic plagiarism norms are considerably more selective. Scholars are expected to cite works published by other scholars in their field whenever those works arguably inform their own. But the devil is in the details. When is a citation required? It depends who you ask. As reviewer 2 reliably demonstrates, scholars are wont to see their own ideas everywhere they look and demand attribution. And senior scholars are accustomed to seeing familiar ideas attributed to themselves. Wise junior scholars liberally cite the giants of their field, save some room for the rising stars, and don't worry too much about the also-rans, irrespective of what they actually read and used.

But everyone agrees the essence of plagiarism is unattributed copying. Proper attribution precludes plagiarism. That's what distinguishes plagiarism from its fraternal twin, copyright infringement. In a nutshell, plagiarism norms ensure authors get credit for their works, and copyright ensures they get paid. For most authors, it's dialectical. Copyright and plagiarism norms both matter, but for different reasons and in different ways. Copyright says your competitors can't create and sell an identical product, and plagiarism norms say that if a competitor creates a similar product, at least they have to promote your brand.

Where it gets weird is when copyright becomes irrelevant, and plagiarism norms replace it. After all, copyright is at least nominally tied to economic realities, and facilitates the transfer of ownership to publishers. Plagiarism norms are pure moralism, albeit in the service of economic interests. The result is predictably extreme, especially in academia, where attribution is all that matters.

So, what is plagiarism? Essentially, the failure to provide a citation when a citation is expected. Expected by whom? Well, anyone who can do anything about it. Or to put it another way, if art is whatever you can get away with, plagiarism is whatever you can't. It's only plagiarism if someone notices and complains. Or rather, it's only

[33] See, e.g., Andrew Carter, *The Case for Plagiarism*, 9 U.C. Irvine L.R. 531, 554 (2019) and Megan Boyd & Brian L. Frye, *Plagiarism Pedagogy: Why Teaching Plagiarism Should Be a Fundamental Part of Legal Education*, 99 Wash. U. L. Rev. Online 1 (2021).

[34] See, e.g., MLA Handbook (9th ed. 2022) (defining "plagiarism" as "presenting another person's ideas, words, or entire work as your own").

[35] Cf. Roland Barthes, The Death of the Author (1967).

plagiarism if the right people call it plagiarism. Once they do, there's no defense. The plagiarism bell can't be unrung. Even the most compelling defense can't wash out the indelible stain.

III LITERARY LANDLORDS AND IDEA TRUSTS

So, why do plagiarism norms present an antitrust problem, and what does antitrust theory have to say about them? It's pretty straightforward. Works of authorship are consumer goods, so antitrust law applies to the market for works of authorship, and antitrust theory should tell us how to regulate that market, if at all.

But actually, it's complicated. While works of authorship are consumer goods, they're a special kind of consumer goods, with special rules. Specifically, the market for works of authorship is governed by copyright, which is essentially a flavor of competition law. Or rather, copyright is obviously anticompetitive. The entire purpose of copyright is to enable authors to charge uncompetitive prices by giving them monopoly rights in their works of authorship. Copyright would clearly violate federal antitrust law, if it weren't authorized by the Constitution and effectively exempt from antitrust enforcement under the *Noerr–Pennington* doctrine.[36]

What about plagiarism norms?[37] While copyright and plagiarism norms are related, and the terms "copyright infringement" and "plagiarism" are often mistakenly used as synonyms, they are actually different concepts that prohibit different actions.[38] Copyright provides that only the copyright owner of a work can authorize its use. It's authorized by the Intellectual Property Clause and created by the Copyright Act, which determines its subject matter, scope, and duration.[39] By contrast, plagiarism norms provide that works of authorship must be attributed to their author. They are created and enforced by the private parties, usually particular discursive communities that determine the metes and bounds of the duty to attribute and enforce the obligations they impose.

Notably, copyright infringement isn't necessarily plagiarism and plagiarism isn't necessarily infringing. Copying an original element of a copyrighted work with attribution but without permission may infringe the copyright in the copied work, but can't be plagiarism, because of the attribution. Likewise, copying a public domain work without attribution is plagiarism, but can't be infringing.

[36] See, e.g., Professional Real Estate Investors, Inc. v. Columbia Pictures Industries, Inc., 508 U.S. 49 (1993) (holding that copyright infringement claims are exempt from antitrust enforcement unless objectively baseless).

[37] See generally Frye, *supra* note 2 at 133 and Frye, *supra* note 2 at 294.

[38] See, e.g., Sheldon v. Metro-Goldwyn Pictures Corporation, 81 F.2d 49 (2d Cir. 1936) (Hand, J.) (incorrectly stating that "unconscious plagiarism is actionable quite as much as deliberate." In fact, plagiarism has never been actionable, because there has never been a cause of action for plagiarism, only for copyright infringement).

[39] See U.S. Const. Art. I, sec. 8, cl. 8 and 17 U.S.C. § 101 et seq.

Anyway, the point is that copyright and plagiarism norms are different regimes with different justifications and sources of authority. Just because copyright is exempt from antitrust enforcement, doesn't necessarily mean that plagiarism norms are also exempt. None of the constitutional and legislative exemptions that protect copyright from antitrust apply to plagiarism norms. Specifically, the *Noerr–Pennington* doctrine doesn't apply to extra-legal property rights. So, there's no reason to think plagiarism norms are exempt from antitrust enforcement, if they violate federal antitrust law.

I think they might. After all, plagiarism norms sure look like an agreement in restraint of trade. They are rules created and enforced by a group of horizontal competitors to regulate commercial conduct that effectively give authors an extra-legal property right in the attribution of their works. Without plagiarism norms, people could copy uncopyrighted works and elements of works without attribution. In addition, plagiarism norms inefficiently limit the alienability of attribution, despite disfavored exceptions like ghostwriting. Why should federal antitrust law permit authors to collusively limit competition in the market for attribution?

Of course, the market for attribution is largely non-economic. Indeed, the salience and enforcement of plagiarism norms seem inversely correlated with economic returns. Who cares the most about plagiarism? Scholars participating in the scholarly gift economy, fan fiction writers, and social media users. None of these authors expect their works to generate an economic return. But that only increases the importance of plagiarism norms. They are writing for attribution, because it increases their status in their discursive community and generates clout.

Academic plagiarism norms, like plagiarism norms in other contexts, are generally framed as ethical rules or principles, rather than anticompetitive collusion. But we are not obliged to accept anodyne self-characterizations.

IV ACADEMIC PLAGIARISM NORMS AND THE ACADEMIC GIFT ECONOMY

While there are many different plagiarism norms, any norm will do, so I'll focus on academic plagiarism norms. Anyone who bothers to read this essay is probably an academic, so academic plagiarism norms will be familiar and relevant, for better or worse.

The market for scholarship is quite peculiar. On its face, scholarship looks like any other literary work, a fundamentally non-rival public good made excludable and thereby artificially scarce by copyright. But in practice, scholarship is largely a public good and increasingly so. Unlike other authors of literary works, academics typically don't expect their works to generate a profit. Accordingly, most scholars don't really care about copyright.

On the contrary, the market for scholarship is an academic gift economy. Academics don't sell their scholarship; they happily give it away to anyone who wants it. They give their scholarship to academic publishers for free, in exchange for those publishers making it available to other academics. Recognizing that academic publishers often charge extortionate rates for access to scholarship, some academics even pay their publishers to make their scholarship available for free.

If the market for scholarship is an academic gift economy, why bother with publishers at all? Academic publishers used to be important, when the cost of publishing and distributing scholarship was high. Not everything could be published, and someone had to decide what qualified and what didn't. But now the cost of publishing and distributing scholarship is nothing. Upload your article to an open-access database and it is instantly available to anyone who wants it, for free.

Academic publishers survive for two reasons: prestige and attribution. Sure, academic publishing is a technological anachronism. Few people want printed copies of scholarly articles, and even fewer are willing to pay the cost. Academic publishers mostly just upload scholarship to a database and let people download it. What a racket! Scholarship is free, copyright provides a monopoly, and academics are a captive audience.

What's in it for academics? Prestige. While they don't get paid directly for scholarship, they do get paid indirectly. Academic publishers confer prestige, which translates into better jobs and more money. If academics only cared about making their scholarship available to the public, academic publishers would shrivel up and die overnight. Luckily for them, academics care about making their scholarship available to the public in a prestigious venue. And academics are remarkably indifferent to what that venue actually costs. Or at least, incapable of doing anything about it, which amounts to the same, given that it is entirely within their control to change.

But that's not all. More than anything, academics care about attribution, and academic journals help make attribution happen. Academics perpetually jostle for prestigious placements, envying those who climb the hierarchy and pitying those who fall. After all, a good placement means citations, and a poor placement means oblivion. Does it really select for quality? Of course not. Who cares, so long as you have enough credible citations to mollify the plagiarism police.

Everyone knows that citations are the coin of the academic realm. As Oscar Wilde famously observed, "The only thing worse than being talked about is not being talked about." It goes double in academia, where irrelevance is as much a feature as a bug. Citations aren't proof positive of relevance, but they're close enough for administrators, which is all that counts. Accordingly, academics gin up countless byzantine systems for ranking themselves according to the number and quality of their citations. It would be amusing, if it weren't so strange.

In any case, academics are jealous of their citations. It's all they have to prove the value of their scholarly labor. So a powerful set of informal rules have developed, which determine what gets cited and what doesn't, not to mention what must be cited and what can safely be ignored. Suffice it to say that they look an awful lot like property rules.

For example, when you are deciding who to cite for a particular idea, you're well-advised to cite the person credited with its first expression. In other words, first in time is first in right. The quality of their expression of the idea is largely irrelevant, as is whether someone else said it better. Academic plagiarism norms say they own the idea, so they're entitled to a citation.

The same is true when it comes to facts. They belong to the academic who published them first. It doesn't matter how they became aware of those facts, or whether they had anything novel to say about them. Priority is key. If you want to address the same facts, you'd better acknowledge their academic owner, or the plagiarism police will come a-knocking.

Of course, academic plagiarism norms aren't formally uniform. Every academic institution has its own plagiarism policy and procedures. But there is considerable commonality. The Modern Language Association (MLA) definition of plagiarism is representative and widely adopted: "Plagiarism is the use of another person's ideas or expressions in your writing without acknowledging the source." And most institutions copy their plagiarism policies from their peers, which is both amusing and sensible. Why reinvent the wheel? The point is to explain a collective policy, not to express a novel idea.

There's a problem. Antitrust law governs commerce, but academics don't sell their work. Or rather, they sell it into an academic gift economy, with no expectation of profiting from the sale. In other words, academics write articles and then give them away. Sometimes, academics give their articles directly to the public, by publishing their articles in open-access databases or journals. Unfortunately, academics often give the articles to commercial publishers, who then proceed to sell those articles at an appalling markup to the few people interested in reading them. It's a truly astonishing grift, and I applaud the publishers for their moxie in making it work. As always, academics know how to solve market failures in every market, except the ones they directly control.

Anyway, the fact that academics publish their work in an academic gift economy, where they're paid in clout, rather than cash, means that antitrust law isn't an obvious fit. After all, antitrust conventionally regulates commercial markets, with a special focus on price. But academics don't care about price and don't expect to profit from their work, at least not directly. Unlike copyright, academic plagiarism norms don't even determine who can sell a work; they only determine who can give it away and call it their own.

I don't think it matters. Antitrust law governs anticompetitive conduct, irrespective of the market, medium, or method. There's no question academics are competing, and there's no question that plagiarism norms are a way of regulating competition among academics. Or to put it another way, antitrust cares about competition, irrespective of the currency. Attribution is the coin of the academic realm, and academic plagiarism norms regulate its ownership and distribution. If a good is valuable and scarce, then antitrust should have something to say about its distribution.

Are academic plagiarism norms an antitrust problem? I think they are, or at least they might be, depending on your theory of antitrust and what it's supposed to accomplish. Academic plagiarism norms effectively enable academics to claim ownership of an idea and impose an attribution tax on anyone who uses that idea. That's pure rent-seeking. Copyright says ideas are in the public domain for a reason. It's one thing for authors to own exclusive rights in what they actually said, but another thing entirely for them to own exclusive rights in what they think. If antitrust is about efficiency, plagiarism norms are wildly inefficient, because they divvy up ownership of public goods for no good reason, other than the selfish interests of academics seeking clout.

What's more, academic plagiarism norms have a distributional equity problem, commonly known as "The Matthew Effect," after a line from the Gospel of Saint Matthew: "For unto every one that hath shall be given, and he shall have abundance: but from him that hath not shall be taken away even that which he hath."[40] The most valuable ideas are already claimed by incumbents, which not only makes it difficult to enter the market, but also forces newcomers to pay an attribution tax. In theory, plagiarism norms could help under-recognized scholars get credit for their ideas, but in practice they force scholars to pay homage to incumbents, whether or not they deserve it. Plagiarism norms tell scholars who owns an idea and is entitled to credit for it, rather than enabling them to identify who explains and develops the idea most clearly and thoroughly.

Consumers usually don't care who published an idea first. They want to know who said it best. Plagiarism norms force scholars to give consumers bad recommendations, based on ownership, rather than quality. Plagiarism norms enable academic incumbents to claim ownership of ideas and harm potential competitors. Ideas want to be free, and copyright says they're supposed to be. Academic plagiarism norms are just academic rent-seeking, scholars claiming effective ownership of ideas, which no one is supposed to own.

How should we respond? It depends on your theory of antitrust law. I suspect the Chicago School would say academic plagiarism norms are fine, because they don't hurt consumers, only competitors. But what about the New Brandeis School? I think it ought to find academic plagiarism norms troubling. After all, they're all about protecting incumbents and preventing competition. Academic plagiarism norms make Big Scholarship possible, as well as the commercial publishing industries it supports.[41]

[40] See Robert K. Merton, *The Matthew Effect in Science*, 159 SCIENCE 56 (1968) (quoting Matthew 25:29). Many thanks to Diana Liebenau for this reference.

[41] Of course, "Defining the market is the first and in many respects the most important question in antitrust." Robert A. Rogowsky & William F. Shughart, II, *Market Definition in Antitrust Analysis: Comment*, Federal Trade Commission Working Paper No. 77 at 2 (1982). "Depending on how the market is defined, a company is or is not a monopolist, or a merger

V PLAGIARISM FOR SQUARES

What does the Chicago School have to say about plagiarism norms? Not much. As Ramsi Woodcock has observed, the conventional wisdom on antitrust doesn't see plagiarism norms as a problem.[42] On the contrary, it sees plagiarism norms as potentially efficient, as they facilitate the communication of information about demand for scholarship and enable institutions to more effectively subsidize scholars who produce work that people want to consume.

From a Chicago School perspective, academic plagiarism norms aren't an antitrust problem, because they don't harm consumers and may make academic institutions more efficient. After all, scholarship is generally free. If the consumer price is zero, it's hard to see how an antitrust problem could exist. Also, academic plagiarism norms could help academic institutions allocate resources more efficiently, by identifying scholars with the most substantial impact and enabling institutions to steer resources to them.

VI PLAGIARISM FOR HIPSTERS

What about the New Brandeis School? I think it ought to find academic plagiarism norms quite troubling. After all, the premise of the New Brandeis School is that market concentration is bad, and we should encourage competition for the sake of competition. Academic plagiarism norms couldn't be more anticompetitive. They exist only in order to regulate competition. In fact, they exist only in order to regulate ownership of ideas, which copyright explicitly says no one can own.

So, academic plagiarism norms are rules created and enforced by private actors to create extra-legal property rights and punish people who don't respect them. Surely the New Brandeis School ought to find that objectionable? Effectively, it's private parties colluding to maintain market concentration by ensuring that incumbents can impose a tax on new entrants. Even worse, Big Scholarship uses extra-legal punishment to force defectors out of the market.

The Chicago School is untroubled by academic plagiarism norms at least in part because scholarship is produced into a gift economy, where the cost to consumers is zero. But a key argument of the New Brandeis School is that free goods can still

does or does not go beyond the market shares required of a *prima facie* violation of the law." *Id.* I use a simple definition of the market for scholarship, in which academics produce scholarship for consumers in exchange for prestige. But there are plausible alternative definitions. For example, perhaps academics produce scholarly works for other academics, who pay for it with attribution, which is valuable to academic employers, and publishers act as intermediaries, ensuring the quality of scholarship. On this account, academic plagiarism norms are a form of quality control, imposed by academics on themselves via their employers. Many thanks to Ramsi Woodcock for this observation, which I hope to address in a future article.

42 See, e.g., Ramsi Woodcock, *The Capital Snub*, Jan. 14, 2020, at https://zephyranth.pw/2020/01/14/the-capital-snub/.

present an antitrust problem. For example, many ISPs provide free services and sell advertising. The New Brandeis School sees that as a potential antitrust problem. Why not academics? They provide free content, but sell attribution. It's a weird market, but it's still a market.

The problem is Big Scholarship. Academic plagiarism norms enable influential incumbent academics to dominate the market for scholarship. And consumers don't care, because they are getting the content for free, and don't realize it isn't as good as it could be.

This is precisely the problem the New Brandeis School was supposed to address. The system is designed to benefit incumbents and prevent competition. It doesn't obviously harm consumers right now. But it might very well harm consumers eventually. The question is what we should do about it.

I think the New Brandeis School answer ought to be antitrust action against the plagiarism police. Academic plagiarism norms are agreements in restraint of trade that should be prohibited. It's fine to criticize someone for plagiarism. The First Amendment says you have a right to your opinion. But it's another thing entirely to privately suppress competition.

Indeed, the Utah Statement calls for the repeal of the *Noerr–Pennington* doctrine, which is the basis for antitrust's copyright exemption. I agree, works of authorship shouldn't be exempt from antitrust enforcement. Let's apply antitrust policy across the board. If competition is good, let's make it happen.

VII IT'S HIP TO BE SQUARE?

Somewhat ironically, I suspect adherents of the New Brandeis School won't love this essay. Why not? Well, for one thing, just because you like the idea of regulating someone else, doesn't necessarily mean you love the idea of being regulated yourself. The New Brandeis School is all-in on regulating Big Tech. But I suspect it may be less enthusiastic about regulating Big Scholarship.

After all, the members of the New Brandeis School are scholars in the business of selling ideas for clout, just like any other scholars. While plagiarism norms are pretty clearly exactly the kind of anticompetitive behavior that the New Brandeis School opposes, it's hard to oppose anticompetitive behavior that directly benefits yourself. Would the members of the New Brandeis School encourage other scholars to use the ideas they have popularized without attributing them? Maybe, but I have my doubts.

In any case, many adherents of the New Brandeis School seem to have the opposite intuition about plagiarism norms and related rules governing competition in creative industries. For example, Hal Singer, a scholar associated with the New Brandeis School, recently published an article effectively arguing in favor of expanding the scope of copyright protection in news in order to benefit journalism.[43]

[43] See Hal J. Singer, *Addressing the Power Imbalance between News Publishers and Digital Platforms: A Legislative Proposal for Effectuating Competitive Payments to Newspapers*,

While his proposal doesn't speak directly to plagiarism norms, it certainly suggests a broad sympathy to property rules designed to benefit authors and publishers.

Similarly, Sanjukta Paul has argued that antitrust law isn't really about promoting competition at all, but is really a way of allocating economic coordination rights.[44] In other words, antitrust law is all about deciding who gets to coordinate economic activity and why. It only looks like it's about competition because we've internalized the allocations of coordination rights that antitrust law has approved and rejected. It's fine for firms to coordinate internally, but not for firms and others to coordinate externally, even though there's no fundamental difference between the two.

And Philip Longman has argued that "small businesses" ought to be able to coordinate for mutual benefit.[45] He points to the American Guild of Organists (AGO), which recommended minimum salaries for organists and created an "ethical code" that prohibited them from competing with each other. Their efforts were not only ineffective, but resulted in an FTC enforcement action. Oops. Longman asks how the AGO is different from a union and argues that antitrust is wrong to prevent them from coordinating their efforts.

Essentially, the New Brandeis School's objection to characterizing coordination as "rent-seeking" is that it unfairly prevents weaker market participants from improving their economic circumstances. After all, if it's wrong for the AGO to coordinate its members and it's wrong for hair braiders to coordinate in support of an occupational licensing regime, why isn't it wrong for unions to organize for higher wages and better working conditions? "Who wants lower prices if it means even lower wages?"[46]

The closest any scholar aligned with New Brandeis School ideas has come to questioning the wisdom and efficiency of literary ownership and plagiarism norms is probably Rohan Grey's work arguing that a job guarantee for authors and artists would be more efficient and equitable than copyright.[47]

I fear this all seeks to prove far too much. After all, unions are regulated in order to ensure they promote the interests of their members and the public. Even if coordination is sometimes in the public interest, it isn't always in the public interest. After all, the problem with occupational licensing regimes isn't primarily that they raise

Oct. 12, 2021, at www.econone.com/news-article/managing-director-hal-singer-releases-new-study-on-the-power-imbalance-between-news-publishers-and-big-tech/.

[44] See Sanjukta Paul, *Antitrust As Allocator of Coordination Rights*, 67 UCLA L. REV. 4 (2020).

[45] See Philip Longman, *The Case for Small-Business Cooperation*, WASHINGTON MONTHLY, Oct. 28, 2018, at https://washingtonmonthly.com/2018/10/28/the-case-for-small-business-collusion/.

[46] See *id*.

[47] See, e.g., Rohan Grey, Who Owns the Intellectual Fruits of Job Guarantee Labor?, in THE JOB GUARANTEE AND MODERN MONEY THEORY: REALIZING KEYNES'S LABOR STANDARD (Mathew Forstater & Michael Murray, eds. 2017). See also, *Rohan Grey on Modern Monetary Theory and Intellectual Property*, Ipse Dixit, Oct. 24, 2019, at https://shows.acast.com/ipse-dixit/episodes/rohan-grey-on-modern-monetary-theory-and-intellectual-proper.

prices, but that they enable insiders to exclude newcomers from the profession. Longman thinks he's describing a union, but he could also be describing the mob, which is all about coordinating economic activity in ways the government disapproves. While it's always tempting to bend the rules to benefit those you favor, you never know who will be making the rules in the future.

Academic plagiarism norms are a perfect example of how this kind of coordination can go sour. As the Matthew Effect nicely illustrates, they benefit successful academics at the expense of unsuccessful academics. And they use a thin and disingenuous veneer of ethics to do it. Plagiarism norms have been around for thousands of years. If they were going to benefit the disadvantaged, they would have done it by now. But they didn't, because it was never the point. Academic plagiarism norms have always been about capturing attention and succeeding in the peculiar academic gift economy, not distributional equity. And if it's true of academic plagiarism norms, it's probably true of other forms of coordination as well.

In any case, it's ok, I get it. I suspect it has simply never occurred to adherents of the New Brandeis School to ask whether academic plagiarism norms are just a nefarious tool of Big Scholarship, an antitrust conspiracy disguised in scholarly robes. But there's still plenty of time! And I would certainly welcome their support.

Index